AF477615

GOD'S PURIFICATION - NOT EASY

BRIDE OF CHRIST IN ACTION

Part II
Chapters 21 – 39

Mariette Do-Nguyen

REBUILD MY CHURCH DIVINE MISSION

The front cover picture and the title were given to me, Mariette in my vision by the Lord Jesus. The Lord Jesus hanging on the cross is symbolic each one of us must be suffer for our souls to be purify before we return to. This purification is weather on earth or in the purgatory. The foot of the cross cut through an onion symbolic of during the process of purification we soft like an onion and God will peel us layer after layer.

GOD'S PURIFICATION - NOT EASY

Printed in the United States of America

Published by
Rebuild My Church Divine Mission
P.O. Box 261550
San Diego, CA 92196-1550
Web Site: http://www.jesusweb.org

The Revelations - Volume II
First printing September 1999
ISBN #0-9652169-2-6

The Lord Jesus told Mariette, "No human's books can teach you of what I am teaching you."

ACKNOWLEDGMENTS

I give praise, glory, and thanks to the Almighty God: The Father, the Lord Jesus, and the Holy Spirit, within me and carrying me through this entire Mission, and forever and ever.

I give honor and thanks to the Blessed Virgin Mother, the Mother of our Lord Jesus, my dearly beloved Mother of my heart, and the spiritual Mother of all human race, for being with me from the time that I was born into this world, for always bombarding to Lord God with prayers for me, comforting me, teaching me, protecting me, and do things for me.

I give thanks and honor to Saint Joseph, the Archangel Michael, Sts Peter and Paul, and all the holy angels and saints who always pray with me and protect me.

INTRODUCTION

God is just and merciful, He forgives all our sins. But we must pay for the damaged caused from commit sins through various kind of suffering, for our souls to be purify on earth, or after our last breath (death of the body) in purgatory.

All things have been handed over to me by my Father. No one knows who the Son is except the Father, and who the Father is except the Son and anyone to whom the Son wishes to reveal him.

–Luke 10: 22

No one who remains in him sins; no one who sins has seen him or known him. Children, let no one deceive you. The person who acts in righteousness is righteous, just as he is righteous. Whoever sins belongs to the devil, because the devil has sinned from the beginning. In deed, the Son of God was revealed to destroy the work of the devil.

–1 John 3: 6-8

"In it he also went to preach to the spirits in prison, who had once been disobedient while God patiently waited in the days of Noah during building of the ark, in which a few persons, eight in all, were saved through water."

–1 Peter 3:19-20

"Settle with your opponent quickly while on the way to court with him. Otherwise your opponent will hand you over to the judge, and the judge will hand you over to the guard, and you will be thrown into prison. Amen, I say to you, you will not be released until you have paid the last penny."

–Matthew 5:25-26

"He then took up a collection among all his soldiers, amounting to two thousand silver drachmas, which he sent to Jerusalem to provide for an expiatory sacrifice. In doing this he acted in a very excellent and noble way, inasmuch as he had the resurrection of the dead in view; for if he were not expecting the fallen to rise again, it would have been useless and foolish to pray for them in death. But if he did this with a view to the splendid reward that awaits those who had gone to rest in godliness, it was a holy and pious thought. Thus he made atonement for the dead that they might be freed from this sin."

–2 Maccabees 12:43-46

Mariette's Responsibility

"Thus says the LORD: Stand in the court of the house of the LORD and speak to the people of all the cities of Judah who comes to worship in the house of the LORD; whatever I command you, tell them, and omit nothing.
"Now, therefore, reform your ways and your deeds, listen to the voice of the LORD your God, so that the LORD will repent of the evil with which he threatens you."

–Jeremiah 26:2,13

Summary of God Calling Mariette

It is hard to believe, but it is a true story of a woman being called by God at the time our nation is in crisis. Mariette Do-Nguyen is a Vietnamese native, who left Vietnam in April 1975. Mariette is the mother of four grown children. She stayed away from Catholic church for nine years, until the Holy Week of 1991, when God silently called her back. On the morning of August 2, 1992, she awoke, frightened, from a disturbing dream. She had, in fact, just experienced her first dream encounter with the Lord Jesus, an occurrence that changed her life as well as the lives of countless others.

In the dream, the Lord Jesus was speaking to her, but Mariette was unable to hear His words. She responded, "Jesus, whatever You want me to do I will do, but do not appear in front of me, and make me prove that I saw You. People will say that I am crazy." Between August 2, 1992 and January 1, 1994, in her dream, Mariette saw the Lord Jesus and the Blessed Virgin Mother about seventy times, and on some occasions the Archangel Michael, Saint John the Baptist, Saint Joseph, Bernadette, Theresa, and the Heavenly Father in symbolic form.

Continually through Mariette, God is revealing to the world of its systems go against God, mental illness such as depression and Alzheimer; and the future of the United States and throughout the world, the revelations come through her dreams and voice of God in symbolism. The task that God entrusted to her, pursue the freedom to worship the true God throughout the world, to minister to priests, unify God's Church, and bring God's peace into the world. She denied her calling many times, but it is a heavenly court order, and she must obey this calling.

Obeying God, for several years, she has been communicating with President Bill Clinton, Vice President Al Gore, and all members of the United States Senate, delivering what God asks of her, to pass laws under God's commandments; to help them to understand the soul and spirit with and in a human's physical body, the life of a human beginning at conception; and the U.S. citizens Civil Right to Freedom of Religion being violated, and God warnings for the lawmakers and high-ranking government officials.

On July 1, 1998, Mariette filed a petition at the United States Tax Court, petitioning for the civil right to freedom of religion in the United States. Based on the grounds of the U.S. high ranking leaders using tax monies to benefit programs that are against God's commandments, these actions add to personal sins lead to tragedies and disasters upon the United States and throughout the world, and destroy the United States citizens' souls. In response, she received over one hundred letters from the members of U.S. Senate, and the U.S. Senate voted 98-0 passing the bill "S.1868 - International Religious Freedom" on October, 1998.

She is petitioning the United States Tax Court requesting the tax laws to be changed, giving all U.S. citizens the civil right to choose the programs that our tax monies are funding. This change would restore citizens' freedom of religion; citizens could avoid committing sins against God and destruction to the nation. Obeying God, she is also calling all religious spiritual leaders to obey all God's commandments: to put their preaching in their daily actions and lead people's hearts close to God, benefiting their souls for heavenly eternal life as well as their earthly life.

INSTRUCTIONS

Then afterward I will pour out my spirit upon all mankind. Your sons and daughters shall prophesy, your old men shall dream dreams; your young men shall see visions; even upon the servants and the handmaids, in those days, I will pour my spirit.

–Joel 3: 1-2

For many centuries to come, God will communicate with His people through dreams and visions. At the same time the devil and his offspring spirits will enter human dreams and visions, as counterfeit gods to those giving their free will to him. This book will assist readers to understand the symbolism in the Book of Revelations, the prophets' visions and dreams in the old testament, and the readers own dreams and visions, plus explain how to interpret the patterns of the Bible. It will help to understand the hidden meaning of God's words through stories and parables. This book will also help to distinguish what is from God and what is from the devil.

It took me nine years to compete this book. Five of these nine years I was alone with God, all day and night, every day and night seeking God, and pray through scriptures, holy rosary prayers, when I am not pray, and do His works I ask Him to help me of what and how to do His works, even while I am sleep I am speaking to God and pray, and completely obeying all His commandments. I made other living sacrifices such as going to daily mass and receiving the Holy Eucharist, going to confession regularly, and fasting.

Ninety percent of my dreams, visions, and words from God, priests, human names, animals, and structures also are symbolic. Because I did not know the Bible when the Lord called me back and entrusted to me this Divine mission; in the early years, the Lord Jesus used Father Joseph Hung Kien Tong in my dreams and visions as symbolism to revealed Himself to me, as Jesus is the highest priest. Later Jesus the Lord used the meaning of Father Tong's name to explain to me of His characters and God's words. Father Joseph Hung Kien Tong's name in the book "My Patient - God's Gift" in the "Acknowledgments and Prayers from Mariette" refers to the Lord Jesus who constantly prays to the Eternal Father for me. The Holy Father always refers to the Eternal Father.   There are times that a priest with a brilliant description is symbolic of the Lord Jesus, priest with ugly face symbolic of spiritual leaders break their vow and serve man not God. The Roman Catholic Church is symbolic of the only God's Church that the Lord Jesus is the head. Vietnam is symbolic of the world, but in some cases Vietnam means a Nation, or tribe of Judah. God uses natural stories as substance to reveal in spirit; and all revelations are revealed to me in spirit. When the revelation comes down to earth will be a lot larger than it was in spirit. Ninety nine percent of these stories will be repeated in later centuries, and I am a witness to all of these stories with my own ears and eyes.

When God reveals to me, He gives to me according to the level of my intellect He teaches me like a child just starting pre-school. When I gain more knowledge, He moves me to the next level, slowly like little child lean to sit, to crawl, to stand, and to walk, and He will not teach me to run. He then teaches me from preschool, elementary, high school, and college. For a person to understand the revelations this book, they must start reading from the beginning in my first book "My Patient - God's Gift" so they can understand of how symbolism meaning changing. The first time of reading of the book must be in order page by page to understand the way God speaks through symbolism and words and formed into a revelation. This symbolism and words will be used from one dream to another in similar symbolism, to reveal one message. Symbolism and hidden meaning are God's language to communicate with man throughout the Holy Scriptures. All of the stories in this book are true stories. The purpose that God uses these stories as natural substance to revealed in spirit; when God revealed to me in spirit they became revelations; these revelation will pour upon the world in future time; the time of the revelations upon the world are various; and they are in God's time, and God's time is different from earthly time. Many of these stories can be applied to each one of our individual lives; they also apply to leaders as well.

The symbolism can be interpreted in different ways to fit each individual, group, or nation. The meanings depend on at least several dreams, visions, and God's words to complete one revelation.

There are times it seems like I exalt myself, but every word in this book and all of my books is given to me by God to fulfill the revelations. Whether God speaks directly or the Spirit of God speaks through me. God always teach each one of us to be humble before Him, not before man. Humble before God is completely obeying all God's commandment, trust and depending in Him

Because of the change in meaning, if a person does not completely obey all of God's commandments, and does not spend enough time in prayer and offering living scarifies, the enemy spirit will twist the words to the wrong meaning. To receive meaning from God a person must completely surrender his life to God, dead to herself.

Each time before read any part of this book, focus your mind to seek God for wisdom of understanding His words. For the beginner, I strongly suggested you ask the Blessed Virgin Mother to assist you, and the holy angels and saints to intercede for you.

Slowly, you will come directly to God, but always keep the Blessed Virgin Mother and Holy angels as your intercessors.

Even at the time I am working on this book, and I will continue to do so all my life, I always come to my beloved Blessed Virgin Mother to help me, and ask holy angels and saints to intercede for me, especially my guardian angel, the Archangel Michael .

As the same time, you must ask God for guiding, protection and discernment. Be very careful because the devil will twist the words and the symbolism, and give you his understanding.

I will intercede for every one whose heart desires and read the books written by me. I am as God's instrument and Vessel, I pray for you to convert to God, exam and repent daily.

God calls all of us for conversion, daily exam and repentance. After each one of us converts and keeps all God's commandments, all our sins are forgiven, and no longer mentioned in front of God. The example is Saint Mary Madelene.

GOD'S PURIFICATION - NOT EASY

Bride of Christ in Action
Part II

Table of Contents

Part II

(After each revelation will be some correspondence to lawmakers, and government high-ranking officials.)

21

THE ANOINTING

Opening Phrase of the Anointing

There are different kinds of spiritual gifts but the same Spirit; there are different forms of service but the same Lord; There are different working but the same God who produces all of them in everyone. To each individual the manifestation of the Spirit is given for some benefit. To one is given through the Spirit the expression of wisdom; to another the expression of knowledge according to the same Spirit; to another faith by the same Spirit; to another gifts of healing by the one Spirit; to another mighty deeds; to another prophecy; to another discernment of spirits; to another varieties of tongues; to another interpretation of tongues. But one and the same Spirit produces all of these, distributing them individually to each person as he wishes.

–1 Corinthians 12:4-11

10:25 p.m. April 18, 1997, close to the end of my devotion, the Spirit of God came upon me, and He said to me, "Get your tape recorder, I will dictate to you. I will send you to meet with Cardinal Ratzinger next year. The Holy Father urgently needs to see you. I will carry you to the Father in heaven. The Father has set aside an amount of blessings for you. The Father will not give you all the blessings at that time, but He will distribute to you a little at a time. These blessing are for the Church, because the church on earth has been empty of blessings from the Father for long time. I charge you to properly deliver each one. The Father will give you their name. The first name He gives to you, you will give them the blessing last. The last name the Father gives to you, you will give them blessing first."

My beloved Blessed Virgin Mother asked me, "What do you say to the Lord? What do you have in your mind? Why do you retain silence in you head?" I replied to her, "The Father told me to think about it." The Lord Jesus said to me, "The Father said your thinking is too long." I then said to the Lord, "Lord, my mind is blank, there is nothing in my thought." Jesus the Lord said to me, "You are lost in your human thinking." I then said to my beloved Blessed Virgin Mother, "Mother, what is the Lord doing here? I do not understand. Everything He said, I did not see that the parts are coming together. It seems to me they are different issues." The Lord then said to me, "Your discernment is working properly, even though they are different issues, they all come from one Spirit." He continued, "This revelation will be in the book named "The Anointing." I then said to the Lord, "Lord, I have not finished the book 'Bride of Christ in Action' yet. Do you want me to do two at the same time? How do I know which one belongs to which?" The Lord said, "These two books, they go hand in hand. One needs another; they can not be separate." I then asked the Lord, "The last phrase you just spoke to me, is that just the instruction or is it a revelation?" He said to me, "That was instructions, but I'll give you a few minutes to think about it, and tell Me what you think." I responded, "Lord, I think I know what You mean. You said to me that You needed me, because I have a broom. You do not have a broom, because You chose not to have one, and I need you, because without You, I can do nothing." Jesus the Lord God said to me, "The people in this world are saying to Me, the Father, and the Holy Spirit that they do not need God, they can survive by themselves." I said, "Lord, I just take a very deep breath; Lord for those that You know who are willing to convert and repent. I ask You, Lord, do not cut that breathing from them, but for those who refuse to convert and repent. Lord I followed the queen Esther, I ask You to cut that breathing from them at this very second, after I finish this sentence."

The very deep breath I physically took was not on my own, the Spirit of God was in me for that deep breath. This breathing is symbolic of the breath of life.

The Lord then gave me an instruction for Father Scott, Rector of the Cathedral of Saint Andrew, "You tell Father Scott to have all the Holy Eucharist Ministers and Lectors wear white robes to serve Me at My sanctuary. I do not want people to wear short sleeves in my presence." In my vision, I saw a small woman wearing a short skirt standing at the Gospel podium. This vision has two meanings, natural and spiritual. On the natural ground, God is directly speaking to the Eucharist ministers and lectors to be in formal dress code, or uniform at His sanctuary to worship Him, and not to distract other people. The sanctuary is a place of worship, not a place for socializing, a picnic ground, or clothes advertising.

The meaning in the spiritual realm: Wearing short sleeves is symbolic of not having God's protection; and not having God's protection means their hearts are impure. White robes are symbolic of pure hearts and serving God with all their hearts and souls.

God revealed to church authorities to be careful when they appoint or select Holy Eucharist ministers and lectors. Priests, Eucharist ministers and Lectors are to serve God in love, with pure hearts.

12:25 a.m. April 19, 1997: I just got up, I heard the Lord say, "The world will say 'God is a living God, they will no longer say God is dead any more."

4:20 a.m. April 1997: The Lord Jesus, God the Almighty just said to me and to you, "The anointing of teaching is very near. Most of the present preachers are under the power of the devil."

The Lord continued, "When the power of God works through a person, whatever that person does is an anointing from God.   But the people do not understand. They are saying they are talented, gifted, and have blocked out the name of God. The post cards that have been made from the anointing from God depends on what image or picture is on those cards. Is the image symbolic of things glorifying God to benefit souls, or to glorify the devil by benefiting flesh? The manifestation that the false preachers proclaimed, this power is from the devil, that manifests among themselves [among false preachers], and within themselves."

I said to God, "Lord, hold me at the center of Your heart, and anoint me with the anointing of listening to the words of God, the living words that will shine upon the world." The Lord Jesus said to me, "The Father said, the second best is the anointing of knowing how to listen to God, and teaching others of the good things you have learned from those who know how to listen. And the best anointing of all is an anointing embracing suffering for the sake of God. The refined anointing oil that you put on yourself every night is symbolic of the anointing of having faith in God. Holding a rosary on your hand while you sleep every night is symbolic of steadfast faith." Then the Lord instructed me, " Place the 'Faith through the Power of Rosary' revelation here, and break the anointing revelations in two parts: Part one, Anointing to serve God; part two, anointing to challenge the world; and title it as: The opening phrase of the Anointing."

Faith Through the Power of the Rosary : February 27, 1997: In my devotion at night, the Lord Jesus asked me, "Sister, what is in your hand?" I replied, "The rosary." He asked me, "Why do you hold the rosary in your hand?" I replied, "It is available for me when I say the rosary when I woke up from sleep during at nights. I also feel safe with the rosary in my hand while I sleep." He said, " You are holding something invaluable in your hand; it is your faith that protects you."

Faith - Holy Eucharist - Holy Water: The 1994 feast of Pentecost, I was on my way driving to church. Suddenly I felt the gentle heat that came down to my face while I was praying. I heard the voice say, "I command you to go to mass every day and receive me." I thought, "Receive me, that must be Jesus." I then obeying the Lord go to mass every day, except two times. I receive the body and blood of the Lord every day, and go to confession regularly.

Through the Holy Eucharist, the Lord Jesus has healed me many times. I couldn't count the number of times He has healed me when writing this book, the number of times the Lord healed me is too many. There is no one in this world that God has healed more than me.

There was one time that was caused by the devil. In March of 1986, I was in an automobile accident, and from this accident I suffered pain in my neck and back for over six years. I was treated for this pain by doctors in many different fields, but no one could relieve my pain. Through the power of God, near the end of 1993, while I was praying, I put holy water on my back and the Lord healed me.

At that time I did not understand why I suffered for over six years, and how the Holy water healed me. But I now fully understand that at the time I was injured from the accident, the infirmity spirit belonging to the devil caused me that long suffering. But the power of God is so great, He delivered me from the spirit of infirmity.

During the two years before writing this chapter in May 1997, every time that something went wrong with my physical body, I normally would find whatever medicine in the house that I had to use. If I didn't have medicine for whatever it caused me, I then asked the Lord if He would allow me to go to the doctor. He then said, "I will heal you." I did not go to doctor, and within a few days I was healed. It took a longer time before He healed me, but I understood that I needed to suffer for the grace of God to work through me.

There is a time that God wants to use doctors as His instrument to heal people, and there is a time He directly heals people without the doctor. Doctors alone can not heal any one; medication alone, can not heal people either. The power of God must be over the doctors and medicine.

Free Will

At the time God created Adam from clay and breathed into him a breath of life, Adam is symbolic of the soul. God gave Adam and everyone of us a free will. At the time of conception the soul is pure. After each one of us is born, as our body grows, the soul also grows with the body. The devil still uses the same trick that he used to convince Eve, the spirit to be disobedient to God.

A person stands straight; to his right is God, to his left is the devil. God leaves him alone and lets him choose to lean to Him or lean to the devil, but the devil keeps pulling him to his left side, the devil's side. Every time a person is disobedient to God's commandments, he is walking toward the side of devil, he is little by little giving his free will to the devil.

The devil attacks us through our thoughts, and from the thoughts will come actions. If a person thinks of things that go against God's commandments, he has sinned against God. If he takes action, he sins against God and whoever the action is toward. There are some cases like sexual alteration, if both parties agree, then both parties sin against God. (Sexual

264

alteration means people who have intercourse outside being married in the present of God, adultery, or sexual acts to avoid pregnancy.)

When priests have renounced everything to follow in the Lord Jesus' footsteps, it means he has completely given himself to God. He must understand that he has promised God that he surrendered his free will to God. If he still keeps his free will, it means that he serves both God and the devil.

Anointing to Serve God

The Lord said, "Serving God as Rectors of the churches, being Eucharistic Ministers, lectors, and altar boys are anointings. When a person serves God, they do it with their hearts and their souls. If a person serves God for their own name, their own benefits, they are under the power of the devil" The Lord means that He only bestowed the anointing upon those serve Him with all their hearts and their souls; on the other hand there is "no" anointing up on those who serve Him with empty hearts and dead souls.

The Lord continued, "These anointed were anointed at the time of the baptism, and the anointing only manifests when a person lives in the life of holiness." The Lord means that at the time of baptism, God anointed every one of us with some anointing to serve Him, but these anointings only result in victory when the person keeps their heart pure. There are many times people serve God at the altar, but their hearts are too far from God, meaning they contain mortal sins and refuse to convert or repent daily.

The Lord continued, "Singing and teaching are special anointings, God has assigned to those as a special calling as a chosen one by God. These anointings manifest slowly in their lives, and these anointings will be fully manifested when a person lives the life of holiness. The chosen ones always have to battle against the devil's spirit in their daily life. Through fighting with the devil, they learn how to embrace the suffering. But many do not understand how to offer their suffering to God, they complain, because they do not understand that they have been assigned by God on a special assignment on earth. But when they fully understand that they are the chosen ones by God, they will be the best in front of God. When they are the best in front of God, they will be opposite the world systems in this age, they will be fighting for the right."

Normally, the devil knows God chosen ones, but the chosen ones do not know that they were being chosen by God. The devil uses other people to create suffering for them, but remember, God allows the devil to do this to make you strong in God, by seeking God daily in your life, God will the do His work through you.

I said to the Lord, "Oh Lord, my God, You are the God of all creation, no one understands Your heart unless they are completely obedient to You. Your love is above all things. The Almighty God has done great things for me and for my family."

Live in the Anointing

Flying Above the Ground: I then saw a man inside the large, low house. I was flying above the ground of an alley behind the house. This man was able to see me through the back window and he was trying to hurry to get out of the house to stop me for conversation. I knew his intent, so I quickly made a right turn at the corner house onto the main street, and geared my strength to fly up high. I then turned to my right, and I saw this man run out the front door, but he could not stop me for the conversation because I flew far away from the house. I saw him stand in front of the house, but he could not see me.

Flying High in the Air: I saw the dream where I was flying up high between tall walls, it looked like an alley. People were on the ground chasing after me, and they touched my legs, I said to them, "Do not touch me," but they kept trying to touch me, and I said, "Not to touch me." This time I flew back and forth, then I flew higher above the roof of these houses.

Velvet Black Divider Rope: I then saw myself laid on the ground of the Gym at Riverwalk Apartments Complex. Behind me was something like a velvet black divider rope, like the divider rope at the public services. I knew that was from the enemies, and I said, "In Jesus' name I rebuke you, get away from me." I then saw this rope move away from me and disappear.

Flying High in the Sky: I saw myself flying high in the sky, and while I was flying up, I saw below a huge open air field, with sand and clay. It was a light brown color, with no trees, no houses, and nothing around. It was in the hot sun, like the desert. In the middle of the field there were some people walking close together, next to a clay high road.

Laid up on the Air at the Side of the Road: I then was laid on the air. My side was next to a very high sparkling rock road. I looked deep down to the ground and I was afraid that I might fall down. I kept trying to roll my stomach on the road so I would not fall down to the ground.

The Lord said, "This dream is Walking in the Anointing. Laying on the ground in the gym is symbolic of when you are in distress. Flying between the walls, people touching you and your telling them 'not to touch you' is the time you are in a tight situation like now, you are trying to do the works, but other people are not cooperating with God. The man you saw in the house and trying to get you is symbolic of your seeing people doing too many activities to please the flesh and you run away from them. Laying at the side of the bridge is security, you are trying to get in the center of God's power. Flying up high looking down on the earth, you saw activities without a house, or tree is symbolic of the time you are happy in the Lord."

8:42 a.m., April 19, 1997. In the morning of my devotion, I just finished the Chaplet of the Divine Mercy, and the Spirit of the Lord was upon me. While the Lord spoke to me, the enemy spirits attacked me from behind. It burned from the upper part of my shoulder, middle of my upper back , and close to my neck, and I could not stand this attack. I broke in the middle of the Lord speaking, and said to the Lord, "Lord, Father, I surrender this suffering to You, Father; through Your beloved, begotten Son, and through the works of the Holy Spirit. If any of this is from the enemies, Father, I ask You to remove them; but if they are from You, I ask you to strengthen me, so I can embrace them to please You, please Jesus, my Lord, my God, and please the Holy Spirit." While I was saying this, in my vision, I saw the dream that I was flying up high between the middle of the two tall walls like an alley, and people were chasing after me, touching my leg. I said to them, "Do not touch me," but they kept trying to touch me, and I said, "Not to touch me." The Lord God, Jesus said to me, "Now you are in the big stream of the big wall in the alley."

I then saw the Lord Jesus just resurrected from the dead. In front of the tomb was Mary Magdelene, standing in front, as she leaned on the triangular rock, she faced the open tomb. The Lord Jesus reminded me and you that Mary Madelene was trying to touch Him, and He said to her, "Stop holding on to me, for I have not yet ascended to the Father." Although I did not see her trying to touch the man, she sat still to the side of the rock, and the man stood firmly behind, facing her. Behind her, next to the rock was a man standing straight. Behind them was a huge open field like a garden, but there was no high tree directly from the middle. At the horizon was a bright light. As I faced Mary Magdelene, to my left, a little up high was a small area with many bushes of palm trees, to my right in the large space was a dark cloud. The Lord just corrected me, "You have been misled; those are not dark clouds, they are iniquities contained in the world.

I then saw a man inside the large, low house. I was flying above the ground of an alley behind the house. This man was able to see me through the back window and he was trying to hurry to get out of the house to stop me for conversation. I knew his intent, so I quickly made a right turn at the corner house onto the main street, and geared my strength to fly up high. I then turned to my right, and I saw this man run out the front door, but he could not stop me for conversation because I flew far away from the house. I saw him stand in front of the house, but he could not see me.

I then said to the Lord, "Lord, keep this man in the house, do not let him come out to stop me or talk to me. I do not want to speak to him. I rebuked him in Your name, Jesus, my Lord, my God." The Lord said, "This is the time that you are in the church, and in the public running errands." While the Lord was saying this, in my vision, I saw myself sitting at the end of the third row, at the right section in the Cathedral of Saint Andrew, painfully fighting with enemy spirits. I then saw myself running home on Chester street, close to the corner of Chester and West Markham. The Lord used the light clouds going back and forth on the southwest corner of Chester and West Markham to make the southwest corner symbolic of holiness.

The Lord said, "Holiness can not mix with impure spirits." God means that His Spirit does not mix with the spirit of the devil. The Lord said, "It is not, it will not, and it was never mixed." God means that His Spirit was not mixed with the spirit of the devil, the Spirit of God is not mixed with the spirit of the devil, and the Spirit of God will never mix with the spirit of the devil. (three forms: past, present and future.)

In my vision, I saw the first time I went to a Charismatic healing service at the Good Shepherd church, and the spirit of the devil jerked at me. The Lord asked me, "Do you understand everything that I just revealed to you?" I replied, "No, I question the charismatic healing service. Lord God, what kind of power was on me at that time? And what kind of power was upon those on the ground?" The Lord said, "For you, it was pressed down on you from the devil, but the Archangel Michael fought against it. There was fighting above and around you. Plus you did not know, you thought it was from God, and you allowed yourself to be on the devil's side. But later, you knew that it was not from God, you completely fought back the devil. Your free will is completely with God, no longer with the devil. Because that one time you allowed in the devil, he attacked you again. The second time was in the mother's room, that charismatic was held there."

While the Lord spoke of the second time in the mother's room, I remembered the event. When I first converted to God, I did not know anything about the charismatics, and there was a woman named Erma, she shared with me that her emotions were healed from going to the charismatic healing service. She asked me to come with her; so I joined them. The second time was in the small room, in the back of the church, where the same group of charismatics prayed. While people were sitting in chairs arranged like an oval, I suddenly kneeled on the floor. The woman was the group leader. A man pulled me out of the room, to the church, and sat me on the last pew. The woman was behind me, the man was to my left and prayed over me. During the time all three of us were praying, these two people prayed in tongues. Then I heard the man say, "My child, I have been waiting for you for a long time." As he said this I thought that God spoke through him, so I said to the Lord, "Jesus, God, I am sorry that I had run away from You, help me to come back to You."

To testify for the spirit in the charismatics: the time I went to this charismatic healing service was in early 1994; within few months the Lord told me not to go there any more, so I stopped. During 1995 and the first part of 1996, Erma called me several times, and asked me to pray for her, because there were too many problems around her, and her emotions got worst than before.

The Lord said, "When a person gives their free will to the devil, the devil has the right to come to the Father to claim the right of what that individual gave to them; whether it was the entire free will or a part of it, a small or large part. In your case, you gave him a piece like 1/100 of a sand grain in the ocean." The Lord revealed that, even though that I did not know, I thought that power was from God, but instead it was from the devil. It was only one time, but the devil had the right to claim what I gave to him. Only one incident and the factor is 1/100 of the piece of sand grain in the bottom of the sea. This symbolizes the life of a person, the piece of a sand is symbolic of a person. The Lord said to Abraham, "Your descendants are like the stars in the sky that you can not count." The Lord Jesus said to John, "The enemies are like the sands in the ocean." Once a person sins against God, then they become a piece of sand in the bottom of the ocean, not a star in the sky anymore. There are two meanings of the sands in the ocean: The Spirit of God is not mixed with the spirit of the devil; the Spirit of God is in the sky, and the devil is under the sea. Heaven is above, and hell is under the earth.

I saw that I was flying very high. Below were some people doing activities in a huge open field like a desert. I said to the Lord, "Lord, I do not think that I have had any moment in my life like this one yet." The Lord said, "Yes, you do, you just do not remember it. There was twice you met with the Bishop Andrew, and he said to you 'all right, how we are going to do this?' And another time he said 'all right.' Both times he raised both of his arms in cheerfulness, and three times you met with the Rector of the Cathedral of Saint Andrew. He sat and focused on every single word that you spoke, there were five times you were flying up high looking down on the desert." The desert is a place that has no water. People need water, and the water here is living water, the Lord Jesus, the Son of the most high living God. In this meeting, the Lord spoke of Bishop Andrew, Father Scott and the church authorities. Every one, except the Holy Father, is in the wilderness.

The Lord continued, "While you up were up high, you were in the midst of the living water." While the Lord was saying this, in my vision, I saw myself floating in the middle of the ocean. Both of my arms were straight to the side, level with my shoulders, and water was up to my underarms, covering my chest. I went up and down, but when I was up, the level of the water still covered two-thirds of my chest. The chest contains the heart, and the heart is the center of my life. When I was up the water still covered two-thirds of my heart, and when I was down the water covered my entire heart. This is symbolic of the anointing of God completely covering me, but when I was up, the one third of the water not covering my chest is symbolic that I still have to endure the physical life. The Lord then gave me credit, and said, "You did an excellent explanation." I said, "Lord, I did not do this on my own. You, Jesus, my God that is in me, help me to do these explanations."

Priestly Anointing

The Priestly Vestments. *From among the Israelites have your brother Aaron, together with his sons Nadab, Abihu, Eleazar and Ithamar, brought to you, that they may be my priests. For the glorious adornment of your brother Aaron you shall have sacred vestments made. Therefore, to the various expert workmen whom I have endowed with skill, you shall give instruction to make such vestment for Aaron as will set him apart for this sacred service as my priest. These are the vestments they shall make: a breastpiece, an ephol, a robe, a brocaded tunic, a miter and sash. In making these sacred vestments which your brother Aaron and his sons are to wear in serving as my priests, they shall used gold, violet, purple and scarlet yarn and fine linen.*

–Exodus 28:1-5

April 16, 1997, 9:45 a.m. During my morning devotion the Blessed Virgin Mother said to me, "There are some anointings that God bestowed upon priests at the time of their ordination, such as not remembering people's sins after they hear confession, and proclaiming the Gospel. But many of them misuse these anointings. To retain these anointings, they must live their life as they completely give themselves to God."

The priestly vestments are the outfit of layers that priests wear in front of God at the time of celebrating mass, hearing confession, or at any time service in the presence of the Almighty. Diocese priests and order priests' uniforms are symbolic of being clothed with the discipline to their vows. God instructed Moses very carefully in detail of how to make these vestments, and to wear them in front of God, the church has to follow these instructions. God chose various expert workmen that He endowed with skill to make these vestments, and that means God Himself pours out His protection, guiding and blessing upon priests. His giving in detail what should be used to make these vestments means that every priest must be very careful of their thoughts and actions. Beyond the anointing God bestowed to priests at the time of ordination, he also bestowed more to those He chose in a special calling. If priests are disobedient to any of God's laws, then some of these anointings will be suspended. When any priests being sustained by the anointing falls, they will be lost in the jungle of enemies, they will no longer be serving God from their hearts. The way they serve God became their duty, and they are performing very poorly. Such a homily out of the Gospel, misleading people or in the confession box can not discern of how to advise people after they confess their sins, and daily communication in the benefit of flesh will not help their soul and souls of others.

This means the priests are leaning to the left side, the side that belongs to the devil; and the vestments that they wear are no longer clothed with the power of God.

ANOINTINGS TO CHALLENGE THE WORLD

The Vessel Holding Special Anointing in Actions

The Lord Jesus instructed me using my oldest daughter, Theresa Thuy-Trang's case and her husband Vincent Huy case as a model. Thuy-Trang is a full time high school mathematics teacher, and Huy works full time selling life insurance for a large insurance company. Thuy-Trang and Huy serve God, through taking very seriously the responsibility as members of a choir at Our Lady of Secret Heart, the Roman Catholic Church in San Diego, California. Thuy-Trang is also one of two female singers in a band. Her husband was the coordinator of the band for several years. They serve God through serving others at wedding receptions almost every weekend.

In the beginning of 1993, there was an advertisement for a Talent Singing contest, organized by Ritz night clubs in Orange county. Thuy-Trang and Huy both entered the contest.

After the second round of competing, Huy withdrew from the list of contestants for the good reason that he didn't want to compete against his wife. Instead, he would groom his wife for the contest.

The final night was competition to rank the winners. Five finalist male contestants competed against each other; and five female finalists competed against each other. The judges board would select five sets; each set a male and female; two first place winners, two second, two third, two four, and two fifth.

During the course of these ten finalist contestants gathering together for rehearsal, Thuy-Trang, her husband, and others contestants experienced the unfairness of the organizers. In front of them and behind them, they complained to the authorities of the club organizers, but these unfair practices still continued. They shared these unfair actions with me, I then advised them that they must do what was right.

The evening of the final contest for ranking, I was in the hotel room with my daughter Thuy-Trang, her husband Huy, and two other female finalist contestants before the contest. They were angry of the unfairness by the organizers, and their dear friends. Thuy-Trang and these two finalist contestants decided to withdraw from the contest, they were trying to figure out how to do withdraw in a proper way. God's strength was poured down unto Huy, my son-in-law to stand by his wife to advise her in this difficult step.

We entered the night club filled with an audiences of about seven hundred in number. Thuy-Trang was the third finalist contestant called. She was carried by the Lord, our God, to the middle of the stage, in her long, black, elegant dress, with her gloves. As she began her speech, the other two female finalist contestants proceeded toward her from the crowd, and stood by her. With the anointing God gave her, in Vietnamese, her soft powerful voice said, " We give thanks to all of you that are here to support us, but unfortunately myself, Thiep Linh, and Hong Phuong will not continue this contest because it is unclean." Immediately after her proud withdrawal speech, the audience said, "OOhOO0." The entire club was silent and shocked by their withdrawal from the contest. While the audience was silent, the family members and friends of these proudly withdrawn finalist contestants brought them flowers, and we all left the club.

That left five male finalist to compete against each other, and two female finalist to complete against each other. One of the two female finalist contestants was that God revealed to me, and my daughter said 'we did not like her actions.'

After the event, Thuy-Trang and her husband were contact by the media, but she refused to speak to them, and left the matter to her husband Huy, with the content, "The contest was unfair, we did not want to continue. We did not want to harm their business, but we hope that this lesson will teach them and others, for the future organizing of contests to be just."

During the time that these ten finalists rehearsed, one night during my devotion, the Lord Jesus told me, "Your daughter and her husband went to a meeting in Santa Ana for video taping. There was a woman in this group carrying a charm." I did not understand the revelation that time; but I did share this revelation with my daughter Thuy-Trang. She responded to me, "Yes, Huy and I went to a meeting in Santa Ana that night; the meeting was held by people organizing the Talent singing contest. We were all happy, except one female contestant from San Diego, we did not like her." God anointing within my daughter fight against the enemy spirits hidden within other contestant.

In another devotion, the Lord told me, "Your daughter Thuy-Trang will be the first winner of the contest." I did not understand the revelation, but I kept this revelation for myself. After everything was over, I thought to myself, "May be the devil lied to me." But I was very proud of my daughter, her husband, and the other two finalist contestants that proudly withdrew.

April 19, 1997. After the Lord revealed that God's anointing was manifesting through Thuy-Trang, Huy, and the other two finalist contestants, I now fully understood the revelation that God revealed to me in 1993, during the time that my daughter Thuy-Trang and her husband, Huy were on God's assignment. She is the first winner in front of God, the winner of speaking out the truth and took actions without fear.

The Lord said, "Singing and teaching are special anointings that God has assigned to those as special callings in the chosen ones by God. These anointings manifest slowly in their life; and these anointings will be fully manifested when a person lives the life of holiness. The singing means speaking out the things that are right according to God commandments, and taking actions. The teaching means to teach others to follow the matters a person brought to the light."

These anointings manifest slowly in their life, and means in our life we must constantly seek God for direction, He will teach us one piece at a time, and these pieces will add up. These anointings will be fully manifested when a person lives in the life of holiness means the anointing is only fully manifested when a person completely surrenders his free will to God. When a person surrenders his free will to God, God will be the one that is running his life, everything in his life is for God. When a person is live in the anointing, the Spirit of God will help him to discern from the actions, words of good or evil. My daughter was on God's assignment so she was able to discern that she did not like one contestant, at the same time the Lord revealed to me a woman carrying a charm, and the charm here is the spirit of the devil.

Thuy-Trang works full time as a high school mathematics: Teenagers are very difficult to teach, they are very stiff necked, and they are symbolic of people in the world. Mathematics is the subject that a very small percent like; this symbolizes how people in the world act toward God. Good high school teachers show responsibility and love for their children representing God toward the world and taking care of us. It is a form of anointing that God bestowed upon those chosen ones to destroy the devil spirit that manifest in those that give their free will him.

Thuy-Trang and Huy are singers, they are both in the choir, singing at the wedding, and competing in the singing talent contest: Singing is a gift from God. With this gift Thuy-Trang and Huy directly serve God through their voices to glorify, and worship Him by singing in the church. They also indirectly serve God through others by singing in the wedding. The Sacrament of Matrimony is obeying God to bring more people in the world, to build the kingdom of God in heaven.

Thuy-Trang challenged the world by participating in the singing talent contest: Through her, God destroys the devil, by bringing his works from darkness to the light, to save His people.

Huy's full time job selling life insurance for the large insurance company: Full time is symbolic of spending most of his time on his job; life insurance represents the security and protection, large insurance company is symbolic of the kingdom of God. Huy is the coordinator for the band: the band symbolizes chanting the praise of hymns to glorify God; the coordinator of the band is taking responsibility for God's kingdom.

Huy's withdrawing from the contest with the decision not to compete with his wife and grooming her for the contest means, as the children of God, we must not compete against each other, but must help each other in love from the heart.

Her long, black dress is symbolic of the darkness of God within a person who live in the anointing. Gloves keep hands clean, it symbolizes God's anointing is not mixed in the devil works. Flowers represent victory. The audience in shocked silence symbolizes works belonging to the devil was destroyed.

God has called Thuy-Trang and her husband Huy to be a model in this assignment; and from this assignment, God then explained to you how to understand His teaching from the old testament. God's commandments are in the new testament, and are hidden in the stories in the old testament. We must really seek God for understanding his words.

The Devil Fights Against God's Anointing

April 23, 1997,1:50 a.m. In my dream I saw a dark bridge over a canyon. This canyon was full of wild bushes. One side of the canyon had something growing out from these wild bushes like an electric base, and on the top it had a dinning room light bulb. This light bulb was only lit at the wire inside, with a little fire around the wire. The fire only flashed around the wire when the voice of a person spoke. If no voice spoke, the light was off. By seeing this light flashing, I knew that it belonged to the devil.

Also in the dream, I saw father Cinnamon. Due to Vietnamese communists torturing him in the education camp, the devil took over his mind, and he turned his back to God. When I saw Father Cinnamon's soul around the light and the light on, I kept saying, "In Jesus' name, get away from me, in Jesus' name, get away from me." I was fighting and very frightened in the dream. I then woke up with my stomach burning, I felt like inside my stomach a big fireball was rolling, and it shot out and burned my entire body. I thought that was the devil doing this to me. I got up and took holy water and sprayed my entire apartment, and prayed asking the Lord to deliver me from the devil.

I called to my God, "My Lord, my God, the Father, the Lord Jesus, the Holy Spirit, deliver me from the devil, to protect me." I then called to my beloved mother, "Mother, the Blessed Virgin, pray to the Lord for me, protect me, send your angels to fight for me." I then called holy angels and saints, "Saint Michael the archangel, all the holy angels and saints, pray to the Lord God for me."

I then said, "Father, I offer this suffering to You Father, in Jesus' name. I ask You Father to remove it, Father destroy it." The Father wants me to record what I went through so others can understand how the devil's power can make people physically sick. The Father told me that it was not from the devil, He only let me feel a very small piece of the attack so I can experience and explain to other people.

Father said to me, "No devil can touch your body, I just showed you how the power of devil can attack people's bodies very heavily." I said, "Jesus, fight them for me. Jesus, Lord, I fight them Lord, You are in me, You fight them for me. Holy Lord, fight them for me. Jesus in Your name Lord, fight them for me. Saint Michael the archangel, fight them for me. Mother fight them for me; all the holy angels and saints fight them for me."

The Lord Jesus said, "That was the word charm that you spoke about in the anointing section. The charm I revealed to you some time ago. Through a charm, the devil can attack people a lot worse than what you are experiencing. The charm is the one that sends out from the devil to those that believe channeling will effect their bodies one way or another. Title this revelation for Me 'The Charm Belongs to Lucifer' "

At this point the pain was a little less burning than it had been, but I still hurt. I said to the Lord, "Lord, You dictated to me what You want to reveal. I know that after You finish revealing to me, I will no longer be burning like I was and I am now." Then the Lord Jesus said, "I promise you this will happen again to you, for you are my sister; this power is not from the devil; this power is from Me, the Lord your God, your Savior as well as your brother. But if this thing happens to others, then it will be from the devil, Lucifer is his original name. The one that My Father cast down to earth." I then said, "Father, Father, Father, wonderful Father, Powerful Father, all the power is in Your hand Father. Lord Jesus, the Father has given to you all the power to execute upon those that are disobedient to the Father's commandments. Lord, Lord, when will this go away; it is getting a little better, but it still burns like a fireball inside my stomach. Lord, Jesus, the blood that You shed at the Calvary, pour up on me, Oh, Lord, the innocent blood, the holy blood, the powerful blood that nothing can fight back."

I then said to the Father, "Father, I offer this suffering to you completely, Father, through Jesus, in his name, Your begotten Son, through the work of the Holy Spirit for the mission that You called me to be Your servant to be complete in victory before I go home to heaven. Amen, amen."

The Lord said, "I am going to explain the dream. The canyon is symbolic of the trap that the devil has built. The bridge over the canyon is symbolic of luxury things in the world. The wild bushes of trees that filled the canyon is symbolic of words coming out from people's mouth, their words sound of protection and care, but they contain the devil in their hearts and in their actions; and this is in the world now. These are from the presidents of the nations down to the teenagers, it seems sweet, it seems to be services, it seems caring of the Lord; but in truth their hearts want for their luxury, for their own benefits, and for the benefit of their flesh. The light bulb flashing is symbolic of the power from the devil put into their thoughts, their heat. When you saw the light flashing you knew that belonged to the devil in the soul of those completely turning their back to God. These souls are being chained in the darkness of the devil. Because you knew that was devil, you said to them 'get away from me, in Jesus' name' means the power of the Father coming through Me is in you, so you are able to discern what comes from the devil, and the devil has to obey what you say to him. The light off means he obeyed what you said and left. But you saw the light on again, and you then rebuked the devil again, he then was gone is symbolic of the devil's persistence to attack people."

In my vision, I saw one of the meetings that I attended. The priests examined some materials that did not belong to God, then the Lord said, "These people enjoy seeing these things more than you did at the at the time you were away from me." God then said to me, "I now release you from the most painful experience that you have to embrace. You were willing to do that for my sake to save other souls."

The power of God was upon me. I stretched my entire body and I prayed, " Our Father, who art in heaven, hallowed be Thy name; Your kingdom come; Your will be done on earth as it is in heaven. Give us this day our daily bread; and forgive us our trespasses as we forgive those who trespass against us; and lead us not into temptation, but deliver us from evil. Lord, deliver me from the devil. Lord I claim Psalm fifty seven, deliver me from the devil; I claim Psalm ninety one for Your protection; I claim Psalm seventy for the Divine help; I claim Psalms forty two and forty three of Your presence within me. I claim all of them ready now, Lord." The Lord said, "The devil can not attack you; this is I, the Lord your God testing you, allowing you to be pained so I can teach you and other people. When I say teach you that I mean reveal to you, you then speak about what you had to go through at the time that I was revealing to you. To teach people, tell them the true heart of the devil, so they will not be trapped by Lucifer." The Lord said to me, "Get the anointing oil to smear on you; I will anoint you with healing power from my right hand." I got up and took the blessed anointment holy oil and put on my self.

2:35: a.m. April 23, 1997. For almost an hour I embraced the suffering, fighting something that the Lord bestowed upon me; through me, he revealed to others the devil's trap, the charm.

I said, "Father, I thank you Lord for using me as an instrument for Your works. I thank you the Lord Jesus that You are in me and with me, and carry me through this journey. I thank you Holy Spirit that assisted me through this fighting. I thank you my beloved Blessed Virgin Mother that suffered with me by watching me embrace the suffering for the works of God. I thank you to all holy angels and saints pleading to the Lord for me that God's will to be done through me as His servant."

I then said, "Lord, my soul is wounded, I ask you to heal my soul, and heal it quickly, Lord." Jesus the Lord said to me, " It is over, you will not hurt any more."

I feel better at my stomach, but my body was very weak from my soul fighting and suffering."

The Lord Jesus told me, "Place this revelation in the anointing section, title it "The devil fighting against God's anointing"

Every one of us receives some anointing at the time of being baptized, the devil then fights against God's anointing by performing some kind of trick when people come to them at the time the devil uses humans for channeling.

When a person has faith in God, the holy water will destroy the devil's power for him/her.

The Lord said, "To restore their souls back to God, they must go to God with sincere heart, reject everything that belongs to the devil. Every material that the devil uses for human channeling must be burned or thrown in the trash. When returning to God, they can not hold on to anything that was given to them through a person using channeling. The power of the devil attaches to these materials that were given to them; they are called "charms". This includes crystal readings, psychics, palm readers, anything that tries to predict the future or find out the past, or tries to understand others people's hearts and actions."

Finally the Lord restored me back to normal, he then said to me, "From your willingness to embrace this suffering, I am giving you a blessing, a mighty blessing, this blessing is in action for My work to be done to complete the Father's will."

The power, anointing of God was bestowed upon each one of us, depending the calling that God calls to serve Him. Normally God bestows upon us through our wisdom. He guides us through our thoughts, feelings toward other people, things, or subject matter of every day in our daily life.

The devil uses his own power to lie to people going against God's anointing by predicting the future, giving them the past of what happened to them and others; giving them the future of other people's actions or hearts that has something relating to them either in work, friendship, family, or anything that they want to know. The devil then gives to them, the lying spirit knows the past, he gave them the past to gain the future, but they do not know the future; it is all with the purpose to destroy their souls and bodies.

Christian Denied God's Anointing

April 23, 1997. During the night, in my vision I saw rain coming down at the side of the Cathedral of Saint Andrew. The street in front of the cathedral, on the parking lot across from the cathedral, on the ground of the parking behind the rectory and side gate was flooded with clear water running from the rain.

Today the Rector of the Cathedral of Saint Andrew was at the Conference at the Diocese, the 12:05 p.m. daily mass was celebrated by the substitute priests.

At 11:35 a.m I entered the Church. No one was in the church, and I was happy that I was alone with God in His temple. Because I was the only one in the church, I said out loud while I was walking up to the seat, "Lord, God, Jesus, I am alone with You." I then felt that the Father and the Holy Spirit were also at the sanctuary, I continued, "Father, Lord Jesus, Holy Spirit, I am here alone with you....... Lord, if any one walks in the door, you stop me from talking out loud......" Then the Lord Jesus said to me, "I want you to copy down what I am going to say." I took an envelope from the pew, and with my pen out, He said, "There will not be many people here today, because their favorite priest is not here today. These people that come here do not come for Me, the Lord their God, the God of all creations. Many of them came for the priests. They are holding on to something that will destroy their souls and their bodies."

The Lord continued, "You are here with Me, and you will be with Me forever. I assure you, those who come here for Me will continue to come; those not here not for Me, will no longer be here."

I said, "Lord, I want to see them here with their hearts for You; but if they are here without their hearts, I would rather for them not to be here."

Jesus the Lord asked me, "What did you just say? Put it down in writing, I will reveal to you to night."

5:17 p.m. April 23, 1997. During my later afternoon devotion, I was physically fighting the enemy spirits, and the Lord carried me to sleep. Even while I was asleep, I was still fighting. While I was fighting, I also dreamed that I saw a woman walking out the side gate at the Cathedral of Saint Andrew. She wore a coat dress that buttoned in the front. The bottom part of the dress was open so I saw inside her left leg at her knee, the dress was khaki color, her skin was tan, with the strap of her purse around her right shoulder. I knew that her tan is symbolic of labor to the devil, because her purse represents her focus on materials. This symbolizes those who come to church regularly, but not from their hearts for God. Her about to go out of the gate represents God purifying His church. I said, "In Jesus I rebuke you; get away from here, this is not the place for you to be here." I then saw over the gate, up high in the air was a little boy face with his neck, no body, very white skin, black hair, his mouth was open little, and some of his teeth were missing. The areas where his teeth were lost was dark. He turned his head to the right side and looked at the top of the rectory. I knew this is symbolic of the spirit of the devil's tongues, counterfeit of the spirit of God, and I rebuked the devil. During the time I was rebuking the devil in my dream, my physical head was fighting the spirit of the enemies. Still in the dream, I petitioned the Lord for protection, and to constantly deliver me from the spirit of the devil.

I then got up and continued to pray, the Lord said, "The teaching of the proper way to come to the Lord is needed at all times, but church authorities lack responsibility to lead God's people."

I said, "Father, it is not easy for me here, Jesus the Lord, this is not easy for me here, the Holy Spirit, it is not easy for me here, that I have to physically and spiritually go through to fight them, even though I know Jesus the Lord, my God, the good Lord is in me and fighting for me."

The Lord said, "The anointing that I bestowed upon a person at the time of his baptism is no longer there in the church. Because the lack of proper teaching from the church leaders and responsible people have been chosen in the church to shepherd my people; almost every single one of them wanted to hear sweet things from the mouth, they fear to speak the truth, they love to please man. How dangerous it is that they are leading My people to go down instead of going up and entering heaven."

The Lord continued, "The false prophets, and preachers claim the anointing, but actually God's anointing is not there; their tongues are being used by the devil to lie to my people. The innocents have been trapped by the devil. Christians these days come to the church because of favorite priests, or favorite preachers, not because they love God, or for the love of God. There hearts are empty for God."

In my vision I saw the outside of the tabernacle at the Cathedral of Saint Andrew. While I saw the tabernacle, the Lord said, "I am here being painfully watching people come here. Repent, if not I will leave this place." I then saw the Ark of Covenant that the Lord instructed Moses have the children of Israel build; a heavy square cubic with four shoulder carriers; the people who carried the Ark were invisible, but I saw Joshua in the shadow standing next to it. He was the one that gave out the instruction of how to cross the river. They then were at the bank of the Jordan river, at first they looked to me for where to cross the river. It then changed that they just arrived at the river bank, they departed and arrived at the same spot. The Lord then said to me, "The book of Joshua, chapter 5 verse 7."

"It was the children whom he raised up in their stead whom Joshua circumcised, for these were yet with foreskins, not having been circumcised on the journey."

The Lord continued, "In this revelation, I the Lord will select my people, and I will lead them to the land filled with milk and honey. I separate goats from the sheep. I am the good shepherd, I will lead my sheep, and my sheep recognized my voice and they follow me; no one can snap them out of my hands. The goats will no longer be in my presence."

The Lord Jesus means this generation means the words He commanded me a few weeks before I left from San Diego, California to Little Rock, Arkansas. God is separating this world into two groups, one that gives themselves to God, He will lead them to eternal life in heaven. The group that holds their hearts away from God, God then is no longer with them; meaning that the devil has power over them.

A few weeks before I actually moved, the Lord told me, " I told Abraham to move out of his father's house, and promised him that I would make him the father of many nations. Now, I tell you to move out of the house that I provided for you, to the land of milk and honey; Little Rock, Arkansas." And "I send you to reopen the St. John Seminary, to bring young men from all over the word to this location. I will teach them through the professors."

Saint John is the only one who stood at the foot of the Cross, a single disciple who had no fear of the Pharisees; the Lord Jesus loved him and revealed Himself to Saint John.

This means the Lord Jesus wants more priests who will obey the vow of celibacy, completely surrendering their lives to God, live a life of holiness, being always obedient to His commandments, without fear of anyone or anything. They would completely depend on God, as they lead His people and help them focus on a spiritual life in preparation for eternal life in Heaven.

Saint John's Seminary in Little Rock was closed almost thirty years ago, and now the Lord Jesus wants it to reopen. God used Saint John's seminary as substance to revealed of God's Church on earth is dead, for they were not in accordance with the way God established them in the beginning.

God has said to Moses, Soon you will be at rest with your father, and then this people will take to rendering wanton worship to the strange gods among whom they will live in the land they are about to enter. They will forsake me and break the covenant which I have made with them. At that time my anger will flare up against them; I will forsake them and hide my face from them, so that they will become a prey to be devoured, and many evils and troubles will befall them. At that time they will indeed say, 'Is it not because our God is not among us that these evils have befallen us? Yet I will be hiding my face from them at that time only because of all the evil they have done in turning to other gods.

–Deuteronomy 31: 16-18.

The Center of Spiritual Life Is God's Anointing

12:37 a.m. April 24, 1997. I my dream I was on the main road Q 15 road in Vietnam. I then was on the road that went directly to the church. Close to the open market, I passed behind a former classmate who was about to enter her home. I then returned to Q 15 road. Walking home late at night alone, to my right all the businesses were closed, except one has a small door was open and I saw a little light inside the business; inside this store was the woman who just won the contest, she was now practicing more of her singing, then she got tired and stopped.

I was thinking that my classmate went to school for a long time. The woman singing won the contest; both women have a good future. But I am here because I left school early, I then went back for a short time, and quit. I am now walking on the street alone at night; I have nothing with me, and no future.

When I got up, the Lord said, "Your walking alone on the street while the other houses on the side of the street were closed; another winning the contest, and singing, some woman classmate just passed by you; your being there without fear in the dark is symbolic of who you are now."

The Lord meant the calling to do His work, He is within me when I speak out the truth; I have no fear while the church authorities are in a safe place singing and others just passed by me. I was a hero in the dream, a hero without a future in this world.

The Lord continued, "That is what you are now thinking of yourself, but your future is in heaven." I said, "Lord, You are within me on the street, that's why I have no fear." The Lord said, "She was singing after the contest, but she got tired after practice, and she stopped and it ended the dream, means when your mouth is open in the public." The Lord revealed when the time comes, through me, He will speak to the public, and those church leaders will stop signing the hymns that they have been singing for a long time. Those hymns please man, not God, and it protects their earthly crowns.

The Lord continued, "They will not like what you say, but they have no power over Me. People will see the truth of what you say, they will agree with you and follow Me through you. The emptiness in the hearts of the church leaders now is exposed to the public." In my vision I saw the naked boy climbing the ladder into the room to take a shower that I saw in the dream few night ago.

After the dream I was on Q 15 road, I then dreamed I was in the long hall of a house, the model of this house is the same model of the house that I lived in Moccasin, San Diego. In the front side of the house was my dad. My father's room had no door, my mother's room did have a door. On the back side of the house, across the hall from my dad's room was another room. That door was closed and my room was the room next to the door that was closed, and my room's door was wide open with the light on.

My parent were asleep, but I was still awake in the hall going to the kitchen. As I passed the dining room , my father woke up from sleep, and was walking behind me to the kitchen. I was flipping the light switch up and down and I said to my father, "Something is wrong with the light." I then saw heavy rain just starting to come in the two kitchen windows, so I closed these windows. My father was quiet and returned to his room.

I then got of out the kitchen and went into the hall to go to my room, but I did not enter my room yet. I heard my mother say "The roof of the house was ripped off." I stepped over to my mother's door, and I saw the ceiling of the room was very dark; I thought it was tornadoes. I needed to notify the city, but I wanted to make sure before I called them. I was on my way out the front door to check the roof, and about to make the turn at the corner, when I saw water dripping around one huge and a few small wooden beams on the ceiling of the dinning room.

I then saw outside the front door was dark. Some large trees were a little further outside the front door. I saw the owner of the neighbor's house next to the kitchen, in front of his house in the dark, looking at his roof. His roof was dark, and I knew that his roof was ripped off, too.

The Lord said, "The house dream is opposite the Q 15 road dream. The father in the dream is symbolic of God; you were calling God 'Daddy', and you also call Him 'father' even though that you do not understand the dream yet, it is the relationship you have with the Father; what you spoke out was from the Father giving to you. The mother in the house is symbolic of the church and it's authorities, she was in the room, the top of the room was dark; her crying out loud that the tornadoes ripped off the roof off her house is symbolic of God in action upon the world."

While I was listening to the Lord and pleading for interpretation, the words came out of my thoughts very fast; I thought that the enemy spirit was attacking me. I prayed for protection, but the Lord was silent and helped me to discern that it was not enemy, but that it was from Him. I then asked Him, "Lord, what is happening to me, I am very hyper?" I then realized that God just poured out a different kind of anointing that I have not experienced before; to teach me, and at the same time He teaches me, He let me go through the experience and reveal messages to me. I then said, "Lord, You are teaching me something here. You are allowing me to feel the tension."

In my vision I saw the scene of Sunday, April 20, 1997, after I entered the Cathedral of Saint Andrew. I saw Father Scott sitting at the end of the last pew in the church, with Deacon Gary standing at the side of the pew next to him. As I walked passed by them, I paused and said, "The Lord Jesus is in the middle of the two of you." Father Scott said to me, "Go pray." I then was giggling in my heart and walked to my seat, because I have been coming to church six days a week since January 12, 1997. He had never said anything in form of authority to me; instead, he was a very soft and listening person; but I already knew that he was struggling for the calling that God just had me deliver to him.

In my vision I saw inside the Cathedral of Saint Andrew was empty, the Lord Jesus asked me, "What do you see?" I replied, "Lord, there is only me at the center aisle, walking up the altar, at the foot of the sanctuary." He then asked me, "Where are the priests and the congregation?" I replied, "Lord, I do not know where are they; now is the middle of the night, they probably are resting at their homes." He then asked me, "Why you are not resting like them?" I replied, "Jesus, why are You asking me all these questions? You know that I am awake, and I am talking to You now. I could talk to you and sleep at the same time, but You chose for me to stay awake and talk to You." He continued, "That is what I showed you in the dream; while other people are asleep and you were walking back and forth to the kitchen, to your room in the hall way."

The Lord Jesus continued, "The Father said to me 'I saw her in the kitchen and trying to fix the light.' "

The Lord Jesus then poured unto me another anointing that made me giggle like little children, I had to turn off the tape recorder, and I said to Him, "Lord, what are you doing here? Lord, if there is any enemy attacking me, please put them away, help me here." The Lord then said to me, "That was how you felt deep in your heart, when the priest said to you 'go pray.' "

Jesus the Lord then said to me, "I am God, I can change a person's feeling very quickly like that, when a person dwells within Me, when a person gives herself to me." As I recorded that, the Lord was speaking of the anointing of sensitivity. The Lord corrected me, "Sensitivity to the Spirit of God, not the spirit of the devil."

The Lord Jesus then asked me, "What do you see on the dining room ceiling?" In my vision I saw the ceiling in the dream, I replied, "Lord, there are some wooden beams, they are big, they are huge, and the water is dripping down from above." He then asked me, "Do you see any water on the floor?" I replied, "Lord, there is no water on the floor, I only saw water dripping from above." He asked, "How can your mother say the roof of the house was ripped off by the tornadoes in the dark, but you saw rain coming down through the ceiling above the dining room with the light?" I responded, "Lord, I do not know. You are the one who gave me this dream. You know the interpretation, I do not know. I am waiting for You to give me the interpretation, Jesus, my Lord. I think, You are very funny today, I think that You are happy today." Jesus the Lord said, "Victory is in my hands, and I have a broom, now I can sweep off all the dirt on the ground." God continued, "Do not give the interpretation on what I just said. Let the readers seek Me, I will then give them interpretation according to their anointing."

Then in my vision, I saw the hall was empty, I then saw the light on the kitchen ceiling, Jesus the Lord asked me, "Why were you trying to fix the light bulb while you can not reach it?" Jesus is very funny today, I responded to Him, "Lord, I did not fix the light bulb, I turned the switch, and the light did not come on like it normally does, it was a very little light and not full bright. So I turned up the switch up and down to find out what was happen to the light." He then said, "You are not going to fix that light bulb, let me do the fixing." He then asked me, "Why did you close the kitchen windows and did not let the rain come in?" I replied, "Lord, I did not want the kitchen to be wet, so I closed the windows." He said, "You are preventing Me from doing my works." I did not realized that I prevented the Lord. The Lord said, "Many times you said 'Lord, how come you are too slow? Lord, how come it does not happen? Lord, why it is not this and that? That means you are preventing me from doing my works through you."

There was some conversation that I did not record, and the Lord shared with Me His happiness. I feel that was so private, so asked the Lord by not recording it. He then gave me permission to not record it. He then said, "Because I love you, you are my little sister. I showed to you that I am the living God; the only difference is you can not see Me like another human person, but I am real, I am the living God. You have been suffering with me for so long, so I showed you how happy it is when you are with Me."

The Lord said, "I do not want you to give them any more than what I have given in "The Anointing" section, let the readers come to Me; I will then give them their share." The Lord Jesus meant that if any one wants the anointing to be manifested, they must seek Him.

God has instructed me not to give the interpretation; I obeyed Him; but I give you the scriptures that He gave me afterward. All these words and questions, and surprised anointing on me are symbolism. In the last two dreams and the Lord speaking, the scriptures below contain everything about God's anointing.

The Coming of Jesus' Hour. *Now there were some Greeks among those who had come up to worship at the feast. They come to Philip, who was from Bethsaida in Galilee, and asked him, "Sir, we would like to see Jesus,*

"Philip went and told Andrew; then Andrew and Philip went and told Jesus. Jesus answered them, "The hour has come for the Son of Man to be glorified. Amen, amen, I say to you, unless a grain of wheat falls to the ground and dies, it remains just a grain of wheat; but if it dies, it produces much fruit. Whoever loves his life loses it, and whoever hates his life in this world will preserve it for eternal life. Whoever serves me must follow me, and where I am, there also will my servant be. The Father will honor whoever serves me.

–John 12: 20-27

22

GOD REVEALED SPIRITUAL AND NATURAL CREATION

Mystery of the Holy Trinity

At 7:25 a.m., April 20, 1997 during my morning devotion, in my vision I saw a globe of bright light at the center of the altar at the time consecration. It was in front of the priest's chest. The Lord Jesus said, "The Holy Spirit is in this very white host. He is the very same one with the Father and Me in the Blessed Sacrament. This is a mystery that the church does not know, because I have blinded their eyes."

He continued, " The Holy Spirit does what I tell Him to do. There are three generations: The Father, the Son, and the Holy Spirit. The Father is above Me, I am above the Holy Spirit, but there is only one God. The Father created Me, then He created the Holy Spirit. This is a mystery, God was, God is, and God will never end." The power is equal, because I do what the Father tells me to do, and the Holy Spirit does what the Father and I tell Him to do."

The Eternal Father, the Creator of heaven and earth: He is the master of the universe. The Eternal Father is the one who has 'all power' over heaven and earth. The Lord Jesus, the only son of the Eternal Father, is the Second Person in the Holy Trinity, or Christ. He was the one who was obedient to the Father unto death on the Cross. The Eternal Father gave the power over heaven and earth unto Him. He is the Only Judge who judges the living and the dead.

The Holy Spirit, the third Person in the Holy Trinity, is the one who receives power from the Eternal Father and the Son and puts it into action. The Holy Trinity has no beginning or end.

In all my writing I normally call the Eternal Father by the name "Father", and in some cases I call Him "Holy Father." And for the Lord Jesus, when I refer to Him as fully man, I call Him "my beloved brother, older brother, or brother." But when I refer to Him as the

The Holy Trinity is 'only' Almighty God, the One that give life and take away life, the One can pour out thunder, storms, rain, floods, and snow. Even when the devil damages people from earthquakes, bomb blasts, wars, murders and other horrors, the devil has to get permission from the Eternal Father before he can take action. And he can only damage those who disobey God and refuse to convert to God, daily exam and repent.

The Eternal Father gave everything in heaven and earth to His only Son, the Lord Jesus, because Jesus the Lord obeyed the Father to die on the Cross. The Holy Spirit receives orders and power from the Father and the Son and puts them in action. When this power becomes action, it is equally powerful to the Father and the Son, because He does what the Father and the Son tell Him.

On the human level, the Blessed Virgin Mary, a lowly young girl, completely obeyed and trusted in God. She was steadfast in faith and humble, she became the mother of our fully man Lord Jesus.

I am a sinner, a convert, and lowly. I obey God without understanding, and humble myself accepting this mission, as God's Instrument. God does His work through me. Therefore, everything that God assigned to me that comes with His power will be completed. Each one of others, God is calling you to convert. If you completely obey all God's commandments, and fear Him, then the things that God calls you to do will come with His power and will be accomplished

Evolution Is God's Creation Revelation

1:34 p.m., November 30, 1996, the feast of Saint Andrew: In my vision, behind the last pew of the right middle section of the Good Shepherd Church, I saw a human body wearing a pair of dark women's pants and shirt, bending over at the waist. Her stomach and her thighs made a ninety degree angle. At first her face resembled that of a Filipino woman I had seen in church, then she changed into one of the Vietnamese women who pushes her husband's wheelchair into church almost every day, while she sits in the pew in front of him. I then saw the face of the Filipino woman again.

Next I saw something that looked like a big monkey standing up, high above the ground. He was about the size of a human, and in front of him was a cave formed with cloud-like dust. Around the monkey and the cave was open air. I then heard the Lord God's voice say to me, "At the beginning, people had no houses or tents, they lived in caves or hutches."

I saw the woman's feet again, and then I saw her lower back with her bottom down to her feet; her thighs and lower legs were monkey-like, and covered with hair. Her feet were also like those of a monkey, with long nails on the floor. I then saw her body, still in same bent-over position, with both her hands on her back, wrists joined on top of her waist. These hands were now monkey-like and covered with hair. I then saw her face—it still had

Asian features—and I saw the lower part of her spine changing from human to monkey, and back into human form again. She stood exactly as a monkey stands, up straight, her left side facing the sanctuary. Then the Lord said to me, "I reveal to you the process of evolution. From the beginning of the creation of the earth in the Book of Genesis, it took several more years."

I, Mariette Do-Nguyen, understand that the Lord's reference to several years symbolizes the seven days of creation in the Book of Genesis. God's time is not the same our time.

The Lord Jesus shepherds His Church through the Holy Father; He speaks through the Holy Father. (The Lord Jesus as fully God, the Holy Father symbolic of the Eternal Father, the Lord Jesus and the Holy Father symbolic of the Father and the Son in One). And through me, He will reveal the seven days of creation to the world, showing how our physical bodies were created as well as our souls. Souls come from God and shall return to God, if they enter into Heaven. Through transformation of our spiritual and physical selves, and through living a life of holiness, souls will enter Heaven, then our physical bodies will be resurrected on the last day and come to Heaven. But the other way—if physical bodies live in sin on this earth, and refuse to convert and repent—those souls will not return to God; instead they will be punished in a place we call hell, and their bodies will be eternally dead.

7:27a.m., August 22, 1997: The Lord Jesus dictated to me, "I then heard a voice come down from Heaven saying, I recognized this voice as the voice of the Almighty Eternal Father. This voice is the same as in the teachings of Jesus, as fully man and fully God. This voice will never end. This voice is in the hearts and minds of those who love God with all their hearts, their minds, their souls, their strength, and their body; as fully man Jesus fulfilled all of these. Because I am a Vessel to the Holy Trinity, I follow in the footsteps of Jesus as fully man. On the feast of the Holy Trinity, through the church, I proceeded to the altar of God; immediately behind me was a priest, Father Scott. He was also the one at the end of the procession to God's altar."

During the night, August 22, 1997: In my dream I entered a very large house. Soon after that I crossed a street, and entered a high dry dirt garden. My duty is to come to this garden every day. The path I take has no tree; [I mean the tree was there, but I did not see it], I only saw dry dirt, and I do the work alone. But today, when I stepped inside the garden, I saw a priest wearing civilian clothes; he was a Navy Chaplain, his rank is major, his name is "Peace." In Vietnamese it means "Binh An." When I saw him, I asked him to help me. I then went to a spot in the garden, where there was a pile of long boards, about four feet from the side of the garden where I had just entered. There was no gate. I took three pieces of wood; two were square, but I realized that there was not enough to build a shelter, so I took two pieces of flat wood to make the top, and the two square boards served as pillars.

I returned with my supplies to where the priest stood. When he saw the wood in my hands, he understood that I wanted to build a shelter. There was a huge, tall tree at the side of the garden. This tree has been here for ages. The Priest told me, as he and I walked toward the foot of the tree "This is the best spot to build a shelter. The tree will provide the shade." After he said this too, I knew that the sun would not shine on the shelter, because the tree would protect it from the harsh rays.

While he was helping me build the shelter I remembered that there was also another person who came here to visit every day. I looked toward the side of the garden that had the tree, at the street, on a lower level, and saw a booth with some people around selling and buying. Because my property was a lot higher than their property, this booth leaned toward the dirt side of my garden. I then saw a heavy woman, standing at the lower level, next to the booth. She looked up at me and spoke to me. I looked at her and saw a lot of makeup on her face; she was very ugly. I recognized her as the one who stopped at the garden every day, then left.

This priest was in love with me. He was taking charge, building this shelter by himself. I was standing there looking at him while he was working. As the same time he was building the shelter, he was hugging and kissing me, holding my body very tight.

He had not finished the shelter yet, but it was time for him to return to his station. Both of us left the garden, walking on the road I had crossed; we turned right, passing the booths on the lower level to our right. The road was now bigger than before, and past the lower property was a large, cathedral-roofed building; the house I had originally entered and quickly left was across the street from the garden.

I followed the priest as he went into this cathedral-roofed hall; at the entrance to the large hall was a restroom. He entered it, standing in the middle of the doorway, his back inside the restroom, facing me, while I was standing next to a column, at the middle of the hall's entrance. Because this priest was so in love with me, even though he needed to use the restroom, he did not want to leave me.

We then were back on the road; he was on his way to his station, and I was going to the building I had entered earlier, to finish my task. While I was walking way from him, I looked back and thought, "He is a Navy chaplain, with the rank of Captain; he makes three thousand dollars each month. It would be very secure if I married him; with his income and the profits from my work, I would be very secure.

I then was inside the house. It was dark and dirty, and the rear part connected to the back yard where there were some dead animals. One was laid in between the concrete foundation and the dirt, a dead rabbit, his skin was peeled back. It was sticking to the side of my trouser leg, head down, and bottom up; I tried to get it off, but it smeared into the fabric.

I then entered a classroom; it had three sections; one at the center, two at both sides, making two aisles. The furniture in the center section was made of high, long wood tables; they were built with strong hard wood, but the iron chairs were weak. I took a seat at the third table in the center section. The two side sections also contained long tables, but they were lower and I could not recognize what they were made from.

This was a law class. The teacher was teaching and students in the center section sat in the front two rows. The other two sides held more students, but they did not pay attention to the teacher, they were looking away from him, toward the center section.

I had a piece of invisible card-stock paper with me, but I needed the second visible one to fill out. I turned to my right, and saw a long book, like a telephone message notebook that had a metal spring. I thought there might be some card-stock paper in there, but when I opened it, I saw that it was the Roman Catholic Church officials directory. I turned to my left, and saw a person close to the end of the side section with a book, like the file index card-stock paper I was looking for; I asked him for one sheet. He handed the book to me, and I took a single sheet from it.

The Lord said to me, "In the Book of Genesis, at the beginning of creation, the garden of Eden is the garden in the dream. Adam's body, formed from clay is the house you first entered. The garden is the earth. Eve is represented by those who sell stuff from the booths below the foot of the garden. The Navy Chaplain who helped you build the shelter is the "Word" that made flesh. The tree in the garden in the dream is the Holy Trinity. The prohibited tree in the Garden of Eden is God's commandments (that every one can not disobey). Building the shelter in the garden is building the kingdom of God. The Priest hugging and kissing you is symbolic of the relationship between God and His priests (the lower case "p" priests are symbolic of those who obey all God's commandments). The Priest entering the restroom and still looking at you is symbolic of Jesus, the fully man sacrificing himself, offering Himself to the Father to cleanse the sins of many. Looking at you means that He loves His priests. When you were thinking of marriage to him, his three thousand plus your profits making you secure means that God is the provider, and He will keep His promise when man obeys all His commandments and generates good deeds. The teacher in the class is symbolic of the Lord Jesus, the Almighty God in a human body bringing humans to the Eternal Father. Those seated in the center section were Roman Catholic Church leaders (Roman Catholic is symbolic of all leaders of God's only Church). Those at the left side are those who came to learn God's words, but not to retain it in their hearts, without action. The one who had card-stock paper represents those who caused division in the Church. When you asked him to give you a sheet, he did as you asked, meaning they will be lost in the battle."

The Lord continued, "In the previous dream you saw six different kinds of animals. This was referring to the creation of the earth. The boa constrictor evolved from the worms. Worms can grow legs, develop caterpillars with many legs, worms also grow two legs and two arms, or two legs. The snake is Lucifer. Snakes can grow into fishes. When the worms grow two legs and two arms, they changed into bears, lions, deer, and camels. You saw the bear change into monkey and enter the house. The evolution from monkey to man was the process of God's creation. In the Book of Genesis, God blew into clay the breath of life, and it became a living man." At the time the woman's egg and man's semen join in one, God breathes a soul into it, and from that time the life of the human grows in the womb.

This is when the Lord created the animals. He gave them spirits and their spirits are a form of supernatural power. For those worms to change into creatures with two legs and two arms, God created them to have souls. In the process, they evolved into monkeys and finally into man. For those animals having two legs and two hands, when they give birth, their offspring is in their image after exiting the birth carnal. But for those who gave birth in the form of eggs which later hatch and bear their image, these creatures not do not have souls."

The Lord continued, "The soul comes from God at the time of conception. The spirit comes together with the souls. God gives free will to every creature."

The Lord continued, "I revealed to you that there was a gap between God and man; this gap will never close because Eve did not repent. The gap between God and His priests was closed, because Peter repented."

The Lord continued, "The people inside the large house where the priest used the restroom are symbolic of God's Church. Through the Church, humans learn God's commandments, and if they obey them they become God's priests in Heaven. (The Lord means that when a person follows in Jesus's footsteps, they will become a priest in Heaven. This includes both priests and laity.) Those outside the building at the booth are those following in Eve's footsteps; they are disobedient to God's commandments, and they refuse to convert and repent. Those who came to the garden without doing the work are those in the house with dead animals, sticking to your trouser leg; they are those who have two faces, serving God and mammon."

The Lord said to me, "Mariette, I love you. You are the first one whom I hugged and kissed in the garden, next to the tree. You are who proceeded to the altar for others to follow behind you. You and the Blessed Virgin Mary are two lowly servants of God. Obey God in faith."

August 22, 1997: Today I served as the Eucharistic Minister; I had to dress properly to enter God's sanctuary. Therefore before I got dressed to go to the church I asked the Blessed Virgin Mother, "Mother, what should I wear today?" I then took out my purple - violet dress and put it on.

On my way to the church, I went to the Little Rock Diocese to drop off an envelope for Most Reverend Andrew, and others envelopes in the mail box. These envelopes contained information from last Sunday's mass, and Monday's communion services. When I entered the Diocese building I saw that the inside door, at my left, to the Bishop's office was open. I looked, and there was the Most Reverend walking out of his office, into the hall, toward where I was standing. I walked toward him, raising the envelope; at the same time, I said, "Bishop, this is for you. I saw the Father. God protects us. I am working on God's creation, souls, and evolution; I have a note in here for you." I am not sure that he heard everything I said, but he replied, "All right."

When I entered the church I found out that today is the feast of the Queenship of the Virgin Mary; and this morning, God revealed to me things about His creation of the earth and evolution. I knew God would take some kind of action today.

The reading in the mass was from part of the Book of Genesis Chapter 3, read by a dark -skinned woman, and the Gospel was part of Luke Chapter 1, "Mary Visits Elizabeth." read by Father Scott.

I then was in the sanctuary to serve the Lord; after Father Scott gave me the consecrated hosts' cup, the Lord told me, "Go and stand in the middle." The Lord meant that I should stand at the center of the lowest step of the sanctuary, to serve Him by giving His body to others.

Father Scott was standing more to the left side of the sanctuary; I then stood close to the center; but during the time I was giving the holy Eucharist, the Lord keep pushing my right arm toward the left; I had to move my feet twice to my left, which was exactly at the center.

The first person came forward, then the second person came out from the third pew, stood up at the aisle, but did not move forward. She let a few others come before her. When Father Scott finished giving the Eucharist to the people in his line, my line still had three more people. Now I knew what the Lord was telling me. The Lord had revealed to me that one of them was possessed by the devil. When this person stood in front of me, I raised up the Lord's body, I said to him, "This is the body of Christ." But when I placed it in his hand, in my thoughts I repeated a few times, "Get away from me, you have no place around me, get away from me."

While I was walking toward the tabernacle, with a ciborium containing the body of the Lord Jesus, I said, "Lord Jesus, I love You. Father I love You. Holy Spirit I love You." Now the ciborium was inside the tabernacle, I said to the Lord out loud in voice, "Lord Jesus, through Your power, I protect Your body." When I returned to my seat the Lord said to me, "Today, the words of God have been fulfilled."

The mass was over and it was time for me to clean up the altar. The Lord told me, "You get the key from the tabernacle first." As He said this, I walked to the tabernacle, took the key, and held it in my hands at my chest. The Lord then said, "Now you bring the empty ciborium and cup and put them away first." I took the empty ciborium and the cup along with the tabernacle key, and placed them inside the cabinet, and locked it. I said to the Lord, "The Blessed Sacrament and ciborium are being protected." He then told me, "Go get the water bowl, towel, wine and water bottles before you turn off the candles." I went to the altar, and brought in what the Lord told me to bring. I found that the water bowl was not the same one that was normally used. The Lord told me, "Put the soap inside the bowl, and wash the inside very thoroughly before washing the outside." I did as He said. He then told me, "On your way to your former seat to get your purse, turn out one candle, genuflect at the center, directly toward the tabernacle, in front of the altar, then turn off another candle." I did as He instructed.

I then gathered my purse and an envelope containing the information from last Sunday's mass, and Monday's communion services. This envelope was for Father Scott, who at this time was in the sanctuary. He crossed by me as I genuflected at the front of the altar. The Lord told me, "Go put the book on the table at the back of the church." I did as He said. While I was on the way to put the book away, I saw the Cathedral secretary inside the sacristy at the back of the church. I was not sure if the Lord wanted me to directly hand the envelope to Father Scott or to his secretary. I then gave the envelope to the cathedral secretary.

These envelopes are symbolic of rewards and punishments. Turning off the last candle was symbolic of the soul of each individual as left he physical body.

In this revelation, God revealed His creation in the Book of Genesis in chapters one and two. The seven days of creation in the first chapter is God's seven days, not seven earthly days. God's time is different from human time. God created heaven before He created the earth. He created heaven and the earth with his words. The words He spoke to create the world were in the spiritual realm, and then manifested in the natural world that we live in. Then the natural living creatures evolved into different body forms, as well other things, such as mountains, rivers, plants etc.

In the second chapter of the Book of Genesis, the "Second Story of Creation", God revealed the spiritual life, the soul and spirit. Because we can not see the soul and spirit, God used natural substance as symbolism to reveal His creation of man.

Everyone in this world is born in human choice, except the Lord Jesus who was born by God's decision. (God's decision means the Blessed Virgin Mary conceived the Lord Jesus as fully man through the Power of God.) Because Jesus is perfect God, during the time He was on earth, His body contained no sin. Therefore, He rose from the dead in less than three days. These three days are symbolic of the Holy Trinity. In the old testament the Holy Trinity was also revealed in symbolism as three columns. (Exodus chapter twenty seven, "Court of the dwelling" is full with numbers of symbolism. In verses fourteen and fifteen, God revealed the road of the Holy Trinity for man to follow.) The fully man Lord Jesus was resurrected from the dead, his body became a glorified body. His glorified body can be in different forms when He chooses to appear to man. Different forms of symbolism exist in the spiritual realm, but it must always be according to the holy scriptures.

We are born by human choice in generations, all of us are sinners. Our physical bodies will depart from the earth one day, sooner or later. But our souls will live eternally. In order for our soul to reenter heaven, all our sins must be forgiven by God, and by one another. Our iniquities must be completed purged by God. When a person refuses to convert, with daily exam and repentance, he contains grave sin(s). As long as he contains grave sin he is under the devil's power.

When he breathes his last breath, his soul will leave his body, and will continue to be chained in the darkness of the devil. His soul will be eternally chained with anger, hatred, and violence, his soul will act in the devil's work to destroy others souls, and that even includes his own family members.   In the revelation God called it "a gap" between God and man because Eve never converted.

Every good work will result in a good deed to benefit the soul, and every sin will result in iniquities. Because God is a just God, we have to pay the damage in the form when we are still on earth; but if we do not pay on earth enough, we will pay in purgatory. The more sin a person commits, the more iniquities result, with more to pay. When a person breathes the last breath with minor sin(s); he will have to enter purgatory for his soul to be purified before he enters heaven. While his soul is in purgatory, he can pray for those on earth, but he can not pray to God for his iniquities to be purged. He has to depend on people in the world to pray and do services in the form of good works on his behalf.

All the souls returning to heaven will inherit the resurrection of the body, through the Lord Jesus as fully man, the first fruit of resurrection. When souls entered heaven, their bodies were destroyed underground, or were cremated. God will give a new body for this soul, that is a glorified body, this body and soul will live eternally with God. The glorified bodies belong to the spiritual realm, and it is higher than the earthly realm. There is a veil between the supernatural and natural. The natural eyes can not see the glorified bodies, but they can see us. I know because I have seen the Lord Jesus, the Eternal Father in the Lord Jesus' image, and the Blessed Virgin Mother at least several times. This is also the way that Bernadette, the three children at Fatima, and people at Lavang saw the Blessed Virgin Mother. This spiritual veil only can be opened by God.

October 25, 1998; the Catholic thirty Sunday of ordinary time. Before the Holy Eucharist celebration, while I was sitting at the end of the third pew, the Eternal Father told me, "The meaning of the words 'first fruit of resurrection is that there was no one resurrected from the dead before Jesus. The people with no sin who left the world physically before Jesus were resurrected after Jesus' resurrection. For less than three days

Jesus remained in the tomb, he was with them in a place that had no evil or light." The Eternal Father revealed a mortal body but not a soul. That includes those who have minor sins with iniquities purged in purgatory; that plus Elija's physical body lifted up by the wind.

And behold, the veil of the sanctuary was torn in two from top to bottom. The earth quaked, rock were split, tombs were opened, and the bodies of many saints who had fallen asleep were raised.

–Matthew 27:51-52

Fossil Wormholes

The San Diego Union Tribune, Thursday October 1, 1998, an article "Fossil wormholes could shed light on evolution of life on Earth," indicated, "By almost doubling the age at which the first multicelled animals appeared on Earth of complicated life forms out of what had been a menagerie of single-celled creatures did not happen suddenly about 540 million years ago, in what biologists call the Cambrian explosion - considered the 'Big Bang' of evolution."......"The traces of wormholes, in rocks that dated to about 1.1 billion years ago, were found in central India, in beds of sandstone that formed when that area was covered by a shallow sea." ...." The new find, if confirmed, would almost double the known age of the first appearance of animals with more than one cell and with differentiated body structures.

Rebuild My Church Divine Mission

(The Lord Jesus gave this name to Mariette)

P.O. Box 261550 ✦ San Diego, CA 92196-1550

October 1, 1998

Professor Adolf Seilacher
Geology Department, Yale University
P.O. Box 208109
New Haven, Connecticut 06520-8109

Sent via facsimile number (203) 432-3134 and U.S. Mail
Re: God's Revelation regarding Evolution of Life on Earth

Dear Professor Seilacher,
I saw your name in the San Diego Union Tribune, October 1, 1998 issue, in the article "Fossil wormholes could shed light on evolution of life on earth."

The evolution of life on earth has been debated for generations. I assure you that human physical life was evolved from worms. I ask you to be patient with me, to read the enclosed revelations from God and you will accomplished your research of the "Evolution of life on earth." I'm also sending "God Summons Mariette Do-Nguyen," so you will understand my life's work.

When I received this revelation, I believed it, and I also mailed it to over 270 Catholic high-ranking leaders as the Lord instructed me; but they may think that I was nuts. For you as researchers, do not give up on me. If you give up on me, your research for life on earth will fail. Through me, God revealed to the world the process of His creation of the living creatures. Each living creature has three parts: physical body, soul and spirit (spirit is the soul's power to work through physical body.)

This is the part of how He created man:

"The Lord said, "In the previous dream you saw six different kinds of animals. This was referring to the creation of the earth. The boa constrictor evolved from the worms. Worms can grow legs, develop into caterpillars with many legs, worms also grow two legs and two arms, or two legs. The snake is Lucifer. Snakes can grow into fishes. When the worms grow two legs and two arms, they change into bears, lions, deer, and camels. You saw the bear change into a monkey and enter the house. The evolution from monkey to man was the process of God's creation. In the Book of Genesis, God blew into clay the breath of life, and it became a living man."

If you need more information or have any questions, please contact me.

Sincerely in Christ Jesus,

Mariette Do-Nguyen

More Meaning of Genesis Chapter 2

The river is symbolic of the Lord Jesus, the Son of God, the source of creation. The river divides and becomes four branches: Pishon, Gihon, Tigris and Euphrates; the four branches and the four sections of land they wind through describe the Spirit of the Son of living God as the source of creation, working through God's predestined chosen ones. The

Spirit of the Son of the Living God later manifested through Noah, the Ark and the contents brought into the Ark. Genesis chapter seven is a historical prophetic revelation to explain of Genesis chapter two, and the future coming in a different symbolism.

In the New Testament, the Book of Revelation, chapter four, God revealed more details of before and after the creation of the earth. This is another revelation of chapter two of Genesis, in spirit as symbolism. The action of the river and its four branches winding through the Garden of Eden is symbolic of the Spirit of God working through predestined chosen ones. The animals in Genesis chapter two are not the natural animals, but the spirit of animals. God created animal spirit souls with less heavenly substance than man; therefore, their spirits are also less wise than man. Eve is symbolic of the Spirit of God in the human soul. After man's physical body was born, Eve transformed into a human spirit. The human spirit is the power of the soul. The supernatural power must always accompany it, either parallel to or immediately before the thought, word, or action of the human physical body.

The Meaning of Chapter Three of Genesis

October 28, 1998. After my afternoon devotion I fell asleep. In my sleep the Lord told me, "Move the altar to the inside front corner of the living room, so you can burn the log at the fireplace." At the time the Lord told me this, my altar covered the fire place. Then I woke up and took out a center piece, a six-pound Duraflame log. (The full box had nine pieces, two pieces were burned last Christmas, with the remaining seven pieces enclosed in the unsealed box.) The box was sitting in the front corner of the living room, it was wide open by the Lord few days ago. I moved the altar to the front corner, opened the fireplace, and set the log on the altar. I set two candle holders with burning candles, one at each end of the log. Then I took a bottle of holy oil from the right foot of the Lord Jesus' statue, pouring oil on my right index finger, I made a sign of the cross at the center top of the log, and prayed, "Blessed Mother and all the Holy angels pray with me." I then pleaded to the Lord, "The Father, the Son, and the Holy Spirit, this log is symbolic of me. I pray for your glory, protection and power within me. Father, I ask you to bless the mission you entrusted to me with prosperity, converting people to Jesus, and to let Jesus bring them to you, to build the kingdom of heaven." I then repeated this petition three more times, making two more crosses on top at each end of the log, and one in the center front of the log. I lifted up the log started to burn at both ends at the same time, and I placed it in the fireplace. I then turned on the gas to help it light quicker. It took about four hours for the log to burn completely.

The next day the Blessed Mother told me, "You have to explain the burning of the log, otherwise they will think you are nuts. When you burned that log, it was symbolic of the death to yourself, the death of yourself for God to work through you. This is the action you saw in the dream you saw before, a long log was burning out side, in front of the Church parking lot. Moses saw burning bushes, the bush was symbolic of him, he did not have the action of burning the bush. But you actually burned the log."

When the log is burning in the fireplace, the Father said to me, " The woman in Genesis chapter three. ('I will put enmity between you and the woman, and between your offspring and hers. She will strike your head with her heel, while you strike at his heel.') This woman is symbolic of Jesus, not Blessed Mary as people understand. Chapter two of Genesis revealed the creation of souls. Adam was made from clay, and Adam is symbolic of the soul. I created Eve from Adam, and she took an apple and ate, and gave to Adam, and he ate it. Eve is the spirit of the human soul. Spirit is power coming from the soul, when the spirit does evil, it will affect the soul. The Garden of Eden is symbolic of the spiritual realm of the world. This is also the spiritual realm of each nation, group, and individual. The spirit of the soul works through the physical body, each one has the free will to plant their garden, what they plant they will harvest. Planting evil will harvest punishment, planting good works in front of God will reap the reward of eternal life, and blessings on earth. The soul came from heaven, but when Adam (soul) committed sin, when the soul disobeyed God, it is under the power of the devil. Adam and Eve were naked, this nakedness is symbolic of not having God's protection, they will not inherit the heavenly tree of life. The tree of life is eternal life in heaven. Man's returning to dirt is being chained in the darkness of the devil. The cherubim are symbolic of God's holy angels. Fire is symbolic of human souls that are being protected by God. This is the revelation of the spiritual life."

Meaning of Part of Chapter Four, Book of Genesis

October 31, 1998. At the end of my late afternoon devotion, the Father told me, "Read Genesis chapter four, I will give you the meaning of it." I then read from verse one to the end of verse sixteen." Then the Father said to me, "Stop there and I will tell you what it means. This chapter has to do with human memory. When a person promises to call someone that night, and he does not call, that is a sin. For other people it will be hard for them to understand this meaning, but not for you. You already know Alzheimer's disease, the soul and spirit within the physical body. Cain was a tiller of the soil. The soil is described by Cain as the dirt, and dirt is symbolic of the physical body. Abel became a keeper of flocks, and flocks are described by Abel as living creatures, so Abel is symbolic of spirit. When Cain killed Abel, it means man's committing grave sins will become spiritual death or cause him to be chained in the darkness of the devil. When a person's spiritual life dies, he will no longer produce any good dead for his soul and souls of other. When no good deeds are produced, this person has cut himself off from God."

The Alzheimer disease in this revelation is symbolic of man turning his back to God;

forgetting that God is the Creator of heaven and the earth and His covenant with man. Everything comes from Him, without Him, man can do nothing. It has led to disobedience of His commandments, a lack of prayer and keeping heart pure. Flocks are symbolic of living creatures, and souls and spirits are alive forever and ever. Soil is symbolic of the physical body and that one day when the soul separates from the body, the physical body will die.

The following prayer is described of earthly offering:

The Pharisee took up his position and spoke this prayer to himself, 'O God, I thank you that I am not like the rest of humanity - greedy, dishonest, adulterous - or even like this tax collector. I fast twice a week, and I pay tithes on my whole income.

– Luke 18: 11-12

Rebuild My Church Divine Mission

(The Lord Jesus gave this name to Mariette)

P.O. Box 261550 ✦ San Diego, CA 92196-1550

November 21, 1997

Ambassador Le Van Bang
Vietnamese Ambassador to the United States

God and Man Relationship

Dear Ambassador Bang,

Thank you for your letter of November 12, 1997. By receiving your letter, I have God's blessing, and through me this blessing will come to the country of Vietnam.

The Creator of Heaven and Earth created the universal church at the time He created the world. When He created people, He gave them His law, called "God's commandments." Some may call it the "Ten Commandments." But people were disobedient to His commandments. He then sent His only Son down to earth, in the form of a human body, the Son of the most high living God, in a fully man's body. He is fully God and fully man. Through the power of the Holy Spirit (the third Person in the Holy Trinity), the fully man was conceived by the Blessed Virgin Mary and He was named Jesus. This name, given by God, it means the "savior of the world," and some may call Him Messiah. At no time before or after the birth of the fully man Jesus did the Blessed Mary have a sexual relationship with any man. Her virginity has two meanings, spiritual and physical.

Jesus began His ministry when He was thirty years old. During His three years ministry He raised people from the dead, cured crippled limbs, healed people from many diseases, and taught the world about God the Father, Creator of Heaven and Earth's commandments.

Because He came down to save the world from corruption, He paid the price for our salvation with His own body and blood. Therefore, He suffered and was persecuted by His own people, the Pharisees and Scribes. They turned Him over to the Roman Emperor's government, who crucified Him to death on the Cross. Less than three days later His body was raised from the dead, and He then ascended to Heaven.

After He ascended to Heaven, through God's power, His apostles continued His mission, which is the Roman Catholic Universal Church.

The Roman Catholic Church is the Church that complies with all God's commandments. The Church's leaders must obey all His commandments and the Holy Father's teachings.   Even though they are Church leaders, they are also human, and they are being attacked by the devil and his spiritual offspring. The Holy Father is the leader of this Holy Catholic Church; his responsibility is to lead his people. He bestows this responsibility upon his cardinals, archbishops and bishops of each diocese. When any of these high-ranking leaders violate any of the Church's rules, the Church's highest committee will warn them to correct their actions. If they refuse to change, he will then excommunicate them from the Church.

I did not choose this calling; God is the One who chose me, I just obey Him. This calling has cost me everything of my life in this world. I must completely obey God and please Him. I must say and do exactly what He asks of me, and everything I say or I do comes through His power.

The Roman Catholic Church has strict rules. It teaches people to obey God's commandments, to do good and reject evil. Therefore, I assure you that the Roman Catholic Church leaders are the ones who teach people to make the world a better place to live, and a place in which to build the kingdom of Heaven.

But they need tools, such as properties on which to build churches and schools, seminaries, and halls; the Church's estate comes from the first fruit of its congregations. Their congregations need to retain what they earn so they can contribute to the Church.

They also need freedom to organize groups where people can learn God's commandments, through bulletins, magazines, and preaching; all of these for the purpose of teaching obedience to God. Through obedience to God, they become good people, so the country of Vietnam can become a better place to live, and a place in which to build the kingdom of Heaven.

Enclosed are copies of a letter and its English translation from Mr. Vu Gia Tham, Acting Chair of the Bureau of Religious Affairs, dated February 2, 1996, and my letter to former Prime Minister Vo Van Kiet, dated September 29, 1994.

I ask you to forward them to Prime Minister Le Van Khai and high-ranking Vietnamese governments officials. As the same time, I ask you, Prime Minster Khai, and Vietnamese government officials and lawmakers, to assist me with these two letters and your letter of November 12, 1997, to implement the real meaning of the words "freedom of religion in Vietnam."

I hope that I may hear from you. I continue to pray for everyone in Vietnam.

Sincerely In Christ Jesus,

Mariette Do-Nguyen,
Ambassador to the Holy Trinity

The Lord had me send this letter to Ambassador Bang, He also used this letter as natural substance to reveal in spirit. Therefore, the majority of the words in this letter are symbolism, such as the Roman Catholic church is symbolic of God's Church on earth; the Holy Father is symbolic of the Eternal Father, and Vietnam is symbolic of the world. The ambassador is symbolic of the Lord Jesus being the ambassador to the Eternal Father.

The name of the Ambassador means the following: In this revelation, the first name "Bang" is Cong Bang, in English it means justice. "Bang" is symbolic that God is a just God. The middle name "Van" is van minh, in English it means moving forward with a fashion within God's commandment. The last name "Le" is le la, in English it means a person moving from one location to another with good attention to sweeping, the hidden meaning is the proclaim the Gospel purification of the world.

Souls Originating

July 11, 1997; In my dream, I saw myself running in a garden behind a high fence. While I was running, I turned to my right to look behind and there was a man chasing me. When I saw this man, I knew that my trousers were just only up to my thighs. I did not want this man to see my bottom, I was trying to pull my trousers up, but the waist of the trousers were too tight to get around my bottom. I pulled harder. I then saw the unlocked wooden door, I quickly opened the door and entered inside to hide from the man.

The man who was chasing me was about fifty years old. He had a strong, light-colored skin, and was wearing shorts and a shirt. He was walking in the way of chasing behind me, like a father ordering a child to do something, but the child stubbornly refused to obey the order; then the father forced the child by threatening to hit him, and the child quickly ran to perform the duty.

Then I was inside a village. Behind me was the dark tunnel that I just passed, and facing the small village, immediately to my left, was a shelter made of dry palm branches. This shelter belonged to a Vietnamese family who had many children. The woman of the house was on the front porch, the mother. She was over fifty years old, sitting on a bench with her little child sitting to her left. In the front wall was a large window.

I was standing on the road in front of her shelter, facing her. She said to me, "My husband and I have already eaten. My children are about to eat dinner, if you want to come in and eat with them." While she said this to me, I saw through the dry palm branches wall her children in the dark shadow form, sitting on the bamboo bed, waiting to eat dinner.

I then was walking forward in this small village. The land to my right was filled with small shelters. At the end of the road were three beasts turning their heads away from the village, these beasts were big like elephants, and the head of each of these beasts had several short, big horns. When I saw these beasts from behind, I was fighting and turned around to my right. After I turned to my right, I saw in the middle of the village a few of the trailer houses, set above the ground.

When I got up the Lord Jesus said to me, "The village you saw in the dream is the earth. The three beasts are symbolic of those who want to be like God. The trailer homes at the center are symbolic of false preachers, and false churches. The woman who sat in front of the shelter with a child is symbolic of God's Church on earth, the child is symbolic of the mission that God entrusted to you. The children in the house about to eat dinner are symbolic of church leaders. Your being in the dream is symbolic of those who do not know God or do not believe in God."

I said to the Lord, "Why you are using me as symbolic of those who are do not know God or believe in God?"

The Lord said to me, "Because you were naked before you came down to earth." God meant in the dream that my bottom was naked before I was entered the village.

I asked, "Lord, why did You show me that I was naked outside the door."

The Lord said, "Because your soul did not believe in God before God sent your soul down to earth."

I asked, "Lord, why did You say my soul?"

The Lord said, "I said 'your soul', meaning I spoke directly to those who do not believe in God or do not know God." In this revelation, God put me in the shoes of those do not know God or do not believe in God, and through me, He revealed to them.

I asked, "Lord, I have a very personal question that I want to clarify. My soul, the soul in the body of Mariette laid here, who was I before You sent me into this body, Your temple now?"

The Lord said, "You are the one that the Father loves the most, and you were very stubborn like Peter before the Father sent you down to the world."

I asked, "Why was I stubborn like Peter before the Father sent me down to the world? Why did You choose me while I was stubborn?"

The Lord said, "I chose you before the Father created you. I knew you would be stubborn, and you would be converted. From that stubbornness the church leaders and other people can not persuade you."

Since the Lord revealed this, I confessed: Before the calling was manifested, I was very stubborn. In the family or as the business woman, I made decisions on my own and stuck with my decisions. I took action, and no one could convince me. But after the mission manifested, I became a soft noodle that the Lord could bend any He wants, and the Lord keeps this stubbornness to apply to other people who are disobedient to Him. I then asked, "Lord, who was the man running behind me and saw me naked, while I was trying to pull my trousers up and run into that door?" The Lord said, "The man running behind you is symbolic of the Father, at the time He sent you to earth. Because of your stubbornness, the Father gave you pants that you would have trouble pulling up, so you would feel shame in heaven and run down to earth. You did not want to go down to the earth." The Lord meant that my stubbornness was to the point that God gave me no choice. He pushed me against the wall so that I had to obey Him."

I now testify that a few years before God took me out completely from the work force to make money, to start work on His mission in the year 1994. In the two years God pushed me against the wall, I could not resist His power. Every place I turned, I was stuck. I then had to obey Him. Now my stubbornness is transferred to the mission. God is the only one I obey. This obedience is through God's revelations to me, God's commandments. Church authorities, leaders or any other who comes to me with things that are not in God's commandments will have no chance to succeed over me.

The Lord said to me, "You have to be careful, do not mix up the nakedness of those who do not believe in God and the nakedness of your stubbornness. They are two different nakedness. Stubborn nakedness of those who believe in God is just stubbornness. Nakedness of those who do not believe in God have been taken over by the devil, they do not believe in God. They are the one third of the angels who were cast out from heaven with Lucifer." The Lord means that when God sends souls down to earth, one third of the souls will not believe in God, or will sin against God and refuse conversion. The souls of this one third of the human race will not return to heaven. God knows everything, He knew everyone of us before He created us, He also knows where each one of us will be after the earthly life. The Lord Jesus said, "You did not choose me, I chose you." The Lord said to me, "People will ask you, if God already knows what will happen, what good is it for Him to tell you to warn them? How you will answer them?"

I responded, "Lord, I do not know. You are the one who gives me all of this. I just copy down what You tell me to say." In my vision I saw the woman who sat in front of the shelter in the dream. He said, "The woman said 'my husband and I have already eaten, and my children are about to eat inside the house, if you want to eat, go inside and eat with them. This means God has love and mercy, God gave those who do not believe in God a chance to convert. If they convert, they will be added to the book of life. There are two sets of books, one is the book of life for those will return to heaven, and the other set of books are for those who will not return to heaven. If people choose to convert, their names will be changed from the book of those who will not return to heaven, and be listed in the book of life. At the same time, God gives people free will. If those whose names are in the book of life sin against God and refuse to convert, daily exam and repent, I will cross their names from the book of life and list them in the book with those who will not return to heaven."

Let me explain why God sends souls down to earth and lets them perish. Earth is the temporary place for souls to lean and earn good deeds for eternal life in heavenly. God respected the free will of each soul, to chose to obey Him and return to heaven, or to disobeyed His commandments and be under the power of the devil and lost their eternal life. Except for very small percent of pre-destined chosen one; even thought, God still leads to the way to chosen Him.

The dark tunnel is symbolic of souls in transition before being in the womb of a woman, and of being born again. Being born again is being reformed a person life from the heart, and through Sacrament of baptism. The Lord Jesus said in John Gospel 3: 5 "Amen, amen, I say to you, no one can enter the kingdom of God without being born of water and Spirit." The dry palm branch shelter is symbolic of God's Church on earth is dry out His present The high trailer homes are symbolic of those depending on human power; the Lord Jesus' iron rod will crush them down. Other shelters along the road to the left side of the road are symbolic of religious people worshipping idols.

Three beasts were big, and their bottom was like an elephant's. The elephant is big, there is no individual who can fight back an elephant; this is symbolic of the devil's spirit controlling people. Human power can not fight that back. The horns on their heads are symbolic of the devil using human minds to damage others, those that want to be like God through their works. This mean do not believe that everything must come from God; but, instead their human wisdom and power.

In the Book of Revelation, chapter 13, God revealed to Saint John of the two beasts. In this dream God revealed to me three beasts; these three beasts mean a counterfeit of God. Man wants to be like God in some area of their works such as researches such as clone human or animals to replaced God's creation.

Any individual who commits mortal sin, or grave sin is under the power of the devil's spirit. The devil uses his body to take actions against God commandments, like Judas. Any individual committing vernal sin is endured by the devil's offspring spirits.

My seeing the back of the three beasts symbolic of the mission which God entrusted to me. I have to spiritual battle, and fighting against the devil and his offspring spirits hiding under people minds and actions; but the Spirit of the Almighty God, the Holy Trinity is within me is fighting for me.

Immaculate Conception Revelation

December 8, 1998. The Catholics reserve today to honor "The Immaculate Conception of the Blessed Virgin Mother". The Gospel reading was Genesis 3:9-15. When this Gospel was read on this day, the feast of Immaculate Conception of the Blessed Mother," I thought of the time I started learning the Bible in the year1994. My understanding was this holy scripture was a prophecy of the devil, to be under the Blessed Virgin Mother's feet; and at the same time I also questioned why they wrote the word "hers" and "he, his heel" in the verse, "I will put enmity between you and the woman, and between your offspring and hers; He will strike at your head while you strike at his heel." Genesis 3:15.

But within the past month, the Father told me that the woman in this holy scriptures verse is symbolic of the Lord Jesus, the Son of God. Then The Lord brought me the dream I saw on December 6, 1998. My legs were stuck on the back of a marine, he was naked from the waist up, and I fought against him; and the Holy Spirit told me that I will grow mature. In the December 6, 1998 revelation, the man was wearing pants and naked from his waist up symbolic of the two beats, enemy spirits. The Lord God just opened to me that through this dream, God revealed that I inherited from the Lord Jesus for the devil to be under my feet, but now I am still young, so my legs caught at his back.

While the young priest at the Good Shepherd Church gave the homily, the Holy Spirit separated me from the natural to be with the Holy Trinity in spirit. He said to me, "You already know that Adam is symbolic of the soul's disobedience to God, and Eve is the spirit of man, the power of the soul. All souls come out of heaven without sin. During the time babies are in their mother's wombs, they do not commit any sin. Your Blessed Mother obeyed God from the time she came out of her mother's womb, that is Immaculate Conception. She told you to use what ever is available, they are come from the Father. In your life you do not hold any hatred against anyone. You inherited your Blessed Mother's estate; her estate includes the immaculate conception." While the Lord was still talking I quickly interrupted, "Lord, I am a sinner." But the Lord continued talking, "And the Father gave you immunity, everything you did wrong before has been wiped off." I interrupted, "Lord, I am a sinner." But He continued talking, "You then surrendered your life to God, and the Father accepted." I said, "Lord, I am a sinner."

Chapter two of the book of Genesis reveals God creating the soul and spirit of man. God used Adam as a symbol of the soul and Eve as symbolic of the spirit. Chapter three of Genesis also reveals of man disobeying God's commandment. He used the same name Adam for the soul and Eve for spirit.   The soul is in the physical body, and the spirit is power coming from the soul. The human spirit alone is not strong enough to think or take any action; therefore, in Genesis chapter three, Eve or the spirit of man disobeyed God, committing sin. Once Eve committed the sin of disobeying God, it affected Adam or the soul. The Blessed Virgin Mother appearing to Bernadette at Lourdes was an action to reveal the Genesis chapter three, her immaculate conception, also immaculate conception of man.

In the New Testament the Lord Jesus also said that we must become like a little child to receive eternal life. The word 'child' means innocent in mind and heart. The Sacrament of Baptism came from John the Baptist calling people to reform their lives, pouring the natural water on their head as symbolic of cleansing of sins. The Lord Jesus taught the apostles, and sent them out to call people to reform their lives. Therefore, in chapter three of Genesis it is not the real Adam who committed sin and man inherited it. Instead, man inherited the disobedience to God sin from our ancestors.

December 10, 1998. I got up at night and the Holy Spirit told me, "Your writing of the immaculate conception is incomplete. You need to tell them who their ancestors are. Their ancestors are their parents and grandparents. It is about the iniquities. The father eat salty foods and his sons will be thirsty. There are some people who question why they have to inherited the original sin, that they did not commit? When parents do not live the life of righteous to teach their children, and instead live a life of sinfulness, their children will inherit iniquities. In the same way, if the parents are wealthy, children will inherit a large estate. If parents are poor, children will received nothing. If the parents are in debt, the children will have to pay the creditors."

> *For I, the LORD, your God, am a jealous God, inflicting punishment for*
> *their fathers' wickedness on the children of those who hate me, down to*

the third and fourth generation; but bestowing mercy down to the thousandth generation, on the children of those who love me and keep my commandments.

–Exodus 20: 5

God's Spirit, Human's Spirits, and the Devil's Spirit

August 17, 1997: before I fell asleep at night, in my devotion; I said, "Father, I have a question for you. Jesus the Lord, I have a question for the Father. Holy Spirit, I have a question for the Father. Please help me to ask the Father." I continued, "Father, my question is I love you." The Blessed Virgin Mother said, "Mariette, that is not the question. If you want to ask the Father, you must phrase it in question form." I replied to my beloved Blessed Mother, "The Father knows what I was asking Him." She then said to me, "The Lord is teaching you something new; just listen." I then said to my beloved Blessed Mother, "Forgive me. I did not know the question, so I just said, 'the Father knows what I was asking Him.'"

During the night, August 18, 1997: I got up during the night, physically fighting against the enemy spirits. As I was struggling suffering in agony, I said to the Lord, "Father, Lord Jesus, Holy Spirit; I do not complain, but last night I was suffering for two hours, fighting against the devil; tonight I am fighting again. Jesus the Lord, You fight the devil and his offspring for me. Holy Spirit, you fight for me. Father, please, You fight the enemies for me, Father, do not give them any more permission." While I was saying this, in my vision, I saw some people and places; I also saw the Lord Jesus hanging on the cross, a crown of thorns on His head, cutting His forehead, blood running down. His right hand was nailed to the cross, blood coming from His hand. I then saw the words the Father said to me at the Church, "Jesus is in you." I realized that Jesus is suffering, and I am sharing His suffering.

I then fell asleep. In my dream I was walking at the side of a low-level, long cathedral-roofed building, and said, "When I see, I will know." I then passed the corner of the house, and saw a woman kneeling in front of the house, wearing a dark, long dress, and a long, thick veil, with both her hands at her chest. I looked up and I saw the Blessed Virgin Mother up in the sky. Somehow she came down, closer to the earth, so I could see her face very clearly, I said, "Mother." As I saw the Blessed Mother, I knew the woman kneeling in front of the house was Bernadette. Facing up toward the sky, to my right, was the Blessed Virgin Mother, to my left, a little higher was Saint Joseph, sitting on his feet, talking to a young child, several years old, who was standing in front of him. Above, and behind him was a large mass of white clouds. Above the clouds the bright sun was shining down.

Crossing the front of this long, cathedral-roofed building was a long dike, and inside this dike was a large naked man, pushing his feet against the round clay fountain. I saw that his toenails were black; he raised his right hand up, and I saw his fingernails were black also.

Over this dike were some people flying colorful balloons. On the other side of the road, over the bridge, in the dike was a man falling down with his balloon; his balloon was deep and small like half of a can, dome top, orange in color.

Then I took the dirt road into a smaller road that was covered with a jungle-like tunnel. There was a man just coming out the gate of a house, to my left side, in front of me; he was wearing a white muddy robe. He seemed to be sexless, and there was a heavy chain attached to his right elbow that he dragged with him as he walked. When I saw him, I was a little afraid of that chain, so I jumped over it as I passed him.

On the same road, I saw another man in torn, dirty clothes. I did not like him but I had to stand in front of him in the middle of the road. I said, "Give me ten dollars." He did not have ten dollars. I then gave him a Vietnamese cone hat; this hat was made from palm branches. It was old, dirty, and had only one layer, with holes. He used this palm hat as his balloon to fly.

The Lord Jesus said, "Those who you saw up high in the sky were the Virgin Mother, Saint Joseph, and you." He continued, "The young child is symbolic of your spirit. You have been adopted into the Holy Family. Saint Joseph is your adopted Father. Behind him was a cloud, and above the cloud is the sun, which is symbolic of God the Almighty, the Holy Trinity. The people you saw flying at the lower level with balloons, the man in the dike fighting against the object with black toenails and long fingernails, the man falling down with his balloon into the dike; they are all symbolic of the human spirit. The one with black toenails and fingernails is symbolic of those chained in darkness. The one just out from the house with a chain is symbolic of enemy spirits. The one who took your ruined hat, and used it to fly represents enemy spirits who have the permission from the Father to damage those with mortal and or grave sins. These sins include intercourse outside of marriage in the church, unnatural sexual acts to satisfy the flesh, prevention of pregnancy, working at nuclear plants, homosexuality, murder, lawmakers who vote to pass laws against God's commandments, and many other mortal and grave sins."

The Lord said to me, "Mariette, put this dream below the one in which you saw the Father [on August 17, 1997]" He continued, "The human spirit is colorful. But when humans commit mortal/grave sins, they are going against God's commandments; they are dominated by the devil's spirit." The Lord continued, "Those who work at nuclear plants, they are unaware that they are committing a grave sin. When they receive the Holy Eucharist their souls become retarded. Those who are paying taxes that the governments uses to fund abortions are indirectly murdering these babies. They have committed a mortal sin. When I revealed to you 'If the world ends today, tomorrow, or within thirty days, ninety-nine percent of the people will go to the place which humans call it 'hell'. "

The man did not have ten dollars, I then gave him torn palm branches. Ten is symbolic of God's Ten Commandments that he disobeyed; the torn palm branches symbolizes permission to damage those who commit mortal or grave sins, or who disobey God's commandments.

All living creatures have a soul. God created man and animal souls out of a different substance, and different formula. Human souls have intelligent substance that the animals do not have.

The Devil's Spirit in the Church Sanctuary

August 18, 1997. I arrived at the Cathedral of Saint Andrew; while I was kneeling, I closed my eyes and prayed; I heard a sound at the side door, like someone opening it. This sound distracted me from focusing on God. As I was trying to re-focus, in spirit, I saw the devil's spirit formed in a heavy, dark smoke coming from a smith's hearth, covering the entire sanctuary, except for a little spot in front of the tabernacle. When I saw this, I could not pray any more, my body was physically being attacked by the supernatural power of the devil. I put my face on the back of the seat in front of me, and sat at the edge of the pew, saying repeatedly, "Father, help me, protect me. Lord Jesus help, protect me, Holy Spirit help, protect me. Get the devil out of this church! Today is the opposite of yesterday." I then heard the Archangel Michael said to me, "Go get the holy water that was blessed yesterday, and put it on yourself." While I heard these words, in my vision, I saw the scene of Father Scott standing next to the baptismal fountain, proclaiming "This is the faith of the Church."

I then lifted my head from the back of the seat with difficulty. The first thing I saw, was Liz standing at the altar, wearing a short sleeved white shirt, like a T-shirt, over it was a medium brown, two-strap robe. I then went to the front of the baptismal fountain, took the holy water, made the sign of the Cross in front of me, and smeared it all over my face, neck, hair, and hands, seeking the Lord for protection.

The Lord Jesus told me, "Copy this down, and add it to the letter you are going to send to the Holy Father, the church officials, and place it on My web site on Internet."

These are the cardinals and bishops that the Father told me to send the information to: Pope John Paul II; Cardinal Joseph, President of the Pontifical Bible Commission; Cardinal Bernardin, Prefect Congregation for Bishops.

Copies of complement to: Cardinal Bernard, Archbishop of Boston Diocese; Most Reverend Jorge, Prefect Congregation for the Divine Worship; Most Reverend Andrew, Bishop of Little Rock Diocese; Archbishop John, Archbishop of Miami Diocese; Archbishop William, Archbishop of San Francisco; Most Reverend Sam, Bishop of Alexandria Diocese; Most Reverend Henry, Bishop of Buffalo Diocese; Father Scott, Rector of Cathedral of Saint Andrew, Diocese of Little Rock.

I saw Liz approach the altar, to perform the communion service, while the devil's spirit still covered the sanctuary. My great fear was for the body of the Lord taken out of the tabernacle. I said, "Lord, what about Your body?" I meant, is the body of the Lord still hiding in the consecrated host, because the spirit of the devil is filling in the sanctuary. The Lord Jesus said to me, "At the time the host is inside your mouth, it will become My body; for others, just the host. They are receiving punishment." As the Lord finished saying this I remember the scriptures in 1 Corinthians.

I was very fearful, and carefully approached the altar to receive the host. When Liz placed a quarter of the priest's host in my hand. I stepped to the side, looking at the host, and said to the Lord, "Lord Jesus, I am receiving You," and I put the body of the Lord in my mouth.

When I got back to my pew, kneeling down, the Lord said to me, "You received My real body; others receive only that of the hosts."

August 19, 1997: Before the consecration, I prayed for the people to whom I am going to give the Eucharist today. I remember what the Lord told me yesterday, and I said, "Jesus Lord, I do not want to bring punishment to people." I meant the body of the Lord becoming just the host. The Lord said to me, " When they come to you, to receive Me with pure hearts, their souls will be nourished. When they come and receive Me with impure hearts, they will receive punishments. All this is taught by Saint Paul."

> *Therefore whoever eats the bread or drinks the cup of the Lord and is unworthy will have to answer for the body and blood of the Lord. A person should examine himself, and so eat the bread and drink the cup. For anyone who eats and drinks without discerning the body, eats and drinks judgment on himself. That is why many among you are ill and infirm, and a considerable number are dying. If we discerned ourselves, we would not be under judgment; but since we are judged by [the] Lord, we are being disciplined so that we may not be condemned along with the world.*
>
> *—1 Corinthians 11:27-33*

Later, in the day, during my devotion, in my vision, I saw that I was putting the ciborium in the tabernacle, and Father Scott gathered consecrated hosts in one ciborium, and the Lord said to me, "When you raise up the consecrated hosts in your hand, and say, 'This is the body of Christ,' at that time it is still My body; but at the time you place it in their hand or tongue, at that time it becomes just a host."

Generation to Generation Inherits God's Blessing

January 16, 1998; In the middle of the night the Lord Jesus said to me while I was asleep, "Your heart is focused on God, in everything you do you are asking Me. You do not want to do any thing wrong and have to fix it. The matter of your older son remaining in the house is the right thing, and that is from the Father. The matter of the priest in Arkansas who asked you to change his name and the name of another was wrong, and you did not do it. The matter of your buying food last night instead of cooking is okay. Your heart is focused in God."

Then there were a few other dreams during the night to support the meaning of the following dream.

In my dream I saw a bright light in the center of the sky, this light was shinning through and spreading like thick fire, like the vision where I saw the Spirit of God inside the Good Shepherd Blessed Sacrament Chapel, on January 14, 1998. In front of the spreading fire were three sets of numbers, each set had two digits: "02 04 05". These numbers were shinning down, upon the world.

Number zero in the front of each other numbers is symbolic of nothing before the next number; number two is symbolic of discernment; number four is symbolic of holiness; number five is symbolic of authority.

In this revelation God revealed, He has bestowed upon His people from generation to generation the grace of discernment, holiness, and power to prevail over the devil. Because all three were set in one line, it symbolizes these three paralleled; it will never be one without another; or more or less of one or another.

After this dream, I woke up, the Lord Jesus said to me, "The Father challenged you." I replied, "Jesus, I am very little, how could I face His challenge?"

Then morning came and the Lord Jesus explained to me, "Embrace your grand daughter in your bosom. She is the first one who opened the womb of the woman who married your older son, like Rebeka. God bestowed that on you and on your granddaughter, and a son from your older daughter. There will always be two: a male and a female in each generation who inherit God's grace. You receive this grace from Me, your brother Jesus. You will bestow it upon your son Chau, and your daughter TuAnh; the next generation will be on your grand daughter Madelene and a son from your oldest daughter. The two corpses your saw in the dream were the first sets of two witnesses in the Book of Revelation, John and you, the second will be your son and daughter, the third is your grand daughter Madelene and your first grandson."

Chau is a Vietnamese name; it has two meanings: precious jewelry or tears. In this revelation he is symbolic of priests. God revealed how He values his priests when they obey all God's commandments. Tuanh is also a Vietnamese name, it means beautiful. Madelene is symbolic of conversion, these two names are symbolic of nuns who are not receiving proper training and will convert. My first grandson is symbolic of church high-ranking officials and leaders. As of today, my first grandson has not been conceived. Because he has not been conceived yet, it means the high-ranking leaders and authorities either have no faith in God or very little faith, and do not depend on God, instead they are depending on human power.

Generation to Generation Iniquities Bounced

Iniquity is the result after a person commits a sin. It more or less depends upon the sin that he committed, such as murder, abortion, hatred, misleading to harm others or to benefit himself, false witness, trapping others, passing laws against God's commandments, and many more. Refer to Matthew 5:21-26 for the Lord Jesus teaching of iniquities.

April 21, 1997, 5:35 a.m.: In my dream I saw some handwriting. I said, "Lord, help me to remember all this." The Lord Jesus said, "I will dictate to you. This revelation is for the Anointing section."

Still in the same dream, I saw the child. He looked like my child. I saw his arm, but the arm was big like a strong adult arm. This arm had three big scars; these three scars covered over a half of his arm. His father showed to me that one of these scars was infected. The father was upset at me for not taking care of him properly at the time of surgery.

The dream then changed, I was in the open air, dialing a telephone, trying to call Dr. Button. In front of me was a telephone up in the air. It was square with a thick, hard, clear plastic large board. The top of it was full of the same kind plastic as the board. They were small and flat like fingers, but three times taller than adult fingers. The sticks at the top made triangles. These sticks were used as the numbers, and the square board was the phone base. When I was dialing, I pushed these sticks down. Some of the numbers were at the bottom of the board and I had to reach at the bottom to pull them. As I looked down at the bottom of the board, I saw there were clear tubes containing a solution that hung down from the board.

I was on the telephone, hearing a medical clerk talking to some one in a very displeased voice. Somehow the other person was disconnected, and I was connected on the line. I told her that I was not the person that she had been talking to; she hung up on me. I tried to call the doctor's office again, and the number was 5052 or 5250.

Then the dream changed. I was outside the door, in front of the doctor's office. Straight away from the door was a hallway, a few steps inside the door was another door to the receptionist. Even though I was standing outside the front door, I saw through the wall that was inside the second door to the left. There the child's father was standing at the counter and screaming at the doctor that he did not do the job right for the child.

Before this happened, in the dream, I knew that the doctor who did the surgery was close to where I was, but the father did not take the child to the same one that did the surgery, he took the child to a different one, but somehow these two doctors shared their responsibilities.

The dream changed, on my way out, outside, in front of the doctor's office was a table, with a nurse sitting there, she said, "Give these pills to the child, but do not let him take too much. If he gets an overdose, the scars will change and be whiter than the skin, and we are trying to keep the scars the same color of the skin." She poured several light green small flat pills into my hand out from a paper envelope like they use at McDonald's to hold french fries. On my way home I heard something that has to do with birth control.

I then saw four white, skinny feet, like toddler's feet. They were female feet because I saw the hems of two dresses, these two women wore dresses above their ankles. Between their ankles and the hems of their dresses on each leg were double flat hooks. Each double hook was one hook chained to the foot, another was opened a little, but I knew that they were chained to invisible hooks. These women were invisibly being chained together.

I then saw the end of the third row, the right section, the same seat where I normally sit at the Cathedral of San Andrew. There was a young woman of about eighteen or nineteen wearing a one-piece black, short sleeve, knee length dress, standing next to the pew. Her body was facing the sanctuary, but her face was turned to her left and looked at the empty seat where I normally sat.

I then saw the sanctuary of the Cathedral of Saint Andrew, Father Earl was standing next to the Gospel podium facing the congregation. His left hand held the side bar of the gold brass Gospel podium, and he was wearing a white chasuble. In front of him, at his chest was a bright globe of light. On the other side of the globe of light was a brass stand that looked like a lamp stand, but I did not see the top of it.

Then I woke up. I had no understanding what the Lord had revealed to me. I said, "Father, sweet Lord, good Lord; Jesus the Lord, the savior of the world, my personal savior, my Lord, my God; the Holy Spirit, the powerful action, show me what you have for me and for others through me. Oh! Lord, sweet Lord. I believe this is a powerful revelation in the supernatural. You are the Almighty God. Everything will come to the light. Jesus the Lord, You are the light of the world, the Son of the most high living God; and this light is shedding upon the world. But the devil has blinded people's eyes, their hearts and their minds. They can not feel that You are the light that is shedding upon them, Lord Jesus because iniquities bounce."

God then said to me, "I solemnly assure you, the things in the world will not be the same like today, what you saw in the dream was in the spirit. The people can not see or hear, they may touch if they seek Me. The four double hooks at their feet are symbolic of those chained in the darkness of the devil. They live the life of mortal sin and refuse to convert. The man standing next to the Gospel podium is symbolic of those living in the light of God. His hand holding on to the brass Gospel podium is symbolic that they depend upon God."

I said, "Mighty God, everything must be in order, we can not take a short cut."

The Lord said, "The woman that was standing next to your seat and gave a dirty look at the empty seat where you normally sit are those people who live the life of judging others. I solemnly say you that this iniquity will never be purged, the devil has the permission from the Father to judge them heavily, because they already have been judged. Do you remember what I said in the Bible? If you judge others, the Father will judge you."

The Lord continued, "The empty seat where you normally sit is symbolic of those who are very careful of everything before they take action."

God continued, "The power of God is upon on those who have a high position in the church, the cardinals, archbishops, bishops, and the priests. They will be heavily liable for their actions, in what they do in their personal lives or in the lives of the community. The arm of the child with three huge scars are their iniquities; these scars are not able to heal because of their actions. The pills poured in the hand with the words 'do not give the child too much, then the scars will be whiter than the skin' means when people hear what I told you to say; they think they will do better than what you say. But I say what things they do; their actions are counterfeit. Their result will never be the same as what I give to you, and the actions that I will take through you."

The Lord continued, "Birth control is limit of human life on earth, it ruled by controlling spirit. In the Bible, the woman Jezebel mislead my people. These days there are many false prophets, they call themselves pastors, preachers, and reverends, and they are misleading my people. I solemnly declare that if they do not convert, repent and pay for their actions, and pay the fine that I have set for them, they will never enter heaven."

God continued, "When I said to you that I will dictate to you; I am the Lord your God and their God, the Almighty God, I am dictating through your actions, not through the tape recorder. Your asking me 'Lord, help me to remember means you constantly say to Me 'Lord, I am not worthy to do this, I am not capable to do anything on my own, but you are in me and with me to do everything, or you say that 'all the words that come out from my mouth must be from you, You take my hand for the actions, use my feet to walk."

Jesus the Lord continued, "For those disobedient to my commandments must open their ears to hear these. They must buy from Me the Q-Tip to cleanse inside their brain so they can see the glory of God. Those who have given their hearts to the devil must get away from my people."

The Lord continued, "The ex-husband laid on the same and trying to have intercourse with you is symbolic of those that associating with the spirit of the devil. You know them, but other people do not; this only can be discerned in spirit through God's anointing."

The Lord means that if you see this person in church you will not be able to know that she associates with the devil's spirit; but if you are sensitive to the Spirit of God, then the Lord will discern for you. You will be able to recognize them through their actions, and their words, and by the things they focus on the issue.

Once a person sins, and comes to God through the Sacrament of Reconciliation from his heart, it doesn't matter how big the sin was, God always forgives. But the iniquities still exist, such as a person who robbed the bank and killed a customer in the bank lobby, whether he got caught or not, when he comes to God from his heart, through the Sacrament of Reconciliation, God will forgive both of his sins. But the damage is to the victim's family, financially and emotionally and the bank employees of that branch live in fear, and cash is lost involving the investors. Beyond this, other things add up, such as the media spreading this devil news to the public, thus giving benefit to the devil's works, by placing the evil news into other people's minds. Because God is just God, therefore; every one have to pay the damaged through committed sins.

God is the only one who can purge these iniquities. For these iniquities to be purged, the sinner must acknowledge his sin, and pay for the damage from his heart. His life must be converted, and he must obey all God's commandments, exam and repent daily.

Reform Each One's Heart for God to Purge the Iniquities

April 25, 1997, 6:58 a.m. In my dream I saw a half of a page written by the Lord in typewritten words. I read all of it after each sentence of His was finished. In the dream I understood every sentence that I read. I said to the Lord, "Lord, help me to remember all this." I then thought to get my tape recorder to tape it, but I could not do it, because I was asleep.

As I got up the Lord said, "You have to wear shorts that have fleas, so you can understand how uncomfortable it is." In my natural life, I have never had any animal in the house; therefore there was no way that I could have fleas in my apartment. I moved into an apartment on the third floor January 10, 1997; but yesterday, I was bitten by fleas twice on my legs, and I found one flea on top of my comforter. I then thought "How can fleas come in this apartment, the neighbor on other side has a very small white dog, but I do not leave my door open, except when I am in and out. I remembered that one time she shared with me that over two years ago she lived in this apartment. I then thought, "Tomorrow, I will go to WalMart to buy some flea killer."

The Lord said, "Place this revelation under the iniquities, with the title 'The iniquities bounce after the abortion laws are passed according to God's commandments'." In my vision I saw the floods and fires coming out from buildings in North Dakota, and the Lord asked me, "What do you see?" I replied, "I saw floods and fires rising out from buildings at the same time." The Lord asked me, "Do you know why two things happened at the same time?" I replied, "Lord, I do not know; but I think that You just revealed to me something about iniquities." The Lord said, "I have revealed to you the iniquities that bounce in this world are tremendously heavy. They are the result of people committing sins against each other and against God, their God, God of all creation."

In my vision I saw the cover letter that Beverly Trainers, my books and correspondence editor wrote. I said to the Lord, "Lord, I do not understand what You are revealing here, but every time Beverly sends me something, she always has a cover letter with some words to me, these words are very nice and comforting." The Lord then said to me, "This woman expressed to you what she has in her heart; there are not that many like her in this world. Many others are the opposite, they speak and write in very nice ways, but their hearts are filthy, and full of hatred."

The Lord continued, "Several people have sets of keys in their hands that you saw in the dream. They are those that have authority, or power in the government. These powers were given to them by the devil. Yet from the president of the United States, down to senators, congress, and city mangers, ninety nine percent of them have filthy hearts.

The Lord continued, "Religious people are filled with teaching using My words, but they are not teaching my words, they are teaching the method of the devil." While the Lord was saying this, in my vision I saw the inside of a Bible classroom of the non-domination. They were wearing Christians outfits, but inside they were filled with the devil's substance." I said to the Lord, "Lord, it seems like I am here to go against almost everyone in this world." The Lord said to me, "They are the ones who go against my commandments. You are my servant, you must say what I tell you to say. The servant must do what the master orders; the servant is not greater than the master."

In my vision I saw a cross up high. There was a man hanging, his body raised up, both of his arms higher than the arms of the cross. His head was covered with a light blue veil and tied with a rope around, outside the veil. While I saw this man on the cross, I also saw the spirit of those Christians teaching on television that teach the words from the Holy Bible. The Lord said, "I solemnly assure you that these people are not teaching my commandments, they are teaching their own human doctrines."

The Lord continued, "Your daughter ate one third of a fifteen ounce jar of red hot sauce in the dream, and you feared that she may get very sick. She was suffering, but she was not sick. You then got up and took her to the back house, for her to go to the restroom. As you got to the back house, your daughter was no longer there with you. You then saw a man and woman inside the back house, and they came from the side gate. They were quick to leave the house and you tried very hard to identify them. In the dream you thought they were robbers, you were watching them. While they were side-by-side they walked out the side gate, then man was disappeared. The woman returned in the front door. You then told the leader at the back house that this woman entered the house without permission; the woman defended herself by saying, "The woman that assisted President Bill Clinton told me to come here and hang up Mr. Clinton's plant at the side of the back house." This woman had some keys in her hand that were given to her by the leader of the back house. Several more people came from somewhere, each of them had a set of keys in their hands."

The Lord continued, "The leader in the back house symbolizes who give their free will to the devil, they do service to the devil by leading people in this world to go down to place that humans call 'hell' to be with the devil."

The Lord continued, "How long can this plant hang at the side of the back house?" I responded to the Lord, "Lord, how long do you allow them to hang it there? If you do not allow them to hang it up there, they can not hang it up there. You are the one that has power over heaven and earth." The Lord then said, " One piece at a time, this entire pot will fall down on the concrete." While the Lord was saying this, I saw the pot was broken on the side, and dirt and plant all fell on the concrete sidewalk. The Lord continued, "This dirt from the ground needs to be cleaned, you can not leave this dirt on the ground." I then saw the dirt was wet and was soaking into the concrete ground. Water came out of the hose and sprayed over the concrete to clean the dirt. The Lord continued, "This means the iniquities must be purged. But I will not purge them until everything is over. I the Lord speak that people must convert, come to Me and daily exam and repent. As long as the iniquities have not been purged, people have to live in the world of suffering."

The Lord continued, "They think that they are rich, they do not need anything, but they are wretched and poor. They need to buy from me the honesty so they can clean their hearts, buy from Me the things that are permanent, and buy from Me the things to benefit their souls forever and ever. Destroy the things that belong to the devil, the one that the Father cast out from heaven."

In private the Lord Jesus said to me, "The Father is on earth now. At the time the Father cast Lucifer out of heaven, He cast him out a little at a time, not at one time like people think. The Father cleaned heaven, He is now on the earth to clean the world. He is here with Me and you to cast out Lucifer dwelling in the bodies of people that gave their free will to him. Those who will convert and repent will be with God, those who refuse to convert and repent will be cast out of this world. Because Lucifer is in them, when the Father casts Lucifer out these people go with Lucifer."

Fleas biting me are the iniquities resulting from over two years ago that the tenant had a small dog in the apartment. After this tenant moved out, the owner put in new carpet, and rented to another couple for the two years before I moved in.

I am going to give a few of the main iniquities that result from the legal abortion law, and abortions, this is murder of innocent babies. The mothers of these unborn babies will never be free in their minds, this will badly affect the rest of their life. It includes their personal relationship with man, friends, children, and business.

Therefore, the result of the abortions, and the legal abortion law alone will bring people of this world, especially the citizens of the United State to live a life of misery. This includes lawmakers, the mothers who had an abortion, the doctors, nurses and everyone involved to support abortions or abortion law; directly or indirectly. These people will have to pay in their life here on earth and especially in the next life. The life of their souls depends on how much of their actions were aware or unaware of the murder of these babies and the iniquities.

Merciful and loving God, He is the only one that can forgive our sins, and He is the only one who can purge our iniquities. But each individual must take the first step. The step of coming to Him with a heart and soul of conversion and repentance, and be willing to pay for the damages. The Lord God will take care the rest.

It is a cycle of iniquities, it takes from generation to generation for them to be purged, and it can be purged by God only. Everything in our thoughts, words we say, and actions we take will affect the supernatural, and then the supernatural will come down to our natural world. When a person does a good deed they will receive a blessing. If they do evil they will receive bad results. Sending out one receives thirty, sixty, or hundred times full in reward or punishment. This includes this life and the life after this.

Cloning of Human and Animal

Every human and animal has a soul. God created human and animal souls from different heavenly substances, and every soul God created from a different formula.

Cloning man and animal are the works of the devil. Therefore, the souls of man and animals born from cloning are reincarnation, these souls were being punished for their rebellion to God and refusal to convert, especially humans. When that person or animal dies, he will be chained in the darkness of the devil.

Men performing cloning are working under the power of the devil. Souls for cloning are sent from Lucifer

When a man eats or transforms cloned blood, he will received part of the spirit from that cloned animal or man, this spirit will affect their life because that spirit is under the power of the devil.

Soul and Spirit within Human Body Revelation

Each human body has three parts: the physical body, the soul, and the spirit. The soul and spirit came from heaven at the time of conception. The spirit is the soul's power, it moves within the body and around the body; the soul remains in the physical body until the last breath.

If a pregnant woman commits a grave sin, her spirit is dominated by the devil. When the child is born, this child also caries with him some of his mother's spirit, or when the mother nurses the child, her spirit also transfers to him.

At the time the spirit joins the soul at the time of conception, both are pure. Growing in the mother's womb or after birth, the spirit and soul are supernatural products. This spirits either comes from God or from the devil depending how each one live their life.

When a person lives in the life of holiness, Spirit of God is within him, and produces good deeds. When a person lives in sin, his spirit is dominated by the power of the devil. His mind is led by the devil's spirit, and he then takes actions against God's commandments to destroy his soul and physical body as well.

The spirit affects the mind first and spreads out over the entire body, causing actions, pain, disease and suffering; what ever may be.

God gave everyone of us free will, whether to chose God or the devil. God respects this free will, but the devil is always pulling everyone of us to his side. When a person chooses God, he must obey "all" God's commandments. The opposite of this is when a person rebels against God's commandments and gives his free will to the devil. A person who obeys God will generate good thoughts, good actions, and will build good deeds. But a person under the control of the devil, their thoughts will be controlled by the devil, their actions will damage people around them, and in the nations, and the world.

We can not see our thoughts, because they are built from supernatural power. Theses thoughts are either built by God or by the devil. From one thought to another, these thoughts could be put away for later use. There are times these thoughts will manifest a similar situation, or will be come actions.

The first thing that the devil does to damage people is to get into human thought. He makes that person think of one things or another, day after day, again and again; this is called desperation. In some cases the devil uses some things that a person either saw, or heard about, and manifests that to new ideas. In some cases he brought the past situation, some cases are the present situation, and in some cases he gives that person imagination.

Sometimes he starts with the bad things right a way and makes a person fearful. Sometimes he starts with the good things and slowly launches to the bad. It causes people to be angry, filled with hatred, sadness, sorrow, or false love. From either way some day will come foolish actions.

There are many ways the devil's spirit can control or interfere with the human mind. From committing a grave sin, or any sin, associating with friends who are controlled by the devil, from the working environment, and co-workers, family members, society, and more. Ninety nine point nine percent of people who deny it are being controlling by or are being interfered with by the devil or his offspring spirits.

These people normally will have one or more of the following traits: they are very stubborn, they are controlling, fearful, or very aggressive, they have no responsibility, are very slick, and will not admit their wrong and accept correction, because the devil stuffed in their minds that they are right and others are wrong. Many times they seem to do the good things, but their hearts are filled with dirt and moss. There are times they are undercover as good Christians, good church leaders, good lawmakers, or good high-ranking government officials. Good students at an age that knows good and evil can be controlled too, for the children at that age know how to lie to their parents etc.

When a person is in the control of the Almighty God, these persons are completely obedient to all God's commandments. They keep their hearts pure, with daily exam and repentance, and live a life of holiness. They go to church, confession and receive Holy Eucharist regularly, pray at least twice a day, after getting up and before going to sleep. They please God and do not please man. They do things from their hearts, accept their responsibility, are filled with love, and embrace suffering. These people normally suffer a great deal. Everything they do is in the name of the Lord, trust in God, etc.. Their hearts are filled with good deeds, building the kingdom of heaven for their souls and souls of others.

The Lord Jesus Stroked His Hair and His Words

October 26, 1998. When I was about to go up to receive the Holy Eucharist, in my vision I saw the dream I had overnight. In the dream I saw the Lord Jesus' face, he was about late thirty years old. His hair was at his shoulders, at the right temple his hair had a cowlick. I saw more of the right side of his face, he was stroking his hair above the right side of his forehead with his right hand; and his did it twice. I said, "That is Jesus." I then heard the angel of the Lord say to me, "This is how Jesus looked when He was on earth."

As I proceeding to the center aisle for Holy Communion the Lord Jesus said to me, "You saw me when you awakened, you were not asleep. I had the priest, Binh An call you early this morning, and say to you that he will be stationed in San Diego for three years. He came to help you. The Chaplain with his ranking has a lot of power over personnel. Call him and share with him what you have done. He will believe you. The Navy will be the one who helps you, not the Diocese of San Diego."

When I received this instruction, my understanding of the Lord Jesus' words is that He uses the priest, chaplain Father Binh An's name as symbolic to pour out His peace down to earth, and uses the Navy as symbolize living water, the Lord Jesus. Testing the spirit, I resisted contacting the Navy Lieutenant Colonel Chaplain Binh An. But the Blessed Virgin Mother kept reminding me to call the Chaplain Binh An. I continued to resist, but God's power was over me, Father Binh An, and everyone on this world. Therefore, this was a Divine meeting and God was in the midst, I finally called the Chaplain for an appointment; while we were arranging an appointment, he invited me to come early to watch the Marine's graduation.

Revelation of Visiting the Navy Lieutenant Colonel Chaplain

October 30, 1998: In my dream I was standing in an open air field, wearing black pants, the back of my pants was up to my waist, but the front was still open. While I was about to pull up my zipper, there was a healthy man coming from my right side. He crossed in front of me, he was naked from the waist up, wearing roomy black trousers that he was holding around his waist with both of his hands. As he saw my abdomen, he stopped and quickly kneeled at my feet. But I pulled up my zipper up and left while he was still kneeling. The meaning of this revelation is symbolic that when people understand God's words through me, they fall in love with God like a man hungry to have intercourse with a woman.

Then the dream changed: In this dream I saw my chest, I was wearing a dress that I was waiting for in a shipment. I then saw the back of my head, my hair was tied up with steel wire, and on top was a black velvet bowl. At the same time I saw this, I also saw the invisible hands of my beloved Blessed Virgin Mother dressing the three flowers made from the same fabric of the dress at the back of my waist; the center one was higher than the two sides. I said, "Mother, I want my purple bowl." She said to me, "The three flowers are mean purple." I then saw around the back of the dress at my waist and the flowers in royal purple.

Then the Lord gave me another dream: In this dream I saw the face of a little child in front of me. She had surgery performed on her eyes, each eye was a double bulbs eye, the one on top was open from the surgery, both eyes were very dark and deep in the two holes. She turned around, I saw her head had a little blonde hair, kind of curly, there were two parallel long wide scars on her head. At the top of each scar was a horn like two cat ears. When I saw this I was very frightened. I then heard the Lord say to me, "Those horns are the beasts." He continued, "Today, you will deliver an assignment to chaplain Binh An. It will not be easy for him, because what you have petitioned in the Tax Court goes against what they are honoring." The Lord meant the system of the United States and the world, going against God's commandments.

The day before I went to visit Lieutenant Colonel Chaplain Binh An, he gave me directions was to take eight east to five south, exit at old town, go straight to the three-way stop sign, turn right to gate number four, left at gas station, right at the end of the gas station, and go to the dead end. I did asked for the address, but he told me that the base that will be difficult to find without following the directions.

At the night before the visit, the Blessed Mother told me, "The directions he gave to you are correct. But you have not put the map back in your car; and you do not have a street name, what happen if you miss the turn?. Call the priest in the morning before you leave the house." Obeying the Blessed Mother, I called the Chaplain, father Binh An's office for a street address. I also spoke to father Binh An for more details of the directions. I thought the Chaplain was at a Navy base, but when I got there I found out that the place is a boot camp to train Marine Corps.

The first time I meet the Navy Lieutenant Colonel Chaplain, Catholic priest Binh An Nguyen, was at the dedication of Our Lady of Lavang mission temple in New Orleans.

320

It was also the first time I had an encounter with the Lord Jesus through my dream on August 2, 1992. From August 1992 until before I left the insurance company to serve God in April 4, 1994; Father Binh An meet me twice for lunch, two different times when he came to San Diego for conference.

When I entered the Navy Lieutenant Colonel Chaplain's office, I looked at him and said, "You still look the same to me as last time." He responded, "No, I am getting old with a lot of white hair." When he said that he looked at me in the way of telling me that I was still young. I told him, "My hairs are dyed." He then shared with me some of his duty in this Marine Corps Recruit Depot. I gave him a 10"x13" brown envelope with materials that the Lord instructed me to deliver to him. He then took me around the boot camp for sight seeing, showing me the business area, commissary, laundry etc.

We then returned to his office. It was very new to me that every time a Marine passed by him they raised their right hand to salute, at the same time he raised his right hand in response. Then both of them said something to each other and it seemed like they agreed, that sentence I did not hear clearly. The Marine pasture is very straight, that made me feel sorry for them each time I saw them salute to the Chaplain; at the same time I was proud of the Marines' discipline. The way I felt was just me, I have never been in the position of other saluting to me, or next to the person having the high ranking in military to witness. I submitted my feeling to the Chaplain, he said to me, "If the children out there are like them, the nation will have peace. When they are at home, they do not listen to their parents, but when they enter here, rules have to obeyed." I said, "Parents have to teach a child from the time he comes out from his mother's womb, but they do not do that, so they fail. Here, they put them in discipline at the first moment they arrive at the camp. But there are many adults who need to learn the good discipline before they teach their children."

While I was in the Chaplain's office. I needed to go to the restroom, but I was not sure what to say to the Chaplain to find the restroom. Because I respected the celibate vows of priest and him, I asked the Lord silently, "Lord, how I am going to find a ladies restroom?" I then asked the Chaplain, "Father Binh An, this is male boot camp, do they have a ladies restroom?" He went to his assistant's office and I followed him. He asked his assistant, "Is there a female restroom here?" He replied, "I don't know, sir, but I'll go check, sir." He then came back, said, "Sir, she can use male restroom, and I will stay at the door as a guard, sir." I then followed the Chaplain's assistant to the restroom, he opened the restroom door, and said to me, "You can go in, m'am; I will stay here." When I finished, I opened the door to get out, and I saw him standing, his with his back against the door, feet apart to covering the entire door, with his hands at his waist as a guard. I then said thanks to him and we returned to the Chaplain's office.

During the time I was visiting the boot camp I went to the restroom twice. The second time was after the graduation, and before the mass. I asked the Chaplain's assistant while he was standing in the Chaplain's office, talking to him, "Would you walk with me to the restroom?" He responded, "Yes, m'am." And immediately he left the office, and I followed him. When we were close to the restroom door, he looked at the hall's corner, opposite to the corner for the restroom, and said to me, "M'am, would you wait here for me to check inside." He went in to check and came out, said to me, "You can come in, m'am." While he was saying this, he also opened the door for me. When I was about to come out of the restroom, there was another woman coming in. I got out of the door and saw him standing with his feet apart, as a guard like the first time. I said to him, "Thank you; would you like me to wait for you?" He replied, "No, m'am." I returned to the Chaplain's office alone. The Marine training taught him these manners, these are perfect manners for each one of us that must serve one another. But for me to receive these services made me very uncomfortable, because the Lord taught me to serve others, not to be served.

Father Binh An and I were crossing the field of the Recruit Depot where the graduation would be held today This field was more than double the length of a football field. While we were walking, the Marine guard prevented people from walking through the center of the field; approaching the Chaplain, said, "Sir, can you move to the side little." He then pointed out the front of the bleachers where people were walking in the front, and said, "They might get you over there, better that you may go behind the bleachers. Father Binh An said thanks to him, he then told me, "Today is an exception because of the graduation ceremony; other days they do not allow any one wearing civilian clothes to cross this field. This field is like heaven to them." I quickly replied, "This is the Garden of Eden". The Chaplain led me behind the bleachers, turned right, and right again to the front of the bleachers, passing a few reserved sections, and he then got up to the third bench from the top of the bleachers. I followed him up with difficulty, because I was wearing a business suit that had a shirt.

We then sat mixing with the audience and waited for about twenty minutes. While we were waiting, Father Binh An shared with me some of the details such that the Marine corps is a son of the Navy; the Navy provides them shelter, medical, food etc.., and in turn the Marines guard the ships. While we were talking I heard the woman sitting in front of me comment about the two Marines who were walking side by side and counting out loud "left, right, left, right." Father Binh An said, "When one man walks alone he does not have to count, but when there are two or more, one of them has to count out loud." He also said to me, "When the graduation starts, on the other side of the field behind the parked cars will be no activities, except inside the hall." I then said to him, "How about if the Messiah comes down, and lands at the middle of the field?" He replied, "That is something from

God." I added, "He will come down from the sky and land in the middle of the field. You will be surprised what God will do." I also overheard Chaplain Binh An and the lady in front sharing that after today, these young men will go home for ten days, then they will go to where they are assigned. When I heard this I said to them, "These young men will bring the Ten Commandments home."

At about ten o'clock the Marine band began the serenade, a few minutes later six platoons marched on, each group with about eighty new Marines in khaki shirts, navy blue trousers, and black shiny shoes. During this time there was one person with a dog sitting at his left foot, on the ground, in front of the stage. Father Binh An pointed this dog to me, and said, "That is the devil dog." I asked, "Why do you call him the devil dog? I oppose that!" He said, "This is an unofficial name, the instructors call them, they call them devil dogs." I asked, "Why do they call them devil dogs?" He said, "This unofficial name came from the fight between the Germans and U.S. Marines, the Germans lost because the U.S. Marines fought so hard. The Germans called them devil dogs." I said again, "I am opposed to that, they are men, they should never call men devil dogs."

People were standing for the Presentation of the Colors and the National Anthem. Before the National Anthem, I asked the Blessed Virgin Mother, all the holy angels and saints to pray with me to the Father, the Lord Jesus and the Holy Spirit for deliverance of all 485 new Marines and everyone present. While people sang the National Anthem, I prayed the Lord's Prayer:

"Our Father, Who art in heaven, hallowed be Your name. Your kingdom come; Your will be done on earth as it is in heaven. Give us this day our daily bread; and forgive us our trespasses as we forgive those who trespass against us, and lead us not into temptation, but deliver us from evil. Amen." I continued, "Hail Mary, full of grace, the Lord is with thee; blessed art thou among women, and blessed is the fruit of thy womb, Jesus. Holy Mary, Mother of God, pray for us sinners, now and at the hour of our death. Amen." I continued, "Glory be to the Father, and to the Son, and to the Holy Spirit. As it was in the beginning, is now, and ever shall be, world without end. Amen."

Then I petitioning, "Father, Lord Jesus, Holy Spirit, I ask you to cast out the devil spirit from all these young men and every one present here. I ask you Lord, deliver them from the spirit of disobedience to you, protect them, guide them, and bless them." I then turned to the devil, I said, "In the name of God, with the righteous of the Almighty Father, through the Lord Jesus, and the work of the Holy Spirit; I command you, devil and all your offspring out of all these young soldiers, and never return." I was standing up high to do this, I was not used to standing up high, and I was scared. I asked the woman standing in front of me, Donna for me to lean my right hand fingers on her left shoulder. (Please see the "**" at the end of the visiting the boot camp section for the reason of this deliverance.)

After the graduation, we returned to the Chaplain's office for a few minutes before we went to the chapel for mass. While we were in his office, Father Binh An showed me his "Minister to the sick kit". He opened it up. It had three metal bottles with different kinds of oil, the Baptismal kit and a ritual book. I went to the restroom a second time. We then went to the chapel for the11:40 a.m. mass. During the Chaplain Binh An's homily, he spoke of the virtue of love, when a person deep in the virtue of love will conquer all obstructions. When I heard this, I knew right away that the Lord Jesus was using Chaplain Binh An to speak to me, reaffirming of His love for me, and that when I love others (and that includes enemies), love will conquer all obstructions.

God spoke to us through His words in the holy scriptures, and through people who have good hearts. God speaks to us through actions in our lives, and through the lives of others, through natural tragedies and disasters. When it is good, we must know and thank Him for it. When bad things happen, we must seek Him through prayer for understanding of why the bad things are existing, and seek help from God. The bad things will bring suffering, but when a person lives with a pure heart, they will embrace suffering in peace. Although God allows bad things happen to good people for good purposes, on the other hand, a person of impure heart will complain of the suffering, with anger and hatred. This anger and hatred will bring violence, destroying the soul and the physical body. In order for each one of us to hear God, we must keep our hearts pure. If a person's heart is impure he will hear from the devil. When a person hears from the devil, he has no peace and no discernment, they act under the devil's power.

At the end of the mass, there was a Navy officer wearing a white uniform at the side entrance of the chapel said out loud to Chaplain Binh An, he said something like, Father Joe, there is an order that next week, you will be a chief Chaplain.(Father Binh An baptize name Joseph) I then reached out and asked, "Excuse me, sir, what did you say?" He repeated the message, but I still did not hear him clearly. After Chaplain Binh An took off the Chasuble, he came out and told me, "You can wait here. I need to find out what is the order." In less than ten minutes, Chaplain Binh An returned to walked me to his mini van. While we were walking I asked him, "What was that the order?" He told me, "There is one of the commanders who passed away, he is Catholic and the funeral service will be held here on Tuesday. Another Catholic Chaplain will be the main celebrant for the mass, I will be the Master of Ceremonies. I need to coordinate for the other religions Chaplains seating (around the altar) in the sanctuary, but they will not be participating in service of the mass."

He then asked me, "Where would you like to go for lunch?" I replied, "I am fasting today, I fast three days each week, I do not eat meat." He decided for the Bay View sea food restaurant in the boot camp. During the short lunch break, the conversion was very limited and short.   I thought that I was going to order fish, but since the Blessed Virgin Mother told me to let Father Binh An pay for the lunch, I decided that I would not get the fish plate because it cost more for the Chaplain to pay. When the Chaplain asked me, "What would you like to order?" I replied, "I am not sure." He then suggested. "Soup and salad for lunch is lighter." I agreed with him. I asked Chaplain "Do you known that Father Hung is in Kentucky, but I think that he does not want people to know that he is there." (Father Hung is former Vietnamese Air Force Chaplain.) He replied, "It was published in the newspaper." I said, "It only said Kentucky, he is at Abbey of Gethsemani." I then said, "My dad was in the military, I was only able to see him twice a year, each time about a week. He was killed in the battlefield by the communists." I asked him, "Did you prepare for today's homily or did it just come?" He replied, "It just came. I only prepare for the Sunday homily, because Sunday has large groups. Sunday mass is about a thousand people, and is held at the theater." I said, "The correct way is that the priest reads the reading and Gospel very carefully, and spends time in prayer. When time for the homily, the Spirit of God will speak through." I continued, "The mass was very short." He replied, "That was long, the mass on the ships are shorter; especially when I see few of the commanders attending I have to shorten the mass to about fifteen minutes." I asked, "Why is that short?" I thought that they only come to say Hi and goodbye to God. He replied, "Because they have to watch out for the attackers." My comment, "I did not know that, where do they come from?" He did not answer my question. I told the Chaplain, "God chose you, and your life will have suffering." He response, "If God chooses, we can not refuse, we have to accept." I then said, "The more you suffer, the more God loves you. Jesus is the only Son of the Father, He suffered to death. He taught us to pick up our cross and to follow His footsteps." Before we left the table, I said to him. "I would like to pay for the cost of my portion. But if you will not let me do this; I will pay for the next time." He gave me a look that he did not agree with what I just said. I then said to him, "If I do not do what the Blessed Virgin Mother tells me, I will be scolded by the Lord."

After we left the restaurant, on the way returned to the parking lot for me to pick up my car. When we got to one of the corners, I saw five young Marine men standing side by side in one line, facing an instructor. These five young men were pulling out their lungs yelling in a very loud voice of something that all I heard was sir, sir, sir and sir. Then one man at the center spoke alone, I was able to see their neck veins rise up. My heart felt sorrow for them, I cried out to the Lord, "Jesus, help them. Lord, my heart is sorrow to see this. " I then turned to Father Binh An and said, "Are these young man being punished? Why do they do that to them? My heart is full of sorrow seeing them punished." He said, "They have to do that to train them, so they can put them in discipline." I then said, "If God applied punishment like that to us, all of us will be punished a lot harder than that. Look at all the floods, storms, fires." He added, "Tornadoes." He then dropped me at field where I parked my car for me to pick up my car to return home. Before I entered my car, I shook the Chaplain's hand, gave him God's protection, guiding, and blessing as God has instructed me during the mass at the Marine Recruit Depot chapel.

October 31, 1998: In my dream I saw one recruit marching, facing the center of the graduation area. While the recruits were marching in place, their instructor was at their left side, he was standing still, resting on his naked huge athletically muscled legs and thighs. His body bent down from his hip, made a corner at his rear end, and his body turned to an empty red iron utility wagon, all rusty inside. I then saw the entire platoon turn to their left, heading toward the audience. Everyone of them turned to the same as their instructor's form. Then the Lord said to me, "Here is how they look in their hearts." Through this dream God revealed that the German cursed the U.S. Marines as "devil dogs."

I then was standing on the opposite side of an ex-spouse extended family table dinner. There was food on the table, some people were sitting in chairs at the table, some were standing behind. I was very angry at them and beat on the table, all their food was spilled, and they stood still and stared at me. I then had another dream: In this dream, I saw some Catholic priests that I currently know were in front of me, from their waist up; and I was yelling at them. Then there was a space of silence, and I asked, "Lord, how come I am so angry at them?" The Father said, "They are symbolic of the world's disobedience to God." (Many time people do things that look good for man, and benefit earthly life, but sin against God, and harm the souls without knowing that.) In this dream, God revealed of the deliverance. The food on the table is symbolic of the hearts and actions that good for man, but are evil in front of God, and God will crush them down.

I then was returned to the area where I was standing in line. I was second in line, but there were two children who were standing at my space. I said to them, "I know that you came here and stood at my spot, this was revealed to me early." Then the dream changed, these two small children grew into two adults, a mother and a daughter. The daughter was standing next to the end of a hallway, with a black iron rail. The end of this rail was at the beginning of the top stair way. Her mother was standing on one of the steps with her head high at the level of the top stairway, while I was standing on the same second floor with the daughter, at the center of the iron rail, and the daughter was at my left. The daughter asked me for a favor, "My mother is going to marry to Father Hung's brother. Would you come to help her get dressed? Father Hung's brother left another woman to marry to my mother." I replied to her, "Go home, I will call you tonight." Then in silence, I did not understand, the Lord told me, "Father Hung is symbolic of the Lord Jesus, his brother on earth is symbolic of you. The daughter is symbolic of those who will accept God's teaching through you. In this dream, the mother is symbolic of government officials. God also warns you, not to let any one to persuade you." When I said, "I will call you." I mean that I need to ask the Lord for instructions; when I heard from God, I will let you know.

When I got to the Good Shepherd Church, I went in to the Blessed Sacrament chapel for just a few minutes. The Father told me, "Go out to the main body of the Church." I left and went to the same seat that I normally sit in. The Glory of the Father was coming up on me more powerfully, I could not kneel, I had to sit down. The Father said to me, "You explain the word 'escort' in detail. The priest, (Binh An) invited you to visit the boot camp not on his own, but that invitation was given to him by God. He served as a vehicle for angels to protect you." He continued, "Where did you have dinner?" I replied, "At the Bay View restaurant." Father asked, "Why did the male servant come to your table and talk to the priest? Why did he suggest soup and salad? Why did you want fish, but not get fish?" I replied, "Father, because the Blessed Mother told me let the priest pay the bill, so I could not order fish." The Father continued, "He showed you the oil supplies to heal the sick, holy water and oil case for baptismal; where is the supply for a wedding? Weddings do not need oil and holy water. Give him the ring at your hand that Jesus gave you." I replied, "Father, I have no ring in my hand to give him." I did not understand and feared that the Father may scold me. The Father continued, "Where is your sword? You pulled your invisible sword out while others presented their National Anthem. Give your invisible ring to the priest, Binh An. It is not the priest himself, but his name 'Binh An'. You are married to God's peace on earth. You are the Emissary of God. In Genesis it was foretold, through you, God would send an angel to the Eden Garden to cast out Adam and Eve, the souls disobedience to God's commandments."

The Gospel today ended with, "For everyone who exalts himself will be humbled, but the one who humbles himself will be exalted." Luke 14:11. When the priest finished reading it, I pleaded to the Lord, "Father, am not worthy for all of these missions, you put me here." At the sign of peace, the Father told me, "Peace comes from Jesus. It is the gift from God that you are married to." I then thought of before the Father told me that the high-ranking church leaders chairs are rocking.

** In my dream I saw the instructor and one platoon standing on their huge athletically muscled legs and thighs, and their bodies turned to wagons. This is symbolic of the time Germans started calling the U.S. Marines by the name "devil dog." They cursed the U.S.Marines, and that curse stayed with the U.S. Marines since.(The Gospel of Mark chapter eleven; Jesus curses a Fig tree.) People do not understand, and thought that it was okay, and some thought it was cute, and continued to accept that curse by using it as a nickname for them. Each time the word "devil dog" was used to call these Marines, it give power to the devil over them. In order for the U.S. Marines to be delivered from the curse by the German, this curse has to be delivered, and they have to know that they were under the devil's power. The cursed effecting many ways in their hearts and actions, that man without discernment from God will unable to discerned. Out side the wagon red symbolic of battle field or battle. Inside the wagon rusty symbolic of things hidden in their hearts or actions go against God's commandments cause by the devil power. They must be deliverance, after they receive the deliverance, they must pray daily for guidance and protection. After deliverance, the devil is still wandering around to attack them. The devil can trick them into doing the good things and lead to evil. When a person is in this situation, he lacks discernment from God, and he will be unable to identify if his actions are good or evil. There are times that other people tell him of right and wrong, and he will not listen, because the devil is controlling him. When I heard the words "devil dog" being use as an unofficial name for them, it frightened me.   Therefore, when I knew that, the Spirit of God used me as His Instrument to deliver them from the power of the devil.

The U.S. Marines also have their prayer, each of these young men to accomplish through the boot camp, they also pray to God, through the Marines' Prayer.   But this Marines' Prayer lacks a major part. Their prayer petition is directly to the Father, not through the Lord Jesus. In the holy Bible, the Lord Jesus teaches, everyone must come through Him and He will lead us to the Father, and everything in heaven and the earth was handed to Him by the Father. The second missing part in this prayer is that the Marine are not praying for their supervisors. They must pray to God to guide, protect and bless their superiors, so they can do what is in God's will. The devil is always attacking them so they can lead others in wrong directions. God measures each ones heart, good fruit comes from good trees, rotten fruit comes from rotten trees.

These young people men gave up their free will to be in the U.S Marine Corps, accepting the rules and discipline. This rule and discipline are started at the first moment they entered the boot camp. If every parent applied this discipline to each of their children at the moment each child got out from the womb, it would partly bring peace into the family, the nation and the world. I know there are also other denominations, and religions that are sharing the boot camp chapel. But, I would like to use Catholics as the front line, for the reason that God is calling me and Chaplain Binh An as His instruments. We were born into the Catholic families. In the Genesis chapters one, two, three and first part of chapter four, God revealed that there is no difference in color, race, or nationality in front of Him.

I am a witness of what I saw: Through the Marine Recruit Depot Commanding General, Major General H. P. Osman, the United States government provides space, personal, and time for these young men in this boot camp, to bring them close to God, making the world a better place to live, and building the kingdom of heaven. But not enough time to be with God as He commanded in the Book of Exodus, chapter 20; God commanded that every one of us must place Him above all things. The word 'above all things' means placing God as the focal point, through spending more time with Him in prayer." Obey all His commandments, keep our hearts pure, and trust in Him. In turn, God will provide the guidance, protection, and blessing, like He did for those that trust in Him in the Bible, 1 King and 2 King, and Gospel of Matthew 6:25-34. God will provide the supernatural protection, when people come to God with sincere hearts, and obey all His commandments.

When I mentioned Father Hung with Chaplain Binh An at the restaurant, I was indirectly saying to Chaplain Binh An that God his name and his earthly title as a symbolism to revealed to me, through the Lord Jesus' mission that God entrusted to me; as vehicle to transport God's peace down to earth. (Binh An is Vietnamese name; in English it means peace).

The name Hung also is a Vietnamese name, in English it means Hero. God is using Father Hung's name as symbolic to reveal to me of the Lord Jesus as a head of the mission that God entrusted to me, like He used Isaac as vehicle to transport the Lord Jesus as fully man born into the world. God loves those who humble themselves before Him, through service and touching the life of the poor and lowly. This can be both through prayer and actual actions of service.

I have no high ranking in the church, government, or private sector. I obeyed God, and contacted Lieutenant Colonel Chaplain Binh An as God instructed me. Since I was obeying God, God poured out His Spirit into the Lieutenant Colonel Chaplain Binh An. The Chaplain serves God, humbling himself before Him, inviting me to the boot camp, to join him at the graduation ceremony. He took me around the boot camp for sightseeing, and provided me lunch. Through the Chaplain's assisting me, the Book of Genesis from chapter one through the first part of the fourth chapter will bring the meaning of God's words, and the meaning of the symbolism in these chapters of the book of Genesis into the world.

I visit the Chaplain and the boot camp, and God deliverance these young men from the devil spirit were predestined by God, I am just an instrument, and I did not know any of these until after God finished He works. There is always, without exception, every time a word or an action takes place, supernatural power pours out before the natural exists. Good comes from God, bad comes from the devil.

23

THE SEVENTH TRUMPETS MEANING

God's Work Through Obedience
The Enemy Spirits Remain within Man After Conversion

February 16, 1998; in my dream I saw a man perched in front of me and he said to me, "I just finished a rehearsal." When he said this I knew that he had just came out from the covered room to my right in the same building where I was standing.

I saw in the distance, a little to my left in front of me, the back of a dance instructor. He was wearing a formal jacket made of soft fabric, shorts, and black dress shoes. His shoes were narrow, pointed at the toes, and very tight. Both his clothes and shoes were old and dirty; he looked ridiculous.

Also in front of me, a little to my right was a group of people. These people were going to a dance function and the dance instructor was going with them. I said to the group of people, "You must be very careful when you dance, he will step on your feet." I meant that the dance instructor would take a lot of space on the dancing floor, and step on other people's feet.

I saw my feet, from my knees down. I was wearing black Levy jeans, and raw leather shoes. My shoes had a strong large base, were round at the toes, and gave my toe more room, it was firm and strong.

The group of people to my right are symbolic of those who have been converted to God, with daily exam and repenting. Dancing is symbolic of worshipping God. The dance instructor is symbolic of those who just converted. His shoes and outfit are symbolic of new converts still being attacking by the devil frequently. The devil will use them to exalt themselves and attack other people who are associated with them, either in group prayer or by association. He said, "I just come out from rehearsal" means that the conversion takes time to learn God's commandments and put them in their hearts and daily life. They learn to constantly seek God's forgiveness and ask God to purge the iniquities. They ask for discernment, embrace suffering, are humble, daily exam and repent, go to church and confession regularly, and keep their hearts pure to receive body and blood of our Lord Jesus, through the Holy Eucharist. Otherwise the devil will lead you to another road that under his control, it is false worshipping.

Real or False Conversion

February 16, 1998. In my dream there were two small children with me, one was in front, and a little distance from me when the child walked with me. The other one was constantly behind me. When we were about to leave the house, this one child carried his hat. I opened a flat large door. This door was like a second wall inside the main wall, this second wall only came up to the middle of the main wall. I pulled out one of the two Vietnamese female cone hats, this kind of hat is made from dry palm branches. While she was standing behind me, I was pulling out one hat, and I said to her, "The is another one in side that you left here from your last visit."

The two children are symbolic of those just after conversion. Palm branches are symbolic of lack of present of God. The one in the distance in front of me is symbolic of those following God's commandments. The one behind me, and wanting her palm branch hat is symbolic of those who convert and go back to the old way, and convert again. Her carrying her hat with her is symbolic of those converts who exalt themselves in the victory of their conversion. They focus on their conversion, and talk about their conversion very often, this could be in private and in the group. There is time a convert needs to talk about it in the way of testimony, but in the way of being very humble before God, and being very careful of the devil using it against them, by being more focused on their conversion than on God.

We must admit that we always sin, and we must remember that after conversion our sins were forgiven by God. When a person talks more of their past sins, they give glory to the devil.

Jonesboro, Arkansas Disaster

Children are innocent and learn very fast. The San Diego Union Tribune indicated below of Andrew Golden's picture: "Father had trained him in practical shooting, a competitive sport." Michelle Johnson's picture: Friend says the 13-year-old had made numerous threats in the days before the shooting." And "Golden's grandfather told The Associated Press that his grandson admitted stealing seven guns from him but didn't remember much about the shootings."

Reasons that caused this tragedy:

a. The anger of Mitchell did not receive attention in conjunction with Andrew has experience of shooting.

b. Guns and ammunitions were accessible for Andrew to steal.

c. Andrew's knowledge of operating guns.

d. The violence on movie, video and television, such as adults murdering adults and murdering children, war, government getting ready for the war etc.

e. Newspapers, books with violent stories or articles.

f. At the time of the tragedy, the media made the situation worse for the children. Too much attention to the tragedy will teach other children to commit more tragedies in the future, either in a same or similar way.

Healing and preventing future tragedies:

1. Never teach children to operate any kind of gun, even toy guns.

2. Never leave guns and ammunitions accessible to children.

3. Parents should not have guns in the home. Likely, if a parent owns or uses guns, then their children will copy from them.

4. Parents daily actions teach their children, because the first place children learn from are their parents, grandparents, members of family, and this learning extends to friends and school, and television, movies, books etc.

5. Do not allow children to watch violent movies, videos, and television programs. That includes news, such as transporting weapons to war, war battle; or read violent and scary books.

6. Little at a time, the devil's spirit is attached to these things and launches in the children minds and come to actions.

7. After each tragedy iniquities result, and these iniquities will affect the victims' family members, community, and nation, even throughout the world. And God is the only one who can heal these wounds. For God to heal these wounds, everyone of us must reform our lives so God can work through each individual within the family, extended to community, nation and throughout the world.

8. More media only makes the situation worse. Because the media is like pizza delivery, they mix other things in to make the story interesting.

9. The process to heals these wounds and prevent more tragedies is to involve parents, schools, community, Church leaders, and government.

The Caused and Prevention of the Columbine High School Shooting, Oklahoma and Kansas Tornadoes

The media called this shooting a tragedy and I called it a disaster. Tragedies come from God to purify each one of us, and each one of us will affect the group, many groups will affect the village, many villages will effect the city, and go on to the nation, and the world. Because the systems of the world are working against God's commandments, ranging from the president of each nation, the members of congress, government officials, spiritual leaders, media, judges, attorneys, police officers and school teachers, down to parents, teenagers, and children several years old.

Disasters come from the devil, the devil only has power over those who give their free will to him. However, the devil must have permission from God before he can do any action, small or big.

When God teaches me, He starts me from the beginning like kindergarten; He did not put me in second grade or higher. He started teaching me how to sit, how to crawl, how stand, and how to walk; I followed His instructions very carefully, and took actions with a lot of caution. He did not teach me to run; in fact He told me, "You will never run; if you run you will fall; be patient." Therefore, I will write out the cause, healing and prevention of this kind as disaster in the way that you as a reader can follow them, and apply them to your own life, the lives of your family members, extending to the community, city and to the nation, and into the world. God gave me these writings, and they will benefit an uncounted number of souls for eternal life in heaven and physical lives on earth. These words come with God's power; but they only benefit those who are willing to change, to convert to the real God, not a god of your own.

In the beginning was the Word, and the Word was with God, and the Word was God. He was in the beginning with God. All things came to be through him, and without him nothing came to be. What came to be through him was life, and this life was the light of the human race; the light shines in the darkness, and the darkness has not overcome it. John 1:1-5.

Jesus said to them again, "Peace be with you. As the Father has sent me, so I send you." And when he had said this, he breathed on them and said to them, "Receive the holy Spirit. John 20: 21-22

The sentence "In the beginning was the Word," the word "Word" means God is the Word, and the Word is Spirit of God. The word "was" is speaking of Jesus as the fully God, He existed before heaven and earth were created. The phrase "and the Word was with God," means Jesus as fully God was with the Eternal Father, the Master Planner of heaven and Earth. The phrase "and the Word was God" means Jesus is God before the foundation of the world. "He was in the beginning with God" means the Lord Jesus was with the

334

Eternal Father before and at the time the Father created heaven and the Earth.

"All things came to be through him." The word "through" in this sentence is everything from heaven come down to earth from the Creator of heaven and earth must come through the Lord Jesus. (The Lord Jesus revealed this in John 16: 15, "Everything that the Father has is mine; for this reason I told you that he [Holy Spirit] will take from what is mine and declare it to you.") The phrase "and without him nothing came to be" Jesus as fully God is the substance for the Eternal Father to created the heaven and the earth.

"What came to be through him was life," the Eternal Father created living creatures from Jesus himself, "and this life was the light of the human race" means human life was created with the light of God. The next part "the light shines in the darkness, and the darkness has not overcome it" means the Lord Jesus is the light of the world; and the devil must subjected under His authority.

"Jesus breathed on them." The word "breath" is speaking of God's Spirit. The Spirit of God is the supernatural power of God, and God does His works with His Spirit, through living creatures. Human bodies are one kind of living creatures. God is Spirit and He heals people with physical disease or mental illness with his Spirit. Vice versa, Lucifer, fallen angels, and souls that passed from this world contained grave sin (s) are in hell, they are spirits of the darkness. The devil and his offspring are also spirits, their spirits are their supernatural power working through people who disobey God's commandments; when a person lives a life of grave or mortal sin, they are under the power of the devil or his offspring.

All souls originate from heaven, coming down to earth with the spirit of God into mother's wombs at the time of conception. If the mother's life is not in God, and lives a life of grave sin, the darkness of evil replaces the Spirit that came with the baby's soul. Because the baby is in the womb of a mother being in the control of the devil. When the mother chose the devil to replace the Spirit of God, her actions affect her child. He is another person inside his mother's womb, but because he eats the food from his mother through his umbilical cord, the spirit of evil within his mother's soul spreads into him. Where the devil lives, there will be no presence of God dwelling there.

Vice versa, if the mother is in God, producing good deeds, then the baby continues to grow in the Spirit of God. After the baby is born, he is separated from his mother, but he is still being breast fed and raised by his parents; the spirits of parents will shadow him, more if the baby is being breast fed. (Receiving natural food is substance to transforming of receiving supernatural nourishment. When a person keep his heart pure and received Holy Eucharist, he received nourishment for his soul.). Therefore, the parent spirits are shadowing him, this baby will copy what the parents do. This baby will learn through hearing his parents talking and seeing his parents action, he may not able to do thing that parents did at that time, but surely, he very well will remember his parents words and actions. If parent actions are good, it will benefit the child's soul and life on earth, if parents have evil words and actions, it will damage the child's soul and his future life on earth.

There are many other ways that the child can learn, from his brothers and sisters, grandparents, family members, friends out of school, friends at school, teachers, and other people that where he hangs around. Besides, a child can learn evil things from many television programs, news with bombings, shootings, sex scandals of famous people, violent or sexual movies, books, magazines, and from violent computer games.

The evil spirits are working through people speaking untrue words and bad actions that we associate with bad televisions programs, sex, violence and war news; books, magazines, and newspapers, and computer games, that benefits flesh and harm souls, etc. After the child (adult) eyes and or ears received them, the evil spirits get in their thoughts and it will manifest through their actions. Vice versa, if a child (adult) hears good and truthful words, or sees good actions from his parent, teachers, friend, etc., the good and truthful words or actions will be engraved in a child's mind and turn to good deeds. The responsibility is laid on parents for a child many years before the time of conception and the rest of his life on earth.

How do you watch your child every moment of his life? It is impossible. You must dwell in God, depending on and trusting in Him. His supernatural power will protect your child, at the same time you ask God to help you to guide your children. The biggest trouble in the world is the majority people have no discernment, people cannot discern between good and evil. From the President of the nations, congress members, governments officials, to teachers, counselors, and parents, they speak carelessly, and take wrong actions.

Parents want the best for their children, but the majority of them are raising their children in a wrong direction, and they think that they do the right ways. Some parents do not even know who their children associate with, and what kind of children that their child associates with. A parent's responsibility is to watch your children's words when they talk, and their actions; not for nagging them, and not to beat them up, for beating the children is to teach them violence; but to discernment, with a lot of love for the troubled child, praying harder for the troubled child; speaking only after a lot of prayer to consult with God, keep you daily prayer. Some time God allows parents to call on police for help, but this must be done with good discernment. With parents love, patience and good examples with a lot of prayer, God will change the child.

School counselors, teachers, principals — how do you monitor every student when they are at the school? Impossible. Do you pray for your students daily, trust in God, and depend on Him? Or are you depending on your training and experience only? The training and experience is helpful, but if you lack discernment, you will be unable to help the

336

students; instead, you will do them harm.

Students suspended from school, or not attending school go to other places to commit crimes. Elementary and high school students are shooting at schools, killing many others students; and this will continue if people ignore the truth of life of depending and trusting in God. Parents are responsible in front of God to raise your children. Principals, counselors and teachers, you are responsible for all your students that God entrusted to you.

As I saw the United States House representatives and members of the senate speak and actions regarding President Bill Clinton's impeachment trial; I found the majority of them lack of discernment, they cannot discern the difference between right and wrong.

The first evil example: The President of the United States committed adultery in the hall of the first office of the nation. "You shall not commit adultery" Exodus 20:14. The Commander in Chief of the United States has lied under oath and still remains in office. During the impeachment hearing of President Clinton, he has no peace, but he changed the trumpet's tone, going to the Middle East the play peace maker, but the accord was false at the beginning. Immediately after he returned, he called to strike Iraq. The enemy spirits are controlling his mind and actions.

The trouble between the Serbs and Albanians has been going on for many years, the mass murder that killed about forty people was about a year ago. But the devil is cunning and destructive; therefore, again the devil's spirit works through President Bill Clinton, using his power of Commander in Chief of the United States to lead NATO press President Slobodan Malosovic to sign a peace agreement, and if they did not get what they wanted they use air strikes against Yugoslavia. Today is May 2, 1999. After 40 days of air strikes hundreds of civilians in Yugoslavia have been be killed by the NATO air strikes campaign, and almost a million refugees have left Kosovo.

Peace only comes with a lot of love and patience, peace is not simple as "if you do not sign an agreement for peace, I will bomb you." In a family, if the husband and wife love each other, they will be patient to each other and will have a peaceful family; but when the husband and wife have less love or no love, the dishes will be flying across the family room.

The air strikes on Yugoslavia are not for defense; it is destructive to property and creates mass murders, forcing almost a million Albanians out of their homes into poverty; many with diseases and mental illness for generations down the line in the history of the world. Who is to blame? The Americans provide more than two-thirds of the total aircraft and have conducted the vast majority of the strikes. The resulting iniquities of all of this are upon the taxpayers, their children, and grand children. The iniquities will transform to tragedies and disasters.

An article "America shoulders the load in air war" in the San Diego Union-Tribune,

April 24, 1999, issue indicated, "after four weeks of NATO's air campaign against Yugoslavia, the United States is providing more than two-thirds of the total aircraft and has conducted the vast majority of the strikes, because of the US bombers' unique ability to hit targets in bad weather."

The San Diego Union-Tribune, March 8, 1998, issue, article "My Lai massacre remembered" indicated, " But this time was different. Within four hours, 504 men, women, and children, by the residents' count, would lie dead after one of the US Army's blackest days." And, "When Quy awoke, the soldiers were gone. They left behind 407 dead and dying, villagers said later. The Americans had moved on to My Lai hamlet No. 2, where they killed 97 more people." And, "The dead bodies piled over me. That's why I survived. I was just lucky," she says. "I managed to pull myself out of the bodies and walked home. It was burned, and all the cows and pigs were killed. We had nothing left." And, "Though the country has no official religion, many Vietnamese believe in spirits. Le and Quy say they and other survivors could hear faint screams and cries for years after the massacre. I think their souls were still wandering around late at night," Le says."

The devil and his offspring spirits have been in the world from the beginning of the world. These evil spirits work through human minds and bodies, conducting various kinds of evil actions, such as violence, bombings, shootings, murder, mass murder and destruction of property, putting people in poverty, and causing physical diseases and mental illness, etc. These evil spirits worked through Adolf Hitler to performed mass murder; through United States lawmakers to pass laws that work against God's commandment, the Presidents and government officials. They joined the former South Vietnam government to fight against North Vietnam. The American - Vietnam war killed over three millions Vietnamese, and over 58,000 American troops of their own. The devil continued on, and currently the United States is bombing Iraq and Yugoslavia.

The taxpayers are participating in generating destructive chemicals and weapons, and salaries for men and women in uniforms. When a person does good they receive a reward; when a person commits a crime, he will be punished. Therefore, the iniquities are upon the United States.

After all the evil actions were committed by the United States President, members of congress, and government officials, and taxpayers participated because the government used taxpayers monies; the result of the evil hearts and actions result in iniquities.   The iniquities will result two ways: a) if people convert to God, they have to pay for what they did wrong to others either here on earth or in the purgatory. b) if people refused to convert it will cause greater disasters and tragedies; this will continue greater until all the elects convert to God.

> *For I, the LORD, your God, am a jealous God, inflicting punishment for*
> *their fathers' wickedness on the children of those who hate me, down to*

the third and fourth generation; but bestowing mercy down to the thousandth generation, on the children of those who love me and keep my commandments.

–Exodus 20: 5

1. San Diego Union-Tribune, April 21, 1999 issue, article "2 gunmen open fire; as many as 25 dead" states, "Students said the gunmen apparently belonged to a clique of outcasts called the "Trench Coat Mafia" who wore long black coats, boasted owning guns and disliked blacks, Hispanics and football players." And "The gunman didn't say anything. When he looked at me, the guy's eyes were just dead." Exhibit S-1, 4 pages

The spirit of disliking some groups or someone is a spirit of division that is controlled by the devil, and this spirit is moving throughout the world, and that includes in spiritual leaders. The gunman didn't say anything, just looked and the guy's eyes were dead; this gun man's body was moved by the supernatural power of the devil; the spirits are destructive and murderous.

2. San Diego Union-Tribune, April 22, 1999, issue, article "2 struck pose of rebels but were seen as losers" indicated, "They talked about Hitler and wore clothes with German insignia. In February they had completed a "diversion program" for first-time juvenile offenders, after their arrest for breaking into a van and stealing electronic equipment, said the Jefferson Country district attorney." Exhibit S-2, 2 pages

Peoples speech and actions speak their minds and hearts. When a child or an adult talks about violence or murder, or destructive stories; that is the symptom of the devil or devil offspring spirits either interfering or controlling, depending on the tone of voice and how often they talk about it. When a child or an adult commits any kinds of crime, and does not convert to God, and does not continue with daily exam and repentance; the evil spirit will continue in his mind, and work harder in his mind, and someday he will rise into action.

3. San Diego Union - Tribune, April 25, 1999, issue, article "Diary tells of planning for "big" indicated, "The diary indicates that Klebold, 17, and Harris, 18, had been planning the attack for a year. The teens had a map of the school that showed where lighting was poor and where it was possible to hide. The diary also reveals they monitored the lunchroom to find out when the greatest number of people would there. They were going to a big kill," Stone said. "This had been on their minds and they've been planning this particular thing and they've been building bombs (and) acquiring weaponry for a considerable period of time."

In the April 27, 1999, article "School gunman wrote of killing 500 students" indicated, "As he planned the assault on Columbine High School, Eric Harris wrote in a diary that he envisioned killing as many as 500 students, going on the attack neighboring homes and then hijacking a jet and crashing it in New York City, police investigators said yesterday."

Exhibit S-3, 4 pages.

A diary is very private and personal and every one of us need to respect it, but there are times the information in the dairy will be disclosed to others; therefore, as parents when we hear something suspicious and dangerous to your child or others; parents must keep your eyes very close on your child, and pray harder, asking God to show to you. That is the responsibility of a parent in front of God. The ideas that wrote in the dairy of killing 500 students and attacking neighboring homes and hijacking a jet and crashing it are the devil working through this boy, not his offspring. This kind of plans are generated from spirits of stealing, mass murder, and destruction. Both of the boys were used by the devil's spirit of destruction and stealing when they broke into a van and stole equipment. These two students received this kind of spirits from others, and they also gave out to others as well. I am very sure that there are more of their friends around them who have the same kinds of thoughts that these two have; their friends also have the thought of mass murder and destruction as well.

4. San Diego Union-Tribune, April 25, 1999, issue, article "Members of Trench Coat Mafia felt the heat" indicated, "We learned about it. We went to the library. You can go to any library and find books about how to do this." And "He said that from the time he was a freshman, jocks at the school called him "faggot," bashed him into lockers and threw rocks at him as he rode his bike home."

April 25, 1999 issue, article, "diary tells of planning for "big kill" stated, "We must do more to keep guns out of the hands of violent juveniles," Clinton said. "We must do more to prevent violence in our schools."

April 22, 1999 issue, article "School safety moves to top of leaders' agenda" indicated, "Some members of Congress are seeking a 'national dialogue' on school violence and asking for more prayer in schools. Exhibit S-4, 2 pages and Exhibit 3, see above

These are two major starting points that the devil uses; the devil uses other students to provoke him; and that same devil spirit worked through them of learning from movies, books, magazines, and television of violent news and war news. This very same devil spirit worked through their minds and focus, then turned to actions.

President Bill Clinton's words of keeping guns out of the hands of violent juveniles contradicts his actions. He as an adult and Commander in Chief of the United States, is untrue under oath, so how can he expect the children to be truthful. He leads NATO in speaking out loud pushing for air strikes on Yugoslavia, causing destruction, mass murder, and a million refugees; how could he tell children not to commit destructive acts and mass murder. The children learn from adults, when adults commit evil and then tell the children not to do it, they will do it behind adults even more stronger. Therefore, when the President spoke of discipline to the children, he has to go ahead to discipline himself to speak the truth, and not to commit this nation with evil actions of murder with air strikes and ground troops in other countries, so his words will be effective, and the American children follow his commends.

5. San Diego Union-Tribune, April 22, 1999, issue. The article titled "Counselors find reaching troubled kids a challenge." "Each of the four counselors in his departments oversees 500 students, but he finds that most of their duties are bureaucratic matters. That leaves little room for one-on-one contact with troubled students." Exhibit S-5. 2 pages

At the level of counselors, teachers, and principals, your responsibilities are almost at the same level of their parents; but you cannot monitor all the students who are under your supervision. You must be a good example and pray a lot, asking God to shepherd them with His supernatural protection.

6. San Diego Union-Tribune, April 22, 1999, issue, article "Students here cope with pain, grief" speaks of various reasons that caused the disaster, and actions to show their pain, grief. The only one that was most important indicated, "Richard Kelly, principal at the University of San Diego High School in Linda Vista, went straight to the heart of it. He got on the intercom at the private Catholic high school and led his students in prayer." Exhibit S-6, a page

The point that I am making is that God is the only one who can heal the pain, and prevent future actions. Yet, the human level has to take action, but each one's action must come from the heart. When actions come from the heart, it will come with God's power. God is the living God, every time class begins, it must start with prayer, asking God for guidance and protection to learn the good and keep them. Beside the learning in class, God will help you to be a better person each day, the school will be less violent and safe. You people do not know how powerful is God's power; but I know, for the last several years, I have completely depended on God every moment, with every action and thought.

7. San Diego Union-Tribune, April 27, 1999, article "Mother of young Arkansas killer feels a double wound," "Where were these boys' parents? How could they not have known these kids were building bombs in their garage" Why didn't they pay attention to the trench coats and other warning signs of trouble? But Woodard had to stop short of taking comfort in the next thought on most people's mind, "My child would never do anything like that. Because, in fact, Woodard's child did, just last year, in Jonesboro." Exhibit S-7, 2 pages

When any child or teenager commits any crime; other parents are quickly blame that child's parents. Yes, the parents of that child are responsible for their child's actions. But the how about the blame, how much do you pray for your child? How much do you keep your eyes on your children? Mrs. Woodard learned the hard lesson after her son's actions caused death. Each one has free will to accept or to reject choosing God for guidance, protection and blessing.

The devil and his offspring spirits use the following actions to transfer their spirit to young children, teenagers and adults that are caused by United States presidents, congress, high ranking officers, and NATO.

a. San Diego Union-Tribune, April 13, 1999, issue, article "Passengers on train fall victim to NATO warplane" indicated, "Serb officials said at least nine people aboard the passenger train were killed and 16 injured when a NATO warplane bombed it. The private news agency Deta said a 10 body was found later and that officials feared the toll would rise even higher."

And April 15, 1999, issue, article "Serbs accuse NATO of raid on civilian convoy" indicated "NATO and Serb leaders clashed yesterday over blame for deaths of at least 64 ethnic Albanian civilians after a NATO bombing raid on a convoy in Kosovo."

April 29, 1999, issue, article "Shocked survivors sift rubble" indicated, "Milic's wife, Verna, 35, also died. So did his mother and his two children, Miljana, 15, and Vladimir,11, all of them killed about noon Tuesday when an errant NATO bomb obliterated their new house and the cellar in which they were seeking shelter." And, "This was a completely new house, three stories, with complete new furniture," he said, still astonished at the jagged pile or refuse where it once stood. "It had a large basement. Everyone felt safe there. But the whole family died." And, "Yugoslavia officials said 20 civilians, half of them children, died in this town of 11,000 people 200 miles south of Belgrade, near the Bulgarian border." Exhibit A-1, 5 pages

Jesus cured a crippled woman on the Sabbath "The Lord said to him in rely, "Hypocrites! Does not each one of you on the Sabbath untie his ox or his ass from the manger and lead it out for watering?" Luke 13:15

The devil's spirit has ruling of the pilot in cooperating with NATO leaders by President Clinton's intentional mass murder of civilians. The devil has given you targets, but when the devil uses pilots to drop the bombs, his supernatural power pushes bombs to miss the target, and to mass murder civilians. Refresh your memory: At the time each of you joined the military, navy, etc., did you sign the agreement to protect the United States? Or did you sign to destroy structures and mass murder? Every time each one of your dropped a bomb; your free will is charged to engaged in mass murders and destroy structures. You are doing the works of the devil, and God is charging against your souls and your life on earth as well. Jesus the Lord, Himself took action to teach us not to obey man's laws that engage to harm others, and to reveal the leaders are hypocrites.

b. The San Diego Union-Tribune, May 9, 1999, issue, article, "Perfect aim; wrong target" indicated, "This time, instead of chanting for democracy, they were denouncing the United State with shouts of 'US killers,' 'US go to hell.' And 'NATO Nazis'. "The San Diego Union-Tribune, May 10, 1999, issue, article "NATO feels new fallout from attack" indicated, "China suspended high-level military contacts with the United States today. The official Xinhua News Agency said talk with the United States on human rights, arms control, international security and preventing arms proliferation also were being postponed." And "China's ambassador to the United States, Li Zhaoxing's aide yesterday that his government would not accept American attempts to "whitewash the atrocity as a mistake." And "NATO Supreme Allied Commander Gen. Wesley Clark insisted the bombing was an aberration and blamed a misstep made by intelligence staff in identifying the target early in planning. 'It wasn't crew error. It wasn't mechanical error.' Clark told ABC. 'It was a case of the selection of the target and the process that was involved there'."

On the same date, May 10, 1999, another article "Chinese mobs vent wrath at foreign envoys" indicated, " Three journalists were killed. More then 20 people were injured, six seriously, a Chinese Foreign Ministry spokesman said." And "....Chinese protester who shattered embassy window with rocks, flung paint bombs and burned caricatures of President Clinton as Hitler." And "Between 200 and 300 Chinese students approached the British Embassy in Beijing today chanting slogans such as 'Pay blood debts with blood' and 'Disband NATO.'" And, " 'America is really a bully,' said Liu Lixia, 37, who bought her 12-year-old son to see the protester. 'I hate Clinton.'" Exhibit A-2, 6 pages.

President Bill Clinton allowed the devil to control him of leading NATO for this airstrikes campaign; and the United States is proud of its bombs hitting targets perfectly. Therefore, the United States is the main country to be blamed. The devil has won using NATO commanders, President Clinton, and those under their authorities of this bombing; the devil then used Chinese peoples to take radical actions full of hatred. The taxpayers are also participating in these entire airstrikes and bombing China Embassy through the United States using taxpayers monies for generating destructive bombs and paying salaries to men and women in the force.

c. San Diego Union-Tribune, April 8, 1999, issue, article "Two weeks of campaign cost NATO $700 million" indicated, "The air campaign against Yugoslavia cost the United States and its NATO allies about $700 million during its first two weeks, a defense analyst said yesterday."

April 24, issue, article "Americans shoulder the load in air war" indicated, "After four weeks of NATO's air campaign against Yugoslavia, the United States is providing more than two-third of the total aircraft and has conducted the vast majority of the strikes, because of the US bombers' unique ability to target in bad weather."

April 28, 1999 issue, article "Clinton authorizes reserve call-up" indicated, "President Clinton yesterday authorized the call-up of as many as 33,102 reservists as NATO warplanes continued to hammer away at Serb targets inside Yugoslavia and diplomats scrambled to find a way to end the 35 day old battle against Yugoslavia President Slobodan Milosevic." And "Clark said Milosevic's forces in Kosovo probably number about 40,000, the same level he enjoyed before the allied war. Those forces, he said, are responsible for driving 700,000 ethnic Albanians out of the province and forced 820,000 to be homeless inside the Kosovo."

April 13, 1999, issue, article "NATO chiefs harden resolve" indicated, "To add muscle to that pledge, NATO's senior commander, Gen. Wesley K. Clark, asked the Pentagon yesterday to contribute about 300 more warplanes to the fight, in what would make possible a rapid and strident expansion of NATO's attacks."

April 27, 1999, issue, article "Reserves could get call today; Apache crashes" indicated, "European officials said the European Commission believes the cost of reconstructing the Balkans after the Kosovo war will be about $30 billion. On Capitol Hill, Congress, despite some criticism of NATO's strategy, was preparing legislation that would exceed the President's request for $6 billion of emergency money for the air war against Yugoslavia. House Republicans were drafting a bill with a price tag of at least $11 billion, according to The Associated Press, quoting unnamed House GOP aides." Exhibit A-3, 9 pages.

The above information proves to the taxpayers that the devil is controlling the President of the United States, and Bill Clinton is leading NATO. This same devil also controls NATO's commanders. The purpose of the devil is to use men's bodies, to destroy their souls and come to their physical bodies. The devil spirit is using President Bill Clinton, NATO's commanders, and United States congress to destroy their souls. At the same this devil destroys them, the devil also destroys the taxpayers' souls, physical bodies and materials. Beyond that, this same devil, the authorities of the Yugoslavia to drive the Albanians out of their homes, put them into poverty, causing physical disease and mental illness. The same devil is using the media to glorify his works to bring this evil news to the in the United States and throughout the world are receiving this news, and the spirit of the devil comes with this evil news. When people receive news the devil manifests in their minds and makes plans, when the time comes, they murder others like the students at Columbine High in Colorado, Jonesboro in Arkansas, at Capitol Hill, post offices, , etc.

d. The San Diego Union - Tribune, May 7, 1999, issue, article "House doubles Clinton's funding request for Kosovo" indicated, "The House last night agree to give President Clinton more than double the funding he sought for the conflict with Yugoslavia, a week after refusing to support the U.S. led NATO air campaign. On a 311-105 vote, House approved spending $13.1 billion to finance American participation in the fighting, assisting refugees from Kosovo, replenish military spare parts, and increase military pay." And "In addition to the approximately $6 billion request by Clinton, the bill includes: * $3 billion for more ammunition, spare parts and equipment identified by the military as needed before the air war began. * $1.8 billion for increasing military pay and retirement benefits, with details to be worked out and authorized later. *1.1 billion for military construction in Europe."

In the same day, May 7, 1999, issue, article "Gunman at large after killing four at nightclub" indicated, "About 20 customers were inside the club yesterday morning when the gunman pulled a semiautomatic handgun and fired a bullet into the first victim. The man then shot the first victim's friend and two other people sitting in the same booth." And "The first victim and his friend both died at the scene. Another victim, a 23-year-old woman who died at a hospital shortly after the shooting, was seated with her sister and two men. One of those men was also shot and died at the club." Exhibit A-4, 2 pages

Taxpayers voted and paid the representative salary to represent us in our best interest, to save our temporary physical lives on earth and eternal life in heaven. But the majority of the House Representatives action in this matter very clearly destroyed the taxpayers interest; instead, they forced taxpayers to commit grave sins of mass murder, destruction, and adding more refugees to the pool of million refugees, bringing more evil disasters and God's purification of tragedies into the United States. The evidence is very obvious; what you sent out, the return will be a lot greater than what you sent out. Good for good, evil for evil. In the case of the United States government using taxpayer monies is majority of evil for evil. Exhibit....

e. The San Diego Union-Tribune, March 8, 1998, issue, article "My Lai massacre remembered" states, "But this time was different. Within four hours, 504 men, women and children, by the residents' count, would lie dead after one of the US Army's blackest days." And "When Quy awoke, the soldiers were gone. They left behind 507 dead and dying, villagers said later. The Americans had moved on to My Lai hamlet No. 2, where they killed 97 more people. Quy found herself in a pile of corpses, including her mother and eldest daughter, in the ditch where the blood was calf-deep. "The dead bodies piled over me. That's why I survived. I was just lucky," she says. "I managed to pull myself of the bodies and walked home. It was burned, and all the cows and pigs were killed. We had nothing left." And "Though the country has no official religion, many Vietnamese believe in spirits. Le and Quy say they and other survivors could hear faint scream and cries for years after the massacre. "I think their souls were still wandering around late at night." Le said. But they say the cries have faded since a memorial was erected in 1978. The spirits seem to be more at rest now."

May 4, 1999, issue, Article Babbitt set to die today by injection" indicated, "Manuel Babbitt, an ex-Marine who survived some of the bloodiest battles of the Vietnam War; was scheduled to be executed early today, 18 years after murdering a 78-year-old Sacramento grandmother." And "To his last moments, Babbitt denied remembering assaulting Leah Schendel, who lived alone in a retirement home between Babbitt's residence and a bar where he spent much of the day drinking before breaking into the woman's home.

April 30, 1999, issue, article "Most patients in mental hospitals criminals" indicated, "Now, the hospital keeps most of its new patients in khaki uniforms, behind a 16-foot-high chain link fence topped with coils of glistening razor wire that was constructed in March. Nearly 75 percent of the 739 residents have criminal backgrounds." And "Part of the reason for the change is financial — the annual state budget for mental patients is $460 million, but few county mental health departments can afford the $100,000 a year it costs to keep a patient at Napa State Hospital said Carla Jacobs, a MAMI board member from Long Beach." Exhibit A-5, 5 pages

There are only two sources of supernatural power and two sides of man in this world, good and evil. Those who do good are receiving supernatural power from God, those who do evil are receiving supernatural from the devil. Everyone who wants to follow God must obey all His commandments. His commandments are filled with love, patience, obedience to God, placing God above all things, serving God through service to others with love, putting others before his or herself. The spirits of disobedience and exult were cast out from heaven. That spirit was Lucifer who disobeyed God and wanted to be like God. That we are calling a devil. God also cast out one-third of the angels who were disobedient to God; they are now fallen angels and they are under the supernatural power of the devil. These evil spirits are searching to act in the murder of souls and physical bodies and destroying structures. The US Army troops that killed 504 people in Vietnam was controlled by the devil; this same spirit of the devil also murdered groups of Albanians in Kosovo, that very same spirit of the devil is either interfering or controlling the NATO commanders, President Bill Clinton, and pilots of airstrikes Yugoslavia. Plant good seeds and receive good fruits, plan thorn seeds and receive rotten fruits. The Vietnamese veterans or any kind of war veterans minds are being interfered with or controlled by spirit of the devil or his fallen angels, which I also call the devil and his offspring. The word offspring includes souls that are in the control of the devil; these spirits are working through human minds and body. The enemy spirits can completely control human minds and bodies like one of the gunman teenager's eyes looking dead, and the US Army troops that killed 504 men, women and children at My Lai within four hours. The minds of people with mental illness are being heavily interfered with or controlled by enemy spirits. The enemy spirits use alcohol to block out people's minds like Babbitt (To his last moments, Babbitt denied remembering assaulting Leah Schendel.) These very same spirits are in the minds of people with Alzheimer disease.

f. The United States government sends uniformed men and women overseas to do the will that belong to the devil, and the taxpayers are paying for destructive chemicals, weapons, and salaries for the uniformed men and women. The US government and taxpayers are planting thorn trees, they receive rotten fruits. The actions of killing people in other countries is not defense; therefore, they do the works of the devil, the devil's spirit got the control of their minds. When they returned to United States, this devil spirit still dwells within them. This is same with people who commit crimes, when they committed crimes, the devil had control of their minds and dwells within them, to harm others, there many times they also harm themselves. The ex-Marine killed a grandmother, or others who committed mass murders like Tim McVeigh are the result of the devil spirits that remain in their minds since they were in the armed forces. This paragraph is a testimony of souls alive after the physical death: (Le and Quy say they and other survivors could hear faint scream and cries for years after the massacre. "I think their souls were still wandering around late at night." Le said. But they say the cries have faded since a memorial was erected in 1978. The spirits seem to be more at rest now.")

g. The San Diego Union - Tribune, May 2, 1999 issue, Article "3 American POWS heading home" indicated, " Jackson organized the trip to Belgrade despite attempts by senior Clinton administration officials to dissuade him." and "Yugoslav President Slobodan Milosevic ordered their release yesterday without conditions "in recognition of Jackson's efforts to achieve peace and understanding between peoples." And "Asked whether the release would bring a halt to NATO airstrikes, Rubin suggested it would not. "Secretary Albright indicated to Jackson our position remains unchanged," Rubin said. On the same issue, another article indicated, "Release is answer to families prayers "We just thank God so much for answering our prayers."

May 3, 1999, issue, article "Clinton rejects airstrike pause" indicated, "This gesture ... of good will cannot obliterate or overcome the stench of evil and death that has been inflicted in those killing fields in Kosovo." Defense Secretary William Cohen said on NBC's "meet the Press." And "Clinton gave little ground, insisted that NATO airstrikes, now in their sixth week, would continue unabated until Milosevic agrees to withdraw troops from Serbian province of Kosovo and allow ethnic Albanians to return under self-rule and the protection of an armed NATO-led force." And "As we welcome our soldiers home, or thoughts also turn to the over 1 million Kosovars who are unable to go home because the policies of the regime in Belgrade," Clinton said in a statement. "Today we reaffirm our resolve to persevere until they, too, can return — with security and self government." Exhibit A-6, 7 pages.

Earlier after these three soldiers were captured, President Bill Clinton called the government of Yugoslavia to release these three soldiers, but his calling was false. The senior Clinton administration officials tried to dissuade Rev. Jesse Jackson; but through prayers of the POWs, their family members and others that have pure hearts, and within God's will; God strengthened Rev. Jackson and other religious leaders to accompany him in the place of life and death next to each other, to rescue others. Because God is within them in this trip, therefore, they were successful.

These are major messages that God is speaking to President Bill Clinton and the NATO's commanders as, "You people should have power to get release for these three POWs; but you have done the evil deeds; twisted your evil actions to good deeds. I will not let you blind my people for you to use one good action to generated hundred evil actions. Therefore, I send my priests to rescue the three young men. Your actions of airstikes cause Serbia to drive a million people out of their homes, putting them in poverty, with physical disease and mental illness; and now you still want to do more destruction by more airstrikes. The Yugoslavia government is evil, you are also evil. You are stronger than them you bombed, they cannot fight back. I have blocked your way with bad weather, but you do not see. You refused to obey my commandments. I love you, I have gave you a lot of time to convert, but you refused. Because I love you I have to discipline you, I am sending my Servant who sent you numbers of letters; but you people ignore Her, I am raising my iron rod at you, so you can be in the shoes of people in Yugoslavia."

h. The San Diego Union - Tribune, May 4, 1991, issue, article "Killer twisters slam 2 states" subtitled "36 die, hundreds hurt in ravaged areas of Oklahoma, Kansas" reads, "Tornadoes tore through Oklahoma and Kansas yesterday, wiping out whole neighborhoods, killing at least 36 people and injuring hundreds. At least 1,000 homes were destroyed in Oklahoma City alone, police said." Exhibit A-7, 5 pages.

God does not make noise with hot air, when He speaks, He speaks loud and clear with His actions, but people eyes are being blocked by the devil spirit. God loves and forgive, but man must obey all His commandments. When man obeys His commandments, it will benefit man's souls and physical life. But men went to the devil's direction, wanting things that fulfill their ego, the things that benefit their temporary body, and destroy their permanent soul. Therefore, God has to discipline man up with His actions for man to convert.

May 5, 1999, in the late evening after the Lord Jesus told me, " Did I tell you to ask the Father for Fatima sun dancing come down to earth? The tornadoes at Oklahoma and Kansas was on May 23, 1997, letter I told you sent to President Clinton and members of the U.S. Senate."

Rebuild My Church Divine Mission

(The Lord Jesus gave this name to Mariette)

P.O. Box 261550 ✦ San Diego, CA 92196-1550

May 23, 1997

Dear United States Senate members and President Bill Clinton,

God the Father, the Lord Jesus, and the Holy Spirit commanded me to send this letter to you. This letter was dictated to me on May 3, 1997, with these instructions. "Mail the letter to United States Senate members and President Bill Clinton, two days before the first Holy Eucharist Healing Service and Altar Call at the Cathedral of Saint Andrew, Little Rock,

Arkansas, on May 27, 1997."

"God commands you to pass abortion laws according to His commandments. His commandments allow abortion only when the life of the mother is threatened of death. He is the only One to give life and take it away.

Tax monies cannot be used to fund for abortions or other purposes that go against God's commandments, such as the production of more weapons, chemicals, training, other than for defense.

God is pouring out more tragedies upon the world to save His people's souls. These tragedies will occur more and more until all the elect convert their hearts and minds to God. No one on earth can stop these tragedies. But people may limit them by obeying all His commandments.

I will be God's instrument, to speak to the public. God's words come with His power, and people will obey His commandments."

On June 6, 1997 the Lord Jesus told me, "Church authorities and government officials, lawmakers are refusing to cooperate with God's plan for salvation of the world. I need you to listen carefully to all my instructions, and take actions as I tell you. Give them My web site address."

The Lord Jesus, Jesus of Nazareth Web site on the internet: http://www.Jesusweb.org

I will pray for you to obey God, to save the people that you are representing. If you do not obey God, you will bring more tragedies upon the people you represent.

Sincerely in Christ Jesus,

Mariette Do-Nguyen)

The above record indicates besides the iniquity resulting from personal sins; the many years that the United State engaged in other countries wars have resulted in the community's iniquities from community sins are up to the foot of the heaven; and this must be purged by God to save man souls, and physical lives as well. God gave each one of you free will to obey Him or to obey the devil; but the majority of the people living in the United States are giving their free will to the devil. I mean of people disobeying God's commandments and acting evil.

I have delivered a number of letters to President Bill Clinton, Vice President Al Gore, and all 100 member of the United States Senate, telling them they must convert to God, and pass laws that go according to God's commandments, but they ignore what God asked me send to them.   Again, the tragedies and disasters will continue, and they will get worse, until people convert to God. All of this was foretold in the Gospel of Matthew chapter 24, and God also revealed to me more clearly. It does not mean that I will tell you of where and when. I do not know of how and when, but many times when the Lord Jesus tells me something, they happen.

Each one of you have the choice of obeying God to limit some of the tragedies and disasters by converting to God: The place thing is asking God to help you be willing to reform your life. Learn God's commandments in their correct meaning, and apply them to you thought and your actions. Pray daily with Holy scriptures, depending and trusting in God alone. It does not mean that you just sit there and do nothing. You must take actions, but do it with God's discernment. Control your thoughts and actions; to reject evil, be a martyr, teach your children, grandchildren and influence your friends and neighbors, co-workers etc.   All of these actions must be filled with a lot of love and patience, and your love for enemies also.

The truth will not make people feel good, but it will save people's souls for eternal life in heaven, and temporary physical life on earth. God the Creator of heaven and the earth entrusted to me this divine mission; I must deliver exactly what God asked of me, and also I love all of you, I pray for people on this world daily for you to convert to God, that your souls can go to heaven after you depart from this world.

The Cause and Cure of Alzheimer's Disease

The Lord uses my younger son to reveal information about Alzheimer's disease, because he is working as researcher on this terrible affliction.

July 10, 1997; I called my younger son, Chau at the laboratory, in San Diego from Little Rock, Arkansas for my DMV sticker. He told me that he forgot to mail it to me. He then asked me, " Mom, can you pray for me to gain more memory."

July 10, 1997. Before I went to sleep I asked the Lord Jesus to increase my son's memory. He said, "I gave him the gift of memory, but because he was drinking alcohol, he forgets. The alcohol decreases his memory. After he stops drinking his memory will revive."

July 11, 1997. In my morning devotion, at 8:50 a.m. I prayed, " Lord, I give thanks to You, Jesus, Father and the Holy Spirit. You have blessed my son: through Him, You will cure those who have Alzheimer's disease, and prevent others from getting Alzheimer's, and to save souls. Lord, I ask you to open my son's mind, and show him exactly how You want him to do, to serve You by service to others."

The Lord Jesus said to me, "The formula, and the cause of Alzheimer's that I give to you, is to give to your son only, not for any other. If anyone tries to take it away from him, I will crush down the formula. This formula needs a lots of prayer. This has been reserved for him as the chosen one. The Father predestined him for this calling."

I asked the Lord Jesus, "Lord, are You finished or You still speaking?" He said to me, "Mariette, how come you are in such a hurry?" I said to Jesus, "Lord, I just want to make sure that I receive everything from You, and deliver to him. In turn, he will deliver to others."

The Lord Jesus said, "Mariette, you are anxious to see he succeeds, because I always answer your prayer, and love you above everything and everyone in this world. But your son is the one who has to pray. He needs to come directly to me. I will give to him in detail. You act only as the intercessor for him, you can assist him, but you cannot do the work for him. He is the one who must labor to Me, the Lord his God, your God, and God of all creation."

Alzheimer's disease is caused by enemy spirits, the spirits work through alcohol. Either that person has been drinking in his life, it could be from drinking a lot or a little, or from the blood line.

God gave everyone various amount heavenly substance as a gift of memory; we also have to ask Him for more in later day in life, this gift can be decreased or lost it. When that person is involved in drinking, more or less depending on the enemy spirit (devil or his offspring spirits) that comes with alcohol, that when a person gets drunk, his mind will not be as sound as when he is not drunk. From his mind comes his actions. A very high percentage of people who drink hard liquor will cause some kind of trouble, because the enemy spirits act through his mind and body. These actions are of various kinds, and may look good in the world, but they go against God's commandments. The enemy spirits use alcohol to enter to people's body and mind; these enemies spirits will transfer to a child at the time of conception from the previous alcohol drinker; and wait for time to manifesting.

The process for Alzheimer's disease to be cured:

a. In many cases a person drinking will not be exposed to Alzheimer's, but will expose his blood descendants many generations down the line. It takes time from generation to generation of avoiding drinking liquor completely to heal the blood line of those who drink alcohol; this also same with Alzheimer's.

b. When the family has an Alzheimer's patient, the family members must pray for the patient as well as for help, that he or she may come to God. Through prayer and the living sacrifices and faith of family members of the person with Alzheimer's, the patient will increase his or her memory. There are some cases when the patient will be completely healed. Everything is possible with God. There are times when God allows this affliction to purify that person's soul, and the souls of those who take care of the patient and members of family.

Jesus the Lord Jesus transformed wine, consecrated it, and as symbolism, transformed it into supernatural as His blood, for the purpose of purification, to save souls for the eternal life. But man is opposite, uses liquor for the purpose to satisfying physical body and ruin souls.

The Alzheimer's Disease revelation also can be understood by people for getting God and His creation, and drinking in the world's system.

The Fish Spewed Mariette upon the Shore

May 6, 1998; Over the last four years, when coming to pray for myself, I asked the Lord for protection, discernment, steadfast faith, how to listen and to hear everything He revealed to me. Also to remember His words, and to put in action exactly how and what He wants me to do, and stay in complete obedience to God alone; everything I asked as tools for the mission that God entrusted to me.

But today for the first time during the mass, I asked the Lord to grant me hope, healing, steadfast faith, happiness in God, and to stand firm and strong as His Instrument. After I finished my devotion to the Blessed Sacrament after mass, the Lord told me, "Jonah Chapters two and three." I then read both chapters.

After I finished reading these two chapters, on the way out to my car, I went back inside Saint Michael's temple, and kneeled in front of the Blessed Mother's statue that was salvaged from the temple when it completely burned several years ago.   Obeyed God, I have been attending the Saint Michael's temple since early March 1998. This is the first time that I came and kneeled in front of her statue. When I saw Our Lady of Grace's statue, I saw a snake at her feet. I hurried to look at her from the waist up and focused at her face, avoiding seeing the snake that lost the top part of his mouth. I asked her, "Mother, I ask you to pray to the Father, the Lord Jesus and the Holy Spirit for me, to grant me hope, happiness in God, steadfast faith, and to be firm and strong, and healing."

After I finished speaking to her, she said to me, "Close your eyes so you will be able to hear." I closed my eyes, and she continued, "The fish spewed you upon on the shore at the time you moved to Little Rock, Arkansas. Today is the time for the city put on their sackcloth. You inherited my estate, the devil is under your feet."

Mariette's Responsibility is to Deliver God's Instructions

May 9, 1998; In my dream I saw I was entering a dark beauty salon. While I was in the salon, I looked out in the dark parking lot where some cars were parking. Immediately in front of the salon, where my car was parked to the door of the beauty salon was some light; I saw people were standing around my car and looking at it.

The dream changed a little, I was walking to find those teenagers who had just stolen my car. I heard the voice from heaven tell me, "They [teenagers] just stole your car. Tell that man, he knows where they keep the car and he can retrieve it for you." While the voice from heaven was saying this, I saw a strong, tall, dark man coming toward me. In my thought, "This man knows where the robbers are and he took money from people to the robbers to retrieve the car. I should report him to the police." While I was thinking, I saw several teenagers outside a poor lower shelter with my car parked to the side. But when the dark man came, I gave him two hundred dollars to retrieve my car.

The Lord gave me another dream: In this dream I saw a small van from behind, with some windows, the inside was filled with passengers. My spirit was higher than the top of the car, I looked and saw this car on its way down a very deep slope. When I saw this I was very frightened for them.

I then saw the same van. This time the van was crushed down on the ground. The top of the van was built with walls, inside this rectangular top were four side walls where four people were laying, in two lines, each line with two persons.

I then heard the Blessed Virgin Mother tell me, "The Lord reveals to you about the abortion. Back in late 1994, you fasted for seventy five days, praying for freedom of religion in Vietnam, and for twenty seven days to pray for stopping abortions. You then gave up fourteen day of each month offering to the Lord for the mission that He entrusted to you."

I then saw the day before when I was at the copy center, and told the owner, "I don't know that Jesus still loves me". He responded to me, "The more He trusts in you, the more He expects from you." I then said, "Lord, I know in my heart that you love me more then everyone in this world; I just said that without from my heart. Forgive me, keep me away from sin, help me to please You."

Recently I met with the second Magdelene at Danny's Restaurant, the Lord said to me, "Let them [second Magdelene and her husband] work out their differences, you have done what you need to do for them." I then saw I was standing at the corner speaking to a woman holding a sign fighting against abortion. The Lord said to me, "They are being sued, let them come to you. The sign they have is not right. The Catholic pro-life will come to you first. These people violate." The Lord means that the sign of babies being cut is causing a violation in spirit.

The Lord continued, "Senator Helms "BILL" gives people some choices to have an abortion. I want you to write a letter to all the members of the U.S. senate, to amend the bill of Senator Jesse Helms, put the discipline of the body to women, responsibility on men, and require parent responsibility for their teen children."

God's Instructions for Mariette

May 24, 1998. The U.S. Catholic celebrated the Accession of the Lord this year on the Seventh Sunday after Easter. After I received the Holy Eucharist, the Holy Spirit told me,

"You can share with her but not the priest. Share with her the reason you can not be an active member. She has been notified by the priest that you are special. Pay close attention to her. She will bring good and bad to the parish. Take her other woman with you on the trip, the Father's glory will shine upon the world through you. She is close to the Blessed Mary. The Blessed Mother's spirit surrounds you and that will draw her to you. She is devoted to the Holy Eucharist. You make the Lord Jesus visible to the world through the Holy Eucharist. You two have a same common ground. There will be some little disagreements at times." The Lord was referring to the disagreement between the church leader's teaching and God's commandments.

The Holy Spirit continued, "Do not let them persuade you, stand firm and strong." I prayed, "Father, Lord Jesus, Holy Spirit, do not give me many choices, but You do your way through me, Your Servant."

Every One at the Right Side Will be Healed

May 26, 1998: About 11:00 a.m. my entire body was filled with God's Spirit, and at the same time I was battling against the enemy spirits. I took blessed anointment oil and put on myself, and went and laid down on the bed to start my devotion. I normally in front of the altar in my private residence during the day for my devotion. I fell asleep close to the end of the devotion. In my dream I saw a wooden window frame, closed from behind. It had crossed teal green blinds, three parts down were divided by two thin bars.

I saw the Lord insert a light cream-colored, dry and clean light palm leaf over the top cross bar with His invisible hand. When I saw this palm leaf already fastened under the two dividers, I looked at the dry palm leaf; to my right, I saw the Lord neatly pushing the end of this long palm leaf under the top corner frame. I looked to the left, and I saw this clean palm leaf coming out of a holder, like a tape measure. I looked at the left corner, the palm leaf went through under the frame's high bar.

The Holy Spirit said to me, "When you walk in the door, anyone you see at your right side will be healed." I saw the wall to my right, and many patients were laying on beds to my left along a hallway. I said, "Lord, there is the wall to my right, but no one is there." The Holy Spirit said, "Make a U turn at the end of the hall." As he said this, I saw myself and a few other people with me had just made a U turn at the end of the hall, and that end door was locked. The Holy Spirit asked me, "Where are they?" I replied, "They are at my right." The Holy Spirit said, "They will be healed." The Holy Spirit continued, "The Father has granted this. From tomorrow, if you see any one physically and emotionally incapacitated, do not tell them to pick up their mat. Talk to them like you normally do, the Word will come through you and they will be healed." While the Holy Spirit was saying this I saw a person in a wheelchair in the public area. I went out in front of Saint Michael's, through the Saint Michael's temple foyer, inside the right side door to the patio.

I then got up. The clock showed 11:35 a.m. I got the black ink pen and tried to copy the dream down, but the Holy Spirit told me, "Get your purple one." He watched me finish copying the dream.

The long room I saw was half of the house, the wall to my right was from the floor to the center beam of the roof. All beds were iron beds with linens, the head of the beds were leaning against the side wall. Every thing was in a light cloud color, except the people with me were a little tinted.

I then went back on the bed and prayed, "Father, Lord Jesus, through the works of the Holy Spirit, I only want to ask you to glorify me so I can glorify You, to build the kingdom of heaven, get people to convert, and have the Church in unity so Jesus' wounds can be healed. The Father's will be done. I ask You for this healing power to come through me without limits."

I fell sleep again. The Lord brought me back to a dream that I had a few years ago in the same setting, except the one before had less beds, no patients and no people walking in the hall.

I saw Mrs. Phong walking at Saint Michael's patio. Close to her left side was a fence wall. While she bent her head down, her hand was fixing my red umbrella hook, and to her right was an empty patio. I knew that Mrs. Phong was symbolic of me, (Phong is a Vietnamese name that means wind in English). I said, "Lord, there is no one at her right." The Holy Spirit said, "They will be filled in at the patio." I then saw some people in dark suits coming out from the right side of Saint Michael's foyer door.

The wall high up to the beam is symbolic of being strong and firm, the wall at the center is symbolic that the strength and firmness was from God, and will endure to the end. The right side is symbolic of the righteousness of God. The righteousness of God is God's power that will destroy the evil spirits inflicted in human minds and bodies.

Physicians- Psychiatrists- Medicine —Mariette on Trial without a Lawyer

Money is not important, but obedience to God is the most important thing in each individual's life. When a person places money above obedience to God, there will be a fall in future days, but obedience to God alone will always result in victory.

On June 11, 1998, under God's instruction when I went to a psychiatric doctor, the doctor told me to take medicine. I asked him, "What will this medicine do for me?" He said, "It will help you to sleep better." I said to him, "The New York Life Insurance Company has not paid my benefits for nearly four months, I have no money to buy medicine." He said to me, "I will give you some samples." I silently asked the Lord, His voice told me, "Just receive it like he told you." I then replied to the doctor, " Okay." He then gave me a small bottle of sample medicine. When I got home I laid it on the second floor with other items that I had on the second floor, next to my bed.

June 12, 1998: I sat next to my bed, and before I started my devotion I saw the medicine bottle. I took one pill before I went to sleep. During the night I got up twice to go to the restroom, both times I fell. The next morning I tried very hard to wake up to go to mass, but I could not get up. While I was trying to get up, I heard the angel call several time, "Mariette, you need to get up to go to church." After I got off the bed, I had to constantly ask the Lord to wake me up. I finally got up and drunk a thick cup of dark coffee so it would wake me up. Driving on free way to Saint Michael's temple, I had to be very careful. During the mass my mind was blank; I was trying to pray, but every time I started a few sentences my petitions dripped away. I left the temple for home immediately after mass, instead of going to the Blessed Sacrament for another half hour.

When I got home there was a message from a woman very dear to me. She had called me twice and left messages, asking me to pray for her, but I had not returned her call. I then called her; during this conversation she complained that her psychiatric insisted her to take medicine; and this medicine made her sleep, she can not take care of her children, and also made her shaking and fear.

After I spoke to her, I went back to bed to pray and fell sleep. I then got up for a few hours, and went to sleep again. In my dream I was laying face up. I saw the sky very dark, it was also dark at both sides from me away up to sky. I said, "Lord, heaven is closed up on me."

I then saw I was standing on my feet, bending down at my waist next to a leather sofa chair. My left hand was holding a holy Bible, my right hand was pushing against the chair, trying to stand up straight. While I was doing this I said, "Tuanh can resign her job as a UC Berkeley Health Service Administration Analyst, with her work experience she is more than qualified for the job at UCSD (University of California at San Diego)." After this dream, I heard the Blessed Virgin Mother tell me, "It is three months from your last confession. You can go to the Good Shepherd Church for the Sacrament of Reconciliation." After she said this, while I still was asleep, I kept hearing the angel call me several times, "Mariette, it is four o'clock, you need to get up and go to confession." I then got up at 4:15 p.m. I thought that confession was from 4:00 p.m. to 5:00 p.m. I hurriedly got dress and left.

When I got to Church parking lot, I saw no cars. I looked at the sign, and the confession time was from 3:00 p.m. to 4:00p.m.. I entered the Blessed Sacrament Chapel to be with the Lord. Just as I kneeled down, I knew that the Lord wanted to speak to me. In my vision I saw Him clean my right ear with a Q-tip dipped in holy oil. I continued my prayer, and the Father asked me, "Why are you here?" I replied, "Father, I came to confession." He asked, "Is there any one to hear your confession?" I replied, "The confession was from three to four, but I am late, I don't think that there is anyone here to listen to my confession." He asked, "Why are you late?" I replied, "I woke up late from sleep."

The doctors and medicine are the way that God uses to heal people. Without God the doctors and medicine can do nothing. Without God, the devil got in and harm people minds and bodies.

God Healed Mariette's Spiritual and Physical Ulcer

May 27, 1998. I was laying at the foot of the altar, facing up at the ceiling with my heat and body warm. I fell half asleep. In this dream I saw a little girl laying face up, and I recognized the face that God normally uses as symbolic of me. I said, "Lord, that is me." I then saw inside a glass front wall, like a living room. I saw a boy from behind. He was about three years old, and I saw the face of a little girl about two years old, they are sister and brother; both of them were sitting inside a long white pine wood box, it was their boat. The width was just wide enough for them to sit, knees touching each other, and under their knees was a center divider. The height of the box around them was to their waist, the divider was lower below their knees. Both of them were wearing white cloud-colored clothes. The girl's hair was dark, the boy's hair was white and was cut close to his scalp so that I was able to see his red head skin. Both of them looked directly at each other's eyes.

I heard the Lord Jesus tell me, "My only dearly sister, you do not have to go to gym and take diet supplement pills any more. Now I will heal your ulcer, heal your weight, cut the fat away physically and spiritually. I will heal all three at one." He continued, "The check will be in the mail slot, take it and cash it and go buy a printer cartridge to print the letter. Mail it out, do not tell any one, surprise them."

The Lord spoke of my benefits check that the New York Life Insurance Company had been holding onto for three months, and a letter to the Bishop and Archbishop petitioning for appointing priests to ordain bishops. The Lord mean that without God, man promised is empty promised; keep you eyes focus on God.

The Lord Jesus Promises of Healing His Church

In the afternoon devotion of May 27, 1998, the Lord Jesus told me, "When I was on earth, I came to the poor, the sick and the sinners, to be with them and heal them. I did not stay in a respectful seat in a high building. You are following me, go out and be with the sick, and the poor that need you. Through you, I will heal them when you minister to them during this mission."

The Holy Spirit Came to Renew the Face of the Earth

May 28, 1998, Before this night the Holy Spirit told me, "You are a daughter of the Blessed Mary, be with the Legend of Mary for short time."

During this night in my dream, I saw a little girl approaching the center of Saint

Michael's temple Altar, and she went to stand at the right side of the altar. When I saw her, she got to the altar and faced the altar joining her hands at her chest. At the same time she faced the altar I saw a huge angel formed from a white cloud above her. The angel's wings were half open, and the angel's leg was at her head, the angel's body tilted to the center of the altar, and the head bowed down at the altar. Both of the angel's hands joined at the chest like the statue of the angels at the right side at the Cathedral of Saint Andrew in Little Rock. The angel is symbolic of the little girl's soul.

Also during this night the Lord Jesus told me, "When you get in the room for the meeting tomorrow, wait for them to assign your seat, take whatever assignment they give to you, I have given it to them."

During the consecration, in spirit I saw the scene of the little girl Julie with the priest and three other boys at the foot of the sanctuary on their first Holy Communion mass, together with the little girl at the right of the altar and the angel again.

When I got in the meeting room, I looked at the altar, the table opposite the altar, and the two long side tables. The two seats at the end table were reserved for Monsignor Joseph, and the President of Saint Michael's parish Legend of Mary. The two side tables had about ten chairs, some with people sitting there and some not. I said hello to some people, then the secretary said to me, "You want to talk to Dorothy." I replied, "I came for meeting." She said, "Take a seat." I asked, "Where would you want me to sit?" She replied, "Anywhere you want." I silently asked, "Lord Jesus, where would you want me to sit?" I was slowly moved by the Spirit of God to the area next to the right of the altar. During the time I was walking, I also looked around, all the other chairs had been taken.

When I got next to the right of the altar; there was a man who had just gotten there, he told me, "You can sit here." He then took a chair and put it at the end of the table, next to the altar. He also took another chair for himself and set it against the wall, behind and to my left. I laid my Bible on the table to my left and sit down. I then turned around said to him, "You can move your chair closer here." He replied, "No, I cannot sit next to the Altar."

Just immediately before the meeting started, I kneeled on the floor, facing the altar, and bowed my head before the two statues on the altar. The center was a statue of our Lady of Grace, and to her right was a statue of a dove with a manifestation behind the dove, and with the Blessed Virgin Mother below.

I prayed, "Father, Lord Jesus, Holy Spirit, I ask you to heal a lady that you told me last night that You would heal today, and to heal all the members of the Legend of Mary here at this meeting." In my vision I saw the Blessed Virgin Mother in her Royal clothes, sitting on a high chair, with the apostles around her. Above her was the Holy Spirit like a dove with open wings, shedding fire mixed with light down into the shape of a triangle. The Lord told me, "Today in lieu of Pentecost Sunday." The Lord meant that instead of the Holy Spirit renewing the face of the earth on Sunday, the Holy Spirit will come down at the

Legend of Mary to renew the face of the earth.

Praying the rosary, reading and many other items were discussed. I just listened, but there were two parts that the Lord had me speak out loud: The President and Monsignor were speaking of the importance to attend the meeting, I heard a number of the reasons. I raised my right hand asked, "Can I say something?" The President said, "Sure, it is free speech."

I said, "We came to this meeting to receive power from God. In turn, we go out and minister to others in the directions of the Lord. If not, you [members] will be led by some things else." The Monsignor nodded his head and smiled in strong agreement. The President also agreed, others just looked around seeming to ask me questions.

When it was time to receive assignments, the President said, "Mariette you go with Bud and Karolyn to the Convalescent Hospital, next to Saint Michael. It will be on Monday, twenty minutes to ten, and the Monsignor will say mass at ten." (June 1, 1998 ,the Monday after Pentecost Sunday,). Karolyn is the lady God used in this revelation over the night, Bud is the man who pulled a chair next to the altar for me. Over a week ago, in spirit, I saw fire mingled with light covering the front of this Manor care.

Afternoon devotion on May 29, 1998, during my devotion the Lord showed me a dream on February 10, 1995. This revelation was published in the book "My Patient - God's Gift" chapter 6, "A clear Zipper Garment bag."

Purple Direction Book

May 29, 1998. In my dream I saw an invisible hand place a book in front of me. This gray hard-covered book was 9 x 8.5 inches. The front cover was imprinted with an Image of the Legend of Mary. The image filled with a bright light at the center, blending out with purple, and outside purple area was navy blue. When I saw this I was not sure, so I asked, "Lord, what kind of book is this?" The Blessed Virgin Mother told me, "Receive it, that [book] is direction from the Lord." She meant that the book contained instructions from the Lord.

I saw the gold pen of my desk set without its base (the base is a light green marble, engraved with two lines. The first line reads"1991 South of the Board", and the second line " Winner".) on the rug area next to the right side of my bed. Still in the dream, the Lord Jesus told me, "The letter you sent to the Archbishop to appoint a Vietnamese bishop for them to look up to for leadership has another meaning. The Bishop is symbolic of you in that the Father had pre-destined you for them to look up to for spiritual leadership, not the bishop." He then explained to me the meaning of the words He used as revelation.

Rebuild My Church Divine Mission
(The Lord Jesus gave this name to Mariette)
P.O. Box 261550 ✦ San Diego, CA 92196-1550

May 28, 1998

Archbishop Agostino Cacciavillan
Apostolic Pro-Nuncio
3339 Massachusetts Ave. N.W..
Washington, DC 20008

Most Reverend Anthony Pilla, President
National Catholic Conference
1027 Superior Ave.
Cleveland, OH 44114

Re: Petition for Appointing Vietnamese Bishops in the United States

Dear Excellency,

I have heard some Vietnamese priests and congregations complain that while the Vietnamese congregation in the United States has over five hundred priests, about seven hundred nuns, and a large number of seminarians and about three hundred thousand in congregations, they have no bishop or archbishop to look up to.   Many priests are divided among themselves, the congregations have formed different groups against each other; especially in San Jose, Santa Ana, Houston, Philadelphia, and San Diego. They also complain of the Catholic high-ranking officials treating them unfairly.

There is only "one" Church, and the Lord Jesus is the head. But the Vietnamese culture and traditional education issues must be taught, and retained from generation to generation.

I request that you appoint some Vietnamese priests to be ordained as bishops, so the Vietnamese priests, nuns, seminarians and congregation may look up for the leadership.

Sincerely in Christ Jesus,

Mariette Do-Nguyen
cc: Monsignor Dennis Schnurr, General Secretary

The Lord Jesus then said to me, "The youngster will come home to be unified with the family. You do not have to go visit her, remain in San Diego for several months, they will be searching for you." The youngster is symbolic of those received improper teaching the meaning of God's words; and through the mission, God revealed to me; they will learn the meaning of God's words properly; and God will dwelling within them.

Then the Holy Spirit said to me, "The Church leaders will come to you with honors, some will reject you. Many national leaders will honor you , some will reject you. The one-third who reject you are the one-third in the Book of Revelation when the seven trumpets blew."

May 29, 1998, about 4:00 a.m. I woke up in a happy spirit and I said, "Lord, I do not remember what you revealed to me in the dream, but I am happy. Please call them back to me." The Lord said, "Seal them up for the appointed time."

When I received the consecrated wine, I was holding a full cup. The supernatural power of the Lord tilted the cup to my mouth, filling my mouth with more than I thought that I was going to receive. Went I went back to my seat, I swallowed the consecrated wine, but the consecrated host was still in my mouth, I said, "Lord Jesus, I swallowed Your blood, now I am going to swallow Your bone. I will swallow it whole, none of it broken." Jesus the Lord asked me, "Who told you that?" In fear, I responded, "Lord, I don't know." He asked me for second time, "Did the Holy Spirit tell you that?" Now I felt less fear and responded, "Lord, it just came through my wisdom." The Lord Jesus said, "The WORD has been said."

I pleaded, "Jesus the Lord, You live in me, and I live in You. Father, the Lord Jesus said, 'You live in Him and He will live in You'. You are living in me and I am living in You. Holy Spirit, the Father and the Lord Jesus are in unity with You. You live in me and I live in You."

I continued, "Father, you answered to Jesus, who raised Lazarus from the dead, healed the sick and cured the lepers. Jesus the Lord is alive in me, He does His work through me. I ask You (I paused and turned to Jesus the Lord, ' Jesus what should I ask?') to grant my petitions as you had answered to Jesus before."

I continued, "Father, Lord Jesus, Holy Spirit, I ask You to glorify me so I can have a spot in the middle of the air, and the center of the earth so I can glorify You. I pray for my son Chau, my daughter Tuanh, all my children, and my granddaughter Madelene. I pray for Monsignor Joseph, the President of Saint Michael's Parish Legend of Mary, and all the Legend of Mary throughout the world, especially at Saint Michael's Parish, all the Church leaders, lawmakers, and government officials throughout the world, especially in Vietnam and the United States. I pray for the conversion of the world. I pray for unification of the Church, and the Lord Jesus' wounds to be healed, to build the kingdom of heaven, and Your will to be fulfilled."

I continued, " Father, through Jesus the Lord and through the works of the Holy Spirit; I came to You with my whole heart, mind, soul, and spirit. This Pentecost Sunday is my son Chau's thirtieth birthday, and not that many people have their thirtieth birthday fall on Pentecost Sunday. Jesus started His public mission when He was thirty. If this petition pleases You, I beg you for my son to be a Catholic monk. I will take him to Anthony's, at the Harbor above the water restaurant for brunch at twelve noon on his birthday. I pray that he will follow in my footsteps, which I am following in the Lord Jesus' footsteps. I ask you to separate him from the world so others can follow in his footsteps while my grandson Michael is still a youth. I pray for my daughter Tuanh to follow in my footsteps, which I am following in the Blessed Virgin Mother's footsteps."

The Holy Spirit said to me, "The son will be like Israel, a deacon, or a priest not saying mass." I asked, "Lord, what do you mean?" He said, "What is in your heart, you ask the Father and He will give it to you."

After the mass while I was sitting on the pew, I prayed, "Father, Lord Jesus, Holy Spirit, I pray for the patients in the Manor care that I am going to minister to, heal them spiritually and physically. All their beds will be set aside, turning the building into a house of prayer." The Holy Father said to me, "When you walk out the door, everyone will follow behind your feet out the door; He then spelled "F E E T." I asked, "Lord, what do You mean by that?" He said, "All of them will be healed physically and spiritually. You have to pray that they will not turn Lavang into a business location like Lourdes and Fatima. This is Lavang. This is the physical Rebuild My Church Mission Center; they have built this location for you. The Catholic leaders will be very disturbed because people from other denominations will come here to worship. Many will convert to the Catholic Church, and many will return to their own denomination. The lot next to the Church is for you to extend into. Copy this down for the world."

The healing of Manor Care is symbolic of the series of healing that God designed for the Rebuild My Church Mission that He entrusted to me, Mariette, and will be bestowed upon my successors, the ministers who will serve through this Mission from generation to generation. And God only can work through the ministers that completely obey all God's commandments; focusing on God alone, and serve God by services through others in love. There is a lifelong living sacrifice to God, and an eternal reward is in heaven. The Lavang is symbolic of me, Mariette; the Rebuild My Church Mission Center is the mission within me not at any physical land location.

Convalescent Hospital Healing Began

May 30, 1998. When I got in the temple before the mass, I prayed, "Father, Lord Jesus, Holy spirit, I offer this holy Eucharist celebration to You for the patients at the Convalescent Hospital to be healed. Blessed Virgin Mother, pray to the Lord for me and for them. Saint Joseph, Saint Michael, and all holy angels and saints pray to the Lord for me and for them.”

After the mass the Holy Spirit told me, “You enter the Blessed Sacrament Chapel through the left door from the sanctuary.” I was then on my way to the Blessed Sacrament Chapel, While I was walking close to the wooden door, the Legend of Mary’s Secretary called me, “Mariette.” She and I stood at the middle of the back part of the sanctuary, she said, “Mariette, Can I have your last name for the meeting’s minutes?” While was she saying this, she was holding a pen and small piece of paper filled with typing, it seems like she just pulled it out from her purse. I spelled my last name to her “Do-Nguyen.” She copied it on the space on top. I then spelled my first name to her, “Mariette.” and told her, “An “e” is at the end of Mariette, it is a French name, the Spanish is an “a”.

Kneeling on the kneeler, pushing my head toward the Tabernacle, both my elbows leaning on the kneeler, my hands covered my face, and I prayed, “Father, I am kneeling on the rock in the Olive garden, in an agony like my Brother Jesus, my Lord and my God. Father, send an angel to minister to me. Jesus the Lord, you are living in me, minister to me. I pray for all the patients at the Manor Care that I am going to visit on Monday, that they will be healed spiritually and physically. I am Your Servant and Your Vessel. Father, Lord Jesus, Holy Spirit, You live in me and with me. You are actually coming to them through me on that day.”

Jesus the Lord said to me, “The Gospel of John was written by John. The chapter contained My prayer that I gave to him before I went on the way of the Cross. Who know the heart of God? Only those He loves and are revealed to by Him. That made John one of the two witnesses. You are a Second witness because I came to you, while I reveal to you during the nights. I gave you all the obstructions that may happen so you can avoid them. While My Word is coming to you, the enemy spirits fight against you from the distance, and make you suffer.”

Before I left, the Lord Jesus told me, “You go to the front of the Convalescent Hospital to see more, and you will find what you are looking for. You can come in the center, who ever you see at the door, just greet him.”

I parked my car in the space in front of the double door entrance. I was trying to open the door, but it was locked for the weekend, and there was a sign that the north side door was open. I was about to take my car, but the Blessed Virgin Mother told me, “You just walk, there is no parking at that side.” I looked and there was no parking as she said. I went to the end of the building and made right turn, and tried to open two single doors, but both were locked. I looked through the side glass at the second door, and I saw a hall way where a person sat in a wheel chair with another person and the vacuum cleaner.

I left and called on the Lord as my brother, “Jesus, how can I get in, Jesus help!” The angel said to me, “Ask a woman at the other side.” I found another door close to the main entrance, there was a door bell. I raised my right index finger about to push it, but the angel said to me, "Mariette, what are you doing? Go to another door." He meant the main entrance. I went out and made a left turn, and as I made this left turn I saw a young female picking up several plastic bags of newspapers at the outside main entrance. Next to her was a large two-level, iron, rectangular utility cart.

I said to her from distance, "Excuse me." She looked at me, and by the time I got to her she finished picking up those bags and loaded them in the cart. I said, "Do you work here?" She replied, "Yes." I said, "I went to mass at Saint Michael's for about three months, today I came here to look around." She said, "I saw you go around so I came out." She introduced herself, "My name is Robyn" I also saw her name tag. I said, "My name is Mariette." I then asked her some questions, she said, "We have ninety nine beds, twenty eight beds for Alzheimer patients, the others are for stroke patients and those that are not able to take care of themselves, they are in wheelchairs." I asked, "How often do they move in and out?" She said, "They do move in and out, but not that often." I said, "I will come back Monday with another two from Saint Michael's Parish Legend of Mary." She said, "They are coming close to ten." I said, "At 9:40 a.m. and have the monsignor say mass at ten." She said, "We have about 20 Catholics in residence. There are some ministers of other religions who come to visit them. When one comes, other ones separate away." I said, " Catholics, Lutherans, Protestants or any denomination have the same God. The Jews worship the Lord Jesus as fully God, but they have not accepted Him as fully man because they have been mislead. When I come to visit, I do not separate any denomination. What happens to those who live in the mountains, they do not have any chance to be in any of these denominations? As long they worship the true God, do good and reject evil." She said, "I like that idea." I asked, "Is there time limit for visitors?" she said, "People love to see visitors. You can stay as long as you want." I said, " I will stay after the mass, and I ask that if you could, take me to visit others that are non-Catholic." She said, "Sure, they are love to see visitors. I will see you Monday." Then I left the center.

At the End of the Trumpet's Blast

Number seven is symbolic of the beginning of the end. Number eight is symbolic of spiritual realms or spiritual life. Number five is symbolic of God's power over the devil's power, or authority over the devil's works through human bodies. Number nine is the greatest number and it is symbolic of the end.

Biblical symbolism has patterns. At the beginning, God created the earth in seven days. In the old testament, God commanded Joshua to march around the city of Jericho for seven days; and on the seventh day he had seven priests to march seven times, and after the seventh time, the priests blew the horns. When they blew five long blasts on the ram's horn, people shouted aloud and the city wall collapsed. In the new testament, seven angels blew their trumpets; the seven angels are symbolic of God's true servants, the seven trumpets are symbolic of God's Words. When God's true servants proclaim the Gospel the city wall will collapse. The city wall is symbolic of an individual, group, nation, or the world.

The collapse can happen two ways, either spiritually or physically. From the spiritual and the physical can have many more meanings, it up to each individual's free will to choose. The convalescent hospital symbolic of the world. The numbers that Robyn gave to me not necessary actual number, but instead, God spoke to her for this revelation to be revealed.

24

UNDERSTAND BIBLICAL SYMBOLISM

God Revealed Mariette's Assignments

January 6, 1995. At the foot of the Monstrance during the adoration, at the Good Shepherd Blessed Sacrament chapel, the Lord Jesus said to me, " I am the Lord Jesus. Today is the first Friday of the year. I take you into the palm of my hand and place in my heart to guide you and protect you. My words will be pounding in your heart like my mother's, and the words will open up one after another. When you depart from this life all of them have been opened. I give you these scriptures: The Book of Revelation, chapters five, six and seven. I will send the Holy Spirit to help you understand them. These chapters are for you and your descendants. I will reward you in heaven to sit at my right hand. For your children, you must speak the truth to them with love, softly, at the right time, and I will do all the works so they can inherit heaven with you. My Father is very pleased with your willingness. He gives you all the power from heaven that you need to do His will. My mother loves you very much. She a has special place for you in her heart, continue to pray rosary. See Father Ediza, Father Chito, and Father Fernando. I have works for all of them. I will bless the Good Shepherd Church. Go in peace."

The three priests name symbolic of God chosen ones on earth. The Good Shepherd symbolic of God's Church on earth.

THE WOMAN AND HER CHILD

Revelations Chapter 12

A Young Man Cleans up His Land

December 24, 1998. In my dream I saw a small rectangle with dry and loose dirt on the surface of the land. While I was hiding behind a dark cloud looking at the land, to my left at the end of the land was a woman and her child was a few feet away from her. In front of me was a young man in his early thirties, he was pulling double long flat bark bars from the air to the right end of the land at my right. He was going to spray water on the land before he did his work, so the dust would not fly up. When he got to the end, he left one of the flat bark bar touched the border of the land; he used the other one to scratch the ground. After he scratched a few times there was a dry, naked long root that popped up from under the ground. This root was from a old tree growing on the land that I had not seen, but its root was laying all the way to the end of the land. Shortly after this young man plowed the ground, there was a white-skinned, black-haired young man laying on his right hip, facing me; I saw his hair had grown down to his forehead. His eyebrows were very thick and black. This man dark haired man was transformed from the naked root popped out from under the ground after the young owner scratched the surface of his land. This black haired man told me, "I had been laying still under the ground for nine years without breathing."

The man in his early thirties working the surface ground is symbolic of the Lord Jesus. The dry dirt is symbolic of the world. The woman is symbolic of the Lord Jesus' mission. The child is symbolic of the mission that God entrusted to me to purify the world systems. The naked root symbolic of people spiritual dead, have rooted in no God protection. This naked root transformed to dark haired symbolic of those come to conversion. He dark haired symbolic of iniquities result from years or generations of sins against God and one another. He did not breathe for nine years: not breathing is symbolic of no life in God, and nine years is symbolic that the Lord Jesus completed crush down the power of the devil.

Spouse and His Car

February 10, 1999. In my dream I was standing inside a large room that had no wall. It seemed like the door was several yards behind me, in front of me was the center of the room. There was a woman who owned the house sitting there, her toddler child was playing nearby her. When she saw me, she said to me, "My husband's car has disappeared, and he feels shamed that his car disappeared and has not returned. After he finds his truck he will return it. All the workers at his auto shop are still working daily from morning to night and go home." When she said this, I was the spirit of her husband and a truck was parked behind him, up high directly at my left forehead.

Then the dream changed. I followed next to the side of a man up in the air, just beneath a round cast metal roof, like a tunnel. It seemed like we were sitting inside an invisible cable car going from one side of a tunnel entrance to the other. While it was moving I read my newspaper, and the man reached over from the other side to read my news paper from the top down. I then started again alone from the same spot, this time my newspaper was a two foot square piece of beef jerky, cut down in flat pieces like mini blinds. This time we went too fast and I was unable to read. I complained, "Last time I was with a man, and the cable ran slow and I could read very clearly. This time I am alone, and it went fast and I was unable to read."

Then the dream changed again. I put on a one-piece outfit. This is like a child's play outfit for an adult. It was white, made from some kind of bath towel material. It had short sleeves, a round collar, and down to before got to knees, it opened at the bottom with three white metal snaps. I thought that I had to sleep outside the house and it would be cold, so I had to stretch the collar and put my head through because the opening at the bottom was not stretching. I then was wearing the outfit and left the place, and went walking on a small road in the middle of a rice field.   Suddenly, I was climbing on the bed with my right side first; in front of me was the end of the headboard, and next to the bed was a two drawers cabinet made of cherry wood that served as a lamp stand. On top of it was a burning lamp that gave me light, so that I was able to see my youngest daughter laying on the bed, inside the blanket.

The next morning I prayed for understanding of the revelation. The Lord Jesus told me, "The woman at the center of the place is My mission, her child is your mission. Her husband is symbolic of Me, the car that turned to a truck is you. Mother and a child, brother and sister. During the time you were in Arkansas, and before that you heard me clearly as you read the newspaper the first time. The second time you were alone is now, I do the work in the supernatural, and you do the work in the nature. My work in the supernatural is too fast for you to catch up with, so you complain of not remembering all your dreams and not fully understanding. Your youngest daughter is symbolic of those who received improper teaching of God's words. Your getting on the bed with her is symbolic that they will receive the meaning of God's words through you, they are laymen and not priests and bishops. The priests and bishops are retaining who they are and what they have; but when they see their congregation leave them they will turn to you. I am slowly removing you from the Catholic Church and having you start your own ministry. You are following my footsteps; I taught in the synagogues, later I separated from them to teach people to follow me. When newspapers receive news they will publish it; no one lights the lamp and sets it under the table, when they light the lamp they must put it on top of the table. If I want to hold this news I will hold it here with you, not to give to other people and hold them there. Go get your hair done. Get ready!"

Mother and Child

February 11, 1999. In my dream I was at the lower level in the middle of a large open air field. As I stood there, in front of me at my feet a lady laid on her left side, her feet were toward my feet. To my left forehead, up high in the sky, God's power was shedding directly at me and the lady, and the voice coming out from this power said to me, "There was an old story, a woman had to die to save her child. This woman [the voice referring to a woman laying at my feet] have a lots of love from above, she does not have to die to save her child, she must embrace tremendous suffering." When I heard this, I thought, "This is a repeated story." I then saw close by me, people were pulling the Lord Jesus laying on a bed sheet, from the foot of the cross to the tomb, while I was laying on the bed asleep.

The woman in the old story is symbolic of the Lord Jesus; her child is symbolic of the Lord Jesus' mission on earth. A woman does not have to die, but has to embrace tremendous suffering is symbolic of me, Mariette, her child is symbolic of the mission that God entrusted to me, as a Vessel to the Holy Trinity.

Winged Ants Cling to Mariette's Body and Head: I saw I was on my way down in the middle of the air, black winged ants were clinging all over my body and head. I dusted them off at the same time I was walking, by the time I got to the ground, only few still clung to the side of my hip.

Winged ants are very tiny, they are black, and they can not hurt people. Winged ants clinging to me are symbolic spiritual battle. They were all over my body and head and that is symbolic of attacking me in spirit. When I got to the ground only a few of them still clinging to my hip is symbolic that there will be less attacking the mission God entrusted to me in the natural.

National Capital and Mariette's checks: I then was walking in front of the nation's capital building doing something. When I turned around, my envelope that I laid on the lawn across the street was not there. It was so full with checks that I was not able to close the flap. I looked and saw several yards away, a big man was holding a little boy walking away from the spot where I laid my envelope. I knew that the little boy took my envelope. When I thought of this, I saw the boy holding my envelope open the flap, full with checks at side. I quickly ran after him to get my envelope back. When I reached them, I grasped the envelope from the boy's hand and told the man, "All of these checks are made out to my name, and I am on my way to the bank to make my deposit." While I was saying this to the man, I also flipped the checks to show him my name on the check.

The nation's capital is symbolic of the world. My checks are symbolic of God's power that He bestowed into the mission entrusted to me. The big man is symbolic of government high ranking leaders and spiritual leaders, and the boy is symbolic of their mission. The boy taking my envelope with the checks is symbolic of when I saw things that were not same as the Lord revealed to me. My grasping it back is symbolic of God bringing victory to the works He entrusted to me.

In the afternoon, after I delivered the article "It is God's Will for President Clinton to Resign" to the San Diego Asian Journal and Philippine Mabuhay, I fell asleep after my devotion. In my sleep, the Lord Jesus told me, "The dream is an old story of a woman and a child. The mother and child were revealed to John about you by using the Blessed Mother as symbolism in the Book of Revelation. There are several chapters in the Book of Revelation revealing about you, chapters 4, 5, 6, and 7. People do not understand the Book of Revelation because it is not revealing about them. I revealed about you, and I give the understanding to you. Add these dreams to the chapter of the woman and dragon."

The First Beast is The World System

Revelation 13:1-10

The dragon in Chapter Twelve is symbolic of Lucifer, whom God cast out of Heaven. The first beast came from the sea. Water is symbolic of God's anointing; ten represents the Ten Commandments; seven symbolizes the beginning of completion. The first beast is symbolic of systems of the world that proclaim good deeds, but whose works are sins against God, which we can identify by name, blasphemous. It looks like a leopard, has the mouth of a lion, and the dragon has its own power and throne, along with great authority. The first beast sat on the throne symbolic of the devil spirit does his work through high ranking government officials.

One of its heads seemed to be mortally wounded, but then it was healed, and the whole world followed the beast. This wounded head being healed is symbolic of the devil power's is in people minds and actions; one evil person dies and another rises; one evil action dies and is replaced by another evil deed.

The beast opening it mouth to utter blasphemies against God is symbolic of the world's system worship idols, glorify man, depending on human power, do not believe in God, or do not trust God, have no faith in God, and want to be like God.

The Book of Life belongs to the Lamb who was slain, the Lord Jesus, the Son of the most high living God. This book's contents names the inhabitants of Heavenly eternal life; the names of the beast worshippers are not in the Book of Life.

Counterfeit Purification

March 19, 1997: In my vision I saw the Statue of Liberty up high, her feet right at my face as I was lying on my right side. Then in my dream, I was standing in front of a kitchen counter that had a double sink with a disposal. The right top corner was a round hole; between the hole and the sink was some trash. I disposed of it by pouring it down the hole. I then discovered that the disposal was at the center of the counter, in the sink, and I realized that I had made a mistake. I looked down at the foot of the corner to find out where the trash had gone. The foot of the corner and the wall next to it formed a big hole, that had been eaten away by moss. I then saw the shadow of the spirit of the psychiatrist in Little Rock, Arkansas, and I saw the late Father Long enter the room through a double glass door with his right hand holding the collar of his jacket over his shoulder. Outside this double glass door was a shopping mall. As I saw Father Long with dark skin, I realized that he symbolized Satan; I said to him, "In Jesus' name, get away from here. Father, Lord Jesus, protect me. Jesus, fight Satan for me."

At 9:34 a.m. the Lord Jesus said, "The dark-skinned late priest's name Long is symbolic of Lucifer who was cast down out of Heaven. His walking in the shopping mall with his jacket on his right shoulder symbolizes the devil wounding people in the world by interfering with their minds and hearts. Using the hole in the counter as a disposal symbolic of counterfeit cleansing. The moss eating away the corner foot of the counter and the wall is symbolic of there being no foundation in the words of God. The shadow spirit of the psychiatrist in Little Rock represents mental disease for those who live in mortal sin. Discovering the disposal at the center of the counter, the middle of the kitchen sink, not at the corner, symbolizes my sending you to open the minds and hearts of people to let them know that they are living in the world with Satan. This has been revealed to John, by the woman and the dragon. The Statue of Liberty is symbolic of people who place human power above God. I will help you to interpret the woman and the dragon."

The name Long is a Vietnamese name, and it means dragon in English. His being a dead priest with dark skin is symbolic of Satan.

In this revelation, God is revealing to the world the fact that Satan and his fallen angels are working hard in the world; they are pursuing people in this age, those who focus on earthly treasury, while putting aside that which nourishes their souls. They will do anything or go anywhere to benefit their flesh; but when it comes to God, they find many reasons to charge against Him. Their free will is given to Satan, then Satan uses this permission to destroy their souls and bodies. The devil either controls or interferes with their minds, their hearts, and their actions. The devil has permission to wreck destruction from the leaders of many nations, from lawmakers, high ranking government officials, spiritual leaders, and business executives, all the way down to teenagers who disobedience to God's commandments and refuse to convert.

The Second Beast's Power

Revelation 13: 11-18

Sunday March 17, 1997: After the vision in which I saw the written words, "Mary of Nazareth bestows to my daughter Mariette my estate," the Lord Jesus said to me, "I will speak about the beasts at the Holy Eucharist services." I silently responded, "I will read this chapter." That night, before I went to sleep, I read the Book of Revelations, Chapter 13. After I finished, I said to the Lord, "Jesus, I understand. 'The First Beast' is the system of the world, but I do not understand 'The Second Beast.' This is Your work, and I am just Your instrument. I ask You to help me understand it." Then, before I fell sleep, I heard the Lord Jesus say, "I will speak about 'The First Beast.' People cannot take both at the same time. I will speak about 'The Second Beast' later."

The night of March 18, 1997: In my dream I saw myself lying on a Vietnamese canopy bed. (The Vietnamese canopy allows one to see through the veil that covers the entire bed.) There were also a few people sitting on this bed, in front of me. I said to them, "I am going to teach the Bible, and tell you about the beasts in the Book of Revelations." When it was time to begin teaching, I looked outside the canopy; in the corner was a woman standing in the middle, facing the front of my bed. Behind, to her right, were two men, and in front to her left, was another man. These three men were wearing messy suits, and looked as if they were very busy running the services. I knew this woman was going to teach the class. I then got up and left the room.

The dream changed; I was standing at the side, behind the same house, in this open patio. In front of me was an ex-spouse sitting on his feet, a cutting board in front of him. On this cutting board was a big round fish, whose top side was very dark while the other side was white. This man held a big, pointed knife (a cleaver) about to slice this fish; I said to him, "It needs to be grilled." I then saw him cut the long face of the fish, and after ward, I saw that the piece of fish was dark with a little white, as if it were already grilled. I thought, "This knife was pre-heated." He then cut another piece close to the tail, leaving the main body of the fish in the shape of triangle. I then left the patio, and went inside the house.

I stood at the side of the same bed, but now there was no canopy. But there was food, and a few people sitting around eating dinner. One of the women gave me some boiled vegetables, raw leaves of spice that are used in dog meat, and some grilled white fish fillets. I picked out the leaves, and only ate the vegetables. One woman sat close to the edge of the bed and gave me a piece of the fish.

Then I was in the same house alone, and I could see through the wall, inside the back patio. Several steps from the back door was a young pregnant woman sitting on the floor on her feet; to her right was a child standing, and to her left was a dog. Behind this child, to the side, was the ex-spouse. I heard her telling him that she used her child and her dog to beat her husband. The ex-spouse told her, "Do not use your child and your dog to beat him."

Next I was out in the covered patio behind my house; the ex-spouse was also there. I hated this man. He then went to the covered patio next door, which belonged to the pregnant woman. I saw them with her child and dog, and I knew that this man lived with a woman without marriage, and was now here with this pregnant woman. I hated him and did not want him to come to my house. I closed the three layers of this wooden door, one at a time, then locked it with a small wooden rod, by placing it on two round hooks, one at the frame of the door, another nailed to the side of the wooden bookcase. I thought, "This man can break through this small rod."

Then I was inside the house, standing next to the front corner wooden table. On this table were two sets of keys; one had belonged to me when I was working for the life insurance company. This set of keys was connected to two key rings and to each other. I could see my black-handled automobile key with a few keys on one ring; the other had twice as many. The set with many keys did not belong to me; all of the keys were on one key ring, and this key ring connected to another which had no keys, and to a huge brass ring, twice the size of my upper arm. A few steps from this corner table was a bed. I knew the ex-spouse was angry at me for locking the back door. I hear the woman tell him, "She does not want you in her home, so do not go over there." In my vision, I saw him coming from her house through my front door with a poison syringe. I did not want him to see the huge set of keys, so I quickly placed them under the mattress. Because my physical body was very powerful, he could not fight me, so he came at me with the poison syringe and pierced my lower left hip, a little to the front. After he shot me with poison liquid, I felt a little paralyzed spot, but the rest of my body was still very powerful.

The woman standing outside the Vietnamese canopy bed about to teach the Bible is symbolic of false preachers; the men in messy suits represent those who work together with false preachers. The people inside the canopy bed with me symbolize the children of God seeking the truth. I, Mariette, am a lowly servant to God's acting on God calling in the Rebuild My Church Mission. My seeing her about to teach and walking away means that God keeps me away from false preachers.

At the time I prayed for an interpretation the Lord told to me the ex-spouse is symbolic of false miracle workers on television, who CNN and Time magazine call "religious super-stars." The fish with one dark side and one white side: dark represents the darkness of the devil; one slice was close to the face and another at the tail of the fish, leaving the middle piece in a triangle. White symbolizes purity, the triangle represents the Trinity. In this revelation, these two symbols are mixed with other symbols of the devil's works, so they became counterfeit of the works of God. One side of the fish was dark, and after he cut the first piece, it was burned, and this is symbolic of the devil's work. A pre-heated knife in his right hand is symbolic of the power of the devil working through him, which people are not able to discern, and this power can destroy their souls and bodies.

Manners at Place of Worship

Behave a like good child from the perfect family in front of your parents' most important guest, and be deserving of a reward from the most strict ruler of the convent.

Every one of us has many hours each day to be with our spouse, children, and others whom we love; but we spend very little time with God, the One who gave us life and all that we have. Everyone must understand that "HE IS ALMIGHTY GOD." Therefore, in

His presence, we must focus on God alone, nothing else.

Upon entering the temple, if there is no Blessed Sacrament, [no sanctuary light] we only need to bow our head to express reverence to the altar. If there is a Blessed Sacrament inside the tabernacle, we only need to genuflect. During the Holy Eucharist Exposition, we must genuflect and bow our head to worship the Lord our God.

** During this time of worshipping God, we must focus our minds on God and His words.

DO NOT think about your spouse, boyfriend, girlfriend, children, business deals, shopping malls, or any objects or events; or talk to your neighbor.

** When facing the altar, close your eyes, or if you open them, look at the crucifix, the tabernacle, or the image of our Lord Jesus; during the mass, focus on the center of the altar, the area that consecrates the bread and wine, (above the corporal).

DO NOT look at the priest, around the sanctuary, around the church, at your spouse, neighbor, boyfriend, girlfriend, other people, or their clothes.

** Your hands should join at your chest.

DO NOT join them behind you, don't put them in your pockets, over your belly, straight down at your waist; do not join hands with other people, even your spouse, at any time, except during the Lord's prayer "Our Father....", do not lean your arm on the back of the pew or behind another person back.

** Sit or stand straight.

DO NOT rock, dance, or waive from side to side.

** Parents with small children: If there is a room for the children, be sure to be there with them in that room. If not, try to stay close to the back of the temple. Every temple must have an area designated for children who are not mature enough to understand the worship service or how to behave in the proper manner.

DO NOT bring children to the front section; children's actions are unpredictable; children's actions and noise will distract others.

** Priests dress for God to celebrate mass; we must dress for God, not for others. Clothes need to be clean, and cover the body for worship; they should not display fashion or your body. Our body is the temple of God; each one must prepare his body and soul before coming into God's presence. The Book of Exodus explains more of how to prepare one's body and soul to worship God.

The devil is the one who attacks everyone through these actions, to distract others from worshipping God. If a person allows the devil to use him to distract others then that person is committing sins against God and against those people whom he has distracted.

The Log and Candle are Burning

January 11, 1998, the feast of Baptism of the Lord. In my dream I was sitting on my feet, at the left, on the church ground, in front of me was a very long, round dry log, and I was finding a way to burn it. Behind me a few middle age women were socializing. I turned around, and I saw one of the woman had dropped a small yellow cigarette lighter, like the one I have, used to light the altar candle every time before I pray. I picked it up and said to her, "You dropped your cigarette lighter." She replied, "It belonged to a very famous man. I took it from him, but I do not want it any more."

I then turned back to my log, and used this cigarette lighter to light the log. Immediately after the fire touched the log, it log blazed like it was soaked with gas. Its skin burned, but the log itself was untouched. Since the woman did not want the cigarette lighter back, I said to her, "I will keep this cigarette lighter."

When I got up, I did not understand. The Blessed Mother asked me, "What is the cigarette lighter symbolic of?" I replied, "The adoption" I meant of me being adopted into the family. The Blessed Mother explained to me a few situations, then she continued, "You are adopted to the Holy Family, but you are not to see it until you come home to heaven. This adoption is not so important to you, but it is very important to the Father." She continued, "The cigarette lighter is symbolic of an anointing to serve God. The famous man is symbolic of God, and those women are symbolic of church leaders. There is only One mission, that mission belongs to Jesus the Lord. God gave grace to [Saint] Peter, to serve Him; this grace passed to church leaders, but they have not kept it. God took it and gave it to you. You explain to them of your anointing to serve God, not just anointing alone."

March 8, 1998. All night I physically and mentally battled with enemy spirits in some dreams, so in the morning I was really exhausted. I heard the Lord Jesus tell me, "Get up, take a shower, dress in your three pieces dress, and go to the eight thirty mass."

I did what the Lord told me. I got to the temple property, and I saw in front of the temple some Knights of Columbus men, and a board filled with sentimental pictures. I was in a spiritual battle through the entire mass. After I received the Holy Eucharist, the Lord Jesus told me, "The Catholic component leaders do not accept you. From tomorrow you no longer have to come here for some time, go to the North Methodist temple, they were the one who received you first before the Catholics, at the time you and your family first got to the United States."

While I was walking out in the center aisle, I heard a voice from a woman behind. She said to me, "Are you a model?" I turned to my left and looked at her and said, "I am God's Servant." She said, "Your dress is so pretty." I turned and looked at her again, and said, "I accept what you just said. I am a role model, God's Servant." She said, 'That is good to be

God's Servant."

Outside of the temple door, while I was still talking to her, I told her that I would no longer be coming to this temple for while. I saw the celebrant of the mass was shaking people's hands, I stopped and shook his hand, and said to him, "I will not come here for awhile. You do not understand it now, but you will understand it later."

As the Lord instructed: I called Betty, who provided space at her home for us, to let her know that I would be at the temple where she was a member. I was glad that the Methodist component also receives Holy Communion, but I was disappointed that they only celebrate the Holy Eucharist on the first Sunday of each month, or sometimes more often, depending on the district or the pastor of the temple. That evening, I went to the Methodist temple to join their worship. I brought with me some revelations for the pastor of the temple.

Even though over twenty years had passed and there had been no communication, when I got to the front of the temple, some of their members who had met me before recognized me with joy that I returned to join them for that evening worship. Then pastor Jim walked by and I gave him the envelope that contained revelations for him.

Passing through, I needed to go to the restroom before the worship, like I normally do before the mass. I asked Don, "Where is the restroom?" He walked with me to the restroom. While we were walking and conversing, he asked me, "How are your children?" I replied, "All of them graduated from college and are working: my little one graduated from the University of Berkeley and works there, my two sons work at U.C San Diego, one is a computer programmer and the other is in the laboratory, the oldest is a teacher Two of them are married, I also have one granddaughter, her name is Madelene."

Concerning the most important thing to the Church and to me, I asked Virginia, who sat next to me, "Are we going to celebrate the Holy Eucharist this evening?" She replied, "You mean communion?" I replied, "Yes," I asked again, "How often is it that we celebrate Holy Eucharist here, I mean communion?" She said, "We have it more often now then before." I explained to her, "Through the celebrant repeated the last suffering words, the bread and wine become the Lord Jesus' body and blood. Also the Lord Jesus said, 'My Father is in me, and I am in the Father.' and the Holy Spirit came from the Father and the Lord Jesus. Therefore, when we received the consecrated host and wine in the supernatural, we receive the body and blood of our Lord Jesus together with His Spirit, the Spirit of the Father and the Holy Spirit as food to nourishment for our souls. Like Israel baked breads and brought them to the altar for blessing, and Spirit of God descended upon the breads. But if any one receives it with an impure heart, they will receive punishment."

The pastor's sermon was obedience and curse, and he used Deuteronomy chapter 28 and the Ten Commandments in the Book of Exodus.

Before the consecration, I asked the Blessed Virgin Mother to assist me if I should receive the Holy Eucharist or not, she said to me, "Listen to what words the celebrant say at the consecration." I then was very careful to listen to the words when the pastor raised up the bread and the cup. After I heard the right words, the bread and wine was now the body and blood of our Lord.

Before delivering the Holy Eucharist, the Pastor invited people from all domination, who love Jesus to come. I then asked, "Lord, I received you this morning, would You allow me to receive You again?" The Lord said, "You are here together with this congregation to partake of My body and blood, you are the role model to unify My Church."

There I was standing in front of the Eucharistic minister, My right hand broke a piece of consecrated bread, and cried out loud, "My Lord, My God, My Savior, You are the Savior of the world." and dipped the consecrated bread into consecrated wine, and I continued to cry out loud, "Father, Lord Jesus, Holy Spirit, You sent me here today, I ask You for the Church to be unified. Bless the pastor of this church, [temple], and through him, others will come to him in unity with You." The pastor put his left hand on my shoulder and said to me, "The blood of Christ, Mariette, that is for you."

When I got back to my seat, the Lord told me, "John, chapter 4 for you and for him." The Lord meant for the Pastor of the North Methodist temple.

When the pastor finished his duty of the worship, he came close to where I was sitting. I raised my hand and called him toward me. He sat next to me, I said to him, "The Lord gave you the Gospel of John, chapter 4. You do not want to hear this, but you will suffer, and the more you suffer, the more the Lord Jesus loves you. I must say what the Lord asks me to say, even if people say that they going to shoot me. I will still say it before they shoot me."

March 9, 1998. During the night I saw a ten inch tall candle burning with a huge flame. While I looked at it, the flame ran down its right side, and trailed like a river of fire. Even the fire was leaning to the side of the candle, coming down to it foot make a fire river, but the ten inches candle still not melt. I said, "Lord, the candle is burning with fire." I know that the fire is presence of God. The Lord told me, "The log you saw on fire was the same way Moses saw the Bush on fire."

In the morning, I went to Saint Michael's temple in Poway for the Holy mass. I was very happy when I saw they served the cup. At my turn to receive the cup, there was only one last drop. I had to turn the cup almost upside down and empty it.

March 10, 1998: I heard the alarm clock on, but I was too exhausted to get up. Still asleep, the Lord told me, "Get up, go to seven thirty mass. The food is on the table for you." I then jerked myself up.

After I received the body of our Lord from the priest, I went to a lady and received a cup, and poured it full in my mouth. I slowly swallowed the blood while I was walking

378

down to my seat, inside the Archangel Michael's temple. Reaching my seat, I kneeled down, and I swallowed His body at last. I pray, , "Father, Lord Jesus, Holy Spirit, I ask you for my sons and my daughters to love You, and love one another, and be obedient to you, through me as their mother and your Vessel." The Lord said, "Today I blessed your household, the children from your womb, the purple and the violet."

After the mass, I was still filled with Spirit of God. God the Almighty said to me, "Dreaming, dreaming, and dreaming all come through from the Lord, except not as a business woman, but as God's Servant. The log burning is you, the burning bush is Moses; the burning bush is you, the burning log is Moses. All of this was written on the tablets given to Moses, but Moses kept them for himself and took them with him. At the transfiguration he will come down and deliver them. Yesterday you drank the last drop of my cup; today you drank your full cup."

I was about to copy down my dream, the Lord said to me, "Why do you have to copy this down, all of it is in Proverbs ten [Book of Proverbs, chapter ten].

After I finished, the Lord said to me, "The burning log is you in your mission, and the fire burning around the log is God's glory, power and might. The burning candle is you who came to the Lord filled with light."

I prayed, "Lord, I give You praise. I give You glory. I give You thanks for ever and ever." After my afternoon devotion, I was very exhausted and fell asleep. In my dream I saw some dark living spirits close to my side, and there were some light living spirits over the horizon. The dark living spirit said, "Call on Monica Trust." I then saw Jesus the Lord with a cross at his shoulder, and Saint Veronica kneeling in front of Him, with a towel laying on her right arm, imprinted with the image of the Lord Jesus' face.

God revealed to me that He gave me another name "Monica Trust." The name Monica is symbolic of spiritual battle through living sacrifices. "Trust" means I, Mariette trust in God that He is the One who is carrying me through this entire mission that God trusted to me. The vision of Saint Veronica wiping the face of the Lord Jesus is symbolic that I serve God with obedience to Him without fear. The face of Jesus imprinted on Saint Veronica's towel is symbolic that His Lordship is imprinted in my mind, heart, and my soul. Monica symbolic of woman of prayer, and trust in God.

Instructions to Modify Mission Name and Build the Center

May 11, 1999, At 4:45 p.m. during my devotion, the Lord Jesus told me, "Add the word 'Divine' before the word 'Mission'. The mission name will be "Rebuild My Church Divine Mission."

May 25, 1999 at 7:40p.m. During my devotion before I went to sleep, the Holy Spirit told me, "The result of the tax petition on June 7, 1999 will be mixed, some in your favor and some still suspended. Let the government officials come and kneel at your feet, and let the people come to surround you." The Lord meant at His feet and around Him, and He used me as symbolism like Jesus used Saint Peter of told him "I gave you the key of heaven". I turned to the Lord Jesus and asked, "Lord Jesus, please ask the Father for your books written through me to sell well." Jesus the Lord said to me, "Not too far from the freeway, between here and Laguna, you will find a large piece of land, put a little down to purchase it, and pay off the balance within one year. After that will be a huge donation for you to build the Center."

Then the Lord gave me His words "Victory in war does not depend upon the size of the army, but on strength that comes from heaven." 1 Maccabees 3:19

May 28, 1999 in my dream I saw the words spelling out "The Mission is healthy, and it is in the hand of the Father" on first line. The second line "Foundation is excellence."

In this revelation God uses the natural substance of selling books as symbolic of preaching His words. The profit from the books is symbolic of God's power. Land is symbolic of Heaven on earth, and not too far from the freeway is symbolic of close to God. The little down payment is symbolic of living sacrifices. A huge donation to build the center is symbolic of the Rebuild My Church Divine Mission building in foundation of God's words and His power.   The word "Divine" added to the mission name means God revealed to us that this mission is under the power of God.

Mariette Do-Nguyen, Founder of "Rebuild My Church Divine Mission"
(The Lord Jesus gave this name to Mariette)

25

PRE-DESTINED CHOSEN ONE

The Father Gave Mariette Immunity

At the beginning and up to today, February 13, 1998, I always felt that I was a big sinner; and that I would never be worthy for this calling. Since I returned to God, every day I ask God to forgive my sins, and purge my iniquities.

During the night of February 13, 1998, while I was asking the Lord to forgive my sins and purge my iniquities, the Lord Jesus told me, "The Father gave you immunity right at the time you returned. All your sufferings are to build the kingdom of heaven." In my heart, I always know that I am a sinner until I depart from this world for heaven.

February 16, 1998. During the night, after I saw the dream of the dance instructor wearing disgusting clothes, the Lord Jesus explained to me in detail the reasons of the spirit environments. While IIe was saying this, I saw a small piece of decayed bone, with many holes through it. As I saw this decayed bone, he said to me, "This is bone that the devil is trying to revive, but I took it away from you this night."

When a person commits any sins, after conversion, each person has to pay for the damage resulting from each sin that person committed. The price to pay depends on what kind of sin; we either pay on earth, in purgatory, or in the place that humans call hell.

While iniquities are bouncing, the devil fights against you, and tries to get you back with him. We must understand that in our daily life after conversion, we still think or do things that sin, that we are unable to know. With our daily exam and repentance, the Lord Jesus is still purging our iniquities until our last breath.

In my case, God sent me down undercover. At the time I returned, the Father granted me immunity. Because the road I went on benefits others in this mission, the devil uses that road, attacking me through other people, such as my children, people that I meet in church or daily life, or those whom I minister to, or any one that I am in contact with.

The devil uses communication with our eyes, ears, smell, etc., to attack people. It can be through such things as television, magazines, newspapers, thing you can see, hear, or touch. He can even just bring sin into your thoughts, and damage people.

Eternal Father Appeared to Mariette in His Son's Image

August 16, 1997. In my late devotion, the Lord Jesus told me, "At the mass tomorrow, you will see something." I asked, "Lord, is it good or bad?" Jesus the Lord said, "It is mixed, a little bad, and mostly good; just ignore the bad, pay close attention, and remember the good. The Father will surprise you with these good things."

At the Cathedral of Saint Andrew, on the seventeenth day, eighth month, in the year of the Lord: At the adoration of the Blessed Sacrament before the Holy Mass I offered this adoration together with my suffering to the Father, through Jesus the Lord; I prayed for God the Father's will to be done, the mission that the Lord Jesus entrusted me, as His Vessel, to unify His church, and build the kingdom of God.

Immediately after I offered these petitions, in spirit, with my carnal eyes, I saw up high, between the original altar and the new altar, behind the monstrance, the Spirit of the Father, in a thick white cloud, formed like a large man. He was sitting, I saw from His waist up to His shoulders clearly. His head was dark round iron and not as clear as His body; the parts most clear to me were the Father's chest and right shoulder. He was directly above the area where the Eucharistic ministers stand at the sanctuary; and today I served as the Eucharist Minister. I said to the Father, "Father, in a little while, I will come to the sanctuary and stand at your feet." I saw the Father during Blessed Sacrament exposition before the mass, and throughout the mass until before I went to delivered Holy Eucharist. When I returned to my pew after delivering the blood of the Lord to others, I no longer saw the Father there.

The mass began with the baptism of an infant, Justin Daniel, at the back of the church. As I heard Father Scott say the child's name, I knew that this was what the Lord Jesus had told me last night because of the name "Justin Daniel." Justin means justice, Daniel is the prophet Daniel, who was thrown into the lions' den and through the power of God, he emerged victorious.

Father Scott, was now at the sanctuary, and said, "Together with the angels, we sing glory to God." As I heard these words in a different tone of voice, I felt the Holy Spirit in Him. The baptism of Justin Daniel continued: During one part, Father Scott was standing next to the baptismal fountain; through his powerful voice, I knew that he was filled with the Holy Spirit. He blessed the water, and before he poured it over Justin Daniel's head, he turned his head twice to the right, facing the congregation, and spoke to the people: "This is the faith of the Church."

Before the mass ended, Father Scott asked Justin Daniel's parents to bring him to the front of the altar, facing the congregation as they prayed for blessings upon the child, his parents, and the congregation. At this time, God took me in spirit, and the Father said to me, "I had been waiting for this baptism today, to bring you to the public. Now Justin Daniel stands in your place today. Through these actions, I pour out my power upon you. Jesus is in you. Go proclaim the words of God." I said, "Father, I am going right now, to the public, for through me, Jesus the Lord speaks and does His works."

After the mass, I was still filled with the Spirit of God, and the Lord Jesus told me, "You must go and touch the child Justin Daniel; and to comfort Father Scott, I will speak through you."

I then stood to the right of Justin Daniel's mother, and asked her, "Can I touch the baby?" She replied, " Yes, sure." I said, "The name Justin Daniel was given to him by God, not by you, and he must be baptized today." While I was saying this, I touched Justin Daniel's left arm and forehead. His mother saw this, and said, "He is gifted." I said, "As you said, he will tear many hearts." In my thoughts I felt that she might think that I was speaking of women's hearts, so I continued, "In a good way, bringing people to God."

I then turned to Father Scott behind me; he was standing out side the opened double glass door, facing the sanctuary. To his right, some people were standing to my right, facing him. I said to him, "You were filled with the Holy Spirit. You said words you have not spoken before. You may not realize what you said, but now you know." He said, "Thank you," twice.

When I got home, I wrote in my note book; I was trying to describe the way I saw the Almighty Father. The Lord Jesus told me, "That is the way you see the Father in the natural."

> *Jesus answered, 'If I glorify myself, my glory is worth nothing; but it is my Father who glorifies me, of whom you say, 'He is our God' You do not know him, but I know him. And if I should say that I do not know him, I would be like you a liar. But I do know him and I keep his word.*
>
> *–John 8: 54-55*

August 30, 1997. Also in my morning devotion, the Lord Jesus explained to me the road of the chosen ones. These chosen ones are being taught by God alone. He pointed out some errors that the church officials approved in the prayer materials, these are from the Saints and the Blessed One. At the beginning, God teaches us a little at a time, slowly, on the road to purification. When the first part of purification is complete, He then begins the second step; at this point He pours out more of His wisdom and discernment. In this stage of God's teaching, He points out the errors that the chosen ones made when they were not awake, these errors resulted from carrying the past teachings that they had learned from man.

He then reminded me of His message, on August 19, 1997, a few days after I saw the Father with my carnal eyes in spirit. He said to me, "You need to explain to the church officials that you saw the Father. Tell them, 'The Father showed himself to me in the image of His Son, glorifying the body.' "

August 19, 1997. Before the 12:05 p.m. mass at the Cathedral of Saint Andrew, the Eternal Father said to me, "I will no longer be with you. I give you to Jesus, but I will always reside in you. The devil will fight against you, because he recognized you from seeing the Father. The Archangel Michael will fight for you."

The Lord Jesus said to me, "You still see the Father in Me. There are times you will see the Father. I am in Him."

Jesus the Lord continued, "The Father and I are in you, and was in My mother in a different way. There is a gap between God and Man; this gap was created by Eve, and will not be closed because Eve never repented. There was also a gap between God and His priests, a gap created by Peter, but Peter repented, and this gap was closed on the day you walked in front of a priest in procession to the altar."

Interpretation of the Baptism of Justin Daniel, August 17, 1997

August 19, 1997. After I had been in agony for some time, the Blessed Mother told me, "Do you want to go get your food [groceries]?" As I got to the supermarket parking lot, I saw there was an empty space under a big tree. The space provided open air in the front and back of my car. The big tree was to the right, and there was another car to the right, and the tree blocked the front of that car. I was very happy that I got this parking space, I said to the Lord, "Jesus, You are the provider, you saved this space for me, so my car would not get hot."

On my way returning to my car, I reached the sewer gate in between two cars. I thought that I could pass it, but I decided not to. I backed up the shopping cart, made a left turn, and went around another way, avoiding the sewer gate to get to my car.

In the evening, in my devotion, the Lord told me that the tree was symbolic of the power of God, and my car was symbolic of the mission. Parking in that shaded space means the mission is protected by the power of God. The sewer gate is symbolic of the enemies that attack me and the Lord Jesus' mission that God entrusted in me.

Jesus the Lord also told me that, on Monday, 18, 1997, when the devil attacked me, Saint Michael told me 'go get the holy water that was blessed yesterday to put on you.' I obeyed and went to the baptismal fountain, took the holy water and made the sign of the Cross, then poured it on my face, my neck and my hand. When the Blessed Virgin Mother appeared to Bernadette, she told her to dig in the ground and take the water and wash her face. Water and dirt was mixed on her face, and people laughed at her.

August 20, 1997. In my morning devotion, the Lord Jesus told me, "The infant Justin Daniel is symbolic of the mission. The name Justin Daniel is the purpose of the mission. You said to Justin Daniel's mother 'The name Justin Daniel was given to him by God. You thought that the name was given to him by you,' means the purposes of the mission are given to you by God; God will tell you what to do. The Father said, 'I have been waiting for this baptism' means through Justin Daniel's baptism, the mission is transformed. I will no longer use your car as the symbol, because the mission was transformed. Justin Daniel's part is done; you can explain this to his mother later. You said, 'He will tear many hearts,' means the mission will tear people's hearts, bringing them to God. Justin [himself] is God's chosen one, he will serve God in the mission. His parent will suffer with him. By your touching the child Justin Daniel, it means the mission is yours." The suffer parent symbolic of God that suffering with me.

The Lord continued, "The priest, Scott is symbolic of John the Baptist. The Baptismal fountain is symbolic of the Jordan river. The baptism of Justin Daniel is symbolic of the renewal of My mission on earth, and you are My main vessel. The Father showing himself to you, formed like a man is in the place of His spirit before like a dove."

In Nature, Mariette Saw the Lord Jesus' Head

April 22, 1997. In my dream, I saw myself laying face up. The Lord Jesus was a little over thirty years old, wearing a kerchief covering His head like people in Europe, His head was bent down. His face was next to my right cheek. I knew that he was my brother Jesus.

I woke up, both of my eyes were open and turned to my left. In nature, I saw in front of the Virgin and Child image that was hanging on my bedroom wall, the same face and head of the Lord Jesus I just saw in the dream, flying very quickly from the right to the left of the image. I said, "Jesus, my Lord, my God." In my thoughts were the Lord Jesus as He appeared to the apostles after He was raised from the dead. They thought He was a ghost, but He said, "It is I" to them. I then heard Jesus the Lord say to me, "At that time, I had not gone to the Father yet, I came to them with my entire body. I am in heaven now; I came to you with just my head. The broom means the physical body."

October 23, 1997. In my dream I saw on the dirt ground a countless number of fish; these fish were dirty, dirt was mixed in between their scales and I took them to wash them. I then was in another place, and I saw in the middle of the air some fish heads only (no body). I was about to clean them, and the dream changed to another dream.

October 24, 1997. In my dream I was standing in the middle aisle, in the end of a mobile home. In front of me was the end wall. Facing the wall I saw two Vietnamese dresses. They were a dark color, both of them were hanging flat to the wall. A small dress for a daughter was at the beginning corner, and a large dress for the mother was close to the right bottom corner of the wall. A woman was sitting next to the aisle of the last bench by the end wall. While I was looking at these two dresses, this woman was very angry and she said, "They changed their plan; they came here for rehearsal and left without telling me." She was referring to the mother and daughter whose dresses were hanging on the wall.

The small dress is symbolic of me, Mariette. The large dress is symbolic of the Roman Catholic church officials. The changed plan is symbolic they are disappointed of God called me and not them.

I then was in a large building, on the telephone talking to a mother of another family, although I saw no telephone equipment. She told me, "I will call you later." I walked to another side of the building. While I was walking I thought, "If I wait for her to call me back, that will be too long. I do not want to wait." I was then on the phone talking to the children of that woman; in front of me was square telephone without a hand set. While I was talking, I saw all her children on another side of the phone, but only one was talking to me. The other children were agreeing with the one who asked me questions. I also saw something long and dark next to them. These children asked me what was different about shipping the long dark thing next to them, and the twelve-sided glass (cup). I said to them, "You need to be careful when you ship your clothes [long dark thing], but when you ship glass, you need to be extra careful in packing it, and pay more for the shipping cost; because glass is very easy to break." While I explained to them, I saw a bright twelve-sided glass in front of me.

The clothing is symbolic of the physical body, the twelve-sided glass is symbolic of the soul. The number twelve is symbolic of the twelve tribes of Israel. The family at the other side of the phone is symbolic of those who are not understand of the soul and spirits within the body, and value of them

Mariette Saw The Lord Jesus Glorified Body with Her Carnal Eyes

September 14, 1997. During the night, the Lord instructed me to wear the three-piece, sky-blue garment that I wore on August 30, 1997, to the morning mass on Sunday, September 14, 1997, the Feast of the Triumph of the Cross. As I entered the Good Shepherd Church, the Spirit of God led me through the middle aisle. When I reached the second pew on my right, I was not sure whether the Lord wanted me to sit in the first or the second pew. Because I was uncomfortable being in the front row, I chose the second pew. But immediately, as I kneeled down, the Lord told me, "Move to the front." I then did as He instructed.

At the consecration, while the celebrant raised up the host and finished saying, "This is My body," the Lord Jesus said to me, "Your suffering and mourning will turn to joy." While the priest raised the cup and finished saying, "This is my blood," the Lord Jesus said to me, "Through the power of God, you are my sanctuary custodian." I then opened my carnal eyes, and in spirit, I saw a tall gold ciborium filled with consecrated host, up high in the air at the sanctuary, to the right of the priest. I then closed my eyes, and the Lord continued, "Open your eyes and look at me." I opened my carnal eyes and gazed at the risen Christ's statue at the center of the sanctuary wall.

388

During the Lord's prayer there was a boy between seven and nine years old who came from my left side, and crossed the center aisle to join hands with me. At the sign of peace, the Lord told me, "You go and bless the boy."

This is part of my discernment. I asked, "Lord, do You really want me to cross the center to bless the boy?" Through the power of God, I said peace to two people, one on my right and one behind me. I then crossed the center aisle and stood behind the boy, with my left hand holding the boy's left upper arm, and my right hand holding the right upper arm of the boy, and I said to him, "The peace of Christ be with you. The Lord Jesus loves you."

Then it was time to receive the Holy Eucharist. The priest [celebrant] was giving the Eucharist at the left aisle; a layman was in his way, giving the body of our Lord to those who needed assistance. I crossed the center, to the priest, to receive the body of the Lord. When I returned to my seat, I said to the Lord, "Lord, if I was wrong for crossing the center of the church to receive You, I ask You to forgive me; but if I did right, I ask You to reveal that to me." The Lord Jesus said to me, "I do not want my body to be interrupted on its way to you." The Lord meant that He wanted His body to remain in the consecrated host for me. He did not want to leave the consecrated host and re-enter. The Lord also meant that His mission in this world from the beginning to the end is without interruption, and the mission that God entrusted to me will not be interrupted, even though God has changed His plan for me, and has instructed me to return to the San Diego Diocese from the Little Rock Diocese.

God revealed to me; the consecrated host in the ciborium up high in the air is the Lord Jesus' glorified body; and ciborium symbolic of me, Mariette, as a Vessel of God.

God Appeared to Mariette the Fourth Time

January 1, 1998, the feast of Mary, Mother of God. During the 8:30 a.m. mass at the Good Shepherd Church in San Diego, California, while singing the "Gloria to God in the highest....." I was sitting at the end of the second row, in the middle aisle to the right side of the altar at the center section. In spirit, with my carnal eyes, I saw the Lord Jesus' glorified body. He was large, formed with a thick white cloud, His long hair touched His shoulder. He flew toward me, above the floor, at the right front corner of the sanctuary. He looked like the one I saw on August 2, 1992 in my dream, except this time He was formed with a thick cloud. The direction the Lord Jesus walking toward is same direction of the Father appeared to me at the Cathedral of Saint Andrew. He was very close, in front my left shoulder was opposite His right shoulder. He revealed to me His chest, right shoulder, upper arm, ear and the right side of his face, even though I saw His entire face. I then looked up above the altar, at the corner of my right eye, I saw Father Earl standing in front of the celebrant chair. I then looked at Jesus again. He was still in the same spot, after I looked at Him for a very short time, I then looked above the altar for a second time. I then looked at the same spot where He had been, but He was no longer there.

The Bright Golden Light Funnel

May 25,1997, the feast of the Holy Trinity. Before the Holy mass, immediately after the Holy Eucharist Exposition and Benediction, I had a vision. I saw a bright golden light suddenly appear. This light was in the shape a cone, it started from the right side door of the sanctuary and extended to the left. It was also at the top of the pillar, in front of the Blessed Virgin Mother statue, and covered the altar, the tabernacle with two cherubim on both side of the tabernacle, and the Blessed Virgin Mother's statue. The end of the cone was under my arms, outside of my ribs. I said to the Lord, "Lord, it doesn't make sense that I am at the top of the triangle." The Holy Trinity responded to me, "No, it is not a triangle, it is a funnel."

After I received the Holy Eucharist the Lord said to me, "Make sure you draw a picture in your notebook. One corner of the cone started at the right door of the sanctuary, another at the top of the pillar, in front of the Blessed Mother. The bottom of the funnel, each side was outside of your ribs. The glory, power, and grace of the Holy Trinity is coming through you for the world. I will reveal in detail to you like the white veil."

May 27, 1997. Before the 12:05 p.m. holy Eucharist celebration, in the Cathedral of Saint Andrew, I said to God the Father, "I accept to be the end of the funnel for the Holy Trinity." The Lord then said to me, "They did not let you speak in this church, on May 27, 28, and 29, 1997. I took you up high to hover down the wind upon the earth." Later in the same day, during my devotion, I saw the funnel filled with bright gold light together with me at the end of the funnel up high, under the sky, and the Lord said to me, "Where ever you go this funnel is in front of you." The Lord meant that wherever my body is, the glory, power and grace of the Holy Trinity is in front of me; or the Holy Trinity is carrying me in every moment of my life in this journey.

May 28, 1997. The funnel was up high, the part immediately under the sky was transformed; I saw one third down from the top, the white cloud and gold light changed into liquor; as I looked down close to the bottom of the funnel, the liquor was thick like melted pure gold waving down into the front of my chest.

May 29, 1997. During the night in my dream I saw the Lord Jesus' side wound very closely and clearly. In the morning devotion, in my vision I saw the back of the Cross facing the funnel, with the Lord Jesus hanging on the Cross, facing away from the funnel, then the Cross with the Lord Jesus was hanging on it, and it slowly went down, leaving the funnel up high close under the sky.

Then Jesus approached and said to them, All power in heaven and on earth has been given to me. Go, therefore, and make disciples of all nations, baptizing them in the name of the Father, and of the Son, and of the holy Spirit, teaching them to observe all that I have commanded you. And behold, I am with you always, until the end of the age.

–Matthew 28:18-20

God the Father Visits the World Revelation

February 4, 1998. I got up at 12:55 a.m., from a dream. In my dream I saw inside the church, behind the last pews; the entire back wall was completely open, like an entrance. On the right side were two dark people standing next to each other, facing the opening. As I looked at them I saw Pope John Paul II, wearing a white cassock, formed from a cloud, his face looking unlike himself; he looked old, suffering, and bent down at the neck while he was walking. He then walked through the two dark people, and as he did so, I walked forward, and pushed myself against his front cassock. When I did this he raised his right hand up. As he raised his right hand up to his belly, both my hands held his hand, and I bowed my head, knelt down at his feet, and kissed his hand. After I finished kissing his hand, I got up, and looked to the left side of the church. There I saw several people sitting on the extra bench, behind the last pew, with two little boys who were playing. I called to the boys, "Come here , to the Holy Father." They came and stood in front of the Holy Father, looked at him, then went back to the side they came from.

Immediately after these two boys left the right side, I went and stood on the Holy Father's left side while he looked out the back of the church, over the street to the lower level. On the other side of this street were many people standing behind the rope waiting for the Holy Father to visit and greet him. I escorted the Holy Father out of the church to the other side where people were waiting for him.

I saw that I was holding a three-month-old child at his belly with my right hand. The child had his head bent down, his eyes closed in sleep. The child and I were facing the same direction. When I saw the child in the dream I knew that he symbolized the mission that God had entrusted to me. I asked, "Lord, why does the baby sleep?" The Lord Jesus said, "You are resting for a few months, let the world be trampled. I will raise you up in May, between Easter and Pentecost, as I promised you before; not last May, but this May. Not between Easter and Pentecost, as you understood, but between the Easter and Pentecost

I then got up. I knew that I had encountered the Eternal Father in my dream. I turned my body around, lying on the bed, facing up, both my hands joined at my chest, and said, "Father, You came toward me in the midst of the world, and showed me Pope John Paul II's image, with a different face, but the world did not see You. The priests looked at You, and they left you. Father, You came to me. I kissed Your right hand. You came to me in the midst of the people, but they did not see You." While I was saying this I thought of El Nino

391

in California, with the heavy rain and storms all day yesterday and through the night. I then saw Pope John Paul II in one of the dreams before, next to the high roof with the Holy Eucharist inside the monstrance. The monstrance was turning; this revelation is in the book, "My Patient - God's Gift." I did not understand that Pope John Paul II in that dream was symbolic of the Eternal Father until later date.

After I copied the dream down in my notebook, I went back to praying, and the Lord Jesus said to me, "Tomorrow show Hanh the window under the hole of the roof. There will be heavy rains day and night, but there will be very little water coming through the hole. Let her, the non-Catholic married to your son, be a witness to your obedience and faith in the Father; so when she sees this in the book, she will talk about it. The Father visiting is different from Pope John Paul II. Tomorrow you watch television, His face is different and He is suffering. He has to raise His rod to discipline the world."

At the Blessed Sacrament I prayed, " Thank you, Father, You came to me in my dream, in the midst of the world. Thank you, Lord Jesus, You came to me in the dream, in the Father. Thank you, Holy Spirit, You came to me in the dream with the Father and the Lord Jesus."

The two dark people are symbolic of government officials and church leaders who live in the darkness of the enemies. The two boys are symbolic of priests and high-ranking church leaders who are not willing to follow in the Lord Jesus' footsteps. The people sitting on the left symbolize Christians and others who refuse to convert, examine themselves daily and repent. Those on the other side of the street, behind the rope, represent souls in purgatory, and those willing to convert, to examine themselves daily and repent. Their standing behind the rope is symbolic of those are waiting for God. The right side of these two people symbolize their right of the Earthly laws that go against God's commandments. The left is symbolic of people in this world who give their free will the devil. Past Easter to Pentecost and future Easter and Pentecost, and the month of May are all symbolic of God speaking of the future. His time is different from ours.

When I saw the Eternal Father's right shoulder and chest with my carnal eyes at the Cathedral of Saint Andrew, it was symbolic of the Father revealing His love, and His righteousness for me to prevail the enemies, and for those who follow in the Lord Jesus' footsteps. At that time I said to the Father, "Father, in a little while I will come to the sanctuary and stand at Your feet." In this dream He raised His right hand up; I knelt down and kissed His right hand. The pope John Paul's right hand raise up in the dream symbolic of the Father revealing to me, that He will raise me up, to serve Him through the mission that He entrusted to me.

The Eternal Father created the world. He is the author of the world, but people go against Him. The tragedies upon the world, such as El Nino bringing storms, heavy rain, heavy snows, and floods, etc. are the Father's actions to discipline man.

The two dark people are those depending on their human power; they ignore God either partially or totally. Priests know that God exists, but do not want to come close to Him. The Christians are proud of their own beliefs and actions do not want to convert to a real belief in God where they must obey all His commandments. The most important is to purify their souls through their daily life in thought and actions. But for those willing to convert, to come to God with all their hearts, their minds, their souls, and their strength, they will see the glory of the Father, through His beloved Son, Jesus.

God's love is mighty, but when people disobey His commandments, and refuse to change; He has to put them in a situation that no human can help them, so they have to come to God, and God will guide, protect and bless them. By disciplining their flesh with suffering, they will gain eternal life in heaven when they come to conversion. God's love is for us, and we must obey all His commandments, embrace our suffering, following in the footsteps of the Lord Jesus to receive our eternal life in heaven.

First Wine and the Last Wine Revelation

August 6, 1997. During my morning devotion, the Lord Jesus told me, "Today, I want you to go get the real estate advertisements, and start looking for a house that has a garage to put your car in; and for you to have a place to live away from these people around you, who are carrying enemy spirits that are interfering with your body."

On the way to 12:05 mass at the Cathedral of Saint Andrew; I stopped by the main post office in Little Rock, there was some advertising for real estate and rentals in a newspaper kind of stand, at the entrance to the post office driveway. I picked up three different booklets, one for apartments to rent, and two for property for sale.

August 6, 1997 is the feast of the Transfiguration of the Lord. After the mass, while I was still in prayer, in my vision, I saw the Lord circling the front stand of a weekly magazine about real estate for sale. I asked, "Lord, what are You showing to me?" The Lord Jesus said, "What do you need to qualify to buy a house?" I replied, "I need a down payment, good credit, and income to assure the lender I will fulfill the monthly obligation." He then asked me, "Do you qualify for that?" I replied, "Lord, I do not have money for a down payment, because the New York Life Insurance company has not paid my benefits, the benefits You had established for me while I worked for them. But I believe that every thing is possible with You, because You are God."

When I got home, the devil used what the Lord revealed to me and attacked me all day. By late afternoon, my right arm and leg were numb with pain; I could not even lift up my right arm, and my right leg was limping.

During my evening devotion, the Lord Jesus said to me, "I give you 'John 2:1-12, [the Wedding at Cana.]" After I finished reading these scriptures the time was 8:09 p.m., Jesus the Lord told me, "I will speak to you of the 'first wine and last wine'."

He then said to me, "Those letters that I had you mail to the church leaders and officials; many of them do not want to hear; but for those who heard them, they will be saved for eternal life in heaven. There is no word in heaven in my speech; you [Mariette] are misleading." He then said to me, "Can you rewind the tape and cross out the words 'in heaven' for Me." I said to Him, "Lord, I am Your servant, it does not matter how hard I try, I'll never be perfect, so I'll just leave it the way it is." The Lord said to me, "Mariette, you are stubborn, this stubbornness is true of you, you are not hiding it from anyone; but for those church leaders, they do not want hear what I had you sent to them. They are hiding the truth of themselves from the public. Everyone that has two faces, they will not be saved. Through the dream that I am going to give to you tonight, it will unveil the future of the Diocese of Little Rock."

In my dream the tornadoes had ripped off the roof of the Diocese of Little Rock building, and the Lord Jesus said, "Now their building had no roof, the sun was shining inside the building, and the rain would wet every part, every material inside the diocese building; except the bishop's conference office, where it was still dark." While the Lord was speaking, in my vision, I saw the actual Diocese of Little Rock had no roof, with light shining down inside the building from above. There were many compartments, and no people in the building; I also saw the conference room still had its ceiling, and inside was dark.

After the Lord spoke, I asked, "Lord Jesus, my right arm and leg are in pain and numb. Can I take a Sudafed or the pain killer that Dr. Strybel gave me?" The Lord said, "Please do not take them, I will heal you tonight."

August 7, 1997, at 6:59a.m. As I woke up, I said, "Lord, keep me in peace, help me to listen to You, and receive everything you are saying, record, and understand them. I ask You, Father, Jesus Lord, the Holy Spirit. I am surrendering this suffering to You, as the suffering offering to pray for the church officials, church leaders for conversion, and daily exam and repentance. Lord, if it is Your will, I ask you to heal my entire body; but if it is not in Your will, I ask you help me to embrace this suffering. I do ask You again, If it is Your will, I ask you to heal my right leg and my right arm from pain and numbness."

The Lord Jesus said to me, "After I finish speaking to you, I will heal your entire body, including the numbness of your hip, your arm, and your thigh. Your leg and your shoulder are in pain and are numb from your fighting against the enemy spirits all day yesterday, and over the night you continued to fight. That caused your body to be painful."

The Lord continued, "In the dream, when you opened the door, and looked on the street to your right, you saw lions, deer and camels proceeding to where you were standing. You were fighting as you saw the lions, and closed the door, went inside the house."

He continued, "The side of the house has no wall. Because the wall has not yet been built; you saw the outside of the wall that has not been built. On the dirt ground, close to the corner was a black bear. You did not want the bear to come onto the floor, so you took a piece of flat wood and placed it at the spot in front of the bear, along the curve of the concrete foundation of the floor of your house, trying to make a wall to prevent the dangerous animals coming onto the floor. When you saw a big rock, the rock had sharp edges around it. At the foot of the rock was a small boa constrictor, covered with mud, he was shaped like a worm, and was trying to overthrow the rock, at the middle of the same dirt ground, along the un-built wall. You hated this boa constrictor, and just walked away."

Jesus the Lord continued, "You then were up high in the air, looking down on the dirt ground; you saw a very thin, light gray, super long snake. You could not see its tail, but you saw its head was reaching up trying to catch you. You were fighting, but you knew that you were up high and this snake could not reach you. You saw on the opposite side of this long snake, another snake, dead for ages. Next to this dead snake was another snake, with a white stomach, dark back, and dots on both sides like a fish, crawling into the hole under the dead snake. A person's hands took a small four sided triangular rock, and hit this snake, by pushing the weight of the rock on top of the snake. While you saw the hands just hit the snake once, and laid the rock on top of the snake, in your thoughts, you wished that this person would crush this snake into many pieces, killing it totally, instead of just hitting it once, and laying the rock on top of it, and letting it slowly die."

The Lord continued, "All of these dangerous animals are symbolic of many spiritual leaders' hearts and actions. They are choosing to let the devil and his offspring either dominate their hearts, and/or interfere with their thoughts. The one whom I love the most is a bear. The one I hate the most is the thin, long gray snake that was lifting his head, and trying to fight against you.   These spiritual leaders and officials have denied the truth, either fighting against you completely, or they are softly loving you, wanting to accept you, but fear others will crucify them. Their love is not for me, but for themselves."

The Lord continued, "The dead snake is symbolic of the victory I won over the Lucifer. The other snake on his way to die is symbolic that, through you, I will slowly destroy the devil before the end of the world. The big rock was set outside the house, symbolic of My placing the authority, the key of kingdom of heaven in Peter's hands; now in the hands of John Paul II. The small boa constrictor is symbolic of the devil's spirit in the minds and hearts of the people, their actions, trying to overthrow John Paul II." While the Lord explained and dictated these words to me; in my vision, I saw all these pictures as he dictated to me for the second time."

The Lord gave me a continuation of the dream: I was in a room, this room was inside a huge building that had a hallway like in a hospital. The only door of this room was at the corner of the room. The room had three beds, two single beds, and one family bed. The single bed leaned to the front wall and the side wall was my bed; one head corner of my bed leaned against the front corner of the front wall. The foot of my bed was to the right of the open door, after entering the room. Directly from the door was another single canopy bed, no one could see inside the bed. The third bed was a canopy family bed, the foot of the canopy family bed was against the back wall, one corner foot of the family bed was against the corner opposite the front door.

On my bed, at the head part, were two of my queen-sized white pillows. Under the side of these two pillows was a pink night gown that had been worn out from washing many times, and some other of my clothes. There was also a large white king-sized pillow, inside a sham cover laid at the middle of my bed. I was trying to use the king pillow to cover the two queen pillows and clothes. I saw an invisible person drop down a black legging, and more clothes on the floor for me to fold them and take with me. While I was trying to fold them; I heard the voice of a woman, speaking out from the single canopy bed, saying, "The alarm went off. It is time to go." As I heard she say this, I hurried to wrap up all my clothes to put in my bag. While I was looking for my long, marine design, nylon bag, I had all my clothes on top of the bath towel on my right hand, ready to put in the bag. I knew that my nylon bag was under the king pillow, but I did not find it.

While I was looking for the bag I saw the woman's spirit leave through the front door. I was hurrying to follow her, I went to the front of the family bed and opened the canopy. I saw there was a child kneeling on the bed, facing my bed. I asked the child, "Have you see my purse?" He said, "Your purse is at the corner." I looked to my right, at the corner was my dark brown leather purse. I took it off the corner; and the dream ended.

The Lord Jesus explained to me, He said, "The single canopy bed with the female voice speaking out, and her spirit leaving is symbolic of My mission on earth some time ago. I then was crucified on the cross. The second single bed you were busy working on is symbolic of your mission in actions. The family bed is symbolic of the Roman Catholic Church. The leather purse belongs to you, and is symbolic of good deeds belonging to you, and will be performed through your mission."

The Lord used Saint Peter as symbolic of the Lord Jesus, to explain of the woman got out the canopy bed direct the door; and pope John Paul II symbolic of me, to explain I was follow the woman out the door. "Trying to overthrown pope John Paul II;" symbolic of spiritual leaders trying to rejected God through me. The Roman Catholic Church is symbolic of God's Church for all religion.

A Young Woman Appeared in the Sky

July 9, 1997. In my dream, I saw a young, very pretty woman, about twenty years old, with short blond hair. She was wearing a big, pure gold crown with diamonds on her head; her tunic and cloak were formed with a thick white cloud. Her right hand held a long sword, the head of the sword rested on the cloud in front of her right toe. While she was standing on top of a mass of clouds, behind and few feet in front of her was covered with clouds. There was a bright light shining to her right face and shoulder.

In the dream, the Lord said to me, "This is how you will look when you return to heaven. The Blessed Mother appeared to several people on earth, like Bernadette and Lucia. But when you go home to heaven, you will be the one who appears to others to continue your mission. The Blessed Virgin Mother is a Queen, she will rest, and let her daughter, the Princess of Heaven and Earth do her job."

Another Rock from Heaven

April 4, 1996. I, Mariette, in my dream I saw a huge rounded triangular-shaped rock laid in the garden. The Lord Jesus was sitting on the heavy side of the rock. His face was very clean, with a beard. His skin was lightly tanned, and He was wearing light gray and brown European-style clothing. His head was covered with a long shroud, His right leg was straight and touched the ground while His left leg was bent and rested on top of the of the rock. His left hand embraced His left knee, His right hand hung straight down beside His leg. The Lord was praying, looking up to a bright light in the sky.

The Key, Rock, Cross, and Shroud Revelations

In different dreams, God placed this same shaped rock in my right palm. This rock was formed from a cloud, but was very heavy, and it filled my hand. The Lord Jesus was standing on top of the metal filing cabinet in the corner of my bedroom. With both hands, He removed the shroud from around His neck, and Jesus the Lord gently put the shroud around my neck, with both tails hanging in front of me down to my knees.

The morning of January 9, 1998, the Father told me, "Jesus came down with His mission. He then gave the authority to [Saint] Peter. After [Saint] Peter went to heaven, Church leaders miscarried the mission by disobeying My commandments. You came down as a Vessel to the Holy Trinity, especially to Jesus with another mission."

The following is the meaning God revealed to me about giving me the key, rock, and laying the cross on my shoulder, and placing His shroud around my neck. Because the Lord Jesus' church is a spiritual church, these are the spiritual meanings: the key is symbolic of God's power to prevail over the devil. The rock is symbolic of standing firm and being strong, the cross is symbolic of embracing suffering, the shroud is symbolic of death to the self and completely obeying all God's commandments, everything for God, to the point that God is a companion of day and night.

At the time the spiritual leaders, especially high-ranking authorities, disobeyed God's commandments, they used their positions to gain power, to serve God and mammon, and to practice sexual misconduct. They served God with pride, with no faith in the immortality of the soul, competing against each other. God then withdrew His power. Without God's power, the church leaders lack discernment, and the devil and his offspring spirits are mixing within the church. The enemy spirits interfere or control the minds, hearts, and actions of many.

Since then until the present, the number of physical churches has grown like weeds, but the obedience to all God's commandments is not there. Many spiritual leaders and officials operate these physical churches by their own will.

God gave everyone free will, and He respects everyone's free will. It up to each one to choose God or choose the devil. When church leaders disobey God's commandments, it means their free will has been given to the devil.

God created the world by the Word, the Word is God's only Son. It means the substance to create the world is God's only begotten Son. Therefore, the world belongs to God's only Son. Before God created the world, He knew that man will disobey His commandments and listen to the devil. The Son freely obeyed the Father to take flesh and dwell among humans to enforce the Father's commandments.

Through the Sacrament of Baptism, water symbolically purifies man heart and actions, and receives the Holy Spirit to strengthen us. Jesus the Lord then died on the Cross, His blood cleanses our sins and purges our iniquities. Before He was crucified He bestowed God's grace upon His Apostles and Saint Peter was the head of His church.

God also knew that after Saint Peter went to heaven, the Church high-ranking leaders would be of flesh. They disobeyed His commandments, and divided His Church into parts. They fought against each other for positions, and focused on materials things. They let the power of the old serpent, the devil control them in many ways. The devil tries everything He can to get people to be disobedient to God's commandments. When disobedience souls refused to convert; God withdraw His present from them permanently. With God's love and mercy; He only withdrew His Grace from His Church. This is like a pregnant woman who miscarried a child because she didn't take proper care of herself.

In God's plan of creation, God pre-destined me, a sinner to reverse the devil's trick. He placed me as an undercover agent. Through God's power, after the time of my undercover work is over, my testimony will open the minds, hearts, eyes and ears of many.

Therefore, when all the church leaders have converted, and practice daily exam and repentance, the spirit of the church will be revived. When the spiritual church is revived, God's power will work through the hearts and minds of the church leaders. Through the church leaders hearts, minds and actions, God's power will radiate to others.

The Lord Jesus will be united in one body; like one family, in love. Every one will place God above all things, serving Him through service to one another, from pure hearts with love.

God's Commandments to His Brides

If, then, we have died with Christ, we believe that we shall also live with him. We know that Christ, raised from the dead, dies no more, death no longer has power over him. As to his death, he died to sin one and for all; as to his life, he lives for God. Consequently, you too must think of yourselves as [being] dead to sin and living for God in Christ Jesus.

–Roman 6: 8-11

April 9, 1997. In my vision I saw a sketch on the front cover of the book, "Bride of Christ in Action," with the Lord adding the sun on both sides of the Bridal cloak. He then said to me, "It does not matter what position you are holding, you are the one who always has authority in this Mission. Now, the Mission has not yet grown large, so it is hard for people to believe this is truly from God. But when the Mission grows big, many of them will come and want a piece of the pie, but they will not receive any; everyone called to work in this Mission was predetermined by My Father."

April 10, 1997 is the three day after the third anniversary of the date when God retired me from the insurance company and gave me the most difficult job in the world. It is has also been three months since God the Father accepted my free will that I surrendered to Him, and moved to Little Rock, Arkansas. While I was asleep, I heard a voice say to me, "You have been in charge of the Mission, doing all the work for 1991, 1992, 1993, 1994, 1995, 1996, and 1997. As of May 1997, Father Peter will become President of the Mission, Father Scott will be C.E.O. [Chief Executive Officer], Darcy will be Treasurer, and Debbie the Office Manager."

I woke up I and said, "Lord, I rebuke this voice in Jesus' name. But if it is from You, please give me the interpretation, and let it happen."

In my morning devotion, I pray to the Lord, "Father, Lord Jesus, I am offering the suffering I am embracing now for the interpretation of these revelations. I only know that Father Scott is the Rector of the Cathedral of Saint Andrew, and he came from Poland; besides that, I do not know anything about him nor the meaning of his name. I only know that Darcy is working on the front cover of "God's Purification-Not Easy," and that Debbie is the wife of Deacon Gary. Besides this, Lord, I know nothing more about them. I know Peter is the head of the Mission, and You are the One who shepherds this mission through him."

The Lord Jesus said to me, "These revelations are not good for the world, but they are good for Heaven. The artist is working on the book's front cover, the artwork represents God purifying the world. The deacon's wife is in the choir, she is singing hymns praising the glory of God. Father Scott is rector of the Cathedral, serving God and leading people to Him. Father Peter is a monk of the Cistercian of the Strict Observance, and he is completely obedient to all God's commandments; Peter's name is used as the head of the Church; the president is the one who enforces all the rules in a company. The C.E.O [Chief Executive Officer] receives rules from the president and enforces them on all the company's officers. The office manager applies all the rules to the subordinates. The treasurer is symbolic of all God's commandments being enforced under God's power, in order for people to inherit the Heavenly treasury. May is the number of authority. Seven is symbolic of the beginning of the completion of actions."

The Lord continued, "In the beginning, God created Adam from clay and He breathed into Adam the breath of life; a soul. The soul will be alive forever and ever, whether in Heaven or in the place that humans call 'hell.' In that place, souls will be chained in the darkness of the devil. Being in charge and doing all the work in this revelation means that God is the One who rules, and does all His works through His servants."

The Lord continued, "The handicapped will refuse to heal, they want to be like Eve, and the iron rod will enforce its will upon them. The seven stars in my hand will shed light all over the world."

While the Lord spoke about Father Peter, in my vision I saw the spirit of the Abbey of Gethsemane nonastery, and I saw Darcy's home in spirit. When He spoke of Debbie, in my vision, I saw her wearing the gold "V" collar on her white gown, walking down the sanctuary with a chalice of Holy Eucharist. As for the handicapped person, I saw a woman who was the assistant to the founder of the non-domination bible class, wearing a brace around her neck, and I then saw Adam and Eve run out of the Garden of Eden. (Adam is symbolic of disobedience soul and refused to convert, the woman Eve symbolic of Adam's spirit)

This revelation had seven number ones, and seven times the double number nine. Seven ones means there is only one true God, and He is the One who is beginning to purify the world. Double sevens and number nine means God's actions will carry out this purification until its completion. The Lord Jesus used the Cistercian of the Strict Observance, Priest, Peter, Rector of Cathedral, the talent of Darcy as an artist, and God's purification of the world, and Debbie wife as the second authority in the family, these characteristics symbolic of Jesus the Lord himself is the head of the mission; me Mariette as His Vessel.

April 26, 1997,12;34 a.m. The Lord said to me, Mariette, "The seals are for the sacraments, the anointings are graces of God upon the people who serve Him." The Lord continued, "I am here with you tonight as the Lord your God with commandments in various areas. I command you to speak the truth about everything I say to you and ask you to reveal. I do not want you to compromise with anyone or anything about what is right or wrong. I am the Lord, these are My commandments, they are decrees. What I have said to you about Church authorities and governments officials you cannot withhold from the

400

public. You must understand, this is the way I do My work, to enforce My commandments. My words come with My power, there is special protection for you. If anyone tries to harm you, he will be dead before he touches you. No one has power over you, unless it is given to him from the Father. I command you to put this revelation at the beginning of the book, "Bride of Christ in Action." The public will know these are My commandments from your God, and their God."

While the Lord spoke, in my vision I saw a press conference, waiting to receive news from the President of all Nations. They were facing a huge powerful dense cloud of Spirit, listening to words coming out from the cloud. I felt that I was sitting there also with the Blessed Virgin Mother. During the time God spoke, there were a few times when He paused; I then put the recorder on pause. During the time the Lord spoke I was feeling some fear of Him, and this is the first time I felt that way in my life. I then thought I could say something so the Lord would take away my fear; but the Blessed Virgin Mother leaned her head to my right shoulder, and said to me, "Do not say anything to the Lord, just listen. The Lord is speaking to you as your God, not your brother. He is officially addressing His commandments. When you want to speak to Him, wait and speak to Him in private."

After the Lord finished speaking I saw the cloud over Mt. Sinai, at the time God gave out His commandments to the children of Israel in the Book of Exodus, chapters 19 and 20.

Through these revelations, God was saying that the Rebuild My Church Mission's actions are under His power. He is enforcing His commandments upon the world. There will be many tragedies upon earth to point out that humans can do nothing, but must come to Him from their hearts, place Him above all things, love Him, and worship Him. When people reform their life, obey all His commandments, and after iniquities been purged, God will then bless them.

In his right hand he held seven stars. A sharp two-edged sword came out of his mouth, and his face shone like the sun at its brightest.

–Revelations 1:16

God Clothed Mariette with Purple: February 5, 1997. In my vision, I saw both of my hands tied behind my back, and I leaned my left face down on the carpet to pick up a paper clip and a piece of cotton. I saw a tight satin, purple gown in my bedroom. I then saw an invisible person put this purple satin gown on me. I saw I was wearing this purple satin gown, and sleeping in a short sleeve satin shirt, and purple satin bra, all three are same fabric.

I then saw the front copy of the State of Arkansas non-profit corporation papers, with the back copy worded, "Rebuild My Church Mission (The Lord Jesus gave this name to Mariette Do-Nguyen), this vision was in the Bishop Andrew's conference room.

I then saw the counter of the Secretary of the State of Arkansas.

Mariette No Longer has Her Free Will: March 19, 1997, the feast of Saint Joseph. After I received the Holy Eucharist, the Lord Jesus said to me, "Besides the Holy Father, you are the only one on this earth in this age that has completely surrendered their free will to God. Your free will was accepted by the Father on January 10, 1997, the day you landed at the Little Rock Airport. You have nothing of your own, not even one word you place in the books." While the Lord said the last sentence, in my vision I saw my monitor screen filled with typing words.

The Copyright of God's Blessing

April 15, 1997. During my morning devotion the Lord Jesus said to me, "I want all the books, artwork, audio cassettes, and video cassettes copyrighted under your name, and bestowed [transferred] to the succeeding founders after you return home to Heaven."

The Lord means that He chose me for this calling, and after I go home to Heaven, the anointing that the Lord bestowed upon me will transfer to my descendants, the succeeding founders. Jesus the Lord God will continue to communicate with her or him to shepherd His mission, the Rebuild My Church Mission. That makes the succeeding founders to have the rights over these materials, to protect them from the devil interfering in other people's minds and trying to take away the blessing from God upon the world by twisting His words in changing these materials.

> *I warn everyone who hears the prophetic words in this book: if anyone adds to them, God will add to him the plagues described in this book, and if anyone takes away from the words in this prophetic book, God will take away his share in the tree of life and in the holy city described in this book.*

> –Revelations 22: 18-19

I have completely surrendered my free will back to God, and God the Father accepted it on January 10, 1997, the day I actually moved to Little Rock, Arkansas. Therefore, I became "God's Instrument," everything I do or I speak is God speaking and doing through me. It means that the Spirit of God is dwelling in me and with me, His power is driving me like you drive a motor vehicle.

The Eternal Father Lifts His Child in front of Him

May 5, 1997. In my dream, I saw God the Father in His Son's Image, standing on a mass of clouds up high, to His left was the Lord Jesus. The Father lowered His hand down to lift me up. I was a little child wearing a round wool white winter hat, and both my hands reached up to the Father's hands. As I caught his hands, He pulled me up; as the same time I pulled all my strength to lifted my feet on the mass of clouds. I got up and stood in front of the Father's legs, I was tall up to His knees. I, Mariette then turned around, leaned my back to His knees, and faced the same direction with the Heavenly Father and the Lord Jesus.

January 28, 1998. After I received the Holy Eucharist, in my vision I saw the risen Christ come down in front of me. Jesus then said to me, "Come here, I will lift you up to the Father. Through you, the world will see the Father's glory like you saw the sky coming down to the earth in the dream."

The Gift of Prophecy

> *To each individual the manifestation of the Spirit is given for some benefit. To one is given through the Spirit the expression of wisdom; to another the expression of knowledge according to the same Spirit; to another gifts of healing by the one Spirit; to another mighty deeds; to another prophecy; to another discernment of spirits; to another varieties of tongues; to another interpretation of tongues. But one and the same Spirit produces all of these, distributing them individually to each person as he wishes.*
>
> —1 Corinthians 12:7-11

April 18, 1997, 3:39 a.m. The Lord said, "Embracing suffering is the only way to increase the power of a gift from God unto a person." The Lord means that His gifts come with suffering. If a person denies or complains of suffering, that person does not have any gift, or will lose the gift. That they embrace it is itself a gift from God, this gift is sharing the suffering with the Lord Jesus.

I asked the Lord, "Lord bestowed upon me the gift that I am able to understand and remember everything You revealed to me, and I am able to discern them, what is in the spirit, and what is in the natural." I then turned to my beloved Blessed Virgin Mother and the holy angels and saints to pray for me. Then the Lord Jesus said to me, "Princess, the gifts you asked for, you already have them. I have bestowed up on you and they will be increasing."

This is to help people in this world understand the prophecy gift. When God chooses a person to bestow the gift of prophecy on, that person becomes an instrument of God. This person's free will is surrendered back to God, she has a life of suffering, fasting, praying and completely obeying all God's commandments. This person is filled with love, is humble, and speaks what God tells them to say, even they have to die for God; the gift itself comes with all these.

God's gifts are to serve Him, a person must have a mission from God before He bestows His gifts. With the true gift of Prophecy in a person, this person is very humble, and very careful of his or her words; she always is in prayer and ask God to discern for her. Words that come out from the mouth of the true prophet hurts people's flesh, very few people are able to accept her, because they deny the truth.

When the Lord said to Moses, "Take off your sandals, this is holy ground," God means that you accept this call, you must remove everything of your own, and live the life of holiness to serve God alone. While the Lord was speaking, I saw Moses bending down taking off his sandals next to the burning bush, together with the holy Bible in the page of the scripture.

The words that come out from her are from the Spirit of God; they are meaning the past, present or future in God's time are the same. Therefore, what this person foretells has no time, things could happen in the near future, or may not happen for many more generations. The future could be the past, and will happen again. The actions in the old and news testaments will happen again in similar forms. Except, the Messiah, the Son of the most high living God, the Lord Jesus will return in the cloud, with His angels, to judge the living and the dead. God called Moses to lead the children of Israel out of the Egypt. This anointing from God still continues calling people to lead other people out of the darkness of sin, but will not be as great as what God bestowed on Moses, less of God's power and glory of the gift.

Saint Bernadette of Lourdes obeyed God to deliver the exact messages of the Blessed Virgin Mother told to say, without fear. She embraced the suffering of her serious illness until her last breath without complaining. The price she paid for those people healed at Lourdes was embracing her suffering, sharing this suffering with the Son of the most high living God.

Saint Francis of Assisi spoke what God told him to say. The church high authorities did not believe him, because Saint Francis obeyed God in faith; and God changed the church authority's minds.

There are many false prophets, these people are lead or control by the lying spirit. The lying spirit is from the devil. Before Lucifer was cast out from heaven he was one of the archangels. God also gave him power, and he can only exercise his power with the permission from God the Almighty, the Father.

The Lord said, "Test the fruit to know the tree, good fruit comes from a good tree, and a rotten tree will bear rotten fruit." The purpose of the gift of prophecy is for those love God and do great works, lead people to God so they can enter Heaven, and for God's will to be done. This gift is not to act like a fortune teller. If people still retain his or her free will, they are not leading people to God, they are leading people to do their will.

Mariette Obeyed God to Relocate

After I met with the Most Reverend Andrew, the Bishop of the Little Rock Diocese, on October 31, 1996, the Lord told me, "Simon is the 'Big Rock.' Saint Peter's Square in the Vatican is the Holy Father. Saint Andrew's Cathedral in Little Rock, Arkansas is the 'Little Rock.' "

Within a few weeks before my actual move, the Lord told me, " I told Abraham to move out of his father's house, and promised him that I would make him the father of many nations. Now, I tell you to move out of the house that I provided for you, to the land of milk and honey: Little Rock, Arkansas." And "I am sending you to reopen the St. John's Seminary, to bring young men from all over the word to this location. I will teach them through the professors." The big rock and Saint Peter is symbolic of the Lord Jesus. Little rock symbolic of Mariette.

"In Little Rock," the Spirit of Saint Andrew dwells in the Cathedral of Saint Andrew, Saint Peter's younger brother; also the Bishop Andrew. God chose the land of Little Rock, where the Cathedral of Saint Andrew was built one hundred and fifty years ago, to gather His true servants, directly shepherded by the Bishop of Little Rock Diocese, the Most Reverend Andrew J. McDonald, and indirectly shepherded by the Holy Father, to prepare for the Lord Jesus' return, and to execute judgments and rewards.

Abraham obeyed God in faith. He rewarded him by making him the father of many nations. God has now said to me, "Mariette, my servant, in faith, move to Little Rock, and do what I have told you. I will reward you with what I had predestined for you." Abraham is also symbolic of Eternal Father.

Saint John is the only single apostle who stood at the foot of the Cross. The Lord Jesus wants His priests to be single, to depend on Him, to have no fear, to obey all His commandments, and embrace His Cross. On the last day, He will reward them with eternal life in heaven.

Saint John's seminary in Little Rock, and many other seminaries through the world will be opened, to train more priests in holiness. The power of God will shadow them, the ones who are willing, to live their lives as holy priests. God needs many more holy priests to lead His people, to help them focus on eternal life in heaven.

On January 15, 1997, I met with the Most Reverend Andrew, and submitted myself under his supervision.

Jesus the Lord Changed Mariette's Name to Michelle

July 2, 1997, before the 12:05 p.m. mass the Lord told me, "Your name will now be called Michelle." I then asked the Lord, "Mariette is the daughter name of the Blessed Mother Mary." The Lord then showed me in my vision "Mariette-Michelle Do-Nguyen." When I saw my name laid out with four words, I understood the Lord revealed to me that Holiness is the strength to fight the devil's power. I then asked the Lord, "Do you want me to change my name as the books author, and on my driver's license?" The Lord Jesus said to me, "I changed your name to Michelle, My power comes with the name. I give you the same power I gave to the Archangel Michael. Whether you are on earth or in heaven, this power remains with you. You are free to use it; it is supernatural power, not earthly power;

you do not have to change your name on earthly papers. Michael the Archangel is your companion through this journey. He is side by side with you."

September 29, 1995. At 2:05AM God anointed My feet, I felt an electric shock for about 3 minutes. God the Father said to me, "Your spiritual name is suffering servant, as a vessel to God the Almighty, the Father, the Son, the Holy Spirit, with a special mission for the Second Coming of Christ." When I heard the Lord give me this name, I did not understand the meaning of it. My only thought was, "Why did God give me this name? This name is too long, I will never use it." Almost a year later, I finally understood. I have used this name before the Lord told me, I now use this name almost every moment of my life. When I use this name, the Lord cleanses my sins and purges my iniquities. The Lord issued me the "Diploma and License to Practice" because I embraced this long name. The name of embracing suffering is a holocaust offering to God, the Lord then changed my name to Michelle. The Archangel Michael is a strong fighter, and when the Lord named me Michelle it meant that I have been fighting, and I am going to fight harder against the world systems that go against my Lord, my God, your Lord and your God, the Creator of heaven and earth.

These two names are also for every one of you, to pick up your own cross, and the cross of the Lord Jesus, and follow in the footsteps of the Lord Jesus, and fight against the devil's power that interferes or controls people's minds and actions. The weapon for this fight is conversion, daily exam and repentance, complete obedience to all God's commandments and the Holy Father's teachings. Also keeping your heart pure, going to confession regularly, going to mass regularly and receiving the Holy Eucharist, taking responsibility to the Lord Jesus' church in labor and financial matters, placing God above all things, and serving God by service to one another in love, praying the rosary and studying scriptures.

My Company Opens the Second Office in the Same Village

February 2, 1997. In my dream, I was outside a huge aircraft with another woman, gathering my belongings to move. This company moved it employees by a huge cargo aircraft, 747 Boeing jet. I then was inside the aircraft, this aircraft was dirty, and almost empty, except there were a few carton boxes next to its tail. Suddenly, I was sliding down from the front to the tail where those boxes were. I realized that the aircraft was taking off from the ground. I then looked through the wood bars, double door, it should be the tail of the aircraft, but there was no tail, just open air. Because I was sliding down, I was trying to use my feet to protect me, but I could not push my feet against the wood door, I then pushed my feet against the corner next the wooden door.

I was then in the village, and I walked past the first office that my company opened some time ago. Next to the office was an empty coffee shop in renovation. I entered the second office that would open soon. This office was at the end of a row of track of houses, to its left, two houses down was my mother's house. Inside the office were three levels. The first level, after I entered the front door, was narrow, a little higher than the second level, and the second level was very large. The third level was a lot lower than the second level, and it was a lot larger than the second that I could only see in the dark. I was standing close to the back corner of the second level, looking at a spot next to the corner and thought, "My desk can be here. At lunch, I can go to my mother's house to have lunch, and come back to work."

The company I work for is symbolic of the family of God. The aircraft is symbolic of God' power carrying me, like the angels being carrying by God. The village is the earth. The first office is symbolic the Lord Jesus came down to earth two thousand year ago. The coffee shop is symbolic of other religious that have not accept the Lord Jesus as the Son of God. Its emptiness is symbolic that they are not in full communion with God. The renovation is symbolic that they will convert their lives, to be in full communion with God. The second office is the mission that God entrusted to me, Mariette; and the Lord Jesus is a head.

> *Standing by the cross of Jesus were his mother and his mother's sister, Mary the wife of Clopas, and Mary of Magdala. When Jesus saw his mother and the disciple there whom he loved, he said to his mother, "Woman, behold, your son," The he said to the disciple, "Behold, your mother." and from that hour the disciple took her into his home.*
>
> *–John 19:25-27*

In this revelation, God focused on the Second Office. This Second Office was revealed to the world at the foot of the Cross through the characters and relationship of people standing around at the Cross. Saint Mary Madelene is a convert; at the foot of the Cross symbolic of the future will have a female convert as God's chosen One, God's Vessel to continue the Lord Jesus's Mission. Saint John is the single disciple, and the one that the Lord Jesus loved most; the Lord Jesus's revealed the future of His mission to Saint John in the Book of Revelation. This Book of Revelation is full with symbolism that no one can understand God's meaning. The hidden meaning of Saint John at the foot of the Cross, and the Book of Revelations that people have no understanding of it means. Yet, people will understand these symbolisms through God's chosen One that revealed in several chapters of the Book of Revelation; and that this pre-destined chosen One will receive the meanings of the symbolism directly from God through more revelations.

The Lord Jesus fully man mother's sister, Mary the wife of Clopas: The sister of the Blessed Mother Mary reveals an adoption of a female into the Holy Family. Mary's (the wife of Clopas) husband not being at the foot of the Cross means that the female adoption into the Holy Family will not have a spouse with her in this journey of the mission. Through God's power, to carry on the Lord Jesus's mission for His return, will be a female sinner, a convert adopted to the Holy Family, taking over the Lord Jesus fully man's family responsibility; this female sister will serve the Lord Jesus's as God's pre-destined God's Vessel. These symbolism in the Book of Revelation are for God's pre-destined chosen One to understand; and that this chosen One will receive proper meanings of them.

Through my dream God revealed; the Lord Jesus chose the disciple John to reveal the future of this world. Saint John belonged to the First Office and the Lord Jesus was a head. God predestined me, Mariette for in the Second Office, and the Lord Jesus also a Head of the office. Through me, God revealed in depth the meaning of the Book of Revelation. This event was foretold in the Book of Revelation chapter 11, The two witnesses.

When the Lord Jesus said, "Woman, behold, your son." He said the word "Woman" not mother; it means this word is from the Lord Jesus as fully God, to man, the Blessed Virgin Mother as spiritual mother all man on earth. He then said to John, "Behold, your mother" which means he commanded every one of us must accept the Blessed Virgin Mother as their spiritual Mother, and honor her. As spiritual mother, through God's power, she takes dirty us as laundry to the Laundromat; to clean us before bring us to God.

The Lord Jesus mother's sister, Mary the wife of Clopas: the relationship of sister means through God's power, there will be an adoption as the sister to the Jesus fully man family. Now, almost two thousand years down the road, God called me, Mariette, out from the crowd, the sinner, for a conversion, and said to me, "I predestined you for this job." The job has a dual relationship of responsibility to the Lord Jesus, as sister, to follow the Blessed Virgin Mother's foot steps. This also means God love the conversion.

There was only man, John, at the foot at the cross, and there were many women. In the old and new testament, God has chosen men in most cases. But in preparation for the Lord Jesus' Second coming, God chooses more women than men in many major areas. Remember the obedience to all God's commandments and the Holy Father's teachings.

Rebuild My Church Divine Mission Center

Before February 2, 1997. More than twice the Lord Jesus told me after I moved to Little Rock Arkansas that the Lord will build a Church, and name it Saint Mary Madelene, for the conversion. On the same property, next to the church will be some big dormitory buildings for a retreat center. Father Hung Tong will be the first Pastor at this church, being responsible for the center, and president of the Rebuild My Church Mission. But I thought, "The Bishop of Little Rock Diocese will be the one who is responsible to build the center and the church, and appointed Father Hung Tong, not my job."

March 26, 1997, Holy Wednesday. In my morning devotion, 8:28 a.m. God the Father commanded me, " I have revealed to you, [Mariette] before. You must build a Center with a church in Little Rock, and name for the Rebuild My Church Mission Center. This name is subject to change after you return home in Heaven; name the Church as Mary Madelene. The Center and the Church will be separate from the Diocese of Little Rock, and owned by Rebuild My Church Mission. I will give you the blue prints: It will have large church, a building to provide offices and bedrooms for Vatican representatives, a building for the Rebuild My Church Mission offices, as a main location for the Mission; dormitories with community showers, and restrooms. It will also have a large building for retreat activities, with a dining hall; a home, small building for the Mission founder and her successors; and a large rectory for priests. Father Hung Tong will be the supervisor of the Center and the first Pastor of the Church."

I said, "Lord Jesus, You give me money to do this things. You send me people to give me land, materials and labors. This is your project, I am just Your instrument."

Mariette is a Servant to the Most High Living God

September 22, 1997. In my dreams I laid on my stomach and cried out to the Lord to pour out the grace of conversion upon His chosen one and the world. The Lord God said to me, "Through the power of God, the big rock in the Vatican and Little Rock in Arkansas, to build Saint Mary Madelene's Church and the Mission Center in Little Rock. After your last breath the Church and Mission Center will change their name to Princess of Peace. Jesus the Lord is the big rock, and you (Mariette) are the little rock. You are the land filled with milk and honey. You are the Saint Mary Madelene's Church and the Mission Center. You are the Princess of Peace." As morning drew near, while I still slept, I heard the Lord God command me, "Let them come to you so they may convert to God."

God Changed the Direction to Fulfill His Will

Saturday, August 30, 1997. I was proceeding to my seat from the back of the Cathedral of Saint Andrew, while Father Scott, the Rector of the Cathedral of Saint Andrew, in Little Rock, Arkansas, was standing outside the sacristy at the back of the church. When he saw me coming, he said to me, "Mariette, can I talk to you for a few minutes?" I replied, "Yes." He then turned around and headed toward the sacristy. I was following behind him, he then took a seat behind the confession window, the seat that he normally sits in to hear confession, I took a seat on a chair opposite him.

We spoke for about twenty minutes, Father Scott focus on the reputation of church leaders and those that serve in the church, and my focus was obeying all of God's commandments, engrave all His commandments in our hearts and actions. I also explained to him of God's chosen ones suffering following in the footsteps of the Lord Jesus. Father Scoot asked me to use artificial names for him and other in my writing that God sent me; but I answered to him that I have to ask the Lord Jesus.

During that night, I asked the Lord Jesus, he told me, "Mariette, you are the eyes witness; if you change their names, how can you testify?" Jesus the Lord instructed me in the first step that He is going to take. He said to me, "Tomorrow, you are going to dress in the three-piece sky blue garment, and use the new hand bag.

August 31, 1997. Sunday mass, after I received the body and blood of the Lord Jesus and went back to my seat, the consecrated wine soaked in the consecrated host; the consecrated host got thicker and tough. At this time in my thought, "I never have received any consecrated host this tough before." I then heard the Blessed Mother tell me, "Swallow it whole." I said, "How do I swallow it without breaking?" she said, "Lift up your tongue." I did as she said, then the whole consecrated host came through in whole. Later the Lord Jesus told me that the consecrated host and wine was turned into His real flesh.

After the mass in the same day, while I was taking an afternoon nap, the Lord said to me, "It is time for you to return to San Diego. You will leave Little Rock on Wednesday." Still in the dream I said, "There are only three days. How could I have enough time to pack up and leave on Wednesday." The Lord confirmed to me, He said, "within a week." I then woke up very excited without understanding the reason of returning to San Diego. The first thing in my thought to call my children to let them know that I would be on my way to be with them.

The Lord also instructed me to send out four letters before I left. I did as He told me before I left. I arrived at the San Diego airport at 9:00 p.m. on September 3, 1997.

September 4, 1997. I woke up at 5:33 a.m. God the Father spoke to me, through His begotten Son Jesus, in the voice of the Holy spirit, "That is the way they have practiced for ages. I separate the equipment from the box, take my equipment, then dump the empty box. I took you and left the one being controlled or interfered with by the enemy spirits. The priest was the only one who was with you close at the time you entered the aircraft."

While The Lord was speaking, in my vision I saw the scene of the meeting inside the sacristy at the Cathedral of Saint Andrew. The fax machine on the right side of the counter was mounted to the wall. Below the counter was the fax machine's empty box, and Darcy's spirit, who assisted me packing up my belongings to move on September 1, 1997. I then saw my Nissan Maxima parked in front of the lawn on September 3, 1997. The trunk was open, and I saw the Lord's hand rearranging the stuff I put in. I saw a rectangular box, a size like the files box, sealed with a security tape that has white grain. The television set was covered with the bathroom floor blanket. The microwave was invisible. The spirit of the computer keyboard was wrapped inside the white linen, with the tool box, the blender and a envelope with a box of works in progress.

I then saw the inside of the Good Shepherd church on the weekday mass, and the Wells Fargo Bank and the spirit of the San Diego Diocese.

410

My Company Connects Two Offices in One Management

August 28, 1997. In my dream I saw I was sitting on the floor of a huge commercial aircraft, my sister was sitting in a chair a few rows in front of me with other people.

I got up and walked through the center aisle to the front of the aircraft, entered the right side door where the pilot was on a high stool like a UPS van driver's chair. On the floor behind him four people were sitting and facing the aircraft's front windshield. There was a cloud-color toilet bowl on the floor in front of these four people. I needed to go to the restroom. I put my right foot inside the bowl and tried to sit, but I realized that I must place my foot at the brim of the bowl. I then finished going to the restroom, and got up, I saw my stool was floating inside the toilet bowl. I did not want those four people to see my stool in the toilet; I took my right foot and pushed the toilet bowl to the side of the pilot's room. I then saw the toilet bowl top, I closed it down and locked it. I then saw a man come and stand at the door, next to the pilot talking to him and at the same time this man gave the pilot some paper.

Then the aircraft took off, it flied directly head up to the sky like a shuttle-rocket to the moon. I thought that I needed to go to the back to be with my sister, but the aircraft was going directly up, I could not walk down, so I decided to stay at the front part with the pilot.

I then heard the voice of Father Scott saying the mass, "Loving God." I saw the Father's image of His Son's glorified body that I saw with my carnal eyes at the Cathedral of Saint Andrew, the Lord Jesus told me, "The Father revealed His chest to you, it means He loves you. He showed His right shoulder to you, it means His righteous is your righteous."

In the morning Jesus the Lord showed me more visions, He then told me, "About the fourteen pages of paper Darcy gave to you... in the year 1947 they brought Bernadette's corpse up from underground, this is telling the world that the Vessel to the Holy Trinity is existing on earth to carry out what God chose her to fulfill in her mission."

August 25, 1997. When I got back from lunch, I was tired and fell sleep. In my dream I saw I was standing at a large double door, and looking on the street, there was a long row of track houses connected from the right end of this double door, making a square corner. Several feet from the double door was an automobile parked next to the sidewalk, facing the double door; behind this car, on the sidewalk was a priest wearing a white alb. Standing and facing the street; there was a woman wearing a white, sleeveless robe. Across the street, raising both of her arms up she fought against the priest, but the priest stood still, but some how the woman had to back up toward the street, and around them were a crowd of spirits who watched this woman attack the priest. I heard a voice from the house behind the priest scolding the woman wearing the white dress. The voice said something like,

"The kind of woman attacking priest is depraved." While I heard this, I also got ready to go out there to protect this priest. I then woke up, and the Lord reminded me of the garment bag in the dream where Father Hoan entered the room. It was not easy since three o'clock; the Lord instructed me to wear the outfit on September 5, the first Friday.

The Lord Jesus reminded me on the first Friday, January 5, 1995. He gave me the Book of Revelation chapter five, six and seven, during the adoration, at Good Shepherd Church in San Diego, and said to me, "I am the Lord Jesus. Today is the first Friday of the year. I take you and the heroes in the palm of my hand, and place in my heart to guide you, protect you. My words will be pounding in your heart like my mother; and they will open up, one after another, until the day you depart from this life; they will all be opened. I give you scriptures, the Book of Revelation chapter five, six and seven. I will send the Holy Spirit to help you to understand. These chapters are for both you and heroes. I will reward you and heroes in heaven to sit at my right hand. For your children, you must speak the truth to them with love and softly at the right time, and I will do all the works so they can inherit heaven with you. My Father is very pleased with your willingness. He gives you all the power from heaven to accomplish His will. My mother loves you and heroes very much. She has a special place for you in Her heart, and continue to pray the rosary. See father Azide, father Otihc, and father Rednanref. I will bless the Good Shepherd Church parish, go in peace."

Obedience and Depending on God

January 6, 1998. In my dream I was at the middle of a three way intersection, in front of the Bui Thai Catholic Church with my daughter. She was five years old, and around her were some other girls. These girls' parents were also around there, but I did not see them. These girls were in a mixture of dark and brown colored clouds. I was almost finished painting my daughter's entire body with white paint.

I was standing at the main street, and at the end of this street was the Catholic Church. I looked at the first room of the building to the right of the church, on the church property, and there was a bed covered with a white bed sheet and my daughter wearing white was laying on top. People were standing around the bed, facing her.

When I saw this scene, I knew these people were about to kill my daughter. I thought, "I have painted my daughter white and given her to them, and then they took her from me and are trying to kill her." I quickly ran over, grabbed my daughter from the bed, together with the white bed sheet, embraced her at my chest, and ran away from them, fighting and crying. When I got back to the spot where I was painting her before, I faced down to look at her, and there I only saw the white bed sheet. I then heard the Blessed Virgin Mother tell me, "Mariette, that was just a dream." She meant that God is revealing to you, it is not on earth yet.

When I got up from the dream the Lord gave me the interpretation. My daughter is symbolic of the mission, and this mission is myself completely obeying all God's commandments, avoiding sin, and to teach others to be the same way I am. The people around my daughter are spiritual leaders, and their daughter are their missions. The majority of them are disobedient to God's commandments so their daughters are mixed with dark and brown. They then tried to persuade me to be disobedient to God like them. But when I knew that, I ran away from them.

God revealed to me that the devil and his offspring are hidden inside many spiritual leaders, and the devil's plan is trying to make me fail.

When I got the Blessed Sacrament before the mass, the Lord Jesus told me, " You are still painting your daughter. Those people are church leaders and officials, their daughters are their mission. They will try to persuade you. Stand firm and be strong." I then said, "Jesus the Lord, Father answered to you to raise Lazarus from the death. I beg you, you are in me and with me, answer by helping me that through you I can hear the Father and understand everything He reveals to me. Keep me always from sins, and stand firm that no one can persuade me."

December 21, 1997. In my dream I was with my child, a little boy about three to four years old, maybe a little older, and we were standing on a huge sandy ground like the beach, but there was no beach. My right hand was holding the child's left wrist; to our right was a one story, large building, in front of us was a high, six-legged shower with three compartments, and my left hand was holding some clothes. I just left the building, looking for water to give my child a bath.

I then entered the shower together with my child. This shower's wall was covered with some kind of material that was very easy for the wind to break through. Wind had lifted off the bottom of one side of the wall. This shower had been built for ages, and people had not used it or taken care of it. After I completed examining the shower, I looked over the sandy field again, and I decided, " I am not going to use this shower to give my child bath, the wind blows sand through the shower.

I then was walking very fast through a park. The park's ground was dry dirt, to my right and at the center was a huge tree, this tree was there before the park ground turned to dry dirt. The first ten feet above the base of the tree had no branches, it was covered with thick dark bark. Above ten feet there were several tiny branches in a different level, without leaves, and there my child was climbing around the body of the tree. I knew that this tree was very tall, but that is all I saw. On the ground, around the tree, a little space away, people were standing watching my child climbing.

I continued walking toward the main street, and passed the bus stop shelter at my right. As I got on the street, I saw the Lord Jesus about one yard away at my left, on the center of the street, walking toward me. When He got in front of me, He asked, " Where is your child?" To the right, I quickly made a one hundred eighty degree turn, looking at my child still climbing on the tree, and said to Him, " He is over there."

Then the Lord Jesus walked to the tree to get my child; I also walked to the tree. While the Lord Jesus and I were walking toward the tree, my child was coming down. The Lord Jesus cut through the crowd into the space in front of them. As this time I got behind a person, looked through the space between two people, and saw my child just getting down on the ground. The Lord Jesus took his hand and led him away from this crowd. When I saw the Lord Jesus take my child's hand, I thought, "I am a very special chosen one, the Son of God favored of my child, and I am his mother."

The Lord Jesus held my child's hand, and led him to the space in between the bus stop shelter and a wall. I followed them. This long bus shelter was covered on the top, four walls were open, and the back and side wall had three square wooden bars nailed to the middle of these poles to make the shelter stronger. I was facing the child already on the wooded bar. To my right between me and my child, the Lord Jesus was standing facing my child teaching him how to climb up high. In my thought, "He will teach the child to fly up very high in the air and go down, that is a miracle." When this came to my thought I also had a vision in the dream that the spirit of the child was formed up high.

When I got up during the night after the dream, Jesus the Lord explained to me. Tne child is symbolic of the mission that God entrusted to me. The shower, sand and ground are symbolic of my life from my birth to the time of my conversion in the Holy Week of 1991. I was walking through the dry dirt park into the street symbolic from the time of my conversion till September 1995. The Lord Jesus coming to me in the middle of the street to the end of the dream is symbolic of the time after September 1995. The tree is symbolic of the Holy Trinity, and the people around the tree are symbolic of God's people. The bus shelter is symbolic of the God's Church.

Through the request from the Lord Jesus, God the Father pre-destined this mission for me, and it came with me at the time of my earthly mother's conception in the town of Lac Nghiep at Nam Dinh, Vietnam, in the year 1946. In the year 1950, my parents took me away from the village where I was born, and we relocated several places after that. When I grew up, we also relocated a number of times. This mission within me went every place I went.

Close to the time that the mission came into action, God opened my eyes so I could see right and wrong; for others it is called "conversion". At this time the devil realized that I was about to come out of undercover, and he fought harder. Every time after a conversion, the devil will attack that person harder in many different ways. At this time it is no longer the devil's offspring that attack you, but the devil himself will go out to get that person back, he is seven times stronger than before the conversion.

Because the devil himself was attacking me, the Lord separated my mission from me. I went to a completely different road. The mission God entrusted in me was pre-destined, I was being undercover; I must come back to finish the work before I return to heaven.

Everyone came down to earth for a purpose. There are many other chosen ones who are "not" pre-destined, God gives us free will to obey or reject Him. When that person rejects and God chooses another person to replace, God judges each one's heart and actions. How do we identify?

WRONG: The devil works through a person's mind and action. This person exalts himself, by joining many groups for services to others. In the church, he prays, and shares troubles and uses these troubles and makes people talk behind another person's back, to make judgment on him. He goes to church more often or everyday, and talks about his conversion frequently in the public. He also fills this person with counterfeit happiness.

RIGHT: We must be filled with a lot of love, and that includes love for our enemies, service from the heart, prayer with a focus in God, not to exalt ourselves in public, and learn and understand holy Scriptures, because all God's commandments are hidden in the old and new testaments. We must constantly "reject sin" and pray for discernment, and ask the Lord Jesus to purify our hearts. Go to confession regularly, do a daily exam and repent, receive the Holy Eucharist with a pure heart, and believe in faith of the body and blood of the Lord Jesus . Seek the Lord through prayer, fasting, and embracing suffering. Offer it to the Father for salvation of the world, pray for others, and to save souls. Do service in the church because you love God, not because of the priest, or for your own benefit, like advertising yourself. We must seek God in everything we do, even joining a group for service in the church. Do not join too many groups and not fulfilled the duties from the heart.

We must always put God in the first place, not money. The first fruit of your income must go to God's works to build the kingdom of heaven. Shopping should be done when really needed. Schedule at least twice each day to pray and learn scripture at home, early in the morning before going to work and before going to sleep at night. When you dress for church, give attention in dressing for God, not for other people to look at you, and wear clothes that will not distract others from focusing in God. Do not watch shows on television or read books that will not lead you to heaven. The devil uses these things to lead you to him without your knowing.

When you are ready, you will know the purpose God has for you in this world. Just wait, let God do the works through you, do not let the devil push you to run ahead. This is the process until your last breath.

Silver Cup

July 10, 1997. In my dream I saw a large, low-footed silver cup up high in the air, and the Lord Jesus said to me, "This is your cup." The Lord meant that this cup is the cup of suffering. Still in the dream, the Lord Jesus explained to me that His cup of suffering has a high foot and is gold, with red wine; and mine, Mariette's, cup has a low foot and is silver, with white wine.

When I got up middle of the night, in my vision, I saw a half glass of red wine in the restaurant on July 6, 1997. This half glass of wine was consecrated by the Father for my drink on my journey. The Lord said to me, "You have drunk from My cup, and now drink your own cup." The Lord continued, "When you drink these cups, the power from heaven transfers into you. Everything in heaven, the Father has given to me. Half of My estate in heaven is transferred to you permanently. Plus you have your estate that the Father has reserved for you, wife of the Lamb of God."

In the Book of Revelation, the Lord Jesus revealed to John two titles; the bride of the Lamb, and the Wife of the Lamb. In this revelation, God revealed the "Wife of the Lamb". The responsibility of the Wife of the Lamb is to God on earth, and God bestowed His power upon the Wife of the Lamb. The earth is a copy from heaven. On earth, when a young woman gets married, the parents give her either money, gold or property to take with her, this called a dowry. The husband she is married to has no share of her dowry; the dowry is to protect her in the case of divorce. She also has a half of the estate that she and her husband built up during the time they live together.

The Lord Jesus revealed: The white wine, I made from grapes the day before, and the Father blessed it at the dinner. My drinking it is my dowry from the Father, and the cup of red wine at the restaurant, the Father consecrated is the Lord Jesus' empowerment upon me.

Before the foundation of the world, the Lord Jesus requested the Father to chose me to be His vessel, the "Wife" of the Lamb, and his only sister. The Father accepted the Lord Jesus request. When my soul came down from heaven, the mission came with my soul. The date the Mission started manifesting is August 2, 1992. That was the first time I encountered the Lord Jesus through my dream. At the time the Father chose me, He reserved for me some heavenly substance. On August 16, 1995, God the Father recreated Mariette's mind with the most substance from heaven. This meant He was sending the dowry upon me. On August 18, 1995, God changed Mariette's name to "Suffering Servant, a vessel to God the Almighty, Second Coming of Christ." The bottom line is during my life until I go home to heaven, I must embrace the suffering, be completely obedient to God, and serve Him, through services to others, to build the kingdom of heaven, for God the Father's will to be completed.

416

Mariette Drank Her Cup, and Finished the Last Drop: April 5, 1997, the second Sunday after Easter. After I received the Body and Blood of our Lord Jesus, my mind was blank and very peaceful. The Lord said to me, "The cup I drank, you will drink to the last drop. The seats at My right and my left were reserved by My Father; and your seat is next to My right hand." I was silent and almost dropped dead with fear without understanding the meaning of the cup for a little while. I then said, "Lord Jesus, You are in me and with me to finish this cup to the last drop."

God's Blessing : June 3, 1997. In my vision, the Lord gave me a number of visions to explain the profit from the "The Lord Jesus website pamphlet." The Lord Jesus instructed "One hundred percents of profit from the website pamphlet will be held in the Rebuild My Church Mission; the beneficiary is Mariette's children, the laity; and their descendants, while they need the money to serve God. Forty percent from the book "Bride of Christ in Action." will be held in the Rebuild My Church Mission to benefit Mariette's blood line descendants, who become priests and religious, sixty percent will go to the Rebuild My Church Mission. One hundred percent of Mariette's share for the book My Patient - God Gift goes to benefit seminarians." All of these are symbolism that God revealed of His power working through my descendants.

Diploma and License to Practice

9:29 a.m., June 1, 1997, the feast of Corpus Christi. In my vision, I saw my oldest daughter wearing a blue graduation cap and gown, and then I saw her a wearing black cap and grown. The invisible hand of the Lord turned the tassel from the right to the left. The Lord said to me, "Last time you graduated from the high school of prophecy, this time it is in action; now you are graduated from college." I said to the Lord, "Lord, have the principal of the high school give me the diploma." The Lord said, "No, the chancellor of the university will give you the degree." I pleaded, "Lord, I do not want a degree from the chancellor of the university; I want the degree from You, the Almighty God." The Lord said, "The Degree, I have given to you before you started school." As the Lord was saying this, in my vision, I saw the "Jesus Delivers a Scroll to Mariette" revelation, November 22, 1993, written in chapter six of the book "My Patient - God's Gift". The Lord asked me, "Do you want Me to read the Diploma to you?" I said, "Lord, yes, please read it to me." The Lord said, "This is the license for you to practice. This license is not issued to you from human authority. This license issued to you by the Almighty God, the Father. Through the Son, and the Holy Spirit you will take action. This license is an eternal license. This license comes with the power of the Almighty God. Every word written in this license was given to Moses before. This license is to practice the Laws of God; at the same time this license will empower the laws. This license has power from God to reward those obey all God's laws; at the same time this license has power to execute judgment on those who do not obey God's commandments. This license was issued to Moses, in the old testament; then issued to Blessed Mary in the town of Nazareth, and this is the third time, this license is issued to you, Mariette, and this is the last time this license will be issued."

Let me give you the interpretation of the last sentence, "This license was issued to Moses, in the old testament; then issued to the Blessed Mary in the town of Nazareth, and this is the third time, this license issued to you, Mariette, and this is the last time this license will be issued." The Lord is speaking of the Ark of Covenant in three generations.

The feast of Corpus Christi first reading: When Moses came to the people and related all the words and ordinances of the LORD, they all answered with one voice, "We will do everything that the LORD has told us." Moses then wrote down all the words of the LORD and, rising early the next day, he erected at the foot of the mountain an altar and twelve pillars for the twelve tribes of Israel. Then, having sent certain young men of the Israelites to offer holocausts and sacrifice young bulls as peace offerings to the LORD, Moses took half of the blood and put it in large bowls; the other half he splashed on the altar. Taking the book of the covenant, he read it aloud to the people, who answered, "All that the LORD has said, we will heed and do." Then he took the blood and sprinkled it on the people, saying, "This is the blood of the covenant which the LORD has made with you in accordance with all these words of his."

Special Minister of Communion Commissioning

He said to them, The harvest is abundant but the laborers are few; so ask the master of the harvest to send out laborers for his harvest. Go on your way; behold, I am sending you like lambs among wolves.... Behold, I have given you the power to tread upon serpents and scorpions and upon the full force of the enemy and nothing will harm you.

–Luke 10: 2-3 &19

A few weeks before Saturday May 10, 1997, before Mother's day, the Lord Jesus told me, "This weekend, there will be a visiting priest celebrate mass with Father Scott. This priest knows that you are here in this town without your children. He will come to be with you on Mother's day." I said Jesus, "Lord, that Saturday is the day I will be receiving the commission as the Holy Eucharistic Minister." While I was in conversation with the Lord I saw the Cathedral of Saint Andrew's altar. I thought, "There will be only Father Hung Tong who knows that I am in this town, that could possibly be him." The day before, my uncle, Father Dominic Nho Duy Do, had his thirty second anniversary of his priest's ordination. During lunch, I told him. "I think Father Hung Tong will be here on Mother's day weekend." My uncle responded, "I have not heard anything from him."

After lunch, during my devotion, I said to the Lord, "Jesus, I do not know who the visiting priest will be on that Saturday weekend; but I told my uncle that Father Hung Tong will be here." Jesus the Lord said to me, "I am the visiting priest, I will speak through Father Scott." I asked, "What will you speak through Father Scott that will comfort me on Mother's day?"

God speaks through His words:

First Reading: The choice of Judas's Successor. During those days Peter stood up in the midst of the brother (there was a group of about one hundred and twenty persons in the one place). He said, "My brothers, the scripture had to be fulfilled which the holy Spirit spoke before hand through the mouth of David, concerning Judas, who was the guide for those who arrested Jesus. He was numbered among us and was allotted a share in this ministry. For it is written in the Book of Psalm: 'Let his encampment become desolate, and may no one dwell in it.' And: 'May another take his office.' Therefore, it is necessary that one of the men who accompanied us the whole time the Lord Jesus came and went among us, beginning from the baptism of John until the day on which he was taken up from us, become with us a witness to his resurrection." So they proposed two, Joseph called Barsabbas, who was also known as Justus, and Matthias. Then they prayed, "You, Lord, who know the hearts of all, show which one of these two you have chosen to take the place in this apostolic ministry from which Judas turned away to go to his own place." They gave lots to them, and the lot fell upon Matthias, and he was counted with the eleven apostles.

–Acts 1:15-17 & 20-26

Second Reading:

No one has ever seen God. Yet, if we love one another, God remains in us, and his love is brought to perfection in us. This is how we know that we remain in him and he in us, that he has given us of his Spirit. Moreover, we have seen and testify that the Father sent his Son as savior of the world. Whoever acknowledges that Jesus is the Son of God, God remains in him and he in God. We have come to know and to believe in the love God has for us. God is love, and whoever remains in love remains in God and God in Him.

–1 John 4:11-16

Gospel:

I will no longer be in the world, but they are in the world, while I am coming to you. Holy Father, keep them in your name that you have given me, so that they may be one just as we are. When I was with them I protected them in your name that you gave me, and I guarded them, and none of them was lost except the son of destruction, in order that the scripture might be fulfilled. But now I am coming to you. I speak this in the world so that they may share my joy completely. I gave them your word, and the world hated them, because they do not belong to the world any more then I belong to the world. I do not ask that you take them out of the world but that you keep them from the evil one. They do not belong to the world any more than I belong to the world. Consecrate them in the truth. Your word is truth. As you sent me into the world, so I sent them into the world. And I consecrated myself for them, so that they also may be consecrated in truth.

–John 17: 11-19

Rebuild My Church Divine Mission

(The Lord Jesus gave this name to Mariette)

P.O. Box 261550 ✦ San Diego, CA 92196-1550

September 2, 1997

Most Reverend Andrew J. McDonald
Bishop of Little Rock Diocese

Dear Excellency,

During the night of September 1, 1997; the Lord Jesus gave me these scriptures:

"You have made void the covenant of Levi, says the Lord of hosts.

I, therefore, have made you contemptible and base before all the people,

Since you do not keep my ways, but show partiality in your decisions."

Malachi 2:8-9

He then told me, "Abraham, Jacob, and Moses obeyed God. They moved and returned to their homeland. That also included My mother and

Saint Joseph. You are following in their footsteps; return to San Diego before I send you to a new land on your journey for this mission."

I obeyed God and came to Little Rock. I'm obeying Him to return to San Diego. I will be leaving from Little Rock in the next few days.

I will pray for you and others in your diocese

Sincerely in Christ Jesus,

Mariette Do-Nguyen

Rebuild My Church Divine Mission

(The Lord Jesus gave this name to Mariette)

P.O. Box 261550 ✦ San Diego, CA 92196-1550

September 2, 1997

Father Scott Marczuk, Rector
Cathedral of Saint Andrew

Dear Father Marczuk,

In our meeting before the vigil mass, on August 30, 1997, you requested that your name and other names be changed in the God's work.

Then the Lord Jesus instructed me to fax to you a letter later in the evening of the same day. The next day after the mass; the Lord Jesus gave me the meaning of His letter. He then told me, "My words have been written; they have been written and they are truth. You are not to change anything until the Church officials in Vatican respond to me, through you."

The Lord Jesus also pointed out to me the reason that my name was on the Preference List, but was not on the September through November Liturgical Ministry Schedule. You are putting the pressure on me so I will do what you ask of me. He then ordered me to move back to San Diego within a week; therefore, I'm obeying God, I will leave Little Rock in the next few days.

Enclosed is the original Special Minister of Communion that was issued to me in May 1997, from the Diocese of Little Rock, Office of the

Bishop.

I will pray for you and others to serve God from the heart.

Sincerely in Christ Jesus,

Mariette Do-Nguyen

Mariette Car is Parking under the Shadow of the Tree: February 20, 1998. In my dream I was entering a parking lot up high, next to the top of a huge tree. While I was pulling my automobile in, there was a sedan parking on the third space, its driver's side front wheel was on the divider between the second space and third space. In my thought was the way he parked and left the second space smaller. I got out my car and looked at my car. Both wheels front and back of the driver's side were lying on the dividing line. I said to my self, "I can not park my car like this." I then saw my automobile parked on the dirt sloping space outside the lot, at the top of the first and the second spaces. The hood was down toward a huge tree, and the car was under the tree branches. I then saw the Lord adjusting the car, moving it back on the top of the hill. The hill was under the car, this hill kept my car from moving forward and backward. I then heard the Lord Jesus said, "Your car is symbolic of you and the mission, no one can persuade you."

Consecrated Hosts Turning : The next morning at mass, at the time to receive the Holy Eucharist, I saw the woman who the Lord instructed me to avoid seeing or talking to her, give the Holy Eucharist at the line that I should be in. I pleaded to the Lord, "Lord, I must obey You, I will go in the other line to receive You." I then got up, turned right, crossed the center aisle, and turned left to the priest for the Holy Eucharist. I then turned left, and used the center aisle to go down to my seat. When I got back to my seat the Consecrated Host was still dry, I used the top of my tongue to turn it five times, I then swallowed it. After I swallowed it, the Lord Jesus told me, "You do not understand what you just did, but you will understand later."

February 21, 1998. After I received the body and blood of our Lord from a priest, who is the main celebrant of the mass, I starting kneeling down. I used my tongue to turn the Consecrated Host ten times before I swallowed it. In silence, I saw a scene from the movie "Jesus of Nazareth" where a woman playing role of the Blessed Virgin Mother was standing outside the eyes wall, looking at the man playing the Lord Jesus in the synagogues, and she repeated the words, " The scriptures are fulfilled." I then saw the title of the revelation "Mariette starting step number ten." The Lord Jesus then said to me, "Who says you are a little woman? A little woman is militant. A militant sent by the Father."

God the Father Restored His Power Upon His Church Minister

When God brought me back from undercover, His completely separated me from all public and personal involvement, including with my own children most of the time. He had all of them move out of the house, and left me alone in a house of over three thousand square feet. He also completely removed me from television, and limited me to one catholic newspaper. I would be alone with the Almighty, so that no one could interfere in His teaching, He then taught me step by step. Up to a point, it is still the same now, and will continue forever and ever that everything that comes to my mind, I ask God. He always answers to me, whether that is for me or not for me. If that thing is not for me then He moves that thought completely away from me. If it is for the future, He files it away, and then when the right time comes, He brings it back for me to do. If that thing is for me to do He pours His grace up on me until I finish that work. But it is not easy as I said to you, I have to fight against enemy spirits constantly.

A very short time before I moved to Arkansas in January 1997, God let me read the daily newspaper, (not magazines) to see how the world was in front of the Almighty God. After I arrived in Arkansas a few months later, He allowed me to watch news on television. Watching the news is for the work that He entrusted in me, (not the show paper).

When I returned to San Diego, in September 1997, I thought that I would be able to watch news on television. But one day He told me not to watch news on television. Screening through the daily newspaper headlines, I did not watch T.V, but one night He said to me, "Tomorrow you can watch TV at five o'clock on CNN to see how your work has effected the world." I thought that was the channel Ten News at five, I did watch TV the next day at 5:00p.m. for less than an hour, and flipping back and forward, I saw something that resulted from the work that I did.

In the first week of February, I thought, "If the Lord allowed me to see the news, I can watch it that night for fifteen minutes." But I ended up watching almost an hour. One thing I will share with you, after about thirty minutes of watching TV I felt the enemy spirits attack me physically. I knew that I must stop watching it, but I continued and wanted to see more news. That night, the Blessed Mother scolded me, she said to me, "You know that the devil uses television to attack people." When she reminded this to me, I knew that I was disobedient to God and watched television that evening. I then turned to the Father, Lord Jesus, and the Holy Spirit and asked for forgiveness. The Lord Jesus told me, "You sin is forgiven, but when you go to the Sacrament of Reconciliation next time, remember to tell the priest."

February 17, 1998, was thirty days from my last confession. After the mass I asked Father Earl, "Can you hear my confession?" He said to me, "We need to set an appointment for your confession." I said, "Can you hear my confession now?" He said, "No, we have to set an appointment; any time tomorrow." I said, "How about after mass tomorrow?' He said, "Yes, I will put it in here." While he was saying this, he had an appointment book in his hands. He is the one that God chose to hear my confession since he was assigned to the Good Shepherd Church after his ordination.

After Father Earl insisted for me to have an appointment for confession tomorrow instead to hear my confession at that time, I knew there was a reason that God wanted this appointment. I prayed on the way home, over the night, and the next morning. This is one of the many ways God speaks to me by letting me know in advance He will do something, so I can pray.

February 18, 1998. I was praying the Chaplet in the church before the mass. While I had my eyes closed and proclaimed the second Chaplet Mercy; Father Earl came next to me, and said, "Ms. Do, can you meet me at the sacristy after the mass?" I opened my eyes, and said, "Yes." I entered the sacristy after the mass, I took a seat on a chair like I did before, but Father Eggleston asked me, "Mariette, can you stand up?" I then got up and walked a few steps forward. In front of me was Father Earl wearing a white alb with a purple stole. After Father Earl started the sign of the Cross, I proclaimed, "Father, Lord Jesus, Holy Spirit, You are here with us. I come to you with all my heart, my soul, my spirit and my strength, to confess all my sins, which you already know..........." At the end, when Father Earl said to me, "For your penance, be in the Blessed Sacrament for a little while. Now you make a good act of contrition." I pleaded to God, "Father, through the Lord Jesus, and the work of the Holy Spirit, I ask You to forgive all my sins, and keep me away from, so I can serve You the exactly the way You want. Father, through the Lord Jesus, and the work of the Holy Spirit, I ask You, Father to pour out Your power upon the minister of the church, Father Earl, so he can serve you the way you want him to serve You. Father, through the Lord Jesus, and the work of the Holy Spirit, I also ask You for the Church leaders, governments officials, and lawmakers the grace of conversion." I then got in the Blessed Sacrament, kneeling down, after I gave thanks to God, and the Lord Jesus told me, "O' Princess of Heaven and Earth. The funnel is opening wide at the bottom. Through you, God's power is restored upon the Church's minister. The Power that was not there for ages is now restored."

He continued, "You are on an assignment, not the confession. The Father blessed you." While the Lord Jesus was saying this, in my vision, I saw the golden funnel opening to a wider flat line, filled with bright light mixed with a little gold.

The Father pre-destined me in this mission, as the Vessel to the Holy Trinity. Therefore God allowed me to invoke His power upon the Church minister in the Father's name. The Eternal Father's name is the most Holy and mighty, we should not use in His name. We must go through the Lord Jesus, by using the name of the Lord Jesus, as He teaches us in the Bible.

When any one asks in the name of the Lord Jesus, obeying all God's commandments, it will be received. But if people ask in the name of the Lord Jesus without obeying all God's commandments, they will not receive from God. Because when persons do not obey all God's commandments, the majority of the time the devil will give them what to ask, and those requests are not in the Father's will.

February 22, 1998. I got up at 4:00 a.m. with a dream. In my dream I followed behind a person, from the right side of a small part of a house, this part was built on the land. We were standing on an iron road, this road was very narrow, just wide enough for one person to stand on, and it was thin and moving like an escalator. This escalator took us in front of this house and entered another building that was built above the water, a floating building. Very shortly after we entered, it took us outside the building, and continued to roll. The person with me was standing facing the building and talking to me, I stood facing him, to my left was the building, on my right was a hand rail, and out there was ocean. I was very frightened when I looked at the ocean. We got close to the front that faced the ocean, and the front was oval. We entered room number 18, and we were still at the right side of the building.

I was at the starting point for a second time, this time I was alone, standing on the same road, but the rolling iron road was not that sharply visible like it was the first time. It was very difficult for me to see the iron road when it was rolling.

I finished the journey at the left side of the building, and I saw the road was a shinning iron rail road, full with oil, it was so clear that I was able to see details of the road.

The road made an "X" between the house on the land and the building above the ocean, the top "X" was the building and I went around it. I started around the house at the right side, and I ended at the center of the "X."

The house on land is symbolic of the church on earth. The building above the ocean is symbolic of the church in heaven. The rolling iron road is symbolic of my journey in this mission. The person ahead of me is symbolic of the Lord Jesus. "X" is symbolic of my cross.

After I saw the building and the house dream, I blacked out for second. I then saw the book "Bride of Christ in Action" already printed in double lines, like the manuscript. The Lord Jesus' invisible hand was turning pages for me. While He was turning pages, He told me, "The book is five hundred fifteen pages." I saw very clearly the title of the "Rebuild My Church Center, and Saint Mary Magdelene's Church" revelation. While I was reading the book, I was happy and said to the Lord, "Jesus, beloved brother, the book is already printed." He said to me, "I printed only one copy for you."

In the dream, I saw I was in the Blessed Sacrament chapel after I got out from confession on February 18, 1998. The Lord continued, "When you prayed to the Father for His power upon the priest, the Father poured out God's power upon you, not on the priest.

I said to you 'you are on assignment, the Father blessed you. This power is upon you and remains with you. Remove that part from the book; put it in your notebook for future use." While the Lord was saying this, he also wrote it down with His invisible hand for me to read.

The same day, after I received the Holy Eucharist, the Lord Jesus said to me, "I am your beloved brother, you are My only sister. Pray for Chamberlain to convert so he can assist you." When the Lord was saying this, in my vision I saw Richard Chamberlain playing the cardinal in the movie "Thorn Birds". He was very old, wearing a cardinal's outfit, sitting on a chair in front of the garden, looking toward his son's tomb while Maggie walked passed him from the tomb. I then said, "Lord, I think You are talking about cardinals, archbishops, and bishops." He then said, "The Father's Power is upon you, and through you will be on others".

The Discernment and Holiness Revelation

February 23, 1998. In my dream I saw a square space, in this space were four different groups of people and spirits. I was laying on my back in one space, to my left was a group of dark living spirits that were sticking to each other. Apart to my right were a few living people, and at my opposite space were some dark death spirits.

I then saw a person come in the building, from the corner of the courtyard at the direction of my left feet. He was carrying a lot of things by hand in front of him, when he was about to meet the group of living spirits, he left these things on the ground. Those living spirits took some of the stuff that the person left on the floor, although I did not see them. When it was over, I just knew that.

I thought, "I'd better hurry to go get some of these things, otherwise these living spirits will take them all." I hurried to sit up, and put both of my feet down like getting out of bed into the area where the stuff was. I then bent down closely, and looked at the things. I saw some knit sweaters, and while I was still searching, I put both of my hands under these sweaters and pulled out two pieces of yucca roots. The two pieces of yucca roots had a nice size body, about ten inches long each. They were cut neatly showing their ends were white and friable.

Ash Wednesday Revelation

February 25, 1998. I entered the Blessed Sacrament chapel to the side of the main Good Shepherd church. At the moment I knelt down, I pleaded to God, "Father, Lord Jesus. Today is Ash Wednesday. My physical body came from the earth and will return to ash. My soul came from You and will return to You. I ask You Jesus, my Lord, my God, my beloved Brother; You are the Only Son of the Father, hear my prayer. Plead to the Father for me on this Ash Wednesday, to destroy all the lying and sorcerer spirits around me and

426

throughout the world, and grant grace of conversion upon the spiritual leaders, governments officials and lawmakers."

Close to the end of my petitions, in my vision I saw the Father's Spirit speaking to me in the Blessed Sacrament, with the dark group of spirits next to my right; and the Lord Jesus pleading to the Father for me. On February 24, 1998 after I received the Holy Eucharist, I then saw the group of dark living spirits in the dream on February 23, 1998. The Lord Jesus said to me, "The living spirits at your feet in the dream are priests, they received God's grace around them, and are in those who live the life of holiness. They have little or no discernment. The Father blessed you with discernment. The high ranking-church leaders are sitting on their high positions; through your writing they recognized that. The secret that has not been opened before, now is opening. Remove yourself from here, go into the Church and copy this down." I then made the sign of the Cross before I left. The Lord continued, "The death spirits are those hungry for earthly power. They are one third of the human race, and they are already dead."

Getting in the Church, I saw the Cross on the sanctuary wall was the same as the Cross I saw on the evening February 23, 1998. The only difference was that the one in the church had a purple short shroud hanging at the Cross's arms, and the one I saw had a super long white shroud wrapped above the arms of the Cross, and the one I saw was up high. I looked at the Cross while I was in communion with the Lord.

When the procession came close to the sanctuary, the Lord Jesus' Spirit descended at the left side of the altar, and moved to the right corner of my forehead. His power came to my face, I felt that I wanted to tell Him of how I felt, but I was not deserving to say how I felt, but I then said to him in a way not worthy for what God gave me, I said "Jesus, I feel that You are my real brother, no longer adopted. You are with and in priests that You chose to serve You in their lives, and they are my brothers." I meant from the same mother's womb. But when Father Earl got to the sanctuary, while I had my eyes closed, I kept seeing his spirit; I then realized that the Lord Jesus revealed to me of priests, they are like my brothers who came from the same mother's womb.

While I proceeded to receive Communion, I pleaded, "Father, Lord Jesus, Holy Spirit, my physical body will return to ash, and my soul will return to You. Father, I will sit at my Brother's right, in front of You, at my throne, next to my Blessed Mother, with all the apostles there, and holy angels and saints around." I got back to my seat, and my Blessed Mother told me, "Sit down." She meant not to kneel like after I received the Holy Communion. The Lord Jesus told me, "Matthew chapter six, verse fourteen, one verse only."

"If you forgive others theirs transgressions, your heavenly Father will forgive you."

After I read it, I said, "Father, Lord Jesus, Holy Spirit, are there people I have not forgiven, but I do not know it? Help me to recognize it and forgive them." The Lord Jesus said, "You have been trying, and you are trying hard. You have been loved. You need to love those who are against you through this mission." I pleaded, " Father Lord Jesus, help me in my personal life and community to love all my enemies, and I ask you to forgive them, and forgive those who curse me."

Kneeling down after receiving the Holy Eucharist, I turned the Consecrated Host one time and prayed. While I was praying I saw the word "INRI" in front of the Cross behind the white shroud and could see partly though it. I then crossed my legs and leaned my bottom to the side of the bench, and the Lord Jesus asked me, "Why did you cross your legs?" I replied, "Jesus, I don't know why I crossed my legs."

He then asked me, "Why do you have that thought? You are no longer a Gentile, you are the Jew, you are my sister, you came from the Father. The Father said, Your brother is the King of holiness, and you are following in His footsteps."

There is no difference of color or nationality in front of God, the Jew and Gentiles in this revelation dictated. Jesus as fully man was a Jew, and the assignment that the Father sent me down for is to prepare for the Lord Jesus' return to judge the living and the dead; therefore, this assignment made me become Jesus the Lord's blood sister from the Eternal Father; the Gentiles are those chosen ones.

Later in same day, after my noon devotion, I fell asleep. In my dream I saw the round metal part of a computer diskette, I then saw the front, it was labeled "Part III & II". This is the diskette that contained the second and third parts of the book "Bride of Christ in Action." I then saw the word "Done" underlined with three lines.

He then gave me another dream. I saw an invisible person sitting at my desk. In my chair, a visible man's right hand held a transparent Bic pen, with a full ink tube. The black cap was opened and put on top of the other end. He had paused from writing and was looking for something. I knew the Lord Jesus' hand, I said, "Jesus, my brother." I was still asleep, and my spirit was lifted lighter, and I saw the front page of the San Diego Union Tribune headline. I heard the Lord Jesus tell me, "They do not need to talk to you, your writing is clear, like seeing through the ink in that pen. Watch out when you are in and out of the church, they took your picture, and they know what you look like." I remembered the time I met with Mr. Bell's Secretary yesterday, the President of the San Diego Union Tribune.

I then got up and I heard, "Go pickup Madelene, the Father wants her." I was trying to get up to go pick up my granddaughter Madelene; but I got pulled back down on the bed. I realized that the Father wants the converts.

Catholic High-Ranking Leaders Rejected God's Servant

December 29, 1997. In my dream, I was in a very poor village. This village was in the middle of a huge open desert. It was on the way to rebuilding, materials were all over the ground. Coming along with me was a man and several seminarians. These seminarians were the size of children under seven years of age. When we got to the front of a house, a man who was the owner of the house came out to greet us, and said, "We only accept Vietnamese young men for the seminary." I reversed his statement, by saying, "We accept young men from every nation."

While we were having a dialogue, I looked across the street, and there were several long buildings. Three main ones at the center, two facing each other, and the third made a layout like the letter "C". The open "C" was to the street, and the rest of the other buildings were behind these three. This section is Bui Thai parish, Father Doan is pastor. [Doan is Vietnamese name, in this revelation doan-trang means formal]. In my thought, "We can ask Father Doan to use one of the buildings belonging to his parish for our seminaries."

The dream changed. I saw Father Doan sitting at the center of a long bench, leaning back. The back of the bench was made with wooden slats, its side armrests were round on top. Behind the bench, a little away from the bench back, I was standing above the ground. To my right was a dark shadow standing above the arm of the bench. While Father Doan was turning his head to his right shoulder, looking at the dark shadow at my right, he also saw me through the right corner of his eye, while his body sat still. To Father Doan's right, behind the back of the bench was a person kneeling on the ground, repeatedly hitting his forehead against the back of the bench, "We have been working very hard....." It seemed like he was begging Father Doan for something. Father Doan said to me, "The people in the rectory do not understand." I replied to him, "All of this is symbolic like in the Book of Revelations, and throughout the Bible." Above the arm on the other end of the bench, a person was standing above the arm, saying to Father Doan, "We believe her." He meant that they believe me, Mariette.

I then said to Father Doan, "When you are ready, you let me know." I then thought, "I will call you."

The dream changed. The shadow to my right and I went back to the side where we were in front of the house. But this time the house was no longer there. Instead, I saw the front of a long building at the end of the lot, in front of me. The dark shadow and I were on our way to evacuate these seminarians early tomorrow morning, between 5 and 6 a.m. Behind me was a helicopter landing, I saw behind me that there was a bench inside, facing the front, and both sides had two doors with two men sitting and holding guns with long ammunition bands that were built at the side of the doors, ready to shoot. The helicopter fan blew up debris on the large spot where it was landing. I went a few step past a bright globe to my left. At the center of this globe was a ball of fire, and around this fireball, filled to the edge of the globe was a white cloud. The helicopter blew up all the debris, but my globe stood firm.

I then thought, the globe is my shell, I have to return to that globe, I can not go to the same building with seminarians. All the seminarians are in this long building. I will not let them know tonight that they [seminarians] be evacuated early tomorrow. I thought, "I will wait until in the morning, I will tell them and have them leave immediately after I tell them before we get in the bus." While I was thinking of this, I saw behind, to my right, at the end of the village, up high was a huge bus, it was formed like a light dark cloud.

Before I got out of bed the Lord Jesus said to me, "In spirit, the Roman Catholic Church will not accept you. They do not understand why I put my shroud over your neck, and placed a rock in your hand, because the "popes" inherited the rock from [Saint] Peter, and the shroud is in the procession of the Roman Catholic Church."

Jesus the Lord continued, "Before, they accepted my works, but they did not accept me as the Son of God until after I was raised from the dead. Church authorities will accept your works that they can see with their natural eyes. In spirit, they will not believe you are adopted to the Holy Family until you depart from this world to heaven. The real prophet will not be honored in their home land, because of a lack of faith. Home land is the earth."

December 30, 1997. After I received the Holy Eucharist, the Holy Spirit told me, "On your birthday [Jan 2], you will enter the shell of the globe. You are no longer in a thin shell. This globe will be in the helicopter. God's power from the Father is around it. Wherever you go, God is carrying you." While the Holy Spirit was saying this, I saw the helicopter in the dream, on December 29, 1997. The shell of the globe moved inside the helicopter. That evening I saw through the front glass of the helicopter two pilot seats, we were taking off from the ground.

The village is symbolic of the earth. The wind is symbolic of the Spirit of God. Through the Lord Jesus, the Father sends His power to battle against the visible and invisible enemies for the mission He entrusted in me. Father Doan is symbolic of the Catholic Church authorities. The shadow at Father Doan's left is the soul of the person who was kneeling of the ground, and he is the same man who greeted us in front of his house. The time he was kneeling is symbolic of the time before her conversion, complaining against God, and when the shadow spoke to Father Doan, it is symbolic of after the conversion. He is symbolic of all the conversions. The shadow to my right and the man with me are symbolic of the Lord Jesus. Seminarians are symbolic of those who will convert.

Through God's Power, God's Pre-Destined Chosen One Prevails

January 31, 1998. In my dream I was with father Hoan's [hoan hi mean happiness] mother, she took me to find father Hoan. We went to the bank of the Jordan river, and as we got there I saw father Hoan at the other side of the river. Both of us were about to cross the river, and I saw my left foot in a small pool of clear water, but as I pushed my toes down, muddy water came up and covered the top of my toes. I then saw father Hoan's mother wearing Vietnamese wooden sandals, I took my left foot and stepped on top of her feet with my toe inside the clear sandal strap. I looked up, and I saw father Hoan run forward with happiness. And the Lord said to me in the dream, "You are Joshua, the church high-ranking leaders are those who carried the Ark of Covenant; those who do not obey God's commandments will be struck dead."

Father Hoan was symbolic of priests who will convert, daily exam and repent. Father Hoan's mother was symbolic of church high-ranking leaders. I stepped on her toes, and that was symbolic of through God's power, the writing that the Lord asked me to do will convert church high-ranking leaders to God.

February 1, 1998. In my dream I checked into the hospital every night, but they did not have a bed for me. I then got out, and on the way out, I was standing on the ground of the center entrance of the hospital's property. I looked back in the direction that I just came from, and I saw a woman standing up high writing large words on the bulletin board, glued to the outside of the one of the buildings, at the center of the property. I went up there and wrote below her words in the same size but in a different style. When I started writing, she got down.

I then went back down to the same spot where I was with my black tote bag on my right shoulder. I was about to go out the front entrance to other area to get my black carry-on suitcase, but I changed my mind about taking the inside road in the hospital, instead I went through the main entrance.

Immediately after I changed my mind, an old, ugly, small woman appeared inside the gate and asked me, "Did you ring the door bell, and call us to pick you up?" I thought that would be denied, but I said the truth, "Yes, I did."

She drove me on her bicycle, and she took off before I got on the seat. My hands were holding the beginning of the rectangular frame iron seat behind her seat, and my body was lifted up high while she was driving. Suddenly, I saw her go up a high straight slope like a waterfall. She stuck her bicycle outside the metal fence of the higher level property. As she stuck her bicycle, I was at her side, I then pushed her bicycle into the fence.

The woman writing on the board is symbolic that what church leaders teach through their newspapers is not in accordance with God's commandments. My writing and her leaving is symbolic of my delivery of what God asks me. Her leaving is symbolic that when they see what they did was wrong, they stop. The hospital I checked into every night is symbolic of my spiritual battle every day and night, and that I embraced my suffering. The black tote bag is symbolic of God's power and glory for me alone. The carry-on black suitcase is God's power and glory that God works throughout the world in the mission God entrusted to me. The old, ugly, small woman is symbolic of spiritual leaders teaching improperly, and this is how they appeared in front of God in the spirit. Her riding the bicycle up fast and high and sticking it into the fence is symbolic of God crushing down the exalted, the exalting actions are from Lucifer. The upper level is symbolic of spiritual life, when spiritual leaders are with the system of the world, they will fail in the spirit.

The Lord then gave me another dream to confirm this dream. In my dream my oldest daughter was standing to my right, in front of us was a supermarket checkout table with a black bell on top of it. On top of this checkout table were five small teddy bears in one row, she was playing with them by changing their positions back and forward. I got angry and slapped her face, and said to her, "Pay the price and go." She cried and handed the cashier one small silver dollar with a quarter on top of it, and took two teddy bears with her. As we were walking away from the cashier, I asked her, "Why did you not buy the other three?" She said, "I bought these two for other two persons, the other three for me, I do not want them."

My daughter is symbolic of church officials, the number five is symbolic of authority. The church officials use their authority like playing with the teddy bears; they do not want to pay the price of suffering and embrace their cross for others in following the Lord Jesus' footsteps.

One small silver dollar and quarter, the silver dollar and quarter are made from metal, a counterfeit of silver. The one dollar has one hundred pennies, it is symbolic of obedience. A quarter has twenty and five, the twenty is symbolic of discernment, and the five is symbolic of authority over the devil's power.

Note: God's power increases when more zeros are added to each number.

The word of the Lord came to me thus: Before I formed you in the womb I knew you Before you were born I dedicated you, a prophet to the nations I appointed you. But do you gird your loins; stand up and tell them all that I command you. Be not crushed on their account, as though I would leave you crushed before them; For it is I this day who have made you a fortified city, a pillar on iron, a wall of brass, against the whole land: Against Judah's king and princes, against its priests and people, for I am with you to deliver you, says the LORD.

—Jeremiah 1:4-5,17-19

The Square House on Top of the Hill

July 1, 1997. After the Lord spoke, I went back to sleep. In my dream, I was inside a square house, this house was built on top of a high hill, and the house was divided in two part. One part was for me and my child, this part was empty, but very rich. I went around the corner of the house and entered inside another part; there was a woman, her mother, and her child. The mother was very old, standing in the middle of the room, this room was also empty, and poor. These three people just moved in, they were very cold, all three of them were covered with a three piece thin jacket, like a lifeguard jacket. I asked the woman, "I have a sweater, would you want to use it?" She asked me, "What kind of sweater do you have?" While I was asking her, I saw my old thick, long, roomy navy sweater. She said to me, "I want a kind that when it is buttoned, it will be tight at the waist." When she said this, I saw her outfit was changed to a lightweight, white cotton sweater. I stood in their room, I was not cold, but they were.

Then the dream changed: We then were in front of the house, toward her side. The part of the house belonging to her was in the front, there was a very large concrete pavement in front of the house. She stood close to the edge of the top of the hill, and looked down. There were some people at the foot of the hill who called this woman to come down and get the cake. This woman called me to come down with her. I turned to my right, toward her and saw there was a ladder at the side of the hill. I said, "No, I am not going down, it so scary down there, tell them to come up here." She then called those people. I saw there was a light skinned young woman, accompanied by a person with black skin and curly hair. Both of them wore light colored clothes, but there was no cake. Then they were on the top of the hill and I said to them, "We can stay here and it is very quiet, the snake can not come here. There is a little grass around the hill, but the snake can not come up high, the snake can only stay at the bottom of the hill."

The dream changed. By the same front concrete pavement close to the front wall, there were two concrete steps. The woman who just got up the hill was sitting on the bottom step looking at me. While I was standing and facing her, she asked me, "What is your name?" I said, "My name is Believe, but in the books it is Michelle." She said, "I called you Michelle."

The dream changed again: Now we were on the other side, in the back of the house, the side that was my house. I was in the middle of the lot walking toward the woman and her mother at the edge of the hill. I saw my child and this woman's child sitting at the corner, in front of them was something dark. My child was holding a plate of cooked sweet rice mixed with mashed yellow beans, sugar, and oil, while he was eating them. My child said, "This is good." My child was a very smart, quick, and talented boy.

To my right, there was something like a dome, or cone top, made of metal. It was very shiny because the metal was polished very carefully. This thing was huge, and around it were many triangle mangers facing up, and connected to the dome. These mangers were filled with the same kind of sweat rice that my child was eating. While I saw this dome, the woman and her mother were at edge of the hill in front of me about to go down to get the sweet rice from those mangers.

The Lord said, "Your name is Believe, but in the book you are called Michelle. The name Believe means your faith in God, Michelle is the female name for Michael. In your writing you are fighting against a world disobedient to God's commandments. A young woman asking your name is symbolic of the church leaders. The man in dark skin, wearing light colored clothes is symbolic of enemy spirits that are attached to them. A woman, her mother, and a child living in the house next to you is symbolic of the Holy Trinity. The life guard vests are symbolic of God saving souls. Their just moving in and being cold and poor is symbolic that everything in heaven must come through you before coming to the world; so if you become rich, the Holy Trinity becomes poor. You offering your old sweater to the woman is symbolic of your offering your suffering to God; and that is transformed into good deeds in heaven. The two children sitting at the outside corner, your child is symbolic of the mission, [Rebuild My Church Mission], and the other child is symbolic of Jesus the Lord; this child is symbolic of Jesus' glorified body in your mission. The round shiny thing like a spaceship with many mangers around it is symbolic of New Jerusalem coming down to earth from heaven. The cooked sweet rice is symbolic of God's words, the manger is symbolic of the Holy Eucharist. It means the world will take in their hearts with God's words and the Holy Eucharist. The roof of the spaceship like a cone is the opposite of the bright golden light funnel, that means the power from heaven will go through the funnel, to the top of the cone spaceship and down to the earth."

The Lord Jesus does His Works through God's Pre-destined

April 3, 1997. In my dream I saw myself walking in the middle of a church aisle in a huge church that was open at the roof. The church pews were in the shape of the letter "V", with the end of the "V" open for the aisle. I took the end of the fifth pew in the right section. Because they were a "V" shape, the end of the middle pews had no kneeler. I thought, "I have to kneel on the concrete ground."

I saw myself standing facing down the section where I sat, with a long rectangular Holy Eucharist, made from corn flour, like the corn chip in my left palm. I took my right hand and placed the Holy Eucharist in my mouth, and standing there for little while, tried to swallow this hard Holy Eucharist. As I saw myself swallow this corn flour Holy Eucharist, I also saw a tiny boy standing in the middle of the aisle giving Holy Communion to two lines of people approaching him. These people were wearing dark outfits. Behind the boy was a priest, kind of sitting on his toes, he embraced this boy inside his chest. The priest's left hand held the outside of the boy's left hand, the boy's left hand held the middle of the foot of a high gold chalice. This chalice was almost as tall as the boy. The priest placed his right hand over the boy's right hand to help lift the Holy Eucharist and place it on people's palm. This boy was too small and too young, and the priest was pouring his strength into the boy's left arm to hold the chalice. The right hand was over the boy's hand to teach him how to lift the Holy Eucharist. The boy bent his head down, and his face almost touched the rim of the cup. The priest was wearing a chasuble, and the boy was

434

wearing a suit. Both of their outfits were in a white mixed with gold .

The priest represents the Lord Jesus. The tiny little boy is symbolic of the mission God entrusted to me. With God's power, this mission will bring people convert to God.

I Support My Brothers and Sisters

May 5, 1997. I got up in the middle of the night and the Lord Jesus said to me, "John 4:9-14."

> *The Samaritan woman said to him, 'How can you, a Jew ask me, a Samaritan woman, for a drink?' (For Jews use nothing in common with Samaritans.) Jesus answered and said to her, 'If you knew the gift of God and who is saying to you, 'Give me a drink,' you would have asked him and he would have given you living water.' The woman said to him, 'Sir, you do not even have a bucket and the cistern is deep; where then can you get this living water? Are you greater than our father Jacob, who gave us this cistern and drank from it himself with his children and his flocks?' Jesus answered and said to her, 'Everyone who drinks this water will be thirsty again; but whoever drinks the water I shall give will never thirst; the water I shall give will become in him a spring of water welling up to eternal life.'*

–John 4:9-14

I then went to sleep. In my dream I saw a child trying to close the window, and while she was trying to close the window, she said, "Tornadoes are coming, close the windows."

I looked out the wide open window. From up high I saw the ground, and my father. He was holding a two edged sword behind him. In front of him was a woman, it seemed to me that she was my mother. I knew that they were fighting each other. I then hurried to the elevator, and went down to the street level, and transferred into another elevator below to go down under the parking garage structure.

I got out of the elevator. There were cars parked on both sides where I was on the way out of the parking structure; there were some people standing in the driveway talking, one of the woman was kind of blocking my way, I said to her, "Get out of my way, so I can go. My parents are about to kill each other." She then moved to the side.

I was then out of the parking structure. I saw some people to my right standing and talking to my father, to my left other people were talking to the woman. I came and stood in the middle, facing the street. As I faced the street the woman and people talking to her were no longer there, they disappeared very fast.

My father was behind me to my right. People were talking to my father and joined him entering the house. As I broke up the fight, people from the parking garage came out and stood at my left. I then said out loud to the public with the purpose that they could hear and use my voice as evidences in the court, I said, "My parents got divorced, and fight against each other. They have no money to support the children. I am the oldest in the family, the only one that has money to support my sisters and brothers."

I then turned my head to my left; I saw my father reach out the window next to the door, to touch a man on ground. He was face up and dead, with both eyes opened.

The child said, "Tornadoes come, close the windows". She is symbolic of the world. The Father in the dream is symbolic of the Heavenly Father. The woman who seemed like your mother is symbolic of those turned their back to God. Divorce represents when a person commits grave sins and refuses to convert is divorced from God. The woman trying to block my way is symbolic of the spiritual leaders try to prevent me from doing the works of God. The people around my father are symbolic of holy angels. People around the woman are symbolic of enemy spirits hidden inside people disobedient to God's commandments. As I broke in the middle and faced the street, the woman and those people around her no longer being there is symbolic of God the Father withdrawn His present from those refuse to conversion. The people around my father who moved behind me and entered the house are the holy angels that remain in heaven. The two-edged sword is symbolic of the Word of God. The man dead on ground outside the window and my Father reaching through the window to help him is symbolic of people in the world sinning against God and later converting to God. He dead is symbolic of dead to sin. He eyes open symbolic of seeing the living God. Me, Mariette myself is the instrument to the Lord Jesus. My parents had no money; money is symbolic of power. Lucifer has no power, God the Father gave everything to His only Son Jesus; and I am a Vessel to the Lord Jesus.

The scriptures said, "How can you, a Jew ask me, a Samaritan woman, for a drink?" (For Jews use nothing in common with Samaritans." These scriptures mean that God has always chosen men, such as Moses, priests in the house, and male apostles, why are you now choosing women?

The scriptures, " If you knew the gift of God and who is saying to you." God means His gifts and He is a just God. The hidden meaning that I am speaking to you is I that will choose a woman in the place of man to prepare for His return.

The scriptures, "Sir, you do not even have a bucket and the cistern is deep." The bucket is symbolic of the physical body, and Jesus the Lord chose not to have a physical body like before to walk on the earth. The deep cistern means the people in the world drinking the water of the world will continue to be thirsty, not permanent. But the Lord Jesus is living water.

The Lord Jesus revealed in the past that God chose males as priests of the house, Levites, priests of the church. In action, God revealed in the book of John and at the foot of the Cross of the women, to prepare for His return to execute judgment and reward.

The Lord brought back to me the high mountain vision "Heaven's Diving Board is

Shinning on Earth. God the Father was flying over Moses's head, landing on my left, and picked me up and hid me under his cloak. This two revelations symbolic of God entrusted this mission to me.

God the Father Commanded Mariette to found Priests Order and Named it "Jesus' Servants"

May 6, 1997, 6:29 am. I got up with some dreams, and I heard the Father say to me, "There are many orders of priests, but I command you to found a priest order as a model and name it Jesus' Servants."

The Lord continued, "I have showed you this before in the dreams." While the Lord was saying this in my vision I saw a dream that I had before, there was one long line of priests wearing white robes with long bibs and uni-sex collars, coming toward me from heaven." The Lord reminded me, and said, "There is a black leather belt." As the Lord said this, He also showed me the waist of a person wearing the black leather belt. There was another dream, after I went under the overhead, I saw two stations giving out food, one to the left, and another to the right. The station to my right had two lines, I joined the line to my right.

I said to the Lord, "Oh! Lord, my God. I am fighting. How do I do all this! It is a lot bigger than what I thought You called me to do."

Jesus the Lord responded to me, "I will do all the works through you and other people. The people that you saw in the dreams, the festival dreams are the ones I chose to serve you, as My servant to put the Jesus' Priest Servants order together." In my thought I did not like the word that the Lord said "to serve you" I was about to change it to "assist you", but the Lord knew my thoughts, He said, "Don't even change the word." I believed this was the revelation, so He did not let me change the word "serve."

I then said to the Father, "Oh! Lord, my God, the God of all creation. I can not do these things. Why don't You speak to the Holy Father and have him to do them instead of me."

The Father said to me, "I command you to do the job, not the holy father. This order I will gather everyone that will enter heaven to be priests in this order; to serve Me, the Lord your God, and their God, and to serve one another."

In this revelation, the Lord commanded me, not the church leaders, because I am the convert. The Lord commanded me to be a model for others to follow in my footsteps of conversion.

The Lord said, "Priests claim that they are Blessed Virgin Mary's priests, but they are not following in her footsteps."

7:03 a.m. may 6, 1997. The Lord had explained to me this revelation; I now fully understand this revelation.

The Lord then said to me, "Many women are fighting to be priests, these people do not understand that everyone who serves God through service to others with their pure hearts are priests in front of God. The church-ordained priests just have their title on earth to help them serve God. I retained you not to have any title in the church, except deacon." Deacon is the helper, make sure the house of God in order.

The Lord continued, "In the dream you saw a group of priests behind you to the right, and that is symbolic of the priests of these days, they are busy doing things that do not belong to God. The several children in front of you that you were taking care of by feeding them is symbolic of the priests that will wear the white robe with black belt. Farther away when you were walking in the midst of those old women, eating cooked pig's blood is symbolic of those who will do not have anything to do with the works of God; these will not have the white robe and black belt." The Lord said these old women who will not have white robes are those who refuse to convert and repent, and will not enter heaven.

The Lord continued, " Those two unclean fish swimming away without the water are the same group of old women sitting around trays of cooked pig's blood."

The Lord continued, "Your coming up to stand in front of Me and looking down at the world is symbolic of your looking after your descendants. You said it was only Jesus alone next to me, but later you saw more people behind Jesus; these were His mother, Saint Joseph, Elija, and Moses."

7:35.a.m. may 6, 1997. The Lord said to me, "I will give you blessing." As His said this, I joined both of my hands in front of my face, and the Lord Jesus made a sign of the cross in front of my face and said to me, "The Father, the Lord Jesus, and the Holy Spirit, bless you with all substance from heaven to do the works of God. The most victories on earth that were never before or after your life on earth, the beginning of the Holy Eucharist Service and Altar Call at Cathedral of Saint Andrew is the bomb exploding in the world. Amen, amen." Cathedral of Saint Andrew is symbolic of the Rebuild My Church in Natural.

Pentecost Sunday

May 18, 1997. Through the night I had several dreams, but only remembered a very little. One was about my son. He was about five to seven years old and had laid on the bed suffering from an injury to the left side of his head for long time. He was in good build, and laid on his left side, the injured side on the bed. I laid in front of him and faced him and used both of my hands to comfort him. I then moved him to the top corner of the bed and laid him face up very peacefully, then I left him.

Another dream was somewhere in a very busy tourist area. I was walking away from the tourists.

I got up in the morning with my left eye red and heavy. My head was very heavy, I never had anything like this before in my life. I put some eyedrops in both of my eyes and

I though about taking some Tylenol. But as I reached for the bottle of Tylenol, the Blessed mother told me, "Do not take them, the Lord will heal you." I then stopped.

A few minutes after kneeling in the Cathedral of Saint Andrew, God the Father said to me, "Today is the second time in world history, and it will never happen again. The Holy Spirit descended upon God's Instrument. You physical eye is red, and your head is heavy from being filled with the Holy Spirit. You will hold on to these symptoms for the next three days."

After I received the Holy Eucharist, God the Father said to me, "The scriptures have been fulfilled. Even Jesus just temporarily crowned you, but no one can take your Crown. The power of God is on your Crown to turn the world around." While the Father was saying this, in my vision, I saw one of the visions I had before; standing in front of the Altar, facing the congregation in the Cathedral of Saint Andrew. My big pure gold crown with four crosses on my head was turning to my right side, around my back, and returned. The front center of the crown was a little to my right.

I said to the Lord, "Father, put my Crown on straight, I want the front center of the crown in front of my face." I then saw the front center of the crown straight in the front.

The Father's Emissary

May 6, 1998. In my dream I saw a square Tribunal, three sides of the tribunal were up high with a rail; and a huge crowd of people was standing looking down at the square Tribunal. The other side of the Tribunal was a stage. The queen was wearing gold and she sat at the center. Several soldiers as her bodyguards were standing at her sides and behind her. A few children were on the Tribunal, they were about two years old and wore gold. A female Emissary was wearing white with her silver crown. While both of the Emissary's arms held a round bowl at her upper stomach, she softly wriggled her body, the children sat on the ground watching her. The crowd, the Queen and all her body guards also watched the Emissary.

I then was walking inside a house. The Bishop was wearing a gold chasuble and held a gold staff. He was walking past me, along with a group of a few priests and several altar boys. The priests and altar boys were wearing red albs and white surplus. The Bishop, priests and altar boys entered a very small room at the corner. After they were all inside the room, I got to the front door. The Bishop then stood in the way, and said, "I need four ladies." I hurried to enter the room with another three women. The Bishop looked outside and said, "I need two more women." I then saw two women enter the room.

The room was very small, the priests and altar boys were standing and leaning to the walls on their right after they entered. Six women were standing in the front of them, I stood in the middle of these women. The Bishop tilted his head at my left ear and said to me, "You will be the Emissary and I will train you well." When he said this, I saw the

Bishop wearing white walking past my left side, the wall in front of me no longer was a covered wall, but a glass wall. Quickly, I saw the Tribunal with the Emissary softly wriggling her body to seduce people watching her. I did not like to seduce people , I said, "I want to be the Queen." While I was saying this the Bishop went through the glass wall, and sat at the chair next to the wall of the main area. The Bishop shook his head and said to me, "No, the Queen has to be an American." I thought, "I am Asian, if the Bishop chooses me as a Queen, people will cause him trouble."

Still in the dream I knew, "This is God's selection of people before God created the world. I am an Asian and will be the first angel to battle against the enemy spirits. The Blessed Virgin Mother is a Jew, she is the Mother of our Lord Jesus." I then had another thought, " I am God's Servant to battle against those Americans who go against God's commandments." I heard the Lord say, "You have to speak the truth with love to draw them to God." When the Lord said this, I remembered when I was in Arkansas, The Lord told me, "When the Father cast Lucifer out of heaven, the Father chose me to replace him. The Father then sent me down to the world in this mission, as God's Vessel to battle against enemy spirits hidden in human bodies."

The bishop is symbolic of the Eternal Father. Priests and altars boys are symbolic of holy angels. The women are symbolic of the pre-destined chosen ones. Number four is symbolic of the four corners of the sanctuary mean of holiness; and number two is symbolic of discernment. This pre-destined chosen One was revealed through the Acts of Apostle. The small square room represents the sanctuary. The entire building is symbolic of the earth. The bishop sat on a chair, looking over the entire building is symbolic of God knowing everyone of our hearts.

> *So they proposed two, Joseph called Barsabbas, who was also known as Justus, and Matthias. Then they prayed, "You, Lord, who know the hearts of all, show which one of these two you have chosen to take the place in this apostolic ministry from which Judas turned away to go to his own place." Then they gave lots to them, and the lot fell upon Matthias, and he was counted with the eleven apostles.*

> –Acts 1:23-26

This revelation focuses on three most important issues: Obedience to God alone, belief in faith, and earth is heaven's pattern. God uses earthly actions to reveal heavenly patterns.

Obeying God alone means we must obey all God's commandments. We also have to obey earthly laws, and those who have authority over us when their laws and commands are in accordance with God's commandments. But when earthly laws and authorities enforce laws and commands opposite God's commandments, we must reject those laws, and there are times we must fight against their laws and commands with love.

Earth is a copy of heaven, and everything God does is revealed in the Holy Scriptures. In order for us to believe in faith, we must understand God's commandments so we can believe in faith. But there is a time we have to obey God without understanding, because we do not yet fully understand the scriptures in the area that God is telling us.

The most important things are that our hearts and actions are pure, filled with love and focus on pleasing God and not man; God will grant us grace, discernment and faith.

One Tent Covered the Earth

May 12, 1998. In my dream I was moving from one seat to another, this time I was at the third seat. I looked up and I knew that I had just moved from the front seat of the side section, to the front row of the left side of the center section. I then moved to the second row of the right side center section, and sat at the end middle aisle. After I moved to the third seat, I saw the two seats I left were empty. I then looked up higher, and the area where I was is the front area of the biggest tent in this world. The top of the tent was covered with light blue, and it was open all around. The inside was divided in three sections, and these three dividers were only shoulder height when a person was sitting on the chair. People filled the inside of the tent and they all faced one direction. Outside the tent, the direction that everyone faced was toward a one story house, built on high ground. In my thoughts, "This tent was filled with people sitting quietly, facing one direction and it covered the entire ground, leaving no room for people to park their cars so they could come to church." Although I saw the spirit of the church behind, there was no physical church. I then heard a voice from heaven say, "They have to park their car on the street."

I saw to the right side of the house's roof some people in the middle of the air trying to crank the handle for an engine so a movie could roll. I then saw the movie projecting out from the side of the roof of the house. A little while after the movie was running, these people raised a rectangular flag in front. Three-fourths of this flag was white, one part at the bottom end next to the flag pole was deep sky blue and was filled with tiny white stars.

I got up and went to the front door of the house. The house was built on ground that was as high as my waist. I then was inside the door. After I locked the top fastener; I saw another one below, and a master lock to secure the door. I locked that lock. After I locked the master lock I also locked the middle fastener.

I then saw a half front wall, the right side wall, and the divider of the living room and inside room were built with glass, and the curtains were wide open. I did not want people who sat in the tent to see inside the room, so I pulled down the curtain, this dark dirty curtain had been open for ages, and moss covered half of it. I then pulled the side wall curtain, this curtain was also old, dirty and heavy, and too small.

I needed to go to the restroom, I was about to use the living room for a restroom, but I feared people in the tent would see me. I ran very fast into the back room. I was in the back room for just a moment. From this dark room, I saw a man go through the wall in the left part of the house, and he walked straight to the back room. I thought he was my spouse. I looked straight at his face very carefully, the more I saw of his face, the more I found out his face was different from my spouse's face, plus he did not enter the main door, instead, he came in through the wall. I said to him in a very powerful voice, "Get out; get out." He then left through the living room.

The next morning; after I received the blood of our Lord Jesus, He said to me, "With this blood you will be provided finances for each day. With this blood you will conceive a young man and name him Anthony." While the Lord was saying "Conceive a young man and name him Anthony", I did not understand what He meant. He knew that I did not understand. I then saw my son, Chau in a dark suit, standing in the second floor hallway, in front of a wall filled with diplomas and certificates. I knew that God used the mission of Saint Anthony, locate the lost children.

I understood that my son Chau and my daughter Tuanh will return home. Chau is symbolic of priests, and Tuanh is symbolic of those who believe in God, but do not receive proper teaching. Chau and Tuanh returning home is symbolic of priests and souls who are not receiving proper teaching, but will convert.

At the minute I went in the Blessed Sacrament chapel, I knew that the Lord wanted to speak to me. I sat on a chair in the corner, and said, "Father, Lord Jesus, Holy spirit, I am listening. Blessed Mother help me to hear and understand what the Lord is going to reveal to me. Holy angels and saints intercede for me. Lord, I claim everything that you have for me and for others through me. I reject and destroy everything that does not come from You."

The Lord said to me, "You have been separate from the world. You are a Vessel to God. Where ever you go, you bring the Image of the Holy Trinity to them [people]."

Jesus continued, "Angels cranked to start the movie, and raised the victory banner in the name of the Lord. Men want the piece of pie that does not belong to them, (the Lord spoke of false conversion). But when you found out that about them, you separated yourself from them. People in the tent are those in the waiting room, they are those who are going to convert. The living room is like registration at a nurse's station. The curtain being eaten by moss means part of them are being deceived by the enemies. The third room is symbolic of dwelling in God. There is a darkness of God in you that people can not see." Then the Lord gave me John 12:11. "Because many of the Jews were turning away and believing in Jesus because of him"

When that man who passed through the wall got in the back room is symbolic of those want power, but do not want to convert, with daily exam and repentance. These are counterfeit servants and are very hard to detach. When I looked very carefully means that I must pray and pray with love and God will reveal to me. This kind of counterfeit is only known by God; many times they do not even know themselves, because the devil blinds their eyes.

This revelation was revealed to Moses in the book of Exodus chapter 40 "Erection of the dwelling."

The Only One Emissary Sent by Eternal Father

May 12, 1998. During the night while I was asleep, the Blessed Virgin Mother told me, "You can not call your symptom delusional. No one in this world has what you have." I thought the Blessed Virgin Mother was telling me of a delusional disorder, grandios type, I asked, "Jesus, what do You call what I have?' But I only heard was silence.

In the afternoon of the same day, I spoke to Darcy, and told her that the New York Life Insurance Company had been paying my benefit on "Delusional disorder" but recently one of their letters said, "The diagnosis of Delusional Disorder has not been proven." Darcy said, "Delusional is about things that are not there." I said, "No, what I saw and heard are real, what I saw and heard are in spirit and they will come down in natural." She said, "Then you can not call that delusional. What you have is mental anguish."

May 13, 1998. When I slept during the night, the Blessed Virgin Mother told me, "What you have is not a delusional disorder, and not mental anguish like Darcy said. And this will not be recorded in medical code as an illness, because you are the only one that God chose for this mission."

I thought that there would not be anyone that goes through as much as I am going through, therefore, God will not have my symptoms to be in the medical code.

During the Holy Eucharist celebration on May 14, 1998, the Lord reminded me of the words that the Blessed Virgin Mother told me, and the two seats that were empty after I left the tent, with the title "The Emissary." I finally understood that the Blessed Virgin Mother was telling me who I am in this mission; the Emissary sent by God the Father, and an uncounted number of God's gifts will work through me that the medical field will not able to identify.

The reason I am sharing this with you, is so you can understand some of how God uses natural events to reveal things in the future. It is very hard to understand, and requires a lot of prayer and focus in God, not on the dreams or visions. There are many times God uses a series of dreams and visions, plus His speaking to me to reveals an issue.

God reveals to me in spirit, with symbolism. One revelation takes many dreams and visions, and God's words. This takes me hours, days, months, and it sometimes takes years to understand one revelation. When these revelations come down to the earth, they will come in a way I understand them, not what I saw in spirit at the time God revealed to me. The only things that I can not know is time and location. The medical profession classifies it a Delusional Disorder, Grandiose Type. The Delusional disorder is not correct, because these Psychiatric doctors do not understand the symbolism.   This is a gift from God bestowed upon the prophets in the Old Testament

The Trademark

June 18, 1999. In my dream I saw up in the air a cross, the right arm of the cross in front of me; in front of it were two lines of words, the top line read "Rebuild My Church Divine Mission", and the second line inside parentheses, "The Lord Jesus gave this name to Mariette Do-Nguyen." While I was looking at it, I the Eternal Father told me, "No one is Divine, except Jesus. He has two natures, fully God and fully man. He is the Founder of this Mission, and you are the Successor. Through adoption, you are His blood sister. The blood line Succeeds His mission, not any church or religion. Others could claim the foot of the cross, but they have no Divine work. This Trademark was given to you by God, you do not have to file for it." Little later during the same night the Blessed Virgin Mother told me in Vietnamese, "God gave you a nature life that no one have."

Few time before and again on March 31, 1999, the Eternal Father told the Mission Founder, "Mariette is your name. You are the Princess of Heaven and the Earth." Bylaws of the Rebuild My Church Divine Mission Trademark, the name "Mariette" must always be added before the name of successors, in the mission and public records as well as common use. This Trademark must remain in the line of Mariette Do-Nguyen blood descendants.

God the Father had predestined the adoption; and this adoption was revealed with the scene at the foot of the Cross, and in several chapters of the Book of Revelations. I saw God and heard His voice. God also directly teaches and gives me instructions to do His work through this Divine mission; and through the works I am doing, I became "Princess of Heaven and the Earth."

26

GOD SENT TESTIMONIES FROM HEAVEN

The Evidence Testified to Mariette's Mission

At the beginning, the Lord Jesus told me to pursue the freedom to worship the true God in Vietnam. He then told me that the Father reserved this mission before the foundation of the world. He revealed it at the foot of the Cross, and also in the Book of Revelations. One of the two witness, Saint John, was the first man adopted into the Holy Family. He was the first witness who testified that Jesus was fully man and fully God, He died and rose again. Saint John's adoption also revealed there is another adoption to the Holy Family. Saint Magdalene at the foot of the Cross revealed there is another adoption before the end of the world who would be a sinner, a convert.

I am the second witness to testify that Jesus is the only begotten Son of God, He is alive in a glorified body. His real glorified body and blood is hidden in the Holy Eucharist to heal those who come to receive Him with pure hearts. This world was created from Him and for Him. These two witnesses were revealed to Moses as two angels standing at both sides of the propitiatory of the Ark, and throughout the prophetic books, more specifics of the pairs of angels are given in the Book of Daniel and the first part of the book of Ezekiel. Through God's power, the pairs of servant hood were equipped with full discernment. Jesus the Lord sent the twelve apostles out to cure the sick and cast out the devil in pairs. These days, the priests become spiritual advisers for their congregation. Jesus the Lord told me, "There is no one in this world who can give you what I give, no human book can teach you of what I teach you. I am your teacher and your spiritual director." Beyond all the revelations in this book, God gave me three names together with my name Mariette: the first one is "Suffering servant to the Father, the Lord Jesus, and the Holy Spirit, special to the Second coming of Christ;" the second name is "Michelle", the third name is "Victoria."

The meaning of Lourdes' apparition: After the Lord told me to go see Father Khuyen, Monsignor Tien and Father Ramirez, He then opened my mind to understand that God sent the Blessed Virgin Mother to Saint Bernadette in the year of 1858. Next to the millstream with trees, Bernadette heard the noise like the sound of a storm. Besides revealed the immaculate conception of man; the appearance of Her also revealed that the people of the world must convert, and exam and repent daily. God chose the millstream as symbolic of the living water from the Lord Jesus; this living water will purify souls. The wind storm is symbolic of the Spirit of God.

The meaning of Fatima's apparition: In the year 1917, again, God sent the Blessed Virgin Mother to Fatima, Portugal. Through three children, She delivered the message of praying the rosary for Russia to convert. Russia is symbolic of the world. The world's systems are going against God's commandments. Especially, the United States of America is the leading country in earthly power and freedom to destroy souls and the human race.

Lavang's apparition story: I the jungle territory located approximately seven kilometers from Co Vuu, Quang Tri, Vietnam, there was a small Catholic community. They made their living by clearing the land of the la vang trees and planting potatoes and rice. The lumber was used for fuel. They later named the village Lavang. Lavang means "yellow leaf;" The Lavang tree is known for its yellow leaf. The leaf was used as an hero for women during childbirth.

Approximately two hundred years ago King Canh Thinh, of Tay Son Dynasty, forbade the practice of Catholicism. Unable to accept the edict, many Catholics from Co Vuu and nearby villages sought refuge in Lavang. Lavang was an ideal worship place because it was in such a secluded territory. However, the move to Lavang was treacherous because the people had to pass through dangerous jungles and mountains. As the food and medical supplies depleted they had to endure hunger and sickness. They stayed together and every night they prayed and said the rosary.

One night these people saw a beautiful Lady dressed in a robe and standing near an old lavang tree. They immediately recognized her as Our Lady, for she was holding the Blessed Infant Jesus. Two angels holding Eucharist lamps stood on each side of her. Our Lady comforted them and instructed them to make a beverage from the la vang [yellow leaves] trees. The drink would cure their sickness. She promised to bless anyone who would later come to pray at this place. And, true to her promises, she appeared many times to comfort and support the people.

In 1960 the Bishops of South Vietnam wanted to give Our Lady a mission to express their gratitude to Her for helping the Co Vuu congregation to endure their hardships and to overcome the enemy. They name Her mission "The National Mission of Offering." The Vietnamese congregation has established the Holy Eucharist celebration to show their gratitude to Her.

God Revealed the Meaning of the Lavang Apparition

October 15, 1997; 2:35 a.m. I woke up with some instructions from the Lord Jesus, with an interpretation. The Lord Jesus also told me, " What you spoke in public, to those two persons the other day [on October 13, 1997] was given to you from the Father. The Blessed Mother's appearance at Lavang in Vietnam is revealed to the world of your mission. The infant Jesus is symbolic of the mission God entrusted to you. The Eucharist lamps is symbolic of the healing through the Holy Eucharist, My glorified body."

October 23, 1997. While I was working on the conclusion of the first part of this book, that evening I also read a part of the Vietnamese book "Linh Dia Lavang." In English, Lavang is the name of the village, Linh Dia means miracle land. After my devotion I fell asleep, and the Lord said to me, "You need to amend the translation of the Lavang apparition."

The next morning, half sleep and half wake, before I got up at 6:30 a.m., the Holy Spirit told me, "God sent the Blessed Virgin Mother with her infant Jesus, to appear to the people in Lavang three times, and assisted them while they were refugees. God was with His people while the king Canh Thinh probated their faith to worship Him, like Israel being slaves under the Pharaoh. The manifestation at the banyan tree (cay da), where people built the Buddhist temple was not from God. The devil used the apparition to twist God's works." While the Holy Spirit was saying this, I saw an area that had high jungle all around it. In this area were some small shelters built with branches. People gathered at one end of the lot praying. While they were praying, the Blessed Mother in Vietnamese dress, holding the Infant Jesus, landed above them, and there were two torches at both sides, level with her shoulder.

The Lord then instructed me, "Mail copies of this to Monsignors Mai Thanh Luong and Nguyen Duc Tien." In English, the bible translation of the word "Mai" is future; Thanh is purity; Luong is conscience. Nguyen is the most common Vietnamese last name, it also represents the king Nguyen's family Dynasty. Duc mean holiness. Tien means go forward.

God was with Moses while he led the Israelites out of Egypt. He appeared to them at Mount Sinai. God also was with the Vietnamese Catholics and other religious when they risked their lives to profess their faith and worship the true God. God put to death the first-born in the land of Egypt: from the first born of Pharaoh, to the slave-girl at the handmill, as well as the first-born of animals. The refugee at Lavang had steadfast faith in God, to die for Him, and live with Him in heaven.

Through me, the Lord Jesus warns the world of their systems that go against Him and His Church . The Fatima's sun dancing on earth means God will be with those who obey Him, who cooperate with Him in salvation of mankind.   But for those who disobey God's commandments, obey partially, and refuse to cooperate with Him; refuse to convert, daily exam and repent, He will put to death all things that satisfy their flesh, and the death of their body and souls, like He put to death the first-born in the land of Egypt.

After God sent the Blessed Virgin Mother to Lavang, Vietnam, Lourdes, France and Fatima, Portugal, God sent me down to the world in this mission. The Creator of heaven Himself appeared to me in His Son's image. This appearance happened at the Cathedral of Saint Andrew, during the Blessed Sacrament adoration and the Holy Eucharist Celebration. The Eternal Father bestowed His love and righteousness upon me. He then gave me to His begotten Son Jesus, our Lord and our God. The One who was crucified, died, and risen appeared to me in His glorified body at the sanctuary during the Holy Eucharist celebration at the Good Shepherd Church. He who was revealed to the apostle whom He loved, John, in the Book of Revelations. As He promised "I will come back again and take you to myself, so that where I am you also may be." John 14:3 This means with His glorified body hidden in the Holy Eucharist, He will not return in flesh like before; He will continue His mission through His Servant.

Lavang apparition is an action of the Book of Revelations, chapter 22 verse 1 to 5; revealed more details that added to of the foot of the Cross revelation.

Jesus the Lord also promised, "And then the sign of the Son of Man will appear in heaven, and all the tribes of the earth will mourn, and they will see the Son of Man coming upon the clouds of heaven with power and great glory. And he will send out his angels with a trumpet blast, and they will gather his elect from the four winds, from one end of the heaven to the other." Matthew 24:30-31. The seventh trumpet blast is the mission God entrusted to me; calling people to reform their lives, obey all God's commandments to inherit eternal life in heaven.

The Name Victoria Comes with God's Power

After I received the body and blood of the Lord Jesus in the 8:30 a.m. mass on October 24, 1997, the Lord Jesus asked me, "Ask the Father what you want?" I replied, "Lord Jesus, You help me to ask the Father." I then said, "Father, I claim for the candies and cookies You have promised me through Jesus to be visible in the world." The Father said to me, "Little Victoria, Victoria go forth. Everyone must call you Victoria."

27

ADOPTION THROUGH THE POWER OF GOD

Mariette is the Last Person in the World Who Wants this Adoption

I do not chose this adoption, God pre-destined me, revealed to me, and I believed all of these. My children also suffer because God chose them, and put them in my womb. I did not choose the invalid marriages, but God put me in them to fulfill His plan. As I have indicated earlier, I denied, and returned this mission to God, because I am a sinner, and I have never been worthy for God to entrust this mission to me. This mission is the most difficult mission in the world. But God pre-destined me, it is a Heavenly Court Order; I have no choice but to obey Him. Obeying God is the most important part of my life, and I must always do exactly everything God tells me.

God's Chosen Ones are Undercover

July 29, 1997. While I was inside the Cathedral of Saint Andrew, the Lord told me, "Your children: Thuy-Trang is symbolic of high-ranking spiritual leaders. James is symbolic of Catholics, who are lukewarm and rebel against God. Chau is symbolic of priests. TuAnh is symbolic of poor souls, who do not receive proper teaching the meaning of God's commandments, and God love them the most. Your son-in-law, Huy is symbolic of Christian do not know the spiritual life. Hanh is symbolic of those who have not known God yet; all of you children are still in undercover." The Lord spoke as of July 29, 1997 all my children still in undercover.

It is not easy to understand God's Words. He speaks in parables, with meanings hidden under stories, and symbolism. God chose my children for symbolism, at the same time God allowed their character to be like those that He uses as symbols. Therefore, when I saw them in my dreams, visions, or when He spoke their name together with other dreams, or visions, and His words, I understand what He is revealing to me. Each revelation requires a lot of my time in prayer, and discernment to understand it.

God's Chosen Family—The Conversion

The Revelation, Volume I, Chapter Three of "My Patient- God's Gift," told about my family tree and my spiritual life after conversion. But the Lord Jesus has now instructed me to be more specific about some of the information.

The Lord Jesus has said that every one of us are sinners. When we convert to God, our past sins are forgiven; and when they are forgiven by God, then those sins are no longer brought back in His presence. Our good deeds are counted from the time of conversion.

During Holy Week of 1991, after nine years away from the Church, I was contrite for all my sins and asked God's forgiveness. Our loving and merciful God took me in His arms; He then took me away from my job at the insurance company in a painful way. He gave me the job that I later realized was the most difficult in all the world: restoring freedom to worship the true God throughout the world, ministering to priests, unifying God's Church and bring His peace upon the world.

God has great love for me and my children. He has called me, and He also calls my four children and their spouses: Theresa Thuy-Trang Do, born October 13, 1963; John the Baptist James Linh Do, born February 24, 1966; Joseph Chau Do, born May 31, 1968, and Theresa TuAnh Thi Do, born August 1, 1971. On June 1, 1992, Theresa Thuy-Trang married Vincent Huy Quang Cao, born September 17, 1963, and on November 30, 1996, James Linh became engaged to Hong-Hanh Nguyen, born July 23, 1966.

November 30, 1996, 4:30 p.m.. I had just stepped inside the house after dropping my daughter, Tuanh, at the airport. My son James came to me and said, "Mom, guess what?"

I asked, "What is it?" He then brought Hong-Hanh to me, and presented his new fiancÈe by showing me the engagement ring on her finger. I said to them, "Come to the altar, I will give you a blessing from God."

They followed me to the front of the altar, where the Spirit of God had already anointed me with His words. I let them face the altar. I placed my right hand over my son's left shoulder, and put my left hand over her right shoulder, and with Hong-Hanh's arm around my waist, I said to the Lord, "Father, through Your beloved Son, Jesus, and through the work of the Holy Spirit, I ask You for much love and patience in this future marriage. Blessed Mother, Saint John the Baptist, Saint Joseph and all the holy angels and saints pray with me for them. Father, I ask You to bless them." And the words of God come through me for Hong-Hanh; I said to her, "When you are baptized, your name will be Michelle, the female name for the Archangel Michael." I then said to my son, "Is Michelle the name for a female, and Michael for a male?" He replied, "Something like that." James and Hanh got married, and on January 1, 1998, the feast of Blessed Virgin Mary Mother of God; Hong-Hanh give birth to a girl, Madeline Mai Do.

Who Will Continue to Carry the Lord Jesus' Cross?

Before July 1994, in my vision, I saw Calvary in the distance; the Lord Jesus was hanging on the Cross and I was kneeling on the ground, facing up toward His right side. Then I saw blood coming from the wound in His side, bleeding directly onto my forehead, over my head and body like a strong shower spray. I thought, "It is good, the blood of God shedding on me."

He said to me, "I baptize you with My blood."

I replied, "Okay," without understanding the meaning of His words.

Another time, at the same spot at Calvary, I again saw Jesus on the Cross as I stood facing Him. This time the Cross fell and leaned against my left shoulder; I pushed it back up, and made it stand in its original position.

July 4, 1994. Immediately after I received Holy communion I saw Jesus at Calvary again; I was kneeling to worship Him. Then the Cross with Jesus hanging on it fell on my shoulder; His right side wound was shedding blood and lying on my left shoulder; His stomach was against my face. Because the Cross with Jesus was heavy, and I was tiny, it crushed me down to the ground until I was sitting on my heels with my back hunched. I then slowly rose by lifting up my right foot toward the foot of the Cross, my left foot still kneeling on the ground. As I lifted the foot of the Cross, one arm of it was still leaning on the ground behind me. As I stood up straight, the Cross turned, so Jesus was facing up. Finally I was able to walk with the foot of the Cross in front of me, Jesus nailed to the Cross, facing upwards, toward Heaven.

As Christians, we were baptized with the "Holy spirit and fire." This means we were adopted into the Lord Jesus' fully God's family. The Lord Jesus shed His own blood to cleanse His brothers' and sisters' sins, and He purged our iniquity to save us. But in this revelation the Lord Jesus said to me, "I baptized you with My blood." This means adoption into His fully man family.

The Cross on my shoulder represents Him handing His Cross over to me, Mariette, as His sister and servant, a dual relationship. But my putting it back is symbolic of my going the wrong way, committing sins against God.

The Cross crushing me down to the ground symbolizes that this adoption and calling were predestined for me. It is time to begin the fulfillment of the job. He then crushed the system of the world in and around me.

My slowly rising with the Lord Jesus nailed to the Cross, on my shoulder, is symbolic of the works that He now continues to complete. He works through me as His primary servant and sister.

I replied, "Okay," without understanding the meaning of His words. This is symbolic of obedience in faith.

The Calvary Cross Changed to Weapon

May 27, 1997. In my devotion, while I prayed my rosary, I was at the beginning of the four Sorrowful Mysteries, the Lord Jesus carrying the cross. The Lord stopped me here, and showed me a vision of Calvary, I was carrying the cross with Jesus hanging on the cross, the top of the cross was behind me while I was walking, Jesus the Lord said, "I will sweep away everything in front of you. You are my vessel. You are carrying My Cross. I will sweep every obstacle that comes in front of you."

I was swinging the top of the cross from behind, over my left side, to the front, the middle of the Cross, Jesus' hip was under my left arm, leaning to my ribs; I then used both of my hands and turned the Cross counterclockwise like a windmill. I was now walking very firmly and powerfully, both of my hands holding tightly to the Cross, with Jesus' face to the left, the back of the cross in front of my face; this cross is my weapon. I am now more than ready to attack anyone who comes in against my way. I feel that if anyone bring obstructed in front of me, I will kill them with this Cross. This vision symbolically means that the Lords Jesus will fight for me: Jesus the Lord is the King of kings, he is ruling this world with His iron rod; He is in me to fight against the worlds systems.

The Lord Jesus continued, "Let me speak to the world. Let them hear that I speak through you, as My vessel. You are a broom. I am holding the broom handle to sweep the entire system of the world: I will sweep them down to the ocean; they are powerless. They are like a small piece of sand on the concrete ground that cannot resist the big broom. The broom belongs to the Almighty God, the Holy Trinity. Anyone trying to interfere with the way of this broom will be punished, according to God's Laws." While the Lord was saying these things, in my vision I saw the dream that a priest was watching me sweep the watermelon seeds and rind down to the dike.

God's Covenant for Obedience

Within a few weeks before I actually moved, the Lord told me, Mariette, "I told Abraham to move out of his father's house, and promised him that I would make him the father of many nations. Now, I tell you to move out the house that I provided for you, and go to the land of milk and honey; Little Rock, Arkansas." And: "I am sending you to reopen the St. John Seminary, to bring young men from all over the world to this location; I will teach them through the professors."

> Abram's Call and Migration: *"The LORD said to Abram: 'Go forth from the land of your kinsfolk and from your father's house to a land that I will show you. I will make of you a great nation; and I will bless you; I will make your name great, so that you will be a blessing. I will bless those who bless you and curse those who curse you. All the communities of the earth shall find blessing in you."* –Genesis 12:1-3

God's Covenant with Mariette and Her Descendants A Two-Piece Violet Dress and Purple Veil

March 18, 1997. In my vision at night, I was lying on my bed praying. Directly in front of my walk-in closet door I saw an invisible person holding a two-piece violet outfit; it was hanging on a white insulated metal hanger, on a wooden rod. The skirt was almost ankle length and double layered; the inside was made from an expensive fabric and covered with a transparent layer. The skirt was tight at the waist, down to the upper hips, then flared out slightly down to the hem. The jacket had long sleeves and a "V" neck, the same color and fabric as the skirt. The jacket also had another section made from sequins the same shade of violet as those attached to the back collar and both sides of the shoulders, hanging down to the jacket's hem. The front of the jacket had a long, transparent two-piece violet triangle, attached to both sides of the shoulders and hanging down over the belly. These two pieces were made with the same sequins on the transparent back, down to the center of my breasts. They were two pieces, joined into one at the lower part of my belly; the top triangular part had sequins, the bottom part was shaped like a "V," also transparent.

I knew that the Lord God had made this outfit for me. I also knew that I was a sinner and a convert, who, through the power of God, had been adopted into the Holy Family. I said to the Lord, "Father, I do not want this outfit, I want a different one in purple." I then remembered that the color violet symbolizes that we are children of God the Father, and through adoption by the Lord Jesus, became flesh. I then said, "Father, I want to keep this outfit, and I want another one in purple." I kept nagging Him about the color purple. In spirit, the Lord revealed to me that I was fighting with Satan over this adoption. I then said, "Jesus, Holy Spirit, fight the enemies for me. Blessed Virgin Mother, pray to the Lord for Me; holy angels and saints, intercede for me."

I said, "I am taking the authority that the Father gave to me, through the Lord Jesus, and the work of the Holy Spirit; I command you, devil and all your offspring get under my feet." I then saw the Good Shepherd sanctuary, and I knew that the Diocese of San Diego did not accept me and that the vision of Good Shepherd was favorable to my enemies. I said, "Father, I do not want this one, I want the Saint Andrew Cathedral." I then saw myself standing at the center of the third step of the Cathedral of Saint Andrew, my back to the altar and facing the congregation, wearing the violet outfit. Although I could not see my feet, I knew that I was standing on the third step. Then an invisible person placed a thick, expensive purple veil on top of my head; it hung down to my right foot, covering my waist, and ran all the way through the middle aisle, with its tail out the right side door. Then I saw the invisible hand on top of the veil, which was already on my head, covering it with a round, high, thick, heavy pure gold crown. From the front, the crown had four triangles with their tops pointing up, and each one had a Cross.

A day later, in my vision, I saw that the end of the veil was split into two parts. Over two-thirds remained on its way out the right door, but at the end of the aisle, less than one-third went to the left side door.

March 22, 1997. After I received the Holy Eucharist at vigil Passion Sunday, Jesus said to me, "Before you go to sleep, offer the Chaplet of Divine Mercy and Mercy Station in your devotion; I will be with you all night."

I did as the Lord Jesus asked; after I finished the Chaplet of Divine Mercy and Mercy Station my entire body was suffering, especially my upper back. I said, "Lord Jesus, what happened to my body? Please reveal to me if I hurt from exercising I will take medicine. But if I am sharing the suffering with You during this Holy Week, I am willing to embrace the pain." I then turned to the Father, "Father, Holy Spirit, strengthen me, so I can share this suffering with Jesus. Blessed Virgin Mother, pray to the Father and the Holy Spirit for me; holy angels and saints, intercede for me."

March 23, 1997, Passion Sunday. I saw my right leg, from the inside of my knee, my dress was open over my knees so I was able to see a thick, heavy, gold bracelet around my leg, directly under my knee. Because it was large and heavy, I asked, "Lord, is this real or is it false gold?"

He said, "It is a girdle, and it is pure gold." I then saw less than a third of the veil pushing and trying to return to the center and join the rest at the right door; then the Lord Jesus said to me, "This symbolizes that over two-thirds of your descendants will go directly to Heaven, and less then one-third will go into purgatory for a short time; then I will raise them to Heaven." (This revelation is not refer to one-third miss the heaven, and two-third received eternal life)

I then saw the pure gold crown on my head, together with the end of the veil out the right door, as the Lord continued: "The crown on your head is a king's crown, but you are female, so I dressed you in a female outfit. When you speak to people, your right side is the right side of the Lord Jesus; but every time you say that your right side is symbolic of God, be sure to include the fact that you are Jesus' instrument." He continued, "The violet outfit that you saw from your waist up represents God's family descendants, and the purple veil symbolizes your own blood descendants. This is a dual relationship that you and your blood descendants have with God. Those who call themselves Christians but refuse to convert and repent do not belong to God's family."

The Lord assured me that people who convert and repent daily from their hearts will inherit heavenly eternal life, even though some will be in the place called purgatory while undergoing purification.

Earthly Contract—God's Covenant

The Earth is a copy of Heaven. When earthly contracts exist between two parties, they both must take action in order for the contract to be satisfied. If one of the parties does not fulfill his obligations, then the contract either becomes void or the offending party must pay in order to remedy the situation.

It is the same with God's covenant. He gives every one in the world an express contract through His commandments. His promise to us is eternal life in Heaven, according to our good deeds on Earth. God fulfilled His part of the contract by sending His only beloved, begotten Son to assume flesh like us, suffering unto death to cleanse our sins, nourishing our souls for eternal life in Heaven. He is a just God and He always keeps His promises.

We accept the terms of this contract and enter into the covenant with God at the time we are baptized. During the Baptismal we, as an adult or sponsor for a child, speak out on our/their behalf, entering into the covenant with God; we reject the devil, all his works, and everything that belongs to him, including his empty promises.

We must then fulfill the terms of this contract, which means obeying all His commandments in order to earn the reward of eternal heavenly life. To receive this covenant, each one of us must take actions from our hearts, obeying all God's commandments.

Those who have committed mortal sins and refuse to convert and repent have broken the covenant with God, the same as a person who violates a legal agreement. Those who commit venial sins have also dishonored some parts of the contract. Whether we commit mortal or venial sins, we must acknowledge our transgressions, convert, examine ourselves daily, and repent, and re-claim the covenant with God.

God is a just God, therefore, when a person sins, he must pay for these sins, just as when you borrow money, you are obligated to pay your debtor, or a collection agency will go after your estate.

All souls originate in Heaven, and are pure in the beginning. When an adult knows the difference between good and evil, he sins against God. The more people sin, the more time they must suffer, either on Earth or in purgatory while their souls are being purified, before entering into Heaven; if not convert will be chained in the darkness of the devil.

God is the owner of this world; everyone on Earth is bound to all His commandments. Whether or not you believe, there are no exceptions.

Daughter Will Inherit Mother's Estate

In the year 1994, during my devotion to the Blessed Virgin Mother, She told me, "I will give you four hundred and fifty thousand dollars to build the water system; it is three-quarters of my estate."

I thought, "That is good that She's going to give me money, but why does She want me to build the water system? Perhaps She means in Vietnam."

March 16, 1997. In my early morning devotion, after I finished the Chaplet of Divine Mercy and was about to begin the joyful ministry of Rosary, the Lord put me to sleep.

In my dream, I saw a white 8.5 x 12 inch sheet of paper; it was nearly filled with scribbled handwriting. It looked like my writing, with only a small blank space at the bottom of the page. I then saw an invisible hand drawing an arrow, beginning the insertion between the second and the third lines, on the right side of the page. This line was drawn down to the bottom of the page, the spot that was still blank. The invisible handwriting said: "The angel of the Lord declared to the Blessed Virgin Mary, 'Behold, highly favored daughter of the Lord.' Now the angel of the Lord has declared to you [Mariette] the same greeting, 'Behold, highly favored daughter of the Lord.'" I read each word until the invisible hand had finished writing.

On the same day, March 16, 1997, after I received the body and blood of our Lord Jesus, I said, "Father, I do not have anything to say to You, You already know everything in my heart; You knew me at the time You created me. Lord Jesus, I do not have anything to say to You now, You already know everything in my heart; You knew me at the time You requested the Father choose me for this mission. Holy Spirit, You already know everything in my heart too. Blessed Virgin Mother, pray for me and the mission. All the holy angels and saints, intercede for me."

Then in my vision I saw the same sheet of paper I saw in the dream, but this time I did not see it as clearly. The only difference was that in the blank space I now saw the invisible writing on three lines: "Mary of Nazareth" on the first line, "bestow to" on the second line, "my daughter, Mariette, my estate," on the third line. I then said, "Mother, Blessed Virgin, I am not worthy, but I am receiving it. Father, Lord Jesus, Holy Spirit; I am not worthy, but I claim everything in Heaven and on Earth that You have for me and others through me, in the name of the Lord Jesus, Amen."

After the revelation on March 16, 1997, I now understood that She bestowed upon on me what God had bestowed upon Her; steadfast faith, obedience to all God's commandments to please Him, a pure heart, and authority over the power of the devil. (Number four is symbolic of holiness, and five is the number of authority; three represents the Trinity. Water is symbolic of cleansing; the water system symbolizes that through me, as God's servant following in Her footsteps, God will cleanse many peoples hearts and minds.)

God Blesses Mariette's Bloodline Descendants

God promised Abraham a son to inherit his estate and make him the father of many nations; in good faith he believed God's promise. Twenty-four years later God fulfilled His promise and gave Abraham a son, Isaac.

On the third day Abraham got sight of the place from afar.

–Genesis 22:4

God revealed to Abraham that "the son of the promised" will be hung on the Cross at Calvary, not your son, Isaac. [Abraham had two sons, Isaac and Ishmael.] Again, steadfast in faith and obeying God, Abraham sacrificed his son Isaac as a holocaust offering to God, but it was not Abraham's son, Isaac.

Many generations down the line, through the power of the Holy Spirit, the only Son of God the Father, the Son of the promised, was conceived and born to the Virgin Mary; He was crucified, died on the Cross, and rose again on the third day.

THEN:

Standing by the cross of Jesus were his mother and his mother's sister, Mary the wife of Clopas, and Mary of Magdala. When Jesus saw his mother and the disciple there whom he loved, he said to his mother, "Woman, behold, your son," The he said to the disciple, "Behold, your mother." and from that hour the disciple took her into his home.

–John 19:25-27

In this revelation, God focused on the Second Office. This Second Office was revealed to the world at the foot of the Cross through the characters and relationship of people standing around at the Cross. Saint Mary Madelene is a convert; at the foot of the Cross symbolic of the future will have a female convert as God's chosen One, God's Vessel to continue the Lord Jesus's Mission. Saint John is the single disciple, and the one that the Lord Jesus loved most: the Lord Jesus's revealed the future of His mission to

Saint John in the Book of Revelation. This Book of Revelation is full with symbolism that no one can understand God's meaning. The hidden meaning of Saint John at the foot of the Cross, and the Book of Revelations that people have no understanding of in itself means that: People will understand meanings of the symbolism and hidden meaning of God's words under the Holy Scriptures directly from God through more revelations. The Lord Jesus fully man mother's sister, Mary the wife of Clopas: The sister of the Blessed Mother Mary reveals an adoption of a female into the Holy Family. Mary's (the wife of Clopas) husband not being at the foot of the Cross means that the female adoption into the Holy Family will not have a spouse with her in this journey of the mission. Through God's power, to carry on the Lord Jesus's mission for His return, will be a female sinner, a convert adopted to the Holy Family, taking over the Lord Jesus fully man's family responsibility; this female sister will serve the Lord Jesus's as God's Vessel. these symbolisms through God's chosen One; and that this chosen One will receive them.

Again, many more generations down the line, after the Lord Jesus was raised and ascended into heaven through the power of God, in the years 1947 an adoption took place.

I was born into a poor human family, a sinner into the Holy Family; I was converted in 1991, and the calling was manifested in the year 1994, forty-seven years later.

March 20, 1997, 9:12 a.m. During my devotion, the Lord Jesus commanded me, Mariette, His servant: "There are two separate positions in the Rebuild My Church Mission; one is inherited from the Mission's founder [God is referring to Mariette as His instrument], to oversee the president who is actually running the Mission. This person must be chosen from your bloodline; at the time the position needs to be filled, choose the one closest to you. If there are no religious females, then choose a priest. [The Lord Jesus means that nun and priest in front of God, not the earthly church nun and priest; single female or male, they then marry to God.] The other position, the president who will supervise the Mission's daily activities, will be chosen by the founder or the founder successor; and this position be held by a single male."

The estate of the Blessed Virgin Mother was bestowed unto me; I then bestowed my estate unto my descendants that choose by God.

The Revelation of the Three Names Meaning

There are the names that God named me, Mariette, "Suffering servant to the Father, the Lord Jesus, and the Holy Spirit, special to prepare for the Second coming of Christ;" the second name is "Michelle", and the third name is "Victoria."

When the Lord told me, "Your name is Suffering Servant to the Father, the Lord Jesus, and the Holy Spirit, special to prepare for the Second coming of Christ." He mean that, "Mariette, You are God's chosen one; your life is to suffer, and you will suffer more while you serve God. Embrace these suffering offerings to God for salvation of the human race.

Michelle is the female name for Michael; this name came from the Archangel Michael, and is symbolic that, through God's power, I battle through living sacrifices and embrace suffering, offering it to God for salvation of mankind.

The name Victoria is symbolic as God's Special Vessel and through His power, I will endure to the end and win victory for the kingdom of heaven.

28

GOD'S CHOSEN ONES

Mariette's Suffering and God's Promises for His Brides

April 11, 1997, 9:35 a.m. I was suffering during my devotion, and I said to the Lord, "Father, Lord Jesus, through the work of the Holy Spirit, I surrender this suffering to You for the Holy Eucharist Healing Services and Altar Call at the Cathedral of Saint Andrew and other churches; that young men and women will respond to Your call, commit themselves to serve You as priests and in the religious life, while others take on the financial responsibilities of Jesus' Church and others pray for these young men and women, with married men serving as deacons. I pray they will convert to you, and receive the Lord Jesus' body and blood through the Holy Eucharist."

The Lord Jesus said," Oh, little one, little one, I have poured into you many substances from God, and I am continuing to place more in you. You are the first and the only one to receive such substance from God." He then continued, "By Sunday you will see the bishop cry out to you for help for the Church and his diocese."

I knew that the Bishop Andrew J. McDonald cries out to God, not to me; so I then asked, "What do you mean? Seeing can be a vision in spirit or in nature. Help me to understand both."

In my vision I saw the Passion Sunday and Bishop Andrew J. McDonald blessing palms. From up high I was able to see the entire courtyard, almost to the gate. The number of people attending was so small, I estimated maybe two hundred. I said to the Lord, "Good Lord, Jesus, I have never seen any place with so few people attending a service that has a bishop, a main celebration. I ask You, next Palm Sunday, to fill this courtyard with people until they stream out through the gate, and onto the street."

The Lord continued, "The bishop has been praying for the church all his life, and for this diocese since he arrived here. But on the day you set your foot in this land, he understood My calling for him, and he prayed even harder. . . .Hold on to what you have, do not let anyone take your crown, and endure your suffering to the end. The living water is running through you. Do not make this difficult for Me, your God, like other Church's authorities." I said, "Lord, I am sorry that I have made this difficult for You, help me not to do this anymore." The Lord Jesus said to me, "I know you are suffering. You are trying so hard, and you are hurting. Your throne in Heaven is decorated with more gold and precious stones."

In my vision, I saw the foyer of the Cathedral of Saint Andrew; the spot at the bottom step of the rectory and meeting hall to the main entrance of the church; when the spirit of Father Scott passed this spot, the Lord said, "This is a holy place, they must purify their hearts before entering God's presence; not as those false miracle workers, false prophets and preachers claim." He continued, "The bishop is suffering with you for Me, and his throne in Heaven is also decorated with gold and precious stones. There are more diamonds being added on top of your throne; more marbles added on to the bishop's arm chair. I am the Son of the most high living God; I am speaking to you, the Princess of Heaven and Earth; Bishop Andrew McDonald, the heavenly host to the Father; and others that have faith in Me."

When I heard that Bishop Andrew is a heavenly host I thought of the Archangel Michael, and I said, "Lord, the Archangel Michael is a heavenly host." The Lord said, "There are many host in Heaven. Bishop Andrew is host to the Father." Jesus the Lord continued, "Peter Joseph Hung Tong is My beloved priest. I am carrying him in my arms. My suffering is also upon him. His throne is brightest, with pure gold. His throne is so heavy that no one in Heaven or on earth can lift it, but God alone is the One who lifts him up. His throne grows more heavy. I am the One standing in the midst of the seven candles, speaking to Peter Joseph Hung and those silently suffering in their hearts and making no complaint for My sake."

"Scott is My precious altar boy; assembling at My throne. He serves Me with delight in his heart. He is the altar boy that My Father loves the most, and He assigned him to serve Me. He will accompany Me wherever I go. He will be visible to many nations. I am speaking to Scott Marczuk and those who serve Me with delight in their hearts."

The responsibility of the position and meaning of the of Bishop Andrew, Father Joseph Hung Tong, and Father Scott are symbolic of me, Mariette; and of them will also be symbolic of each one of you, God faithful servants.

The "God's Commandments to His Brides" revelation and this one must go together to complete their meaning. In both revelations the Lord Jesus has indicated some names of the chosen ones and their calling, He is charging us with our responsibilities to pay for the debts we owe to ourselves, the inheritance that was given to us before we came down to earth. We will receive more treasures in Heaven than the price we pay on earth. On the other hand, the more sins a person commits, the more punishment he will receive after

460

death, if he does not convert and repent daily.

Even God spoke through His words, these words are symbolic. God wants each of you to seek Him for an understanding of His words in detail. I am only giving an overall view of both revelations. God is speaking to the world regarding His pilgrim church on Earth and Heaven, and those who the Father has predestined before the foundation of the world. Now it is up to each one of you to seek the Lord Jesus, to find out if your name is on the scroll. In order to hear Him you is must first seek Jesus and ask Him to purify your heart. If your heart is not pure, the devil will give you his calling.

Obedience to God Results in Victory Revelation

February 15, 1997. In my dream I was standing up high, facing the right top corner of a huge billboard. It was made like a wall, going from one corner almost to another corner of the room, dividing the room in two; it was filled with typewritten words. To my right, immediately outside on the left, in front of the billboard on the ground, was a square wooden high chair and a dark, muscular man. This man flexed his muscles frequently, and sparks of light came out as his muscles moved.

I faced the right top corner of the billboard; at this corner, I saw the first word of the top line; below this word, at the beginning of the second line was a long black spot. It seemed as if the word had been crossed out with black ink, and the first word at the beginning of the third line. While I looked at them, I explained to the dark man the difference between the first word on the top line and the first word on the third line. I said to him, "These two things are separate. The spiritual leaders say 'They go together.' I could change what I saw and tell them that they came together like the Church authorities understood, but I can not change; I must tell what I saw."

The man walked behind this billboard, and Father Hung Tong came from above down behind me, and crossed the room to join this man behind the billboard to do some research. I then saw Father Hung come back from behind the billboard and pick up the chair. I thought, "The research takes too long; he came to take the chair behind the billboard so he can sit down." But Father Hung picked up the chair and brought it to the middle of the bottom of the billboard and placed it there. As Father Hung moved the chair, I saw that a man was standing behind the billboard leaning against a counter like a cubical that was built into the wall, talking on the phone. Up in the ceiling, directly up from this counter a light was shinning on his head. In my thoughts, I knew that it was past eleven p.m. here and that it was daytime in the Vatican; this man was talking to someone in Rome, seeking assistance with his research."

The huge billboard represents the mission for which the Lord is calling me. The fact that the billboards are normally hung at the side of freeways is symbolic of God's commandments originating at the time He created the earth. The type written words are symbolic of God's commandments being clear in the Holy Bible, both old and new testaments.

As I saw and distinguished the first word of the top line; below this word, at the beginning of the second line was a long black spot symbolizes that God equipped me with a gift of clear discernment.

Father Hung is a Cistercian priest of strict observance, at the Abbey of Gethsemane: The name Hung is Vietnamese and it means "hero" in English. An order priest is symbolic of obedience to all God's commandments. Cistercian of the strict observance is symbolic of living a life of holiness, and his life is filled with prayer, fasting, and embracing suffering as he follows in the Lord Jesus' footsteps, carrying his cross and the cross of the Lord Jesus. The Abbey of Gethsemane represents clergymen who must always seek God for discernment before taking any action, with complete obedience to all His commandments, to please God, not to please man, and are always ready for their last breath. In this revelation, Father Hung is symbolic of the Lord Jesus. The Clergymen must always put these things in their thoughts and actions to follow in the Lord Jesus' footsteps.

The strong dark man is symbolic of [all] Church authorities, clergymen who lack discernment. His strong muscles that move frequently symbolize the things they do in this world to satisfy their flesh, and that their thoughts and works belong to the devil. The sparks of light coming from him represent good deeds. His strong muscles moving and the little sparking light are symbolic of spiritual leaders who focus on earthly things the majority of their time, and spend little time in spiritual pursuits to benefit their souls and the souls of those they serve. They mix good and bad together. His standing on the ground, to the side of the board, is symbolic of their lack of understanding of God's commandments, as they allow the devil to blind their minds, their eyes, and their hearts. When he heard my voice, his walking behind the board to do research is symbolic of God opening their hearts and minds, through me, that they might see the truth of God's commandments, and begin seeking Him. Their free will is now given to God, and is no longer given to the devil. His going behind the billboard and Father Hung's appearance is symbolic of their complete surrender to God, and His taking control over their lives like the light from above shining on this man's head. Talking on the phone at night to someone on the other end of the line in daytime, seeking assistance in his research, is symbolic of communion with God, walking in faith, completely trusting the Lord, and depending on Him.

The chair represents the Cathedral of Saint Andrew as well as Bishop Andrew. His placing the chair in front of the bottom of the billboard is symbolic of the Cathedral of Saint Andrew in Little Rock being the place God chose to gather His true servants for the Lord Jesus' Second Coming. And the Bishop Andrew is the first chosen one, the first Roman Catholic Church authority, to shelter me, Mariette and shepherd others in this mission to serve God. He is the first one in the Roman Catholic Church to clearly see this mission. In this revelation, Bishop Andrew is symbolic of the Lord Jesus; and the Roman Catholic is symbolic of God Church.

My saying, "These two things are separate," symbolizes that good and evil cannot mix together. "The Spiritual leaders saying 'They go together' " means that spiritual leaders thoughts and actions, plus what they teach their congregation, mixes the devil's works with God's works. "I could change what I saw and tell them that they go together, as the Church authorities understand, but I cannot change; I must tell what I saw." This means I cannot say things spiritual leaders want me to say just to please them. I must always say what God tells me to say.

My thought, "The research takes too long; he [Father Hung] is moving the chair behind the billboard," is symbolic of through me, God's mercy and love coming upon people; people will come to God, and begin to focus on eternal life in Heaven sooner than I thought.

During the night of February 16, 1997, in my sleep, I was in communion with God all night; but when I woke up, I remembered very little. I then said, "Lord Jesus, I claim everything You have for me and for others through me." I then felt the inside of my head shaking right and left, and I said to Him, "Lord, You said 'no'. What do you mean by the word 'no'? Lord, my head is shaking right and left. Jesus [as fully man] I am Your only sister in this world [by adoption through God's power], I ask You to whisper in my ears, and help me to remember the things You said, and to understand the ways that You spoke to me." The Lord said to me, "These priests are refusing to follow in My footsteps; they are going the wrong way; these cardinals [all churches] lead them opposite from the way I teach them. They are stabbing more wounds into My side." When the Lord said the words "more wounds into My side" in my vision, I saw the Lord Jesus hanging on the Cross, with the wound on His right side wide open. I then saw the revelation "Obedience Results in Victory" that the Lord revealed to me in my dream the night before.

And the Lord said to me, "Deliver this revelation to all the cardinals, archbishops and bishops in the United States of America, and place it in the third book, "Bride of Christ in Action" so Christians can read it; then pray for these clergymen to discern good and evil, and to follow in My footsteps."

Sun Shining on God's Servants

April 30, 1997. In my dreams I heard the Lord Jesus say, "I will separate the sheep from the goats." The Archangel Michael said, "Let go and see the goodness of the Lord." I then saw clear water running on the street in front of the Cathedral of Saint Andrew, and the rain coming down made the water on the street splash up high. The Lord Jesus said to me, "You move things through your thoughts, other people move things by their hands."

In another dream I was standing in the air above a snowy area. In front of me was something that looked like a tall, round, dark green mannequin. It was bigger in the middle, the top was round, and it had many straight hands around sticking out from the body. Suddenly, I saw a spirit enter the mannequin and give this mannequin a life. After the spirit entered, I saw these arms start dancing and waving up and down, there was only one arm at the back that did not move. I then said, "Oh, the one behind does not move." After I said that, the hand started moving, but it pointed down, while the others gently went up and down repeatedly. Somehow the one behind that was pointed down was formed like a chicken tail.

This mannequin turned into a living human body with many hands and the chicken tail then changed into a small white private airplane. This plane ran on top of the snow like skating, with the highest speed that no one in this world could compete with. The entire airplane was skating on top of the snow, it always had three wheels on top of the snow, and it was skating around me. I saw it in front of me skating from my right to my left, then it was hidden behind me, and then it was there again skating from right to left many times. Close to the last few rounds, I saw the pilot standing outside the airplane to control the aircraft, in the part between the fuselage and the tail. It then came again at my right side. While this plane was proceeding like the previous rounds, suddenly something came from behind me. It looked like a smaller airplane, and these two aircraft crashed. In front of me, at other side of the airplane that had been circling around me were some people on the snow. I got up and recorded the dream.

I fell asleep again. The Lord give me more dreams to help interpret the dream of the green mannequin tree turning into a human, and about the white airplane. These dreams were more grounded in nature; one of them was my book "God's Purification - Not Easy" inside a white plastic bag, tied with insulated metal wire. The plastic bag was white, but we still could see the front cover of the book.

The green tree mannequin is me, Mariette. The spirit entering the mannequin is the Spirit of God. It then changed to form a white private airplane; the aircraft is me, Mariette, the pilot inside is God. At first the pilot was inside, and that is symbolic of people only being able to see my physical body. Close to the end the pilot was outside the aircraft, and that is symbolic that close to the end of my life, the actions of God upon on the world will be more visible to people. The time the two aircraft crashed is the end of my life, and the anointings will be transferred to my blood line descendants. People on the other side of the aircraft are symbolic of other faithful servants to God.

I then got up, in my visions I saw a tall gold ciborium at the middle of the altar, on the center of the corpus, this ciborium stood in the middle of the crown of thorns. The Lord gave me this vision for the last several days. This means that at the altar, people can not see the host inside the ciborium. People only can see the white host, they can not see the

Spirit of the Holy Trinity hidden in the white host. The crown of thorns is symbolic of the gift of suffering that God's true, faithful vessels must embrace.

The Lord said to me, "Now I release you from the suffering that you shared with me all day yesterday and over the night. I love you more than everything in this world. Michael the archangel is your guardian angel, and by watching you, he also suffers with us. None of this suffering is from the devil, it all comes from Me, the Lord your God, God of all creation. With the love that you have for Me, I will never forsake you. For the next few days to several weeks you will have the sun shining on your face; from the East all the way to the West. The high authorities will see how the living God works through the poor and the lowly. The very same sun will shine on those who trust in me and have faith in Me to assist you.

The dream of the green mannequin transforming into a human and an airplane is symbolic of God in me that people can not see; they only can see me, Mariette. God also revealed that He is inside other of His faithful servants; in various callings, and also, the Lord revealed the Spirit of the Trinity is hidden in the Holy Eucharist. God is hidden inside His true and faithful vessels.

God the Father Clothed His Pre-destined Chosen One with a Sequined Pure Gold Cloak

May 4, 1997. In my dream I was wearing my green silk dress backward, the zipper was in the front and the bow tied at my back. As soon as I knew that my dress was on backward I searched for a restroom to turn my dress around. I went in two restrooms, but they were too narrow, and did not have enough room for me to move my arms to take my dress off and put on the correct way.

I then was sitting at the side of the street and two people were also sitting on the ground. In front of these two people was a monsignor. The two other people and I were facing a track of houses that were built on higher ground. The monsignor was holding the collar of a cloak, and another one was laid on his left arm; these two cloaks were made from cotton wool feathers. I was still wearing my green silk dress backward, with a gold cloak. The grain of the fabric inside my cloak was a very delicate net, each of the long oval flat pure gold pieces had a hole at the end, and was sewn to the net; the collar was standing up like a queen's cloak.

While the monsignor was fixing the collar of the cloak in his hands, he told me, "The scriptures the Lord gave to you were outside. You can ask Him for another scripture to be inside; He will give it to you."

I then stood up and walked to the door in front of me; I had to step up a few steps to enter the house. The room I entered was empty, I went to a corner and put my green dress back on the correct way. I then went out the door and while I was stepping down, somehow the back of my cloak covered these steps; I saw the middle of the hem was a triangle, with the point up. This triangle part was made from white dove feathers. This cloak was heavy because of the gold and diamonds on top of the sequins. Then the dream ended.

Chosen One on Earth and Beyond

April 2, 1997. In my dream I was at the side yard of the house, with my middle aged mother and my brother, about four or five years old. At the corner of the property was a food case was made from a wooden frame with a screen. It was as big as a wardrobe. The inside contained many bowls of food on the top shelf, in front of the door was a large bowl of noodles. My brother wanted to eat them, so I took the bowl down and put some noodles in a small bowl for him. I returned the large bowl back where it was, I did not eat any, although the major portion in the large bowl was for me. While my brother sat on the ground, my mother was standing, and I saw the spirit of the microwave oven on top of the food case. I knew that I had to leave this property to go another place, and my concern was, "While I am here should I do all the cleaning for my mother and take care of my brother? After I left this property, who will take care of the house?"

Property is symbolic of spiritual realm over the world. My mother represents the Lord Jesus's mission on earth. My brother symbolizes the mission that God entrusted to me. The food in the case is symbolic of God's commandments. The microwave oven is symbolic of supernatural power.

I then was in a classroom with a man, he was the school counselor. In my hand I had a long form with triple copies, the top copy was white card stock, the second and third copies were thin and yellow with carbon. The counselor assisted me in filling out this form. He did not understand the purpose of this form, but I knew I had to complete it to transfer the real property.

The counselor is symbolic of false ministries. Real property is symbolic of spiritual life of human His not understanding the purpose of this form means those false preachers think that they are rooted in God words, but they are not, because they are being blinded by the devil. They do not completely understand all God's commandments, they do not obey, and teach others not to obey God's commandments. They have denied celebrating the Holy Eucharist, and receiving the Body and Blood of the Lord Jesus, as spiritual food for their souls. They do not obey God's commandment. They do not believe that the Virgin Mary is their spiritual Mother, and that She is a Virgin. They also teach others disobedience to God's commandments.

I then approached the road to the high school, as I entered the road I saw the end of the soldiers property to my left. I saw a crowd of high school students on the road with some teachers, teaching them how to battle, to fight against those soldiers who just left. The students faced a row of track houses and used this house as a target to learn to shoot.

466

I thought, "The soldiers left before they learned to battle with them." I took one more turn to directly face the line of students on the road, I saw some were standing, some were sitting on blocks to rest. Then I was with my oldest daughter, she gave me two robes she made, one pure white, and another light gray, almost the same style. I was then outside the gate of the elementary school in Vietnam, holding my brother in my arms, with these two robes that wrapped at his hips. I put my brother on the ground. At the same time I was trying to separate the robes from him, but I accidentally pulled down his dark pants; he called my attention and I pulled his pants back up. I then left him outside the gate and entered one of the classrooms, but it was the wrong one. I entered a second classroom; there were a few teachers around the teacher's desk, I gave the gray robe to one of the teachers and another teacher introduced me to the rest of the teachers, saying, "She is an interpreter."

The teacher in this revelation is symbolic of false ministries. Giving the gray robe to those teachers means that God uses me to point out those commandments that they have denied to obey. Some admitted that they did not understand those commandments and explained to others.

I then stood at a little open space in between the trees. I looked down and very deep below were some children in the white water like clouds; next to the bank was a little girl related to me. She was holding a rectangular clear water jar in front of her. I looked up at the tree in front of me and there were some ripe fruits; the shape of this fruit was oval, and colored like dark plums when ripe. I was trying to find the very best one to throw down to her. I found a few that were ripe, but not really ripe, and smooth, and ate them. Finally, I found the very best one and threw it down to her. While I was doing this, I saw the church that I was on my way to. Both sides of the road were full with the same kind of trees.

Through these different dreams, God teach all of us to discern between good and evil.

The Woman and Three Beasts in the Jungle

April 26, 1997 3:31 a.m. In my dream I was up very high, looking down at the jungle. This jungle was like an illustrated picture where I saw a woman very clearly just entering the jungle, to her right, at her feet was one beast, directly in front of her in the middle of the map was another beast. The animal's faces looked like pigs, and each of the beasts had two horns. They were very big and fat. Then directly ahead on the straight road was another beast at the end of the map. These three beasts were on one main road and they were spaced almost from one corner of the map to another; both sides of the road were filled with big trees, and the trees stood separately.

I asked the Lord, "Lord, how come the woman is all by herself with three beasts in the jungle?" But I heard no respond. The Lord is warning His faithful chosen ones that the enemy spirits are within those people around you, those who reject the truth, even the ones that you love the most, such as a spouse, children and best friends. Therefore, they are all around you in the natural, but in spirit you are alone with God. The three beasts are symbolic of false worshipping.

The Relationship of God with His Obedient Servant

April 26, 1997, 8:23 a.m. In my dream I saw a president of the most powerful nation sitting on top of a small rectangular cherry wood table, the table leaned to the wall. He crossed his legs and his right shoulder leaned against the wall while his right leg leaned to the side of the table, his left thigh was over his right thigh. He had something like a layout for a presentation. It had three headlines and artwork at the bottom of the three lines, some blank spaces, and then the body of the presentation. This map was very big and colorful and sparkled with bright light, he hung it on the wall at his right shoulder. I came and kneeled at the foot of the other corner of the table, my right hand embraced his left thigh. To my left at the end of the wall was a room that was very dark. While I did this I felt that I really loved Him, and I wanted to have intercourse with him tomorrow. I knew that his wife was in that dark room, but he didn't like his wife that much. I then went to the restroom, this restroom had two pipe holes for sewers. I sat at one, and then changed to another and faced opposite the one I just used. I saw thick dark blood raining down both sewer holes by the water. This is symbolic of suffering and purification. I then went in the church, there was a Vietnamese priest with something. It was gold, and it looked like a lamp to me, because he was cleaning the lamp wick, but it was supposed to be a censer, while he was talking to me he walked toward another section in the church, I followed him; during the conversation, he called out my name "Believe". I entered another church, I saw some pews at the back section filled with big strong elders wearing blue jeans uniforms. I came in at the center aisle, passed these uniformed strong elders and went to the front section where some people were sitting. I got to the end of the third pew and I was exhausted, I could not walk anymore, so I sat at the end of the third row. I saw some children wearing white come in from the back of the church.

The Father said to me, "Hold on to what you have, do not let others take your crown. I am speaking to you. Endure to the end, there will be many tribulations that come upon the world. You are the only one who understands why these things are happening. I gave them my commandments, but they are ignoring my laws. I give you to Jesus, my beloved Son and He will give you the meaning of your dreams."

The Lord Jesus said, "The president is symbolic of Me, the Father and the Holy Spirit. You held on his thigh and wanted to have intercourse with him represents the love that you have for God, the Almighty, your Lord, your God, sweet God, merciful God, loving God. The restroom that you entered was not yours, it symbolizes the world will be cleansed, and the people will suffer. The military uniform of the elders at the back section of the church symbolize those who have been dwelling in God and live the life of holiness. The front section in the church represents those on the way to convert and repent; you are there to assist them. You are battling with the devil to the point that you are exhausted; when you are weak, you are strong in God. Children coming in are the holy angels fighting for them. The priest that played with the gold censer is not a priest, he is symbolic of the archangels, who consume and consecrate good deeds from those that believe in God."

Broken Water Pipe

3:15 a.m., April 22, 1997. In my dream I saw the title "The Vessel holding Special Anointing in Actions." At 5:49 a.m. The same night in my dream I was flying up high looking down at Cantrell road, and part of it was flooded with clear water. The Lord said to me, "Those who believe you will be live in the anointings. When they believe you they believe Me, when they believe Me they will obey all My commandments. The anointing works through a person when that person obeys all my commandments; if a person intentionally disobeys some of My important commandments, they are under the power of the devil." I said to the Lord, "Lord, in my dream I saw myself in the middle of the house, and was sitting on something like a bed. My ex-husband brought in some mail and laid it there and I went through it. I saw two square envelopes, they had a blue and red spotted border, one was from the Vietnamese government prime minister, and another one was from the United States senators. I opened both of them, but I do not remember what they contained. In the same house there was a square tank of water, in the middle of the tank was a hydrant, but it was broken at the top and water shot up high. I called the repair man. He came on a bicycle to fix the hydrant."

The Lord said, "I solemnly say to you that the broken water pipe will never be fixed." I said, "I am here to listen to you, and understand everything you say, this understanding is for my knowledge and my obligation is to deliver what you say to others as well." The Lord said to me, "You saw the baby giggling and went to the restroom inside the dark green triangle on the firm mattress bed, and you took care of the baby." The Lord continued, "I will not give the interpretation, if those who love Me want to know, they must read these books that I write with you through from the beginning, they must understand and remember the meaning of the symbolism."

For those who want to enter heaven, if you want to understand of the meaning of symbolism, the way of God's teaching, you must read from the "The Revelation Volume I" and so on, so you can understand, because symbolism is God's language; and if we want to hear God, we must lean His language from the begin.

Passed the Exam, Receive the Diamond Rosary and Diamond Cross

April 8, 1997. In my dream I saw there was a square on the ground, out in the open air, filled with people who laid on their stomachs. I laid on my left side with my teenage child, he also laid there with his face up above my head, next to the wall. There was a man wearing a military uniform holding a machine gun, walking in between people to make sure everyone laid flat on the ground. If any one raised up, he would shoot that person. I was afraid of him because my right shoulder was raised higher than everyone on this ground. The military man stepped his foot on the ground, directly by my stomach, but he did not say anything to me. I then sat up and leaned my back on the wall with my teenage child to my left; all the people on the ground were no longer there, except one line in front of me; there was a military man questioning each one like a verbal quiz or contest. When he came in front of me, people in the other half of the line were no longer there. He then said to me in the form of an answer instead question, he said, "There are over ten thousand poison medicines." I said to him, "What is a poison pill?" He then said out loud, "She is the winner." As he said this he walked very quickly to get the prize. When he came to the end of the property, he stopped there and talked to others in spirit to find more questions and returned to test me. He found some sheets of questions, but they had already been used. He then declared again, "She is the winner."

He came toward me with a single camping tent, inside this tent was the prize. I got up and saw both sides of the tent were open; I put my head inside the tent and saw a big crucifix. I was very happy that I won, I bent down and picked up the prize. As I held it in my right hand, it got smaller and looked like a pole in front of a house with a "For Sale" sign. It then changed, one side was a cross with Jesus engraved deep in the wood, around the Lord Jesus' body the cross was decorated with steel and diamonds; I turned it over and the other side was a regular crucifix with twelve pure diamonds in the cross, made like a rosary. I then turned the crucifix one more time, and it changed again. I opened a small door to see inside a jewelry box; in my thought, "I will build an altar for this crucifix next to the main altar, against the wall, just inside the entrance of my house." While I was thinking of this, in my vision, I saw a single door entrance to the house, inside the entrance were three steps, and the top step was higher than the other three. I then was walking with my teenage child on a dark road. This road had three different kinds of ground, the left side was highest with some iron mixed with the dirt, next to the iron was high firm ground, and to the right was low and muddy. We went inside the church where there were some people. Then the dream changed to my child and my going home to heaven. And the dream left me here.

In this revelations, God revealed the road of conversion from the heart, and God's reward the obedience.

God Warns Mariette of False Servants and Prophets

May 8, 1997, The feast of the ascension of the Lord. Just before I woke up, still in my sleep, the Lord Jesus gathered some dreams in the same revelation, then he said to me, "I pointed out in the dreams to show you every step you take will be difficult. And you always succeed at the end."

As I woke up, the Lord said to me, "Everything you ask is in the Father's will. The Father loves you, I love you, the Holy Spirit loves you, and My mother loves you. Every step you take is difficult, and you do not know how large the result will be. I love Bishop Andrew; he needs to suffer, and he is going to suffer a great deal. He will not suffer as much as you, but he will suffer more than he has in the past. If there is no suffering, there will be no trust in God. If there is no suffering and no difficulty, then it is not from God. The Bishop Andrew loves you, and he loves you dearly. I the Lord allowed all these difficulties to happened as well as allowing him to handle the issue for you; so the result can be more victorious for both of you. The Father said 'I have My hands on everything that My Princess takes actions about, I the Lord do everything My way, so My way is always victorious at the end; and My Princess will suffer. She knows that she needs to suffer; I will pour unto Her more strength, courage, and power to finish everything I called Her to do before She comes and sits next to Your right.' " Bishop Andrew symbolic of the Lord Jesus as fully man in glorify body. The Princess symbolic of me, Matiette.

In my dream I was walking in the open market; one of the booths was on the ground, a woman was selling a lot of small children's clothes, they were white and for girls, some were wool, some were polyester. Some people were standing at the front of the booth soliciting them, but I was not sure that they would buy anything or not. I purchased one little girl's polyester dress for nineteen dollars. It was size three, tight at the chest and loose from the under arms down to the hem, with light green trim at the seam between the chest and the body of the dress, and had long sleeves. I then asked her, "Do you have any size threes in wool?" but she did not find any. The people searching for their design left; I then changed my position from one side in front of the booth to the other side of the front of the booth. I then saw a small one; I picked it up and saw the label was size three; the seller asked me, "Where did you find it? I was looking all over." I replied, "Right there." I asked her, "How much?" She said, "Eighty six dollars." I offered nineteen dollars, but she did not sell it to me; I then left her booth.

I saw a woman sitting behind one of the booths selling something; she was eating beef jerky, the big round end of the beef jerky had almost run out; she asked me, "When you go out to the market, would you buy some more beef jerky for me? This beef jerky was delivered to me by a young girl, but I ran out of supplies before her next delivery." As she said this, with her hand, she cut out a piece of the beef jerky in her hand and gave it to me, but I did not take it from her. I then quietly walked away from her shop, thinking that she asked me to buy the beef jerky for her, without paying too much money.

I was in the open market again; I was standing far away and saw a booth with a counter; above the counter on one of the poles hung some plastic bags of small round sticks of beef jerky to sell. I recognized that was the kind of beef jerky that the woman asked me to buy for her, but I did not buy any.

I then woke up, and the Lord said to me, "I am saying to you, all these dreams are counterfeit of God. They are showing services to God, learning the words of God; but these actions only exist in public, not in their hearts. The woman did not see the size three polyester, and your showing it to her symbolizes people who serve God without seeking God in their hearts. The white polyester dress that your bought from her for nineteen dollars is symbolic of the mission; I the Lord chose you to obey all God's commandments to complete the assignment at the end of the world; but the people in the church do not see this from God; they are going to claim their own rewards in the end, at the judgment. Some of them serve me to assist you from their hearts, they will receive rewards, but those who pronounce they are serving Me by assisting you, they do so externally, not from inside their hearts, and they will receive zero."

The Lord continued, "I order you to place this revelation and the Father's statements to you at the end of the book in progress, the purpose is that I alarm them to convert and repent. The title is "The warning from God."

The Lord continued, "The dream about your standing at the side of the street and trying to get the public transportation; you were almost a hitchhiker; people went by driving bicycles, motorcycles and other kinds of vehicles, but they can not give you a ride because they have no room, and because they ignore you, they went by fast without knowing that you were on the street. Yet, you did find one that had room for you to get in, it had only two passengers inside, the vehicle was almost empty. He made a very quick stop for you. He then quickly took off. Both of your hands were at the two corner side bars, with your feet on the step, and he was driving recklessly. You told him to stop for you to completely enter the vehicle, but he did not stop. You then give up on him and stepped back down on the road. You again stood at the side of the road like a hitchhiker; one after another passed you by, some of them had room but they did not stop to pick you up. Yet, at the end there was one that stopped for you; this driver waited for you to get inside and sit in the left end corner of the vehicle. While the vehicle was running, two other people sat still, but where you sat rocked terribly because of the reckless driver. You held tight onto your belongings; these belongings God has entrusted to you - your address book and calendar [inside the leather Day Runner], and your uniform. You embraced them, you were fighting so you wouldn't lose them on the road. You even wore double pants and put the wallet inside your tight black exercise shorts to protect it. But the wallet was too

472

big, it stuck out in front of you making you look like a pregnant woman. It did not seem right for you, so you took it out. You held on to protect the wallet and your uniform to the end."

The Lord continued, "The driver stopped to load plants from the nursery. You went in the nursery to check the plants, while others purchased them. These plants were expensive; you were interested in a pot, its leaves had two veins and hairs on top and fig fruit. You thought the leaves that had sections would be symbolic of the Trinity; you then asked the driver, 'How much for this plant?' The driver said, 'Almost one hundred dollars.' You bargained, 'Twenty dollars.' You then asked, 'Will you continue to go on this road?' He said, 'Transporting these plants is my business; I have to do my business. I will not continue on the road that you want to go.' You knew that you were close to your home; you entered the parish gate to take the inside road; but the inside road had many turns and would take a longer time to get home than the main road. You got back to the right side of the road trying to get another vehicle, but there were none going on this dark road. In front of you was a road that you must take to go home, but it was all dark, and you could see nothing." While the Lord was saying this to me, in my vision, I also saw of everything He said.

I said, "Jesus the Lord; Father, my God; the Holy Spirit, my advocate, My Lord, everything is in Your hands. I have nothing to do with all of this; but You, Lord, God, You have everything to do with every action. I am just You instrument, nothing else."

The Lord said, "These vehicles are symbolic of the church authorities toward you; the way it was and the way it will be in the future. My beloved, the more you suffer, the more victory you have at the end. The more you stand firm on your feet, the more these churches authorities will suffer. Their suffering is to pay for their sins, the sins of not obeying of all God's commandments; the sins of holding tight to their earthly crown; the sins that make everything difficult for God's chosen ones; the sins of exalting themselves in public and in private; these sins are almost unforgivable. But, I the Lord, loving and merciful God; I forgive every sins that they commit against Me; but the sin against the Holy Spirit will not be forgiven; these people do not understand what sins are against the Holy Spirit. The Holy Spirit is a person, being sent by My Father and Me; He is in you and with you to do this work. When these church authorities are against you, they are against the Holy Spirit, they sin against the Holy Spirit."

The Lord continued, "They want discernment, more discernment and more discernment; but their hearts and their actions are not pure enough to receive discernment from God. Some of them have almost no faith in God; if there is no faith in God, no pure heart, no service to God with their heart and souls, then there is no discernment in them. Many of them would like to have discernment; the majority of them have no discernment; they mix good and evil. This is happening in the church these days, from the cardinals down to priests, to deacons and religious people. They lead my people without discernment of good or evil. They are liable for the sins of misleading my people."

The Lord then said to me, "Suffering Princess, none of them want to hear this. But, I command you to disclose everything I told you to publicly deliver to them. Give them every possible chance to reach at My words. They have ears and eyes, they are out to open and hear this. Put these words in their hearts, and put this in their actions, obey all My commandments."

*The public transportation the Lord spoke of is the Lambretta, one kind of public transportation in Vietnam before the fall in April 30, 1975. It has three wheels and two benches at the side. The maximum capacity is ten passengers for the old model, and twelve passengers for the new model. It was open around was with a few iron bars, and an iron roof. The new models have two corners between the driver's cabin and passengers compartment. The entrance was from the back, it has two higher oval corner bars at the end of the benches for the security of the passengers. The entrance has no door; the new model is higher than the old model, so the new model has a small step below the floor at the center of the rear end.

God's Faithful Servant Visits Heaven

May 8, 1997, 10:04 a.m. The feast of the Ascension of the Lord. The Lord Jesus said, "I am the Lord God of all creations. The Father created this world from Me and for Me. I have a lot of love for all the living creatures that the Father created. The first time you visited heaven, the Father poured out a lot of love unto you, and mercy unto the world. He is very firm on all of His commandments. No one can escape from His nest that covers the entire world. Everything He has revealed to you is true and will be in the world. I assure you, many will repent and convert, and many will refuse. You saw in the dream one driver that refused to give you a ride to finish the road; another was a reckless driver so you decided to walk alone in the dark of the main road. You are not alone; you are walking in the darkness of God. In this darkness, you must always completely trust in Me, the Father, and the Holy Spirit."

The Lord Jesus said to me, "In the dream you visited heaven. The Father was symbolically sitting on the couch in the living room, behind Him was the dining room, and at the corner of the counter inside was the kitchen. The other side of the wall by another couch had a bedroom."

The floor plan in the dream was the same plan of my apartment on the third floor at the Riverwalk apartment complex. Except in the dream we were up high in heaven, the living room had two couches, my living room was empty; the bedroom was dark, and my bedroom had some light. It had the same kitchen counter, and the same bathroom. The Father I saw in the dream was formed by a white cloud, and I only saw from His belly down to His feet. He sat with his left leg crossed over His right leg. To his right was another long couch; behind this long couch was the wall and this wall divided the living room and the dark bedroom.

Mariette Gathers Laundry to Wash

May 22, 1997. In my dream, I saw myself standing on highway Q15 road, on the same side and the same street that I saw in the dream of May 8, 1997, the feast of Ascension. In this dream I was a little ahead from the previous dream. A man was with me on the side of the road, but I only saw a shadow, he was the driver of a lambreta, and he assisted in bringing dirty military uniforms to wash.

Above the village, to the same side we just passed, I saw the ex-spouse spirit trying to prevent me from taking these clothes to wash; I feared that if I did not hurry, I might not be able to pick up all of these long military bags full of dirty clothes.

The vehicle was parked at the right side of the road. Directly across from the side of the vehicle was a small residential street; in front of the third house from the street, there were three to five bags; while I was loading them on the vehicle, I told the man, "about two houses from here, there are another two bags that we need to pick up." He walked toward these two bags, and I said to him, "No, you can not walk, we will drive there and pick them up, after we finish loading these bags."

I saw the vehicle parked at another small street, the driver sat in his seat, two houses away from the first location. The first house had its side facing the street; in front of this house were two bags of the same kind of military uniforms, some of them were loose outside the bags. I picked up these two bags together with the loose uniforms.

I then saw the vehicle change to a big and high transport truck. In the large cab of the truck an ex-spouse sister-in-law sat next to the driver. I stood between the ex-spouse sister-in-law and a large plywood passenger door, this door was locked with a metal hook to the outside of the cab. My back faced the corner of the windshield, and my right hand held onto the back of the passenger seat. My left hand tried to keep the door closed, but it stayed open while the vehicle was running. Because I was in a standing position, I was able to look at the road in front, the driver, the ex-spouse's sister, and through the back window in the cab. I saw the truck go very high and it had a part attached to the end of the truck; this long narrow part was made from plywood, and it was empty. All the dirty clothes were in the main body of the truck; there were some people spirits moving around in this narrow tail, and it seemed like these spirits were doing something.

I said to the ex-spouse sister-in-law, "Can I bring this laundry to your house to wash?" She replied, "I may move out from that house shortly." This woman wore a dark Vietnamese triangular hat made from palm branches.

I saw the road curve around a square corner, turning to the right. Before the road turned into the square, the left part outside of the square had some shelters with banana trees. These shelters were for people to take a break while they were working in the rice fields. The top of the shelter was made with dry rice straw. I heard a voice come out from above the shelter, even though I did not see anyone, but I feared the ex-spouse was still following and trying to take away my laundry. At this time the vehicle returned to the lambreta like it was when we started, with only me and the driver.

Somehow, the vehicle no longer existed. After we turned the corner; I saw some dark colored horses standing to the left side of the street, on the outside of the corner. I sat on the back and shoulder of a white horse, but the horse's body was like a lamb with curly hair; the head of this white horse had a lot of very long hair. My white horse faced the dark horse, he lowered his head, and kept his head still, and bent his knee down, but his back was raised very high. He pushed with great strength against his head; while the bottom of the horse was jerking and wanting to leave. I had to use both hands and hold very tightly to the hair on his head to keep sitting on the horse.

I then saw myself sitting on the passenger side of the lambreta, with those dirty clothes that we picked up in the beginning. The road now had houses on both sides. While the driver was driving, I stuck my head to the side, looking in the alley to find Mrs. Glass, the ex-spouse cousin, to have her wash these clothes. I did not find the first alley, or the second alley, but I saw her at the plaza, surrounded with houses. People were there to pick up military clothes to take home and wash, and then bring them back. I was very happy. I got out of the vehicle and said to Mrs. Glass, "I have more clothes for you to wash." She follow me to the lambreta and helped me unload them. While I unloaded these bags, I held a Discover card in my right hand and was about to use this card to pay the driver after we finished unloading.

I returned to the vehicle after the last trip of unloading to pay the driver; but the vehicle and the driver both turned into a globe of light clouds, I said, "He is an angel." I turned back to the plaza and saw this plaza also turned into a globe of light clouds. I said, "They are angels." I said this twice at the end of the dream.

Later in the same day, in my vision I saw the white horse jumping up high in the air with both of his front feet higher than his head and going forward on the road. I then saw I was driving the white horse, while the white horse was taking time and walking in front of the other dark horses.

The dirty laundry is symbolic of people coming to conversion. Military uniforms are symbolic of a spiritual battle. The long wooden tail attached to the back of the truck with spirits of people doing something around is symbolic of counterfeit servants. The dry rice straw shelter with banana trees and the voice coming out from above the shelter is symbolic of the world's media system. Dark horses symbolize the spiritual leaders. I, Mariette am myself; the white horse is symbolic of power, glory, and the grace of God carrying me. The white horse with his head down means humbleness, his back moving powerfully is symbolic that through my prayers, God pours out His power to do His works through me. The white horse jumping with his front feet higher than his head is symbolic that God works in spirit. Driving the white house in front of the dark horse is symbolic of God's plans being fulfilled in the natural world. The square corner bend in the road is symbolic of holiness, the inside corner is better than the outside corner. The ex-spouse is symbolic of those refuse to conversion.

29

LOOKS LIKE GOD, BUT NOT FROM GOD

Discernment is the Most Important of our Life

In my dream, I was flying over a long road with the members of my family and other people. This road was covered with many different kinds of crafts hanging over the road. I came to an end, in front of me at this end was a woman who purchased a purse made out from craft material from this road; and behind me others also bought other things out from the road we were flying on top of it. But I did not find anything that I liked; I wanted a transparent scarf to tie my hair back with. I looked around and I saw some hair decorations on the wire fence, but they were not what I wanted.

This dream is symbolic of life on earth, there are many things that attract us away from God. People either have no discernment or very little discernment; they then fall in the trap of the devil.

After the dream on the road, I saw in another dream a long line of people waiting to get in the cruiseship at Disneyland. I also wanted to get on this cruise ship, but I did not join this line at the end. I came out from the large, bright empty building up high and stepped down on the ground, at the beginning of the line where everyone just stood and leaned to the wire fence. I was walking at a very fast speed, and there were some people also walking along, these people walked faster than me. We entered the theater gate; this gate was like the gate between the border of two countries. As I entered, I saw this theater was huge, it was divided in two parts; to my left was a huge area, I only saw it was dark, and the ground was way below the part that I was standing on. Another part was the part that I was in, it was up high and had some light. The concrete floor was empty before we entered. To my right was a high stage; in front of the stage was a row of black plastic vinyl chairs with metal frames; these chairs seemed like they were connected together at their arms. People were running for their chairs from both sides of these chairs. There were two that were connected together by a counterfeit pearl bracelet. I took off the bracelet, sat on one chair, and saved the chair to my right by leaning my right palm on the seat, for my older brother; they were scattered up high in both parts of the theater.

I then put this imitation pearl bracelet on my left wrist; the main pearl was as big as my wrist, and it had some smaller pearls around the bracelet. I looked at my real gold diamond bracelet on my right wrist and compared these two.

I then saw a group of boy scouts come through in front of us. The boy scouts were wearing white shirts, navy blue shorts, a light green triangular sash, with their gold-colored triangular flag on a wooden pole. They walked all the way to the corner, and stood in a triangle formation, the pointed end to the corner, and faced the stage. Their flag was held by one person at the right.

And then more people came and sat on the floor in front and behind us. I saw female teenage dancers coming out from behind the stage, proceeding onto the stage. These dancers' outfits were made like angels wings, with the same kind of counterfeit pearls that I found on the chair and put on my left wrist. While these dancers were proceeding out, but before they got on the stage, I heard the woman sitting in the chair to my left call out to them. I turned to her and asked her, "Are these dancers your children? I mean are you their teacher." She denied it, "No, I did not call them; a person at the end of the row to our left was calling out to them." While she was saying this I saw a spirit shooting from her left shoulder to the end of the row.

Then there was a man who brought over a small rubber snake and gave to the boy sitting to the woman on my left; it was frightening me to death. I cried out loud, but this boy and the woman at my left kept playing with this snake in front of me; I continue to cry out louder and louder. Then a man came from the corner entrance and took away this rubber snake.

This large building is symbolic God Church. The boy scout group is symbolic of those who go anywhere for God, even if they have to die for Him, in humble hearts. The dancers are symbolic of those who serve God in the sanctuary without their hearts for God, but for their own name, their earthly crown. The woman to my left is symbolic of those throwing rocks and hiding their hands, like the man in an early dream that proclaimed that "she is not the winner". Playing with rubber snakes is engaging with the work that belong to the devil. Outside and inside the building like a theater is symbolic of the actions that a majority of the people in God's Church are making shows in front of God.

The Book of Revelation, Chapters 12 and 13 Meaning

On June 10, 1997 I went to the Guardian book store in Little Rock, Arkansas, to purchase a Jubilee card for a Cistercian of the Strict of Observance, and also a copy of Our Lady of Fatima's peace plan from heaven. While I was searching for the pamphlet "Our

Lady of Fatima's Peace Plan from heaven;" I saw some books regarding Medugorje; and at the time I paid for the pamphlet and the card, I saw the enclosed "Chaplet of Our Lady of Medugorje;" I picked it up and read it. Quickly the Spirit of the Lord spoke through me to a woman at the bookstore check out, about the Chaplet of Our Lady of Medugorje, "This chaplet is counterfeit of the Chaplet of Divine Mercy. Today, many of spiritual leaders are lack discernment to understand the visions and apparitions."

When God open the veil between the natural and supernatural to any one in this world to see His glorify body, the Blessed Virgin Mother, or any saints must have to real purposed. The mission that God entrusted to he or she is not simple like just go out and be a speakers to delivery messages of what they heard. But the mission that God entrusted to he or she is impossible for man to achieve, and God works through that person alone. The mission that the church leaders or spiritual leaders will go against, and he or she have to fight against them with God's power, at the end will be victory to build the kingdom of heaven, and spiritual leaders will follow.

Over two years ago, through my dreams and visions, the Lord revealed to me that the Medugorje phenomenon is a counterfeit illusion of the Spirit of God. But I asked the Lord, "Lord, you speak to the church authorities." Since then I did not hear from Him until June 10, 1997. Before this information was revealed to me, I heard from women who said that Our Lady appeared to some children at Medugorje, some that went away later got married, some still see her.

The deep secret of Satan and his works are introduced the "Announce the First Mystery" in the chaplet of Our Lady of Medugorje. This deception means the devil is saying the messiah will come in the flesh, or Lord Jesus will return to earth in the flesh. The serpent's trick later will induce someone and say "I am Jesus, or I am the messiah;" and he will go against the Lord's teaching, which is:

> *If anyone says to you then, 'Look, here is the Messiah!.' or 'There he is!'*
> *do not believe it. False messiahs and false prophets will arise, and they*
> *will perform signs and wonders so great as to deceive, if that were*
> *possible, even the elect.*
>
> *–Matthew 24: 23*

Yet, the Lord Jesus will return in a cloud at the end of the world, to judge the living and dead, not in flesh and working on the earth to teach like before.

> *And then the sign of the Son of Man will appear in heaven, and they will*
> *see the Son of Man coming upon the clouds of heaven with power and*
> *great glory. And he will send out his angels with a trumpet blast, and they*
> *will gather his elect from the four winds, from one end of the heavens to*
> *the other.*
>
> *–Matthew 24:30-31*

June 11, 1997, in my dreams the Lord revealed to me more of the occult spirits; spirits that belong to the devil. In the morning, the Lord Jesus explained to me that the apparitions at the Medugorje were occult, from the lying spirit:

> *The LORD asked, 'Who will deceive Ahab, king of Israel, so that he will go up and fall at Ramoth-gilead?' And one said this, another that, until a spirit came forward and presented himself to the LORD, saying, 'I will deceive him.' The LORD asked, 'How?' He answered, 'I will go forth and become a lying spirit in the mouths of all his prophets.' The LORD agreed: 'You shall succeed in deceiving him. Go forth and do this.'*
>
> *–2 Chronicles 18:19-21.*

The morning of June 11, 1997, before the 12:05 mass in the Cathedral of Saint Andrew, the Lord Jesus told me, "Write a letter to Archbishop Agostino, Apostolic ProNuncio regarding the Medugorje apparitions. The spirits that belong to the devil are manifesting there, church leaders have no discernment; they are misleading My people."

> *Why do you glory in evil, you scandalous liar? All day long you plot destruction; your tongue is like a sharpened razor, you skillful deceiver. You love evil rather then good, lies rather than honest speech. You love any word that destroys, you deceitful tongue.*
>
> *–Psalms 52: 3-6*

My responsibility to the Lord is to deliver what the Lord Jesus asked of me. The above revelation come with instruction from the Lord Jesus, delivery this revelation to spiritual leaders and to the public.

God's Spirit, Enemy Spirits and the Charismatic Movement Revelation

August 9, 1997, at 4:22.a.m. The Lord Jesus said to me, "Princess, would you send this tape [cassette tape number 443], and the previous tape [cassette tape number 442] to two cardinals in the Vatican for Me. These are the two who must know all this information to lead people in the correct ways to come to Me; Cardinal Ratzinger, and the Cardinal that is in charge of the Congregation of the bishops, Cardinal Bernardin Gantin." I responded to the Lord, "Lord, I thought, You told me that they will ask me for these tapes." The Lord Jesus said, "They will ask you [for them], but it will take too long for them to come to you. It is quicker to save souls for you to send to them; instead, you are waiting for them to come to you. Send these tapes together with the "First Wine and the Last Wine" revelation. Tell them what is contained in these tapes. I will dictate the letter to you."

The Lord Jesus continued, "Here is how you are going to say in the letter, 'Dear His Eminence, the Lord God, Jesus Christ, the Son of the Most High living God, commanded me to send this letter to you. Enclosed are copies of: the "First and the Last Wine" revelation; a letter to Most Reverend Andrew J. McDonald, August 2, 1997. August 2 is the most important day for the Church, of the last phase of the Lord Jesus' mission. In these two tapes, the Lord Jesus revealed, the dangerous animals are symbolic of the church leaders' hearts. The future of the church leaders; and its congregation of conversion. Some will refuse to deal with the truth; [those who] fear to deal with the truth will not be saved. In the second tape, the Lord also revealed of the charismatic movement. The devil exalts himself through the people who accept him, through the charismatic movement. Jesus the Lord had revealed this [charismatic] to Saint John, in the Book of Revelations about the power of the second beast. I enclosed it here for you of the interpretation, that the Lord had revealed to me some time ago.' "

The Lord then said to me, "Now you end the letter, tell them that this letter was dictated to you. Put in exactly what I told you to put in the letter. Saying, I am just an instrument of God. I fear for the life of the Church. I urge you, quickly to take the most important step; get Lucifer, and his offspring out of the Roman Catholic Church. I will pray for you to have courage, take the most important step in your life, to shepherd your flocks."

Note: The contents of the "God's Spirit, Enemy Spirit and the Charismatic Movement Revelation" was mailed to Cardinal Joseph Ratzinger, President of the Pontifical Bible Commission, on August 10, 1997

The Meaning of the Second Beast

April 8, 1997. In my dream I laid on my left side asleep on the bed; the sound of an electric typewriter machine rolling woke me up. I rolled my stomach down on the bed, raised my head up and I saw the invisible hands of my earthly parents put some kind of form inside the typewriter on a small table next to my bed. On the other side of the table was another canopy bed.

Printed in the middle of the instant carbon paper were six boxes in two rows, and the typewriter filled in those boxes. I then saw three names on three lines, the first names were more clear and they read "Nha Trang," the earthly father's name, the second line was the earthly mother's name and the third line was their children's names, but the second and the third line I do not remember their names. I saw this form on the table, next to the typewriter, and the hands of my earthly father had written more names in these six boxes.

I then saw these six boxes projected up high, between the ceiling and the top of the wall. In the middle of these two rows were two boxes, one on the top row and another on the bottom row that was filled with names of the two dogs, they were spelled the same, but I knew that there were two different dogs. I complained to some people walking by in this room, "These people filled their dogs name in these boxes and projected them up high." It means that they exalt their dogs

I stood on the grounds of a huge piece of property that I owned, next to me were several thatched cottages. I saw people freely entering and walking on my property. I saw in spirit in the middle of the property, people were doing business, they claimed my property in their name, and they blocked out my name. I was very angry that they encroached on my land, and did not let me put my name on. I said out loud to all of them, "You do not let me put my name in with you. The only place that has my name alone is on the legal paper, the Grand Deed."

I then was standing in front of the oval corner of a fake, high wooden counter. I tried to put three pure gold rings in three different sizes on my right little finger, but my finger was too big for the smallest ring, I could not put them on yet. To my right, a little in front, next to the counter was a young woman with tan skin. She wore three gold bracelets on her right wrist, in different sizes. Up high on the other side of the high counter were two statues hanging on the wall, these two statues were two women, both of them were fat. Behind the statue that was closer to the corner, it looked like this statue had been nailed on cross; her right waist had no clothes and I saw her white skin.

I then said to her, "I will go visit Father Cinnamon in Dinh Quan. (Dinh Quan is a village in Vietnam. Before the year 1975, at the time I was in Vietnam, the communists hid in this village. Father Cinnamon was locked in a communist education camp for thirteen years, and he had been tortured by the communist soldiers. He ended up with several serious diseases and his faith had completely turned against God.] But this woman did not know this place, I continued, "The place has a Marian day each year." She replied, "He is dead, he died from a terminal HIV disease, he was constantly going out of the camp to have intercourse with prostitutes. After he died, they found the disease all over in his clothes."

I then heard a spirit in the open air in front of the counter, little behind, to my right, singing the verses in Vietnam, "Ngay xua tren doi Golgotha"[in English means formerly day on Golgotha hill]. The tan woman sang with them; I knew this song when I was teenager, so I sang one verse with them. I then quit while this woman still sang with them.

I woke up in the middle of the night praying for the interpretation, and the Lord Jesus said to me, "That is the deadly sins. This man will explain to many others about the second beast in the Book of Revelations, I chose him for this calling. He joined other people in this kind of worship. When the owner of the printing company, and others understand the meaning of the second beast they will go out and rescue others from the deadly sin." He continued and said to me, "In the dream, you did not know that Father Cinnamon was dying, because you did not know that the action of the devil use people body to performed false healing is a deadly sin, but the tan-skinned woman knew that it was a deadly sin, a mortal sin; she then told you that "the priest is dead." Once a person goes out and has intercourse with a prostitute they have committed a deadly sin."

The Lord continued, "You joined them at the time you first converted. Those who come and join them are not committing a deadly sin; the deadly sin is only charged to the founders of the ministries." In my vision I saw the Bible class, the founder operating in a charismatic revival, that I attended from May 1994; but in September 1995, the Lord sent the Blessed Virgin Mother to take me completely away from associating with them.

The Lord continue, "This is spiritual death, this sin will not be forgiven, until it is completely revived in spirit. I will show you in the scriptures and explain to you. In the Gospel according to Saint John the first Chapter said, 'He came in flesh among his people, but his people did not accept him.' When they did not accept Me, they did not accept God, but not all of them will go down to the place below, some of them will convert and they will get to heaven. If they get in the Heaven, there is still a drawback on them, they will not receive a position in heaven."

I went back to sleep, and got up in the same night, the Lord said to me, "Read John chapter one," He stopped me at John 1:5 "The light shines in the darkness, and the darkness has not overcome it."

The Lord continued, "After I went home to Heaven, the darkness of the devil still continued. To those who believed in his name means those who crucified Me, after they did they knew that I am a Son of God and believed in Me, that means revival."

He came to what was his own, but his own people did not accept him. The Lord gave me John 1:11

The Lord Jesus gave me John 12:42-43 *Nevertheless, many, even among the authorities, believe in him, but because of the Pharisees they did not acknowledge it openly in order not to be expelled from the synagogue. For they preferred human praise to the glory of God.*

The Lord said, "Many of them may have been aware that the spirits were not from God, but they preferred human praise to the glory of God. This means people believe humans and are against God's commandments. I will help you to put this in the next book, the title is 'Charismatic is second beast'

The printing shop owner is also symbolic making more copies, and in this revelation is symbolic of generating more followers and actions. The tan-skinned woman is a symbolic spirit of the enemy spirits. The Lord is saying many people in charismatic movements hearts are impure, and the devil or his offspring hidden in their bodies raise up their flesh, the devil knows this is a deadly sin, he then pushes more power into it to make more people to follow them. This is counterfeit of the Holy Spirit, and it is blasphemy to the Holy Spirit, as the Lord Jesus said, all sins will be forgiven, except the sin of blasphemy against the Holy Spirit. There are also some people with their hearts are pure in the charismatic renewal, but the percent with pure hearts is very small.

Those who commit deadly sin (s) and revive, with the mercy and love of God, these souls enter heaven, but they will not be rewarded with any position in heaven. The Lord Jesus said in the Bible 'sitting to my right or my left is not Mine to give, it was reserved by My Father.' The Lord explained to me about the founders of some ministries in detail so I can clearly understand and deliver this revelation to others to save their souls; the details of the explanation.

The Teenager with a Deformed Arm

I then I saw myself standing in the middle of group of people, these people were facing me, with their hands at their chest, keeping their eyes very closely on me; these people wanted me to pray over them so they could get healed. I very quickly saw behind these people, a teenager child with a deformed right wrist and hand. I knew that the Lord did not want me to pray for these people, He wanted to use me to heal that teenager's deformed wrist. I had to turn around to find this boy; when I found him, I grabbed his deformed arm with both of my hands and prayed for him. After I finished praying, I saw his right wrist and hand grow like normal, even looking more pretty than his regular hand. Two thirds of his arm and hand was healed, one third of his arm that was close to his elbow was still deformed.

God is searching for those founders that are being led by the devil to bring them back to Him. The hand was healed, but the part still deformed is symbolic of revival, but he will not receive any compensation in the way of rewards for building the kingdom of God.

Keyboard and Monitor without Computer

April 10, 1997. In my dream I was sitting in front of a table high up to my breast, with the keyboard on it. On the other side of the keyboard, directly in front of me was a monitor, to my right, at the corner of the keyboard were two more monitors, all three monitors seemed like they were fighting for each other's spot.

All ten of my fingers were on this keyboard, each finger took its position according to the typing rules. I then saw all ten fingers slide off these keys to the right. I then somehow stood up and moved all my fingers back to their positions, and pushed all of them down at the same time, as I did this, my female organ felt the satisfaction of sexual intercourse. I quickly thought, "That is a sin. How could this happen to me?"

As I woke up after this dream, during the night; the Lord said to me, "The dream I gave to you, is to complete the revelation that you do not fully understand of intercourse in the spirit." He continued, "To the rule of typing all ten fingers, each of them have their own position on the keyboard. In the dream when you saw all ten fingers slide off their own positions to the right symbolizes breaking the rule of typing. The three monitors that stand close together to your right, at the corner of the keyboard without a computer are symbolic of a counterfeit Trinity, because their is no computer. Pushing all ten fingers down to the keyboard and feeling the satisfaction of sexual intercourse without another human body is symbolic of intercourse in spirit. This dream symbolizes intercourse in spirit that I gave to you to help you to understand those dreams that you had the night before. The false healer ministers operate by the power of the devil, just as I revealed to John as a second beast."

Conclusion of the Meaning of the Second Beast

In the year 1994 and 1995, at the time I went to Bible study, the people raised their hands, some of them really shook their hand very strongly. I asked some of the people that attended there for a long time the reason for their actions, but none of them knew the reason.

I remember the first time I attend a healing service at the Good Shepherd Church in San Diego, the enemy spirits jerked me to the point that the woman, a Charismatic leader and another man had to hold me down and pray for me for a while before the spirit released me.

March 1997, on Larry King live, CNN broadcast an interview with a man that Larry King called a religion superstar miracle worker. Larry King asked this man, "Do you know why they [the people attending a crusade] fell on the ground?" The man [religion superstar miracle worker] replied, "I don't know. There was a time I felt when I was alone."

The Lord God called me as His instrument to reveal to the world. He also teaches me by letting me go through what He is teaching me, so I can speak what He told me to tell you, with the experience that I went through.

God's power is very gentle, peaceful and calm, and is very powerful. When God's power is upon a person it will "never distract" any one from focusing on Him. God is the Almighty God, the Creator of heaven and earth; we must always be in the good manner of worshipping before His presence, focusing on Him, not at a party, dancing function or socializing. Therefore, any actions that draw people away from focusing on God comes from the devil. The devil has the purpose of exalting himself through human bodies; and distracting people from focusing on God.

The gift of discernment is the most important. This gift only comes to those who obey all God's commandments, daily examine and repent, and who try their best to keep their hearts pure, with love, their works are benefits other not themselves.

If any one is disobedient to any of God commandments or/and the Holy Father's teaching then there is a devil's spirit interfering or controlling that person's mind, and will come to his actions.

God Reveals Enemy Supernatural Power Manifesting .

On June 17, 1997, at 4:28 a.m., the Lord Jesus said to me, "I need you to send Cardinal Ratzinger a package regarding the events that are happening at Medugorje; send him exactly what I am going to dictate to you."

The Lord continued, "The odor of Medugorje is from Lucifer. He wants to be like God. He has been cast out from heaven. He is now creating the earth as heaven for himself." The Lord stopped and gave me some instructions, then He continued, " The package will include: (1) a letter to Archbishop Agostino, Apostolic ProNuncio; (2) the interpretation of two chapters of the Book of the Revelations: the dragon and the beasts; (3) and the copy of the [My] Web site. I am going to give you dreams to go with the instructions."

At 5:28 a.m. I woke up with these dreams: In my dream I saw myself inside a large building like an aircraft hanger; I walked into the right side of the front entrance, and there was a small area close to the corner that was built out of concrete barriers, like the ones used between the lanes of a freeway.

This area was filled with square and rectangular shapes. One side and the back were the walls, one wall was made from the concrete barriers, and the front of the area was also made out of these concrete barrier pieces, and they were about 30 inches high. Between the front of this area and the front wall of the building was an empty space for people to either stand or sit and shop for their products. This area was added onto the building, therefore its back and one side used the walls, the other sides of the walls were outside the building.

As I reached the front corner of the area, I saw a green, cone-shaped cluster of grapes hanging in the air, above the barriers. I came close to the wall, and sat on the balls of my feet and leaned my legs on the top of the short concrete wall. While I was sitting there, I saw some people working. In front of me was the back side of a woman named Ngam. (Ngam is a Vietnamese name; in this revelation is Ngam nghia; in English to gaze.) In front of the Vietnamese woman, on the floor at the center of the area was a big, clear white rectangular plastic container with a lid on it. It was filled with strawberries and a few long pieces of crackers. The crackers had some sugar on them. They had just brought this container back from the commissary. Somehow I knew this woman named Ngam. I saw her open the lid of the container, and I leaned over the barrier and asked her, "Can you give me a few of the crackers?" But she did not want to give me any, she ignored my request.

There was another person who gave me some crackers. Miraculously, as she handed the crackers to me, they changed into office supplies. Next, to my right side, I started a little fire by putting a few pieces of charcoal inside the concrete barriers, on the ground, and lighting them; the wind was blowing and it made the charcoal fire burn fast. I turned around to my right to find some dry small branches to help light the charcoal, and while I was looking behind me, the front wall of the building was no longer there. I saw in front of the building a park, with short green grass cut neatly, but barely growing. There were some trunks of trees without leaf, and on the other side of the grassy lawn was a big man-made pond, but no dry branches I could use for my fire. I then turned back and looked at the charcoal fire, and I heard an invisible person tell me, "Why did you start a fire next to those boxes, it will burn that stuff!" The trunk in this revelation is opposite Moses saw God through burning brushes. The trunk is not burn symbolic of no present of God.

I then turned back to look at my burning charcoal; I saw a few piles with boxes of small black binder clips, paper clips, and small staples at the foot of the fire, about to burn. I said, "I just bought a box of the black binder clips at the Office Supplies store." I reached over and took some of the staples and put them inside an empty envelope box on the ground to my right. While I was busy trying to choose what I should get, there was a woman on my left who took a lot of these office supplies. I looked again at the staplers and clips in the envelope box, they no longer had a box, and they were rusty. As I looked to my left, that woman was no longer there, but there was a small iron office desk, both sides of it had many flat drawers like a tool box. This desk was rusty like it had been left in a junk yard for ages, and it also tilted to the front. Above the desk in the air, were two boxes of thumb tacks having colorful plastic on their ends, and one box of nails. The nails had no base at the bottom, and they are in clear plastic boxes.

Then I went outside the building on the way home. To my left was the same man-made pond, but it seemed big like the ocean to me. To my right as I was approaching, were three military buildings, like bungalows. The one in the middle is lower than the other two. These buildings have cathedral roofs, and these roofs were a light color like clouds, but I knew that they were not clouds. While I was walking home, I was thinking that I must cook dinner for my spouse. As I thought of him, I saw a taekwando teacher. On his left was a child, high up in the air, inside the middle bungalow building. This Taekwando teacher worships Budda. He came to my house with nothing, he contributed nothing, and I am no longer obligated to make food for him. I do not like him.

I was then walking back on the concrete sidewalk. To my right is the same man-made ocean, to my left was the building that I saw before with the Taekwando teacher and the child. A little behind to my left was a boy dressed in the same cloud color as the roof of the building. Suddenly, he was standing in front of me, with a very long skinny snake. He took the snake and wrapped it around my waist several times. I was fighting, and my right hand crushed the head of the snake. My left hand pulled the snake off of me, and threw it very far behind me.

The snake is symbolic of the devil either in spirit or hidden inside human bodies; symbolic of obstructions in the journey of this mission. I crushed the snake head symbolic of through God's power I will destroy the devil hidden within man bodies. I pulled snake off and threw it behind me symbolic of I will overcome obstructions, won victory.

I then saw myself laid down on my stomach on the sidewalk, at the same spot where I was standing. The ground with grass on my right side was high, and there were more snakes. At the end of the high ground with grass, on my right, level to my shoulder was one big snake, and its head was smashed. On my left, behind, was the same boy, trying to pull a small boa constrictor from a hole in the grassy ground. I was fighting and shouting out loud. This is same version of prophet Daniel in the den of lion.

I got up, still fighting, but the Lord calmed me down. I remembered that the Lord revealed to me about Medugorje.

The Lord said, "There were three parts of your dream: the first part was about a man, a Taekwando teacher inside a military compound building. He is symbolic of the devil, Lucifer that has been cast out of heaven, now he is in the world. The child is symbolic of the devil's mission, or his works. He came down with nothing, and he is eating the food. The food that you thought to bring to him is those people being around the false miracles in Medugorje. The child wrapping, a snake around your waist is the same child inside the building with the Taekwando teacher, he is symbolic of the devil's mission The snake, serpent, and the skinny one that wrapped around your waist are all symbolic of the enemy spirits that attack. You have to fight to rescue people that are unable to discern, they are coming to Medugorje. Other snakes are on the ground and are the people that the devil influences or controls their minds, and do the works for the devil. The boy who tries to get the boa constrictor is symbolic of the devil working to bring his false miracles into the systems of the world."

The Lord Jesus continued, "The corner behind you is the corner of the earth in the Book of Revelations. The person that spoke to you from behind you is an angel. His saying, 'You charcoal fire is on the way to burn those office supplies boxes' is symbolic of the works of God on the way to destroy the devil's works. The old rusty supplies inside the new boxes are symbolic of its looking good on the outside, but inside are evil works that other people cannot see. They are taken in and keep on being taken in; but when they came to you, you discerned very quickly; because, I the Lord have given to you. When you took the staplers and put them inside the envelope box, it no longer had a box. Naked staplers are symbolic that you see inside the hearts, dirty hearts, the works of the devil that can not hide from you, because I the Lord have given this to you. You compare the clips that you purchased at the store and these ones. The ones you purchased at the store were paid for with money, and the other ones were free. The money is symbolic of suffering, and sacrifices to God. Free, no charge, no cost: people these days want the benefits from God but they are not willing to suffer so their souls can be clean. The container is full of strawberries with just a few crackers. The crackers are made with flour, sugar, and oil, and it takes work to make crackers. They are sweet with sugar, and standing in front of the container is symbolic of the outside looking good. It seems that God sent His mother to save souls, but there are only a few crackers. The other parts are strawberries. Strawberries are grown from the ground, the fruit lays on the ground, the berries are dirty from the dirt and the vine is filled with hairs. This is a counterfeit of grapes. Grapevines grow up high, grapes make wine and are offered to the Lord at the altar. Strawberries have no seeds, there are no future plants. The grape has seeds inside and these seeds are transferring into guava seeds. Guava is firm and strong, it has a lot of seeds, and it is symbolic of the words of God that will multiply. I leave this interpretation here for the Cardinal [Joseph Ratzinger] that is charged with the Doctrine of Faith, to come to me in his prayer: I will speak to him of the real food from God. But I am going to give him the interpretation of the rusty tool box, that built the table, this rusty tool box is counterfeit of the altar."

While the Lord was speaking of the counterfeit altar, in my vision, I saw the rusty desk in the dream, with the Cathedral of Saint Andrew's altar up high afar and covered with a white table cloth. The rusty iron desk symbolic of impure hearts. No base nail symbolic of proclaim the things without of the mission and foundation of God's commandments.

Obeying God, I mailed the content of this revelation to Cardinal Joseph Ratzinger, on June 17, 1997.

30

1997 HOLY WEEK

Passion Sunday

I indicated at the beginning of this book, and now I clarify it again: I am just the Holy Trinity "instrument."

March 23, 1997. Since that first Sunday, January 12, 1997, I had been attending mass at the Cathedral of Saint Andrew. Day by day I saw how few people attend weekdays and Sunday mass. I have seen the cathedral almost empty, and it tore my heart for Jesus, and for you, Father Scott, and for others devoted to God who serve Him in this holy place.

Today, Passion Sunday, while I was standing on the top step by the side cathedral door, looking directly at the center of the Saint Francis's courtyard where the Bishop and Andrew McDonald were blessing palms, I saw you and Deacon Gary beside them. From up high I was able to see the entire courtyard, almost to the gate. The number of people attending was small, maybe only two hundred. It tore my heart even more, and I said to the Lord, "Good Lord, Jesus, I have never see any place with so few people attending a service that has a bishop and a main celebration. I ask You, next Palm Sunday, to fill this courtyard with people until they stream out through the gate and onto the street."

After the Holy Mass the Lord Jesus told me, "I ask you to be here in the cathedral with me, an hour before the washing of the feet on Thursday."

Later today, after the mass, in my devotion, I saw the spirits of many people filling the courtyard, through the gate and out into the street in front of the cathedral.

Chrism Mass

After moving to Little Rock, Arkansas on January 12, 1997, according to the Lord Jesus' instructions, I registered at the Cathedral of Saint Andrew, and have been attending the cathedral ninety-nine percent of the time. One of the commandments the Lord Jesus gave to me is that I must go to mass and receive Holy Eucharist every day.

Usually when I attend this cathedral, I sit in one spot, at the end of the third pew, right section, side aisle, in front of a huge pillar, where people cannot see me from behind.

On March 24, 1997, Monday of Holy Week, the Chrism Mass was held at 5:30 p.m. I went in the cathedral's front door at 5:10 p.m. and saw that it was filled with people. I looked for my usual seat, but it was already taken, so I found some empty pews, at the side, in the corner close to the sanctuary. I sat there for a few seconds, then I saw a place in the front pew on the right.

I was uncomfortable sitting in the front row, so I said to the Lord, "Father, Jesus give me peace and calmness; I am not comfortable in the front row, but other people are sitting in the place I normally sit, and there is no other space for me." Immediately I was at peace, and I felt the Spirit of God very powerfully. I prayed, "Holy Spirit, teach me to come to the Father and the Lord Jesus. Blessed Virgin Mother, my beloved Mother, pray for me. Holy angels and saints, intercede for me. Father, Lord Jesus, You brought me to this land. I am not worthy to be here as Your chosen one, but I am obeying your instructions. I ask You, Lord, to send all the heavenly angels to this church, to surround us today, as we offer You our hymn of praise. I petitioned You earlier today, for You promised me you would bestow the gift of discernment upon all the priests here today, as well as others in this Diocese of Little Rock who were unable to attend. I ask You again to open their minds and hearts, to focus on You, and live a life of holiness, serving You through service to others."

After the blessing of the oils, about a hundred people from the sanctuary came down to proclaim the sign of peace. The Lord Jesus had reserved this seat for me, and used me to deliver His peace to several priests. Early in the service a priest approached the second woman on my right and said, "Did you bring me any meatballs?" Then he gave her a hug. Silently I said, "Lord help him, he does not know what he said here." And a little later, to my left, another priest came up from behind, hugging another woman at the edge of the front pew. As he was about to step into the sanctuary, he said to her, "I just bought a boat." I said to the Lord. "Jesus forgive him, he did not know what he said." During this time, my uncle came down from sanctuary to gave me huge with blessing, and there also about four priests shake my right hand

All the priests joined the Bishop, speaking out loud at the consecration; in my head, I also joined them the proclaim the holy scriptures to consecrated bread and wine. I then questioned myself: "I am not a priest, why I am joining them, and not just listening as I always do?" I then gave myself the answer: "I am not a priest on earth, but in front of God I am."

Throughout the entire service of blessing the oils, and during mass, I was surrounded by the glory of God. The presence of the Holy Trinity was so powerful covering me and connecting to the altar that it radiated to the sanctuary. The Lord has bestowed upon me the gift of sensitivity to His Spirit; when I am in public I am able to feel what He wants me

494

to do, even without hearing His voice, dreams, or visions.

That night, during my sleep, I prayed Chaplet Divine Mercy. After I finished, in my vision, I saw I myself standing at the same spot where I was at the Chrism Mass, in the front row. On the other side of the kneeler was the Lord Jesus, as fully God (invisible), wearing an expensive gold satin cloak, like the one priests wear at the benediction. Around the collar, and on both sides down in front and around the hem, were three lines of pure gold. He was at that time twenty-five years old. He brought me back to the moment when I had silently joined the bishop and priests at the consecration, and He told me, "I was within you, and I consecrated the bread and wine into my body and blood, by saying 'This is my body. This is my blood.'"

I have been constantly begging the Lord to carry me during this mission, and I asked the Lord to remove my own thought and actions. The Lord Jesus has told me, "The Father accepted your free will on January 10, 1997." The January 10, 1997 is the first day I moved to Little Rock, Arkansas.

In this revelation God revealed the presence of the Trinity at the time of consecration, which people cannot see, but can only feel. That feeling depends on our faith and the degree to which we live a life of holiness. (Remember that every one of us are sinners until we enter into Heaven.) He wants us to focus on Him alone, from each of our hearts, as well as externally, by worshipping the Almighty God; not in a den of thieves, or on the playground, or while socializing.

Priests are God's instruments to consecrate the bread and wine into Jesus the Lord's body and blood. They must understand that when they are at the altar or any part of the church, they should absolutely not be thinking or talking about meatballs, boats, or any activity that feeds the flesh. Priests must completely surrender their lives to God and focus on Him as their spiritual leader in order to guide people in the proper way to receive the body and blood of the Lord Jesus with a pure heart, to nourish their souls. A priest has a responsibility to himself and to his congregation's spiritual life in front of God. The Roman Catholic Church bestows the title "Father" upon priests because they are the fathers of responsibility to their congregations.

The devil causes people's minds to focus on things that satisfy or benefit their flesh and go against their souls. Whether a person's heart focuses on God or on material things is revealed by the words that come out of their mouths and actions.

My responsibility is to deliver the exact contents of God's messages to others; there is no difference between addressing a teenager, an adult, a priest, a bishop, a cardinal, a president of the nation, or even my own children. When I do this I please God, and I love them, and this love is for the purpose of saving their souls.

The Lord reveals Himself to priests, and to all of us. During each consecration the Spirit of God is at the altar, more or less depending on the holiness of the priest who is presiding over the service. The Lord Jesus uses that priest as an instrument to consecrate the bread and wine into His own body and blood.

The Lord Jesus chose for me that seat in the front row, so I could hear the two priests talking about things that feed their flesh in a place of worship. This means they are focusing on earthly, not heavenly matters. Priests must focus on spiritual life and not on that which satisfies the flesh. The Church is the house of prayer, a place to worship God, not a place to socialize or talk about worldly things.

Jealous Church Authorities Try to Destroy the Rebuild My Church Divine Mission

March 25, 1997. In my dream, I entered a huge building that was being renovated, and I was immediately greeted by a woman who escorted me for awhile, then let me walk in the building alone. As I passed by the outside round corner of a high wooden counter, I saw a man pushing a small, false wooden portable counter in the shape of a "Y." He was holding the bottom of the "Y" and pushed one of its arms against my hip, and the other arm against my lower belly. He then pushed me all the way to the high round corner. I was stuck there, and I said to him, "The woman checked me out before letting me in the house." He then left me alone with his false "Y" counter.

I then heard the Lord telling me in my sleep, "The man is symbolic of jealous Church authorities."

The Lord Jesus Said, "The Rebuild My Church Mission is My Mission."

The same day, March 25, 1997, Holy Tuesday, before the Holy Mass: I was surrounded by the Spirit of God, and I said, "Lord, Father, the Holy Spirit is helping me to empty myself into Jesus." In my vision I saw that the gold satin cloak had been moved from beyond the kneeler and placed over my left side and across my shoulders. I then saw a black bow tied around my hair and around the collar of the black jacket I wore at Chrism Mass.

The Lord Jesus said to me, "I emptied Myself into you at the time you were born, but you rejected Me. Later you returned to Me. Again, I emptied myself into you by showing you that I hung on the Cross at Calvary, came down, and entered your body, but you did not understand. Then I covered you with my King's cloak, so you would understand." As the Lord was saying this, in my vision, I saw a vision that the Lord had shown me before at the Good Shepherd Church.

The man pushing the Y-shaped false counter represents the future when there will be jealous Catholic Church authorities claiming that the messages the Lord told me to deliver are not holy. But what he claims to be holy is counterfeit, merely external, and not from the heart. The woman in the dream is symbolic of the Roman Catholic Church examining and accepted the words that I deliver to the public.

The invisible God entering my body and placing the gold satin cloak with pure gold trim on my shoulders represents the power of God working through me in this mission.

As I pushed the "Y," I said, "The woman checked me out before letting me in the house." Those words are symbolic of the Lord Jesus saying, "This is my mission, and I do all the work through my servants; Mariette is only my instrument." He then crushed them down.

The Lord revealed that in the future there will be some spiritual leaders who will be jealous, and they will choose a counterfeit form of following in the Lord Jesus' footsteps. They will allow the devil to control them, and their preaching will go against the Rebuild My Church Mission.

Each One Have the Free Will to Feed His Soul or Abandon It

March 27, 1997, Holy Thursday. The Cathedral of St. Andrew's parish has a tradition of celebrating the Lord's Supper with a dinner at 6:00 p.m., before the Mass of the Lord's Supper at 7:30 p.m.

The Lord Jesus instructed me to register with the Cathedral of St. Andrew, and I obeyed Him, registering on January 12, 1997. Every time I saw an announcement I asked the Lord, "Jesus, is this one for me? Or can I join them?" One time He told me, "You can assist in a few of their activities, but not many."

I arrived at the cathedral at 6:05 p.m. and found that it was still closed. I came to the hall where the parish members held their traditional dinner and asked Deacon Gary to let me in the church. At the moment I kneeled, I felt the glory of God surrounding me. I then started praying, with the Holy Spirit leading me and the Lord Jesus spoke to me for over twenty minutes. Although I'm not able to remember everything He said, it was something like, "The Princess of Heaven and Earth, my beloved sister . . .the voice came from the desert. . ." My soul was filled with His spirit; God's power came with His words; whenever I need them, the Lord will bring them to me.

After the mass, Jesus the Lord said to me, "Stay here with me another fifteen minutes." I then sat down and said to Him, "Jesus, I will be here with You as long as You want; but please let the church allows me to stay."

He replied, "Matthew 4." I knew He was referring to the Gospel according to Matthew. I read verse one through verse seventeen, then stopped. I understood that enemies were attacking me, but the Lord Jesus is always within me, fighting for me, and I will prevail.

That night in my dream, I saw myself from behind; I was wearing a jacket that was formed by a white cloud; in the middle of the cloud was a long snake, thin as a pencil. Its tail was at my right shoulder, its head at my left hip; holding the head in my left hand, I tried to pull it out of my jacket.

Almost the entire the night of Holy Thursday, through Good Friday, I was fighting hard against the enemy spirits. The devil kept bringing to my visions a scene of the Heaven's Gate mass suicide in Rancho Santa Fe, California that I saw on television.

March 28, 1997. I arrived at the cathedral at 11:30 a.m., in time for the 12:05 Veneration of the Cross and Holy Communion. After I received the Holy Eucharist, the Lord Jesus said to me, "Princess of Heaven and Earth, the highly favored daughter of the Father, My beloved sister; I bestow the power of God upon on you. I will make Lucifer your footstool from this day forward."

Friday evening the devil was still trying to lure me into watching CNN for more news on the suicides; but I knew I was being attacked by the devil, so I said, "In Jesus' name I will not watch the news. Jesus, my Lord, my God, my savior, You are the savior of the world; tonight is the night You were hung on the Cross to die for the world; I will be with You." The devil then attacked me by giving me a good reason to call people in San Diego; but I knew that he was trying to draw me away from Jesus. I then began my devotion to the Lord by reading Scriptures and praying to the Blessed Sacrament; the devil was still trying to distract my mind, while attacking my body.

I struggled for awhile, then I said, "Mother, Blessed Virgin, I am Your only adopted daughter, teach me how to come to the Lord. Holy angels and saints intercede for me. Holy Spirit, You are God the Almighty, You are my advocate; teach me how to come to the Father, the Lord Jesus, and You. Lord Jesus, teach me how to come to the Father. Father, I come to you through Your beloved, begotten Son Jesus, in His name, and through the work of the Holy Spirit. Reveal to me which of my thoughts, words, or actions have displeased You, the Lord Jesus, and the Holy Spirit. If I have offended You, help me to repent and not to do it again." The Lord said, "You have not done anything wrong. You are fighting against the devil, and you will prevail in victory."

Then in my vision I saw the Scriptures concerning the temptation of Jesus; Matthew 4:1-17. I then saw an invisible hand pull out the snake from my jacket that was formed by a cloud. I saw the right bottom corner of the hem's outside layer open up when the Lord pulled out the snake. Then this corner flattened down; the jacket was now thicker than before. I said, "Lord God, I thank You for Your protection. You always answer my petitions." Then I said to the devil, "To fight the spirit of mass suicide, I am taking the authority given me by the Father; I am the Princess of Heaven and Earth, and you are my footstool. In Jesus' name I command you to get down under my feet." After that there were no more attacks.

The Lord's main purpose in allowing the devil with his spirit of suicide to attack me was so He could reveal His message to the world: Every time a tragedy occurs or anything deceitful happens, the devil receives more power from the Father to damage others, through broadcasts that include television, newspapers, and word-of-mouth.

Because the Spirit of God the Father, through His beloved Son, and through the workings of the Holy spirit are residing in my body, my body is a temple of God. God then fights the devil for me. Everyone who watches these deceptive news stories will have their lives affected. Those not dwelling in God will never be able to fight off the devil because he is spirit, and he is stronger then you in the natural.

Good Friday

I arrived at the church at 11:00 a.m. for the Veneration of the Cross at 12:05 p.m.. This included the Communion Service by Bishop Andrew, scheduled to finish about 1:15 p.m. I thought I might stay through the stations of the Cross at 2:30 p.m., although I hadn't eaten since dinner the night before. But the Blessed Virgin Mother brought me out for a quick lunch. I then returned to the church at 1:50 p.m., and as I went inside, I saw that two or three people were already there. I then saw the Crucifix that was used for veneration; it was lying on the ground. The top of the Cross was touching the second step of the sanctuary, and more than half of the crucifix was up in the air, with the foot on the ground.

I looked at it and wanted badly to come and kneel at the foot of the Cross; but I feared that I might distract others from focusing on God. I stood there for a moment, trying to determine whether it was Jesus who wanted me to kneel at the foot of the Cross or the enemy spirits who were attacking me. I knelt down on my heels for about five minutes to be in communion with Jesus, without fear of distracting people, then returned to my seat.

I continued my devotion, and the Lord Jesus said to me, "Sister, do you know what you did over there?" I replied, "No." He said, "You were weeping at my feet like Mary Madelene."

During the stations of the Cross, I walked to the foot of the Cross and remained at that spot, looking at Jesus each time it changed from one station to another, while almost everyone else was moving from station to station. At the first few stations a man and a woman stood in front of me, the Cross lying on the floor between them, their hips facing it. I felt angry because they should have known to move their hips away from the Cross.

Good Friday night before I went to sleep: During my devotion the Lord told me, "You stayed at my feet the entire time during the stations of the Cross."

It may seem that this story merely describes my communion with God. But through my actions that were led by the Spirit of God, He revealed this to the world: The Crucifix on the ground, and the man and woman facing it are symbolic of people whose hearts turn toward God, the way that many people's hearts treat God the almighty. My standing in one spot and keeping my eyes on the Lord Jesus' image as He hung on the Cross symbolizes God wanting us to focus in our daily lives on His dying on the Cross for our sins. The others moving from one station to another represents the fact that people's hearts are focusing on the things that satisfy their flesh. To them the stations of the Cross are only pictures on the wall, but the Cross lying on the floor is the one that was venerated just two hour ago, and the point of the Sanctuary. My wanting so badly to kneel at the foot of the Cross, and Jesus later revealing to me that I wept at His feet like Mary Magdalene, means that the love He wants us to have in our hearts for Him must be demonstrated in our daily actions.

Holy Saturday

Before I left the church on Good Friday the Lord told me, "Tonight, I will be with you all night, and show you the vision of Heaven being opened, angels descending, and the Son of Man coming in the middle of a cloud." After the Lord said this, I thought that He would show me the same vision He revealed to Apostle John in the Book of Revelations, Chapter 4, that was first given to me on August 31, 1995, and many times later. But what I expected was different from what He showed me in the dream, although the meaning was the same.

March 29, 1997 Holy Saturday. In my dream I saw a huge power pole like a tree that has no bark; it was so tall that I could not see the top. Up high, before I lost sight of the tree top, there were two arms like a cross, and on them were double power cables lying on each side. At the end both cables disappeared inside the cloud. As I faced the power pole, on my right, under one of the arms was the face of a man, about thirty-five years old; a triangular scarf covered his head and was tied under his chin. He had tan skin, and his face was oval at the forehead, then became slightly smaller at his chin; it was a powerful face. As I saw him, I knew this was the Lord Jesus, and I cried out loud, "Jesus, my Lord, my God, my brother." I then questioned myself; maybe this was a ghost, so I said, "Jesus, protect me." I then saw the entire pole again, and I understood that this was truly the Lord Jesus.

I then saw the auxiliary bishop of New Orleans, sitting in the only chair at a beauty salon, facing the door. His front was covered with a white gown, and behind him was a hairdresser, working on his hair. A friend of mine was standing by the door, and the bishop looked at her, fell in love, and married her in the Roman Catholic Church. She was a young girl, and in her heart she knew what was happening, but she had nothing to do with the bishop choosing to marry her.

After the marriage she stayed home doing housework. The bishop went to work at the parish office every day, and came home every night. But she became jealous of the women who worked with him at the rectory, knowing how they focused their eyes on him. But she was the wife, so the bishop came home to her, not to those women. The bishop knew that his wife was jealous, so he brought her to the rectory for awhile, for her legs were painful from walking all day. Then the bishop stood to her left, his right hand embracing her back; his secretary sat at a desk in front of them. The bishop said to his secretary, "Her legs are painful from walking all day. I will take care of her." As he made this statement the secretary listened carefully.

I then saw myself standing on the ground, to the side, in front of the Bui Thai Church. At the center of the grounds was Bishop An, wearing a black cassock. Several women were grabbing both his shoulders from behind, trying to push him down. As I saw these women mocking him, in my heart I thought, "I want to marry Bishop An, and after I marry him, he will change like the bishop who married my friend."

As I walked closer to the women and the bishop, I saw a woman inside the church to my left, with her two children, but I could not see her clearly. She said to me, "Can you tell the Bishop [of New Orleans] that my husband beats me?" But I did not answer her.

I then passed the church's grounds, sitting on my heels; to my right was my friend who married the auxiliary Bishop of New Orleans. She had with her many green bows in a line; these bows were made from one ribbon, without being cut apart. She laid them on the ground and explained them to me.

I remained in the same spot, but my friend was no longer there. Replacing her, on my left, was a woman with a rectangular box. She opened the box and showed me one object, but I could not identify what it was. I knew that she would leave the box here and go into the beauty salon to buy more supplies. I looked up and saw that the salon was closed. There was a man working inside taking orders from several people outside, but these people had to climb up to reach inside the store, through a small opening between the wall and the roof.

As I got up, praying for an interpretation, the Lord said, "The Alpha and Omega is the huge tall wooden power pole whose top you could not see. The Almighty is the two power cables paralleled, lying on the arms of the pole. I am the Son of Man whose face was next to the pole, with a scarf tied at My chin." He then continued, "The bishop being mocked by those women is symbolic of the Church today, which is being persecuted in many different ways. Your wanting to marry him and make him a better person means that after you help the Church by being active in the ministry, its future will be brighter. The woman with two children who was beaten by her husband, who asked you to speak to the Bishop of New Orleans on her behalf, represents spiritual leader who left the Church, and who now convert to God, asking Him to plead in their favor." (The Lord meant that they want God's commandments to change to suit their ways of living and preaching.)

The Lord continued, "Your friend who does housework, to whom the bishop comes home every night, is symbolic of you. The bishop represents Me, the Son of most high living God; I am in communion with you every night, you are My main servant. Her jealousy of others in the church is symbolic of the love that you have for Me. Your (her) coming to the parish rectory means you will soon be speaking to the public. Your painful legs represent your suffering; and every time you call on Me, I am always there for you.

The secretary is symbolic of the Church authorities; My telling her about your pain represents my telling the Church that 'She is My suffering servant; embrace her in your arms and take care of her.' The secretary listening attentively symbolizes that the Church authorities believe that you are suffering because of Me."

During the night, in my dream, I saw myself from the waist down, wearing expensive black silk pants; the trousers were wide and my bare feet were walking in a hurry. After the Lord dictated this interpretation to me, He then put me to sleep. In my dream, I saw inside the foyer of the Good Shepherd Church; there was a light blue desk, and in front of it was a woman who was also wearing black pants with bare feet. She was standing on her right foot, her left foot resting behind it, on its toe. I saw a cut on the inside of her left ankle, but it was on its way to being healed. Then the Lord said to me, "You are on the way to appearing in public."

> *In the beginning was the Word, and the Word was with God, and the Word was God. He was in the beginning with God. All things came to be through him, and without him nothing came to be.*
>
> *He was in the world, and the world came to be through him, but the world did not know him. He came to what was his own, but his own people did not accept him. But to those who did accept him he gave power to become children of God, to those who believe in his name, who were born not by natural generation nor by human choice nor by a man's decision but of God.*
>
> *And the Word became flesh and made this dwelling among us, and we saw his glory, the glory as of the Father's only Son, full of grace and truth.*
>
> –John 1:1-2, 10-14

On this Holy Saturday, through me, Mariette, the Lord Jesus revealed to the world that He is the holy One of God, the One who was, who is now, and who never ends; the almighty God. He is the Word, the Word became flesh; obedient to the Father unto death; the One knows no sin, but who died for our sins on the Cross to save those who obey Him. He then rose from the dead.

The Church that He established almost two thousand years ago is now being divided into many factions. Those separated from His Church want it to act according to their own ways; those who remain in His church have become rebellious and mock his faithful servants.

He is the Word; God the Father created the earth from the Word; that means that God the Father used Jesus the almighty God to create the world. But His own people have not accepted Him and continue to reject Him by worshipping idols and material things that satisfy the flesh.

He is a loving and merciful God; He has now sent His suffering servant to make this known to the world, before His return to execute judgment and reward.

Lo, I will send you Elijah, the prophet, before the day of the LORD comes, the great and terrible day.

–Malachi 3:23

Easter Vigil Mass

In this Vigil Mass adults were baptized and then joined the Roman Catholic Church in full communion with God.

I sat in the fourth pew, behind people who were baptized in that mass. During the entire time of the Holy Celebration, I had to fight against enemy spirits. Although there was the glory of God at the sanctuary, I felt there was something missing in the area where I was sitting. Near the end of the service and after I got home I was exhausted from fighting against the devil's spirit. During the mass these enemy spirits had been trying to make me think that the Bishop Andrew does not like me, because I came to this diocese and asked him to help me with the Mission. The spirits also tried to make me believe that the people in the Cathedral of Saint Andrew do not like me; but I knew the devil was attacking, and I asked the Lord to deliver me.

Easter Sunday

Holy Saturday night, before I fell asleep: In my vision I saw the Crucifix lying face up on the steps of the Cathedral of Saint Andrew's Sanctuary.

March 30, 1997. In my dream I was up high above the spot where I normally sit, in the third pew, to the right. I saw Bishop Andrew J. McDonald carefully step down from the sanctuary to where the first station of the Cross begins. He was wearing a small round pushia cap on his head, a light colored chasuble with a sash over his arms and shoulders, and his hands held the foot-high gold chalice, with a Cross on top of the lid as is done at the time of Benediction. I could not see inside, but I knew it was filled with Holy Eucharist.

I then saw him at the other side of the sanctuary; I knew that he had just finished going around the fourteen stations of the Cross, and this was the fifteenth station. He was standing next to the baptismal fountain, both his arms stretching up high over his head, his left hand holding a cup, and his right hand holding a priest-size Holy Eucharist. The power of God radiated around the cup and the Holy Eucharist, covering the bishop and the area high above him; close around the Eucharist the air was a light gold color, and beyond this halo the air was white like a cloud.

In another dream I saw myself and one of my children, about three or four years old, lying on the floor of a building, doing sit-ups. It looked as if people were holding a festival inside the building. We then moved backwards to the middle of a three-way walkway, to the center of the "T"-ways. At the foot of the "T" was a revolving glass door. My feet were touching the inside of a two-piece divider, made in the shape of "V." It then separated a little, and I used my feet to put it back.

My child and I got up, and he ran out the door ahead of me. I saw the spot where we were first lying, and saw a Bible with some toys. I went over and picked up the Bible, brought it to the clerk at the counter next to the door and asked, "Can I have this Bible?"

She responded, "I need to check." As she said this I noticed that the Bible's spine had changed from perfect binding into comb binding. I then turned around and saw the clerk entering the glass door, saying, "You need to go the high school to pick it up." I understood what she told me. "The high school is across the street, and is owned by the same people who own this festival and its building. They have this festival once a year, and they won't have another one next year, so they do not need this Bible."

Then I was outside walking home, holding my child's right hand in my left hand. I said to him, "I forgot to bring your milk bottle that I had the day before yesterday." I thought to myself, "Yesterday he was not drinking milk, but eating adult food, so he does not need the bottle."

He said to me, "I dreamt that I prayed in my sleep, and while I prayed I touched your nipples."

After I returned from receiving Holy Eucharist on Easter Sunday, I said to the Lord, "Jesus, I am happy that today is the memorial of Your resurrection from the dead. I do not have anything to say to You now, but I always claim that I am Your instrument." I then felt His power pressed in my mind, and I continued, "Your servant, Your sister, and highly favored daughter of the Father; when I return home I will claim that I am a Princess of Heaven and Earth."

The Lord Jesus said to me, "Today you have entered into the center of my heart. Your life in me will be happy. You are my precious stone. Today is the first day that I have been happy since I returned to the Father."

The Lord Jesus has revealed to us that after He ascended to the Father, He was still suffering because His church was so divided. Holy Week is the time for us to look back on His being crucified and dying for our sins. In turn He is silently asking us, "Do you love Me as you proclaim? Then follow in My footsteps through these celebrations: the washing the feet, the stations of the Cross."

This celebration is for people to convert and repent, and to follow Jesus, our Lord, our God, and not to just socialize and exalt their flesh. Instead, deep inside each person's heart and soul, they must obey all God's commandments to unify His Church.

31

RECEIVING THE HOLY TRINITY'S SPIRIT THROUGH HOLY EUCHARIST

God Revealed The Lord Jesus' Real Body and Blood Changing

At about 10:a.m., August 10, 1997 the Lord Jesus said to me, "When I said to you, 'When I am not in heaven, I am in the Holy Eucharist.' This sentence has two meanings."

He continued, "I said, 'when I am not in heaven', I mean for those false churches, churches that are not obeying the Holy Father. In front of God, they do not belong to My Church; they are dominated by the devil and his offspring. The Charismatic movement is also dominated by the power of the devil and his offspring. Therefore, any place that is dominated by the power of the devil and celebrates the Eucharist, these hosts and wine are not consecrated into My body and blood."

He continued, " When I said, 'I am in the Holy Eucharist', I mean that My flesh is hidden in the consecrated hosts and wine. Hosts and wine become my glorify body and blood after the consecration. My glorified body, I can be every place. I am in heaven, I am also on earth. When I am on earth, I hide myself in a very few people; these are the ones who I love the most in the world, they completely surrender their lives to God, obeying all God's commandments, they are even physically ready to die for Me, without fear."

In this revelation the Lord uses Charismatic movement as symbolism of the operation of those church as business; that using the name of God through the church to benefits individuals earthly life, not benefits souls, and build the kingdom of heaven.

The Holy Trinity Hidden in the Holy Eucharist Resurrection of the Bodies; Ark of the Covenant

Jesus said to them, "Amen, amen, I say to you, unless you eat the flesh of the Son of Man and drink his blood, you do not have life within you. Whoever eats my flesh and drinks my blood has eternal life, and I will raise him on the last day. For my flesh is true food, and my blood is true drink. Whoever eats my flesh and drinks my blood remains in me and I in him.

–John 6: 52-56

April 17, 1997, at 5: 13 a.m. In my dream I saw an open field in front of the church where an event, a play, was being held late at night without lights. I was sitting next to the front church wall, eating and eating red cooked sweet rice, Vietnamese call it xoi gac; with sesame mixed with salt. I did not have to pay for it, the sweet rice was provided by the church.

At the other side of the ground opposite where I was sitting; there was a skinny, short man, that was divorced by his wife, directing the play. Behind me, a little to my left was the younger brother of this skinny man. He was glorifying his ex-sister-in law, who was living with another man without marrying him after she was divorced. I turned to him to shut him off with a louder voice than him; he then stopped speaking.

Suddenly a heavy rain came down and some people were transported away by a big dark van that came and left in front of me. The rain almost stopped, but not completely; some people came out to continue to watch the play. I got up and walked to my right side of the field; the director's area had some people sitting on metal folding chairs inside the shelter.

I returned next to the front wall of the church, there was a lady sitting there with a big basket of red cooked sweet rice, but not as red as the rice I ate before. I asked her, "Is this free?" She replied, "Yes, it is free." I had a party plate in my hand to put some on my plate, together with sesame mixed with salt. She gave me some of what I asked for. I then mixed the sweet rice with sesame and salt with my own right hand; it became like bread dough. I felt embarrassed by eating too much, because this woman knew that I ate red sweet rice before.

I then was walking into another area next to this church ground. My mother said to me that we had invitations for three people to a concert by a famous Vietnamese religious singer for her event; and asked me if I wanted to come. I was happy that we were invited, because it was very hard to get to see this singer in person, because she was very famous.

It was about time to go, five minutes to twelve. I was still outside the house where a girl showed me the invitation for her group, and she said to me, "It is very close to here, it only takes few minutes. I saw on the inside of her invitation, a light print and a handwritten bold black "12 x 25 x 12"; but my invitation was different. On the front was a picture of two wooden wheels, like a wagon on cream paper, and the inside had a similar light print like hers, with a hand written bold black "3."

In the dream the Lord gave to me that was my mother, but she was a young girl wearing a Vietnamese dress, following me in the house where we lived. I said as she followed me in the house, "I will come with you," because at first I thought that I would not go, but I changed my mind and decided to go with her.

I hurried to the back yard go to the restroom because I ate to much. I did not want any one to see me through the door; I moved to the corner of the outside of the neighbor's wall next to my house, but their wall was sticking to the back. I sat on my feet to go the restroom on the ground; I saw soft stool in bright colors with a few dead leaves, and there was a lot. I had to move my feet two or three times. While I was going to the restroom, my mother came at the back door and looked at me and said, "You ate a lot of chicken yesterday and that is why you must go to the restroom." She meant about the soft and light color of my stool.

I knew that my mother was checking on me because she did not want to be late for the event. In the dream, I saw she was sitting inside the open window, at the rectory, wearing a white shirt. I then said to my mother, "She is still sitting in the rectory practicing her singing, we are not late." I thought, "Because she is the host, she must be there before the guests arrive."

I woke up and prayed for the interpretation. In my visions I saw the Purification Image that I laid on the counter of Rose Wood's Frame Shop yesterday, with a velvet red mat trimming the top left corner; the invisible hands of the Lord moved this mat together with the trim, from the left down to the left side, and kept the corner facing the image, stopped a few times, down to the bottom corner and stopped. He continued at the bottom, and the right side of the image and did the same at the left side. He then rested the mat with its trim at the top right corner of the Purification Image. I then saw the Purification Image transparency for the front cover of this book.

Then the Lord said to me, "You have finished the perfect job that I assigned to you." I replied to the Lord, "Lord, God, I thank you for raising me, giving me credit of what I have done, but not. I am just Your servant, Your instrument, I did what You told me to do; and yet Lord I was very careful to follow Your instructions, step by step; and I will continue to try, but everything I did was from You, nothing of it was mine; I am not worthy for anything that You assigned to me. I just obey You." Then the Lord asked me, "Do you understand what you see in the dream?" I replied, "Lord, I understand very little, and I am not sure what I understand is the same as what you said to me or not." He asked, "What part do you understand?" I replied, "When I went to the restroom it meant purification, and you are still cleansing me." He then said, " I solemnly assure you, I will continue to cleanse you until your last breath." I said, "Lord, I thank you for purging my iniquities constantly, that is the only way I am able to enter heaven immediately after my last breath, and my soul will join my body at the same time." He then asked me, "How do you know that your soul will join your body and enter heaven?" I replied, "Lord, I have been trying very hard, beyond obeying all Your commandments, by constantly trying to please You. For my effort to do all this, You will reward me after my last breath, and you will raise my body up on my last day." The Lord corrected me, "You forget what I promised you. I promised you that I will raise your body on your last day with your soul."

The conversation between the Lord God and me reveals the way that God purifies us; and He promised long ago that those who obey all His commandments show their love for Him. For loving the Lord through obeying all His commandments, He will reward our souls in heaven, and raise our bodies on the last day. When this revelation is interpreted in detail, each individual will be different in the way each soul enters heaven, the body is resurrected, and rewarded.

The Lord God then said to me, "I want you to title this chapter the resurrection of the bodies as God promised, or you can change the words around, God promises the resurrection of the bodies."

There are different meanings in the way the Lord said this revelation, do not understand just the way He dictated to me. You want God to fulfill His promise of raising up your body on the last day or you just say, "yes, my body will be resurrected as God promised." They are completely different meanings, and I will put them in the correct way.

The Lord said, "The play performed in the dark is symbolic of the actions of people in the world these days. You spoke louder than the boy's voice and he was stopped: The boy is representing those who glorify the evildoers; but you proclaim good news of God, and you will have victory at the end. The rain in the middle of play means God purifies the world, with many tragedies coming upon the world, while they were happy with earthly things; their earthly treasure will be destroyed in the hour that they are not expecting."

I then said to the Lord, "I am one of the sinners that You brought me back to You, I ask You to open the minds and hearts of other sinners to convert to You." The Lord said, "Those people sitting on the folding metal chairs inside the shelter represent those being saved by God. Your eating more and more red sweet rice mixed with sesame symbolize you are embracing more and more suffering." While the Lord was saying this, in my vision and in my thought I was thinking of the Book of Revelations 12:15-16.

"The serpent, however, spewed a torrent of water out of his mouth after the woman to sweep her away with the current. But the earth helped the woman and opened its mouth and swallowed the flood that the dragon spewed out of its mouth."

I heard the voice say, "She has said she loves the Lord, how does she prove the way she loves the Lord?" I responded to this voice, "I love the Lord by my complete obedience to all His commandments and I constantly try to please Him, that is the way I proved that I love the Lord." As I said this in my vision I saw the dream I saw on my birthday, January 2, 1996. I was exhausted after picking many coins and bills out of my left ear and mouth. I said to my spouse, "I am going to sleep and rest." I then got up, made a right turn, went to the corner and made a left turn. Outside of the left corner there was the devil asking the Lord Jesus, "How about her?" and pointed his finger at me. But I saw Lord Jesus was standing there defending me; I scowled at him and continued on my way to my bed in the exclusive room. The voice is symbolic that the devil will continue to claim our souls until our last breath, because of our sins. But the Lord Jesus will defend those who convert and repent daily, obeying all God commandments. From the time we convert and continue to be obedient to all God's commandments, Jesus the Lord will always be there to defend us. But if a person returns to their old ways of life, then the devil will gain more power over them before their conversion.

The Lord continued, "The van represents God evacuating people out of the tragedies." While the Lord said this, in my vision I saw the March 1, 1997 tornadoes in Arkansas. The Lord said, "The dead are dead, the living are alive, who will be evacuated by the Lord, or who will not; no one knows but God alone." The Lord means in these tragedies: For those physically dead, some will enter heaven, some will not get to heaven. For those physically alive, for those who convert their hearts to God and repent daily, then they are evacuated, they are alive in front of God; for those refuse to convert and repent daily are spiritually dead, they were not evacuated.

The Lord then said to me, "Princess, you love the world by being very careful to explain to them of what I said so they can be saved." The Lord continued, " The invitation is symbolic of a ticket to enter heaven. The wagon in front of the invitation is symbolic of the Ark of Covenant. He means those who enter Heaven must receive my body and blood with a pure heart." The inside of the invitation to my mother and me has the number "3"; the number three is symbolic of the Holy Trinity. The Lord said, "Receive my body and blood;" during the celebration of the Holy Eucharist, at the consecration; through the power of God, the host supernaturally becomes the body and blood of our Lord Jesus, with the Spirit of the Father and the Holy spirit. The Lord Jesus said in scripture, "I am in the Father and the Father is in Me." In another scripture the Lord Jesus said, "I will ask the Father, and he will give you another Advocate..... The Advocate, the Holy Spirit that the Father will send in my name, will teach you everything and remind you of all that [I] told you." When we receive the Holy Eucharist in pure heart, we supernaturally receive the body and blood of our Lord Jesus, together with Spirit of the Father and the Holy spirit.

The Lord continued, "The other invitation that has many numbers that multiply means they receive the Lord [Holy Eucharist] their God with impure hearts."

The Lord said to me, "You went to the restroom before you went to the event means you make sure that your heart is pure before you receive the Lord your God. The mother that checked on you symbolizes each one has a guardian angel to assist them. But for you, Princess, you are chosen for this calling; you have the Lord your God, the God of all creation checking on you." The Lord means that His presence is within those who have a pure heart; and He will do His works through them.

God continued, "You saw the singer practicing; you knew it was not late; while others were in a hurry to go, represents the world systems they are fighting for to satisfy their flesh, but for you, you very carefully discern what God has for you."

God revealed of people living in the systems of the world, and this system has led them to spiritual death. God pours down tragedies up on the earth. At the same time, God opens the hearts and minds of those who choose to convert and repent; and on the last day of their breath, they will receive eternal life in heaven, and their bodies will be resurrected on the last day.

The Lord Jesus Birthday Revelation

December 10, 1997. In my devotion to the Holy Eucharist in the Blessed Sacrament before the holy mass, the Eternal Father told me, "You bring the infant Jesus out tonight, get the three-drawer cherry wood chest and place Him on top. Do not put the cherry wood chest under the stairway; place it in your bedroom, the light and the holy Bible on top of the chest."

Immediately after I received the body and blood of our Lord Jesus, I prayed, "Lord Jesus, the Father answered to you when you asked Him to raise Lazarus from the dead; would you pray to the Father for me?" Then the Father said to me, "What you see and what will be happen are not the same. You are seeing the real apple; but when it comes it is real gold."

At 11:25 p.m. the Lord woke me up from sleep, He explained to me many things in the Bible, He then said to me, "The Word you proclaim in the Second Glorious Mystery, 'Our Lord Jesus ascended into heaven, sits at the right hand of the Father. Now He is on earth as the Second Coming of Christ, brings souls and dead bodies to the Father; through me as His main Vessel.' Go back and correct your name that I gave you. You are the suffering Servant, as a vessel to God Almighty, the Father, the Son, the Holy Spirit, a special mission for the Second Coming of Christ. This is your spiritual name. Do not change it, because you do not understand."

He continued, "The Church official will not certify for you to testify in the Church, but you are testifying away. They are fearful of not knowing what will come out from you. The Pharisees, elders and scribes did not accept Me. It happened to Me, it happened before, it will happen again to you. You are undercover to bring out the truth. The church leaders will certify you after you leave the earth. They will use your teaching. The church will be divided into two parts. One third will not accept your teaching. The two thirds who accept your teaching will be saved for eternal life in heaven. This is the Second Coming of Christ. This is the time I come back to bring people to the Father that I promised. I will be at the end of the world to judge."

At 11:44 p.m. After I copied down in my note book, the Lord told me, "Almost two thousand years ago, December 10 was my birthday." After He said this, I started to look in the Bible for His birthday; He then said to me, "It was not written in the Bible.

In the first part of the revelation, the Eternal Father revealed to the world that each one of us must embrace our cross, and make it shine like cherry wood. The Holy Trinity is before everything in our life, we must obey all God's commandments so the presence of God is important as we sleep each night.

In the second part of the revelation, the Lord Jesus revealed that we must believe in faith. Faith and obeying all God's commandments are parallel.

In the third part of the revelation, the Lord Jesus revealed His birthday in the manger at Bethlehem. December is symbolic of the twelve tribes of Israel, ten is symbolic of the Ten Commandments, means the Lord Jesus obeyed His Father to die, and resurrected from the dead to save the world.

The Lord Jesus is Real Flesh in Holy Eucharist, Not Memory

December 12, 1997, the feast of Our Lady of Guadeloupe. Immediately after I kneeled down from receiving the Holy Eucharist, I said, "Jesus Lord, I received Your soul and Your body." He asked me, "Why did you say, 'My soul and My body?'" I replied, "I don't know, but I said it." He explained to me, "Your soul is in your body, your spirit is loose. You received My body, My soul comes with My body." I then said to Him, "If other people receive Your Body with a pure heart, they also receive Your soul."

The devil twisted the word "memory" in the scripture, regarding the Body and Blood of our Lord Jesus to deceive many. [Luke 22:19].

There is no commandment where God said the world must celebrate His birthday. But for almost two thousand years, the world has celebrated the Lord Jesus' birthday each year. The last supper means the food that your physical body needs daily, and also this means that our soul needs food.

Our physical body is a vehicle to carry our soul and spirit. The consecrated bread, the Holy Eucharist is a vehicle to carry the soul, Spirit and glorified body of the Lord Jesus. As the Lord Jesus said, "My Father is in Me, and I am in my Father." The Holy Spirit is the action, proceeding from the Father and the Son; therefore, the Spirit of the Father and the Holy Spirit come with the Holy Eucharist.

Each time a person receives the Holy Eucharist with a pure heart, he or she receives the actual glorified Body, Soul, and Spirit of the Lord Jesus, together with the Spirit of the Father and the Holy Spirit. But if a person receives it with an impure heart, he or she will receive punishments.

God's Power Rises up from Priestly Host like a Heat Wave

May 13, 1997. I am testifying, these things are the truth. I saw a globe of heat waves, rising up and spreading around the priest's Holy Eucharist, inside the gold paten, on top of the corporal, in front of the celebrant. I know that it was God's power, the power is like heat coming out above a strong fire. I knew that was the Spirit of the Trinity, I squinted my eyes so I could see it more clearly. Yet, even though I was standing a several steps away, that small amount of God's power I saw pressed on my face and my chest. God's power was gentle and powerful. I feared that I might fall, and I said in my thought, "Jesus keep my physical stand firm and strong." I then stood still, and I continued to see God's power spreading over the altar, and the sanctuary. I also felt it through my body.

Returning to my seat, God's power grew stronger in my body; I had to sit there for a while after the mass.

I went to deliver the "God's Purification - Not Easy" manuscript to the layout person for correction. More than an hour after I got home, I was still drunk in the power of God, the vision of above the paten almost constantly in my head. I then went into my devotion, I heard the voice say, "The community saw you alone with the priest." I thought the community at Cathedral of Saint Andrew saw me at the sanctuary with Father Scott, the mass celebrant. But the Lord Jesus said to me, "The heavenly community saw you alone with the priest; that priest is Me. You saw the glory of the Father radiate from the host. The host is my body and blood. With your natural eyes, you saw the power of God above the corporal."

The Lord Jesus continued, "You saw the glory of the Father in His power at the altar. The Father's glory, can only be seen symbolically as a cloud. You saw the power of the Father like power coming out of a strong fire. The Father's glory was in me at the time I was on earth. Today is the first time the Father descended His glory on the altar since I went back to heaven."

I then fell asleep. In my dream I saw in front of me a big oval ball of clouds in the middle of the dark.

How does a person discern seeing the true power from God with natural eyes? The road for a person to truly see God's power, God's grace, and His glory is very difficult and brings a lot of suffering. He must always be willing to embrace this suffering, and be completely obedient to all God's commandments, and have a lot of love for others, and this includes enemies. He must seek God daily through prayer; daily exam and repentance to keep his heart pure. This is God's gift; God's gifts are not cheap; this is the gift of suffering. God's gift does not come in to look pretty; God's gifts only come for service.

And there is another way of seeing God's power, God's grace, and His glory, that is through other persons, or through yourself.

God Revealed the Lord Jesus' Glorified Body Hidden in the Holy Eucharist

June 24, 1997. In my dream, I heard the Lord Jesus say to me, "After I was resurrected from the dead, before I went to heaven to the Father, sometimes people saw me, and sometimes people did not see me. There were times I wanted them [apostles] to see me, and they could see Me. If I did not want them to see me, they could not see Me." While the Lord was saying this, in my dream I saw inside a tomb, this tomb was like a hole in the middle of a huge rock. Jesus the Lord was sitting on something like a single bed, that was in the same piece of rock carved in the center of the rock. There was a long cloud color shroud wrapped over His shoulder, and across His chest, down to his right waist, and covered His thighs. I then saw the upper room that He appeared to the apostles, then I saw He was walking along with a few men on the road.

The Lord still continued talking in the dream, "After I went home to the Father, sometimes they could see Me, sometimes they could not see Me." While the Lord was saying this, I saw a King's plaza from afar. This king's plaza had concrete pavement in the middle, and around this concrete ground were big, tall ancient buildings. The main one was like a dome at the top. These buildings were built with clouds, but no one was there.

I asked, "Jesus, when You are not there [in heaven] where are you?" He said, "When I am not in heaven, I am in the Holy Eucharist." I asked, "Lord, I know Your body was resurrected, but I only see the host; I believe that the consecrated host comes with Your Spirit." He said, "Mystery. There is one host turned into My fresh flesh." I remember that some time ago, someone told me in nature that, a host turned into fresh flesh. While the Lord was saying these things, I saw a white host at the sanctuary at the Cathedral of Saint Andrew, I also saw some place very far with a dark area, and I knew that the dark area contained the consecrated host turned into the Lord Jesus' fresh flesh.

July 25, 1997. God the Father said to me, "I have showed you the door of heaven is opening for you. You saw legions and legions of holy angels coming out from heaven to battle against the enemies on your behalf. Jesus the Lord is the Commander. You will see many responses to your calling them to convert and repent." He continued, " I want you to add this revelation to the letter you are going to mail to Catholic Church officials in the Vatican."

This is the evidence of the church clergymen's and people's hearts toward God. If any of you love God from your hearts, I urge you to cooperate with God, "take immediate action" to serve Him as you promised Him at the altar on your ordination.

When God sent me down to earth in this mission, He equipped me with many gifts, as the tools for me to fulfilled the job in this journey. But everything that I have belongs to Him, I have nothing.

I am testifying that all of these happenings are the truth. I pray that you and others may believe the same as my belief so you can receive blessing.

Holy Eucharist Healing - Altar Call Revelations

On February 18, 1997. In my dream, I was called to organize the Holy Eucharist Healing Services. I sat at the side of the concrete ground; on my left was a young man, about thirty years old, sitting on his heels, trying to copy the instructions from me, to prepare for this service. I looked across the small lot, at the back of Saint Andrew's Cathedral (outside the church, behind the sanctuary). This cathedral was carved from a huge piece of iron; the inside was not touched. In front of the cathedral was a small road, leading to a three way street; far away from the main road. I realized that this cathedral was in the middle of the village and very hard to locate.

I said to the young man, "From the main street, we must have people standing along the road, to give directions to the Church; if not people will get lost. This Healing Service is an all day event. People will come to the church in the morning; at noon they will go out on the concrete ground next to the cathedral for lunch and activities, and then come back inside for more prayers."

I then moved to the side of the cathedral, sitting on my heels, facing the same young man, who also sat on his heels. He wore eyeglasses, his right hand held a pen, and his left hand held a clipboard, which he laid on his knees. The clipboard was clear and about an inch thick; it looked like a sheet of clear, hard plastic; on it was some type-written words, which were engraved at the center of each line, leaving room on both sides. Some of the lines contained more words than others.

I was about to tell this young man how we were going to serve God at the Holy Eucharist Service. He was anxious to hear what I was going to say. I said to him, "There will be an altar call in the middle of the Holy Eucharist healing services. God will call young men whom He has chosen to step forward to commit themselves to the priesthood, and young women will commit to becoming nuns. We can plan one session a week, each week at a different parish, through the entire diocese." The man asked me, "How many young men will commit to the priesthood at each service?" I responded, "We do not know, but maybe two at each service."

While we were talking, a woman came over and bent down by his left side, interfering, and said, "I can recruit young boys to be priests." I continued talking to the young man; "I can get permission from the Bishop for Holy Eucharist healing services throughout the diocese." The woman said, "You cannot do these things; there are not enough boys; you cannot do this; you are not qualified to do this [job]." She got up and walked away. Then the young man turned to her, and said, "She [Mariette] is different; she can speak English, you only speak Vietnamese." She continued walking away, while looking back us.

The Bishop is symbolic of God; the parishes represent nations. My saying, "I can get permission from the Bishop for Holy Eucharist healing services throughout the diocese," is symbolic of God choosing me for this job. The young man's eyeglasses symbolize people seeing things more clearly and they represent the gift of discernment; he is symbolic of the spiritual leaders who God has equipped with that gift of clear discernment. The two man symbolic of discernment. The clear clipboard and engraved words represent the fact that one of the Roman Catholic Church's main focus is very clear; it needs more holy priests to lead people on earth toward spiritual life.

The cathedral symbolizes the mission God entrusted to me. Its location away from the main street means at that time was still in private. The playground for lunch and activities also have meanings. Lunch is symbolic of the words of God; eating lunch is symbolic of learning God's commandments. Activities represent living sacrifices and service to God, through service to one another with love from our hearts.

The Holy Eucharist healing in the cathedral is symbolic of time spent seeking God in prayer, listening to God's words, with His glory and grace upon us, as we heal.

My words, "From the main street we must have people standing alongside the roads, to give directions to the Church; if not people will get lost," means that God calls me to speak to the spiritual leaders so they will be sure to lead their congregation, in details of how to come to God in the correct way for Him heal their souls.

Vietnam is a communist country without the freedom to worship God. The woman speaking Vietnamese who interrupted our conversation with negativity toward me and our conversation represents spiritual leaders who have no faith in God, and who do not believe that God calls me, Mariette, a lowly person, as His instrument. The devil has blinded their eyes, and because their eyes are blinded by the devil, their works are mixed with good and bad. English in this revelation is the Eucharist Healing Service symbolic of power's power will rule the world, and heal those convert, examine daily and repent.

It does not matter how hard we try to please God; we still are sinners until our last breath.   But those God has predestined as His instruments to bestow the gifts of exorcism, deliverance, and healing will embrace the Cross of the Lord Jesus. Their bodies and minds are attacked by enemy spirits, trying to harm their bodies; they are constantly fighting with these enemy spirits through prayers. They are sharing the Lord Jesus' suffering; in this suffering they are happy because the Lord Jesus is within them and fighting for them. I am one of those persons.

The world's system is going against God's commandments. The words that come from the mouth of God's true instruments will cut people's flesh, and will hurt them; but later they will convert and repent, and focus on God for their eternal life in Heaven.

God's true instruments for these three gifts have to battle with enemy spirits constantly; there is much spiritual battling before each healing service. People who receive the healing must also prepare their hearts before the services.

If the ministers who act as healers contain mortal sin, it does not matter if they know or are unaware of it; the devil has the right to come to the Father and win the case by refusing to leave the person who came for the service, and that makes the situation worse.

The Ark of the Covenant and the Cathedral of Saint Andrew's Cherubim

Saturday, July 12, 1997, I went to the Church of the Immaculate Conception for the vigil mass. The mass was held at the Community Hall.

Besides many other things, I saw on the platform to the right were two chairs, the one closest to the tabernacle was a priest's throne chair. Under that chair the couch pillow was stored, and another chair was lower to the left of the priest's throne chair.

Before the priest came to the center of the altar to celebrate mass, one of the four altar servers picked up the pillow from under the priest's throne chair. He placed it at the left side of the altar [right side of the priest], and put the "Roman Missal - The Sacraments" book on top of the pillow, with other supplies at the foot of the book.

Before the priest made the sign of the blessing at the end of the mass, I saw the pillow on the floor of the platform, in between the foot base of the tabernacle and the feet of the priest's throne chair.

At the end of the mass, Jesus the Lord told me, "You need to give him a few seconds so he can get his soul back into his body before you speak. I need you to go to the rest room, let the other people get out first, and he [the priest] will be there when you get out." I went to the rest room before I came and stood in front of the priest, Father Francis, pastor of the Church of the Immaculate Conception.

There I was standing in front of Father Francis shaking his hand, and I said to him, "I am a visitor here. My name is Mariette, I came from San Diego." He said something like, "Welcome to the Immaculate Conception Church." Now I was no longer shaking his hand, but standing directly in front of him, and I said, "Did you receive my letters?" He replied, "Yes." I said to him, "You are the theologian, and you know that God needs the natural actions to pour down His grace and blessing. The Immaculate Conception renovation is for God to purify the Roman Catholic Church's leaders." He said, "I hope so." I then left to return to my apartment in Little Rock.

During the night of July 12 to July 13 morning, while I was asleep, my soul struggled to fight against the enemy spirits all night for the priests. In my dream I kept seeing the pillow under the priest's throne chair, a big pillow in the altar with gold cups. Also in my dreams, God told me that I must deliver these messages out to church leaders, to let them know that His presence is at the altar, do not treat Him with a disgraceful manner like Father Francis treated Him.

Because my soul was fighting all night for the church leaders against the devil and his offspring's spirits, I finally got up 8:15 a.m. I heard the Lord Jesus, Son of the most high living God say, "I am the King of heaven and earth. The terms to 'look over' and 'surrender' are two different things. 'Look over' is just watching and making sure that person do things on his own correctly. 'Surrender' is a person doing everything not from his own, but from whoever entrusted to him to do and finish the job. The priest's sermon yesterday was a disgrace to the Father and to Me. His actions at the altar must change. These changes must be from his heart, and will be shown to others. He sat on a chair above the pillow; the pillow was then placed on My altar, then again the pillow was on the floor at his feet. These actions are disgraceful to God's presence at the sanctuary, in front of his congregation. You were not the only one to spot these actions, there are others who felt the same way you feel. They just spoke among themselves. The bishop has not been aware of this priest's actions. I command that you must bring these actions into the bishop's heart, not just his mind and eyes, but deep in his heart. His responsibility is to correct and make sure none of these actions will be on My altar or My sanctuary again. You then send a copy to the priest, the one that you saw celebrating mass last night. I will speak to him as I had sent you to tell him."

Then the Lord Jesus said to me, "Mariette, My faithful Servant, I will see you in heaven, when you return on your last day. These priests are not aware of their actions. They sin against God, because the devil blinds their eyes." Because Jesus spoke in this revelation, He also means that He wants His priests loyal to Him, and respond to Him as faithful servants.

In the Arkansas Democrat & Gazette, Saturday, July 5, 1997, there was an article headed "Notion of angels is intriguing, appealing to many". It had a picture of the Cathedral of Saint Andrew's original altar: Tabernacle, crucifix above the tabernacle, and two cherubim. Words below the picture, "These two angels, missing from the Cathedral of St. Andrew, 617 S. Louisiana St., since the 1950s, were discovered in a parishioner's basement in 1994. Originally terra-cotta, the 1,000-pound statues were painted and marbleized before being returned to their rightful place on the altar on Oct. 2, 1996."

July 5, 1997, after 4:30 p.m. vigil mass, I asked Father Scott, "I have a question about the missing cherubim that I saw in the newspaper today." He asked, "The angels at the altar?" I responded, "Yes." Father Scott said, "In 1950, during the renovation, they deliberately took them out; and in 1994, a lady called Father Francis, and told him these angel statues were in her basement; she said to Father Francis, 'They are yours, if you want to come and take them.' Father Francis said 'yes', he then brought them back here, painted and put back at the altar; and that was the time I came here [Cathedral of Saint Andrew]."

I said to Father Scott, "These angels were missing in 1950, and found in 1994. I was born in 1947, and left the village I was born in 1950; and the Lord took me out from work in 1994; this has to do with the Cathedral of Saint Andrew cherubim . Little Rock is the land God chose to gather His true faithful servants, and with me to be in Little Rock." Father Scott, "It is time for fulfillment."

Exodus 25:18-20 "Make two cherubim of beaten gold for the two ends of the propitiatory, fastening them so that one cherub springs directly from each end. The cherubim shall have their wings spread out above, covering the propitiatory with them; they shall be turned toward each other, but with their faces looking toward the propitiatory."

God sent me into the world in the year 1947. After three years of my existence in the world, the year 1950, through my earthly parents, God took me away from the village where He put me, and in the same year, 1950, God had the church remove the two angels at His altar and hid them in the basement.

The removal of these two angels from the original was symbolic of God saying "This Cathedral is the physical church I chose for my Messenger to be here in the future to serve Me. She is on the earth, but she now has turned her face away from me."

Placing these angles back to the original altar is symbolic of God saying, "My Messenger is returning to worship Me. Prepare this Cathedral for her to be here to fulfill the first step of her 'Mission' that I sent Her."

The actions of placing the angels back at the original altar of the Cathedral symbolic of fulfills what the Lord told me few weeks before I left San Diego, " I told Abraham to move out of his father's house, and promised him that I would make him the father of many nations. Now, I tell you to move out of the house that I provided for you, to the land of milk and honey; Little Rock, Arkansas." And "I send you to reopen the St. John Seminary, to bring young men from all over the world to this location; I will teach them through the professors."

April 7, 1994, was the date God took me out from work to serve Him completely, and the year 1994 is the year that Father Francis found these two angels, repaired them, and placed them back to the altar on October 2, 1996. October 1996 was also the month that Jesus told me to prepare to move to Little Rock; and my actual moved took place on January 10, 1997.

The Interpretation for Exodus 25:18-20: The two cherubim fastened at the end of the propitiatory, at the ark of the covenant are symbolic of God's Messenger, who God equipped with the full gift of discernment as sanctuary custodian. The Spirit of the Holy Trinity hidden in consecration host/the Blessed Sacrament inside the tabernacle is replaced the Ark of Covenant in the old testament. These facing cherubim can also symbolic of

518

those filled with God discernment, worshipping God day and night, and God's laws as the center of her heart

Actions Show the Heart

September 27, 1997, 8:30 a.m. mass with funeral service at Good Shepherd Church in San Diego, California.

Immediately when the young priest arrived at the floor, next to the lowest step of the left side of the sanctuary, I saw a consecrated host fall down from the paten. I silently prayed that several people in front of me would not step on it. One more person was ahead of me in line, and then it would be my turn to receive the body and blood of our Lord. I saw the consecrated host laying on the ground, about three inches from the priest's right toe.

I was still focused on the consecrated host on the floor, then it was my turn. I quickly called the priest's attention, saying, "Father." At the same time I kneeled my right knee down, looking directly at the Holy Eucharist and cried out loud, "My Lord, my God." While I was saying this, the young priest bent down and picked it up. I then looked at the paten filled with the consecrated host in front of my face, and said to the priest, "Give me that one [the one that was on the floor]. As the young priest placed the body of the Lord Jesus in my left hand, I cried out loud for the second time, "Jesus, I love you." I then returned to my seat. As I got back to my seat; I felt that I was in the middle of heaven.

32

THE WORLD IN FRONT OF THE ALMIGHTY

The Lord Jesus Shepherds the Rebuild My Church Divine Mission

April 6, 1997. The Lord said to me, "I want you to record these things like black and white to the world, because many deceivers have entered the Vatican. I knew this before the Earth was formed. I then chose this land for you to establish the second location that will completely obey all God's commandments. I also give the successors of the Founder authority of the Mission. The persons to inherit the Mission are your blood descendants; they will have authorities above the president of the Rebuild My Church Mission. The presidents of the Rebuild My Church Mission must be appointed by the founder or successors of the Founder; they must be under the authority of the successors of the Founder. The successors of the Founder are the ones that I the Lord will be intimate with and give them instructions to run My mission; she or he will deliver the instructions to the presidents of the Mission. You as the Founder, you must put all these instructions in writing for human laws to comply, so no one can deceive others like they do in the Vatican."

The Vatican in this revelation is it self, it also symbolic of the world

Virtue of Love : God the Father loved the world by sending His only Son to save us. Jesus was freely obedient to the Father, and loved the world to His death. The love God has for the world is mighty, He forgives our sins, purges our iniquities, and rewards us for our good deeds. God is a just God; therefore, we must pay the damages that caused from our committed sins to purify our souls. The Lord Jesus said, "If you love me obey My commandments." Respond to God by loving Him and obeying all His commandments in each heart and action.

I did not chose this calling, it was God who chose me, I obeyed Him. I am, and I will always do and say everything exactly what God asks me to do or to say. I am pleasing God, I will not please man; even though I have to physically die for God. This means I love God first, I then love each one of you. If any one of your actions is evil, I still love you, but I hate your actions.   I hate the devil and his offspring; the devil and his offspring are those who give their free will to the devil, and the devil lives within them.

God proves his love for us in that while we were still sinners Christ died for us.

–Roman 5: 8

Steadfast Faith in God

Abraham believed God, and it was credited to him as righteousness. A worker's wage is credited not as a gift, but as something due

–Roman 4: 3-4

Jesus said to them in reply, Have faith in God. Amen, I say to you, whoever says to this mountain, 'Be lifted up and thrown into the sea and does not doubt in his heart but believes that what he says will happen, it shall be done for him.

–Mark 11: 22-23

Faith is a gift from God, and it only comes when a person wants it, and it requires a lot of prayer, living sacrifices to the Lord, and keeping the heart pure for the gift of faith.

I believe that God's words come with His power. I believe everything in the Bible. I believe all my dreams and visions are from God, and I recognize the voice of God; because everything I saw and I heard was foretold in the Bible. My thoughts and my actions benefit souls, and bring them to eternal life in heaven.

Standing by the cross of Jesus were his mother and his mother's sister, Mary the wife of Clopas, and Mary of Magdala.

–John 19: 25

Then the kingdom of heaven will be like ten virgins who took their lamps and went out to meet the bridegroom. Five of them were foolish and five were wise. The foolish ones, when taking their lamps, brought no oil with them, but the wise brought flasks of oil with their lamps. Since the bridegroom was long delayed, they all became drowsy and fell asleep. At midnight, there was a cry, 'Behold, the bridegroom! Come out to meet him!' Then all those virgins got up and trimmed their lamps. The foolish one said to the wise, 'Give us some of your oil, for our lamps are going out.' But the wise ones replied, 'No, for there may not be enough for us and for you. Go instead to the merchants and buy some for yourselves.' While they went off to buy it, the bridegroom came and those who were ready went into the wedding feast with him. Then the door was locked. Afterwards the other virgins came and said, 'Lord, Lord, open the door for us! But he said in reply, 'Amen, I say to you, I do not know you.' Therefore, stay awake, for you know neither the day nor the hour.

–Matthew 25: 1-13

One of the seven angels who held the seven bowls filled with the seven last plagues came and said to me, Come here. I will show you the bride, the wife of the Lamb.

–Revelation 21: 9

Through the Lord Jesus, Father Commanded

June 29, 1997, the feast of Saint Peter and Saint Paul. After I came home from attending mass at Saint Edward's church, in my devotion I said to the Lord, "Lord, I will lay out everything that You asked me to lay out. Tell me what would You want me to put in the book? How do you want your people to do?" The Lord said to me, "Here is what I want you to put in the book; word by word exactly what I said, and how I said it to you. Man will be confused by what you put in. Man will see these things do not make sense to them, because their thoughts are so out of order. They need to learn from Me, the Son of the most high living God, and buy from Me holy oil to smear on their eyes, so they can see clearly the glory of God."

The Lord continued, "I do not want to see any Eucharistic minister and lector wear shorts in the sanctuary. The children to serve as altar servers, the priests must train them well, so they will be in order. What I said are My commandments, and they are My decree. If any one doesn't obey, they will be subject to trial on their last day. Now I let you teach them what I have taught you."

The word "wear short" have two meanings; spiritual meaning is live in sins and have no God's protection; natural meaning is dress in short at the sanctuary will distracted other from focus in worship God

The Perfect God — Mighty God

April 24, 1997, 7:43 a.m. After I got up the Lord revealed to me that I am not walking, but I am living in the midst of God's anointing. These anointings give me everything that I need to service my Lord, my God, God of all creation.

The words of the Lord came to me, "The woman in the house in the dream said 'I have paid over one hundred and thirty thousand dollars to the old woman to support her; these words came from the cross at Calvary; the Son of the Promises purchased everything for us, those that are obedient to all of God's commandments." I then heard, "What is coming, what is going, what do we get?" That was the question Saint Peter asked the Lord, and the

Lord said to Saint Peter, "Your throne is in heaven, next to my throne to judge the living and dead." I then said, "Perfect Lord, mighty Lord, sweet Lord, Loving Lord, give me like you gave Saint Peter. The whole world will say, 'What is this woman saying, that we have such difficulty to understand her thinking?' " The Lord said, "Who can reach up to the sky to touch the Lord's feet. The Lord's feet only can be touched by these chosen ones. The price the chosen ones must pay is very high. For all their sins have been forgiven and the iniquities are constantly being purged. Crowns for the chosen ones are not on earth, but in heaven. Even when they are in heaven, they still take their crowns and put them on the floor and worship the Lord of hosts."

The Lord continued, "The dead are under the sewer, so that no one can get close to their tombs; this dream is symbolic of those church priests and church authorities trying to prevent others from obeying God's commandments. Even those are not that many, but there are some that are proud of themselves in church. They are serving God with the dignity of the devil." I, Mariette said to the Lord, "Lord, my feet are distracted me from hearing You, my stomach is rising up with heat, and my upper back straightens me with discomfort. I offer these to you, Lord God for my sins and the sins of those who serve God with the devil's dignity; I ask You Lord for them to be willing for conversion. Because, You have taught me and others to forgive the enemies; and yet Lord, some where on the road, I crossed this individual too. Lord, You are the mighty God, perfect God, You know my heart, my heart is not held against this individual, and You know that I pray for this individual. I ask You, Jesus, for the blood that You shed at Calvary to clean our sins, and purge our iniquities." The Lord said, "Buy from me a white garment to put on so you will not be exposed, and buy from me refined oil to smear on your eyes so you can see the living God."

The Lord continued, "The woman outside the building depended on her naked husband, who was running across the field, the plaza. She and her husband are those who come to church every day with empty hearts. 'Who says that I have empty' was what she argued with you in the dream; while you saw her naked husband run across the plaza; these are those who never admit their sins in front of God, they always defend themselves in front of Me the Lord God of all creation. But the eyes of the mighty God see everything, in and out of the plaza. They call the plaza the holy place to worship the Lord; but these plazas are not holy, they are filled with murders and hatred. Men and women called themselves holy, yet they are friends of the devil. They pronounce who can judge. God is the only one who can judge, but they are judging others themselves. Come and I will show you the sacred place." He continued "Those who are faithful and believe in God will sit at the center of God's heart, they are the ones you saw in the dream that were sitting inside the building, facing the front door; and the man came and called them 'believers'. They then all got up to follow that man across to the holy place."

The Lord continued, "The garden that needed to be edged, bushes of flowers needing to be trimmed so they can grow perfect next spring, that is what you saw in the dream; and you helped the lady work in this garden. The Garden of Eden had been violated for centuries and centuries; now is the time to clean up and fertilize it so the trees can grow green, instead of being dead. These are the onions that I am peeling with my own hand; my own sword. When the Lord rewards, the rewards are mighty. The mighty deed you have done is on earth, and the pay is in heaven."

God continued, "Over three thousand dollars is the price that you had to pay for the garments. The two pieces of garments were embroidered with silver and gold. This two piece garment is the power of God, the glory of God, the grace of God, and an anointing from God. In the dream you focused your mind on an appointment at noon to go pick up your garment, while others interfered and tried to give you something else; but you said, 'I have an appointment at noon to pick up my garment. I went at ten, but they said that the garment was not ready, I have to come at noon. Every one who enters heaven must be obedient to every single commandment of God."

The Lord said to me, "I give you this to conclude this chapter. Hold on to your crown, let those judging be judged by the Lord."

> *Because you have kept my message of endurance, I will keep you safe in the time of trial that is going to come to the whole world to test the inhabitants of the earth. I am coming quickly. Hold fast to what you have, so that no one may take your crown.*

–Revelations 3:10-11

God the Father Speaks the Truth

April 29, 1997. In my dream I was washing a car, using a washing glove with soap. There was a man formed with a cloud standing behind me spraying water on the side of the car that I was washing. Behind this man was a woman wearing dark clothes. With us in this group was another man who went out to get more cars for us to wash, it seemed like the dark shadow woman was supervising the group.

I got up and prayed for the interpretation, I heard the voice say, "That was members of Jesus' family on earth." Then the Father said, "The Father is speaking to you, not a voice." I said, "Father, I am sorry that I did not recognize your voice." He then said, "I have a different voice, My voice is in the sick, the lowly and the poor. The woman standing to supervise is your Blessed Mother. The man spraying the water is your brother. The one who went to get more cars from the public is Saint Joseph. You are yourself, putting soap on the cars. Cars are symbolic of people, washing with soap and water is symbolic of washing their hearts and minds, an internal washing."

The Father continued, "They said to Me, Father, I love you, but where is the love these people on earth can prove to Me these days. They love themselves, not God. They are preaching , they are preaching, and they are preaching, all of this is for their own flesh. I am sick and tired of what they are offering to Me; I have not enjoyed what they are offering to Me for a long time. Your pure heart that I purified for you, it is not for My sake, but it is for you and for the sake of the world."

In my vision I saw Larry King of CNN interview retired General Colin Powell. The Father said, "Silver and gold are their own benefit. The living God sees that there are no benefits for the world."

I then said to the Lord, "Living God, Merciful God, loving God, please change their hearts and minds to benefit the world."

The Father said, "I the Lord God have light to shine on the world." While the Father was saying this, in my vision I saw the first part of the Gospel according to Saint John; this means the Father was referring to the Lord Jesus as the light that shines on the world.

The Father continued, "My words have been twisted by those who call themselves preachers, and ministers to serve God. They mislead my people and serve themselves."

I then said, "Lord, I am your own. Father, You have anointed me with the blood of Your only beloved Son."

The Father said, "Besides you, there is no other person in this world that has, had or will be anointed with the blood of My begotten Son. The people in this world anointed themselves with the grace of the devil, from the priests down to ministers."

The Father continued, "Very few of them asked me to anoint them with the grace of God." While the Lord was saying 'very few of them asked me to anoint them with the grace of God', in my vision I saw Father Scott standing at the Gospel podium giving a homily; although I did not see his face very well, and it meant the Father was speaking about ministers of the church. The Lord continued," These are the ones that I love, and I will love them for ever. They have showed Me their sincerity and love for Me, and for My Son. They are speaking and they are taking actions; they are not speaking without action. The number of people that speak and take action is very small in the church today. These are the one that I circumcised after they got out of their mother wombs." While the Father was saying this I saw the spirit of my older daughter, Thuy-Trang.

The Lord continued, "I speak of her, she is also symbolic of other laity; these people that have died for Me in their hearts. Through the grace of God, they have been fighting for the truth."

I said to the Father, "Father, Jesus is the hero; He fought and fought to the end, to the death on the cross; to help me and those that You have chosen to fight for the kingdom of God, so we can fight and fight to the end of our last breath."

The Father said to me, "You are drowning in the suffering for Me; through this suffering, I will raise you up on your last day."

In this revelation, God the Father revealed to the world the hearts of many people are disobedient to His commandments. Larry King on CNN symbolic of media, and General Colin Powell symbolic of those proud of their own human power. Father Scott symbolic of church ministers. My oldest daughter, Thuy-Trang is symbolizes other laity in this world that speaks right according to God's commandments and take actions of what she speaks. [Reference of her actions on The Anointing Phrase.]

Everyone of us must follow in the footsteps of the Holy Family. I was in the dream, and that means I am following the in the footsteps of my beloved Blessed Virgin Mother. Serving God through service to others from the heart, with love. Obey all God's commandments; preach God's commandments, not your own doctrine. Put your teaching in your daily life, do not preach God words and do the opposite of what you are preaching. Speak the truth without fear. Be humble, speak and live the life of God's true servants; embrace your suffering for the grace of God to work through you.

God Chooses Earthly Church to Fulfill His Plan

God chose the following churches as examples to reveal to all American Christians. I am an instrument of God, I only put down what I see and hear, whether in nature or supernatural. After the resurrection of our Lord Jesus; through Saint John, the Lord Jesus revealed these messages to His seven churches. The number seven is in the Book of Revelation are symbolic of the beginning of the completion. The Lord Jesus revealed the entire Book of Revelation through His servant, Saint John, in symbolism of the future of God purifying the world systems, and before the end of individual world.

Throughout the Bible, from the old to the new testaments, and especially in the Book of Revelations, the stories in the old testament, the parables and actions of the Lord Jesus, apostles, and others contain many hidden meanings. Even the words spoken also have hidden meanings.

God has predestined me as His servant for this mission; through me, He reveals to the world the meanings of His words in both old and new testaments.

God chose some physical churches, and sent me to each church, to be mingle with its congregation; with my eyes witness, he then explained what is wrong and right with each church in front of God. These wrongs or rights of each church can be interpreted into each group or individual. The church and its fixtures are symbolic of the focus of the heart in that parish, its organizations and the majority of the parishoners hearts, either towards God, or towards their own name and benefits. Through me, every word God has me write in His books has more meaning than it sounds.

> *A good person brings forth good out of a store of goodness, but an evil person brings forth evil out of a store of evil. I tell you, on the day of judgment people will render an account for every careless word they*

speak. By your words you will be acquitted, and by your words your will be condemned.

–Matthew 12: 35-37

Avoid Man's Creations, Because Man wants to be like God

Toward the morning of July 11, 1997, in my dream I said to God, "Lord, I do not want to have intercourse with the human anymore, because this mission is very sacred." I then saw an invisible person showing me two open sheets of paper stapled at the top left corner. This person asked me something, I said, "Can you wait? I need to ask my boss." I thought that I would go into the next room to see my boss, but I did not; instead, I closed my eyes and said, "Lord, this person came in and asked to see the man to meet with him; I think this time they will reach an agreement." I then saw an invisible hand and pen, writing the words, "The agreement is approved, sign at the bottom line." When I heard sign at the bottom line, I was physically trying to lift up my right hand to sign, I then saw the invisible hand sign my signature "Mariette Do-Nguyen"

The Lord said to me, "In the dream, you asked not to have intercourse with the human, and you did rot know what was said in the agreement, but you signed your name."

I said, "Lord, I trust you, everything that You tell me."

The Lord said, "It was not what you think the meaning of it. It is different than what you think and what you said. This is not about human physical intercourse; this is symbolic of human actions to be involved in the future, those actions that are created by man, not by God." While the Lord said this I saw the three beasts I saw in a dream. This means God said, anything people create to deny God or want to be like God I will never get involved in. The intercourse with man is symbolic of those trying to get to Mars, Mir, mass murder, or who want to be like God, under the power of evil.

The Gap Between God and Mankind

I said to the Lord Jesus, "Lord, when You left the earth, You left a gap between God and priests, because You are God and we are human. But for me I am human, what do you mean when I go home, there will be a gap between me and the church leaders?" While I was asking the Lord, in my vision, I saw the "White Veil" revelation in the first part of this book.

The Lord Jesus said, "When I left the world to go home, people were disobedient to me, because the disobedience created the gap between Me and priests. At the time you go home, if the church leaders and people do not obey what I told you to teach them, this disobedience will create the gap between you and them. Your responsibility is to make them know if they are not following your teachings, they will create the gap between you and them." The Lord charged me of the responsibility, to make sure people in the world know well that I, Mariette, am just God's agent, God's Ambassador. Any one not following what comes out from me, that person will create the gap between him and God; because everything I speak and wrote are from God revealed to me, and is already in the Holy Bible.

The Lord said, "These commandments were revealed to John in the Book of Revelation chapter 4, [Vision of Heavenly Worship.]" The heavenly worship means people on earth worship God like in heaven.

The reason the Book of Revelation is full of symbolism is that God's words are almighty, and His language is symbolism. This symbolism can be interpreted in many different situations; because depending of what dome after or before it To understand God's language, that person must keep his heart pure and seek the Lord Jesus for the interpretation, but people refuse to keep their hearts pure and seek God. They allow the devil's spirit to blind their eyes, and complain that the Book of Revelation is difficult to understand. The Vision of Heavenly Worship in natural symbolism interprets the supernatural actions of God's commandments. The natural daily actions will transform into supernatural power; then supernatural power will come down to natural.   When people obey God's commandments, and do good deeds, the good deeds will be transformed to God's power, then God's blessing will come down to earth. Opposite of that, when people are disobedient to God's commandments, and obey the devil, evil actions will be transformed to supernatural disasters, then the disasters will come down to earth.

Before Moses went to heaven, God said to Moses in the Book of Deuteronomy chapter 31: 16-7

> *"Soon you will be at rest with your fathers, and then this people will take to rendering wanton worship to the strange gods among whom they will live in the land they are about to enter. They will forsake me and break the covenant which I have made with them. At that time my anger will flare up against them; I will forsake them and hide my face from them, so they will become a prey to be devoured, and many evils and troubles will befall them. At that time they will indeed say, 'Is it not because our God is not among us that these evils have befallen us?' Yet I will be hiding my face from them at that time only because of all the evil they have done in turning to other gods.*

When many people in the world are disobedient to God's commandments, and refuse conversion for a period of time, God will hide His face from the world. When God hides His face, the gap occurs.   When the gap is created, people will petition to God what the devil gave to them, these petitions are not in God's will. When people submit petitions to God and those petitions are not in God's will, it will create problems in the supernatural;

then the supernatural power will come down to natural, which will be actions on earth.

I refused to disclose who I am in front of God while I am still on earth, But God ordered me to disclose what He told me of who I am in front of Him, and charged me with the responsibility to disclose the "GAP" between God and the world at the beginning of my mission, and not wait until the end of my mission like Moses.

Soul Journey On Earth

July 12, 1997. In my dream I was on the road to school, but there was no public transportation. There was a young man, he was kind of short, who gave me a ride on his dark motorcycle. The motorcycle seat barely was large enough for me to sit behind him, I had to hold around his waist for security.

He and I were then inside a house; the front of this house was a right angle corner, and the inside was divided in two parts. Facing the front of the house, to the right was the motorcycle driver's mother, where he and his sister lived; to the left was the communist officers station.

While he and I were inside his house, his retarded sister was standing at the middle of the front door. His sister was being sexually molested by others. I was married, and knew this man loved me, he took care of me and tried to convince me to get a divorce and marry him.

I then saw we were several yards in front of the house, it seemed like a convenience store shopping center. The communist officers station was behind us, I saw some of the officers outside the station door, wearing khaki uniforms. He was sitting on a different motorcycle, and I was sitting behind him. To our left was a gas station with two gas pumps. This motorcycle was a light color and a bigger, newer one than the one before.

The dream completely changed. I was in front of a huge building trying to find my classroom. I then was inside the building, between two groups of bleaches, and these bleaches were for people to sit and watch volleyball. They were filled with students. Facing the center of the building, to my left, was my class. The students in my class were about twelve to fifteen years old, but I was a little older than them. I put my overnight bag on the second bench from behind, with my jacket on top of my overnight bag, and sat on the bench lower than the one where I set my overnight bag. On the other side to my left was a man standing up to do his work, he was a teacher.

I saw the teacher come in front of me, to the spot where I was standing and laid my bag before I sat down. He came to this spot with nothing, but as he got there, I saw he had three awards, one of them was a trophy, and he gave it to those students who were sitting on the benches to my right. The trophy was silver; the top and bottom were two pieces of a triangle, and three pillars connected with them to form a triangle at the corner.

It was time for a break, I pulled out a huge blue sheet of paper from my bag that had my class schedule on it. It had two groups of rectangles with many dots, and another half that connected to the one on the right. I knew that I had finished one class, and that was the class on the right that had another part connected to it; I still had another class on the left to finish after the break. I needed to go to break and find another building for my class.

I faced a high shelf that was built into the wall. A little behind me to my left was a young woman waiting for me, while I was trying to put my overnight bag and jacket on this shelf and go out the door to my right for break. I would come back for the bag to go to another class.

I then was outside the building, on the concrete ground, and some students were passing me while I was trying to tie my belt. My belt was a big white rope, the same kind of rope priests wear around their waist while they celebrate mass. Sadly, I looked down and my long, black, tight satin trousers were damaged badly. The front part was completely cut off and my entire lower belly was showing. I then tried on roomy trousers, then pulled both sides at the waist to cover the front, but there was not enough to cover the entire front belly. I then pulled down my long black sweatshirt to cover my front belly and my bottom. I could walk without people seeing my front lower belly.

I then woke up and prayed, and the Lord Jesus helped me understand the dream, He said, "The communist officers wearing khaki are symbolic of the church leaders. The young retarded young woman is symbolic of people in this world. The man who gave you a ride is symbolic of Me, Jesus."

The church leaders are bad, so the Lord gave them to me like communist officers. The man who wanted me to get a divorce to marry him; this divorce is the sinfulness and stubbornness that needs to convert to God.

The badly damaged trousers are symbolic that I will be torched with suffering to pay for my sins: that I was stubborn to the Father and refused to come down to earth for this mission, the Father had to force me to come down. On earth, I was bad until I came back to God in the year 1991.

The Lord Jesus said to me, "When the Father cast Lucifer out of heaven, before He created the earth, you replaced Lucifer's position. You were an Archangel before you came down to earth for this mission." While the Lord was saying this, I saw the dream where I was standing in the midst of a cloud in the sky wearing a white tunic and cloak with a long sword in my right hand.

Jesus the Lord also said, "At the time Father sent you down to earth, He sent Michael the Archangel with you as your guardian angel. Through your earthly parents, the Father gave you the name at baptism of Maria Tin [in English it means Mary Believe]"

The Lord continued, "When you were in heaven, you saw Me suffering; and you knew if you came down to earth you too would suffer. You were stubborn, and refused to come down to earth; the Father had to force you, you had no choice, but to come down to the earth. All this was foretold in the old testament, open the Isaiah chapter 44 and Malachi chapter 3."

> *It is I who confirm the words of my servants,*
> *I carry out the plan announced by my messengers;*
> *I say to Jerusalem: Be inhabited; to the cities of Judah: Be rebuilt;*
> *I will raise up their ruins.*
>
> –Isaiah 44:26
>
> *Lo, I will send you Elijah, the prophet,*
> *Before the day of the LORD comes,*
> *the great and terrible day,*
>
> –Malachi 3:23

At the time the Lord revealed this to me, he gave me the choice to record or not to record it on tape. But His power silently moved my entire body and I then did record it on the cassette tape, and now it is in the book.

Tight and Roomy Trousers

In one dream I wore tight trousers that I could not pull up to cover my bottom, I felt shame while the man was chasing me in the garden. It is written in the "Souls Originating" revelation of July 11, 1997. These tight trousers are symbolic of heavenly rules God the Father set for me. Tight is symbolic of strict rules to obey for others to follow; these tight rules were to prepare me to come down to earth. But I was afraid of suffering on earth, I refused to accept the job. But the Father showed me those wrong things I made; I was ashamed and accepted and came down to earth with no choice.

Roomy trousers in the "Soul Journey on Earth" revelation, on July 12, 1997: This roomy pair of damaged satin trousers are symbolic of God's commandments and the church rules being abused. Part of the front of my trousers being cut is symbolic of God's commandments and church rules being deliberately ignored. I pulled from both sides of the waist to cover the front of my lower belly is symbolic that through God's power, I will assist them, pointing out the areas they have been deliberately ignoring.

Shopping for Christmas Gift and Its Meaning

The following shopping story is an action transformed into revelation, both my daughter and I were on assignment that led by Spirit of God. Therefore each word that we spoke or an action that we take, the items that I purchase, and color are symbolism.

December 11, 1997. About 4:00 p.m. my daughter, Thuy-Trang came and asked me, "Mother, would you like to go to Christmas shopping with me?" I said, "Yes," I continued, "while I am getting ready, I made rice and fish, if you want to eat?" She said, " Yes. I am hungry. I will eat before we go so I won't munch other things." She continued, "This is the kind of fish that I like, but I do not know how to make them. What do you put in? They are so good every time you make them."

While we were shopping, she said to me, "Mother, cinnamon rolls are good." She meant that she wanted to get some for us. I said, " I can not eat now, I am fasting, but I can save it until dinner." But we didn't buy any, instead she bought a cup of cafÈ mocha and shared with me. When she just received the cup, she handed it to me and asked me to drink it first, with the warning, "Mom, just taste a little, it may be very hot." We then shared the cup to the end.

After three hours of shopping, she bought nothing, I bought an ash color "V" neck sweater, open in front, with double rows of white trim at the end of the long sleeves, for my youngest daughter, TuAnh; a velvet navy blue turtle neck blouse for my son's wife, Hanh; and a light blue striped dress shirt for my oldest daughter's husband, Huy.

The next day, December 12, 1997, was the feast of Our Lady of Guadeloupe. After I came home from morning mass, I went to the foot of the altar and asked the Lord, "Father, Lord Jesus, Holy Spirit; I am in the world, but I belong to you. Mother, Blessed Virgin, help me. All the holy angels and saints pray with me. Lord God, I do not want to do anything that is not from You, I need Your direction. Jesus the Lord, You are my brother show me; should I go to shopping for the children or should I not. If you want me to go, I will go, but if You do not want me to go, I will stay home."

Then the Lord lifted me in spirit, in my vision I saw a checkered, four-pocket jacket with a belt, in a light brown color that my daughter looked at the day before at the Ann Taylor store. I then saw an ash color, round neck, not open in the front or back, good quality man's sweater. Then the Father told me, "Go and do what needs to be done. Pass through Nordstrom department store, and shop in the mall."

Before I went to Mission Valley, I went to the Sporting Goods store, and got a pair of running shoes for my son James, the same brand and style that I have, and a youth red and white sport outfit for John. I then got to Fashion Valley, and I walked through Nordstrom's, went to Ann Taylor, the store where we were last night to get the four-pocket jacket for my daughter, Thuy-Trang. I also got the black velvet turtle neck blouse that the Lord told me last night to get for me.

While I was walking in the mall, I saw a group of children about to entertain people with Christmas carols. I then stood behind an adult doing the set up of the music instruments, and I saw a sign on their equipment "Nazareth school." I then said out to myself, "They come from the same village as my brother."

While they were singing, I looked at the faces of each individual child, they were American, Mexican, Asian, and others. I counted them, a total of 24 children, with three adults. The three adults were a nun, and two women. The nun was the director, two women played instruments with one boy, the 23 other children sang. The 24 children wore school uniforms, they were wearing the same shirt with a sweater jacket; the two boys were wearing navy blue pants, the other 22 were wearing navy blue short roomy skirts.

While I look at the hair and faces of the 23 children singing, I knew for sure that 22 of them were girls; one of these 22 girls had damaged teeth. One of the 23 was standing in the middle of the front row; his face and hair looked like a boy, but he was wearing skirt, his face showed a lot of suffering while he was focused to sing.

While I looked at them, they were like angels to me. I wanted to give them ten dollars, but I was not sure what the Lord wanted me to do. I then silently prayed to ask the Lord Jesus for direction. I took ten dollars out of my purse, very carefully hidden inside my right hand, and walked to the young woman at the back, at the side playing music and said to her, "Do you allow me to give these children some cash to get water or soda?" She referred me to the other woman, I asked this woman, "Do you allow me to give these children some cash to get water or soda." She said, "Ask sister Cathy, she is the Principal." I went to the right side of Sister Cathy, and asked the same question, she said, "We do not take it, but the director will take it, give to her." She referred to the woman standing in the front playing a music instrument.

I went to her and said, "The sister said, 'give this to the director and she will take it." I then carefully opened my right palm, handed the ten dollar bill to her hand, she then placed it under the music sheets, at the music stand. I then went back to Nordstrom, bought a round neck ash colored sweater that the Lord showed me in my vision for my son, Chau. Before I purchased these gifts, I already bought a car seat for my first granddaughter, Madeleine who were born January 1, 1998; the Catholic holiday obligation, Mary Mother of God.

Ten dollars are symbolic of the Ten Commandments. The Nazareth school students are symbolic of the people in the world. The director is symbolic of church authorities. The principal is symbolic of world leaders. The girl with several damaged teeth is symbolic of deception through false teachings, false prophets and others through their words and actions and will convert. The boy wearing the shirt is symbolic of the Second Coming of Christ to lead people to the Father, He is hiding in the form of a female. The other students in uniform are those whose name in the Book of Life belong to the Lord Jesus. Singing is symbolic of praising and serving God through service to one another, and preaching the Gospel.

Uniform is symbolic rules. The turtle neck is symbolic of completely obeying all God commandment. The baby car seat is symbolic of being carry God's power. Black velvet is symbolic of the darkness of God that the world can not see through. Navy blue is a symbolic God's anointing. Ash color is symbolic physical body will return to dirt. The double striped sweater is symbolic of a uniform, meaning discipline, but open in the front means they do not receive proper training. A dress shirt is symbolic of the outside being formal, like the systems of the world, but refusing to learn and accept the truth from God. The jacket with four packets is the uniform for the officers, the number four is symbolic of holiness; the color brown is symbolic of labor, and the checkers design is symbolic of gambling. This means spiritual leaders are preaching of live in the life of holiness, but not putting their preaching in their daily life. Running shoes are symbolic of competition in labor, this means serving God by trying to be ahead of others for their own benefit, not from the heart and love for God.

God the Father Takes Actions to Purify the World

4:00 a.m., May 1, 1997. God the Father said to me, "May will be a month of victory for you. The House of Representatives, the Senate and President Bill Clinton will see the power of God upon the world. They have heard My words and have refused to obey My commandments. I will strike them down on the floor of Congress. There is no other power than the power coming down from Heaven. Nuclear and chemical weapons will be at the bottom of the sea. Citizens of the United States will see the glory of the living God upon them. This glory is the glory of suffering by those who convert and repent. I have no power to give to those who worship the devil and his false luxuries. I will help My servants win over those who refuse my commandments; when the tragedies upon the world consume them, they will not receive pay after the play is over."

The Lord instructed me, "I want you to place these two revelations in the book, "God's Purification is Not Easy." While I prayed for the interpretation, the Father said to me, "It is a revelation. It is not a revelation. These are my commandments. It may sound contradictory to you, but not to Me."

I said to the Lord, "Lord, the devil is in the world. He has hidden himself; now You are exposing him to the public." The Father said to me, "It is true; but beyond that, people are giving their free will to the devil. I am sick and tired of people treating Me badly; I am the Lord their God, the creator of Heaven and Earth. The Israelites built and worshipped the golden calf; the same spirit of the devil came down on many generations of descendants." The Father continued, "Those who have ears, are out to hear." While the Lord was saying this, in my vision I saw the Book of Revelations being opened; this means that God will give me more detail for the public.

After God the Father spoke, in my dream I was in a house. This house was divided into two parts, front and back, and there was a door to the side of the divider wall. I was in the front section, and at the corner opposite the door was a pile of old, dirty clothes, that had not been washed for years. Right next to it were eight pairs of socks in different colors, all soaked with mud; I was putting these socks together with the clothes. As I was doing this, my son, about three years old, said to me, "You are militant."

I did not understand the word militant, so I asked him, "What is militant?"

He explained to me, "A small woman like you, very poor, who suddenly becomes rich; there was another small woman like you before."

As he said this, I recalled a woman from the old days. I said, "We need to finish cleaning the house. I am leaving tomorrow."

I then went to the back part of the house. This area was small like the front, and in the middle was a rectangular concrete tank. This water tank measured five yards in length, three yards wide, and its edges were ten inches thick; it was filled with clear water that came up to my knees. My husband was sitting on his feet fixing the foot of the wall at the top of the water tank. On the other side of the top corner of the tank was a washing machine; it looked twice the size of a five gallon gas tank. On top of the washing machine was a huge funnel, with large, round edges, a little bigger than the body of the round washing machine. The inside of the funnel was lined with a dark plastic trash bag, and the outside was metal.

Water was transferred from the water tank to the washing machine from the corner of the tank to the side of the washer through a long, black rubber pipe; the pipe was so long that its middle was hanging from the ceiling by a string. The inside of the washing machine was filled with clothes going through the wash cycle, and air was coming out from the bottom of the funnel, as the water ran out from the bottom and soaked into floor.

I, Mariette, was myself in the dream. My son represents the mission that God entrusted to me. The man who was my husband is symbolic of the Lord Jesus, and this signifies the responsibility that each one of us has toward our God.

Apply for Heavenly Citizenship

February 1, 1998, the feast of Presentation of the Lord. In the law of Moses, this is the feast of the purification of a woman after giving birth to a child. The Roman Catholic Church tradition is presenting the Lord Jesus to the Father in the temple, with a blessing of candles; Jesus the Lord, begotten Son of the Father is the light of the world.

In my dream I was in the hall at the side of the mansion, looking for a restroom. I then found a lounge, this room had a divider in the back part, this back should have had a toilet, but there was no toilet.

Then in another part of the hall, I continued to search for a restroom. This hall was underground, built out of clay. The side opposite the mansion wall had several midgets up to my knee entrances. There was an oval topped entrance, and this entrance had no door. Some people went in and out, but this entrance was too small for me to enter.

I was then inside the main mansion, walking on the left side toward a huge stage. I knew that this stage had a judge's bench. To the left of the foot of the stage was a long table, parallel with the lounge outside the door. My second cousin was sitting behind the table, and her son sat in front of the table. I knew that she was waiting for the judge to hear her case of applying for citizenship; her son was the one who assisted her in the process, and act as her interpreter.

After I chatted with them for a few words, I turned around and saw, at the center of the mansion, a larger and longer table, set parallel with the side table. As I walked to it, I saw some people sitting around the hall area of the table close to stage. The other side had three strong men wearing dirty clothes, they were interpreters. The famous interpreter had not yet arrived. They were talking to one another about me, they said, "She is not qualified to interpret." I responded to them, "The language I am interpreting, you do not even understand."

The inside of the lounge room without a toilet is symbolic of the church leaders do not teach their congregation of road of purification, emphasis on to conversion, daily exam and repent; instated, they are teaching them be relax on God's commandments.

The hall, with several midgets entrances and the oval top door built underground from clay is symbolic of the system of the world. Their power is like clay, it comes from below the earth, they are under the power of the devil.

The stage is symbolic of God's throne without God's presence. People at the side table are symbolic of those who are trying to come to God. My extended cousin is symbolic of those who needed help to come to God. Her son is symbolic of preachers, ministers, and church leaders are willing to help. The interpreters are symbolic of those interpreting the earthly laws. Those were sitting around the top part of the table are symbolic of lawmakers and government officials.

God Reveals the World Against the Almighty

January 24, 1998. In my dream I entered the government building door, to my left was an open door to the military offices. About five steps from the door was a public handicapped restroom; its door was about seventy percent closed, or thirty percent open. I saw Adam, a former worker at a large bank in California, sitting on the toilet; I said to him, "Adam, I need to talk to you after you are done." As I walked forward a few steps, about to turn right, I saw him sitting on the floor in front of the toilet, naked, exposing his entire male organ. As I saw this, I quickly hid my face outside the divider, next to the restroom. I screamed for help, the military officers came out from their office, and asked me what had happened. While Adam was still inside the restroom I told them what I saw and asked for Adam's superior. But all of them shrugged their shoulders, and responded that they did not know Adam's immediate superior. I then said to them, "I am going to the highest superior." While saying this, I saw the highest superior up high to my right.

I then heard the Lord said to me, "The male penis (organ) is giving birth. The officers have denied their responsibilities. Adam is the Adam who disobeyed God's commandments. The bank is the power of money to protect liars."

I then saw two old, dirty, light coffee-colored bed sheets, and the Lord continued, "Those belong to her; she fears you and denied them yesterday. Bring them down and leave them on the floor of the second family room for her." He continued, "They denied their responsibilities." I said, "Lord, my responsibility is to hear You, to understand them, and delivery to them exactly the contents of your message."

I got up, and while I was praying for a deeper meaning, in my vision I saw next to the corner of my left face the right of David's face, a clerk for the largest life insurance company. He told me that when he was little, one time in a dream, he saw an angel. In the dream, David was wearing clear eye glasses with dark-tinted frames. I asked, "Lord who is this man?" I remembered King David and I said, "King David prayed for me and for them." Then the Lord said, "One wrong added to another wrong makes the situation worse." He meant that we must deal with the truth to resolve the problem.

I then saw in the distance, in front of me, my purple pen. The outside color of the pen was very shiny and pretty; but the ink came out in bad form; the Lord said, "Humans replaced God's commandments with their laws; they made the world violent with their abortion law; people march to protest, even killing adults." God means that legal abortion brings church people with no discernment, involving marching and protest and causing adults to be killed, like the purple pen that looked good when I looked at it, but I when wrote with it ink sometimes came out and some times not.

The name Adam symbolizes souls disobeying God's commandments. His sitting on the toilet on the floor exposing his male genital symbolic of counterfeit repent expose to other. Because they did not repent from their hearts, they gave the devil permission to be seven times stronger in controlling that person's mind and actions.

The office to my left represents the nation's governments. The officers who shrugged their shoulders are symbolic of lawmakers, government officials, and church leaders. They shrugged their shoulders symbolizing one blaming on another, denying the truth and responsibility, using other people's donations to gain power, making the matters worse; and costing the taxpayers money, and American citizens shame. The superior above the earth is symbolic of God the Almighty.

The two dirty bed sheets are symbolic of those who deny responsibility to the foundation, and this has been crushed down by God.

The World Pays for Crimes Against the Creator

January 22, 1998. In my dream I saw a few steps directly from the front opening of the door an altar setting on the floor. The top was made with four pieces of triangular-shaped red cardboard; joined with something gold making four dragons face away from the center of the roof. The back altar was covered, the front and other two side had no wall. Inside

538

was a pot filled with sand, with several sticks of incense burned to the bottom. While I looked at this altar, I was very angry; I then took both of my hands and lifted the entire altar and threw it outside the door.

I turned to my left, and I saw at the center of the back wall the throne of God formed from a white cloud, firm and strong. While I faced the throne of God, I saw to my left beside God's throne was another throne, it was formed with loose white smoke. I knew the smoky throne was the kind of altar I just threw out the door.

I saw myself just left of a high basement; my right hand held a round hollow metal pole. The top of this pole was like the back of a big snake's head. Walking away from this basement in firm and confidence, I looked for a canyon to throw this pole down into. Inside the basement some clothes hung to dry; some people were trying to follow me, but I walked too fast. Their shoulders touched the bottom of the clothes, these people were looking at me, trying to catch up with me. The house symbolic of spiritual realm, the loose white smoke symbolic of man good deeds.

The altar on the floor is symbolic of sins that people focus on or are married to; idol worship in the world such as murder through abortion, generating destructive weapons, researchers who want to be like God, such as cloning humans and animals. They terminate the virtue of love for one another, and destroy the human race and souls. The basement symbolic of the earth.

The pole in my hand that I was on the way to dump: metal is symbolic of authority, the top of the pole like a snake's head is symbolic of world leaders thoughts filled with evil. The hollow pole is symbolic of empty promises.

The clothes are symbolic of protection; hanging to dry is symbolic of God purifying the world. People standing at the bottom of these outfits symbolize future conversions.

January 30, 1998 was the third day of celebrating of the Vietnamese New Year, it was also my first grand daughter Madelene 30 days old. Besides having other food, I went to a Chinese B.B.Q. store.   After I got out of my car, about two steps forward to the front door, I saw an altar on the floor, and I commanded out loud, "In Jesus name, I am a Princess of Heaven and Earth, I come to destroy you. Get under my foot." I then prayed to the Lord, "Father, Lord Jesus, Holy Spirit, I did what You sent me. I ask You for protection during the time I am in this store, and forever." The altar that has four dragons I saw in the dream was revelation in spirit; today is in the natural; these four dragons symbolic of false holiness.

> *Then God delivered all these commandments: "I, the LORD, am your God, who brought you out of the land of Egypt, that place of slavery. You shall not have other gods beside me. You shall not carve idols for yourselves in the shape of anything in the sky above or on the earth below or in the waters beneath the earth; you shall not bow down before them or*

worship them. For I, the Lord, your God, am a jealous God, inflicting punishment for their father's wickedness on the children of those who hate me, down to the third and fourth generation."

–Exodus 20: 1-5

Many people do not understand the difference between the two words "worship and honor." God is the only One we worship: God is the Eternal Father, creator of heaven and earth; His only Son is Jesus, the fully God and fully man, the Holy Spirit is the third person in the Holy Trinity.

The holy saints and holy angels we only honor. Saints and angels only can do what God gives to them. We ask them to pray to God for us, like we ask other people to pray for us. The difference of holy saints and angels is that they will pray for us according to God's will, and God will accept their petitions.

Other invisible enemy spirits belong to the devil, they only do harm to our souls and physical bodies as well. They are hidden inside all kind of statues.

The visible idols are things that people place above God to satisfy their physical life, and doing so damages the spirit and the soul. These things are such as material goods, careers, money, cars, hobbies, sex hatred etc...

January 23, 1998. In the Blessed Sacrament Chapel, God the Father told me, "The newspaper that you subscribe to, screen its article headlines only. Their accusations and allegations are the earthly system. The world must pay for their crimes against God. John, chapter twenty, verse seventeen."

"Jesus said to her, "Stop holding on to me, for I have not yet ascended to the Father. But go to my brothers and tell them, 'I am going to my Father and your Father, to my God and to your God."

The world system went too far away from God's Commandments. The earthquakes, storms, heavy rains, snow, floods and such are God's warning. These warnings will not stop until we let go of the earthly things that benefit flesh. It mean the material things are not the top of the list, stop evil thoughts and actions, convert, daily exam and repent, and build good deeds to benefit souls. These warnings are just the start, and will not end until all the elect are converted.

Saint Mary Madelene was a convert; after her conversion, she placed the Lord Jesus above everything in her life, and was at the foot of the Cross without fear. After the Lord Jesus was resurrected from the dead, she did not want Jesus to leave the world. But the Lord Jesus told her not to hold on to Him; He meant that He came from heaven He must return to heaven. There is a lot greater for you and me in heaven, the eternal life. Do not hold on to the earthly treasury and evil works; they are empty promises, and will destroy your souls. We must focus in God, generate good deed and return to heaven some day.

Settle with your opponent quickly while on the way to court with him. Otherwise your opponent will hand you over to the judge, and the judge will hand you over to the guard, and you will be thrown into prison. Amen, I say to you, you will not be released until your have paid the last penny.

–Matthew 5:25-26

God is a just God; He forgives all our sins, but we have to pay for the damages that are caused by committed sins. For example, the Oklahoma City bomb blast took away over one hundred and sixty lives. The Vietnamese war killed millions Vietnamese, and over fifty thousand American troops. The Oklahoma City bomb blast was by an individual; the Vietnamese war was by two nations governments, and both destroyed the human race. Both of these actions are murder, and create hatred among people; iniquity high up to the foot of heaven.

The court in the scripture is God's court, Jesus is the only Judge. Every one of us must pay for our sins, either on earth, in purgatory before being released to heaven; or chained in the darkness of the devil for ever. Therefore, we must acknowledge our sins, convert, examine ourselves daily, and repent. Scriptural reference 1 Samuel 24:3-21.

January 24, 1998. After I received the Holy Eucharist, I pleaded to God, "Father, what do I need to do for You to protect me from hearing the enemies voices? They have been attacking me for the last several days. I promise You that I will do for You to put Your shield over my heard. Jesus, Lord, what would You want me to do, or what do I need to do so the Father will stop the enemies from speaking around my ears? Holy Spirit, help me, pray to the Father and the Lord Jesus for me. What do I need to do for the Father to seal my head from hearing enemy voices. Mother, Blessed Virgin, Archangel Michael and all holy angels and saints pray to the Lord for me."

I then saw an old soldier afar, his right hand held a sword, his left hand had a large round bronze shield raised high in front to his left. This person was formed with a white cloud, then move closer to me. While he was moving, his head grew a helmet, and this helmet got thicker. I said, "Father, Lord Jesus, Holy Spirit thank you for answering my prayer. You always help me when I come to You."

I then saw the Spirit of the Blessed Virgin Mother in from of me, she said to me, "You can not live in the case. You will go out in the public to serve the Lord. Live the life of holiness." She mean that for me an you. When a person lives in the life of holiness, by obeying all God's commandments, God will protect that person from enemies both visible and invisible, and to gain the gift of discernment.

January 25, 1998. In my dream I saw myself in the middle of the jungle, with a super-long worm chasing me. It got behind my back, and I used my right hand to pull it to the side and dumped it on ground. I saw behind me were some very small worm pieces left on the ground, and my back had slippery stuff on it from out of the worm.

I then saw myself sleeping on my left side, on my own bed. The Lord placed a helmet on my head, this helmet get thicker after the Lord put it on my head.

The worm is symbolic of the devil's offspring hiding inside human minds and actions; the slippery liquid is symbolic of iniquities. The helmet is symbolic of God protection. In my journey in this mission enemy spirits attack me in spirit, they also works through others will try to persuade me to disobey God; but God will keep me firm and strong to fulfill His way.

Meaning of the "Cup", Deceiving Church Authorities and Christians

April 6, 1997. In my dream I was working in a very small square garden; behind me on some other ground that wasn't part of my garden was an old woman, she was my ex-mother-in-law. She sat on her feet. In this garden, in front of me, to my left was a rectangular cardboard box, it contained dry soil with some spice plants that were almost dead. To my right front was a person laying on my garden spice bushes, the leaves of this plant are eaten with dog meat. As he laid the pot down, the old woman behind me told me to plant this bush in the empty corner of the cardboard box. Then the person who brought this plant picked it up and I saw that it had no root.

I then was in the middle of my garden turning this box upside down; I saw the bottom of the box was soggy and dirty from too much water for a long time. I thought, "Plants can not grow if the bottom of the box covers them, I need to cut out the bottom of the box." I then thought, "If I cut out the bottom of the box, this box would have no bottom to hold on to the soil and plants." I went to the end of the garden and took a dry rectangular carton, and scooped up some dry soil mixed with spice seeds.

The dream changed, I was standing above the ground, and my feet did not touch the ground. To my right, I saw something like a well, but there was no water, only wet soil at the middle and around it. Outside the wet soil around the well, some big, fat, long worms were crawling. I saw some hands pick up these worms. I was already fighting, seeing these worms and they were moving, then I fought even more when I saw human hands pick them up. I ran by using both of my hands to hold a cable high above my head, to get away from these worms. I then saw a skinny long worm stuck to the back of my thigh, part of it was inside my birth canal, and it was trying to enter more deeply. I fought the hardest fight I ever had in my life. My right hand grabbed the middle of the worm and pulled it out, at the same time I gathered all my strength to make a great effort like a woman giving birth to a child. I got all of the worm out of me, and it left a very small part behind my thigh, I dumped it away; I then used my right hand to peel the rest of the worm off my thigh and dump it on ground.

In the morning, while I prayed for interpretation, the Lord said to me, "Now, I give you the interpretation of the dream: Your sister that you only saw in spirit, in the dream, that glued a worm to your thigh, and part of a live worm crawling inside your birth carnal, is symbolic of the many you will see who do the works in the church that look great externally, but the inside of their hearts are against Me, the Lord, Your God. Sometime I will reveal to you these people; as you know that they are deceivers, you will be suffering. The elderly woman sitting on the ground is symbolic of the church authorities who give out their orders against My commandments. The spices plants in the box that were almost dead, and her giving you orders to put another dying spice bush in the box, and your recognizing immediately the plant had no root; this action is they are trying to persuade you. Your turning the entire box and replanting them means your know their actions are wrong; you are cleansing their systems, and their actions, by those words coming out from your mouth, which are words from Me that I put on your lips. The words from out of your mouth come with my power; and the systems will be changed. The symbolism of the systems being changed in the dream is that you cut off the wet dirty bottom of the carton box, and replaced it with dry clean cardboard to separate the ground and the soil in the box."

He then continued, "The second dream when you saw worms mixed with good soil; the worms are symbolic of the demons and devil; they are weeds among the wheat. There are times I will reveal to you who are the weeds; when you see them in natural, you will be fighting, you will run away from them like when I revealed to you some before at the Good Shepherd Church. You knew their hearts when you saw them, you will not speak to them, and you rebuke the devils in your mind when you see them walk by you, or say hello to you, because they will not enter heaven, their free will is completely given to the devil These will not convert and repent, people are not able to know from their actions, they even look better than the wheat. Their tongues are prey of sword; their words are sweet but they are poison. The part of the worm inside your birth canal represents those who try very hard to destroy words that come out from your mouth. Gathering all your strength to pull out and dump it away is symbolic of through your obedience and labor to God you will have victory over them. The small end part of the worm stuck to your left thigh, you then peeled it off and dumped it on ground making you feel free symbolizes your complete victory. The feeling free is symbolic at your last breath."

God Revealed the Heart of False Worshippers

In the morning of January 9, 1997, I heard the Lord say, "Tell them, I don't bark, but when I bark, I bark loud and clear. I don't preach, I bark through my actions."

When the dog barks, people are scared and run away, if that person does not avoid the dog, he will damage that person. Preaching is symbolic of proclaiming the Gospel, to help others to obey God's commandments, and make the world a better place to live and build the kingdom of heaven. Dogs barking are symbolic of those who disobey God's commandments, bringing an evil tongue and actions to others, creating more evil actions, and destroying souls.

January 10, 1998. In my dream I was in a room with an open door at the corner to the front wall. Across from the door was a high mail box, similar to a U.S. mail box on the street to collect mail. There were seven telephone buttons on top of it, one at the top row, and the second and third row each had three buttons, and one big hole at the bottom of these buttons. Through this hole I saw the inside was empty and very dark. These telephone buttons were for auto dialing. I dialed a few of these six buttons and I received an answering machine. When I looked at them, I knew all the people would not answer these six buttons, these six lines are always answered by the answering machine. Next to the top button was a small square piece of paper, like the button, with the number 11. I knew that this top button was the only one that would have a human pick up the phone; but I was afraid to dial the top button, because I just pooped (go to toilet) into the hole, and my stool was in the box.

The inside of the box is symbolic of the heart of those who refuse to convert, exam daily and repent. Going to the restroom, and the poop staying inside is symbolic of the sins adding up. Dark in this box is symbolic of the darkness of evil. Six auto dialing buttons are symbolic of humans habit allowing the devil to use them. The top button with the number is symbolic of discernment, some refuse to convert, daily exam and repent, or deal with the truth. When a person dials the telephone and receives the answering machine; he is the only one talking, he is the only one controlling, but if he gets a person answering the phone, this person will say their view.

False worshipers are coming to church, singing, reading, praying the rosary etc... Participating in the worship service "WITHOUT" focusing in God or the words they sing and read, their hearts contain spiritual murder.

The meaning of spiritual murder is that they place other things more important than God; they spend their time to benefit their physical bodies; and give their time to God only when it is convenient for them; when a person does this kind of action, he is naturally rejected God.

The cause of spiritual murder comes from: families that do not have a foundation of obeying God's commandments; from false or improper teaching, and from friends, or co-workers that do not have a foundation in God. They committed sins, go to confession and committed same sins again, refused to reject those sins they had confessed. They received the Holy Eucharist with impure hearts.

These thoughts and actions lead to lack of discernment; serving God to please the priest, for their own name or benefit; to obey the devil, reject the truth, accept murder, being too lazy to fight against flesh, carelessness, no faith in God, disobedience to God's commandments, and obeying earthly laws that go against God's law. Practicing or associating with fortune tellers, channeling, or associating with friends or co-workers that associate with fortune tellers or psychics also leads to the above, as well as rejecting to place God above all things, improper sexual acts, or out of marriage in the church, etc.....

Life on Earth, Body Resurrection after Death

Close to the end of the year 1996, my 1993 Nissan Maxima started making some noise. I took it to one of the Vietnamese auto repair shops, and they told me that a fan in front of the radiator made that noise, I could bring it back later so they could fix it.

A few days before I left San Diego for Little Rock, Arkansas, this noise increased became a big concern to me, because I do not know anything about cars. I was dependent on my two sons. I told my older son, Linh-James to replace the fog light, and repair that noise. He replaced the fog light, but the noise was from inside the engine. He told me, "There is not enough time to fix this noise in San Diego; but when you go to Arkansas, find a Nissan dealer and have them to fix it for you." He also asked me about the guarantee of the car. The car did not have even forty thousand miles at that time, and the guarantee I bought with the car covered up to either 75,000 miles or the year 1999.

There were a few times I was about to take the car to have it checked, I had even made an appointment, but I did not take it there. Friday, June 20, 1997, the Lord Jesus told me, "Monday, you will take the car to be fixed."   Monday, after I got out from 7:30 a.m. mass from the chapel at the Saint Vincent hospital, I took the car to Premier Pontiac and Nissan. The woman at the service desk took some information, and asked me to come back the next day at the same time, because they could not work on my car that Monday.

Tuesday, June 24, 1997, the feast of the Birth of Saint John the Baptist; I took my car back to the Premier dealership, left it there and went to Enterprise rent-a-car to make arrangements for a rental car. As I walked out their door to pick up the car, a rental agent told me, "This car is brand new." I saw the new car sticker at the window. The rental agent asked the service man, "How many miles?" The service man said, "Seven hundred and three." The rental representative asked, "Why are there that many miles on a new car?" The service man said, "It depends on where it came from." I then asked, "Is this the first time you have rented this car out?" The rental agent replied, "Yes, you are the first one rent it." Now I felt that God was saying something to me through this new rental car; I said out loud, "Jesus, what are you saying to me, Jesus." The rental representative asked me, "This is a brand new car, we carry our own insurance coverage, only twelve dollars per day; if something happens to the car, you only give us the key." I thought this car was covered by my car insurance, but there may have been something that the Lord wanted to use the extra insurance for as a substance for a revelation; I then turned my face away from the agent, and asked the Lord, "Jesus, what would you want me to do." I then said to the agent,

"Okay." He said, "I'd like you to initial at these spots."

While I was driving home, I knew the Lord was using this new rental car as a substance to transport supernatural power down to earth. I entered the bedroom, seeking the Lord for the interpretation, the Lord said, "You car is symbolic of yourself. This rental car is symbolic of the mission." I said, "Lord, this rental car doesn't have strong power like my car." The Lord explained, "When you are weak, you are strong in God."

After I came back from the 12:05 p.m. mass at the Cathedral of Saint Andrew, in the afternoon devotion, I was on the way to being completely asleep, I asked the Lord, "Jesus, as a fully man body, You were resurrected from the dead and went home to heaven. As you are in this body in heaven, do you see me? And the Blessed Mother, with Her body in heaven, does she see me?" I then slept.

In my dream, I heard the Lord Jesus say to me, "After I was resurrected from the dead, before I went to heaven to the Father, sometimes people could see me, sometimes people did not see me. There were times I wanted them [apostles] to see me, then they could see Me. If I did not want them to see me, they could not see Me." While the Lord was saying this, in my dream I saw inside the tomb, this tomb was like a hole in the middle of the huge rock. Jesus the Lord was sitting on something like a single bed, that was in the same piece of rock cave as the tomb, in the center. There was a long white cloud shroud wrapped over His shoulder, across His chest, down to his right waist, and covered His thighs. I then saw the upper room where He appeared to the apostles, and He was walking along with a few men on the road.

The Lord still continued talking, "After I went home to the Father, sometimes they could see Me, sometimes they could not see Me." While the Lord was saying this, I saw a King's plaza far off, this king's plaza had a concrete pavement at the middle, around this concrete ground were big, tall ancient buildings, the main one had a dome at the top, these buildings were built with clouds, but no one was there.

I asked, "Jesus, when You are not there [in heaven] where will you be?" He said, "When I am not in heaven, I am in the Holy Eucharist."

I asked, "Lord, I know Your body was resurrected, but I only see the host; I believe that the consecrated host comes with Your Spirit."

He said, "Mystery. There was one host that turned into My fresh flesh." I remember some time ago, someone told me in nature that, a host turned into fresh flesh. While the Lord was saying this, I saw a white host at the sanctuary of the Cathedral of Saint Andrew, I also saw a dark places very far away. I knew that dark area contained the consecrated host that turned into the Lord Jesus' fresh flesh.

Jesus the continued, "After they put My mother in the tomb, I raised her up. I will raise you up before people put you in a tomb. Her body now is in heaven, she is sitting at the Queen's throne. Saint Joseph also resides in the King's plaza as her companion. There is no marriage in heaven. Moses and Elija are also in heaven. She is watching angels working at your throne." While the Lord was saying this, in my dream I saw a spirit of a tomb, and the queen's throne in the King's plaza.

I asked, "Jesus, angels do not have a body like humans that we can see; how does Mother watch them working at my throne?" While I was asking the Lord, I saw to the right of the queen's chair a globe of spirits in action.

The Lord said, "Your good deeds will transform into supernatural, together with your prayers, angels take them to heaven and build your throne."

The telephone rang, and I woke up. On the other side of the telephone was Debbie from Premier Nissan; she told me, "We found the noise you told us about, it is VTC in the engine. We will not be able to fix it today. I will get you a rental car." I said, "I already have a rental car." She said, "I am only able to authorize it for one day." I said, "I will get another day. Does the guarantee cover it?" She said, "Yes."

The rental car was not approved by the dealer insurance at the time I pick it up, and later the dealer representative let me know of she authorized to pay for it symbolic of trust in God, He is provider.

This is an actual story of my car, and the Lord Jesus spoke to me in my dream, He also allowed me to ask questions, like those stories in the old testament; and parables in the new testament, they are symbolism. Almost all the conversion between me and the Lord are symbolism. The Lord used my car as symbolic of me, Mariette; the insurance as God's promises. The new rental as the mission, God entrusts His power in my hand, and my responsibility is to receive, take care of and distribute it properly.

Cloud and Fire are Lamb Language

7:03 a.m. May 7, 1997. In my dream I saw myself lying on my back, up high in the air, close to the sky. I saw the entire sky filled white clouds; between the sky and me, at my chest was a globe of fire with a fire fighter's helmet next to it. Still in the dream I remembered that I had seen this before, except the last time I was on the way flying away from God throne to the gate of heaven, not lying on my back; I thought that was after I went home to the heaven.

I then saw myself lying on my back in bed, the back of the white lamb touched my left cheek, I said to the Lord, "Lord, this is the Lamb of God touching me; I want Your real face to kiss me." I then saw my right arm was straight out to the level of my shoulder; my five fingers and another five fingers of another hand were embracing each other, the two arms were in same direction. I knew this was the Lord Jesus' hands, my dear brother, my God was holding my hand; He said, "I will hold your hand while you are standing at the Gospel podium; I will speak into your ears, go into your thoughts, and come out of your mouth."

I then asked Jesus the Lord, "Will May 27, 28 and 29, 1997 really be the Holy Eucharist Healing Service?" I then saw in the dream a vision "100%" YES. He then said, "The church will gently agree with what the Lord ordered."

I then saw my left arm across my upper stomach, with the shadow of the Blessed Virgin Mother, she kissed me at my arm, like a mother kisses a little child while she sleeps. I physically lifted up my arm. I then saw her face lift up in front of me like the virgin and child image; she said to me, "You set fired at Scott twice yesterday; you will set fire at him harder tonight. He will then set fire at the Bishop, as well as you set fire at the bishop." She means, through the power of God, I will set fire at people's hearts and minds with God's commandments; they in turn will set fire at the spiritual leaders.

I then saw the right turn spot of the concrete road with high barricades, both sides have houses that seem like community townhouses, and the end of the road was curved like a snail's tail. This is symbolic of the true foundation of God; we must place our trust in him; none of us will see His entire plan, and there are many times we see nothing in the future, but we must obey in faith.

Visiting the Most High Priest

I heard the women married to the New Orleans Bishop that I saw in a dream before, say to me, "She visited Father Hero in the compound, He lived there alone." I was looking for him, but I could not find him.

I was in the public, outside the building asking this woman to give me Father Hero's address; this woman came out of the building which was built with clay like a tomb. She had two American Airline brass logos, each of them in an individual plastic bag; she gave me one from her left hand, this one was bigger than the one she held in her right hand. I opened it up, in front of the left side of the logo wing was number 6496. She retained the one on her right hand for herself, this one had no number, the front of the eagle wings were smoother than the one she gave to me. This symbolic of people refused to obey God, carrying their cross, choose the easy way to get around.

I then turned around and went to look for Father Hero, this woman followed behind me. She stopped at the hot food counter in the open air to buy a lot of hot food for Father Hero; she knew exactly what to get for him. I thought that since I had not seen him for long time, I also needed to buy something for him. I was looking at fire sauces inside the glass case, but I did not know what to buy so I did not buy anything.

I then looked up at the front of the round corner triangular booth to see how far it was from here to Father Hero's apartment. I saw the number 696 at the front. I then saw the number I had in my right hand was 6496. I thought that we had a long way to go to get to Father Hero's place; I saw his place up in the air in a remote area. I then thought we needed to get a car to drive there, it was too far to walk. Now the woman was finished paying for the food she bought for Father Hero; she took the lead, I was walking behind her to a small house at the right side in that complex with number 696. We were then in front of Father Hero's small house. While I was walking behind this woman, I saw Father Hero walking out of his house after he closed the wooden door behind him. This front door was at the corner of the house, to his right was a long carport, making a corner to the house. A big light-colored bath tub with no water was on the porch that connected to the front wall of the house. While Father Hero was walking out, he wore a white T-shirt with large white polyester shorts; these shorts were too large for him because he look old, skinny and ill. He was happy to se the woman, but he did not seem happy to see me. I feared that he might disappear on me; but he told the woman in sign language, "Bring her inside the house," while he continued to walk outside. The woman was confident to walk in the house, and it seemed like this was her own home, but I was afraid to enter Father Hero's house.

I then stood inside this small house with only one room. This woman laid the bag of food on the high counter. She stood at the end to open it; I was standing behind her, there was a space between her and me. Father Hero was standing to the right and about to cross the space in between the woman and me. As I looked at his face, he did not look like the face that I saw before; he now looked too old for his age at fifty five, with skin and bones. I thought, "I wish that when he speaks to me, his voice would still be sweet like before."

After the dream while I was still asleep, the Lord gave me the interpretation, and slowly brought me up in spirit to finish the interpretation before I got up. God reveled to me the hearts of the spiritual leaders. The woman was symbolic of their congregation. Father Hero in this revelation with old symbolic the church systems are mingle of good and bad together when they come to services or worship. It mean counterfeit God. Food is a holocaust; and there is no suffering as a holocaust that they offer to God.

God's Power Comes With His Word

January 28, 1996; 8:46 a.m. In my devotion I was too concerned of opening to the public the truth of my responsibility, that the Father predestined me for. The Father said to me, "You fear to speak the truth, but do not be afraid; it is from God. I did the same to Abraham, Jacob, and Moses, and now to you; there is no difference between you and them. Every one must say the truth of what they heard from God, and who they are in front of God."

It was now 18 days after I left San Diego, California to be in Little Rock, Arkansas. Even though my children were young adults, this was the first time in my entire life that I left my children and moved this far away from them. I love God above everything, I also love my children, and miss them. Beyond missing my children, I had not seen anyone respond to me as God had promised me. All day I was homesick; around six o'clock, in my devotion, I asked God, "Jesus, what I am here for? Can I go back to San Diego?" I went on and on with God, then fell asleep.

In my sleep, I heard the Father say to me, "I predestined you for this job. You are here to fulfill it. You are not to go back to San Diego yet." I then woke up, crying out loud, "That was the Father speaking." I looked at the clock and it was 11 p.m.

April 14, 1997, 5:10 a.m. In my vision I saw my black purse next to my Bible, on the floor next to my head, then the purse moved by itself above my head. The Lord Jesus said to me, "The Father granted that now is the right time for you to learn of everything. Go see Scott tomorrow or the next day. He is anxious to see you, so you can assist him in understanding God's calling for him. In this meeting he will give you the dates for the Holy Eucharist Healing Service and Altar Call. He has spoken to the bishop, and the bishop told him, 'I have prayed and discerned, everything she [Mariette] gave to me is from God. This woman is hearing from God. She will be a great treasure for our diocese.' While the Lord spoke, in my vision I saw the Cathedral of Saint Andrew and the rectory, with bishop Andrew's face in spirit. Still in prayer, I heard the Father call, "Abraham." Abraham replied, "Ready." I said to the Lord, "Lord, I am ready too." The Lord said to me, "Go to sleep, I will tell you exactly what to do." Then in my vision I saw my notebook was open at the page I recorded yesterday, and the front and back cover were folded inside. The Lord turned back one sheet, and He said to me, "In the past I have done some works through you, for you are mighty, but compared to the future it is still nothing. I will send you to all nations to proclaim My words, the same commandments I gave to Moses on Mount Sinai. The children of this age will be in the wilderness like the Israelites in those days. They have been built the golden calf and worshipped it. Now is time for you to come down the mountain Sinai like Moses before, to destroy that golden calf."

The bishop in this revelation symbolic of the Father. Father Scott symbolic of the Lord Jesus

The Power of Credit Cards and Channeling are the Devil's Trick

After the Father spoke, in my vision, I saw a buffet counter without a cover on the top, there were arms crossing over the mashed potato container, in his hand was a VISA credit card. This hand was giving out VISA cards to others, I said to him, "I do not want this, In Jesus name, get under my feet." Then this hand and VISA disappeared. I then saw a man who does channeling, and the Lord said to me, "I have sent you in the jungle with wolves, now you can understand the trick of the devil."

The Lord God mean that credit cards are one of the tricks that the devil uses on people in this age. These credit cards drive people to be in debt, and from being in debt they must spend more time working to pay for their bills; not as time for God. This is as bad as the devil using the human body for channeling.

The Lord God then said to me, "Now you understand that I do not allow you to use credit cards anymore. While you need a piece of plastic for protection, have the bank issue you a VISA that links to your account, where you are using your own money, you will not be in debt like VISA." The Lord spoke about the 'debit card.'

I then saw the Christian television where many ministers sell their books on TV for people to call in and charge to their credit cards. The Lord said, "These people are in the system of the devil, they are not serving God; they are in the system of getting people in debt, so people turn their back to me.

April 1996, was the time I published the book "My Patient - God's Gift." The Lord Jesus did not allow me to put credit card information on the on the books order form; but the man who did the layout put it in anyway, and explained to me that it would be easy for people to order; but I did not understand that this system was the trick of the devil. But in the second book "God's Purification - Not Easy" He silently told me to write send me money and I will send you books. God revealed of people used God's blessing without pay their due for eternal life.

Then in spirit, I saw a Catholic woman who taught a non-domination Bible class. I asked the Lord, "Lord, is this woman operating under the spirit of the enemy, but you called her to teach me Your words. What is happening here?" The Lord God said to me, " She does hear some from me, but most of the time, she hears from enemies. I sent you there because there is no other better than her, to teach you to take the first step to learning the basics of My words."

I then went back to sleep. In my dream I was sitting on a chair at the desk, inside the front door of my earthly mother's house. In front of me on the ground was a military man who just brought in a military, long, heavy dark bag I was suspicious that this bag contained a dead body. I reached to the spot light on the wall to my right, I thought that I could make the light shine on his bag so he could see. As I was trying to turn it on, I found that this spotlight was only half made, not a full bulb, and this electric bulb was taped to the wall with office Scotch tape, it did not have a source nor wires to connect to the electricity. I was a little scared of the dark bag. I then looked to my left, there was another man with many more bags containing dead bodies. I was fighting and ran out the door, and crossed the ground between the house and the kitchen.

I stood next to the well outside my earthly mother's kitchen. But this well no longer had any water. A square container was built in the middle of the well and filled inside with pig food. On the ground, next to the pig food container was Mrs. Binh, sitting and facing my earthly mother who sat inside the kitchen, while there were children taking the pig food out of the container and eating it. It looked gross to me.

I then was inside another room that was next to my earthly mother's kitchen. I saw a big huge man, who looked strong and had dark skin. The Lord gave to me that he was the father of the family, the same Mrs. Binh who sat on the ground faced that father. The father was eating burned rice, and he still had more that he was holding in his hands, this piece was as big as the bottom of a five quart pot. I liked the burned rice, I asked him to give me some, and he gave me a piece that was as small as my two fingers. The father sat behind Mrs. Binh, his right hip was next to her back, and he leaned his right face at her right shoulder. I knew that this woman was very dangerous, I separated the father using my hands to pull him away from the woman's shoulder. He laid his back on the ground, behind her. I saw the father's upper and lower body was separated by a line, and it was filled with disease.

In my afternoon devotion, in my vision I saw a huge Chinese gate that was very colorfully decorated, each of the four corners of this gate was built with a dragon head looking away, and their tails connected to the main beam of the gate. In front of the gate, close to the top step, was a man formed as a cloud, holding his jacket at his shoulder. This man fought against the wind to pass many steps, and he was trying to enter this gate.

I then saw the Chinese gate at the entrance of the Vietnamese business center, in Bolsa in Westminister, California. I then saw another Chinese gate at the center of the military cemetery in Vietnam.

The Lord said, "The Chinese gate entrance to the business represents the spiritual dead, and the gate at the military cemetery is the physically dead." The Lord continued, "The military dark bags are symbolic of spiritual death. Your trying to turn the spot light on them, but with no wires to connect to the electric means you were trying to help them, but you could not do it alone, they have to raise themselves up to God. The pig food symbolizes enemies. The burning rice symbolizes the world systems. The woman name Binh represents the devil. The woman facing the earthly mother and father is symbolic of the devil watching peoples every step. Your separating the man from the woman means you try to help people to get away from the devil. The disease in the stomach of the father represents the world's systems are a disease that lead to the dead."

God is just, loving and merciful, He does not want souls that he created to die in the darkness of the devil forever; but people must help themselves in cooperating with God. He is now saving them by placing this world in the wilderness. The Lord called Moses to lead the children of Israel through the wilderness in the Book of Exodus, and now in actions in this world. During the period of wandering in the wilderness, people will experience a lot of tragedies and human power can do nothing. People must take their steps to obey all God's commandments; each person must destroy their own golden calf. This wilderness has two periods; first is conversion to God, and the second God purging their iniquities. How long will the wilderness last? It will last until all the names in the Book of Life iniquities are purged.

Pride to Serve God

You have defied me in word, says the LORD, yet you ask, "What have we spoken against you?" You have said, "It is vain to serve God, and what do we profit by keeping his command, and going about in penitential dress in awe of the LORD of hosts?" Rather must we call the proud blessed; for indeed evildoers prosper, and even temp God with impunity.

–Malachi 3: 13-15

April 14, 1997. In my devotion before I went to sleep, I pleaded to the Lord for the Holy Eucharist healing Service and Altar Call at Saint Andrew's Cathedral. I the said to the Blessed Mother, "Mother, I am desperate to have the date for the Holy Eucharist Healing Service and Altar Call at the Cathedral of Saint Andrew and other churches." Because I used the word desperate to her, she said to me, "You ask the Lord what you just said to me." I then said to the Lord, "Jesus, the Blessed Mother told me to ask You, the first time she asked you to do something for her was at the wedding in Cana, and now is the second time in her life to say this to you; she is not tempting God, but she interferes here as the mother, you are her son, and I am her daughter, your sister; she asks you like fully man when you were on earth, but now You are God, to plead to the Father for me, for the Holy Eucharist Healing Service and Altar Call at the Cathedral of Saint Andrew to be in action." This revelation is symbolism, not as what the words are saying.

April 15, 1997. In my dream, I walked inside the lower level of a big house. I do not live there, but I have authority over this property. I saw the ex-father of the two sons standing in the middle of the ground. When he saw me, he left. I then saw him again; he left again. I knew that the two sons gave the key of the door to the ex-father, and I was very angry at these two sons.

I was up on the second level, standing in front of these two son, and scolded them about giving the key of the house to their ex-father. I told them, "I will change the locks on all eight doors, and each of them will have a different key. I will give you one key for one door to enter the house, and I will have the master key to open all eight doors (these two sons would only be able to open one door, each of them would have a different key.)

I then saw myself beating up my oldest daughter's head very badly; while her husband sat there and watched me beat up his wife, without saying anything or doing anything. I beat her head for a while; I then thought, her head will be ruined from me beating her on her head; I then hit her at the side of her lip then on her thigh. At this time her husband got up and walked behind me and said something to me, but I did not remember what it was.

I then was standing away, I saw the two same sons standing outside the fence, in front of a house and urinating inside the fence, on the lawn. Their was a little child inside the house looking through the window watching these two sons urinate on the lawn like they were sprinkling the lawn.

I woke up and prayed for the interpretation. In my vision I saw the table of the custom frame shop at Hobby Lobby; then I saw two parts of my key chain put together, and the Lord said, "Not to trust them, not to believe them. Many people are saying who they are, and what they will do; but they are not who they are, and do not do what they say. These business professors are coming here to recruit more business, they are not coming here for the benefit of the church." While the Lord was saying this, in my vision, I saw the first row of the members of the Health Care Ministry on Sunday April 13, 1997." The Lord means the Hobby and Lobby store and custom wood frame shop represent these professors like service to God is their hobby.

I said, "Lord, Jesus, You are the spirit of the truth, You are really truth, not the truth like people take and oath at court." I was led by the Holy Spirit to say this to the Lord Jesus. The Lord said, "Everyone of us when come to church and service to God, must serve Him from our hearts and our souls. Not like people sworn in the court to speak the true and lie. The kind of people all over the world, they come to serve in My church, but for their own benefits."

He continued, "Priests lack discernment because they are away from me, they are not able to discern what is true good, and what is evil behind, who really comes to serve God in the church, and who comes for their own benefit. Those proclaim their talent, they have high pride, and they look down on others. When they come to serve in the church they feel that they are better than priests, because of their profession. But I the Lord, I declare to you, I will lift up My priest and crush down those who have high pride."

In the scripture at the wedding at Cana, the Lord turned water into wine. The head waiter and others did not know why the good wine was served at the end; but the servants that poured water in the jars knew that a miracle was performed by the Lord Jesus. The Lord Jesus said that He now will perform more miracles by raising up His priests and those who serve Him with their hearts and souls will understand God's heart. He is speaking of having faith in the Lord Jesus, this faith that we inherited from the Blessed Virgin Mother; she has faith in her son, and her son is God, by telling those servants at the Cana wedding "do whatever he tells you to do."

The Lord continued, "The Blessed Virgin Mother's faith is from God given to her, she does not have it on her own. Anyone who pronounces that they have talent on their own; doing things on their own, they belong to the devil.(John: 15:15:5 ... without me you can do nothing.) As the Lord said this, in my vision, I saw Father Scott sitting at the sanctuary, bending his head down, showing much suffering. This scene was at the Sunday mass when the Health Care Ministry introduced themselves to the public; and the Blessed Virgin Mother told me, "They [enemy spirits] are attacking Scott." The Lord God means we must be humble before God, and depend on Him; this humbleness must be from the heart as well as proclaimed in the public.

I said, "Lord Jesus, these are your works, I just do what You tell me to do, not what other people tell me to do. I only hear from You, I will not hear from other people."

The Lord God continued, "Working together with the devil is like this telephone with the open back battery cover." While the Lord saying this, in my vision, I saw my Panasonic wireless phone KX-T9500 - the handset cover of the battery on the back was laid on carpet floor, next to the hand set facing up. Even with the handset facing up, I still saw the battery on the back without a cover. The Lord means that people are proud of themselves in a profession and think they are better than lowly people. These people are hiding their pride in their hearts; but sooner or later it will be open to the public. Things done in the darkness will come to light, such as those doing illegal things will be exposed in the public, in the court of God. Lucifer was cast out of heaven because of pride, pride is a great sin against God.

The Lord said to me, "This is a separate Chapter, and it is a continuation of the Health Care Ministry; with the title 'Service to God full of pride is not depending on God.'"

The Lord continued, "The two sons in the dream symbolize of those who do service to God in the darkness, and will be exposed in the light." In the dream these two sons giving out the house key to their father behind me; their father represents the devil; but I knew their action means God knows everything; God will bring these actions to the light.

He continued, "Beating up the daughter is symbolic of them receiving punishment for their sins. Service to God not from the heart and without humbleness is a grave sin." While the Lord was saying this, I saw the dream that I beat up my oldest daughter's head very badly. The Lord spoke about the first and the last to enter heaven, because they have to pay the damages caused from their sins before they enter heaven.

The Lord continued, "Many people come to church regularly from the time they were baptized. They believe that they will enter heaven, but they live a life without having faith in God, without depending on God, without giving their heart to God. That is who you saw in your dream and beat her up. You will beat them up through the words that I speak through you." The Lord means that His words coming out through me together with His power, and through supernatural power will beat them up."

The Lord said to me, "Thank you for being patient with Me. Your reward on earth is the result of the Holy Eucharist Healing service and Altar Call at Saint Andrew Cathedral in victory."

Jesus the Lord continued, "Changing the lock in the house means I will blot out the names in the Book of Life of those who do not convert their hearts and actions to me." The Lord means those who will not convert and repent daily will not enter heaven. God revealed I was acting as God's Vessel.

He continue, "Urinating on the lawn, then turning to hold a cup, and walking on the rough road are those who will convert and find remission from their sins." Urinating is symbolic of purification; the cup and walking on the rough road represents embracing the cup of suffering to pay the damaged from they committed sins. While they are suffering, the Lord Jesus will purge their iniquities, and make their souls pure.

He then said to me, "You will see many people hate you because you bring what I said to you, you bring in the public. They will hurt, the more they hurt the more they suffer, and the more they suffer the more they come to Me."

In this revelation, God revealed to everyone involved with service in a non-profit group or organization, and that includes groups that belong to the church. These people provide service for their own benefit in some way, they do not provide service because of love God first. Secondly they do service with pride, not with humbleness before God; they are independent and proud of their experiences, their experiences, but not dependent on God.

God is calling them to convert and repent so they can receive heavenly eternal life. For the elect must wake up quickly before God pours His power up on you; if you wait for God to pour out his power, then it will be a lot worse than if you come to Him first.

Note: Every time I am in prayer or devotion, I only can say what the Spirit of God gives to me. Because these are the times that God is revealing to me the truth of people's hearts or events in the spirit. These could be past, present or future.

Enemies Traps

May 27, 1997. In my dream I was approaching a bridge. I was about to make a left turn on the bridge before I entered a house that was built above the ground. I saw an occult, American attorney standing on the left side corner at the beginning of the bridge. He also saw me, and he knew that I must pass through this bridge to enter the house above the ground. He tried to trip me by walking very fast across my path and hoping that I would collide with him and fall, but I quickly paused for him to pass. I then went by him very fast. He turned around and saw that I passed him. I then increased my strength and walked faster and stronger, and entered the house.

In the morning, the Lord explained to me of the dream: the occult, American attorney trying to trip me is symbolic of those who tried to prevent the Holy Eucharist healing services and altar call at the Cathedral of Saint Andrew. Pausing for him to cross and passing him symbolizes the Lord changing the Holy Eucharist healing and altar call from natural to supernatural. I had increased power and walked faster and stronger is symbolic that after God changed His direction, God will do His works more powerfully.

Miracles do Happen

June 3, 1997. In my dream, I was walking on a small road, seeking for the house to pray; following behind me was Natty Nanane and several people. I made a right turn into a huge dry ground, in front of a church. To my right were some houses that faced the church ground. I then made another right turn into an alley. Immediately as I turned, to my right there was a house shining with light mixed with fire. The front of this house was behind the other house facing the dry church ground. I stood in front, and looked at the front door, with a group of people standing behind me.

I turned around to my right, and returning to the church ground made a left turn, passed the front house, to the second alley, made another left turn, and this alley led to the same house that had the light in front. This time the door was open. I stepped inside the door, and I saw a woman who sat in the middle of the front room, facing the back wall. There was some empty space between her and the wall, to her left was a stairway to the upper room. On the other side of the empty space a few people sat and leaned their backs to the wall, facing the woman in front of me. I asked, "Can we come in here and pray?" She did not say anything to me, but she raised up from the position of sitting to kneeling, so I knew that she wanted to pray with us. I kneeled right behind her back, she was physically bigger and taller then me, so my face was facing at her mid-back, this woman was constantly facing the wall, she did not say anything. I asked "Can we pray the rosary?" Those people following were kneeling behind me to pray the rosary.

While we were praying the rosary, I heard almost everyone there speaking at the same time, "Light is falling down into the empty space. Miracles!" There was joy and surprise. I looked up over the left shoulder of the woman and I saw people once leaning to the wall were now standing, looking up and among themselves, and talking; I then looked to the right side of the woman, and I saw some clouds falling down.

While these people were sounding so excited for the miracles, the woman and I continued to pray. I felt God's power pour down into the empty space in front of this woman, and pressing into her body made her body hard like iron; she became immovable. After we finished praying, we left the house.

God Calls His People to Pay Their Tithes

November 17, 1996. In my dream, I was walking inside the upper room. In this room some people were making something on a square quilt, using soft white cotton fabric with little small burgundy flowers printed on it, like I saw before in a dream that children wearing to sleep, and they are symbolic of angels. I sat on an iron student chair that had a small wooden table, like in the classroom, to make this square quilt with them. Both sides of me had some people sitting on floor to make pieces. I saw the person to my right more clearly than I did on my left side. I thought to myself, "I can cheat when I count the number of things that I make on these square cloths to catch up with others, or even more."

I then sat on the floor in front of this chair with two huge square clear strong plastic quilts that belonged to me, one was folded in two. While I was trying to open this folded plastic, from the floor of this upper room, to my right, I heard the voice of the Archbishop Thuan Van Nguyen, Vice President of the Pontifical Council for Justice and Peace, in Vietnamese, say, "Goi tien cho cha". In English it means "Send money to me." I replied to him, "Cha can tien cho chung sinh. Con se dien thoaãi lai cha thu Hai." Translated means, "You need money to raise seminarians. I will call you back Monday." That day was Friday, and in my mind, I thought, "Saturday and Sunday I will go and collect money and call him Monday before I send it to him.

The two huge clear strong plastic quilts in my hand are symbolic of protection. The archbishop vice president is symbolic high ranking spiritual leaders. The voice of the Archbishop telling me to send him money is symbolic of the Lord Jesus commanding me to take care of seminarians. In turn, seminarians will service to God. The money is symbolic of God Power. The voice raising from the high floor is symbolic cry out to God. My thoughts about collecting money on Saturday and Sunday is symbolic that the Lord will call every one of us to pay our tithes according to His commandments to support His Church. Calling him back Monday and sending money is symbolic that I will take action on God's commandment.

> Consecration of First-born: *The Lord spoke to Moses and said, Consecrate to me every first-born that opens the womb among the Israelites, both man and beast, for it belongs to me.*
>
> –Exodus 13: 1-2

> Collection of Materials. *This is what the LORD then said to Moses: "Tell the Israelites to take up a collection for me. From every man you shall accept the contribution that his heart prompts him to give me.*
>
> –Exodus 25: 1-2

> The Sanctuary Light. *The LORD said to Moses, "Order the Israelites to bring you clear oil of crushed olives for the light, so that you may keep lamps burning regularly.*
>
> –Leviticus 24: 1-2

Through the children of Israel, God commanded all of us, from our hearts, that we must set aside some first percents of our income, to take care of His Church finances before our own expenses; or put time to do service to God before our own needs.

The sanctuary light is symbolic of the presence of God. God ordering children of Israelites to bring olive oil for the light is symbolic that God will be in their presence, because they are obedient to God by taking responsibility of God's church before their own bills.

We must understand this is God's commandments, when each one of us obeys His commandments, He then blesses us one hundred fold. If anyone does not obey God's commandments, it will be a sin against Him. Love God by obeying all His commandments in actions.

God Speaks to His Servant through Her Actions

In the morning of August 24, 1997, I took a shower and put on my purple dress. I brought with me the "God Reveals Evolution is the Process of His Creation" to give to Father Scott.

Driving to the church I was blocked by a train in front of me for about two minutes, on Riverfront Drive. I then had to stop at the red traffic light immediately after that. As I made the right turn on Chester Street, the Lord told me, "Give the envelope to the priest before the mass." I said, "Lord, You make Father Scott be inside the front door of the church for me."

I entered the front door of the Cathedral of Saint Andrew; standing in the foyer, I saw Father Scott sitting at the end of the last pew to the right section reading some paper. I walked over and gave him the envelope, and said to him, "This is for you. It is good. The Lord Jesus loves you."

The mass today was a continuation from the last Sunday, August 17, 1997. Beginning with the second baptism of an infant, I heard from the back of the Church, Father Scott ask an infant's parents, "What is the child's name?" He then announced her name "Maria." As I heard the name "Maria" I knew that the Lord has made this baptism an action to pour out His glory, power and grace upon the Rebuild My Church Mission.

We continued with the reading from the book of Joshua 24:1-2,15-17; and Gospel of John 6:60-69.

The infant baptism continued at the right side of the church, next to the same baptismal fountain where Justin Daniel was baptized last Sunday. The Father of the child was the one who carried the child, instead of the mother; I noticed this was different from the Vietnamese custom. Twice Father Scott spoke out during the baptism the name of the child "Lily Maria." I understand the word "Lily" is the flower for Easter, and "Maria" is the name of the Blessed Virgin Mother. One time the priest said, "This is the faith of the church and the child to be baptized." As he said, "The child to be baptized" he turned his face to the congregation.

Before the end of the mass, the same as last week; Father Scott asked the parents to bring the child to the middle, in front of the altar for the blessing. Lily Maria's father was holding her, with her mother following him to the middle of the sanctuary, in front of the new altar. While they were on the way, Lily Maria's mother stumbled and almost fell in front of the Gospel podium. Lily Maria's father stopped to assist her to the sanctuary; then they stood facing the congregation. Father Scott faced them, and raising his right hand above Lily Maria's mother's head, said, "Special blessing for the mother...... for her to be in one with her daughter." As I heard the words, "To be in one with her daughter" I knew that the mother have not be baptize.

On the way out of the church, I stopped in front of the child's mother, and I asked her, "Why didn't you hold the child during the baptism?" but she did not know what to answer to me. The infant's father came from behind me, I asked him, "Normally the mother holds the baby during the baptismal, why did you hold Lily Maria?" He replied, "She was too tired, she gave her [baby] to me." I then said Lily Maria's parents, "Through you, God gave the name Lily Maria to her. At the time Father Scott prayed for her [mother], I knew the reason that she was not holding the child. I know that she [mother] will be in one with her daughter. Both of you will be happy." I then said to the father, "You think that you will be the one that is happier, but she [mother] will be a lot happier then you." I then said good bye then left.

August 27, 1997, during my devotion, in spirit, the Lord told me, "Lily Maria is symbolic of you [Mariette], her mother is symbolic of the church leaders and authorities. Lily Maria's father, the word "Father" is symbolic of the Eternal Father.

The envelope of "God Reveals Evolution is the Process of His Creation." means that this baptismal will be a continuation of Justin Daniel's baptism. The Blessed Virgin Maria, obeyed God, and through the power of the Holy Spirit, she brought the Lord Jesus, as fully man on earth. The name "Lily Maria" and the name "Mariette" are symbolic of, through the power of God, His choosing another lowly woman, a sinner adopted to the Holy Family, as His Vessel to continue His mission.

Our Good Deeds are Sent to Heaven Before our Arrival.

February 5, 1997. In my dream, I was in a compound of commercial buildings, but it also looked like an elementary or a high school. This compound had three stations to collect the mail. Two were on the ground level, and one was on the top level. The mailman had to go on the roof of the building to get the mail out from the box on the top level.

I was searching for Father Hero's mail in the upper mail box. Somehow, I was up high, inside the spot to open the upper mail box. I was opening the white plastic, trying to vandalize it and get into the mail box, because I knew that Father Hero's letter was inside this mail box. I wanted to get his letter out. Under this plastic were three pieces of steel, I slid all three pieces of steel to the side. These three pieces of steel were one size, they were a little bigger and longer then an adult finger. Under these three pieces of steel was another layer of steel that sealed like the drinking fountain. While I was up high doing this, there were some children standing on ground watching. I had no fear, I just did not want them to know that I was trying to vandalize the mail box. I then went down.

Down on ground with these children was a mailman who came to gather mail from the two stations on the ground level. I asked him, "Do you also pick up mail from the high station?" He replied, "The mail from that high station is only picked up by their employees [not by the mail man]."

I then saw a woman coming down from the top of the roof, the place where the company employee gets mails out; she said to me, "I was up there, on the roof. I saw a person, his face was covered with raw blood. I was afraid, and came down." Then, another man came and walked in front of me to the corner of the inside building; I knew this man would take the mail out from the upper mail station. I thought, "I could write a quick note and give to him, and ask him to put it together with the mail he is going to collect from the upper mail station." While this man was doing something at the corner of the building, inside the middle of the area, I said to him, "I have quit my old job, and was hired for the new job. The arrangement for me to start the new job was made."

I then had a handful of white rosebuds. I laid them on ground and cut them to keep only the parts with flowers, and threw away the extra bottom stems. These children still followed me and watched me. In my thoughts, " People who worship Buddha also offer him these kinds of flower, but they use the stems to put in the vase. I cut away their stems, this part is not good. I have no fear of enemy spirits mixing with people who worship idols."

God is the Only Way

In my dream I was standing in front of something like a target on the ground. There was something on the ground in lieu of carpet. There were two bowls on this carpet, each bowl had some pieces of fish deep in flour and deep in fire. One was used as a target, another contained fish to be purchased and placed in the target bowl to shoot. Directly in front of me, on the ground, on the other side of the carpet was a man facing me. To my right, a few steps away, another man faced these bowls.

I bought without pay, a back head of a fish from a bowl for sale, and was about to put it in the target bowl. I then changed my mind, I laid the head piece on the carpet in between these bowls; and took a different piece, this piece was a complete whole piece, from the back around to the stomach of the fish, everything inside its stomach was taken out. I laid this piece on top of the fish in the target bowl. To win the game, I must shoot at the piece of fish I laid on top, and this piece must remain inside the bowl. I aimed and shot at the piece I put on top. As I shot, I saw a spirit from outside the target bowl fly to the right side of the man standing opposite me. This man said something like "she does not win." But the man that stood a few steps to my right came forward close to the bowl, and said, "Her piece is still inside the bowl." While this man was saying this, the invisible hand dug my piece of fish up from the center of the bowl; this piece was under other piece because I shot too hard on it.

As I got up the middle of the night, the Lord explained to me that these two men are symbolic of the two priests in the diocese of Little Rock, the one opposite me was trying to prevent the works of God through me; another at my right was fighting for the works of God to be done through me. The Bishop of the Diocese of Little Rock believed what I delivered to Him was from God; but stayed silent because these two priests were opposite each other; the silence of the Bishop is wrong actions. The priests and bishop are symbolic of spiritual leaders not believe God is living or have no faith in God

A Narrow Door to the Mansion

May 15, 1997. In my dream I was inside the front entrance of a mansion. An ex-spouse was standing in front of me, wearing a dirty white outfit, I saw his male organ was cut of from his joints. It fell in a small bag, and this bag was hanging from his joints, inside his pant, some of the blood soaked through his dirty white pants.

Then, somehow, I had this light-colored plastic bag containing this man's male organ; I was afraid, but I must find a way to dump this male organ. I put it in a plastic grocery bag, and while I was putting this male organ inside the bag, I saw something moving inside the grocery bag. Even though I did not see it, I knew it was a mouse. I then put this bag in another grocery plastic bag; and got out to the side of the mansion, and put it in the big trash can. The trash can was moved from the front of the mansion to the side by an ex-spouse brother.

I then saw myself back in the mansion, the spot I where I was at the beginning. I was with a lady, the owner of the mansion, and she is the seller of the mansion. She said to me, "This house was purchased for you for six hundred thousand U. S. dollars; some of the money was paid, and the loan balance is over one hundred thousand. The monthly payment is over one thousand dollars." In my thoughts, "I have over five thousand dollars income monthly, and a monthly payment over one thousand is a good deal for me."

She then took me in the hallway to examine the mansion. I knew that this mansion is round, and the hall way was around. My right side had a solid wall, to my left I saw a man fixing a metal door fastener. A few steps forward, I saw a wooden door with three hooks, but one of them was loose. I said to the lady, "This thing needs to be fixed." Even though I had not see the inside yet, I knew this mansion was huge.

I was then back in the front of the mansion with a child. I was very fond of this little girl; she will come to visit me some time in the future. I will live in this mansion alone. I told her, "This mansion has too many doors, all of them are locked so the ex-spouse can not enter. There is only one door that is always open, and I will show you that door to you so you can come and visit me. Be sure you come to that door, and do not tell the ex-spouse the door was open."

We were at the back of the mansion to show this little girl the door that was not locked. While I was walking on a large concrete backyard, I saw there were two wrecked cars on the dirt ground next to the concrete ground. I thought, "The old owner will have to move these cars to clean up the area. On the other side of the concrete ground was an auto repair shop, the front of the shop was facing the mansion's backyard.

While I was standing in the same spot; suddenly the geography changed; the mansion was up high, with many doors around the mansion. I showed the little girl the unlocked door, and said to her, "When you come, ring the bell, and wait because the mansion is huge. I live on the high level, some times I do not hear the bell, and it takes me time to get down to the lower level and answer the door."

Then I was in the hall way with the lady owner, in front of the back door of the mansion. This door was larger, and higher than the double garage door. Inside the door was covered with a white carpet with a light green design, an expensive, elegant carpet. I then turned, and across the hall of this back door was a large open entrance to the center of the mansion. Standing in the hall, I saw three shining cedar wooden beams cross from the right to the left of the mansion. The middle was higher than the two sides; and shining cedar pillars came down from the cathedral ceiling and joined with cross beams. This made the triangular shape above the floor. On the floor was shining marble, the middle was higher than both sides, and it made a triangle to match the ceiling. The air between the floor and these cedar wooden beams was filled with loving, gentle, powerful, sparkling light.

The lady told me, "This mansion is over one millions dollars. I built it for nine hundred dollars. I will sell it to you, and build another at the district near by." I thought, "This too expensive for me; I can not afford to buy this. I thought she said that I only had to pay over one hundred thousand dollars, and the mansion cost six hundred thousand." In my vision in the dream I saw another mansion in the next district.

Meaning of the symbolism: The mansion is symbolic of the mission that God entrusted to me. The ex-spouse is symbolic of Lucifer or those refused to conversion. The cut-off male organ is symbolic those live in sins, no longer participating in building the kingdom of heaven. Another mansion being built symbolic of more God works send down in the natural. Wooden beams and pillars are symbolic of cross. Light is symbolic of God's glory and power are pouring into the mission God entrusted to me . One door open is only one way to heaven; the other locked doors were the wrong ways. When the little girl comes, I will come down and answer the door is, through the power of God, I will assist people to come to God in the correct way. The man fixing the door is works are in progress. The hook needing to be fixed are works need to be done. I, Mariette, am in the hall, looking at the carpet covering the double garage door. The lady symbolic of God. The two wrecking cars symbolic of the world lack of discernment. Six hundred thousand is symbolic of the mission on the earth. One hundred thousand as the price I have to pay is complete obedience to God. Nine hundred thousand is symbolic of completing the job. The mansion being worth over one million is symbolic that the reward will be more than the price that I have to pay.

While I was praying for the interpretation, in my vision I saw the invisible hand of the Lord draw a square at the back corner of the Cathedral of Saint Andrew's Rectory. The Lord said, "This rectory will be torn down and will build a new corner. The corner of holiness in God. Your suffering is the price to pay to build this corner."

I then asked, "Lord, what you mean of the corner for the rectory?"

The Lord said, "The rectory of the universal church."

I asked, "Lord, You said one corner or four corners?"

The Lord said, "I said 'four corners of the universal church. The rectory means of clergymen. Ministering to priests is your calling."

I said to my beloved Blessed Virgin Mother, "Mother, I am offering these sufferings to the Lord for the people's conversion and repentance. I ask you to pray to the Lord to strengthen me."

The Blessed Virgin Mother said, "The Lord is strengthening you. Jesus is suffering with you; the Father is suffering with you; the Holy Spirit is suffering with you. You are not alone."

The Power of God Comes when a Person Embraces Suffering

May 17, 1997. I woke up in the morning remembering my dream. I heard the Lord Jesus tell me, "This dream and the early dream are the same revelation. Just write down the same exact words that I am going to give to you. In the dream, I went in the small dormitory, wearing a white silk blouse, and black pants that God put on me. Before I entered this dorm, a priest told me, 'That dorm is not for you,' because I was wearing the darkness of all God's commandments, with and in my black pants. Around my waist was a large plastic belt, with big counterfeit gold buckle. After I was inside the room; I took my belt off my waist and laid it flat on the counter.

This room was divided in two parts; there was a door that covered the lower part of the door. Looking through the top part of the door, I saw the back part had some single beds. These beds belonged to a young man and woman who came and greeted me at the inside of the entrance, they were also for others too.

I then laid on the bamboo dais to the my right side of the front part. These two people were still in the front part doing their study. I was bleeding at my bottom, I was able to see the napkin inside my pants was soaked in blood; I was bleeding heavily, there was not enough room on the pad, so blood ran down and soaked my pants. I did not want anyone to see my blood stained pants. I needed to get up to get changed, but it was so difficult for me to got up because I was almost glued to this dais because my body was exhausted. These two people came to assist me to get up, but I told them, 'Just leave me here, I will get up when I can.' These two persons went back to study. While they were studying, they shared with each other regarding the Catholic church and its priests. I overheard them, and I said to them, 'Do not believe all priests in what they say, many things they say they do not do. They are not the same as what they look.'

I then got up and went in the open restroom for a new pad. While I was holding the soiled pad, blood got on my hand and on both side walls at the corner of the restroom; I folded the soiled side of the pad in and used the outside to wipe the blood off the wall.

I left this open restroom with new pad on me. There was a metal trash basket outside the door of the restroom, I disposed the pad in it. This trash basket was made with round wire; it was square, ten by ten inches, and three feet tall. Each of the four sides of the basket had three square eyes, the corners of the three eyes bent at the middle. The basket was filled with clear, used plastic bags. When I dropped the napkin, it fell down to the middle of the basket."

I saw this dream twice in the same night, and the Lord then dictated to me. Because the Lord dictated to me, this revelation has the meanings of each word, and the meanings of the symbolism on the dreams.

The bleeding symbolized tremendous of suffering upon the world to purify it systems. The bamboo dais symbolic of the truth, firm of God commandments is foundation of life. The two students symbolic of angels. The trash bin symbolic of iniquities need to be purge.

33

RESTORE FREEDOM TO WORSHIP THE TRUE GOD ON EARTH

Earthly Laws Must Be Based on God's Commandments.

February 6, 1997. During my devotion, in my visions, I saw the invisible hands, holding a stack of white legal paper. In front of it was one sheet of a regular size that looked like it had some writing on it, on top of the new typewriter, about to put in the typewriter. I then saw the image of the Lord Jesus, and Our Lady of Perpetual Help; the Lord Jesus was holding with His right hand pointing up to heaven, His left hand holding a Holy Bible with the words "I am the light of the world. He that follows me shall not walk in darkness, but shall have the light of life." These two images connected together at the side; and it set at the top of a legal sheet of paper filled with typing, in four paragraphs. And the Archangel Gabriel said to me, "They will pass the laws according to God's commandments, as thy showed them."

Restored Freedom to Worship the True God In Vietnam

Rebuild My Church Divine Mission

(The Lord Jesus gave this name to Mariette)

P.O. Box 261550 ✦ San Diego, CA 92196-1550

October 6, 1998

Archbishop Fx. Nguyen Van Thuan, President
Pontifical Council for Justice & Peace
00120 Vatican City
Rome, Italy

Re: The most Blessing from God will be upon His chosen Ones

Dear Excellency,

The Lord Jesus asked me to send the following copies of letters to you. He also said that after you read them, this evidence will strengthen your faith in the "living" God, and explain to you the reasons Vietnamese Christians have been persecuted for their faith many years.

Because you are God's chosen one, the communists placed you in prison for 13 years. While you entered the prison, God peeled off all the earthly treasury from you. During this prison term, God purified you, (and He will continue to purify you.) When you were discharged from prison, you had more trust in God than you did before you entered the prison. Therefore, after thirteen years purification, God used the communist to deported you out of Vietnam, and He now promoted you to President of the Pontifical Council of Justice and Peace for the Catholics, this is higher in church ranking then the Archbishop of Saigon Diocese. The position in the church that God entrusted to you is for services, bringing conversions, daily exam and repentance, for justice and God's peace into Catholic's spiritual leaders and its congregations.

God sent me into the world, born in the land of Vietnam, and the Catholic family. My family is a victim of the misconduct Catholic authorities, I lost trust in Catholic spiritual leaders and separated from the church for nine years. Then the Lord Jesus called me back to God, and to attending Catholic physical churches.

God uses me as His Vessel to Unify His only Church and bring His justice and peace into the world. Therefore, I am not in physical prison 13 years like you, but my life held suffering from the time I came out of my mother's womb. I suffered even more since I returned to God, He placed me in a very small invisible box, and that's all the room I have to move. If I attempt to hit the wall, I will fight against something that is even worse than the communists who guarded you while you were in prison 13 years. I accepted all of these afflictions to please the Father, the Lord Jesus, and the Holy Spirit, and made my beloved Blessed Mother happy; and to benefits souls and build the kingdom of heaven. I am looking for my eternal life, be with my Lord and my God in heaven.

Enclosed are copies of: (1) a letter to Vice President Al Gore and 8 member of the U.S. senate, September 30, 1998, (2) letters to Vice President Gore and President Bill Clinton, September 14, 1998, (3) letters to and from Vice President Gore, January 27, 1998 and February 25, 1998; (4) letters to and from President Bill Clinton and Paula R. Jones, December 23, 1998 and February 12, 1998, (5) letters to and from first lady Hillary Rodham Clinton, June 21, 1996 and June 25, 1996

I would like to share this with you, and I will also share this with Cardinal Pham Dinh Tung, and that God's blessing will be upon you, me, and all the people of Vietnam in very special way, and so the world will also be benefit from all of these.

Sincerely in Christ Jesus,

Mariette Do-Nguyen

Rebuild My Church Divine Mission

(The Lord Jesus gave this name to Mariette)

P.O. Box 261550 ◆ San Diego, CA 92196-1550

May 13, 1997

Mr. Peter Peterson
U.S. Ambassador to Vietnam

Re: Freedom to Worship the True God in Vietnam

Dear Ambassador Peterson,

Congratulations on your recent appointment as the United States Ambassador to Vietnam.

Enclosed are copies of: (1) my letter to the Vietnamese Prime Minister Vo Van Kiet, September 29, 1994; (2) a letter from Vu Gia Tham, Acting Chair of the Bureau, February 2, 1996, and translation; (3) the book "My Patient -God's Gift;"(4) a letter from Dennis G. Harter, Director's Office of Burma, Cambodia, Laos, Thailand and Vietnam Affairs, United States Department of State, September 5, 1995, responding to me and to all the people of God in this world, on behalf of United States President Bill Clinton.

In the letter Mr. Harter indicated, "We want to assure you we will continue to press for Vietnam's full compliance with internationally recognized human rights in the area of freedom of religion." I received almost thirty other letters from the U. S. State Department officials and senators who wrote and promised the same things that were indicated in Mr. Harter's letter. I have published some of them in my book, "My Patient - God's Gift," in chapter four.

It is now over twenty months from the date of Mr. Harter's letter, and I have not see any action regarding the promise made to me and the people of God in this world, by the officials of the U. S. State Department, on behalf of President Bill Clinton.

I did not choose to do this job; God has chosen me. I am only obeying Him. I must deliver exactly what God has instructed me to say. We have seen many tragedies upon the world; Arkansas tornadoes, North Dakota floods, and the Qaen, Iran earthquake, where at least 2,400 people were killed, over 6,000 injured, and about 40,000 left homeless. These tragedies were acts of God, to cleanse the world systems, the systems that go against His commandments, and they will continue. No one knows what is coming next, or where it will be; human power can do nothing; the tragedies will increase until all the elect convert their hearts and minds to God. All of this was foretold by the Lord Jesus, in the Gospel according to Saint Matthew, chapter 24, and the Lord also revealed this to Saint John in the Book of Revelations chapter sixteen.

I feel the emotional pain for the MIA family members; God is the only one who can heal their pain. Therefore, the freedom to worship the true God in Vietnam is more important than finding the remains of these service men. I believe that when the freedom to worship the true God in Vietnam is restored, God will heal the MIA families, the American citizens, and the Vietnamese people.

God gave everyone a free will, to choose Him or to choose the devil. The Vietnamese lawmakers are giving their free will to the devil; the devil is controlling their minds and actions.   I assure you that the country of Vietnam will not be blessed until there is complete freedom to worship the true God, and the people of Vietnam's hearts and minds are converted to God.

God's words come with His power; I pray to God that you will take the proper actions on this most important issue, to save your soul and the souls of others, as well as your physical body and the bodies of others through whom God has chosen for you to serve Him.

Sincerely in Christ Jesus,

Mariette Do-Nguyen

cc: President Bill Clinton
    Madeleine Albright, Secretary of State
    Members of the United States Senate

You shall love the Lord, your God, with all your heart, with all your soul, and with all your mind. This is the greatest and the first commandment. The second is like it: You shall love your neighbor as yourself.
–Matthew 22:37-39

Rebuild My Church Divine Mission

(The Lord Jesus gave this name to Mariette)

P.O. Box 261550 ✦ San Diego, CA 92196-1550

June 9, 1997

Ambassador Pete Peterson
U. S. Ambassador to Vietnam

Dear Ambassador Peterson,

Thank you for your letter, May 28, 1997; I also thank you for your effort of working with the Vietnamese officials on the issues of freedom to worship God.

In a same letter from Dennis G. Harter, September 5, 1995, he indicated, "In December 1993 the government of Vietnam agreed to conduct a human rights dialogue with the United States."

Enclosed is copy of a letter to Mr. Nguyen Manh Cam, Minister of Foreign Affairs, March 1, 1995: A "Request for Religious group visas for Triumphant Pilgrimage"; but the Vietnamese government denied my request at that time.

The United States of America, as the older brother, stepped forward to appointed you as U.S. Ambassador to Vietnam, for Vietnam to follow in the United States footsteps. You are represent the President of the United States, and the whole American citizens. God ordained you for this job, He saved your physical life from prison of war, and sent you back in the same country to serve Him, to represent God's people in this world.

I ask you to take actions: to press the Vietnamese government to fulfill their agreement of conducting a human right dialogue in the area of freedom of worship the true God, and to honor my request for the group religious visas to accompany the International Statue of Our Lady of Fatima in the year 1998.

The Freedom to worship the true God in Vietnam, and your later dated May 28, 1997, is enclosed on the Lord Jesus, Jesus of Nazareth Website on Internet; and this is Jesus's web site address, http://www.Jesusweb.Org

I am just the instrument of God; I speak of what God tells me to say; therefore, my letter comes with the power of God to fight for you.

Sincerely in Christ Jesus,

Mariette Do-Nguyen

Rebuild My Church Divine Mission
(The Lord Jesus gave this name to Mariette)
P.O. Box 261550 ◆ San Diego, CA 92196-1550

July 25, 1997

Ambassador Pete Peterson
U.S. Ambassador to Vietnam

Dear Ambassador Peterson,

I have not yet received a response from you regarding the letter I sent you, dated June 9, 1997 .

The Lord Jesus asked me to call the archdiocese of Ha Noi. I am obeying God, I spoke to a priest at the Archdiocese of Ha Noi in the evening of July 24, 1997.

Through the conversation, I found out the following from the hearts of the Vietnamese people toward Americans.

Many children have diseases caused from chemicals that the Americans used in bombing North Vietnam before 1975; and many churches were also destroyed from the same actions of the American bombs.

You are the U.S. Ambassador to Vietnam; you represent the President of the United States, and the American citizen. I am an American citizen; I request that you examine these cases throughout the North Vietnam, that were caused by the American government with your own eyes; and send the evidence to the U.S. President and senators to repair for the damages. From the past bombings, they are fear of American is big in body, and country will harm them. Please come to them with a lots of love.

For your convenience to locate the evidence, the priest I spoke to is under the supervision of Cardinal Pham Dinh Tung. You may contact Cardinal Tung for the assistance: Cardinal Pham Dinh Tung, at the Ha Noi Archdiocese, 40 Pho Nha Chung Road, Ha Noi, Vietnam, Telephone number, 844- 8-254424.

I will pray for you, your staff, your family, and everyone involved in this matter to serve God, through services to one another. I also request that you will take this action immediately to save these children from disease.

Sincerely in Christ Jesus,

Mariette Do-Nguyen
cc: Cardinal Pham Dinh Tung; President Bill Clinton; Madeleine Albright, Secretary of State; Senator Dianne Feinstein, California; Senator John McCain, Arizona

Rebuild My Church Divine Mission
(The Lord Jesus gave this name to Mariette)
P.O. Box 261550 ✦ San Diego, CA 92196-1550

October 24, 1997

Prime Minister Phan Van Khai
Vietnamese Prime Minister

Dear Prime Minister Khai,

I congratulate you on your new election. I pray to God that He will open your heart and mind to do what He is commanding you through me in this letter.

Enclosed are copies of: (1) letter to the Roman Catholic Church high ranking leaders and officials, October 24, 1997 and it attachments; (2) letters to U.S. members of senate and President Bill Clinton, and letter to Ambassador Pete Peterson, U.S Ambassador to Vietnam, October 24, 1997.

I ask you review these materials, you will understand that Vietnam is the country chosen by God. The people of Vietnam are being persecuted for their faith, many of them became martyrs. God predestined me for this mission before the foundation of the world; He chose Vietnam as the land of my physical birth.

I pray to God that you will gather all the Vietnamese government officials and share these materials with them. The Roman Catholic Church is universal Church; please leave the Vietnamese Roman Catholics under the leadership of the Holy Father John Paul II.

I guarantee that after you and the Vietnamese government officials put God's commandments in actions, He will bless the country of Vietnam in many ways.

Sincerely in Christ Jesus,

Mariette Do-Nguyen
Note: The Roman Catholic Church symbolic of God's Church on earth.

Rebuild My Church Divine Mission
(The Lord Jesus gave this name to Mariette)
P.O. Box 261550 ✦ San Diego, CA 92196-1550

October 24, 1997

Ambassador Pete Peterson
U.S. Ambassador to Vietnam

Dear Ambassador Peterson,

Enclosed are copies of: (1) letter to the Roman Catholic Church high ranking leaders and officials, October 24, 1997 and it attachments; (2) letters to U.S. members of senate and President Bill Clinton, and letter to Prime Minister Phan Van Khai, Vietnamese Prime Minister, October 24, 1997; (3) an unsealed envelope containing a letter to Cardinal Pham Dinh Tung, October 24, 1997, and it's attachments.

God instructed me to deliver the above materials to you. If you can make a trip, I ask you to visit Cardinal Pham Dinh Tung and give the envelope to him. If not, would you send some one to deliver this material to his office at the Archdiocese of Ha Noi, So 40 Pho Nha Chung, Ha Noi Vietnam, telephone number 84-48-254424.

This is the calling that God called you. He saved you from prison of war, He brought you from the least, and raised you to above all, in the same country.

Trust in God, obey all His commandments, cooperate with God, serve Him by services to the people of Vietnam; He will continue to raise you on earth and in heaven.

Sincerely In Christ Jesus

Mariette Do-Nguyen

Rebuild My Church Divine Mission
(The Lord Jesus gave this name to Mariette)
P.O. Box 261550 ✦ San Diego, CA 92196-1550

November 4, 1997

To: President Bill Clinton,
      Members of the U.S. Senate,
      Ambassador Peterson,
      Secretary of State Medeleine Albright.

Dear.........

I would like to thank to you for assisting me in laying down the groundwork for the "freedom to worship the true God in Vietnam."

Enclosed are copies of letters to Vietnamese government officials, Most Reverend Robert Brom, Bishop of San Diego Diocese, dated November 4, 1997. I ask you to serve God by assisting me and others in urging the Vietnamese lawmakers and officials to make this "freedom to worship the most high living God" a visible and viable policy, so this pilgrimage can take place in June, 1998.

Sincerely in Christ Jesus,

Mariette Do-Nguyen

Rebuild My Church Divine Mission

(The Lord Jesus gave this name to Mariette)

P.O. Box 261550 ✦ San Diego, CA 92196-1550

November 4, 1997

Phan Van Khai, Vietnamese Prime Minister
Nguyen Manh Cam, Minister of Foreign Affairs
Le Van Bang, Vietnamese Ambassador to United States

Dear Mr...

Obeying God, I request 30 day visas for 100 to 200 people to enter Vietnam, in June, 1998.

This pilgrimage is strictly for the purpose of worshipping the true living God. We will depart from California, arrive at Ha Noi Vietnam, and stay at the archdiocese of Ha Hoi from June 7 to June 13, 1998 We will then travel to Lavang, Quang Tri, and remain in this location from June 15 to June 20, 1998. We then will travel to the Blessed Virgin Mother (Nha tho Duc Ba) Cathedral in Saigon archdiocese, and Fatima in Binh Loi, Ho Chi Minh City. We will then depart from Ho Chi Minh city for California on June 28, 1997.

We are in the process of gathering people who are God's chosen ones for this pilgrimage, and will submit individual applications to you for individual approval.

Sincerely in Christ Jesus,

Mariette Do-Nguyen

Freedom to Worship the True God in Vietnam Revelation

May 1, 1997, 3:26 a.m. God the Father said, "After the Abortion Law passes according to God's commandments, you will receive a letter from Vietnamese government officials, responding to your letter to the Vietnamese Prime Minister, regarding the pilgrimage you request. They call the statue a picture. 'We have concluded our decision to approve your request to bring the picture to Vietnam. Let us know the date you request so we can arrange security. We have also invited Archbishop Thuan to return to Vietnam as the Archbishop of the Saigon Diocese.' When you receive this letter, make a copy and arrange an appointment with Bishop Andrew, and give it to him. He is your supervisor. Have him send this letter to the Holy Father.

Interpretation of the symbolism: The Holy Father represents God the Father. Archbishop Thuan is symbolic of Mariette Do-Nguyen; Thuan is a Vietnamese name, in English is means "agreement." The Vietnamese communists disagreed with the Holy Father's appointment of the Archbishop of the Archdiocese of Saigon, and deported him from Vietnam after his release from an education camp. The pilgrimage represents the Rebuild My Church Mission. The Vietnamese government is symbolic of Catholic Church authorities in the United States who are trying to prevent Mariette from doing God's work. Vietnamese government officials are those assisting Mariette as she serves God. Bishop Andrew represents the Lord Jesus; his congregation is symbolic of those who come to the Holy Eucharist Healing Service and Altar Call to convert, repent and proclaim the Gospel. United States Catholics are symbolic of those who convert to God, daily exam and repent.

Restored Civil Right to Freedom of Religion in the United States

Rebuild My Church Divine Mission
(The Lord Jesus gave this name to Mariette)
P.O. Box 261550 ✦ San Diego, CA 92196-1550

December 6, 1994

Honorable Christopher H. Smith
2353 Rayburn House, Room 2353
Washington, DC 20515

Dear Honorable Smith,

Thanks to God that He chose us as instruments to accomplish His will, and thank you for your letter of November 30, 1994, and copies of resolutions. H. Con.Res.215 "Expressing the Sense of the Congress Regarding Human Rights in Vietnam," and H.Con.Res 278 "Expressing the Sense of Congress Regarding U.S. Policy Towards Vietnam.."

I have read them very carefully, and prayed for this letter. I would like to testify what my eyes witnessed during the weeks of July 4 - July 19,

1993. During this time, I visited Vietnam after living over 18 years in the United States.

1) July 10 and 14, 1993. I met with Rev. Le Thanh Que at Thu Duc Vietnam, and my heart broke at the sight that he had totally lost faith in God, and had many serious sicknesses in his body. He was the one who had been my consultant for years before I left Vietnam, but on these days I was the one consultant for him for over three hours. Satan used the government of Vietnam, and officials put the 60 year old priest (60 years old in 1993) in education camps for over 13 years. It turned the very intelligent priest, who gave his life to God, and served other people for God, into someone against God, with many serious sicknesses..

2)   July 14, 1994, I visited the 84 year old Archbishop Nguyen Van Binh of the Saigon Diocese, in Vung Tau, Vietnam. The archbishop was on leave for illness of old age, and could not totally hear me. Every time I spoke, a priest companion of the archbishop would repeat my words in a very loud voice. Father Viet Chau, and other sources in U.S., informed me in September 1994 of The Holy Father's appointment of Archbishop Nguyen Van Thuan to replace Archbishop Nguyen Van Binh prior to the fall of Saigon in April 1975. After the fall of Saigon, the devil used the communist government officials to put Archbishop Nguyen Van Thuan in an education camp, and after they released him they deported him from Vietnam and will not allow him to return. The Holy Father appointed Bishop Nguyen Van Nghi from Central Vietnam to be an Administrator for the Saigon diocese, the devil again used the Vietnamese officials to prevent Bishop Nghi from transferring to Saigon. At this time, the Diocese of Saigon has no shepherd to lead the sheep.

3) July 15, 1994. I visited Bishop Nguyen Minh Nhat, President of the Vietnamese Catholic Conference, in Ho Chi Minh City. In conversing with Bishop Nhat, I gathered that every young man needed permission from the government of Vietnam before entering seminaries, and after many years of school, they again needed permission to be ordained. There are hundreds of young men who have dedicated their lives to God and are waiting for permission to enter seminaries.

I urge the U.S. Congress to press the Vietnamese Government officials as soon as possible to obey God and follow His law. If the Vietnamese Government officials choose to obey the devil, then reinstate the U.S. embargo against Vietnam.

The following regarding the United States:

As a vessel to Jesus and instrument for God, I always have to speak the truth, and deliver His messages under His instruction. Regardless of the cost, sometimes people have to die for God to gain eternal life in heaven.

On August 25, 1994, at about 9:35 am, at the Blessed Sacrament Chapel in the Good Shepherd Church of San Diego. Jesus the Lord gave me a day vision. Letters spelling out "White House" appeared, and at the end corner of the word "House," a row of several ambulances with lights flashing, heading toward the White House from the horizon. The entire horizon was on fire. After a couple of minutes, two-thirds of the ambulances in front disappeared. Jesus then said to me "Mariette, deliver this message to Clinton. The Freedom of Religion in Vietnam must be contained in the aviation agreement between the United States and Vietnam. The final hours of the earth are coming. He must choose whether or not to lead his country on earth into heaven by choosing whether or not to obey me. Send a copy of this message to the head of the Vietnamese government." I prayed for discernment for few days and I sent a letter to President Bill Clinton on August 29, 1994. (Copy enclosed.)

A few days later, while praying I heard the voice say " Just watch me. The warning is coming to Clinton." I thought that was from devil because it sound like a threat. I rebuked the voices..

In first and second weeks of November 1994, I saw Jesus in my night vision. He landed on the dining table, with a big crown, wearing a red coast, and I heard a voice say "Jesus is King of kings, He is ruler, and He is imposing His law". After this dream, there was another. I saw the steps in front of the congress building, and at the lowest step there was a priest in white vestment, both hands at his chest. I saw him take a few steps, then turn to the left. After he turned, I saw that he wore a high cap like that of a bishop during mass, and God gave to me that Jesus takes over congress.

these messages, Jesus told me that He will choose the next president of the United States, and Congress members to accomplish the Heavenly Father's will. Of course there will be some deceivers like Judas, one of the twelve apostles. Last week, God told me that the two incidents at the White House were physical warnings for President Clinton. Many others, such as earthquakes, fires, and etc..... were warnings for the world, I rebuked the message. But this morning at about 7 am in my prayers, He ordered me to write this letter to you, with a copy of complement to the Honorable Phil. Gramm, and President Bill Clinton. He instructed me to fax and mail by registered mail, to have you and the Honorable Phil Gramm make this letter known to all congress members. He stated that "the legalization of abortion law must be revoked immediately", it is murder to all those babies whose souls begin at the first day of conception, and told me to enclose those warning messages. I always rebuke devil's spirits in the name of Jesus when I receive messages that sound strange, and ask for discernment before I act on any message, and some times I test God.

None of us know what God is going to do. God does things in His time and in His way. Remember that. God used a donkey to carry Jesus. He can use any human, animal, or thing to accomplish His will.

God chose me to communicate with Him to accomplish His will. I only want the reward that comes when I depart from this life to eternal life in heaven. For this reward, I must always listen, obey and act for His will. I spend most of the time God gives me in prayer for everyone in this world, especially those God has chosen to do His works, and leaders of religions and nations.

This paragraph is not one that God has spoken to me, but one He has revealed to me by wisdom. The United States is the leading nation for the world. Every nation looks up to the United States. I urge all congress members to pray, listen, obey, and act to save the United States first and then other nations.

I pray that God bless all congress members, their families and the world.

Mariette Do-Nguyen
cc: Honorable Phil Gramm
    President Bill Clinton

Taxpayers Indirectly Murder Unborn Babies Through Tax Moneys Funding Programs to Benefit Abortions

Rich or poor, everyone in this world must depend on God, and, whether you believe or not, you are no exception. He gave us our lives, and He can take our lives away any time He wants. He gave us material things, He can make us rich; He also can make us loose everything.

> *I am the vine, you are the branches. Whoever remains in me and I in him will bear much fruit, because without me you can do nothing.*

–John 15:5

It is a two ways street; God has blessed you with many things. In turn, you must pay Him back with the first dollars you received just as in business, we must pay our expenses before realizing our profits. Every one of us must set aside a percentage of our incomes to support the Lord Jesus's Church before paying our bills.

He gave us life to live; life on earth is time on earth; in turn, we must designate a time each day to worship Him and serve Him in pray before we serve ourselves and others.

> *Consecrate to me every first-born that opens the womb among the Israelites, both man and beast, for it belongs to me.*

–Exodus 13: 2

God is the one who blessed us with things on earth, we must obey all His commandments. We cannot use our money for purposes that work against God's commandments. Many times we allow the devil to blind our eyes by refusing to admit our sins. Whether or not we admit these sins, we are subject and liable for our actions in front of God, according to His commandments. Even though God is merciful and forgiving, but we must pay for our sins, either here on earth or in purgatory, to cleanse our souls before entering into Heaven; If we do not convert and repent we will be go to the place we call hell.

Our souls are the breath of our lives; the body without a soul is dead. Human life is begin at the time of conception. Anyone who participates in any way in aborting a baby is participating in murder.

> *The Lord God formed man out of the clay of the ground and blew into his nostrils the breath of life, and so man became a living being.*

–Geneses 2:7

The Government uses tax monies to benefit abortion through family planning clinics. As taxpayers you are contributing to the murders of these babies.

> *You shall not kill*

–Exodus 20: 13

God commands us to always obey human laws, unless these laws go against His commandments. The abortion law allows the murder of unborn babies who are unable to speak for themselves.

Taxpayers must demand that lawmakers pass laws according to God's commandments. If taxpayers continue to participating in programs that go against God's commandments, His punishment will be upon those continue to participate in the devil's works, specially the murder of babies. Punishment will come after their last breath, as well on this earth.

Whoever sacrifices to any god, except to the Lord alone, shall be doomed.

–Exodus 22: 19

Spiritual leaders cannot participate in politics, but they are responsible for teaching your congregation to obey God's commandments to save their souls. If you are not firm and are lax in your teaching, you will be partially liable for your congregation sins. In the case of abortion law, you are sinning against God by helping to murder these babies, by paying your taxes, for some of your tax monies are benefit abortion through family planning clinics. You are also liable for your congregation's sins as taxpayers.

On May 21, 1996, God the Father revealed to me "Abortion is murder," and on August 21, 1996 "Tax monies that benefits programs that go against God's commandments are an indirect sin by the taxpayers." Whether a sin is grave or venial depends on the purpose. In the case of abortion it is a grave sin.

The Lord God has instructed me to deliver these revelations to President Bill Clinton, Vice President Al Gore, and all members of U.S. senate. After praying to discern the meaning of these revelations, I then delivered them as God commanded me, and I urge you to obey all His commandments to save your souls.

Tell us, what is your opinion: Is it lawful to pay the census tax to Caesar or not?" Knowing their malice, Jesus said, "Why are you testing me, you hypocrites? Show me the coin that pays the census tax." Then they handed him the Roman coin. He said to them, "Whose image is this and whose inscription?" They replied, "Caesar's." At that he said to the, "Then repay to Caesar what belongs to Caesar and to God what belongs to God."

–Matthew 22: 17-21.

God created the heaven and the earth and He is the owner of the both.

Rebuild My Church Divine Mission

(The Lord Jesus gave this name to Mariette)

P.O. Box 261550 ✦ San Diego, CA 92196-1550

February 3, 1997

To: This letter addressed to 100 United States senators, and to Vice President Al Gore.

Re: Abortion Law

Dear ....

Enclosed are copies of "Taxpayers indirectly Murder Babies through Tax monies benefit abortion through funding family planning," and "Heavenly Court Summons Writ for Mariette Do-Nguyen."

As an Ambassador to Christ Jesus, I must say what the Lord Jesus instructed me to say, because His word comes with the power of God.

On January 20, 1997, President Bill Clinton laid his hand on the Holy Bible and took a solemn oath as he began his second term as President of the United State of America.

This means that all United States laws must be passed according to God's commandments.

President Clinton and all lawmakers are under God's power to run this country. The President and many of the lawmakers have allowed the devil to either blind their eyes or twist the meaning of God's commandments. But He is a merciful God; He has instructed me to point out His commandments with regard to abortion, and the fact that taxes monies are being to used to fund for programs that go against His commandments.

In order to limit some of the tragedies on earth, I urge you and members of Congress to revoke the Abortion law and other laws that go against God's commandments; and pass laws that are in accordance with God's commandments.

I pray to God that you obey His commandments, and act on them. If you need more information, please contact me at Rebuild My Church Mission - P.O. Box 1077 - Little Rock, AR 72203.

Sincerely in Christ Jesus,

Mariette Do-Nguyen

Rebuild My Church Divine Mission

(The Lord Jesus gave this name to Mariette)

P.O. Box 261550 ✦ San Diego, CA 92196-1550

May 23, 1997

Dear United States Senate members and President Bill Clinton,

God the Father, the Lord Jesus, and the Holy Spirit commanded me to send this letter to you. This letter was dictated to me on May 3, 1997, with these instructions. "Mail the letter to United States Senate members and President Bill Clinton, two days before the first Holy Eucharist Healing Service and Altar Call at the Cathedral of Saint Andrew, Little Rock, Arkansas, on May 27, 1997."

"God commands you to pass abortion laws according to His commandments. His commandments allow abortion only when the life of the mother is threatened of death. He is the only One to give life and take it away.

Tax monies cannot be used to fund for abortions or other purposes that go against God's commandments, such as the production of more weapons, chemicals, training, other than for defense.

God is pouring out more tragedies upon the world to save His people's souls. These tragedies will occur more and more until all the elect convert their hearts and minds to God. No one on earth can stop these tragedies. But people may limit them by obeying all His commandments.

I will be God's instrument, to speak to the public. God's words come with His power, and people will obey His commandments."

On June 6, 1997 the Lord Jesus told me, "Church authorities and government officials, lawmakers are refusing to cooperate with God's plan for salvation of the world. I need you to listen carefully to all my instructions, and take actions as I tell you. Give them My web site address."

The Lord Jesus, Jesus of Nazareth Web site on the internet: http://www.Jesusweb.Org

I will pray for you to obey God, to save the people that you are representing. If you do not obey God, you will bring more tragedies upon the people you represent.

Sincerely in Christ Jesus,

Mariette Do-Nguyen

Rebuild My Church Divine Mission
(The Lord Jesus gave this name to Mariette)
P.O. Box 261550 ✦ San Diego, CA 92196-1550

June 26, 1997

This letter mailed to Governor Fife Symington, and thirty members of Arizona State Senate. (Listing attached)

Enclosed is a copy of a letter from Senator John McCain, dated June 19, 1997, responding to my letter of May 23, 1997, regarding legal abortion and taxes monies that funded programs against God's commandments.

I ask you to read my letter very carefully; God has dictated this letter to me, and instructed me to mail it to all the members of the U.S. Senate, and to President Bill Clinton.

The same day I received the letter from Senator McCain, the Lord God also dictated this letter to me, and asked me to mail it to the members of the Arizona State Senate.

Jesus the Lord said, "Church leaders, lawmakers, and government officials are disobedient to God's commandments; They refuse to cooperate with God in the salvation of mankind."

The "V" shape with lights in the air, above Arizona homes, in March, was a warning from God.

I ask you to review these letters in detail and take action to save mankind.

Sincerely in Christ Jesus,

Mariette Do-Nguyen

cc: Most Reverend Thomas J. O'Brien
    Bishop of Phoenix Diocese

Rebuild My Church Divine Mission

(The Lord Jesus gave this name to Mariette)

P.O. Box 261550 ✦ San Diego, CA 92196-1550

July 3, 1997

Senator John McCain
United States Senate

Dear Senator McCain,

Thank you for your letter of June 19, 1997. May God bless you with strength to serve Him as you fight for these unborn children who are unable to speak for themselves.

Enclosed is a copy of a letter to Governor Fife Symington and thirty members of the Arizona State Senate, dated June 26, 1997.

In February 1997, the Lord Jesus revealed to me the Hubble Space shuttle; He said, "Man wants to be like God; they are following in Lucifer's footsteps. I the Lord will crush them down." The Lord God means that He created the earth for humans; we should not try to be like God by violating the rules He has commanded. The devil is on his way to trick NASA like Eve in the Book of Genesis.

In God 's love and mercy, He only cut the trip short for the Hubble spacecraft, and brought it back to earth safely. But the world did not see the warning. The Mir was also struck down by God.

The taxpayers' monies which fund for NASA go against God's commandments, man is trying to be like God, while the poor in the United States and all over the world are starving.

God allowed the Vietnamese communists to put you in prison. As a prisoner of war you forgave the enemies and fought for normalization between the United States and Vietnam. God also called Pete Peterson, a prisoner of war in Vietnam, and sent him back to that same country as an ambassador.

God revealed to me that He is on His way to unify the world's legislators into one party. It is impossible for man, but it is not impossible with God.

I must deliver to you and others what God has asked of me in His time. They are the words of prophecy, they are true and trustworthy.

I will pray for you to be firm and strong, so God can use you.

Sincerely in Christ Jesus,

Mariette Do-Nguyen

587

Rebuild My Church Divine Mission

(The Lord Jesus gave this name to Mariette)

P.O. Box 261550 ✦ San Diego, CA 92196-1550

September 30, 1997

To President Bill Clinton and all the U.S. Senate members

Re: U.S. Abortion Law

Dear ......,

The Lord Jesus instructed me to deliver the "Only exception to no-Abortion in God's commandments" to the Roman Catholic Church high ranking officials, 287 United States cardinals, archbishops, bishops, President Bill Clinton, Vice President Al Gore and all the members of the U.S. Senate.

The airplane crashes, tornadoes, floods, fires, earthquakes, death, violence etc. are God's warning to the world. God is taking actions against those who are disobedient to His commandments, the same as He did to Israelites and others in the Book of Judges, in the old testament. The actions God is taking now was foretold in the Book of Revelation, especially in chapters 6, 16, 18 and Saint Matthew's Gospel, chapter 24. I also enclosed a copy of my letter to the Roman Catholic church officials and leaders, September 30, 1997, and it attachments.

Abortion is against God's creation, destroying the human race. I pray that you as the lawmakers, and all our nations leaders to obey God's commandments, to limit some of the tragedies up on the world.

Sincerely in Christ Jesus,

Mariette Do-Nguyen

Rebuild My Church Divine Mission

(The Lord Jesus gave this name to Mariette)

P.O. Box 261550 ✦ San Diego, CA 92196-1550

October 24, 1997

To: The U.S. Member of Senate and President Bill Clinton

The world is full of things against the Creator of the heaven and earth. He allowed the darkness eclipse the sun, the veil of the temple was torn down at the middle on the day of His begotten Son being crucified on the Cross. The sun was dancing at the Last time God sent the Blessed Virgin Mother, Mother of Jesus to appeared to three children at Fatima, October 13, 1917. And there are many other physical warning, such as earthquakes, tornadoes, floods, weather etc. upon the world these days.

Through me, God warns the world in words. My responsibility is to speak out loud and clear to the world every words that God asks of me.

God told me to go to the Roman Catholic Church officials and leaders, not to ask them, but to command them to cooperate with God, do the will of the Creator of heaven and earth. I take the same authority from God and command you to vote all human laws, pass them according to God's commandments.

Enclosed are copies of: (1) letters to the Roman Catholic church officials and leaders and it attachments, October 24, 1997

God answered to Moses every time His people consulted Him. God also answered to Queen Esther to save her people and destroy the enemies. I obeyed the Lord Jesus to ask the Father for Fatima's sun dancing up on the world. It means I pray to the Creator to punished those who disobey His commandments and save those who are obeying Him.

Therefore, if you obey God, He will bless you; if you disobey His Commandments, He will take away the things in your possession that you place above Him, just like He did to Pharaoh and people in the land of Egypt.

I pray to God for you to obeyed Him, serve Him through services to your people. The world will be come the better place to live, and build the kingdom of heaven.

Sincerely in Christ Jesus,

Mariette Do-Nguyen

589

Rebuild My Church Divine Mission

(The Lord Jesus gave this name to Mariette)

P.O. Box 261550 ✦ San Diego, CA 92196-1550

October 31, 1997

To: President Bill Clinton and members of the U.S. Senate

Re: IRS Officer who asked a taxpayer to sign a Power of Attorney over to the IRS

Dear ....

God has commanded us to obey all of His commandments and human laws, when those laws are in accordance with God's commandments. But when human laws go against His commandments, we must not obey them.

In March 1993, the Win First Association at 2097 E. Washington Blvd. Colton, CA 92324, told me that, "the IRS is a private corporation incorporated in Delaware, July 11, 1933," I enclosed some of their information for you.

Why do I have to pay taxes to a private corporation, when the monies are not benefiting American citizens? I decided not to pay.

In 1994, after I was no longer working, Ms. Mariam Quinones came to my home to investigate on my finances. She agreed that I could make installment payments. While I was making those payments; she broke her agreement, and sent a notice of Levy to the bank. Immediately after, I received a copy of that notice. God told me that taxpayers were indirectly committing grave sins, because of tax monies which fund for the abortion to murders babies, and other destructive programs.

At this point I must obey God, and through His power, I fight to save my soul and the souls of others so they may have eternal life in heaven, and save the life of those babies who are unable to speak for themselves. I retained the tax attorney Jeff C. Swartzlander, to represent me, and on September 26, 1996, Ms. R. Lauridsen, Revenue Officer, went behind my attorney's back and came to my home with a woman who asked me for the copy of the trust to my house, bank records and proof of my income. I told her, "I can not pay taxes when tax monies benefit abortions to murder babies and other programs that kill people. I have explained all these to Mr. Swartzlander. Has he given you those papers that I faxed to him?" She replied, "Yes." I then said, "He must, because he is representing me." She then said to me, "Do you remember the Power of Attorney you signed for Mr. Swartzlander?" I replied, "Yes." She then asked, "Can you sign for me the same one you signed for him?" I said, "No, I signed it for Mr. Swartzlander because he is representing me." They then left my home.

That night, God told me to see my attorney, and tell him that Ms. Lauridsen, Internal Revenue Officer, asked me to sign a Power of Attorney for her. She violated the law by asking me to sign it over to the IRS. God also told me to have my attorney ask her two questions: Why had she asked me to sign the same Power of Attorney that I signed for him? Why did she come to my home when I was represented by an attorney? I told my attorney exactly what happened. As of the date of this letter, I have not received an answer from Ms. Lauridsen.

After I refused to sign the Power of Attorney, she then placed liens on all my life insurance policies and my house. As an immigrant, I have been working hard since I entered the U.S. The IRS officer is trying to sweep away everything I worked hard for by going behind my attorney's back and coming to my house without an appointment, served a Summons and asking me to sign a Power of Attorney over to her.

I believe that the United State is a country that has freedom to help each of its citizens, and that Congress is passing laws to protect American citizens. I would like to know if there is any law passed by Congress or the Senate which gives IRS officers the right to ask taxpayers to sign a Power of Attorney over to the IRS, and which allows them go directly to the taxpayer's home while the taxpayer is represented by an attorney. At the same time, I ask you as a lawmaker to resolve this matter for me and for other victims, and passed laws to make the United States of America is a better place to live, and to build the kingdom of heaven.

Sincerely in Christ Jesus.

Mariette Do-Nguyen

Rebuild My Church Divine Mission
(The Lord Jesus gave this name to Mariette)
P.O. Box 261550 ✦ San Diego, CA 92196-1550

December 4, 1997

To: President Bill Clinton, Vice President Al Gore, all U.S. senate members; Secretary of Treasury Robert Rubin; U.S. Department of Treasury General Inspector Valerie Lau; IRS Chief Inspector Gary Bell.

Dear ....,

Enclosed are copies of: (1) a letter to President Bill Clinton, Vice President Al Gore, and all members of the U.S. Senate, dated October 31, 1997; (2) a letter from Senator Trent Lott, dated October 21, 1997; (3) a letter from Senator John Glenn, dated November 10, 1997, and (4) a letter to Internal Revenue Service Commissioner Charles O. Rossotti, dated November 25, 1997.

As I indicated in my letter to the U.S. Senate members and President Bill Clinton, "God has commanded us to obey all of His commandments, and to obey human laws when those laws are in accordance with His commandments. But when human laws go against God's commandments, we must not obey them." This commandment dictates that everyone must pay taxes. However, the tax monies must be spent on the programs determined by human laws to benefit the citizens, their physical bodies and souls, and to build the kingdom of heaven, NOT to benefit works that destroys the human race and individual souls.

God uses people from the Win First Association to notify me of the huge numbers of Americans who did not file tax forms or pay income tax for a number of reasons. In my case, God opened my eyes and showed me that since 1975, when I entered the U.S. as an immigrant, the majority of the tax monies I have paid have supported works against God's commandments. Also, IRS agents who came to my home, unannounced, were abusive and guilty of serious misconduct.

Each American citizen has a right to the nation's monies. Taxpayers are contributing to the United States of America, not paying a debt. The Internal Revenue Service officers must respect taxpayers' rights, for we are paying their salaries.

When God poured His power upon me, I was told not to participate in the works against His commandments. Through His power, I must speak loud and clear to others, to open their eyes, to encourage them to obey God's commandments, and not obey human laws that go against His commandments, to save their physical bodies and souls. This also applies to those who have not filed and paid income taxes when the human laws are in accordance with God's commandments.

I ask you to assist me with all my requests in the letter to Internal Revenue Service commissioner Charles O. Rossotti, to remove the liens on my life insurance policies, bank accounts, real estate property, sources of income, including credit reports to the credit agencies, in the time frame that I have requested the abusive actions of the Internal Revenue Service officers must be terminated and punished. I also request that lawmakers pass laws so that all taxpayers will have a say in how their tax monies are to be spent each year when they file their returns. Therefore, those who have not been filing and paying taxes will join others in contributing to building the United States of America.

If you need more information or have any questions, please contact me.

Sincerely in Christ Jesus,

Marlene Do-Nguyen
cc: Charles O. Rossotti, IRS Commissioner

Restricted Order Revelation

On February 4, 1998, under restricted order, the Lord Jesus's voice was speaking out from the congressional building; "You send this letter to five people: John McCain, Jesse Helms, Christopher Smith, Phil Gram, and Al Gore."

He continued, "These five men will see that this revelation is contradictory to them, but not contradictory to the Almighty God. They are dividing themselves in to different groups and parties, and fighting against each other. Who can escape the Almighty God's hand? Who is innocent enough to cast the first rock? My words for them are not easy to swallow. They have the choice of volunteering or I will force them into it. The Vietnam, Arkansas, Florida, and California; you have been against the Son of the Most High Living God. You must swallow God's purification painfully. The mermaid is rising out of the ocean, crossed the freeway; this is just the beginning. The Armenian president resigns and the White House crisis is just the beginning of God rocking their chairs of out it spot."

He continued, "People interpreting God's law into the true shining words is not for men whose heart contain evil. The evil is twisting the words for man."

The restricted order is meant for God's chosen ones, God's chosen ones will suffer with Him, fighting for the truth to benefit souls and man. The five names: the Biblical symbolic, five is authority over the devil; the devil is working through man. Dividing into groups and parties to compete with each other means the devil uses humans to compete against each other, and leads them to sin against God, destroying souls, and physical life. These are hidden behind abortion, people killed in bomb blasts, and destructive weapons in the war between nations, that kill one another, and innocent people. God has control of the world that He created; He also gave each one us free to choose Him or the devil. The mermaid is symbolic of destruction of the devil to whom God gave permission to destroy those who refuse to obey Him. Tornadoes in Arkansas, Linda storms in Vietnam, El Nino in Florida and California is God's visiting the world, to discipline us.   God loves us; He gave us every chance to convert, but the world is playing deaf and dumb, and now is the time He raises his rod to correct us; those who refuse to convert will perish. When a person perishes, he will lose his earthly possessions, physical life, and eternal life in heaven.

Rebuild My Church Divine Mission

(The Lord Jesus gave this name to Mariette)

P.O. Box 261550 ✦ San Diego, CA 92196-1550

February 17, 1998

This is letter mailed to 74 U.S. senators , same letter to 27 senators, dated February 9, 1998

Dear ....,

Enclosed are copies of God the Father Visits the World, and Restricted Order revelations. After God dictated to me the Restricted Order revelation, I asked Him, "What do You want me to do with this?" He reminded me of a letter that He had me sent to Congressman Christopher H. Smith, with copies to President Bill Clinton, and Senator Phil Gramm, dated December 6, 1994, regarding Freedom of Religion in Vietnam and God's Law. In the Restricted Order revelation, God spoke of "unity in one with Him."

Over three years ago God spoke to three persons. The one who goes against Him is the most visible to the world. President Bill Clinton approves of legal abortion involving mass murders of unborn babies. Congressman Smith and Senator Gramm have been trying to save these babies, but have not tried hard enough, and not for the correct reasons. God gave souls to each one of us at the time of conception, before we grow in our mother's wombs.

God ordained you for the job that you do, and He is with you to the end; in this job He is charging you with "responsibility" to protect human life from the time of conception to a natural death. Over three million Vietnamese, and more than fifty thousand American troops were killed in Vietnam; this is mass murder. The Cuban embargo caused people to suffering and die; this is a form of murder. You are in a position to work harder to save people from death in Cuba. If you are not trying hard enough to save them, you are responsible for the their death in front of the Almighty God.

When earthly laws go against God's commandments, they will cause death; we see this in practices such as legal abortion, court ordered death penalties, destructive weapons, and research, such as cloning cattle to generate blood, to replace the human blood. There is evidence that destructive weapons have killed over three million Vietnamese and more than fifty thousand Americans in the Vietnamese war; now weapons are on the way to Iraq. Donating blood is an act of love; when man replaces human blood with the blood of cattle, man removed the virtue of love from one another.

There is no difference between color or nationality in front of the Almighty God. Killing people in wars, abortions, and court ordered executions are acts of murder. When human laws give license to murder, to destroy souls and mankind, God will pour out His power to discipline each one of us; it means that human law must be under God's law.

God disciplines people through heavy storms, rain, snows, and floods; and He will continue until human power can do nothing but return to obeying Him. God's discipline will cause much suffering and at times of physical death.

When lawmakers pass laws against God's decrees, they are placing embargoes upon their own people. U.S. lawmakers place embargoes upon American citizens. When church leaders mislead their congregations, they destroy God's people's souls and some time their physical bodies as well.

In order for you to fulfill your responsibility, your personal life must be in compliance with all God's commandments; your personal obedience to God will be extended to your job. There is no way to have a personal life against God and serve God in public life. Each one of us must put what we preach into our daily life.

I continue to pray for you. If you need more information please let me know.

Sincerely in Christ Jesus,

Mariette Do-Nguyen

Rebuild My Church Divine Mission
(The Lord Jesus gave this name to Mariette)
P.O. Box 261550 ✦ San Diego, CA 92196-1550

April 17, 1998

This letter mailed to President Bill Clinton, Vice President Al Gore, and all members of the United States senate

The U.S. Constitution Human Right; Freedom of Religion being Violated

Dear ....,

Beside some other important issues in a letter from Senator Carl Levin to me, March 24, 1998, I would like to bring up the main issue, in a letter indicating:

"While I am personally opposed to abortions (unless they are performed to save the life of the mother, or are performed as a result of rape or incest), I also support a public policy which permits women to decide whether or not to have an abortion. I have taken this position because there is an absence of religious and medical consensus on when 'human life' begins. In hearing held on Senator Helms' bill to establish that human life begins at the moment of the conception, the American Medical Association and the National Academy of Sciences testified that there is no consensus in the medical community on this question. Religious leadership is also very divided."

I would like to answer to the above paragraph as follows:

"The LORD God formed man out of the clay of the ground and blew into his nostrils the breath of life, and so man become a living being" Genesis 2:7. This scripture is symbolism, and it has two meanings: The soul and spirit within a physical body from the time of conception; and Adam also symbolic of disobedience soul, Eve symbolic of disobedience spirit.

a. "Formed man out of the clay" is symbolic of the time a man spermatozoon meets the woman's egg. This fetus is grown in the womb of a woman and becomes man.

b. "Blew into his nostrils the breath of life" is symbolic of a soul; this soul will remain in each human life until the physical body dies. It means the soul will leave the physical body, and will return to heaven immediately, or be in purgatory to pay for the damages he caused during his earthly life, or be punished in a place that humans call "hell" forever. Hell means a place for souls to be punished for the crimes committed on earth, and refusal to convert.

c. Besides the soul and the physical body is the spirit. The spirit is the supernatural power of the soul "in" and "with" physical body. When a person obey God's commandments, then his spirit mixes with God's Spirit; but when person disobey God's commandments, his spirit mixes with the devil's spirit. This human's spirit will affect the human mind and body. During the time a person contains grave sin, the devil's power will be either controlling or heavily interfering with his mind and actions. God respects each individual's free will to accept Him or the devil, but the devil is pulling all of us toward him; we must fight against him. Although the devil must have permission from God.

"You shall not kill." Exodus 20:13

Because for the mercy of God, there is only one exception to have an abortion, and that is when the life of the mother is threatened to die.

Enclosed is a copy of the meaning of Saint Peter's key & Unify the Church revelations. Many Church leaders do not understand the hidden meaning of the holy Scriptures. They allow the devil to interfere or control their minds, and act to gain their earthly life benefits such as title, money, and life's pleasures like elders and Pharisees. They refuse the truth, like politicians, point fingers against each other.

Many Church leaders, lawmakers, and government officials focus on saving unborn children from partial- abortion, but not all unborn children through abortion. They either do not fully recognize the human body has three parts, and how these three parts are formed, or they want to please man to protect their title. To understand of human body forms and functions, requires the life of holiness, for fully understanding the hidden meaning behind the holy scriptures.

Referring to the attachments of my letter to you, dated April 14, 1998, these materials explain false beliefs of the medical science. They refuse the truth, the One who created the heaven and earth, He is living, and understands the supernatural power existing.

"Whoever sacrifices to any God, except to the Lord alone, shall be doomed." Exodus 22:19

Using taxpayers monies to fund programs against God's commandments such as, Parent planning, providing services for abortion and birth control; training medical students for abortions, researches that against God commandments, generating destructive weapons to create war between nations etc.... These programs benefit the work of the devil, destroying the human race.

The U.S. lawmakers and government officials are violating the U.S. constitution human right in the area of freedom of religion, passing laws allowing the Internal Revenue Services to levy taxpayers wages, checking accounts, life insurance policies, foreclosure citizen's first resident. They are spending over forty million tax dollars to investigate the Whitewater and President Bill Clinton's personal sex scandal.

Jesus the Lord said, "Who among you have no sin, throw the first rock at her." I have told Paula Jones and President Bill Clinton, I now say to you, and everyone in this world, "Do not be the judge" because there is only one Judge, the eternal Judge is Jesus, the only begotten Son of God.

"Stop judging that you may not be judged. For as you judge, so will you be judge, and the measure with which you measure will be measured out to you. Why do you notice the splinter in your brother's eyes, but do not perceive the wooden beam in your own eye? How can you say to your brother, 'Let me remove that splinter from your eye,' while the wooden beam in your eye? You hypocrite, remove the wooden beam from your eye first; then you will see clearly to remove the splinter from your brother's eye." Matthew 7:1-5

Only sick people need doctors, and Jesus the Lord ate with tax collectors. If any one said he has no sin, by saying he has no sin, he committed the greatest sin, exalting himself like Lucifer that wants to be like God. God calling all of us to conversion; our free will is either to admit our sins, and ask God for forgiveness; in order for God to forgive us must forgive others. If any one does not forgive another, God will not forgive that person.

God loves the world that His created; but the world goes against His commandments. To save the world, He is raising His iron rod to purify its system.

God speaks to people through holy scriptures and actions. On April 16, 1998, after Paula Jones announced her appeal of her case against President Clinton, God poured out twisters in three states, Tennessee, Arkansas, and Alabama. The San Diego Union Tribune indicated "Tornadoes rip Nashville; 10 die as storms hit three states." The Biblical symbolism for three is the Holy Trinity, and ten represents the Ten Commandments of God. These three twisters with ten deaths are actions symbolic of God saying "obey all My commandments."

These tragedies will be getting worse, and they come suddenly, human wisdom can not predict; man's power can do nothing. It will only get better when people convert their hearts and actions toward God.

If you have more questions, or need assistance for deeper understanding, in serve God through services to people you representing, please contact me. I pray for you.

Sincerely in Christ Jesus,

Mariette Do-Nguyen

Rebuild My Church Divine Mission
(The Lord Jesus gave this name to Mariette)
P.O. Box 261550 ✦ San Diego, CA 92196-1550

June 12, 1998

To: President Bill Clinton, Vice President Al Gore, Senator William V. Roth Jr., Chairman of Financial Committee; Robert Rubin, Secretary of Treasury, U.S. Department of Treasury, Charles O. Rossotti, Commissioner for Internal Revenue Service

Dear ....

On the following dates: October 31, 1997, December 4, 1997, December 25, 1997, February 1, 1998, February 17, 1998, and April 17, 1998, these letters were mailed to you through the U.S. Postal Service.

On June 11, 1998, 11:05 a.m. I found a letter in my mail box; this mail slot has a box inside my residence's garage. I saw that sender was the "Internal Revenue Service, ESP: 90 Day Suspense Unit, PO Box 30218, Laguna Niguel, CA, 92607-0218." A round red stamp read: "Laguna Niguel, Ca, June 9, 1998," and a rectangular stamp read: "U.S. OFFICIAL MAIL, US POSTAGE, ... 02.13, H METER 474603," and a black hand-stamp read: "June 09, 1998— CERTIFIED MAIL NO. 363616."

The first thing I thought was, "There was no mail in the box after yesterday delivery. Who put this piece of mail here? The mail carrier normally comes in the afternoon. The certified number and stamp did not look like those I had signed for when I received certified mail, plus the numbers were different." I than immediately noted the time I removed it from the box, and left a note for my mail carrier outside mail slot, "Mail carrier, please let me know when you are here. I have a question regarding a piece of mail I received."

At 3:15 p.m. the U.S. mail carrier came, and I asked, "What does this certified number mean? I did not sign for this mail." He said, "It may be UPS." I said, "This mail slot is only for U.S. postal mail, for deposit by its mail carriers only." While I was saying this I pointed to the mail slot at the garage wall in front of my house. The mail carrier filled out a yellow slip, handed it to me and said, "You can sign this and I will check it out for you." I said, "This piece of mail was inside the mail box, inside this slot, before you got here, and I brought it here. I am not signing for it because you did not deliver it. I just asked you write on the front of the envelope that you are delivering mail on this route today and that you did not deliver this piece of mail." He then wrote: "Not delivered by carrier, 6/11/98, C.J. Bantist." Inside the envelope a letter from Marilyn A. Soulburgs, District Director, IRS, dated June 9, 1998, indicated at the top "Certified Mail", notice of deficiency -waiver and its instruction; Income tax examination changes with explanations of adjustments; enclosed is a letter only.

I would like to condense the contents of all the letters I sent to you. As you already know, communist countries have no freedom of religion. To retain my civil rights and freedom to worship the One who created the Heaven and Earth, before South Vietnam fell into the leadership of communists; I came to the United State as an immigrant and became U.S. citizen for this purpose.

With God's help, I understand His commandments and I am obeying Him. I find that the United State's laws sometimes contradict each other: On one hand there is freedom of religion, and on the other hand, freedom of religion is restricted, when citizens are forced to pay taxes, and then those monies are used for purposes that are destructive to the nation, leading to violence and destruction of the human race.

Tax monies benefit programs that go against God's commandments; funding family planning, advising people to seek abortion and birth control, and supporting medical students who learn to perform abortions. Generating destructive chemicals and weapons engaged in the killing of women and children; the evidence is over three million Vietnamese and more than fifty thousand American troops who were killed in the American - Vietnamese war. Unlimited funding and tax monies are spent for investigations; (While our own national demands have not been taken care of properly, such as: the safety of children at schools, such as grandparents and parent contents weapons in the home to accessible to children, education for adults to teach children, children being abused, problems of the elderly, homeless, diseases, move welfare receipt to work.) the evidence: President Bill Clinton's sex scandal and Whitewater in Arkansas, placing shame on its citizens, and, creating mental suffering to friends and acquaintances of President Clinton. This suffering also has caused key witnesses to die; this shameful news has also caused U.S. citizens to committed backbiting and judging sins.

The third hand is using tax money to pay Internal Revenue Service officers to violate my civil right for freedom of religion, right to privacy in my own home, to my residence without an appointment, trespassing on my property, placing unauthorized mail in my mail slot that has restricted authorization for U.S. mail carriers only. They have cheated me by asking me to sign a Power of Attorney. The IRS conspired with New York Life Insurance Company and made unauthorized loans from my life insurance policies cash value to benefit programs violating my civil rights and freedom of religion.

I know that my tax contribution to build the nation, is like one grain of sand in the ocean, but I cannot disobey God by participating in the works that destroy mankind. Therefore, when the United States Congress passes laws that give me freedom to choose tax programs that benefit the citizens, I then I will participate and pay my share to build the nation.

The holy scriptures said, "Repay to Caesar what belongs to Caesar and to God what belongs to God." God created this earth, not the lawmakers or Internal Revenue Service officers. Therefore, I request that the United States lawmakers protect me and U.S. citizens' right to privacy by preventing unauthorized strangers from trespassing on individual property. I also ask that to restored my civil rights for freedom of religion, and civil rights for freedom of religion for all the American citizens.

Sincerely In Christ Jesus,

Mariette Do-Nguyen

Rebuild My Church Divine Mission

(The Lord Jesus gave this name to Mariette)

P.O. Box 261550 ✦ San Diego, CA 92196-1550

June 29, 1998

Mary Ann Cohen, Chief Judge
United States Tax Court
400 Second Street, NW
Washington, DC 20217

Via: Return Receipt Register Mail

Dear Honorable Cohen,

I know that this letter may seem strange to you, but please be patient with me, and you will understand why I am writing.

I.   Since early 1994, I have retained a tax attorney for various services, but mainly to represent my connection with Internal Revenue Service officers who have been contacting me for over four years. After I received a 90 days suspense letter from the Internal Revenue Service, dated June 6, 1998; in this letter indicated, "You have 90 days from the date of this letter (150 days if addressed outside the United Stated) to file a petition with the United States Tax Court for a redetermination of the deficiency." I met with my tax attorney twice, on June 16 and 26, 1998, He then prepared for me my 1992 and 1993 tax return; at the second meeting I asked him to represent me in tax court, regarding my civil right to freedom of religion. He told me that if a situation arose years before, he would handle it, but at this time he does not wish to do so.

II. I have called a number of lawyers referral services in San Diego, trying to find a civil rights attorney who specializes in freedom of religion. But I am unable to find anyone willing to represent my case involving the Internal Revenue Service. Therefore, I am writing to you to ask you to allow this letter and its attachments to be filed in Tax Court, and to allow me to represent myself.

III. As you already know, communist countries have no freedom of religion. (Although when I left Vietnam it was not clear that I left the country for freedom of religion.) On April 28, 1975, I left Vietnam in an evacuation to the United State, as an immigrant, and became a U.S. citizen for this purpose.

IV. Then I learned that U.S. tax monies have been funding programs that harm United States citizens and lead to the destruction of mankind, causing physical and spiritual violence, and at times physical death and lost souls, such as:

1. Funding for family planning, offering abortions and birth control

2. Support for medical students to learn how to perform abortions

3. Generation of destructive weapons,(not for defense), for example the Vietnamese - American war, which killed over three million Vietnamese and over fifty thousand American troops; these actions slowly destroy the human race.

4. Unlimited funding for investigations and that harm to citizens and bring shame to the nation.

Other areas are improperly serviced, such as:

a. The safety of children at schools; preventing shootings and violence.

b. Teaching adults so adults can teach children; the first place children learn is from parents and grandparents.

c. Moving welfare recipients into programs, providing assistance in transition from welfare to work, not just giving out money and food stamps.

d. Providing spiritual aid for patients with diseases that can not be cured, and elderly in wheel chairs; because these people are depending on God's grace daily to live; the correct spiritual aid will lead them to heaven.

e. Homeless teenagers; these young adults have been rejected by their parents and society; they need love, comfort, and guidance to become better persons in the future. If not, they will join gangs.

f. Limiting gang violence; these people need understanding as to why they became gang members; love them and help them to get out of this system in various ways; they need God in their life to bring them back to society.

g. Lawmakers must pass laws to benefit the U.S. citizens, and not contradict each other.

V. Obeying God, for over four years, I have been communicating with President Bill Clinton, Vice President Al Gore, and all members of the U.S. Senate, to help them to understand the soul and spirit with and in a human's physical body, and that the civil right to freedom of religion in the United States is restricted. In response, I have received over a hundred letters.

Enclosed are copies of a few from: (1) from Senator Arlen Specter, dated March 12, 1998, (2) Senator Tim Hutchinson, dated June 18, 1997, (3) Vice President Al Gore, dated November 21, 1997, (4) Senator William Roth Jr., dated March 31, 1998, (5) Senator John Ashcroff, dated May 20, 1998, (6) Senator John Gleen, dated November 10, 1997, (7) Senator Carl Levin, dated March 24, 1998, (8) a letter from Marilyn A. Soulsburg, District Director, IRS, dated June 9, 1998, (9) an outline of the history of God Summons me and works in two compelling books.

I also enclosed copies of my letters to: (a) seven letters and its attachments to President Bill Clinton, Vice President Al Gore, Senator William V. Roth Jr., Chairman of Financial Committee; Robert Rubin, Secretary of Treasury, U.S. Department of Treasury, Charles O. Rossotti, Commissioner for Internal Revenue Service, dated October 31, 1997, November 25, 1997, December 4, 1997, December 25, 1997, February 1, 1998, February 17, 1998, April 17, 1998, June 12, 1998,(b) a letter and its tax related attachments to Harry Horn, Chairman of the Board, New York Life Insurance Company,(c) and in faith, I trust the Court will protect my civil right to freedom of religion, a signed copies of from 1040, U.S. Individual Income Tax Return for 1992 & 1993 that I have not reviewed.

VI. I know that my tax contribution is small, like a grain of sand in the ocean, but I cannot participate in destroying the nation. I ask you, the Tax Court to grant my petition for taxpayers to have the right to choose where their tax monies go.

1. The Congress should pass laws with a list of account numbers showing what the monies in each account will be funding.

2. Tax return forms should have box (es) for taxpayers to fill in the account number(s) showing what their contributions will fund, similar to the one on the 1040 for "Presidential Election Campaign."

I petition the tax court for these tax laws to be passed, giving me and all United States citizens the civil right to choose the programs that our tax monies fund, restoring citizens' freedom of religion, and to protecting the citizens' privacy at home and abroad.

Respectfully Submitted,

Mariette Do-Nguyen

Rebuild My Church Divine Mission
(The Lord Jesus gave this name to Mariette)
P.O. Box 261550 ✦ San Diego, CA 92196-1550

July 10, 1998

This letter sent to 30 Church leaders, and some pro-life groups

Re: Restored Freedom of Religion and bring God's Peace into United States through Reform Tax Law Revolution - United States Tax Court's Petition Docket No. 11892-98

Dear ....

Enclosed is a copy of a letter to United States Tax Court Chief Judge Mary Ann Cohen, dated June 29, 1998. I ask the Court to grant my petition to give taxpayers the right to choose how their tax monies are spent.

On July 6, 1998, I received a letter from a U.S. Tax court clerk, dated July 2, 1998; a copy is enclosed.

The amount on the notice of tax deficiency that the Internal Revenue Service sent to me for 1992 & 1993 was almost four times greater than the amount of my actual obligation. I will contribute these dollars to the tax fund from my own pocket, when the U.S. Tax Law passes, giving U.S. citizens the civil right to choose the program (s) of their choice; and I will also pay for my own tax attorney's expenses.

This "U.S. Tax Law Revolution" will give its citizens the civil right to choose how their tax monies are spent, as well as freedom of religion. They will have the right to reject indirect participation in murdering unborn babies through abortion, killing civilians in third world countries, and many other areas for which the U.S. government uses taxpayers' dollars that works against God's commandments.

This "Reform Tax Law Revolution" will bring conversion to many, and the nation's iniquities will be purged. And when the iniquities are purged, God will pour His peace and blessing upon the United States.

This "Reform Tax Law Revolution" will benefit uncounted numbers of U.S. citizens. Therefore, in serving the Almighty God in truth, with love and living sacrifices, I ask you and your congregations to assist me in praying, hiring a legal team that specializes in constitutional issues, and to pay their expenses.

It is URGENT because the Court's time is expiring soon, I ask that you respond to me at your earliest convenience. If you need more information or have any questions, please feel free to contact me.

Sincerely in Christ Jesus,

Mariette Do-Nguyen

God's Blessing for those Accepting God's Servant

August 20, 1998. Mr. Thien, a member of Our Lady of Vietnam in Silver Spring, Maryland dropped me at the Heart building at about 11:30 a.m. for the 2:00 p.m. appointment. I was wandering in the building, and called from the street level to the third floor to see if I could change the appointment to an earlier time, but I was unsuccessful; because it was lunch time, and Ms. Kris Ardazzone, Senator's Liaison was out to lunch. For over two hours I walked from one hall to another on the street level to see the structure of the senate buildings. I then went in a lounge room and prayed the rosary; and after I finish praying, the Lord helped me to sort out the materials I brought with me to give to Ms. Ardazzone. I got in the elevator to go the top level, got out of the elevator, crossed the bridge to the same side, but above Senator Ashcroft's office. On my way to return, before I crossed the bridge to the elevator, the Lord brought to me one of the dreams where I was crossing the water bridge on my stomach. I then went down to the street level before I went to the third floor for my appointment. My shoes were killing my feet from the long walk.

The first comfort to me on this trip was from a clerk sitting inside the door of Senator Ashcroft's office. She said to me, "You were the one I gave instructions (to get here)" I said, "Yes." I told her of my purpose to meet with Ms. Ardazzone, and she said, "I am Christian." Then a few minutes later Ms. Ardazzone came out to greet me, and invited me to come in her office.

The moment after both she and I sat at the round table in her office, I felt the Spirit of the Holy Trinity in the room. I prayed, "Father, Lord Jesus, Holy Spirit, I know Your are here in this room with us, and the Blessed Virgin Mother pray for us. The Lord sent me here to deliver this materials. I ask you to do Your work through Kris." She said, "I do believe God works through many of us."

During the meeting I delivered to her some materials and my book "My Patient -

God's Gift" for the purpose of tax laws to be passed allowing the citizens to choose the programs where our moneys will be spent. There were a few times Ms. Ardazzone commented and questioned me of the holy scriptures, such as when she asked me, "Do you know how many people can be saved?" I replied to her, "The Bible said one third of the human race will not enter heaven." I also explained to her that the earth is a copy of heaven. When God cast Lucifer out of heaven, he took with him one third of disobedient angels out of heaven.

She also told me, "When God calls us, if we do not want to do His works, He will make us do like Jonah." She then told me the story of Jonah's denial to do God, but God made him do it, he was cast inside the stomach of a whale for three days. I said, "Yes. There are some people that God chooses to do His works. If they deny to serve God, He will make their situation worse, so they have to do His works.

She then said, "My mother told me 'God chose you'" I asked, "Did you show your mother the paper I faxed to you?" She replied, "Yes; and she said 'God choose you." I then said to her, "My responsibility is to get here, and deliver to you what God asked of me. I now charge you with the responsibility of what God calls you to serve Him. Instead of Him telling you what to do, He sent me here and to give you these materials and charge you with responsibility." She promised me, "I will read them." I requested, "After you read them, please give them to Senator Ashcroft, and God will reveal to you of how to do them." She replied, "Yes."

When I got up, she also got up to walk me out; just as I walked out her office's entrance, she gave me a good bye hug. While my face was at her right shoulder, I then prayed, "Father, Lord Jesus, Holy Spirit. In Your name, I bless everyone work in this office. I ask You, Lord to protect them and guide them." I then left Senator's Ashcroft's office

Rebuild My Church Divine Mission

(The Lord Jesus gave this name to Mariette)

P.O. Box 261550 ✦ San Diego, CA 92196-1550

August 27, 1998

Senator Orrin G. Hatch
United States Senate

Dear Senator Hatch,

Thank you for your letter of June 17, 1998. Yours is the first letter I received from any lawmaker indicating to me to follow "God's commandments."

I know it is very difficult to follow God's commandments. His commandments are full with "truth, love and forgiveness." When a person follows God's commandments, God always protects him or her. But on the other hand, if a person does not deal with the truth and has no real love, they will have to pay for his or her actions, because God is just God.

Enclosed is a copy of a letter to U.S. Tax Court Chief Judge Mary Ann Cohen, dated June 29, 1998; filed on July 1, 1998 and amended on July 29, 1998, serving as a petition for the civil right to freedom of religion in the United States.

To follow God's commandments in serving Him through service to others, help the U.S. citizens not to be forced to commit sins through the government programs using their tax dollars for programs that work against God's commandments. Because the personal, national, and the worldly sins against God, and one another, are causing iniquities. Throughout the world, God is purifying human iniquities, through heavy storms, floods, fire, and other tragedies; and these tragedies will not end until people convert their hearts to God.

God is calling for conversion. I pray that God will give you strength to serve Him, take your actions and help the U.S. Senate members to deal with the truth, admitting some of the tax laws passed contradict other and violate the civil right to freedom of religion, and make the correction. Do not conceal this issue, or wait for another seven months like President Bill Clinton did of the Monica Lewinsky matter. If you need more information please contact me.

Sincerely in Christ Jesus,

Mariette Do-Nguyen

UNITED STATES TAX COURT
WASHINGTON, D.C.

MARIETTE DO-NGUYEN,　　　　　　)
　　　　　　　　　　　　　　　　)
　　　　　　Petitioner,　　　　)
　　　　　　　　　　　　　　　　)
v.　　　　　　　　　　　　　　　) Docket No. 11892-98
　　　　　　　　　　　　　　　　)
COMMISSIONER OF INTERNAL REVENUE,　　　　　)
　　　　　　　　　　　　　　　　)
　　　　　　Respondent.　)

REPLY TO ANSWER TO AMENDED PETITION

1.　I hereby acknowledge the main part of item No. 3.　Tax dispute for tax return years ending 1992 and 1993.　Forms 1040 will be present at the trial for evidence.

2.　I deny the addition to tax: I.R.C. 6651 (a) (1) and I.R.C. 6654 for years ending 1992 and 1993.

This denial is based on the Constitution of the United States, the Bill of Rights, Freedom of Religion, Speech, and Press, and the Right to Assembly and Petition.

CONSTITUTION OF THE UNITED STATES

FIRST AMENDMENT

" [Section 1*.] Congress shall make no law respecting an establishment of religion, or prohibiting the free exercise thereof; or abridging the freedom of speech, or of the press; or the right of the people peaceably to assemble, and to petition the government for a redress of grievances."

Based on the Bill of Rights, the First Amendment; the I.R.C. 6651 (a) (1) and I.R.C. 6654 are invalid.

3. GOD'S COMMANDMENTS

a. "The Lord God formed man out of the clay of the ground and blew into his nostrils the breath of life, and so man became a living being." Geneses 2:7. ** Human life begins at the time of conception.

b.　"Consecrate to me every first-born that opens the womb among the Israelites, both man and beast, for it belongs to me." Exodus 13: 2. **

The "first born" is the first percent, and the "womb" is symbolic of the income. Every one must set out some first percent for the works of God to benefit souls and human lives. Tax is the first percent of taxpayers' income.

c. "Whoever sacrifices to any god, except to the Lord alone, shall be doomed." Exodus 22:19. ** The words "any god" mean any works that go against the Creator of the Heaven and the Earth's will.

d. "You shall not kill" Exodus 20:13. ** Tax dollars that benefit programs that works against God's commandments result in destroyed souls and human lives .

e. "Tell us, what is your opinion: Is it lawful to pay the census tax to Caesar or not?" Knowing their malice, Jesus said, "Why are you testing me, you hypocrites? Show me the coin that pays the census tax." Then they handed him the Roman coin. He said to them, "Whose image in this and whose inscription?" They replied, "Caesar's." At that he said to them, "Then repay to Caesar what belongs to Caesar and to God what belongs to God." Matthew 22:17-21. ** In the Holy Bible, the first and second chapters of the Book of Geneses recorded the fact that God created the world and He owns it (not any government on earth).

I petition the Court for tax laws to be passed, giving me and all United States citizens the civil right to choose the programs that our tax dollars to be fund, restoring the Civil Right to Freedom of Religion in the United States; and the invalid penalties on my 1992 and 1993 tax returns should be removed from my records. I also petition the Court to protect me and the United States citizens' privacy at home and abroad.

Dated: September 14, 1998   Mariette Do-Nguyen,

Rebuild My Church Divine Mission
(The Lord Jesus gave this name to Mariette)
P.O. Box 261550 ✦ San Diego, CA 92196-1550

September 25, 1998

Senator Barbara Boxer
United States Senate

Re: Civil Right to Freedom of Religion in the United States

Dear Senator Boxer,

Thank you for your three letters of August 12, 1998, September 3, 1998, and September 17, 1998.

As you indicated in your letter of September 17, 1998: "I believe that all citizens should become involved in our legislative process by letting their voice be heard."

My voice God has given to me, and that voice is "Civil Right to Freedom of Religion in the United States." This voice is a pending case at the United States Tax Court. I ask you, as my Federal level representative, to assist me that my voice to be heard at the U.S. Senate floor.

Because my voice is from God, and when this voice (Reformed Tax Laws Revolution) be passed by the U.S. lawmakers, God will withdraw some of the pending tragedies and disasters upon on the United States, and throughout the world.

Enclosed are copies of: (1) a letter served as "petition" to United States Tax Court Chief Judge Mary Ann Cohen, dated June 30, 1998, was perfect file on July 29, 1998, (2) Answer to Amended Petition, dated September 4, 1998, and (3) Reply to Amended Petition, dated September 14, 1998 as the evidences of my voice case is pending in the U.S. Tax Court.

If you need more information or have any question, please contact me at (619) 689-0445.

Sincerely in Christ Jesus,

Mariette Do-Nguyen

Rebuild My Church Divine Mission

(The Lord Jesus gave this name to Mariette)

P.O. Box 261550 ✦ San Diego, CA 92196-1550

September 25, 1998

TO: Senators Orrin G. Hatch Chairman Judiciary Committee, John McCain, John Ashcroft, Tim Hutchinson, Carl Levin, Trent Lott, Jesse Helms

Re: Civil Right to Freedom of Religion in the United States

Dear Senators......,

I believe that majority of lawmakers want their citizens' voice be heard. The Civil Right to Freedom of Religion is the voice of all the U.S. citizens. This voice is also for the citizens of the United States and throughout the world, who are praying to God for His peace, to avoid tragedies and disasters.

That voice is "the Civil Right to Freedom of Religion in the United States." This voice is a pending case at the United States Tax Court. I ask you, the Federal level representative for your State, to assist me for "Reformed Tax Laws Revolution" to be heard at the U.S. Senate floor.

Because this voice was given to me by the Almighty God, therefore, when the (Reformed Tax Laws Revolution) are passed by you and other U.S. lawmakers, God will withdraw some of the pending tragedies and disasters. These pending tragedies and disasters can be upon on the United States, and throughout the world, no one can predicted neither time or place, and they just come suddenly. All of this was foretold in the holy scriptures. But, they can be limited by people converting their hearts and actions to God, and obeying all His commandments..

Enclosed are copies of: (1) Answer to Amended Petition, dated September 4, 1998, and (2) Reply to Amended Petition, dated September 14, 1998 as the evidences of my voice case is pending in the U.S. Tax Court.

If you need more information or have any question, please contact me at (619) 689-0445.

Sincerely in Christ Jesus,

Mariette Do-Nguyen

Rebuild My Church Divine Mission

(The Lord Jesus gave this name to Mariette)

P.O. Box 261550 ✦ San Diego, CA 92196-1550

October 1, 1998

To: Vice President Al Gore, Senators Orrin G. Hatch Chairman Judiciary Committee, John McCain, John Ashcroft, Tim Hutchinson, Carl Levin, Trent Lott, Jesse Helms

Re: Evolution of Life on Earth

Dear ....,

Enclosed are copies of: (1) a letter to Professor Adolph Seilacher, Geology Department at Yale University, dated October 1, 1998; (2) an article "Fossil wormholes could shed light on evolution of life on earth." and (3) "God reveals the evolution of the process of His creation."

In my letter to you of April 17, 1998, I explained to all the member of the U.S. Senate of how life started at the time of conception. The information was from God, given to me to deliver to you; now God asks me to deliver to researchers for life on earth, so they can continue their research.

I pray to God that you will accept the revelations, passing laws against the legal abortions. Life is started at the time of conception, not when the babies are at age twenty weeks. Like the electric bulb, when you turn the switch, the light is on then, not 20 weeks later.

President Bill Clinton admitted that he misled the American citizens. I open to you the spiritual leaders have misled people they are leading; through fighting against abortion. They are fighting for partial abortion, not for all abortion. You did not understand when human life started, but the spiritual leaders do know that human life starts at the time of conception, and they are refusing to fight for these unborn babies before they are 20 weeks old.

You now know that the human life starts at the time of conception. As God's agent, I am charging you to bring this information to the U.S. Senate floor, and to reverse the legal abortion. If you refuse, you are intentionally murdering the unborn babies through all abortions, and God will charge this against you and all the lawmakers of giving a license to murder.

If you need more information or have any question, please contact me.

Sincerely in Christ Jesus,

Mariette Do-Nguyen

Rebuild My Church Divine Mission

(The Lord Jesus gave this name to Mariette)

P.O. Box 261550 ✦ San Diego, CA 92196-1550

October 21, 1998

TO: Seven Senators, author of the Bill "S.1868 - International Religious

Dear Senator...,

I would like to express my thanks to Senators Don Nickles, Connie Mack, Joseph Lieberman, Larry Craig, Dirk Kempthorne, Tim Hutchinson, and Mike DeWine for introducing the bill on International Religious Freedom within the National Security Council and for other purposes. The bill was read on the U.S. Senate floor and passed.

Enclosed is copy of a pending petition at the United States Tax Court in Washington. In this petition I am asking the U.S. Tax Court to restore the United States citizen's civil rights for freedom of religion. Through reforming tax laws, the U.S. citizens will be given the civil right to direct where their own tax money will be spent, by indicating on the tax return of each year, form 1040. This reform also releases the responsibility of the government in using tax money to benefit programs that work against God's commandments, forcing the taxpayers to commit sins indirectly. It gives the free will to the citizens to practice their faith, and to make them liable in front of God for every one's sins in directing their tax dollars spending; limiting some tragedies and disasters, and will bring God's peace upon the nation, and throughout the world.

This Reformed Tax Laws giving the U.S. citizens civil rights to direct each citizen's tax money will work parallel with the bill "S. 1868" that you and other senators have introduced, and the bill was passed in favor of all the members of the U.S. Senators.

I ask that you and other senator members assist me to complete the last part of the bill "S.1868" by passing this Reformed Tax Laws. When the Reform Tax Laws are passed, restoring the civil right to freedom of religion in the United States, the United States lawmakers and government officials take the first step to enforce the bill S. 1868, and it will give power to the bill for other nations to follow. If you need more information or have any questions, please contact me.

Sincerely in Christ Jesus,

Mariette Do-Nguyen

Rebuild My Church Divine Mission

(The Lord Jesus gave this name to Mariette)

P.O. Box 261550 ✦ San Diego, CA 92196-1550

December 4, 1998

To: Vice President Al Gore, and all members of the United States Senate

Re: The U.S. Citizens Civil Right to Freedom of Religion in United States is Violated

Dear Senators.............,

I would like to express my thanks for your vote to support the bill "S.1868, International Religious Freedom" which passed unopposed 98-0.

President Bill Clinton admitted that he misled Americans of the relationship with Ms. Lewinsky. The members of congress also are misleading the United States citizens in the "civil right to freedom of religion in the United States of America."

When U.S. Lawmakers pass laws using taxpayers dollars for various purposes that go against God's commandments, such as benefits for legal abortions, generating destructive chemicals and weapons to engage the third world countries, (not the defense) it forces U.S. citizens to indirectly commit the sin of murder. This grave sin is against God and against one another, and the lawmakers violate the citizen's civil right to freedom of religion.

These community grave sins, the national systems, and individual lifestyles are bringing down natural tragedies from God, such as heavy rains, floods, hurricanes, fires, thunderstorms to purify the iniquities caused after these sins were committed. Beyond this, the devil received permission from God to bring disasters such as bombings, shootings at school, on the streets, in homes, in the places at work, suck as Capital Hill and post office; airplane crashes, violence, murders, and other horrors, to damage citizen's life on earth and destroy their souls.

These tragedies and disasters will come suddenly and man can not predict them, they will increase more and more until lawmakers pass all laws according to God's commandments, and people convert their hearts and actions to God.

Enclosed are copies of: (1) a letter to Tax Court Chief Judge Mary Ann Cohen, dated June 29, 1998, (2) proof of filling, dated July 29, 1998, (3) Answer to Amended Petition and Reply to Answer to Amended Petition, (4) letter from Christine V. Olsen, November 18, 1998, (5) my letter to Ms. Olsen, November 28, 1998, (6) Evolution is God Creation Revelation, and meaning of the Book of Genesis, chapters 1,2,3, and partial of chapter 4, (7) article from San Diego Union, "Fossil wormholes could shed light on evolution of life on earth."

President Bill Clinton has admitted he misled Americans of his relationship with Ms. Lewinsky. I urge that the U.S. Lawmakers admit they are misleading the U.S. Citizens in the civil right to freedom of religion in the United States, correct the "Tax Laws," give taxpayers the freedom to choose where our tax dollars are to be spent, and restore the civil right to freedom of religion in the United States, leave the free will to each individual, to choose to obey God or disobey Him, to choose to receive peace or reject peace.

Sincerely in Christ Jesus,

Mariette Do-Nguyen

White House Crisis Turned to National Crisis

See, the earlier things have come to pass, new ones I now foretell; before they spring into being I announce them to you.

–Isaiah 42:9

Rebuild My Church Divine Mission

(The Lord Jesus gave this name to Mariette)

P.O. Box 261550 ✦ San Diego, CA 92196-1550

June 21, 1996

sent via Federal Express

Hillary Rodham Clinton
White House

Dear Mrs. Clinton,

I give praise, glory, and thanks to the Lord our God who is guiding me as I write this letter to you. I'm asking you to thank Mr. Clinton for his letter of June 14, 1996, regarding the Abortion Law for me. After I received the letter, I placed it on the altar and gave thanks to the Lord for using the President as His servant in this matter. The Lord Jesus said to me, "[Mr. President] My beloved slave to the Lord." I was so happy to hear this message from the Lord, and I thought of what Saint Paul said in Colossians 3: 24 " Knowing that you will receive from the Lord the due payment of the inheritance; by slaves of the Lord Christ."

I, too, am a slave to the Lord God the Almighty, and served as His instrument in the writing of the book, "My Patient—God's Gift." The Lord Jesus instructed me to send a copy of the enclosed book to you and Mr. Clinton. Co-authored by Dr. Gerald E. Nelson, it contains God's truth. I am His servant, nothing else, and following His calling is not an easy path.

I pray for you, your husband, and your daughter. I trust in Him that you and Mr. President will be able to accept His call to you. As a slave to the Lord God one must always act from the heart, and please Him [God] by obeying all His commandments, rather than the laws of man. This means regular prayer, asking Him to cleanse our sins and purge our iniquity, and loving God first and loving others as ourselves. It also means forgiving and loving our enemies and constantly discerning between good and evil, for the devil is cunning and often appears as God.

I know that your life and the life of Mr. President has been difficult and will continue to be so. I will keep on praying for you, for your husband and family; and for Vice President Gore, his family, and the White House staff.

In Christ Jesus,

Mariette Do-Nguyen

Rebuild My Church Divine Mission

(The Lord Jesus gave this name to Mariette)

P.O. Box 261550 ✦ San Diego, CA 92196-1550

December 23, 1997

sent via U.S. Certified Mail

Mrs. Paula R. Jones
P.O. Box 7482
Charlottesville, VA 22906-7482

Dear Paula,

I received your undated letter and read it carefully. In my devotion that day, I asked the Lord Jesus for direction.

In this matter, you and the President of the United States are dealing with each other in front of the Almighty God; and through this matter many will receive a lesson. Therefore, the result is in the hands of God.

Jesus the Lord came down to the world to save, not to condemn us, but His own people crucified Him to death. He teaches us to deal with the truth, acknowledge wrong, to convert and not commit the same sin again. He also teaches us to forgive others seventy-seven times.

Through the power of God, I am heading a mission to prepare for the Second Coming of Christ, when he will judge the world. As the Messenger of the Holy Trinity, I send this letter to you and a copy to President Clinton. In God's love and mercy, I encourage you, your husband, the President and Mrs. Clinton to sit down privately and resolve this matter with love and forgiveness from each person's heart; avoid the media and convert to God, so that you may be saved for eternal life in heaven. Win or lose in this world —- will not profit in heaven.

I will pray for you, your family, the President, his family, and everyone involved in this matter to be united in God's love. If there is anything I can do to assist you, do not hesitate to contact me.

Sincerely in Christ Jesus,

Mariette Do-Nguyen

Rebuild My Church Divine Mission

(The Lord Jesus gave this name to Mariette)

P.O. Box 261550 ✦ San Diego, CA 92196-1550

December 23, 1997

sent via U.S. Certified Mail

President Bill Clinton
White House

Dear President Clinton,

Enclosed is a copy of my letter to Mrs. Paula R. Jones, dated December 23, 1997. I know this matter is very difficult for you as the President of the United States, and for the First Lady. The public places judgment on Mrs. Jones and you; this also is effecting on Mrs. Jones' husband, their marriage and their children, the First Lady and your daughter. Everyone must overcome the iniquity and be healed. Each one must come to God for He is the only One who can purge the iniquity and bring about healing.

In the letter to Mrs. Jones, I make no judgment on you or Mrs. Jones, because Jesus the Lord is the only Judge. I only give Mrs. Jones the Lord Jesus's teachings. I also give to you exactly what I gave to Mrs. Jones.

I strongly encourage you, just as I encouraged Mrs. Jones. If there is anything, beside praying for all of you, that I can do to assist you, do not hesitate to contact me.

Sincerely in Christ Jesus,

Mariette Do-Nguyen
cc: Mrs. Paula R. Jones

Rebuild My Church Divine Mission

(The Lord Jesus gave this name to Mariette)

P.O. Box 261550 ✦ San Diego, CA 92196-1550

September 14, 1998

President Bill Clinton
White House

Dear President Clinton,

You may not remember the letter I sent to you, via the first lady Hillary's address, and a letter to Paula R. Jones, dated December 23, 1998, and your letter of response, dated February 12, 1998. In the letter to Mrs. Jones I indicated, "Win or lose in this world—- will not profit heaven." And in a letter to you, I indicated, "I only give Mrs. Jones the Lord Jesus' teachings. I also give to you exactly what I gave to Mrs. Jones."

Obeying God, I must deliver what God asks of me. In the same way, continuing as the President of the United States the rest of your term will not benefit heaven.

God instructed me this morning, September 14, 1998, to send a letter to Vice President Gore, tell him that He said, "It is God's will for President Bill Clinton to resign." A copy enclosed.

I also enclosed a copy of my letter to first lady Hilary, dated June 21, 1998. The meaning in this letter is that God is calling you back to him, like He called Saint Paul. Your statements to American citizens on August 17, 1998 is the same as at the time God struck Saint Paul blind for three days.

I will stand with you and pray for you, the first lady, your daughter, and the U.S. citizens to be healed.

Sincerely in Christ Jesus,

Mariette Do-Nguyen

God Calling President Bill Clinton and First Lady Hillary for Conversion

> Saul's Conversion. *Now Saul, still breathing murderous threats against the disciples of the Lord, went to the high priest and asked him for letters to the synagogues in Damascus, that, if he should find any men or women who belonged to the Way, he might bring them back to Jerusalem in chains. On his journey, as he was nearing Damascus, a light from the sky suddenly flashed around him. He fell to the ground and heard a voice saying to him, 'Saul, Saul, why are your persecuting me?' He said, 'Who are you, sir?' The reply came, 'I am Jesus, whom you are persecuting. Now get up and go into the city and you will be told what you must do.' The men who were traveling with him stood speechless, for they heard the voice but could see no one. Saul got up from ground, but when he opened his eyes he could see nothing; so they led him be the hand and brought him to Damascus. For three days he was unable to see, and he neither ate nor drank.*
>
> – Acts 9: 1-9

This is the scripture that the Lord used and instructed me to sent a letter to the first lady Hillary Rodham Clinton, on June 21, 1996. The letter indicated, "I trust in Him that you and Mr. President will be able to accept His call to you."

The word "murder" can be interpreted as the spiritual death or physical death:

Spiritual death: President Bill Clinton is President of the most powerful earthly nation in the world. From his thoughts transformed into actions causes spiritual death to many U.S. citizens, and this will influence to caused death in other countries. Actions such as tax moneys that benefit programs that go against God's commandments, force citizens to commit grave sins against God and against one another. He was untruthful to the American citizens, and lied under oath causing many people to commit the sin of judging him. This untruthful action is a bad example for children and adults. Through this letter, and being published in this book, God indirectly speaks to government officials and lawmakers throughout the world.

Physical death: He used the power of the President of the nation to put immorality into the laws. These laws give the right to murder people, such as the legal abortion laws, (human life begins at the time of conception), and generating destructive weapons and chemicals. Engaging in other countries issues with strikes cause death to civilians. This takes away their right to life and the opportunity to generate good deeds for their reward in heaven. Through this revelation, God also directly speaks to lawmakers, high-ranking government official, and presidents throughout the world that voted for or vetoed the laws working against God's commandments.

When the first lady Hillary received my letter, she thought that the works President Clinton was doing at that time was serving God; but the letter was prophecy. Even though her understanding of my letter was incorrect, she accepted my letter; it meant that she accepted that God was calling President Bill Clinton and her for conversion. Through this acceptance, God's power strengthen her to go through with her husband, specially on August 17, 1998, the night he admitted his and Monica Lewinsky's relationship. And because of the husband and wife relationship, God will also help President Clinton slowly on his journey of conversion.

After the conversion, there is a journey of iniquities to be purged. Every time a sin is committed, it will result in iniquity. God is the only One who can purge our iniquities. More sins committed means more iniquities to be purged; more iniquities to be purged means more time is needed. This can called a purification process for the soul to be pure before entering heaven. The purification can be on earth or in the purgatory. If a person does not convert back to God, he will be punished eternally by being chained in the darkness of the Devil. The start of the purification is acknowledging the wrong, sorrow from the heart, and not committing that sin again, dealing with the truth at all time. Yes means yes, and no means no, not in between.

God Calls to Speak the Truth and Forgiveness in Love

Then Peter approaching asked him, "Lord, if my brother sins against me, how often must I forgive him? As many as seven times?" Jesus answered, "I say to you not seven times but seventy-seven times.

–Matthew 18:21-22

But I say to you, love your enemies, and pray for those who persecute you, that you may be children of your heavenly Father, for he makes his sun rise on the bad and the good, and causes rain to fall on the just and the unjust.

–Matthew 5:44-45

The letters that God had me send to President Bill Clinton and Mrs. Jones, dated December 23, 1997 were warning letters. God told me to emphasize the virtue of love, truth, and forgiveness, and call them to convert to Him. In the contents of a letter to President Bill Clinton, dated September 14, 1998, God asked me to deliver to President Clinton of his disobedience to God's warning, resulting in a crisis for himself and for the nation. The September 14, 1998 letter served two purposes; God calls him to conversion; and the present crisis was God purifying him for sins that he committed during his life against God and others, especially during the vetoes of legal abortion, and twice called for military to the Gulf and strike. These are acts of indirect murder, but he did not listen to God.

God's commanded us to deal with the truth; if we wish to deal with the truth, each individual must obey all God's commandments. When an individual obeys all God's commandments they will be filled with love, forgiveness and truth. His commandments must apply to the personal life and bring to the public life. Both the private life and public life are hand in hand and subject to be judged in front of the Almighty God.

Rebuild My Church Divine Mission

(The Lord Jesus gave this name to Mariette)

P.O. Box 261550 ✦ San Diego, CA 92196-1550

January 27, 1998

Vice President Al Gore
White House

Dear Vice President Gore,

The Lord Jesus asked me to send the enclosed materials to you: (1) a letter to the first lady Hillary Rodham Clinton, dated June 21, 1996; (2) letters to Paula R. Jones, and President Bill Clinton, dated December 23, 1997, and (3) God Reveals that the World is against Him.

Jesus the Lord came to save sinners. He is calling all of us to convert, to deal with the truth from each of our hearts to pay for what each one of us has done against Him, the creator of the heaven and earth; and no one can escape His nest of purification.

As the Lord revealed; the world's systems leads people to deny their responsibility. Therefore, the Lord asked me to send this letter to you, charging you with the responsibility in many areas, including the White House crisis regarding President Clinton.

The earthquakes, heavy rains, storms, and floods are just the beginning of God's purification of the world's systems.

I will pray for you, your family, the White House staff, and lawmakers to take actions within God's commandments. Obeying God will limit some of the tragedies upon the world, and make the land of American a better place to live and a place in which to build the kingdom of heaven.

If you need more information or have any questions, please contact me,

Sincerely in Christ Jesus,

Mariette Do-Nguyen

Rebuild My Church Divine Mission

(The Lord Jesus gave this name to Mariette)

P.O. Box 261550 ✦ San Diego, CA 92196-1550

September 14, 1998

Vice President Al Gore
White House

Dear Vice President Gore,

You may remember a letter that the Lord asked me send to you via Federal Express, dated January 27, 1998. This letter indicated "As the Lord revealed in the revelation, the world's systems lead people to deny their responsibility and truth. Therefore, the Lord asked me to send this letter to you, charging you with responsibilities in many areas, including the White House crisis regarding President Bill Clinton." Copies of the letter and proof of receipt are enclosed.

The United States citizens went through seven months of shame with President Bill Clinton's denial of the truth. As time went by, the situation got worse, no longer just the White House crisis, but the national crisis since the Independent Counsel Kenneth Starr's 445 page report was posted on the internet. This situation has done great damage to the citizens, especially the children and young adults. This event is very shameful to the nation. The length of the impeachment procedure will put more damage on the nation and its citizens

The Lord told me this morning that it is God's will for President Bill Clinton to resign, and for you to lead the nation with honor and truth, facing the troubles and results of them. The real conversion and repentance, the apology and contrition for President Bill Clinton can only happen after he leaves the office as the President of the United States, and this will take many years to come.

Therefore, again, the Lord Jesus asked me this morning after I received the Holy Eucharist, to send this letter to you, charging you with the responsibility of obeying God's commandments, and leading the nation so He can heal this nation and its citizens.

I pray to the Lord that He will strengthen you to fulfill what He call for you. If you need more information, please contact me. I also enclosed a copy of letter to President Bill Clinton, dated September 14, 1998.
Sincerely in Christ Jesus,

Mariette Do-Nguyen

625

Rebuild My Church Divine Mission

(The Lord Jesus gave this name to Mariette)

P.O. Box 261550 ✦ San Diego, CA 92196-1550

December 14, 1998

Vice President Al Gore
White House
1600 Pennsylvania Ave.
Washington, DC 20500

Sent via facsimile No. (202) 456-7044 and U.S. Mail

Re: God's will for President Bill Clinton to resign

Dear Vice President Gore,

When God uses someone to do His works, it is never been easy; in fact is very difficult. You are in one of the most difficult situation, but God will strengthen you, and help President Bill Clinton to be strong when the time comes for him to fulfill what is the most important for his soul, the souls of his family and the citizens of this nation, as well as the nature future of this nation.

President Clinton said the other day when he was walking away form the podium, "I read in Isiah said 'do not be afraid, I have redeemed you.'" This is the word that God spoke to him; God had redeemed him, but he has to obey God to resign so he can convert to God.

In President Clinton's mind, he thinks he has converted to God, but God told me that he will not really convert until he resigns as the President. President Clinton's true conversion will only come when he loses the thing that is most valuable to him, and that is his presidency. This time he has no one to cling to, only God.

God is speaking to the President, but the devil is blocking him from hearing God. He needs substance from people who have real love for his soul, no for his presidency, so he can hear God. When he receives this substance, he will hear the voice of God himself.

God asked me to write this letter to you, therefore, I ask you to seek God for direction.
Sincerely in Christ Jesus,

Mariette Do-Nguyen

After the day of President Bill Clinton's deposition of the Paula Jones case, on January 17, 1998, the President disobeyed God's warning, and spoke untruth. Therefore, a letter to Vice President Al Gore, dated January 27, 1998 informed Vice President Al Gore to prepare to lead the nation. A letter to Vice President Gore on September 14, 1998 was God's command to the Vice President to take over the leadership.

Rebuild My Church Divine Mission
(The Lord Jesus gave this name to Mariette)
P.O. Box 261550 ✦ San Diego, CA 92196-1550

September 24, 1998

Honorable Henry J. Hyde, Chairman
Judiciary Committee
United States House of Representative

Dear Honorable Hyde,

During the night of September 20, 1998; The Lord Jesus told me, "The Immortal body listens to mortal sins." I asked, "Lord, what do you mean?"

He said, "You know that I am within you, and you watched the gossip of President Clinton on television, focusing to see President Bill Clinton's resignation. You must trust in God that His work through you will be done." (The Lord means that when God is dwelling with and in a person, that person must not gossip or listen to any gossip. And the contents of the letters He commanded President Clinton to resign is done. Note: I know that the devil uses bad television to attack people; but, since the White House crisis broke out, I watched a little of the news, and sometimes other people are judging President Clinton and Independent Council Kenneth Starr on television).

The Lord Jesus continued, "The pending Tax Laws Petition is the one that the Father will bring you visible to the world to speak of what I am giving to you, to tell the world that God is purifying its systems." (The Lord means that the prophecy of President Bill Clinton's resignation hidden in the letter to Vice President Gore in January 27, 1998 is not the one that the Father revealed the mission that God entrusted to me to be visible to the world.)

Jesus the Lord continued, "You need to send a letter to the Judiciary Chairman committee, Congressman Henry Hyde, and tell him that 'his past sin is no longer to be mentioned.'" (The sins committed before the conversion are longer used against.)

Enclosed are copies of letters to: (1) a letter to Vice President Al Gore, dated January 27, 1998, and a letter response from Vice President Gore, dated February 25, 1998; (2)letters to Vice President Al Gore and President Bill Clinton, dated September 14, 1998.

If you have any question or need more information, please contact me.

Sincerely in Christ Jesus,

Mariette Do-Nguyen

Rebuild My Church Divine Mission

(The Lord Jesus gave this name to Mariette)

P.O. Box 261550 ✦ San Diego, CA 92196-1550

December 11, 1998

Honorable Henry J. Hyde, Chairman
Judiciary Committee
United States House of Representative
Washington, DC 20515

Sent via Honorable James E. Rogan facsimile No. (202)225-5828, and Federal Express

Re: God's will for President Bill Clinton to Resign

Dear Honorable Hyde,

This may be very strange to you and to many members of the House of Representatives, but I ask you to be patient with me, to finish reading my entire letter, and its attachments, and you will see it is very real.

I am speaking out as an immigrant and United States citizen, and of what God asked me to deliver to you as the Chairman of the Judiciary committee, and all the members of the House of Representatives. The contents of this letter are full of love and truth, and I am accountable in front of God for them.

President Clinton is the Commander in Chief of the most powerful nation, either he or any other President of the United States or any nation, must always obey every single law of God and hold themselves as a mirror for its citizens to follow. The actions of President Clinton's untruthful testimony under oath in front of God, and hi actions are teaches the United States citizens to lie under oath like him, and have extramarital causing destructive to family and nation. He made the worst example for the U.S. citizens to follow in breaking the laws of God, laws of the nation, asking God for more tragedies and disaster.

For the benefit of the United States citizens, and for President Clinton himself, and the members of his family and friends he must resign. The reason is that as long as he is still the President of the United States, he will not convert to God. He will only convert when he loses everything, then he will sincerely turn to God. Because he has not converted to God, his actions will add more natural tragedies and disasters upon the United States. His resignation will teach future leaders of the United States that they must always hold themselves in the highest standard for the entire nation to follow, and this will bring God's peace upon this nation.

I received this commandment from God, and God asked me to deliver it to you. In turn, I am charging you to deliver this letter and all the attachments to all the members of the House Representatives before the beginning of the House Impeachment Hearing.

Sincerely in Christ Jesus,

Mariette Do-Nguyen

Enclosed are copies of:

1. Letter to and from first lady Hillary Rodham Clinton, dated June 21, 1996 and June 25, 1996

2. Letters to Mrs. Paula R. Jones and President Bill Clinton, dated December 23, 1997, with proof of mailing and delivery.

3. Response letter from President Bill Clinton, dated February 12, 1998. President Clinton changed the trumpet tone in this letter.

4. Letter to and from Vice President Al Gore, dated January 27, 1998 and February 25, 1998,

5. Letter to Vice President Al Gore, dated September 14, 1998
6. Response letter from Bill Mason, Director of Correspondence for the Vice President, dated September 25, 1998,
7. Letter to President Bill Clinton, dated September 14, 1998
8. Outline of God summons Mariette Do-Nguyen,
9. God's Revelation in two compelling books.

Things (Sins) Happen for Reasons

Letters to the first lady Hillary Rodham Clinton, Paula Jones, President Bill Clinton, Vice President Al Gore are the messages of God calling for conversions; and letter to congressman Henry Hyde is confirm of iniquities of pass sin was purged by God.

Sunday, September 20, 1998. During the night in my dream I was searching for my shoes, and I did not find them. I got up a few times to pray for understanding. Close to the morning, in my dream I saw the altar at Saint Michael's, and the right lower arm of the mass celebrant, and his hand was holding a gold paten. This arm was old bones, the skin was peeled off, and looked like an arm of death. This was fearful to me, I pleaded to the Lord for understanding of the revelation. When I saw this arm, I thought it was something that I did terribly wrong, that was in my thought or my actions; or other people had done, and the Lord revealed to me and I would have to deliver to them.

He told said, "Immortal body listen to mortal sins." I asked you, "Lord, what do you mean?" He said, "You know that I am in you and with you; and you watched the gossip on television, focusing to see Bill Clinton's resignation. You must trust in God that His works through you will be done. (He means that when God dwells within a person, that person must not gossip or listen to the gossip, and in the letter He commanded President Clinton to resign. Note: I know that devil uses television to attack people; therefore, since the White House crisis broke out, I watched television very little in the news and some times people judged President Clinton and Independent Council Kenneth Starr). The tax laws petition is the one where the Father brings you out to the world. (The Lord means that the prophecy of President Bill Clinton's resignation was hidden in the letter to Vice President Gore in January 27, 1998 and is not the one that the Father revealed this mission to the world.) You need to send a letter to the Judiciary Chairman committee, Congressman Henry Hyde, and tell him that his past sin is no longer to be mentioned."

The Lord then pointed out to me by showing me some visions, He said, "Congressman Hyde's extramarital sin was over thirty years ago. He converted, and when the matter was revealed to the public he asked the House Speaker Newt Gingrich to resign the position as the Chairman of Judiciary Committee. But God's will is not for him to resign his job, but instead he must stay to finish the job. While President Bill Clinton announced contrition, and repentance, he refused to resign; as long he has not resigned he is not yet converted."

The Lord continued, "You need to go to confession, and return to the Good Shepherd church for 8:30 mass this morning. Today is the third day after Saint Michael's statue arms have been repaired. This repeats the pattern of when you were in Little Rock; I told you to return to San Diego the third day. (This is a repeated pattern of Abraham having a vision of the third day, the Lord Jesus rising from the dead on the third day. It is not suspicious, instead, the Lord uses natural to reveal the supernatural. Saint Michael statues arms being repaired are symbolic of being ready to battle for victory.)

I was very humiliated of my sins against the Lord, I pleaded, "Lord, forgive me that I listened to the gossip and focused on President Clinton's resignation. I know that when I come to you from deep in my heart, pleading for forgiveness and my sins will be forgiven. The Sacrament of Reconciliation serves as counsel with my spiritual director. You are my spiritual director, my Master, my Teacher, my Lord and my God."

I then got ready for the 8:30 a.m. mass. Getting out of the car at the church parking lot, and walking toward the Good Shepherd physical church, I was very humiliated, and not worthy to enter the church. I was trying to enter the side door to the Blessed Sacrament chapel, but the Lord told me, "Take the way to the main entrance." I then turned to my right, and walked toward the main right entrance. After I walked few step, I saw father Earl opening the door to get out. As he saw me, he said, "Hi Mariette." I replied, "Good morning Father." He said, "How are you?" I then shook his hand, looked at his face and said, "Jesus loves you." He said, "Have a good mass." I did not like what he said, I said, "While I was not here, I prayed for you." He said, "We are united in prayer." I asked, "I need to have a confession." He said, "You need to come on Saturday at three or call for an appointment." I said, "I will call for an appointment." He said, "This week will be bad, because all the priests will be in retreat. Pray for us." I replied, "Sure, I will pray for all of them." He said, "Have a good mass." I did not like what he said 'have a good mass', but I said, "Thank you." And entered the church.

Entering the right main entrance, then I proceeded to the Blessed Sacrament chapel. After I was inside the Blessed Sacrament chapel, I asked, "Lord, where would you want me be?" He said, "On the ground, next to the kneeler." I did as He commanded me.

I then got up, and the Lord said, "Take the door into the baptismal fountain." I was then inside the main church, and I asked, "Lord, where would You want me to sit" He said, "Sit in the second row."

During the entire mass I was feeling very bad for my sins and focused on the Lord, asking God for forgiveness . I also asked the Blessed Virgin Mother, Saint Joseph, Saint John, and all the holy angels to plead to the Lord for me for forgiveness.

After the consecration in my vision, I saw one of the dreams I saw before: The Heavenly Father up high, He looked down on the large stage where Jesus was standing and preaching. Around the stage were people standing all the way to the horizon, and there was a line of light coming from above the Father's right shoulder down to the Lord Jesus' left. Then the Holy Spirit said to me, "The sun will shine on people through you. God works like a puzzle, and you are the last piece. You need to wait for all the other pieces to be put in before you."

After I received the Holy Eucharist, the Lord Jesus said to me, "You are apostles Peter, Paul and John, and they are those women accompany them to proclaim the good news."

Rebuild My Church Divine Mission
(The Lord Jesus gave this name to Mariette)
P.O. Box 261550 ✦ San Diego, CA 92196-1550

September 30, 1998

TO: Senators Trent Lott, Majority Leader; Orrin G. Hatch, Chairman Judiciary Committee; John McCain; John Ashcroft; Tim Hutchinson; Carl Levin; Jesse Helms; Barbara Boxer.

Re: God's will is for President Bill Clinton to resign

Dear Senator........,

In my letter to you earlier this year; I enclosed copies of three letters. The first item was a letter to first lady Hillary Rodham Clinton, dated June 21, 1998. In this letter God revealed He calls President Bill Clinton and the first lady Hillary for conversion. President Bill Clinton's admission of August 18, 1998 was like the time the Lord Jesus struck Saul (Saint Paul) blind for three days. And the response from the first lady's letter of June 25, 1996. The other enclosures were a letter to President Bill Clinton, dated December 23, 1997, via the first lady Hillary's address, and a letter to Paula Jones. These two letters were a warning to both President Bill Clinton and Paula Jones.

You may not understand why I sent the above letters to you at that time. But God has His reasons for you to have them before President Bill Clinton's admission on August 17, 1998.

Today, I am enclosing copies of: (1) A response letter from President Bill Clinton, dated February 12, 1998 to my letter of December 23, 1998. In this letter, President Clinton changed the drum's tone. (2) A letter to Vice President Al Gore, date January 27, 1998. God's messages to the Vice President prepared him to take the leadership of the nation. And the

Vice President's response letter of February 25, 1998. He is sharing his faith in God. (3) A letter to Vice President Al Gore, dated September 14, 1998; God commanded him to lead the nation. (4) A letter to President Bill Clinton, dated September 14, 1998; God revealed that His will is for President Bill Clinton is to resign. (5) An outline of God summons me (Mariette) and God's Revelations in two of my compelling books.

Monica Lewinsky and Paula Jones are just a very small fraction of President Bill Clinton's works against God. But His actions of vetoing legal abortion laws, calling for strikes Iraq to change the drum's tone, using tax benefits for abortions, generating chemical and destructive weapons to murder civilians are actions that force taxpayers indirectly to commit the sins of murder.

I warn you and all the U.S. lawmakers, the longer the President and all members of the U.S. Senate who have not "admitted the whole truth" of the laws passed against God's commandments, and take steps to correct these errors, the longer, and more strongly storms, heavy rains, floods, fires, earthquakes, and other tragedies and disasters will come upon on the United States; and they will come suddenly, no human can predict. The sooner the lawmakers correct the laws, the quicker people will turn their hearts and actions to God, then God will withdraw some of the pending tragedies and disasters. The disasters, such as shootings, bombings, murders, and airplane crashes are caused by the devil, although, the devil needs permission from God . The tragedies are natural actions to purify the world systems, and they come from God.

The Israelites cried out to God, God heard their voice and sent Moses to rescue them from Pharaoh. The U.S. citizens and others throughout the world are crying out to God, and He is answering them. Each individual must convert to God first before receiving blessing.

All the congress represents the U.S. citizens, you and they are responsible to do the best for the U.S. citizens interest. President Clinton has admitted his personal wrong action. I ask you and members of the U.S. Senate to assist the President with love to resign from the office. After the President resigns, he will convert, the congress can correct those laws that work against God's commandments, and God will heal the President, the members of his family, and the U.S. citizens. If you need more information or have any questions, please contact me.

Sincerely in Christ Jesus,

Mariette Do-Nguyen

God Calls Government Officials and Lawmakers Throughout the World for Conversion

The Call of Tax Collector: *As Jesus passed on from there, he saw a man named Matthew sitting at the customs post. He said to him, "Follow me." And he got up and followed him. While he was at table in his house, many tax collectors and sinners came and sat with Jesus and his disciples. The Pharisees saw this and said to his disciples, "Why does your teacher eat with tax collectors and sinners?" He heard this and said, "Those who are well do not need a physician, but the sick do. Go and learn the meaning of the words, 'I desire mercy, not sacrifice.' I did not come to call the righteous but the sinners.*

–Matthew 9:9-13

The same Jesus the Lord of those days is in our midst; He is calling all the nations' presidents, lawmakers, government officials, and all sinners. The only difference is in those days people saw His un-glorified body. We are more blessed than people of those days. The blessing is our faith to believe Jesus the Lord's glorified body is hidden in the consecrated host and wine; and His Spirit is always in our midst; and He is calling all of us in this world like He called the Tax Collector Matthew, other tax collectors and sinners.

Note: There are more details repeating Saint Paul's conversion in my note book, dated September 20, 1998.

God, United States, Iraq

November 14, 1998. Before the mass I repeatedly prayed, "Father, through the Lord Jesus, and the work of the Holy Spirit, the situation is very difficult for me. I am alone on earth. I am ready to go home. I know the works You entrusted to me have not been finished; but I am too weak. I ask you to take me home, and send other stronger than me to accomplish this work." The Lord Jesus said to me, "Your prayer is answered. At seven o'clock tonight you will return to heaven." I then asked the Blessed Mother, "Blessed Mother, prepare me to return home tonight at seven." Then the Lord Jesus said to me, "Tonight when you are in bed, the glory of the Father will be upon you, and lift you up from the bed." He continued, "Your soul will return to heaven, but your body will still be on earth. You will see millions of roses in front of you." I replied, "Lord, what you said does not make any sense to me, but let it done; I received everything from You, happiness and endurance for great suffering." He then told me, "The gospel today is for you." Luke 18:1-8 "The parable of the persistent widow."

In the afternoon devotion, the Lord gave me Daniel chapter 4, the King Nebuchadnezzar vision of the great Tree. I fell asleep, and while I was asleep I heard, "Lord, the boat is about to sink, and you are asleep." My understanding was that the world is going to sink, and the Lord entrusted this mission to me, but I am in peace laying here sleeping. When I got up and continued my devotion, the Lord gave me Mark 4:35-41 "The Calming of the Storm at Sea." Then the Lord Jesus said to me, "You soul is sorrowful like I was in the Garden of Gethsemane. Tonight the Father will pour upon you great power, you will see that in the nature."

I went to sleep at 7: 00 p. m. after I finished my devotion. While I was asleep, the Blessed Mother told me, "You will not feel that much different at the time the Father pours out His glory upon you. You did not understand the Father's words. In the morning you will see in nature, what you send out will return in double." She was referring to the works that God asked me to deliver to President Bill Clinton, and to all the members of the United States Senate, regarding destructive weapons and chemicals.

I woke up at 1:04 a.m. on November 15, 1998 with some dreams. In my dream I was walking. To my right was a small concrete pool, about the size of a single bath tub above the ground in an open air field. There were four people there; one was in the human body of a young adult female, she was sitting at the edge of the pool; one large, bleak dark spirit was above the top of the pool, and two other human spirits in front of her were above the middle of the pool. The young woman and the two sharp dark spirits were in conversation. I overheard them, the woman said, "I want to hire someone to kill him." She referred to two of her boyfriends. One of the two dark spirits responded to her, "If you want to do that, then do it." Just after this man finished his words, fire raised up in the middle of the pool and the woman in the middle of the fire, I saw from her waist up, she was raising both of her arms to her sides. I thought, "She is being burned." While I saw all of the above, I also saw in the distance, on the other side of this pool, a big building. This concrete building was a rectangle and had four walls and an open roof. I saw heavy dark smoke coming out from its roof.

I made a left turn to a high building, this rectangular building had five levels. This five-level building had no front entrance. I then was at the back of this building; on the last step of an aluminum ladder. I only saw myself, the top part of the ladder, and two windows of the fifth floor. The window at my left was a large square. The window in front of me was about one-fifth the size of the large one, and had a rectangular shape. Its top was at the same level of the large one, and it was covered with flat bars of wood. I was trying to reach the large window at my left to enter the kitchen. While I was trying to do this, the hood of a military vehicle came against this window, its engine blowing air at the window blind. The blinds flew up, and when these blinds flew up, I saw a spider's web hanging in the window. Inside the kitchen was a chef wearing a white coat, behind him was military kitchen steel equipment. Then the vehicle left, and I was still trying to enter through this large window; but the young woman inside told me, "I will open this side for you." She removed the flat wood bar, and told me to enter in. I then put my feet in, but when it came to my chest, the window was too thin at my right. The woman told me, "Move to your left; this side is larger." I did as she asked me, then I was inside the kitchen.

Next, I was at the side of a store in the business park. There was a bench parallel with the side wall of the store. Between the store wall and the bench were several martyr's dark, long-sleeved breastplates with helmets. The helmets and breastplates connected together, and were laying on the ground. I picked up one and put it on. Making the way to the right, I went to the front of the building. Before I got to the front entrance of the first floor, there was a wooden stairway to the top floor. This stairway had many steps, with rails at both sides. It turned to the right before entering the top floor. The top stairway was above the front space of the main double door entrance.

I then just got out of my room. In the narrow hallway of the third floor, I remembered that I had a list of my district congressional candidates that I was going to vote for at the end office, in the same direction of Mr. Yale's office, to the west. I then was at the office at the end of the hall. Looking inside, to my left were high shelves, to my right was a bulletin board with some papers there, and a long desk below the bulletin board. I picked up my list and left. While I was walking in the hall, I opened it, there were two sheets of papers in triple spacing. The first sheet was filled with ten names; the second sheet was half, with five names. There were two names on the second sheet that were crossed out.

I got up to pray for understanding of the revelations; the Lord Jesus told me, "The young woman who got in the pool of fire is symbolic of U.S. missile aircraft pilots. The two thick dark human spirits are symbolic of other nations being attacked by the United States. The large spirit above the pool is the devil's spirit. The cubic building like a tank with dark thick smoke coming out of it is symbolic of the devil himself sending out his offspring spirits to damage the souls and physical bodies on earth. The five-level building without a front entrance, and your entering through the back window was heaven on earth. The woman who removed the flat wood bar for you to enter is symbolic of your Blessed Mother. The martyr's breastplates are symbolic of predestined humans fighting for the kingdom of heaven through God's power and having no fear. The congressional candidate list you hold in your hands is symbolic of God's predestined chosen one for the mission, that God entrusted to you. Those names crossed out are symbolic of those who went the wrong way and will convert. Other lists still hanging on the bulletin board in the office are also predestined chosen ones that belong to different denominations."

The Lord Jesus continued, "While you were asleep the Father lifted your soul to heaven....... For Chaplain Binh An, God made arrangements for him to serve Him at the boot camp, so he doesn't have to be engaged in this war with Iraq. God protects His predestined chosen ones. You have been at your right with God alone. Now is time for you to slide a little to your left. The thought you had about helping at Jacquelyn's store without receiving pay; the Father gave that to you, you need to mingle with her. She is one of the predestined chosen ones. She will bring you to meet the business association members, as she had told you that she wants to help. God chose her to be the President of the large business association. They are the ones who have money. God has prepared all of this for you." Jesus the Lord continued, "John the Baptist came down and did not eat and drink.   I ate and drank with the sinners when I was on earth. You are following my footsteps. I am in you." The Lord Jesus continued, "The United States citizens do not know what happened in the Iraq. They only heard from the government officials that Iraq has destructive chemicals. They have to look at the facts that the United Nation inspectors were in Iraq for many months, and they have not found what they were looking for, the dangerous chemicals.   The Iraqis do the same as the United States, generate chemicals. Does the United States allow other countries to come in to their secret bases to inspect them? The devil uses Bill Clinton and others, in the matter to gain power, because Iraq has oil. Iraqis have their own privacy like other countries in the world; but they have allowed the United Nation's inspectors in their country that long. They got tired of other nations trying to control them. Iraq has the kind of chemicals that the United States has."

I then went back to sleep. In my dream I walked in a house in the daytime, this small house was owned by a woman, and she had a child with her, although I did not see the child, only I saw her through the shower door.

Then the dream changed. I was in another house, this house was smaller than the one before and darker. Against the corner was an old bed. The wall at the side bed had a large window to the patio. I stood at the head of the bed, and looked through the window; I then looked at the bed. It had a very old mattress with a valley in the middle, and two pillows. The mattress and pillows were covered with old dirty white bed linens.

I then was sitting on the dais in one part of the house. To my left was a man who just finished half of his white chow main noodles with beef at the side plate. He pushed the other half plate to me. I was about to eat; but a man at my right, more like God to me in the dream, told me, "Let him finish his food. Here is your plate." While he said this, he laid in front of me the same kind of noodle, while in oil, with five pieces of fried fish sticks laying at side of the noodles. I got up and stood by the window at the middle of the divider of the house. From the other side of the room, a dark-skinned, short teenager with curly hair stuck his forehead through the window and challenged me. I raised my right hand and pushed at his forehead. He immediately turned around to leave. Just as he turned around I reached through the window and hit him on the back of his head with my right hand.

I then got up, and the Lord Jesus told me, "The woman in the shower is no one else, she is symbolic of you. Her child is symbolic of a mission God entrusted to you. The bed is symbolic that the system of the world is unclean. The short curly-haired, dark-skinned teenager is symbolic of the one-third of the world who refuses to convert will attack you; but with God's power, you fight against them. The man sitting at your right on the dais is your nanny, the Father. The one at your left symbolizes those who believe in you, they heard and received the words of God."

Most of us in this world know that, when we have a good friend, we have no difficulty to learn the good; but if we have bad friends, it is likely we will learn evil things from them. Of course there is an exception for those who want to learn good and reject evil. These people, when they meet the bad people they will avoid them. Or in another example, a person playing with fire will get burned some day. For example, if teenagers hang out with a gangster, it is likely these teenagers will become either gangsters or a character similar to it.

The majority of people in this world do not know the supernatural power affecting the natural thought and actions. The soul and spirit with and in the body was created by the Creator of Heaven and Earth. This was revealed in the Book of Genesis, chapters two, three and part of four. If a person lives the life of completely obeying all God's commandments, dealing with truth in love in the family life, the personal life will carry to the public or business life. Therefore, these good people from the heart will dwell in God, the Spirit of God will help them through their thoughts with good discernment, to choose good and reject evil. On the other hand, the devil and his offspring spirits will either control or interfere in the minds, then manifest actions for those who disobey God's commandments, dealing with untruthfulness, hatred, and controlling others, for his personal gain.

Therefore, the United States high-ranking government announces to its citizens that Iraq produces destructive chemicals. Everyone of us must collect all the facts and analyze them. I will look at President Bill Clinton, the Commander in Chief of the strongest nation in the world, lying under oath at the deposition in the case of Paula Jones, and admitting to America that he misled the United States citizens about the sexual relationship with Monica Lewinsky, the young White House intern at that time. When he lied under oath, and misled the citizens from his personal matters, surely he will carry the untruthfulness to his public services. Especially during the time his misconduct is the top topic for the media, he changed the drum tone for the media to shift their attention to Iraq, by calling for a strike on Iraq. President Bill Clinton teaches the United States citizens and others throughout the world to lie under oath through his actions. There will be some of the high-ranking United Governments officials who lie to gain their own benefit and get ahead. If any nations want to get ahead, they must have their leaders dwelling in the Almighty God.

The Iraqis do not wear model clothes or manufacture model buildings etc. like the United States does; from the way they dress, they look like very simple people. Because they are simple, God blesses their country with oil. Disagreement and fighting between neighbors on the same street or nations is the same, the only difference is between individuals or nations. The United States is too far away from them, why did the United

Nations have to stick their head in to create war? The matter of inspections in Iraq and trying to strike them is that other nations do not have oil and they want to control Iraq. I am warning all the nations in this world, God is ruling every country with His iron rod. Now is the beginning of the completion. All of this was foretold in the holy scriptures; if any country does not obey all His commandments and refuse to convert, they will receive punishments.

December 16, 1998. During my early afternoon devotion, after to Lord Jesus gave me the "God Revealed the Meaning of the Book of Revelations and Genesis," He continued, "I love you, you are my little sister. The Father allowed your children to separate from you and follow the one who goes against God. The Father is hurt when he allowed you to be sick, I am hurting, and Mother has been crying for the last few days for seeing you sick. The Father allowed them to do that, and when they convert it will be a miracle." When I heard Jesus the Lord say this, I thought he was speaking of my own children, but at 7:00 p.m. I watched the news and found out the United States made a strike against Baghdad. While I was watching this, the Lord brought to my mind that my children are symbolic of President Bill Clinton and his support to strike Baghdad. He put me in the place of suffering because of the way my own children treat me because I obey God, and uses me as symbolic of God Himself to pour out His hurt unto me, so I will be able to explain to the world of how God hurts when people sin against Him. My suffering is only a very tiny fraction of God's suffering as the world sins against Him.

Hot Air Balloon Kite Crushed Down (United States Strike Iraq Result Revelation)

December 17, 1998. I got up at 5:30 a.m. with some dreams, and the Lord Jesus explained to me the meaning of the dream. In my dream I was standing in front of a house, my back was against the front wall. I looked up, there were several cables up in the air. On the highest cable a man was trying to open a closed balloon laying on the same cable where he was standing. He pulled it backwards, while people in the house behind were pulling the ropes attached to the balloon kite, and trying to open it up to fly. When I saw this, I walked forward, moved one separate rope that connected the balloon over several lower cables, to the same air space with the bundle of ropes. Those people pulling these ropes now were on the top of the roof, they bent down and gave the entire bundle to me. I then saw the dark hot air balloon kite laying flat on the ground while people surrounded looked at it. In this crowd was an old, tall woman with dry skin.

Still in the dream the Lord Jesus said to me, "The man walking on the highest cable trying to reopen the huge hot air balloon kite is the devil in Bill Clinton. Those pulling the ropes, trying to get the kite up again are those who support Clinton, the devil's offspring is in them. You moved one separate rope that connected the balloon over several lower cables, to the same air space with the bundle of ropes; and these people on the roof bent down to hand the bundle of ropes to you. You then pulled this huge dead balloon down to ground is symbolic of the recent letter you just mailed to all members of the United States Senate and Al Gore, [letter dated December 4, 1998]. These senators have not read their letters, but they will hear from their assistants.   For those who spoke to support the strike last night, the more they talk the more they are wrong. You will see senators come out and pull back the strike. They strike at night to avoid people on the street, they can not see the ground so they strike the other nations close by Iraq. The face of a woman next to you at the scene, the President's wife is symbolic of church leaders saying to you, 'Thank you for your help.' But you said to her, 'That all was Jesus, and He is over all.' She looked at your hands that were no longer attached to those ropes, and said, 'You are out already?" Look at the heavy woman behind her holding a coat at her belly that shoots out silver sparks. You know the tall woman servant. You turned around and left the scene, that tall woman also followed you, you said good bye to her with, 'I may see you tomorrow for breakfast; but I am not sure [if the Lord allowed me]'

The Lord continued, "You do not need to go out in the public to do anything. You only have to send letters to all members of the United States Senate. People do not know your works now, but when your books are published they will know your works. Place yesterday's revelation and this revelation in the same book."

The Lord continued, "Yesterday I told you the Father allowed the strike and He is hurt, I am hurt, and Mother has been crying for the last few days, but you did not understand. I had you mail copies of letters to all the members of the United States Senate and Al Gore, December 4, 1998 with its attachments, to four high-ranking Catholic leaders on December 15, 1998, for Bishop Brom to receive it on December 16, 1998, the day the United States struck Iraq. During this night I told you to call Jackie because she had some good news for you. This Jackie is symbolic of the Father. You speak to the Father, He has good news for you. On earth, the Father called Jackie to help you." Jackie is symbolic of those serve God with their heart in love.

After the Lord finished speaking, in my vision I saw up in the air in front of me, a little girl wearing a burgundy velvet dress with a white lace collar. She was held by her Father, I only saw her from her front neck down to below her knees. This little girl is symbolic of the special assignment God entrusted to me, this special assignment is in the control of the Almighty God. This assignment is like a puzzle and God put all the pieces in himself.

After I received the Holy Eucharist, the Blessed Virgin Mother told me, "The devil's spirit is in many people, but he is the most strong in Bill Clinton. Every one wonders who is symbolic of number "666" in the Book of Revelation. Now this has been revealed, he is dead." Bill Clinton will convert, and have to pay dearly price for his sins. December 19, 1998 in the evening while I was asleep, the Blessed Virgin Mother told me, "The senator is the lawmakers, the senator is symbolic of God. From the time that the United States military began the air strike against Iraq, turmoil started in the United States. This turmoil will cost the United States and the whole nation suffering."

The Blessed Virgin Mother spoke of the iniquities after the United States and Britain air strike against Iraq that will be placed upon the United States and Britain .   This air strike was contributed by the taxpayers through tax dollars to generate destructive weapons and pay for personnel. Therefore, the whole nation will have to pay the price of their actions, whether they know it or not. The strike against Iraq is a mass destructive action of murder, wounding people, damaging people's materials and causing suffering; this is a grave community sin. The suffering will be upon these two countries, and the United Nation officials. Suffering will come in various forms; such as terrorism, more violence, and shootings. These kinds of suffering will circle between the United States, the United Kingdom and other nations involved, adding more and more grave sins, and generating more iniquities. These evil actions will not end until people convert their hearts to God. After each person converts to God, individual iniquities must be purged by God. The iniquities to be purged by God is the price that each one must pay for damages in order for their souls to be purified. The purification of iniquities will come in various forms such as heavy rains, floods, hurricanes, storms, tornadoes, and other natural tragedies. This purification can also be individual trouble in family, work, finances, disease, tragedies, disasters, etc....

Everyone must pay for the damages; the more that individual is involved, the more price to pay before each one can enter heaven for eternal life. If not completely paid on earth, they will continue to pay in purgatory after the last breath. Those who refuse to convert will be chained in the darkness of the devil eternally, continuing under the power of the devil. Their bodies will never be resurrected, because God is a just God.

*Continued in the book "The Only Petition at U. S. Tax Court"

34

THE WORLD'S BUSINESS SYSTEM

God Revealed the Media's Hearts and Actions like Pizza Delivery Men

October 11, 1996. In my dream, I was in a conversation with a little boy, although I only saw his left shoulder and top part of his arm sleeve. I put something like fabric next to his sleeve, and as this piece of fabric touched his sleeve, magically, he flew up.

I then saw the same shoulder with a very light gray arm sleeve again. I took a very small square thin piece of fabric the same color, and laid it on his sleeve to compare. As I compared these, I lifted him up by the piece of square fabric in front of me, he was about three to four years old. He had light-colored hair, a baby face, looked healthy, and was a sharp, quick talker. He was filled with a happy light on his face, and the light shone on his face and the area where he sat. I said to him, " You need to be good, and study hard." He responded to me, " I deliver pizza full time, every day; and they called me to go to the Academy School." I knew that he went to school full time and worked hard.

I then was in a spirit body, cleansing the rust off three small edges with my fingers, from a very long iron bar. There was an American boy sitting in front of me, about three to four year old. He had light-colored hair, a baby face, looked healthy, and was a sharp, quick talker. He was filled with a happy light on his face, and the light shone on his face and the area where he sat. I said to him, " You need to be good, and study hard." He responded to me, " I deliver pizza full time, every day; and they called me to go to the Academy School." I knew that he went to school full time and worked hard.

The three times I saw this little boy is symbolic of God working through this boy. Two time his flying up is symbolic of God lifting him up to a higher level of service, and it also gives him more discernment to choose the right things to serve Him. This boy delivers pizza is symbolic of media. The pizza is hot, but pizza of many other things is symbolic of news have been mixed with other things that belong to the devil and delivered to the public. He said, "They called me to go to the academy school" and that is symbolic of God's calling the media and teaching them His way of discerning good and evil, delivering the good to the public, destroying evil interfering in their minds by only thinking of themselves and not the public benefits. My cleaning long iron bars is symbolic of God's calling for me. Iron is symbolic of the Lord Jesus is ruling the world with His iron rod, through me as one of His primary servants.

Before this dream in the middle of the night, I was seeking the Lord regarding of the communication with Cardinal Joseph Ratzinger through John Thavis at the News Catholic services in Rome, Italy. Therefore this dream was Jesus answering my question. It is also symbolic of others having been in service to the Lord. The Lord Jesus reveled that He lifts up his servants higher, to a special level of service to Him.

In this revelation, God revealed the media, this includes television news broadcasts, interviews, shows, and newspaper writers. Everyone in this world is judged under God's rules; there is no exception of whether you believe in God or not. New carriers are responsible in front of God to deliver news as it is exactly, no more or less. Beyond that, media must discern to feed more good news to benefit audience's souls as well as their physical lives. Not harming the public, or creating more suffering for the victims will benefit the media individuals.

I have seen with my own eyes, some Catholic newspapers that must deliver the words of God to benefit souls, but they do not do what God calls them to write; they do not write things to glorify God and benefit souls, they write things to glorify man, supporting the works of devil, such as a priest participating in the Olympics. The priest's life is surrendered to God, the priest vows to spend all his time in prayer and ministering to people to feed his souls and the souls of other with God's words, and the body and blood of the Lord Jesus, not spending time to practice sports and participating in the Olympics to glorify himself, and satisfy his flesh and the flesh of others.

Professional broadcast networks, televisions, and newspapers are focusing on things to bring more evil ideas into the minds of adults and children, creating more emotional suffering to the victims, damaging their souls and sometimes to their physical lives. Adding more salt and pepper to the matter is like more topping of the pizza, or twisting the words, to make the story hot. This is a sin against God and against those being harmed through the untruthful media. It creates more iniquities to gain companies a financial profit, and glorify their image. Such as O. J Simpson's trials, the Oklahoma City bomb explosion, and President Bill Clinton's crisis that turned into a national crisis.

The victims were dead and buried under the ground, their families suffered for the loss. Can the media bring these victims back by broadcasting the story again and again? Are the victim's families emotions healed by writing in the newspapers again and again? Or by the media digging up more suffering to the victims family members?

You people do not understand the dangers of the iniquities after any sin is committed, such as a murder. The result after the murder is that the iniquity will bounce, or return again and again, and this hatred will transfer from one generation to the next generation. To be healed, the iniquity can only be purged by God alone. Coming to God is the only solution, God is the only one that can heal victims family members, and raise the dead to life.

The media members will be accountable in front of God for every untrue word (singular) written and published to the readers, or broadcast to the viewers.

Profit and Non-Profit Corporations

The insurance industry is also symbolic of Church systems. The New York Life Insurance Company in this revelation is symbolic of Catholic components, and other insurance companies are symbolic of other Church components.

The New York Life Insurance Company and the Catholic Component are called by God to deal with me in the natural world. Through me, God uses the these natural substances to reveal that the spiritual leaders disobey God's commandments. They are lack of discernment, mislead people, and it shows the corruption of the insurance industry, governments, and religious..

February 25, 1997. In my dream I was in the front yard, where someone's invisible hand gave me a letter. It was folded into four parts; the outside was red foil paper, the inside was white with handwriting filling two of the four sections, and the other two sections had only a line and a half. This handwriting was like that of a second or third grade child and was very difficult to read. I knew this letter was written by two of Father Hero's nieces, little girls who lived in the same house with the Father and His parents. I had a feeling that these girls might not like me because they knew that Father Hero loves me. His loves for me shows in his actions. Therefore, these two knew little and wrote this letter to me.

There was a man living in my house, my ex-spouse, and also my oldest daughter. The former spouse was very jealous of Father Hero, so I hid this letter in the left side of my bra. I continued to gather more of the used Christmas wrapping paper; although it was used, it was not wrinkled; it laid like fabric on my left arm. As I was gathering this paper, the ex-spouse followed behind and tried to find the letter.

Before I entered my house, I saw three big cardboard boxes sitting outside the corner of the house, next to the door. I then was inside the house, the ex-spouse still following me. Deep inside the house I saw my oldest daughter standing next to the washing machine, washing clothes. She said to me, "There is a letter for Father Hero from two of his nieces, they said nice things about you." I did not want the former spouse to know about the letter, but after my daughter said this, he knew that I had it. I thought, "I need to find a place to hide myself so I can read this letter in private."

I then was walking in the back yard, turning right at the corner of the my house to a portable restroom owned by my neighbor, which my family shared. This restroom was square, divided into two sections, and the actual toilet was built up high. The section that I was going to use only covered a standing person up to the chest. I saw a young woman inside the restroom about to take a shower; but when she saw me coming she got out and let me use the facility.

I was inside, trying to go to the restroom, but I had trouble. While I was trying, I was able to see the other side through the bottom of the divider, and there was some kind of food. I then looked up and I saw the young woman standing outside, leaning her chin on the wall and watching me. I then stood up, my pants still down, and I saw some of my soft stools behind my leg. I left the restroom where the woman was on her way to take her shower. I then stood on the ground, outside the restroom with my pants still down. I did not want the woman to see me like that, so I tried to clean myself.

I then went to my neighbors' back yard where a field of grass had died, leaving a few old trees whose tops I could not see. As I was walking away from the toilet I saw to my left some very dirty portable restrooms which no one had used for ages. These restrooms only had two side walls, another two side walls were torn down, and leaving only the rotten wood poles in the between. I was able to see the main section of these restrooms.

Next I saw myself walking along the wooden fence. Another young girl called me from the other side of the fence, the side she was standing on was the side of my house. I was at the side of my neighbor's property, and she said, "You need to go home, they are violating your house."

Then I was inside the patio, built at the side of the house. I saw a dark man's back; this large man was the former president of the Indo-Chinese Chamber of Commerce. He faced the wall of my house, with a big heavy tool box lying on the floor to his right, he was trying to ruin my house. I asked him, "What are you doing here?" He responded by saying that he wanted to take something out of the wall. Then the ex-spouse came into the patio; as he walked in I knew that he had hired this dark man to take things from my house and to ruin my house; I saw some huge television sets, broken in front; I knew that the ex-spouse was angry at me for hiding the letter from him.

I exercised my rights and seized the former spouse's collar, pulled him out of the house, into the middle of the street. As I was dragging him I said, "I am the owner of this house, you are ruining my home; I am going to call the police and have them arrest you." I thought, "I can dial 911 to call the police, but I do not need a telephone;" I then saw the number "911" appear in front of my face.

I then woke up. With the Blessed Virgin Mother's assistance, I offered to the Lord God the Chaplet of Divine Mercy and the Holy Rosary, and prayed for the interpretation. I said, "Lord, Father, through Your beloved Son Jesus, and in His name, and through the works of the Holy Spirit; that my beloved Blessed Virgin Mother is here with me, together with all the holy angels and saints, I offer You this devotion, Father. I am asking You, Father, if it is not too much for You, this is for Your works and for the sake of the name of the Lord Jesus, it is not for my sake. I beg You, Father for the Spirit of the Lord Jesus is mixed with my spirit like water poured into flour, mixed together like dough to make bread. This is for Your works, not for me." While I was petitioning to the Lord, I saw in my vision the invisible hands making bread dough.

The Father said, "I am going to give you the interpretation for the dreams now." As He said this I reached for the tape recorder; it was 8:10 a.m., February 25, 1997. He continued, "Those dirty portable toilets in the field symbolize the insurance industry. The first one you entered, is symbolic of the New York Life Insurance Company. The woman who was inside and who left the restroom so you could enter symbolizes the Blessed Virgin Mother, the mother of all Christians. She is there to assist you in cleaning the system of the New York Life Insurance Company. The person on the other side of the wooded fence calling to you represents the holy angels and saints who are constantly interceding for you, through their prayers, and fighting enemy spirits. Through the power of God, they are reminding you with every single action. The man with the tool box represents the devil. The ex-spouse is symbolic of New York Life Insurance Company and other insurance companies in the world. Your seizing his collar and pulling him out to the street symbolizes that through the power of God, you are making their actions known to the public. Your saying 'I own this house' symbolizes that this world belongs to God, and you are God the Almighty's Ambassador. Your saying 'I am calling the police, you are violating my house,' is symbolic of evil insurance company actions and your calling the power of God upon them. All this is revealed to you from the Almighty God, the Spirit of Prophesy. The letter with red foil paper is symbolic of God's call for you. The two young children are nieces of Father Hero, and they symbolize the holy angels. Father Hero represents Lord Jesus, Son of the most high living God. The woman who was your daughter in the dream, standing next to the washing machine symbolizes Christians. The three boxes at the outside corner of the house represent the Trinity."

Note: The two little girls are symbolic of holy angels. Father Hero represents the Lord Jesus. His parents symbolize God the Father and the Holy Spirit. This is symbolic of God's family in Heaven. The New York Life insurance company is it self, it also symbolic of business, non-profit organization, religion, nation, and the world. My daughter symbolize the spiritual leaders, washing clothes symbolic of outer conversion. Go to the toilet symbolic of conversion from the heart. I seized the man collar symbolic of God's power will bring the evil actions, system in to the public. 911 symbolic of urgent calling for conversion.

Insurance Companies' Laws and Practices

On March 3, 1995, I was on my way to print some letters to send to the United States Senate members regarding freedom to worship the true God in Vietnam. As I was driving my almost new Nissan Maxima on Interstate 15, a GMC 7000 hit me from the rear, damaging the back end, almost half my car. An investigation by my insurance company certified that the accident was 100 percent the fault of the GMC driver.

On March 6, 1996, the adjuster for the GMC driver, Nationwide Insurance Company, questioned me about my injuries, and tried to settle out of court, offering to pay for the car's repair. And, he said, "We'll give you $500 for your suffering." I replied, "I want to settle the property damage first," and he agreed. On March 14, 1995 an agent told me on the telephone, "Your car was worth over $20,000; we're offering $8,550 to repair it." I went to my Nissan dealer, and was offered $12,000 for my car, after repairs, because of depreciation after collision. It was in the shop for over three months, and I had to pay over $2,000 for a rental car because my insurance would not cover that expense.

I was also suffering from numbness in both my legs, my arms, part of my wrist, and my entire back. The medical bills were over $5,000, some of which was paid by my insurance company, and I was liable for the rest.

October 29, 1995. Shortly after eight a.m., I was using the hip-flex machine at the gym. The Lord Jesus told me, "I am going to heal your back." I said, "Okay," and then I felt a gentle heat travel down my head and across my face. I then heard my lower back crack a few times as I continued to exercise. After forty-five minutes in the gym, I left with my back completely healed by the Son of the most high God, and later He healed my wrist.

With the love of God within me, I have given Nationwide Insurance Company, (the GMC 7000 driver's carrier) every chance to settle, but their free will is allowing the devil to influence their minds by controlling their system of doing business. God the Father granted this request from the devil. I did not understand much at the beginning, but the Lord Jesus told me, "You need to suffer, and at the same time I will teach the attorneys (the one representing me as well the opposing lawyer and others)."

A few days before they took my deposition on August 26, 1996, in my prayers, I pleaded with the Lord God, "Lord, I ask that this deposition be done according to Your will, not my will nor that of the attorney representing me." The Lord Jesus said to me, "This deposition must take place in order for you to complete one chapter of the book "God's Purification - Not Easy."

August 27, 1996, the day of my deposition: The Lord God had control of the entire proceedings. One of the questions the Nationwide attorney asked me was about my claim for loss of wages. I told him, "I work for God, I do not receive (monetary) pay, but my injuries are slowing the work of God. I do not claim anything for myself, but if Nationwide Insurance Company wishes, they can give this money to the poor." During the break in the conference room with Nationwide Insurance Company's attorney and the court reporter, I said, "I do not care about money." The Nationwide attorney responded, "We are here to discuss money, if it weren't for money we wouldn't be here."

September 17, 1996, the day of arbitration: At the opening of the hearing, the Arbitrator explained the procedure, saying, "The defendant has admitted fault; it means you've already won."

I replied, "I do not like the word win or lose; Mr. Rogers, (the GMC driver) did not want this accident to happen; I am here to do what is right."

The hearing continued with my chiropractor testifying about my injuries. After his testimony Nationwide Insurance Company's attorney asked him some questions, and at the end he brought forth reasons not to pay for the damages. At that time I said to the Arbitrator, Nationwide Insurance Company 's attorney, and the attorneys representing me and the GMC driver, "God sent me here to do what is right; to reveal what He has told me. I am not here for the money, maybe that's why some other people are here. Although this accident was not my fault, I am the one who is suffering a great deal."

I continued, "You [Nationwide Insurance Company 's attorney] said that your company refused to reimburse me for car rental expenses because I did not mitigate this expense by instructing my insurance company to initially pay it. Why should my company have to pay for repairing my car, since the accident was not my fault? Nationwide Insurance Company had agreed to pay, then refused, and backed out. While I was renting, I had three rental cars that broke down on me, and once a police officer had to drive me home, and another time I had to walk almost an hour in the dark to get home from the gym. But the fault lies with Nationwide Insurance Company, who refused to pay for depreciation and backed out on fixing my car, which was almost new before the accident. A few days after the accident, Nationwide Insurance Company 's adjuster told me, 'Your car was worth over $20,000 and the estimate for repairs is over $8,000.' He also offered me $500. for personal injuries and asked me to sign off on liability. After I spoke to the adjuster, I went to my Nissan dealer, and found out that there is always depreciation on cars after an accident."

I continued, "You asked the chiropractor, 'From your standpoint, do you believe that she was healed by God?' God has healed me many times; in October or November of 1993 He healed my back and neck from injuries resulting from an accident in March, 1986. I had suffered for over six years, and my health insurance had paid for many doctors, chiropractors, therapists, and an acupuncturist, but no one could help me. God healed me from cyst in the middle of 1992. This time He healed my neck, back, and wrist. Do not think that you are better than God, for He has power over us. I am here to say what God has told me to say: The legal system and insurance practices are wrong. And this accident case will be reported in my next book."

The entire liability fell on Nationwide Insurance Company 's client, and their system caused the cost of repairs on my Nissan ($8,031.78), medical bills ($6,615.00), rental expenses ($2,748.75), depreciation of my car ($3,535.00), and appraisal fees ($390.00) to fall on my insurance company, who paid $8,031.78 for repairs, and $5,000 for medical expenses. Nationwide Insurance Company reimbursed car rental expenses of only $868.80. I suffered from my injuries for one year, six months and twenty-four days, and the arbitration awarded $7,962.50. From this amount I paid my attorney 2,627.00 plus $307.23 in advance expenses. I was reimbursed just $2,000.00, (negotiated down from 5,000.00) from my automobile insurance company, and the balance of the medical bills, $1,615.00. I paid $1,879.95 out of pocket for car rental expenses, which left me with a deficit of $5,391.68 plus pain and suffering.

Beyond the money lost, I have suffered physical pain for over a years. But I offer all this suffering and monetary loss to God for the salvation of the world. I forgive and love these people as individuals, but I hate their evil actions. I pray to God the Almighty for those who act against God's commandments in this matter, and for the United States legal system to be cleansed as God has commanded, to save souls.

The United State's legal system allows Nationwide Insurance Company and other insurance companies to refuse to take responsibility for what they have promised on their policies, in exchange for their collected premiums. The legal system gives the devil power to roam within the minds of insurance adjusters, so that all they can see is money to benefit themselves, not responsibility to their clients actions, or those who their clients have unintentionally injured. These companies cause the victims even more suffering. And the Devil roaming in attorneys' minds causes actions that twist the truth in return for money. God has revealed to me through dreams and visions the fact that there are many more of His children who are being victimized by the legal system. It is time for Jesus Christ, the Son of the most high living God, to cleanse this earth. He is the King of kings, and this earth was created from Him and for Him.

God's love for the world will never end. No matter how sinful we are, God always forgives us when we come to Him from our hearts. God is calling all of us to convert and repent before our last breath. Young or old, be prepared for the unknown hour, for none of us know the time of our last breath. Physical life on earth is temporary. Our inheritance in Heaven is eternal; there is resurrection of the body after the end of the world for souls in Heaven.

Rebuild My Church Divine Mission

(The Lord Jesus gave this name to Mariette)

P.O. Box 261550 ✦ *San Diego, CA 92196-1550*

February 19, 1998

Harry Horn, Chairman of the Board
New York Life Insurance Company

Insurance Company Violates Citizen's Civil Right to Freedom of Religion

Dear Chairman Horn,

In response to Mr. Daniel L. McGuigan's letter of February 9, 1998, I never requested the two loans, totaling of $4,219.00 (132.00+4,087.00) to pay the IRS. I do not owe the IRS. Income tax is a contribution to build the United States, but the government uses tax money to fund programs that go against God's commandments, violating the freedom to worship the true God. The New York Life Insurance Company is cooperating with the IRS in violating my right of freedom to worship the true God, and the right to the money in my life insurance policies. Therefore these two loans were made illegally. I charge against you and the New York Life Insurance Company the amount of $4,219.00 which must be put back into my life insurance policies immediately, plus all the interest by New York Life insurance Company's actions.

As the Chairman of the Board for New York Life Insurance Company, I request that you instruct New York Life Insurance to pay me in full, plus interest on the two policies: NYLIC/N6 Contract No. 528705, and Group policy No. G-610, Claim No. GZ 33695-5.

Enclosed are copies of: (1)God Revealed the New York Life Insurance Company, and the Insurance Industry Systems, (2) letter to President Bill Clinton, Vice President Al Gore, all U.S. senate members; Secretary of Treasury Robert Rubin; U.S. Department of Treasury General Inspector Valerie Lau; IRS Chief Inspector Gary Bell, dated December 4, 1998, (3)God the Father Visits the World and Restricted Order revelations, (4) letter to President Bill Clinton, Vice President Al Gore, and all members of the U.S. Senate, dated February 17, 1998, (5) letter to Gloria Fox, dated September 10, 1995, (6) letter to you, dated November 8, 1994, (7)

Heavenly Court Summons Writ for Mariette Do-Nguyen, and the Almighty God appeared to Mariette.

The New York Life Insurance Company must pay for their unjust actions against me and others, and that includes principal and damages. The world is against the Almighty God's commandments; God is purifying them with suffering caused by heavy rain, storms, and floods; this purification will not stop until people convert to God. God is dealing with the New York Life Insurance Company concerning this matter and others in the same way that He is dealing with the world.

These words are trustworthy; they are from God, and they are prophetic words. I pray to God for New York Life Insurance Company employees and agents to hear God's voice, so they may be saved for eternal life.

Sincerely in Christ Jesus,

Mariette Do-Nguyen

Rebuild My Church Divine Mission

(The Lord Jesus gave this name to Mariette)

P.O. Box 261550 ✦ San Diego, CA 92196-1550

May 10, 1999

Seymour Sternbert, Chairman of the Board
New York Life Insurance Company
51 Madison Avenue, 13th Floor
New York, NY 10010

Sent via U.S. Certified Mail

Dear Chairman Sternbert,

In late 1997 and early 1998, I received letters from Daniel L. McGuigan, Accounting Consultant at Policy Information Center, New York Life Insurance company, notified me of New York Life Insurance Company cooperating with the Internal Revenue Service; violated my civil right to Freedom of Religion by taking out and authorizing loans from two of my life insurance policies.   I filled a complaint with Chairman of the Board Harry Horn, but the matter has not been resolved.

Therefore, I filed a petition at the United States Tax Court. At the time I responded to Respondent's Request for Admission, I included the New York Life Insurance violation as Exhibit L-1. Recently I filled a Motion Request for Judgment, again including New York Life's violation as Exhibit II.

Enclosed are copies of:

1) Letters of communications to New York Life Insurance company

2) 2) My declaration that includes the violation of New York Life Insurance Company and Petitioner's Motion Request for Judgment.

3) Handout and audio tape of the Rebuild My Church Mission conference, rally for civil right to religious freedom in the United States on April 11, 1999.

The trail for this case will be started at 10:00 a.m. at Federal Court House in San Diego, California, on June 7, 1999. I ask that would you have the New York Life legal department contact me.

Sincerely in Christ Jesus,

Mariette Do-Nguyen

Rebuild My Church Divine Mission
(The Lord Jesus gave this name to Mariette)
P.O. Box 261550 ✦ San Diego, CA 92196-1550

March 3, 1998

Seymour Sternbert,
President, CEO, and Chairman of the Board
New York Life Insurance Company

Appeal to Insurance Company denied Claims by Using False Doctor Reports

Dear Mr. Sternbert,

Enclosed is a copy of a letter to California Insurance Department, dated March 3, 1998. A report from my physician, Doctor Walter Strybel is being prepared and will follow shortly under separate cover.

The Almighty God, Creator of Heaven and Earth, and His only Son Jesus, and the Holy Spirit is the One who is speaking to me, and giving me orders.

I was away from the church for nine years; then God called me back; He appeared in my dreams, my visions, and in front of me so I could see Him with my carnal eyes. He told me to be His instrument to prepare for the Lord Jesus' Second Coming to judge the living and the dead. His supernatural power is upon me as it is upon the world. This supernatural power developed the winds, storms, rain, floods, sunrises, sunset, and the moon. This supernatural power also creates birth and takes away life from all living creatures.

God is the only One who is controlling my mind, my physical body, my soul, and my spirit; He puts decisions into my thoughts; I have no power of my own to any portion of my mind. This is reality, not mere belief.

God told me what to write in the books, and to print them; but He does not permit me to sell any of them yet.

I will have an independent CPA audit all my financial and records, and send the result to you, together with the cost of the audit, and attorney fees incurred by Mr. Harry Horn actions and those of the New York Life Insurance Company.

God's words come with His power, I must obey Him at all times. His words also produce physical and emotional suffering that the Social Security Department authorities have recognized and honored, but which New York Life Insurance Company still deny.

God's prophetic gift is in me, and it comes with suffering every moment of my life, day and night, sometime to the point that I ask Him to take my life; but to bring salvation to mankind, I must embrace this suffering and pain.

New York Life Insurance Company suddenly stopped all my benefits, and this adds to my suffering. I request that all my benefits and accrued interest be paid immediately.

I continue to pray for you and New York Life Insurance Company; if you have any questions feel free to contact me.

Sincerely in Christ Jesus,

Mariette Do-Nguyen

Rebuild My Church Divine Mission

(The Lord Jesus gave this name to Mariette)

P.O. Box 261550 ✦ San Diego, CA 92196-1550

March 29, 1998

Lynne Cohn, Vice President
Client Services
New York Life Insurance Company

Dear Ms. Cohn,

Enclosed are copies of: (1) a letter to Joan Wong, Associate Insurance Policy Officer, California Department of Insurance, March 16, 1998; (2) a facsimile transmittal to Darryl Wright, New York Life Insurance Company, March 16, 1998; (3) a letter to Joan Brady, Disability Claims Division, March 21, 1998; (4) two letters from Walter F. Strybel, M.D. March 4, 1998 and March 26, 1998; (5) a facsimile transmittal to Mike Abriola, March 26, 1998 with a copy of social security disability benefit check, dated March 3, 1998.

Both of my doctors, General Nelson and Walter Strybel that I have been meeting with at least one or twice each month for over four years, have fully reported to New York Life Insurance Company at the request for an update status. But the New York Life Insurance Company employee did not understand, or refused to understand these reports. They are based on the two doctors that only saw me three times.

My services to build the New York Life Insurance Company for over seven years, and now at the time I need their help to process my claim for the benefit that I entirely to them, but many of the New York Life Insurance Company employees create severe emotional suffering in addition to the suffering that God already put on me. I called number of times, even to Seymour Sternbert, Chairman of the Board, they only took messages, no one has either returned the calls, nor solved the trouble, except one time by Mr. Abriola, and he gave me wrong information.

The love that God pours upon me, I have in return, been pouring out to everyone at New York Life Insurance Company, including those who have mistreated me. But I can continue doing this only up to some point. If they continue to refuse to see the truth; obeying God, I have to take some action so this kind of misrepresentation will not happen again to others.

Therefore, the last person in New York Life Insurance Company, who knows me by my face during the time of my services at the Company is the former San Diego Managing Partner, Phillip Hildebrand. I spoke to him on March 26, 1998 asked for help, but he told me that he was not able to assist me, because the company did not allow him to interfere in this area, then referred me to you.

I pray to God that you will understand the contents of this letter. Because of the love I have for the New York Life Insurance Company, and I want the best for it, and to receive the best; but the Company has to fulfill of what it promised. Like the father to his children; but if his children refuse to obey, the father has to raise up his rod to make his children obey him.

As of today, March 29, 1998, all my living expenses bills for the month of March 1998 are past due. It is urgent that would you give me a call today regarding the status of my individual disability income benefit check for March 1998, and the Nylic QN6-82 agent benefit.

Sincerely in Christ Jesus,

Mariette Do-Nguyen

Rebuild My Church Divine Mission

(The Lord Jesus gave this name to Mariette)

P.O. Box 261550 ✦ San Diego, CA 92196-1550

April 1, 1998

Phillip Hildebrand, Senior Vice President
Agency Services
New York Life Insurance Company

Dear Mr. Hildebrand,

I remember very clearly that during the time I worked for New York Life, agents were told by trainers that during the selling interview, the largest percent is the agent selling himself and the company's reputation, and very small percent of the selling is the products.

They also told us that seventy five percent of Social Security applications would be denied, and the New York Life Insurance individual disability always pays the benefits, and the requirement is clients physician's statement. In the case of class 4A, they will not have to take any other jobs that lower pay until returning to the professional occupation, such as the physician, the physician is class 4A, and my individual disability income policy is class 4A.

The Social Security Department is currently paying my disability benefit, but New York Life Insurance Company denied benefits, enclosed is copy of the benefit check, dated March 3, 1998.

The New York Life Insurance Company denied my Nylic QN6-82 physical incapacity benefit claim request, with reason that I filed a claim after I left New York Life, and this reason is wrong. The copy of a five minutes home video I mailed to Joan B. Brady, Disability Income Claims Division, dated March 21, 1998, showed the evidence of the beginning of my physical disability, and that date was July 12, 1993, over eight months before I left the company on April 7, 1994.

God took me off from work in very a painful way; I do not chose to be who I am now, I have denied it many times and I still continue to deny, because twenty four-hours a day and everyday I have physical and emotional suffering.

Doctors Gerald Nelson and Walter Strybel have meet with me at least one or twice each month since January 12, 1994, they use diagnostic criteria 297.10 Delusional Disorder; they know my symptoms that I am suffering, this is God's choice, not my choice.

"Grandiose Type: delusions of inflated worth, power, knowledge, identity, or special relationship to a deity or famous person" a copy enclosed.

The "Power and knowledge" are coming from God. Again, God chose me for His works, I have no choice. But the three doctors referred by New York Life Insurance Company, two of them only saw me one, and another twice. In these one or twice meeting, how much do they know of my symptoms? According to their result, how much do they remember of their training? How much do they understand of God's power upon the world? That, compared to my two doctors who have been seeing me at least once or twice each month over the course of four years to diagnosing the symptoms.

These three doctors do not believe in God, do not understand God's power, and made their conclusion with lack of information. People with mental illness are increasing very rapidly because of those doctors who do not believe in God and know His power. Doctors Nelson and Strybel are being chosen to work with me in research to understand soul, spirit, the supernatural power upon human physical body and mind, and the spirit's voices.

I have no choice, God has power over me, I am being forced by God to obey Him, like the world has no choice to accept or deny heavy rains, storms, floods, tornadoes, and other deadly tragedies etc.... President Bill Clinton, a president of the most powerful nation in the world has no choice, but he has to accept what God put on him.

The examination result from those three doctors are wrong, they wrote a report with lack of information, and insufficient knowledge of their training or experience. They are causing the New York Life insurance company a great deal of confusion and misrepresent their products.

In the letter from Donna M. Midgley, February 23, 1998 indicated, "Since we no longer consider you totally disabled according to the definitions of "total disability" as cited above, we will be terminating your Long Term Disability claim with the next payment which will be released on or about March 5, 1998. This covers the period from February 12, 1998 through March 11, 1998." The NYLRACare health Plans check benefit for $982.22 dated March 4, 1998 was sent to me after I received the letter and appealed; but when Mike Albriola returned my called on March 26 & 31, 1998, he kept telling me that there is no Long Term Disability benefit check pay to me after the letter from Ms. Midgley. Mr. Albriola and all those works on my claims are confusing by these three independent doctors.

I know that I am not perfect, and there is no one in this world is perfect, but I always try to do my best, I will not do things that I do not want another people do to me. When I found out I make a mistake, I admit it and will not make the same mistake again. God calls everyone to deal with the truth and come to conversion.

Enclosed are copies of: a letter from Donna M. Midgley, Claims Analyst, February 23, 1998 and the NYLCARE Health Plan explanation of the benefit, March 4, 1998, copy of Social Security check, March 3, 1998, and two letters from Doctor Walter Strybel, March 4 & 26, 1998, letter to Joan Brady, March 21, 1998, and her response March 25, 1998.

I ask that the New York Life personnel to admit their wrong actions, convert, and pay me the physical incapacity benefit of the Nylic QN6-82 contract up today, to continue to pay my individual disability income policy, and Long Term Disability together with the different amount that short of monthly payment since July 1994 until when God releases me from this physical and emotional suffering.

Sincerely in Christ Jesus,

Mariette Do-Nguyen

Meaning of the Delusional Disorder Grandiose Type & Paranoid Schizophrenia

The Delusional Disorder, Grandiose Type is the gift from God for prophets in the old testament, it comes with the gift of discernment. The gift of discernment will discerned what comes from God, and what comes from the devil, and the devil has no power over them. Because the life of prophets includes much suffering, they must completely obey all God's commandments. They only obey God, not man, and their lives are very peaceful in tremendous suffering. Because God uses the natural environment as symbolism to reveal to man in spirit, prophets have to pray to understand the meaning of these symbolism. When these revelations come down to earth, they come as the way the prophets understand, not what they see or heard in the spirit. Doctors do not understand the symbolism, and the medical profession calls it "Delusional Disorder, Grandiose Type."

The following is Mariette explained a delusional disorder, grandiose type to a psychiatrist: "Some people see things in spirit with spirit eyes that others can not see. What we see in spirit is symbolism. I have to pray for understanding. For example, if I saw you sitting now in my dream or vision, I must understand it as: You are looking at the calendar; this is symbolic that you are planning. You are wearing vertical (navy blue) stripes that do not cross, this symbolizes plan to go up high. You are wearing eyes glasses, not sun glasses, this is symbolic of discernment. Your leaning back is symbolic of your relaxing when you plan for the future. Your watch also adds to the calendar, planning for time in the future. Your navy blue pants... navy has to do with water, and water is purification. Your gray hair has to do with being elderly, meaning respect. Because people do not understand the symbolism, they said delusion, and it is in medical code." The psychiatrist replied, "That made sense."

The people diagnosed of paranoid schizophrenia are hearing supernatural voices, seeing visions, and they also feel supernatural power, and there are some time in their imagination. (The imagination was control or interfering human's mind by the devil or his offspring spirits). These people have no discernment, they do not understand the symbolism. The devil's power is come with voices, visions, feeling, and imagination, and force people to take actions as the voices told, or what containing in their thoughts. These people have no peace, and their actions are harmful to others, sometimes even harming themselves. But they always believe they are right and other are wrong. These people are either not believe in God, or not obey God's commandments, or obey part that benefit themselves only. They are not dealing with the truth to themselves and to other.

Rebuild My Church Divine Mission

(The Lord Jesus gave this name to Mariette)

P.O. Box 261550 ✦ San Diego, CA 92196-1550

April 14, 1998

Mr. Chuck Quackenbush, Commissioner
California Department of Insurance.
300 South Spring Street, South Tower #201
Los Angeles, CA 90013

Via: Federal Express

Re: Your File Number: CSB-5217772
       New York Life Insurance Company

Dear Mr. Quackenbush,

This letter serves as a complaint of the California Insurance Department system. After I sent you the letter of March 3, 1998 by Federal Express, I received a letter from Joan Wong dated March 6, 1998. I responded to her request by letter via Federal Express dated March 16, 1998, and a second letter by U.S. mailed dated March 21, 1998. I also spoke to Ms. Wong, she indicated with me that my complaint was handled by J. Craig Collins. I spoke to Mr. Collins. He told me that since I have been helped by an attorney, the California Department of Insurance is not able to help me unless he received the release from my attorney. I told him that Mr. Koler only assists me for legal grounds and some letters to New York Life Insurance Company. I also had Mr. Koler faxed the release to Mr Collins the same day I spoke to him.

As of today, April 14, 1998, I have not heard from either Ms. Wong or Mr. Collins. During the conversation with Ms. Wong, she told me that the work load is heavy and some citizens have not heard from her for months.

The heavy work load is not an excuse for those coming to the Department of Insurance with an urgent need.   I had to use Federal Express mail to insure the quality of their service, and it is urgent for the next day's mail. My complaint is not only for me, but it is also for uncounted numbers of U.S. citizens in the State of California being harmed by the insurance industry and unqualified psychiatric doctors.

The New York Life Insurance Company acted in bad faith, using unqualified psychiatric doctors to breach the contracts, suddenly stopped paying three of my benefits. My bills are currently past due; even the New York Life Insurance Company Chairman of the Board, Mr. Sternbert ignores my appeals, at the same time Ms. Jennings, Director Claims Division continues to send me more and more letters denying my benefits.

This matter also deals with those people who have emotional suffering (mental illness), that are being harmed by those unqualified psychiatric doctors.

Enclosed are letters to Executive Director Ron Joseph, Medical Board of California, April 13, 1998, a letter to Phillip Hildebrand, Senior Vice President, New York Life Insurance Company, a latest letter from Anita Jennings, Director Claims Division, April 7, 1998, this is one of several letters denied my benefits from New York Life Insurance Company.

I request you enforce the law of services at California Department of Insurance, bring this matter to the public, to protect insurance agents and people who own insurance policies in the State of California, and to people with emotional suffering so they may come in the right direction to be healed, and prevent the suicide cause.

If you need more information, please contact me.

Sincerely in Christ Jesus,

Mariette Do-Nguyen

Rebuild My Church Divine Mission

(The Lord Jesus gave this name to Mariette)

P.O. Box 261550 ✦ San Diego, CA 92196-1550

April 15, 1998

Honorable Pete Wilson,
Governor of the State of California
State Capitol, First Floor
Sacramento, CA 95814

Dear Honorable Wilson,

I am writing to you to ask you, the Governor of this State, to pass laws, and enforce the laws, to clean up the corruption of the insurance industry and Psychiatric doctors systems.

The reason I am writing you is because of the personal experiences I have had with the New York Life Insurance company and the California Department of Insurance. The Independent Medical Examinations have issued false examination reports to New York Life Insurance Company. The New York Life Insurance refused to hear my doctors, who I have seen over dozens of times, and fully understand of my symptoms. They are licensed and doing business in the state of California, all these violations are accrued in the State of California.

The original date of this matter was filed at the California Department of Insurance on November 28, 1994, and was assigned to J. Craig Collins; Mr. Collins left the matter unresolved, allowing the New York Life Insurance Company to continue a breach of their contracts. In an act of bad faith earlier this year in February, New York Life denied my individual disability policy benefit, and on the same day also stopped paying the long term group disability, and waived the premium on my life insurance policies.

I filed a second time on March 3, 1998 for the lack of results of the complaint. As I have indicated in an enclosed letter to Commissioner Chuck Quackenbush, of the California Department of Insurance, during the conversation with Ms. Wong, after I responded to her letter, she then refused to handle my case, telling me that the case is the same matter, and it was handled by Mr. Collins previously, so she gave it to Mr. Collins; and because her case load, and some of citizens do not heard from her for months.

For whatever reason, Mr. Collins left my complaint unresolved. This time when I spoke to him, he told me because I have been represented by an attorney, the attorney has access to the laws, the Department of Insurance has no access to it. I explained to Mr. Collins that I came to attorney Duncan Koler for advice of the law and for him to write some letters to New York Life Insurance Company. He then asked me to get a release from Mr. Koler, and this request was fulfilled the same day by fax.

Mr. Collins did not finish my complaint the first time, therefore I can not trust him and allow him to handle my complaint a second time. I called the Department of Insurance at least twice and asked to speak to a supervisor, seeking another officer besides Mr. Collins, but their answer to me was that it is Ms. Wong's choice to handle my complaint or not. There is no supervisor, all complaints came are assigned to officers by the receivers. I told them that I had talked to Ms. Wong and she refused to help me.

Before I mailed the April 14th letter to Commissioner Chuck Quackenbush by Federal Express, I also faxed Ms. Wong's letter. I called the Department of Insurance again asked for Commissioner Quackenbush's telephone and fax number, a man answered and told me that Commissioner Quackenbush is in Sacramento, and gave me his telephone number (916) 322-3555. I was unsuccessful in reaching him.

Again I request of you, the Governor of this State to pass the laws, enforce the laws, and to clean up this corrupted system. Protect your constituents, the insurance agents, policies holder and beneficiaries. Persons with emotional suffering (mental illness) patients need to be healed, to limit some of the suicide causes.

For me, I indicated in an appeal to New York Life Insurance Chairman of the Board that I do not chose to be in this position; God put me here, He has power over my physical body and mind. I have to accepted the physical and emotional suffering twenty four-hour each day, and every day.   This is God's choice for me to do His works for the salvation of mankind.

It is urgent because all my living expenses bills are past due; would you or some one in you office contact my doctor by telephone for the full symptoms of my body and mind suffering; and enforce the New York Life Insurance Company to fulfill all of their contracts. Walter F. Strybel M.D.

If you need more information, please contact me.

Sincerely in Christ Jesus,

Mariette Do-Nguyen

Rebuild My Church Divine Mission

(The Lord Jesus gave this name to Mariette)

P.O. Box 261550 ✦ San Diego, CA 92196-1550

April 14, 1998

To: President Bill Clinton, Vice President Al Gore, and 100 all members of the United States Senate

Complaint Against the Insurance Industry and Psychiatric Doctors Evil Practice Systems

Dear ....,

I request that the U.S. Citizens who purchase any kind of insurance policies, and people with emotional suffering (mental illness) in the United States must be protected by the Federal Laws, and these laws must be very strict upon the insurance companies and psychiatric doctors, and heavy penalty upon them when the "trust" is being violated.

Enclosed are copies of: (1) a letter to Commissioner Chuck Quackenbush, April 14, 1998; (2) a letter to executive Director Ron Joseph, Medical Board of California, April 13, 1998;(3) a letter to Phillip Hildebrand, Senior Vice President, Agency Services, New York Life Insurance Company, April 1, 1998; (4) a letter to Seymour Sternbert, President, CEO, Chairman, New York Life Insurance Company, March 3, 1998;(5) a letter to Honorable Pete Wilson, Governor of the State of California, April 15, 1998.

If you need more information or have any questions, please contact me.

Sincerely in Christ Jesus,

Mariette Do-Nguyen

Rebuild My Church Divine Mission

(The Lord Jesus gave this name to Mariette)

P.O. Box 261550 ✦ San Diego, CA 92196-1550

April 24, 1998

Walter F. Strybel, M.D.
San Diego, California

Dear Dr. Strybel,

Enclosed is a letter from Donna M. Midgley, April 16, 1998. This is the number twelve letter of denying my disability benefits from New York Life Insurance Company since February 23, 1998. I have never seen any insurance company send out this many denied claim letters within a two month period.

They are shipping the denial reasons of my benefit because they have not receive the inquiry from you.

Each time I received the denial letter, the enemy spirits attack me very strongly for at least a day or two; and this is very painful for me. Yesterday I asked to Lord to permit me to hand these matters to the attorney; and then I got an appointment with an attorney on May 1, 1998. If I do not receive my March and April benefits checks from both individual and Long term disability by April 29, 1998, I will turn these matters to a law firm, so I can serve God more effectively; because the world needs me; I can not let the devil controlling the New York Life Insurance Company employee's minds and actions to keep attacking me, pulling me away from services to the world that needs me.

I need the report from you before I meet with the attorney. Thank you for explaining my disability symptoms to Anita Jennings on April 22, 1998.

Sincerely in Christ Jesus,

Mariette Do-Nguyen

Rebuild My Church Divine Mission
(The Lord Jesus gave this name to Mariette)
P.O. Box 261550 ✦ San Diego, CA 92196-1550

April 24, 1998

Seymour Sternbert, President, CEO, Chairman of the Board
Phillip Hilderbrand, Senior Vice President, Agency Services
Lynne Cohn, Vice President, Human Resources
Anita Jenning, Director of Individual Claims Division
New York Life Insurance Company

New York Life Sent out Twelve Denial Letters within two months for three policies

Dear Mr. Sternbert,

Enclosed is a facsimile to Doctor Walter Strybel, dated April 24, 1998, confirming Doctor Strybel called Joan Brady, and Anita Jennings called him back on behalf of Ms. Brady on April 22, 1998.

Doctor Strybel told me on April 22, 1998; he spoke to Anita (you) about twenty minutes, explained to her (you) of my symptom.

From that conversation, the New York Life Insurance is no longer blamed of his did not responded to your inquiry. Prior to this conversation, there were number of attending physician statements from Doctor Gerald Nelson, and Doctor Walter Strybel, indicated the diagnosis and my concurrent conditions as, "Delusional disorder 297.10." The New York Life Insurance company's employee must understand this type of symptom.

When this symptom is not on the independent medical examinations reports; it means that report is false; New York Life Insurance company should never have honored the false reports and stopped my benefits, plus sending out twelve letters of denied claims.

As I indicated on facsimile to Doctor Strybel; if both of my benefits checks for March and April, 1998 are have not arrived at my home by April 29, 1998; I surely will turn this matter to a law firm. This is courtesy note.

Sincerely,

Mariette Do-Nguyen

Rebuild My Church Divine Mission
(The Lord Jesus gave this name to Mariette)
P.O. Box 261550 ✦ San Diego, CA 92196-1550

May 1, 1998

Walter F. Strybel, M.D.
San Diego, CA92123

Psychiatric being persuaded by the enemy spirits

Via facsimile

Dear Dr. Strybel,

Enclosed is a letter from Anita L. Jennings, dated April 27, 1998, that I received yesterday. She is still waiting for your comments on the results of the Independent Medical Examinations.

On your letter to her, March 4, 1998. You indicated, "I do question whether she would be able to function in the work place. I also would question whether she would be able to adhere to any type of schedule or routine." As I indicated on my most recent letter to New York Life Chairman of the Board, Seymour Sternbert, they have set their minds on not paying my benefits; when they read these paragraphs, the devil gave them understanding of his way, to harm the New York Life and you; and to added more physical and emotional suffering upon me.

I ask you to write to them a short letter, as you have promised her and me that you would do within a week. Give her black and white as you have told me at last appointment, that you said to her, "You can call her delusional. You can call her intelligent. You can call her what ever you want to call; but she is disabled."

As you know that I must suffer to follow in my brother's footsteps, the Lord Jesus as fully man. Therefore, the Father allowed the devil to let the New York Life add more suffering on what I already endure. When you gave the New York Life March 4, 1998 report, the devil led them to understand the evil way, that untruth, to added more physical and mental suffering on me.

I have an appointment with an attorney at 12:15 p.m. today, May 1, 1998. You told me not to see an attorney. If you fax this short letter to me by or before 11:00 a.m., I will cancel an appointment. If not, I must see attorney to battle against them. I can not go on any more with number of days either eating very little, or skipping a number of meals; during the night losing more sleep, and the devil uses the situation to attacking me heavier.

If you have question, please give me call, I will return from mass about 9:00 a.m.

Sincerely in Christ Jesus,

Mariette Do-Nguyen

Rebuild My Church Divine Mission

(The Lord Jesus gave this name to Mariette)

P.O. Box 261550 ✦ San Diego, CA 92196-1550

May 3, 1998

Seymour Sternbert, President, CEO, Chairman of the Board,
Phillip Hildebrand, Senior Vice President, Agency Services,
Lynne Cohn, Vice President, Human Resources,
Joan Brady, Assistant Vice President, Disability Claims Division,
Anita Jennings, Director, Individual Disability Income Claims Division,
Donna M. Midgley, Claims Analyst,
NEW YORK LIFE INSURANCE COMPANY

Re: Individual Income Disability & Long Term Disability

Dear ....,

In response to Anita Jennings' s letter, dated April 27, 1998, her letter indicated:

"We currently await Dr. Strybel's letter providing additional comments on the results of the Independent Medical Examinations you underwent with Dr. Bergsma and Dr. Melendez. Upon receipt of this information we will contact you."

Enclosed is a letter from Dr. Strybel, dated March 4, 1998, that Joan Brady indicated of receiving it on her letter, dated March 16, 1998. Ms. Brady's letter indicated, "is not due to a mental illness but is a matter of choice." Since that, I have explained to New York Life's insurance Company that I have no choice, but am being forced by God.

Dr. Strybel's letter, dated March 4, 1998, already gave the comments to New York Life Insurance Company of the Independent Medical Examination. The last two paragraphs in his letter was very clear that I am unable function to any schedule or routine daily.

My mortgagor sent me a note for foreclosure proceedings on April 30, 1998 for payment past due; my Homeowner's insurance policy will be canceled on May 4, 1998, due to not paying the premium; and my car payments is two months past due; and my automobile insurance payment is due immediately.

From the day of this letter, May 3, 1998, the New York Life Insurance Company is fully responsible for all my financial loss, and that includes myself and all members of my family's emotional suffering, and all other damages that may be because the New York Life Insurance Company acted in bath faith, and stopped paying my disability benefits.

I have requested early that the New York Life Insurance Company continue paying my benefits while the State and Federal investigate. Again, to limit some of the future damage, I request the New York Life Insurance Company pay all my monthly benefits while the litigation is in process.

I request my monthly benefits mail direct to me, and all the correspondence are to my attorney, Mr. Eugene P. Yale at the Law Offices of Eugene P. Yale, 501 West Broadway, Suite 1350, San Diego, CA 92101.

Sincerely in Christ Jesus,

Mariette Do-Nguyen

Rebuild My Church Divine Mission

(The Lord Jesus gave this name to Mariette)

P.O. Box 261550 ✦ San Diego, CA 92196-1550

May 8, 1998

Seymour Sternbert,
President, CEO, and Chairman of the Board
New York Life Insurance Company

Re: Nylic QN6-82 Physical Incapacity Benefits

Dear Mr. Sternbert,

Since Mr. Wright's letter, dated November 3, 1994, the New York Life Insurance Company denied my claim with untrue reasons. Many times I appealed to the retired Chairman of the Board, Harry Horn, but he ignored my appeals.

Enclosed is a five minute home video that was taped in Vietnam, on July 12, 1993. This portion of the video shows the end of my parent's memorial service; we visited their grave after the service. Accompanying me in the video, from the United States were my oldest daughter and her husband, my son-in-law who is New York Life Insurance Company's agent. In one scene in this video, I was torched by a supernatural power; the Lord God was breaking through my physical body and my mind, although at that time I did not understand.

Since then, God's power has continued to manifest in my physical body and mind. God also allowed the enemy spirits to attack me very heavily; causing my body many different symptoms, and stretching my mind number of time each day to maximum. Through all of these sufferings, God revealed Himself to me, He then told me to put my story in writing to benefit mankind.

The New York Life Assistant Vice President Ann Ford's letter, dated April 30, 1998 indicated, "The diagnosis of Delusional Disorder has not been proved." The Lord Jesus told me some time ago, "There are no human books that can teach you of what I am teaching you." He is God, His word is truth, and come with God's power; there is no doctor or theologian in this world that has learned and go through of what God has put me through. God instructed me to put these events in writing to benefit mankind. Therefore, in the second book I have written which will be coming out soon; and the following is short summary of the book

"God's Purification - Not Easy," by Mariette Do- Nguyen will be Published in the third quarter of 1998. This book contains God's revelations, and explains the details of God's purification upon the world. U.S. Constitution right-Freedom of religion being violated. It is a guide to understanding God's commandments hidden in the scriptures, explaining the symbolism in the Book of Revelations and in the old testament and God's anointing.

Through a biblical pattern, this book will assist ordinary people to interpreting their dreams, and how to understand symbolism in their dreams, and messages from God to them, in conjunction with the Holy Bible. The book is also a key to discerning visions, apparitions and voices, knowing that evolution is a process of God's creation; and to understand supernatural power that causes physical and emotional suffering, and God's healing power.

Within the last year, the Creator of Heaven and Earth appeared to me in His Son's image. The Lord Jesus appeared to me in His glorified body, and God's Throne was formed with a mix of cloud and fire. At these times, I saw God with her carnal eyes. All the stories in this book are actual events. In some cases, God placed me through intense suffering; she is God's suffering Servant, God uses her as His Instrument to purify the world system.

Through me, God speaks to the world, purifying it systems, by beginning with the United States government, and the United States Catholic leaders, to unify them in one with Him."

Enclosed is a partial manuscript of chapter 9, God revealed of "Discernment and Supernatural Realms;" and chapter 34, "The World Systems against Him" written of the actual actions in nature of how the supernatural powers rule the human mind and body.

The onset of my disability is July 12, 1993, not after I left the New York Life Insurance Company. I request that you instruct the New York Life supervisor at the Agent Benefit Division to honor my Nylic QN6-82 Physical incapacity Benefits partial disability as of July 12, 1998, and total disability as of January 12, 1994. I also request my benefit be paid up till today, plus the interest.

The Lord God instructed me only to ask Mr. Eugene P. Yale at the Law Offices of Eugene P. Yale to represent me on Long Term Disability and Individual Disability, retaining the Nylic QN6-82 contract for me to deal with the New York Life Insurance directly.

If you or any one have questions of the Nylic QN6-82 matter, do not hesitate to contact me.

Sincerely in Christ Jesus,

Mariette Do-Nguyen

Rebuild My Church Divine Mission
(The Lord Jesus gave this name to Mariette)
P.O. Box 261550 ✦ San Diego, CA 92196-1550

May 8, 1998

Phillip Hidebrand, Senior Vice President
Agency Services
New York Life Insurance Company

Re: Appeal of the denied decision on the Nylic Qn6-82 Physical Incapacity Benefits

Dear Mr. Hildebrand,

Enclosed is copy of a letter to the New York Life insurance Chairman of the Board, Seymour Sternbert, dated May 8, 1998, with attachments.

Besides my appeal to Chairman Sternbert, I also appeal to you, because you were the Managing Partner for the San Diego Office at the time I was serving at New York Life Insurance Company. You also know my son-in-law who still works for New York Life Insurance Company. My two children were witnesses the first time that God poured out the supernatural power unto my body and mind in the public on July 12, 1993 were my son-in-law, Huy Cao and his wife, my oldest daughter, Thuy-Trang.

God has put me in one of the most difficult positions in my life , to tose between my son-in- law, my daughter and the Almighty God. I love my son-in-law and my daughter, I also love people at New York Life; but I must obey God. I have been praying a lot for God's decisions on this journey, especially in this case I even pray harder. I must follow the decision that God puts in my mind. If I go against it, I will suffer more than I can endure. The decision that God puts in my mind on the New York Life matters not only for me, but also for others in the area of insurance industry, medical field, and governments systems throughout the world.

The decision that I have an attorney representing me for the Long Term Disability benefit, and individual disability income were made by God few years ago. Through my dream, God showed me the map of these attorney's office together with His presence. I did not know this until the night after I left Mr. Eugene P. Yale's office, God brought it back to me, this revelation is also in the book, "God's Purification — Not Easy."

God also has reason to retain the cases of Nylic Qn6-82 and the New York Life Insurance as violations to my right to the U.S. Constitution —

Freedom of religion, (by taking out the loan from my life insurance policies and paying the IRS. By paying these taxes, New York Life forced me into participating in murdering unborn babies, and civilians when the U.S. engages in war with another nation.)

God is calling all of us for conversion; and all of these are to purify the world's systems, come to salvation of the mankind, building up the nations, the world, and for souls to be saved for eternal life in heaven.

I request that my benefit for Nylic Qn6-82 be paid up to today. If you have any question, please contact me directly in these two matters.

Sincerely in Christ Jesus,

Mariette Do-Nguyen

Rebuild My Church Divine Mission
(The Lord Jesus gave this name to Mariette)
P.O. Box 261550 ♦ San Diego, CA 92196-1550

June 8, 1998,

Brent Moore, Managing Partner
Howard Fowler, Office Manger
San Diego General Office
New York Life Insurance Company

U.S Returned Receipt Mail

Re: The New York Life Insurance Company Violated the Word "TRUST"

Dear Mr. Moore and Mr. Fowler,

I feel that I owe to all my colleague agents at New York Life Insurance Company, especially San Diego General Office agents if I do not sent this letter to you. Therefore, I request that you have "the entire contents" of this letter be known to all agents at San Diego Office and all New York Life Insurance Company's agents in short time limit.

To all my colleague agents at New York Life Insurance Company, I owe to you if I do not send this letter to you. But I am sending this letter to you so I do not owe you the love and care for your future, and future of your family after you left the company. The words "Do not believe what they promised, but stand firm and do what need to be done so it will not happen to your future, and your colleague's future."

This letter will open the truth of how the New York Life Insurance Company executive's officers, the company you had served with your heart and soul, will take care of you; the time that you will be on the street any day from your house in danger, all your bills are past due; you life insurance policies been canceled, and how the New York Life Insurance Company executive officers fulfill their written promises.

All of us make mistakes, if anyone does not make a mistake, that person is a saint; and some time that single mistake becomes the most important one to save uncounted number of other, agents, insurance clients, and mental suffering patients that are being taken advantage because of the word "TRUST".

After I served the New York Life Insurance Company for seven years and ten months; I made an honest mistake; after the investigation, the high authority found that I am not guilty to the murder charged against me by the New York Life Insurance Company.

At the same time the New York Life Insurance Company charged me with murder, they also acted in bad faith, not paying me any penny of my Nylic QN6-82 Physical Incapacity Contract benefits. They paid my Long Term Disability and Individual Income Disability for four, and suddenly stopped both benefits, by ordering and using their Independent Medical Examination false reports, blocked out the symptoms that I have been physically suffering and mental anguish. I have written to them over dozens of times within two months, told them that in January 1994, my first doctor, Dr. Gerald Nelson, and all my other doctors Attending Physician's statements diagnosis my symptoms is not in their report, but all of them are ignoring the truth. Then after two months, one of their Assistant Vice President wrote to me and said that my symptoms have not been proven.   I then sent them my Independence Medical Examination's report, but as of the day of this letter, my benefits have not been reinstated.

I have given the New York Life executive officers and representative all the opportunities to do the right things, but they rejected and forced me to file claims against the company and them with California Department of Insurance, and engaged in a litigation against the New York Life and it executive officers of acting in bad faith and violated the work "TRUST."

For the love of God, to protect all agents in the insurance industry, clients, and patents with mental suffering that are being taken advantage of by their doctors; all my communications with New York Life Insurance Company representative will be published in my forthcoming book "God's Purification - Not easy."

Because the matter as in litigation, I am not allow to speak in detail, but when it is over, you will hear the matter in more detail.

Sincerely in Christ Jesus,

Mariette Do-Nguyen

Note: The word murder has three meanings: physical, spiritual, and reputation. The murder meaning in this issue is harming earthly reputations and causing confusion in spirit.

Rebuild My Church Divine Mission

(The Lord Jesus gave this name to Mariette)

P.O. Box 261550 ✦ San Diego, CA 92196-1550

May 27, 1998

J. Craig Collins, Associate Claims Officer
California Department of Insurance
Consumer Services Bureau

Via: Certified Return Receipt Requested

Dear Mr. Collins,

In response to your letter of April 21, 1998, sent to my old address, please note the new address on the appeal of your decision, dated March 3, 1998. P.O. Box 261550, San Diego, CA 92196-1550.

The New York Life Insurance Company stopped contributing premiums to my account at the State of California Disability Insurance; they have kept the money and replaced their own carrier, Nylic - QN6-82. They then denied my benefits. I have been providing them with all the requirements, and appealed numbers of time to the company Chairman of the Board and its executive officers, but they are ignoring me, and continue to deny to pay my benefits.

The New York Life had paid my individual disability income policy and long term disability benefits on my doctors diagnosis condition of 297.10 Delusional Disorder, Grandiose Type for four years and two months. This diagnosis was found by Dr. Nelson and reported to them the first time on April 19, 1994; since, all Attending Physician Statements from my doctors to New York Life Insurance Company indicate the diagnosis is "297.10 Delusional Disorder, Grandiose Type".

In bad faith, they then honoring their Independent Medical Examinations report that left out the "297.10 Delusional Disorder,

Grandiose Type;" stopped paying all my benefits since beginning of March 1998. Dr. Walter Strybel sent them two letters, one was a comment of the Independent Medical Examination, and another was about how their actions caused me severe depression; but they continued to ignore Dr. Strybel's comments.

In three months time, I had written them over a dozen letters, telling them that my doctors diagnosis is a condition as "297.10 Delusional Disorder, Grandiose Type" that their Independent Medical Examinations left out; in bad faith, they refused the truth and honoring the untruth. Then Ann Ford, the Assistant Vice President of NYL letter of April 30, 1998 wrote: "The diagnosis of Delusional Disorder has not been proven."

To protect other Insurance agents, clients and mental suffering patients (mental illnesses patients) I have written to the Governor of California Pete Wilson, Ron Joseph, Executive Director for Medical Board of California, President Bill Clinton, and to all members of the United States Senate, to prevent the insurance industry and psychiatric doctors when the "trust" is being violated.

Enclosed are copies of: (1) Request for Assistance, dated March 16, 1998, (2) a letter from Ann Ford, Assistant Vice President, NYL, dated April 30, 1998, (3) Attending Physician's Statement from Dr. Gerald E. Nelson, dated April 19, 1994, (4) a Medical Report from Dr. Roy Resnikoff, dated May 21, 1998. (5) a letter to President Bill Clinton, Vice President Al Gore, and all members of the U.S. Senate and it attachments, dated April 14, 1998.

Dr. Roy Resnikoff's report was sent via Federal Express on May 21, 1998 for next day delivery services. As of today I still have not heard from them.

I request that the California Department of Insurance take proper actions against the New York Life Insurance company to prevent this happening again to other insurance agents and clients in the insurance industry.

Sincerely In Christ Jesus,

Mariette Do-Nguyen

Rebuild My Church Divine Mission
(The Lord Jesus gave this name to Mariette)
P.O. Box 261550 ✦ San Diego, CA 92196-1550

August 13, 1998

Seymour Sternbert
President, CEO, and Chairman of the Board
New York Life Insurance Company

Via: U.S. Certified Mail Return Receipt and facsimile No. (212) 576-4545

AND
Phillip Hiderbrand, Senior Vice President Agency Services,
and former Managing Partner, San Diego General Office
New York Life Insurance Company

Via: U.S. Certified Mail Return Receipt and facsimile No. (212)447-4267

Re: Nylic QN6-82 Physical Incapacity Benefits

Dear Chairman Sternbert and Mr. Hilderbrand,

On July 1, 1998, through my telephone conversation with Mr. Collins, from the California Department of Insurance, he notified me of the New York Life Company claim that I am being represented by attorney of several policies. In response, I sent Mr. Collins a letter, dated July 1, 1998, and copies to you, (Chairman Seymour Sternbert and Senior Vice President Phillip Hilderbrand), Assistant Vice President Michael Abriola, and my counsel, Mr. Eugene P. Yale.

July 16, 1998. I spoke to Mr. Collins, he told me that he was sending New York Life a letter. On August 5, 1998, Mr. Collins informed me that New York Life still claimed this policy (Nylic N6) is in litigation, and my attorney, Mr. Yale had not responded to New York Life's attorney's letter regarding this policy.

On July 14, 1998, the Early Neutral Evaluation conference, in Judge Aaron's chamber; was held in front of the New York Life attorney, Mr. Thomas P. Ackland and J. Ronald Ignaruk, Ms. Joan Brady, and another woman from New York Life. Included in Mr. Yale's statement to Judge Aaron, he said, "I represent Ms. Do-Nguyen for the group Long Term disability and individual income disability. I am not representing her on the Nylic contract of one thousand four hundred dollars benefit." During this conference, one of the New York Life's attornies brought up the

$4,200 loan from my life insurance policies and sent that monies to the IRS, and to the Lord Jesus web site. Also, I was notified by Judge Aaron that New York Life wanted to keep the settlement confidential.

I have written to you, Mr. Hilderbrand, Mr. Abriola, and the California Department of Insurance before, telling you that God has instructed me to have Mr. Eugene P. Yale only represent me for the group Long Term disability, Individual Income policy, and waiver premium on my life insurance policies. The issue of how the New York Life Insurance Company treated me will be open on the books to protect insurance agents, insurance policies holders, and how their actions cause mental suffering (illness) throughout the United States and the world. I delivered this instruction from God to Judge Aaron on July 14, 1998.

Obeying God, I filed complaints against New York Life for the Nylic QN6-82 Physical Incapacity Benefits with the California Department of Insurance to protect insurance agents; the loans from my life insurance policies in the United States Tax Court, because these loans caused a violation of my civil right to freedom of religion, seeking civil right to freedom of religion for myself and all the American citizens..

There were four letters from New York Life written by Sr. Benefits Associate Darryl C. Wright, November 3, 1994, Assistant Vice President Donna O'Driscoll, CLU, December 27, 1994, Assistant Vice President Paul Platz, January 10, 1997, and Assistant Vice President Michael Abriola, May 29, 1998 denied my claim. The reason they denied my Nylic QN6-82 Physical Incapacity Benefits was that my disability started after April 7, 1998 when I was no longer working for New York Life. This reason was untrue; because my total disability started from January 12, 1994, and New York Life had been paying me benefits for group Long Term Disability and Individual Disability effective January 12, 1994.

The New York Life representative have set their mind with "DO NOT WANT TO PAY MY BENEFITS". They changed the denied reason from the total disability after I was no longer working for the company to the policy that is in litigation.

Through me, the New York Life Insurance Company is dealing with God; and God calls all of us for conversion. I pray that you and your employees choose the free will of hearing God's voice of justice and convert to God. I request that my Nylic QN6 benefits and interest be paid immediately.

Sincerely in Christ Jesus,

Mariette Do-Nguyen

cc: Craig Collins, California Department of Insurance; via facsimile No. (213)897-5891

Eugene P. Yale, Attorney at Law; via facsimile (619)234-0369

Michael Albriola, Assistant Vice President; via facsimile No. (212) 447-4168

Rebuild My Church Divine Mission

(The Lord Jesus gave this name to Mariette)

P.O. Box 261550 ✦ San Diego, CA 92196-1550

September 22, 1998

Eugene P. Yale Esq.
The Koll Center
San Diego, CA 92101

Sent via facsimile No. (619) 234-0369 and U.S. Mail

Dear Mr. Yale,

This letter is regarding my deposition request by the New York Life Insurance Company. Enclosed is a copy of a "Reply to Amended Petition" that I filed at Tax Court, Washington, that the Lord God asked me to send to you regarding His commandments.

Because God's commandments are above man's law; and the mission that God entrusted to me as a head; I must always obey all of His commandments. This also applies to every human being alive in this world, with no exception in any area of the laws, nation, or group.

Based on God's laws pertaining to this deposition, I only answer the questions directly regarding the Insurance business practice, my health symptoms and psychiatric practice systems, and God's calling man for conversion.

At this time, my health does not permit me to drive from San Diego to Orange Country for over an hour and then sit for hours in the deposition. Therefore, I request that my deposition be taken in San Diego.

I ask you to inform the New York Life Insurance company's counsels as soon as possible. If you need more information, please let me know.

Sincerely in Christ Jesus,

Mariette Do-Nguyen

Rebuild My Church Divine Mission

(The Lord Jesus gave this name to Mariette)

P.O. Box 261550 ♦ San Diego, CA 92196-1550

February 3, 1999

Seymour Sternbert, Chairman of the Board
New York Life Insurance Company
51 Madison avenue, 13th Floor
New York, NY 10010
Via Facsimile No. (212)576- 4545 and U.S. Certified Mail

Re: NYLIC Contract , QN6 No. 528705

Dear Chairman Sternbert,

J. Craig Collins, Associate Claims Officer, from the California Department of Insurance notified me today, February 3, 1999, He said, "The New York Life insurance company sent me a letter, they said your matter was result."

I do not understand what "the matter was result" means while I have not receive any penny from this benefit. I asked him for a copy of the letter from your company, but he refused to give it to me; instead, he told me, "I sent you a letter on January 7, 1999, and it was returned. I sent to 6755 Mira Mesa..." I told him, "That was my old mailing address. I notified you at least twice that my mailing address changed to P. O. Box...." He then told me, "I will fax to you a copy of my letter." I then gave him my fax number.

The New York Life insurance company deducted premium from my income account, and paid to the California Disability fund for the first three years, 1986- 1988. Then the company replaced the QN6 Agent contract as short term disability. I became partially disabled on July 12, 1993, and totally disabled January 12, 1994.

At that time I filed claim for my individual and long term disability policies benefits, I also filled a claim for the QN6 benefits, the New York Life Insurance company is paying for the individual and long term policies benefits, but denied the agent contract QN6 benefit. I had to filed a complaint at the California Department of Insurance; during these five years, all I heard from Mr. Collins was New York Life Insurance Company's changing different reasons to deny paying my benefits. For over five years, the New York Life Insurance Company put a lot of pain in my heart.

With the love of God within me, I gave the New York Life Insurance representatives many chances to resolve this matter, but you refused them. This is the last time, I request New York Life Insurance company to pay my benefits within five days from the date of this letter.

Sincerely in God,

Mariette Do-Nguyen

The Meaning of Quail and Manna

April 2, 1998, 3:40 a.m. The Archangel Michael asked me, "What is quail in the old testament symbolic of?" I replied, "I don't know." He said, "Quail is symbolic of suffering, hurting human flesh." He asked, "What does manna mean?" He continued, "Manna is tragedies. Through you, Dr. Strybel received quail, [because he received quail]and he asked you to come back next week. Through you, Phil Hilderbrand received quail; he shared it with Lynne Cohn. He saw that you are suffering, have no money, and bills are past due. He felt that the last time he called your son, this time he also does the same. You are a person that holds suffering for yourself. For these reasons, your daughter called you last night. Your son pretends that he does not know, but these children are speaking. The way that Heavenly Father tells your children is by having someone else to tell them instead of your tell them yourself. The older asks the younger 'Do you see anything changed in her?' You hide your suffering.

Through you, the priests at Saint Andrew Cathedral received quail. Bishop Andrew and church high-ranking leaders are receiving quail

The staff turned into blood; blood is symbolic of suffering. The frog is symbolic that man can do nothing. The snake is symbolic of those who refuse to convert. The funnel you saw above the Cathedral of Saint Andrew's sanctuary means through you, these things come down upon the world.

The meaning of Saint Peter's key is important for them, they are sharing to each other. They know where you go to mass. That monsignor already knew before you met him, that is why when you asked him to see the bishop on your behalf; he responded 'no' twice in a firm voice. Just think that he is under the bishop's direction, when you ask him something like that, if he doesn't want to do it, he will give you a soft answer. Priests have office clerks to schedule appointments so you can see them. Have you seen any priest allowing the office to set appointment for them? The Eternal Father allowed you to cancel an appointment with Father Paul. He [Father Paul] called you just to tell you about the Eucharistic Minister assignment. Be visible to them, and let them come to you. They know the meaning of Saint Peter's key will come to the public. They are trying to change your plan. Do not let them persuade you."

The New York Life Insurance Company, and its employees are being called by God in conjunction with me as natural substance; through these natural substances, God revealed the falseness of the insurance industry, government officials, and psychiatric doctors.

Although God gave everyone of us free will of choosing Him or the devil, God has pre-destined me for this mission; therefore, the employees of the New York Life Insurance Company had allowed the enemies spirits to interfere in their minds and actions and made wrong decisions toward me. They are dealing with the Almighty God through me; and up to some point God turned the situation to the right direction for His plan to be fulfilled.

God knew before the New York Life Insurance Company started acting out of their promises and training for agents during the time I was there; their actions are my enemies. The Lord Jesus told me many times, "You need to love them [New York Life Insurance Company employee] the Father had put you to work for the Company; and uses them as the source of financial contributions to support you in this mission." God means that their wrong actions will add more to my suffering; but I must love them. New York Life Insurance Company is one of many other business that God calls to participating in building the kingdom of heaven. God calls each one of us to serve Him by service to one another in love and truth, so they can inherit the heavenly eternal life.

God revealed that many medical doctors do not believe in God, and His power existing in this world. Many psychiatric doctors have not treated their patients properly; and the percent of people with mental illness increases daily. Because those who do not believe in God and His power, the enemy spirit causes them to lack training, forget their training, ard do not have all patients symptoms information. They are careless, irresponsible to their patients, or the people who they exam; they do not understand the three main elements, the soul, spirit, and physical body, and how they are function; and this leads them to improperly treat their patients and issue false reports.

The names, titles, business type among other things also symbolism. God calls everyone to conversion. The conversion normally starts after that person or a business makes the worst mistaken in their life. Consequently, that business or person has to pay for the damage from that worst mistake, this is called the iniquities; the biblical symbolism is quail or blood.

Jesus the Lord used the earthly court judgment penalty to transform to spiritual penalty. The spiritual penalty will be paid during the earthly life or the soul retained purgatory after each individual last breath until all the penalties are fulfilled, or be punished by being chained in the darkness of the devil forever.

35

MARIETTE'S SPECIAL ASSIGNMENT

On Monday June 29, 1998, the Lord Jesus told me, "It takes too long for your attorney to file a motion for New York Life to resume your monthly and past due benefits. You need to go see the judge that the case is assigned to. During the night of July 3, 1998, He told me, "Retype the declaration draft you received from Patty, make copies of all the exhibits, make three sets of copies, take all three sets and ask the judge to let you file it. Send one copy to the New York Life attorney, keep one for you; and let the judge call your attorney in."

Before I got up on Monday, July 6, 1998, Jesus the Lord told me, "Call your attorney before you go to mass, leave the message with his answering service, and ask Patty to spare you a few minutes between nine thirty and ten, and you go over see him before you go see the judge."

After the mass I went home instead, to see if Patty called me, but there was no message. I then went to Mr. Eugene P. Yale, my attorney's office. Patty brought me a declaration to sign, and told me that Mr. Yale was not in that day. The Lord told me, "Ask her to make you a copy of it and go to the court." She asked me to read it and sign it, but I told her, "Would you give me a copy of it, I need to go home pray, read it, sign and bring it back." She did. Before I left, I told her, "You may be surprised." I then went to the State Superior Court to see the judge.

Footnote: The word "judge" alone in this revelation is symbolic of the Lord Jesus. God uses Earthly Court actions to transform His justice upon the world.

Declaration of Mariette Do-Nguyen in Support Motion for Preliminary Injunction

I, Mariette Do-Nguyen, declare:

1. I am the plaintiff in the above-entitled action. I make this declaration in support of my application for a preliminary injunction restraining the defendant from terminating my disability insurance benefits and from terminating the waiver of premium benefits for my life insurance. I have personal knowledge of the facts stated herein, and if called to testify. I could and would competently testify thereto.

2. Prior to and in 1994. I was an independent contractor insurance agent affiliated with New York Life Insurance Company. In connection with my profession, I purchased individual disability income insurance, life insurance, health insurance and group Long Term Disability Insurance from New York Life. A true and correct copy of the subject individual disability income policy is attached hereto as Exhibit 1

3. On January 12, 1994, I became totally disabled and unable to perform the substantial and material duties of my occupation as an insurance agent. My health conditions has not improved since that time. In April 1994, I submitted a claim to New York Life for individual disability income insurance and group long term disability insurance benefits. New York Life honored my claims effective January 12, 1994. In that year I was being treated by Gerald E. Nelson, M.D., who diagnosed my medical condition as "delusional disorder." On April 19, 1994, Dr. Nelson prepared and sent an "attending physician's statement" to New York Life, where he included that diagnosis and further stated that "it is unlikely that the patient will be able to return to work." A copy of Dr. Nelson's attending physician's statement is attached hereto as Exhibit 2. New York Life started pay benefits.

4. In September, 1995, New York Life required me to be examined by a psychiatrist of their choice. Dr. Abrams. After Dr. Abrams examined me, New York Life continued paying my benefits.

5. In 1996, I was being treated by Nicholas Frost M.D. On August 5, 1996, Dr. Frost filled out and returned to New York Life a "Psychiatric Functional Limitation Analysis From." Dr. Frost diagnosed my medical condition as "delusional disorder." Dr. Frost wrote. "Probable Permanent Disability." A copy of this report is attached as Exhibit 3. New York Life continued to pay benefits.

6. In 1997, I was being treated by Walter Strybel, M.D. Dr. Strybel submitted "attending physician's statements to New York Life, wherein he diagnosed my condition as "delusional disorder" New York Life continued to pay benefits.

7. In October 1997, New York Life directed me to submit to a medical examination with a psychiatrist of their choice, Dr. Bergsma, and also required that I submit to an

examination by a Psychologist of their choice, Dr. Fernando Melendez, I attended both examinations.

8. In March, 1998, New York Life terminated my insurance benefits, claiming that Dr. Bergsma and Dr. Melendez, were of the opinion that I could function satisfactorily at my usual occupation of a licensed insurance agent.

9. Later, Dr. Strybel advised New York Life that I was still disabled, and was unable to work. Despite this, New York Life did not reinstate my benefits. A copy of this report is attached as Exhibit 4.

10. In early May 1998, I received an April 30, 1998 letter from Ann Ford, a corporate officer of New York Life, again denying my insurance benefits. Ms. Ford stated that the reason for the termination of my insurance benefits was because: "The diagnosis of Delusional Disorder has not been proven."

11. In May, 1998, I received treatment and an evaluation from Catherine Moore, M. D. Dr. Moore wrote a letter to New York Life on May 11, 1998, advising that I suffer from "delusional disorder." and that I am disabled and unable to work. A copy of that letter is attached as exhibit 5.

12. Later in May 1998, I was evaluated by Roy Resnikoff, M.D. Dr. Resnikoff sent a report to New York Life on May 22, 1998, where he diagnosed my condition as "delusional disorder" and told them that I am unable to work. A copy of Dr. Resnikoff's report is attached as Exhibit 6.

13. Because Dr. Moore charged for cash payment before each visit, and she submitted to Medicare for payments, I do not have money to continue treatment with her because New York Life discontinued paying my benefits. My current psychiatrist, Ronald H. Gold, M.D. is also of the opinion that I suffer from "delusional disorder," and that I am unable to work.

14. Despite the fact that at least seven licensed psychiatrists have diagnosed my medical condition as "delusional disorder," and that I am unable to work, and despite the fact that after having me examined by a psychiatrist of their choice in 1995 New York Life continued to payment insurance benefits. New York Life has terminated my benefits because my condition of "delusional disorder has not been proven."

15. Because of my disability, my life insurance premiums have been waived by New York Life. When they terminated my disability related benefits as of March 1, 1998. New York Life also terminated my life insurance waiver of premiums benefits. I cannot afford to pay my life insurance premiums. I request that the court enjoin New York Life from terminating this benefit and that they be ordered to reinstate my life insurance protection until the trial is completed in this case.

16. New York Life terminated my disability related benefits with knowledge that I have qualified for and receive Social Security Disability benefits due to my "delusional

disorder" medical condition. I received $ xxxx (the actual amount filled in court) per month from Social Security, which is not enough for me to pay my bills. A copy of a check for July 1998 is attached as Exhibit 7. My monthly income from my New York Life insurance benefits was in excess of $4,200 per month. I have no other source of income.

17. On June 17, 1998, my mortgage lender started foreclosure proceeding against my house. A copy of the notice from them is attached as exhibit 8.

18. On June 13 1998, my automobile insurance company canceled my insurance for non payment of premium. A copy of that notice is attached as Exhibit 9.

19. On April 24, 1998, my homeowners insurance company canceled my homeowners insurance. A copy of that notice is attached as Exhibit 9.

20. I own a five year old Nissan car. My car payment are about $475 per month. My payments are more than two months past due. I am worried that the lender will repossess my car, leaving me with no transportation.

21. My car registration past due on June 20, 1998. I do not have the funds to register my car. A copy of vehicle registration renewal notice is attached as Exhibit 11.

22. I want a second independent medical examination report, but I have no money; Medicare only pays for therapy. On July 1, 1998, I went to Dr. Sleem Ishaque at xxx Washington Street, suite xxx, San Diego, California 92103, his telephone number is (619) xxx-xxxx. He gave me three samples of "Risperdal," each sample contains ten tables, for a total of 30 tablets. There are the same kind of medicine that Dr. Frost prescribed to me.

23. Unless New York Life is restrained and enjoined from stopping my $4,200 + per month insurance benefits until trial in this case, unless New York Life is restrained and enjoined from terminating my waiver of premium benefits for my life Insurance (and ordered to reinstate my life insurance), and unless New York Life is ordered to pay my benefits that have been withheld since March 1, 1998. I will lose my house, lose my car, lose my life insurance, lose my liability insurance, and have my credit rating ruined. I do not have anybody to financially support me.

I declare under penalty of perjury under the laws of the United States that the foregoing is true and correct. Executed this 9 day of July, 1998, at San Diego, California.

Signed by Mariette Do-Nguyen

Rebuild My Church Divine Mission

(The Lord Jesus gave this name to Mariette)

P.O. Box 261550 ✦ San Diego, CA 92196-1550

July 6, 1998

Eugene P. Yale, Esq
Law Offices of Eugene P. Yale
San Diego, CA 92101

Dear Mr. Yale,

This is something I am not eager to do, but I must protect myself. I have been trying very hard to comply with everything you asked me to do to obtain a hearing and requesting the judge to order New York Life to resume my monthly benefits. But after a number of promises, I see no action of the motion being filed.

Early this morning, July 6, 1998, I left a message with your answering machine saying I would come by to discuss the matter of filing a motion and hearing date for New York Life to resume my monthly benefits; but you were busy and not in the office today. Patty told me that the motion may be filed this week. I know this will not happen if I do not take steps to protect my interests. I went to the Superior Court with my declaration and tried to see Judge Vincent P. Di Figlia, to see if he could help me. I approached Mr. Fong Vu, Court Marshall at Judge P. Di Figlia's Court, department 42, and asked him if I could see Judge Di Figlia. I explained my situation; he refused, but he saw I was crying, he went to the Court Clerk for information, then returned and told me that there was no answer from New York Life on file. I kept insisting to see the Judge, so he then went to the Court Clerk a second time. The Court Clerk came and explained to me the form that needs to be used. She then told me to find a substitute attorney, and gave me the telephone number for the San Diego Bar Association. I asked her to clarify what the Court Marshall told me about there being no answer on file, and she told me that the case is new and that the defendant has not file the answered.

When I got home, I called your office to find out if you had received an answer from New York Life. I learned from Patty that your office received the answer a few weeks ago.

Regardless of whether answer has been filed or not, New York Life must resume my monthly benefits, so I can bring my house out from foreclosure, pay my car registration, my car payments, my automobile and homeowner insurance, and all other bills that are months past due.

Therefore, I must take action: If I do not have the hearing within 10 days from today, June 6, 1998. Would you kindly sign the substitution of attorney form and mail it to me.

I am very sorry for any inconvenience, but I must protect myself, otherwise I will be the victim for the second in the same matter, and I will be homeless.

Sincerely in Christ Jesus,

Mariette Do-Nguyen

Rebuild My Church Divine Mission
(The Lord Jesus gave this name to Mariette)
P.O. Box 261550 ✦ San Diego, CA 92196-1550

July 7, 1998

Mariette Do-Nguyen
San Diego, CA 92126

Sent Via Facsimile and U.S. Mail

Re: Do-Nguyen V. New York Life

Reference your July 6 fax. Your case has a high priority in my office. As you know, I have other clients with pressing legal problems who also need my assistance. I understand the urgency of your financial pressures. That's why I started preparing an injunction motion as soon as you showed me the foreclosure papers and other documentation of your financial status. I need your cooperation so we can put our best case in front of the judge when we attempt to require New York Life to reinstated your benefits pending trial.

I have represented insured against insurance companies for twenty years. I taught insurance law for ten years at the University of San Diego, School of Law. I am very knowledgeable about insurance litigation matters. I need you to allow me to represent you to the best of my abilities. In my professional opinion, you may jeopardize your case by going to the courthouse and asking to see the judge.

As we discussed in our initial office conference, defendants who are "residents" of states other than California have the right to automatically transfer lawsuits filed in the Superior Court of California to the Federal

District Court, and that New York Life probably would exercise that right. New York Life did transfer your case to Federal Court in San Diego.

I have obtained the earliest available hearing date for our motion for an injunction. In Federal Court, you cannot obtain a hearing date until your pleading are ready to be filed. We have to file and serve your pleading by next Monday. As I explained, it is difficult to obtain an injunction requiring a defendant to de something affirmative (such as the payment of past benefits). I believe we have a good shot at having the court prohibit New York Life from refusing to pay currents and future benefits until trial, but it will be more difficult to persuade the judge to require them to pay you the past due benefits from February to the present, although I will make every effort to obtain that order.

In Federal Court, the remedy of a Temporary Restraining Order is available, but, unfortunately, the judge will consider this type of request only be the submission f written pleadings. The Court usually does not allow the plaintiff's attorney (or the plaintiff) to appear in person. We are preparing an ex parte application for a temporary restraining order on your behalf, but I do want to discuss this with you in more detail when we meet tomorrow. Basically, I recommend that for the temporary restraining order, we request that the court prohibit New York Life from withholding your monthly benefits that are presently due and will be due in the future, pending a trial on the merits. Then, in the injunction motion, I suggest that we request that New York Life has to pay the past due benefits as well.

I believe in your case. I believe that New York Life has done you a terrible injustice. I have already invested considerable time, effort and expense in representing your interest. I need your assurance that you will cooperate with me and allow me to persecute your claims without have to worry about your going to court and asking to see the judge. In my experience, judges have very little patience with plaintiffs who do these things. I certainly understand your fear and frustration about what New York Life did to you, but please remember that you and I are on the same side and need to work together in order to have the best opportunity to prevail in this lawsuit.

Very truly yours,

Eugene P. Yale

God's Teaching vs. Man

On July 8, 1998, Dr. Gold informed me that my symptom was paranoid schizophrenia. I then met with him again on July 13, 1998, and I asked him, "Dr. Gold, what is the difference between Delusional Disorder, Grandiose Type and Paranoid Schizophrenia?" He replied, "That is a very interesting question. They are similar."

I then read an article "Paranoid schizophrenia defies nation's efforts" in the San Diego Union Tribune. It was regarding Russell E. Weston Jr. , the suspect in the fatal shooting of two police officers in the nation's Capital. In this article, psychiatrists speak of Mr. Weston Jr's. mental suffering as paranoid schizophrenia. This article indicated, "More than 4 million Americans suffer from schizophrenia in a variety of forms. It typically is a lifelong condition that waxes and wanes even with ongoing treatment." After I read this article I knew of the cause and how to heal the paranoid schizophrenia.

July 30, 1998, I met with Dr. Gold again. I told him of this article, and explained to him that the Delusional Disorder, Grandiose Type is the gift for the prophets in the old testament, it comes with the gift of discernment. The gift of discernment will discern what comes from God, and what comes from the devil, and the devil has no power over them. Because the life of prophets includes much suffering, they must completely obey all God's commandments. They only obey God, not man, and their lives are very peaceful in tremendous suffering. Because God uses the natural environment as symbolism to reveal to man in spirit, prophets have to pray to understand the meaning of these symbolism. When these revelations come down to earth, they come as the way the prophets understand, not what they see or heard in the spirit. Doctors do not understand the symbolism, and the medical profession calls it "Delusional Disorder, Grandiose Type."

On August 12, 1998, I repeated the above information to Dr. Gold for a second time. I also told him of his diagnosed my symptoms of paranoid schizophrenia. Because I was meeting with him in the middle of litigation with my insurance company. New York Life caused me tremendous suffering by stopping the payment of my benefits; and these visits with Dr. Gold were so short that Dr. Gold did not have the information of what God told me and the works He asked me to do. For example, I have to petition the U. S. Tax Court for the civil right of freedom of religion. Asking the court for tax laws to be passed, allowing U. S. citizens to choose how our monies are to be used in funding government programs. This will restore freedom of religion, voiding the U.S. government's forcing citizens to sin against God and one another. It will benefit souls and earthly life, bringing God's peace into the world; and to build the kingdom of heaven

The people diagnosed with paranoid schizophrenia are hearing supernatural voices, seeing visions, and they also feel supernatural power. These people have no discernment, they do not understand the symbolism. These voices and visions also came with the power

690

of the devil, and force people to take actions as the voices tell them. These people are filled with fear and their actions are harmful to others and themselves, lead to destruction.

On July 31, 1998, I was at Mr. Yale's office. Patty Santos handed me a letter from Joan E. Brady, Assistant Vice President for New York Life Insurance Company, dated July 20, 1998. In this letter she indicated, "On July 13, 1998, one of your treating physicians, Ronald H. Gold, M.D., submitted a declaration to the United States District Court wherein he opined that you were suffering from paranoid schizophrenia. This is the first time that we have received a diagnosis of paranoid schizophrenia. This diagnosis, when compared with Drs. Moore, Resnikoff and Strybel's opinion that you were totally disabled from the distinct condition, delusional disorder, caused concern that you have been misdiagnosed for a number of years." I left to Mr. Yale a note as follows:

Rebuild My Church Divine Mission
(The Lord Jesus gave this name to Mariette)
P.O. Box 261550 ✦ San Diego, CA 92196-1550

Dear Mr. Yale,

Paranoid schizophrenia and delusional disorders are similar. The paranoid schizophrenia has voices that are unidentified; the delusional disorder, grandiose type also manifests supernatural voices, but they can be identified. My case is delusional disorder, grandiose type, not paranoid schizophrenia. But if people do not believe what is delivered to the world, they will call it paranoid schizophrenia. For those do not understand the symbolism, they will say "delusional disorder." The New York Life people are trying to be my "doctors," and their doctors are trying to be the "judges."

If you need more information, please let me know.

Sincerely in Christ Jesus,

Mariette Do-Nguyen

Doctor Gold's Appointment

On August 18, 1998. Immediately after I entered Dr. Gold's office, he said, "You did not bring the report from Dr. Bergma." I replied, "The Lord told me to give you the answer, 'you will not have the report from Dr. Bergma, because on that report he acted like a judge, not a doctor. The Lord wants you to be a doctor and not a judge. He did answer your prayer when you sent the request to Dr. Bergma and New York Life. Both of them did not send a report to you. God now told me not to give it to you. God's answer to you is that you will not have this report." Dr. Gold then said, "God did not answer to me that I want the report." I said, "You asked Him for the report, and His answer is 'no'." He was sad that God did not let him have this report.

He then asked, "Tell me about your trip." I replied, "I have not gone yet." He said, "I know, tomorrow. What time you are leaving?" I replied, "Around noon. I go for three purposes: first, I will meet with an Archbishop, he is the President of the Pontifical Council of Justice and Peace, a Catholic, he comes from the Vatican. He is Vietnamese, I have been writing to him, and the meeting is about asking him to speak of Catholic leaders needing to convert, to obey all God's commandments, so they can lead people in converting to God. Secondly, I will be meeting with Senator John Ashcroft's representative. I will talk to her of how Congress passed laws that contradict each other. On one hand they say "freedom of religion in United States", on the other hand the government uses tax monies for purposes that go against God's commandments. This action violates the civil right to freedom of religion and forces the citizens to sin against God and one another. They said President Bill Clinton obstructed the justice, and they are violating the citizens freedom of religion.   I will also speak to them of other issues............Thirdly, when I am there, I will spend some time with priests and laity attending the commemoration of the 200th anniversary of the Mother of Our Lord Jesus appearing to people in Vietnam."

Dr. Gold then said, "I have to go to a deposition on Wednesday on your case with five other doctors. Do you know anything about this?" I replied, "Mr. Yale is away, so I have not heard from him yet." He then said, "What are they going to ask me?" I said, "The lady from New York Life wrote me a letter and said, 'Drs. Nelson, Strybel, Frost, and other have diagnosed my symptom as Delusional Disorder, your diagnosis is paranoid schizophrenia. She said that I was misdiagnosed. But actually when I came to you in the middle of the New York Life benefits problem, that situation put a tremendous amount of suffering on me. All the time we spent was talking about New York Life, so you do not have enough information for proper diagnosis."

I continued, "Some people see things in spirit with spirit eyes that others can not see. What we see in spirit is symbolism. I have to pray for understanding. For example, if I saw you sitting now in my dream or vision, I must understand it as: You are looking at the calendar; this is symbolic that you are planning. You are wearing vertical navy blue stripes that do not cross, this symbolizes plan to go up high. You are wearing eyes glasses, not sun glasses, this is symbolic of discernment. Your leaning back is symbolic of your relaxing when you plan for the future. Your watch also adds to the calendar, planning for time in the future. Your navy blue pants... navy has to do with water, and water is purification. Your gray hair has to do with being elderly, meaning respect. Because people do not understand the symbolism, they said delusion, and it is in medical code." He said, "That made sense."

New York Life Name on Yellow Banner

July 15, 1998. In my dream I was in a room of a military track housing; between my house and the next door neighbor we shared a glass wall. Look through the wall, I saw a lady was sitting on the bed, and her husband was walking back and forward in the room, close to her bed. She was arguing with her husband, and her husband was also talking to her, it seemed like he was trying to explain to her so she could calm down.

I then was on my covered patio, looking through the glass wall that we shared, the couple was also at their covered patio. The man was walking back and forward, but now he was standing in one spot, on his head was a large bowl that curved at the rim, like the bottom of a squid, it was up side down like a turban. Next to him his wife sat on ground, she was complaining, " I have brought this matter to you a number of time during the week in the house, but it did not end." She then spoke louder, " Now I have to bring this matter to you on Sunday so it can have a result."

When I heard she said, " Now I have to bring this matter to you on Sunday so it can have a result" I said something to her, she then stopped.

The dream changed: I was in a huge one story hanger, at the center wall of the room was a king size water bed. While I was standing close to its foot, I saw a small yellow cloth with the words "New York Life" in navy blue dropped on the ground and unfolded. I then saw another piece, in the same fabric and color, a lot larger that unfolded laying on the ground, at the foot of the bed; I went and picked it up, it was a large and long banner. While I was folding it, I saw the words "New York Life" also in navy blue.

The next morning, at the Holy Eucharist celebration, immediately after I received the body and blood of our Lord; I was filed with Spirit of God, I proclaimed, "Father, I proclaim in front of You, the Lord Jesus, and the Holy Spirit. Also in front of my beloved Blessed Virgin Mother, all the holy angels and saints, and the world. I am the Eternal Father's Emissary. The only Emissary sent by the Father in this mission, as a Vessel to the Lord Jesus and the Holy Spirit." I then heard the Blessed Virgin Mother's voice come from Her statue that was salvaged from the temple that burned, she said, "What you have in your thoughts is from the Father, use them, keep them in secret, let the attorney do all the talking."

An attorney symbolic of the Lord Jesus, New York Life Insurance company is it self and also symbolic of earthly business. Yellow color symbolic of empty; in this revelation symbolic of the earthly business's system will be crushed by the Almighty God.

Rebuild My Church Divine Mission

(The Lord Jesus gave this name to Mariette)

P.O. Box 261550 ✦ San Diego, CA 92196-1550

July 17, 1998

Eugene P. Yale, Esq
Eugene P. Yale Law Offices
San Diego, CA 92101

Dear Mr. Yale,

Thank for your fax yesterday. As I have shared with you for the last few days, God entrusted to me the most difficult position in the world. God works through me, and there is much love that I have for every one, that includes enemies. Therefore, I pour out a lot of love for people at New York Life who are treating me as criminal with injustice. The more they wrong me, the more God's power works through me. If they do not convert, there will be huge damage to the company in a number of different ways, that God has not revealed to them through their thoughts yet; and these words are trust worthy.

God entrusted to me the mission to purify the world's systems. Over the last several years, God has put me through different tasks, and asked me to record in the books, for uncounted numbers of generations in the future. The situation of New York Life will be recorded the same like others; I must record exactly what happened, together with God's revelations. Therefore, I have embraced all the pain and suffering so the New York Life people can be converted.

There are uncounted numbers of people being betrayed or taken advantage of by insurance companies and/or psychiatric doctors. The New York Life is dealing with God, and I am just His agent, my responsibility is to deliver loud and clear of exactly what God asks of me. With God's power with and in me, I will bring justice into insurance systems, the nation, and throughout the world. God knows everyone's heart, and He respects free will. These people have the choice to obey or not to obey. If the New York Life people convert, each individual will be blessed as well as the company; but if they refuse, then this blessing will fall to others; these are prophetic words.

I want to deliver them a message, "Do to others as you want them do unto to you."

Thank you for serving God in assisting me in this case. By the way, would you help with an attorney specializing in constitutional issues.

Sincerely in Christ Jesus,

Mariette Do-Nguyen

Each Step God Bestowed on His Servant is Firm

July 17, 1998, was the Early Evaluation and settlements conference of the case against New York Life, at United States Judge's chamber. New York Life requested the settlement dollars amount to be confidential, and for me not to talk about New York Life. I responded to the Magistrate, "This matter is not for New York Life Insurance Company alone, it is for the insurance industry, they have been treating people before, and me, unjustly. I am in this case to let people know, so they can protect themselves. I cannot accept their request of not talking about New York Life." The Magistrate asked my attorney, Mr. Yale of the amount for settlement of the case so she can relate it to the New York Life people and their two attorneys. On my behalf, Mr. Yale used the present value of my benefits to age 65 and five months past due of my two policies, he arrived at $500,000, and his fee at this time is $166,000. The total of the settlement demand is $666,000.

After the Magistrate met with the New York Life representative, she told us that the New York Life said that was too much money, and offered a settlement of $300,000. She also informed us that the New York Life attorney and their representative want to keep the settlement confidential; they do not want me to speak about New York Life. I rejected their offer. I asked the Magistrate for New York Life to resume my monthly benefits, and pay my past due benefits. The Magistrate told us that the New York Life people said my Group Long Term Disability policy was sold few days ago. I said, "Why did they sell my policy?" she said that they properly sold them with other policies. In my thought, "What does that have to do with me? Their problem." Then my attorney, Mr. Yale said, "That is interesting that the policy sold; they can settle the case, but can not resume her monthly benefit."

After I rejected the New York Life offer; Magistrate Aaron commented about the three number sixes. I said, the three number sixes was revealed in the Book of Revelation. After

Mr. Yale and I left Magistrate Aaron's office, I explained to him a little of the meaning of three number sixes.

On the first day, the New York Life Insurance Company attorney brought up the Lord Jesus web site, and a $4,200 unauthorized loan that New York Life took out from my life insurance policies' cash value and sent to the Internal Revenue Service, violating my civil right to freedom of religion.

When I got out of the U.S Court House the enemy spirits attacked my physical body and mind heavily, and became physically powerless. My appetite left me, I ate very little all day, and went to sleep.

The next morning, I went to the Blessed Sacrament chapel in a spirit of physical weakness that I had never experienced before. Immediately after I kneeled on the kneeler, and leaned my elbow on the panel and said, "Lord Father, Jesus, Holy Spirit, I can not talk any more." The voice spoke out from the tabernacle, "The revelation you received yesterday is not about New York Life, not insurance companies, it is you, you were charged with murder by the world." He paused, I asked, "Lord, what do you mean the world." The angel said, "They crucified your brother, and the Father raised Him up. You stood at the foot of the Cross. The Father raised you up today. Give them a week or two. There will be another set of people, whom you know will come and meet with you." I asked, "Lord, the another week or two of your time or nature. I am the handmaid's lowliness of God. I follow my beloved Blessed Virgin Mother's footsteps. God has done great things for me. Holy is His name. All ages will call me blessed." I then saw the angel to the right, above my head departed from me.

When the Lord said "The revelation you received yesterday is not New York Life, not insurance companies, it is you, you are being charging by the world with murder." He mean that the devil works through human bodies. The devil used people before to crucify Jesus the Lord. Because God sent me down as the Vessel to the Lord Jesus, for Him to continue His mission, then the devil, his fallen angels and souls are under the devil's authority are using humans, charged me by twisting my words, to harm me; but God is the most powerful. He raised me up to serve him, through services to others in love.

In the same day afternoon, I was exhausted and fell asleep. In my dream, I saw my son and his wife about several feet away from me, they were holding my granddaughter Madelene. On their way out, both of them turned to their left and looked at me before they left. I heard, "Madelene, you go with your parents, and come back later." Madelene is symbolic of conversion; but her parents took her away, and she will return is symbolic that there will be a lot of conversion after they go through many tribulations, and problems that humans can do nothing about, then they will convert to God.

The Only Electric Sky Cable Car

July 18, 1997. In my dream I was standing on the ground, there was a road as high as my belly dividing this house in two, both sides of the road were open. There was a double iron rail on the ceiling above the road. At the time I saw an electric cable car just pass the center of the sky railroad; after this cable car passed, it left several heavy iron bars, like horse shoes with a tail, hanging on both ends of the sky rail, and their tails were swinging back and forth. This cable car was like a table, and had a box built below it, there was no wall, and was hanging to the iron sky rail with invisible cables. When I saw this, I was afraid for two people who were sitting on it because the cable car was on its way to leave the house again. I heard the angel's voice say, "They came from another Island, and only come once in a while." I then looked toward the side that the cable car entered, it was white cloud sky, I knew this cable car came from heaven, but the voice called it an island.

I then was walking in the huge bank lobby, when I got in the waiting line next to the rope, suddenly people got in front of me, and there was a dais in front of them. I then saw some people carrying a very expensive coffin in at the middle of the lobby; the top and the rim of the coffin was open about six inches; I was afraid of the dead body when I was in that open area, I backed up a few steps; they then laid the coffin on the dais, next to a dead body laying on a huge dry dark banana leaf. I knew they were transferring the dead body into the coffin; I feared the dead body more than seeing a hole around the coffin. I then hurried and turned around and ran out the door. After I left the bank door, I passed a large dry dirt ground, to another building opposite that bank lobby building; I turned around, and I saw a dark young woman had just pulled the dead body from the dais out the same door I just left, and laid at the door step. She raised both of her hands and screamed as loud as she could.

I then was standing inside my bedroom on the second floor, to my right was the entrance to my bedroom, in front of me was young girl in light colors. This girl was waist high to me, she leaned the back of her head at my belly. I looked in front of her, she wore a long skirt that had a slit at her right front thigh; her male genital was long and stuck out at the slit. I told her, "You have changed your sex recently." While I was saying this, both of my hands examined her breasts, her breasts were flat like a man. Then her male organ got inside her skirt.   A big dark woman entered my bedroom door, passed into my bathroom in angry voice saying, "Trying to save the marriage." I replied to her, "How about there is no marriage to save."

The island is symbolic of heaven. Several iron horseshoes are symbolic of God turning the earthly church systems around. The very expense coffin is symbolic of businesses, non-profit organizations, governments officials, and lawmakers advertising themselves in good standard, but in front of God they are stink. The coffin not closed all the way is symbolic of their evil deeds leading to the public. The dark dead body laying on a dark banana leaf and being pulled to the door step is symbolic of God bringing all the evil doers works to the light. A dark big woman being angry and passing by me into my bedroom are the same dead body laying on dark dry banana leaf, their works are against God's commandments, generating unjust actions, harming people. Now God opens it to the public.   Saving the marriage is symbolic of trying to hide the unjust action to save their reputation. Her going to the bathroom is symbolic of their coming to conversion. The young adult leaning her head to me is symbolic of those preaching the good things, but when it come to actions they are mixed of good and evil. I responded to her, "How about there is no marriage to save" means through me, God revealed that they have not done any good deeds to deserve a good reputation.

Wallet and Ruler

July 19, 1998. In my dream I was walking in a circle on a huge concrete ground open field. I saw a black small wallet laying next to a damage spot on the ground, next to the wallet was a U.S. fifty dollar bill folded in fourths, and three dollar bills in one stack also folded in fourths. I picked them up, held them in my left hand. At my right hand was a wooden ruler; I used this ruler to press the wallet and money tightly to my palm. I continue to my walk, there was a man looking on the ground and walking at the same time; he was looking for something that he lost. I called him over, showed him the wallet and money with the ruler pressing at my palm, I said, "Are you looking for this?" He shook his head. While I was saying this to him, I saw the fifty dollar bill change to a one hundred, and became two but in one fifty and hundred. I then heard, "Mariette, do not give it to him." It seemed after I heard this the dream was ended, but the dream continued.

I heard, "They [wallet, cash, ruler] are you, do not give them away.   Fifty, three, one hundred, three, ruler, and wallet. Add five to three to equal eight means the supernatural realm. The ruler is the Father's righteousness for you to rule the devil within the human race. One hundred is obedience; three is the Holy Trinity. One has five must have three, has one hundred also must have three."

The Lord continued, "In your dream you saw a man passed away and his wife still on earth. They made people who see God filled out a form and turn it in the same day. But you did not follow their rule. You told them you would bring it back tomorrow. He then told you early in the morning, and you knew that you would not bring it in early the next morning, but you did not respond to him. To avoid arguing, you kept silent. Do not let them persuade you."

The Lord continued, "There is an institution in U.S. searching for people who see God and understand. There are a few others who see God, but do not recognize Him, many are seeing the devil. They do not understand the symbolism, so they are called delusional. All others said you are delusional, but God gave to the last one who called you paranoid."

The Lord continued, "You are doing things that are different from them. You understand the reasons of what you do; they do not understand so they call you crazy. The man searching for the lost symbolic spiritual leaders. They thought they had God's power working through them, but now they understand that they are not......"

Church's Bell Blast

July 14, 1998. In my dream I saw a Church, to its right was a square bell tower, it was built with four concrete columns. Up high at the middle of the four sides, a bar connected the four columns. The roof was four triangular pieces of red title. While I looked inside the roof, the bell was ringing very fast with a loud voice. I then saw the lower levels of the tower, there were two white sheets of papers full of printing, with a large bold title "Settled out of court".

Before I left Saint Michael's temple, I went in front of the Blessed Mother's statue, (only this Blessed Virgin Mother statue and a cross from the top of the temple were salvaged from Saint Michael's temple was destroyed by fire,) and asked her to pray to the Lord for me and be with me at all time, especially at the conference that I going to at United States Court House. She said to me, "When the Lord called me, I was very young. I used what had been available to me at the time, and all of them were from the Lord provided for me. I became who I am. You use the sources that you have; they are come from the Father. They will give you what you asked on your declaration." When she said this, in my vision, I saw the paragraph number 23 on my declaration.

"23. Unless New York Life is restrained and enjoined from stopping my \$4,200 + per month insurance benefits until trial in this case, unless New York Life is restrained and enjoined from terminating my waiver of premium benefits for my life Insurance (and ordered to reinstate my life insurance), and unless New York Life is ordered to pay my benefits that have been withheld since March 1, 1998. I will lose my house, lose my car, lose my life insurance, lose my liability insurance, and have my credit rating ruined. I do not have anybody to financially support me."

Later in the same night I saw the Federal Superior Judge's chamber where I was during the morning for the Early Evaluation Conference of case "Do-Nguyen v. New York Life Insurance Company"

There was the Judge's desk, to the right of the Judge was a sofa, I sat on one side of the sofa, and my attorney, Mr. Yale sat at my left, behind me was the Our Lady of Guadeloupe Image. The sun behind the Blessed Virgin Mother in the Image was shinning out fire mingled with light. Facing the Judge's desk were four people; two of New York Life representatives, and two of their attorneys; were sitting in four separate chairs. Our Lady of Guadeloupe image behind me is symbolic of through me, they are facing the

Almighty God, many people will convert to God.

Flaming Heart Embraces Cross

After I returned from receiving the body and blood of our Lord; in my vision I saw the front of Our Lady of Lavang temple in New Orleans. The last spot I saw the Lord Jesus in my dream on August 2, 1992. This time I only saw His heart in the mid of the air. The heart was more clear: the cord, and flame was rising on top, and then a cross was added in front of it, and then the Lord Jesus was hanging on the Cross. The Lord said, "This is not an apple, it is gold." I kept silent, and then I saw the heart in front of my physical body, and it slowly entered into my heart. This is symbolic of the cross that I am carrying, God will rewarded me with His fire of love in me.

I then went to the Blessed Sacrament chapel; immediately I kneeled on the kneeler, laid my head on my arms on the panel, and I pleaded, "Brother Jesus, help me to listen, remember, and do everything exactly as the Father revealed to me through You." My brother Jesus said to me, "You do not need to copy this down, I will remind you. Go home; your son will find no house to buy, he will ask you to remain in the house for several months." I knew that Jesus did not talk about my son, but instead, he talked about me. He continued, "He is you, you stay in the house until the legal litigation is completed. Mattha being score, and Madelene has been rewarded. Mattha is Church leaders, Madelene is you. Be careful of what you say, stand firm."

July 20, 1998, at about 1:42 p.m. Mr. Yale's paralegal called and said, "Mr. Yale said New York Life will reinstead you benefits, you will received a check within a day or two. Mr. Yale will call you tomorrow when he comes in. They [New York Life] may also reinstead the six hundred policy as well." After I hung up the telephone, I went to the front of the altar, and gave thanks to the Lord. He gave me 2 King 4:7

She went and told the man of God, who said, "Go and sell the oil to pay off your creditors; with what remains, you and your children can live."

Before I fell asleep for the night I prayed, "Lord Jesus, I know that I have see you and heard You, but still it is not enough for me. I wish that I could see You and hear your voice like two people talking in the nature. You have promised "Who seeks will find, who asks will receive, who knocks the door will be opened." Jesus the Lord said to me, "Have faith in me, your wish will be fulfilled." Today during my afternoon devotion the Lord Jesus told me in a different statement but same meaning. "I take care of you, answer to your needs by sending other people, from church and government in high positions to assist you. When you speak, those who don't want to hear you, they just laugh at you and leave; those want to hear they will bow at your feet. If I came down as a man they would try to kill me. (The Lord meant as a human physical body with no title and do the work that He entrusted to me.) I said, "Lord, they are not bowing at my feet, they are bowing at your feet. I anointed your feet with the most expensive oil, wiped it with my tears, and smeared it with my heart."

July 21, 1998. In my dream I saw the Blessed Virgin Mother statue at the altar in my house. Fire started from the left hem of her white silver veil and raised up to the back of her left shoulder."

Later in the same day, I received the Independent Medical Report from New York Life order through Dr. Bergsma. I read the major part of it, and the Lord Jesus told me, "I have told you, they crucified me, and they are trying to murder your reputation. The servant is not greater then the master. Did I tell you before, the world came to videotape you outside the Church. They came to your house to do reports, and offered to cause troubles to others, but you refused their evil actions."

He continued, "Just swallow that report for me, put it away. Michelle had swallowed something by a priest, and later the priest would be the one who delivered to her an award "Woman of the Year." ....The devil's spirit works through doctors, and the New York Life. I will have them to pay your full benefit, your attorney, and assist you with Tax Court expenses."

Brother and Sister Responsibility to God

September 10, 1998. In my dream I saw my light soft cream blouse. The wide round back neck was laying from one shoulder to another, and the front neck was laying lower next to the back, they were parallel.

I then saw my cafe cappuccino cast iron strainer had cafÈ after being strained laying on its side in the kitchen sink, next to it were two small glass cafÈ pots. They had black handles and metal around that was glued to the handles, one was clear glass and another light tan.

I then saw I was holding a loaf of unleavened bread, at the other side was an invisible hand holding a bowl of cotton dry meat. I was about to use the cotton dry meat to make a sandwich, but I remembered I was fasting and do not eat meat. I then decided not to make a sandwich. I saw I was eating unleavened bread alone. (The unleavened bread symbolic of humble).

When I got up the Lord Jesus told me, "You came down to serve, through you, I will purify the world systems. You are obedient to the Father. You do not need to send a letter to the Nationwide Insurance company chairman of the board; instead, change its name to Nation Fire and Casualty Insurance Company. For New York Life Insurance's settlement, take whatever it is. You are not to argue like the world systems do. The Father will bless you in many ways."

The front neck is symbolic of me, Mariette that people can see with human eyes. The back neck higher than the front is symbolic of God is the one pouring His power upon me,

He is working through me, but people can not see Him with their natural eyes.

The café from the cast iron strainer is symbolic of the same mission. The clear glass pot is symbolic of the Lord Jesus as fully man never having any sins. The light tan glass pot is symbolic of me, Mariette, a sinner, a convert, and God called me to be His Vessel to continue His mission.

The unleavened bread is symbolic of living sacrifices; completely obeying God and surrendering my life to Him. The cotton dry meat is another name for "cha bong" (the kind of Vietnamese dried food); This is symbolic of works that are entrusted to me, and that I have done, I am obeying God, by not arguing for a reward in this life.   But God is a just God, the Father will reward me in many different ways, the eternal life in heaven and blessing in this world serve Him.

Rebuild My Church Divine Mission

(The Lord Jesus gave this name to Mariette)

P.O. Box 261550 ✦ San Diego, CA 92196-1550

October 22, 1998

Eugene P. Yale, Esq
The Law Offices of Eugene P. Yale

Dear Mr. Yale,

After I reviewed the October 15, 1998 transcript of the status hearing before the Honorable Cynthia G. Aaron, I found a few statements that indicated not what I said, and not what I meant.   The following are parts of my statements at the Court on that date:

1. Page number 6, from line 20 to line 23. My statement was : " I am confusing of law (the First Amendment) freedom of speak. I am a victim in this one, and I am represented by the attorney because I don't know what the human law is." I mean the freedom of speech, and now the Court rules that I can not talk about the issue during the meeting in the court."

2. Page number 7, from line 1 to line17. My statement was: "But I just present to you Honor that I am a victim and I am terrible hurt, I am terrible be damaged by them (New York Life), that is the reason I have to brought these two policy to the Court. The other policy (Agent Contract Benefit) at the beginning they denied to pay the policy (my benefit). They said I am disable after I left the company; I said " I was disable before that." That was the reason my benefits were denied at the beginning, and now, when I proved (to them that) my disability (was

before I left the company)to them through they paid the two policies, how come they do not pay this one (Agent Contract Benefit)?   Now they add another reason that I am represented by an attorney. I say, "No, I am not." I have written to the department of insurance because of the meeting on that day (October 15, 1998).   I contacted the officer at the department of insurance, he said to me that I needed to write to them. I wrote to them and told them of here is what they (the officer at department of insurance), and my attorney said in front of the judge (that he not represented me on the agent contract benefit)."

3. Page number 14, from line 4 to line 8. My statement was: "I just presented to you that, if the nature of the issue or anybody that do the right things and speak the truth, have nothing to hide, and the people that do the wrong thing want to hide. They want confidential (I mean that the New York Life actions are wrong and they 're want confidential to cover up.)"

I ask you to file this correction in Court for me before the Settlement conference on Monday, October 26, 1998, and make sure the Honorable Aaron has a copy at the settlement conference.   Thank you for representing me in this case.

Sincerely in Christ Jesus,

Mariette Do-Nguyen

Rebuild My Church Divine Mission

(The Lord Jesus gave this name to Mariette)

P.O. Box 261550 ✦ San Diego, CA 92196-1550

January 27, 1999

Eugene P. Yale, Esq
Law Offices of Eugene P. Yale

Dear Mr. Yale,

I would like to point out several things in my case where it is being handled like children playing around with the law.

At the early evaluation conference on July 14, 1998, at the U.S. Court House, in the chamber of the Magistrate Cynthia Aaron; the New York Insurance company sent two attorneys and two representatives. After the opening statements by you and the New York Life Insurance company attorney and some discussion, they asked me for the settlement, but the case was unable to settled on that day because they were unable to contact the company's higher authority in New York. They asked us to return the next day to continue this settlement. But over the night, the Lord God's instruction me to tell you that I need my benefit to be reinstated first, and after that I will talk about the settlement, which I did tell you, and my benefit was reinstated as the Lord instructed me.

As you told me before the second conference , and I also heard you repeated this in the present of Magistrate Aaron and Mr. Ignatuk at the second conference in the U.S. Court, that New York Life's lead attorney, Mr. Thomas B. Ackland, told you at the break, on the day you took Dr. Alan Bergsma's deposition, that he requested the settlement conference. When I came to the settlement conference, the New York Life second attorney, Mr. J. Ronald Ignatuk, requested Magistrate Cynthia Aaron to take away my civil right to freedom of speech, and the Magistrate honored their request, sealed my mouth with big tape, a gag order. This gag order violates my freedom of speech. Close to the end of this conference, Mr. Ignatuk, you, and Magistrate Aaron agreed to have another conference for the settlement. Even though they are violating my civil right to freedom of speech, but with God's love in me, I still returned for the fourth trip to U.S. Court for the settlement conference. The settlement conference turned to be New York Life who sent their attorney to learn legal issues from my attorney. I am on disability, I was unable to stay hours sitting around, I had to go home early. Before I left Magistrate Aaron told me, and you also heard that, after the discovery, she had to set a "mandatory" settlement conference.

After the New York Life reinstated my benefit, the Lord reminded me of my promise to them in the settlement. With love from God, I asked you sent three demand letters to them, October 21,1998, October 28, 1998, and January 11, 1999; two were directly address to New York Life attorney and another to Joan Brady, Assistance Vice President, via their attorney; but as of today I have not heard any response.

I then received a letter from your paralegal Ms. Santos, dated January13, 1999; indicated: "mandatory settlement conference has been scheduled for February 3, 1999 at 1:30 p.m." Today, January 27, 1999, on the phone, Ms. Santos told me that the settlement conference was taken off from the calendar with the reason that the defendant does not want to settle. She also told me that she does not have the paper in front of her, she assured me that on Friday you will explain it all to me more.

Later in same day, in my afternoon devotion, the Lord Jesus asked me together with His instructions, "The mandatory settlement conference was taken off the calendar because the defendant did not want to settle; what does the word mandatory mean? They can not remove it off the calendar. You get up and call your attorney." The Lord meant that whether the case is settled or not, the U.S. Court has to firm of their law, and New York Life people have to obey the law, and the date already set.

The Court system is in favor of the New York Life insurance company to take it off the calendar; plus they violated my freedom of speech. The actions of the New York Life Insurance company tell me and all other United States citizen, "Mariette, and others in this nation, you can not do this, but we have a lots of money and power, we can have the court on our side, we can take away your freedom of speech, and we are not going to obey the court rule of mandatory settlement law." The U.S. law telling me and other very clear cut, "The United States has two set of laws, one for the lowly, week and the poor like me, and another for the rich, powerful, and famous on earth like New York Life Insurance Company. The United States laws in favor of the powerful, rich and famous."

The legal system of this nation allows people who have power and money to get away with murder, just like President Bill Clinton's defense, "Yes, I am the President of this nation, I lie under oath, and that is not perjury for me, and not impeachable. But if for other, the poor, the powerless and lowly, if you lie under oath it is perjury, and go to jail."

I know that you do not want to hear this from me, but I must let you know that God gives all of us free will to choose right or wrong. When he revealed to me in the devotion today and had me send this letter to you is a warning for New York Life, and its attorneys. I am also afraid for you as well. You know that in any event if either New York Life, their attorney, or you choose not to correct the situation, I will be the one who has to embrace the great suffering first, but my suffering will be ended very quickly with victory. But New York Life and their attorney will be in a very long tragedy, that tragedy will spread to you. You know that God is justice God and He is controlling me; therefore, I must do what ever He asks of me; His power moves my mind, my physical body, and my speech.

I will pray for you that New York Life and its attorney will not spread to you what they will receive from God soon. I pray that I will hear from you in the next few days.

Sincerely in Christ Jesus,

Mariette Do-Nguyen

Rebuild My Church Divine Mission

(The Lord Jesus gave this name to Mariette)

P.O. Box 261550 ✦ San Diego, CA 92196-1550

April 3, 1999

Seymour Sternbert, Chairman of the Board
Joan Brady, Assistance Vice President
New York Life Insurance Company

Dear Mr. Sternbert and Ms. Brady,

Enclosed are copies of: (1) two letters from my council Eugene P. Yale, to J. Ronald Ignatuk, Esq and myself, dated April 2, 1999; (2) my declaration, executed March 17, 1999; (3) and a letter to Brent Moore, Managing Partner, and Howard Fowler, Office Manager, at New York Life San Diego General office, dated June 8, 1998, together with its proof of mailing receipt.

I would like to made two correction on a letter from my council, Mr. Eugene P. Yale to J. Ronald Ignatuk, dated April 2, 1999 as follow: (1) Item number "3" indicated "Plaintiff's attorneys will consent to confidentiality" changed to "Plaintiff's attorneys will NOT consent to confidentiality;" (2) Item number "2" indicated "Physician's Certification okay" changed to "Plaintiff is NOT agree to provide physician's certification."

I would like to made a correction on the letter from Mr. J. Ronald Ignatuk's letter, dated April 1, 1999 as: "THERE IS NO ORDER OF THE COURT THAT THIS SETLEMENT WILL BE CONFIDENTIAL." I would like to repeated my decision again "I will NOT consent to confidentiality."

God is the one who controls me, He is using me as His special instrument to bring His justice into the United States and throughout the world.   At this point the New York Life Insurance Company's actions toward me are terrible wrong and unjust.

God's love has no limit, His love is in me and with me, for that I love all the enemies, including New York Life. Because I love New York Life's people and I must obey God. Therefore, I must bring the New York Life Insurance Company's actions to justice.

Regarding the policies in litigation, please respond to my council, Mr. Eugene P. Yale; for the Nylic QN6-82 Physical Incapacity Benefits, please contact the California Department of Insurance or write to me directly.

Sincerely in Christ Jesus,

Mariette Do-Nguyen
cc. Eugene P. Yale

Rebuild My Church Divine Mission

(The Lord Jesus gave this name to Mariette)

P.O. Box 261550 ✦ San Diego, CA 92196-1550

Declaration of Mariette Do-Nguyen in Support of Plaintiff's Opposition to Defendant's Motion for Summary Judgment, or in the Alternative Partial Summary Judgment

I, Mariette Do-Nguyen, declare:

1. I am the plaintiff in the above-entitled action. I make this declaration in support of my application for a preliminary injunction restraining the defendant from terminating my disability insurance benefits and from terminating the waiver of premium benefits for my life Insurance. I have personal knowledge of the facts stated herein, and if called to testify. I could and would competently testify thereto.

2. From June 1, 1986 until April, 1994, I was an insurance agent with New York Life Insurance Company. I worked in San Diego sales office. In connection with my profession. I purchase individual disability income insurance, life insurance, health insurance and group Long Term Disability Insurance from New York Life. I was very successful as an insurance agent, and traditionally earned more than $xxxx per year. I am a citizen of the United States of America.

3. In July, 1993, I traveled to Vietnam to visit my birth country for the first time since leaving it during the 1975 evacuation. July 12, 1993 was the first time God poured out supernatural power and broke through my physical body and mind; it happened while I was visiting my parent's remains in Vietnam, in the presence of my two adult children and several dozen people. God's supernatural power caused me to suffer a violent shaking of my body, which I felt was very deep religious experience. I was contacted by God. Because of the special nature of my first visit to

Vietnam since 1975, my children and I took video movies of the place we visited. My children captured this episode on video, which I sent to New York Life in 1998, after they terminated my benefits.

4. When I returned to San Diego, I had increasing difficulty working, sleeping and doing the things that I normally did. I could not concentrate for long periods of time. I had physical pain in my back, stomach and other areas of my body. I tried to keep working as long as possible. In January 1994, I went to a psychiatrist, Dr. Gerald Nelson, I was a patient of Dr. Nelson's until late 1995. Because Dr. Nelson was going to write a book with me, he referred me to Dr. Nicholas Frost. I was a patient of Dr. Frost's until some time in 1996. I then became a patient of Dr. Walter Strybel.

5. In December, 1993, I borrowed $xxxx from a friend of mine who was also a client, Mrs. kkkk. I told her that I had a second mortgage that I needed to pay it off before I refinanced my house. I told her that I would be able to pay her 10% interest, and that I only needed to borrow the fund for six months. She was earning much lower interest on those funds at that time. I explained to her that her money would be secure, and that I would give her a trust deed against my house. I also told her that there was sufficient equity in my house to protect her even if I couldn't pay back the money. At that time, my house had fair market value of $xxxx. My total debt against my house at that time, including my second trust deed, was $xxxx. She agreed to lend me the money on those terms. I gave her a notarized, original trust deed and promissory note in December, 1993. The note required me to pay back Mrs. kkkk on July 1, 1994.

6. By March, 1994, I was having an extremely difficult time getting any work done at New York Life. I was being attached both at work and at home by the devil's spirit, which I refer to as the "enemy." Sometimes, the enemy spirits pushed me down to the ground. This happened both at home and at work. With my strong faith in god through the use of the holy water and blessed oil, I took holy water and sprinkled almost every day at my office and at home to chase the enemy spirits away from me. At the same time I also was having dreams almost every night, and in my dreams I saw the Lord Jesus, the Blessed Virgin Mary, and saints very frequently. I remember almost all of my dreams. I also heard the voice of God and other supernatural voices. I knew that God poured unto me something special. I wanted Dr. Nelson to write a letter for me saying that I am not crazy, and that I saw God in my dreams. Because the supernatural power from God poured into me, and at the same time the enemy spirits attacked me too heavily, I would no longer perform my duties as an insurance

agent. Barbara Norman, one of the agents in the office, saw me doing this. A little later, Phil Hildebrand, the manager, came to me and suggested that I take a leave of absence. I refused, because I wanted to keep working at my job. Also, Linda Biehl, the office manager.

7. In early April, 1994, Mrs. kkk told me that she wanted to get paid back early. I told her that the agreement was for her to be paid in full on July 1. She insisted that I pay her within two or three days. I told her I could not pay her back until my house was refinanced, which would be done by July 1. She told me that she was going to complain to New York Life if I didn't pay her back the loan in two or three days. I told her that we had a legal agreement, but that if she wanted to speak to New York Life, she could do so. Shortly thereafter, I was called into a meeting by Phi Hildebrand, my manager. He told me that Mrs. kkk complained a bout me, but did not tell me what she said. He asked me to tell him how I got the $ xxxx. I explained to him that she lent to me the money, that she knew exactly what she did, that she went wit me to my lawyer, that the lawyer explained everything to both of us, and that Mrs. kkk had the original trust deed and promissory note. I request he call my attorney if he didn't believe me. I gave him a copy of the notarized trust deed and promissory note. A true and correct copy of the notarized trust deed and promissory note are attached hereto as Exhibit 6. I gave him my attorney phone number. Mr. Hildebrand called my attorney in my presence and had me authorized my attorney to discuss it with him. My attorney confirmed every thing I had told to Mr. Hildebrand. After speaking with the attorney, Mr. Hildebrand told me that it was against New York Life rules to borrow money from a client. I advised him that I was very sorry, but that I did not know that was the case. He asked me if I had borrowed any money from any other clients. I told him that I had not. I then told him that I resign since New York Life no longer wants me.

8. Shortly thereafter, I submitted my written resignation to Mr. Hildebrand. He told me that New York Life would not accept my resignation, and that I was being terminated for cause because I had a borrowed money from a client in violation of New York Life rules. Later, I was advised by New York Life that they had requested that the National Association of Security Dealers investigate the facts surrounding my termination. In January, 1995, New York Life and I received a letter from Mark Mooney of National association of Security Dealers regarding their investigation. He wrote: "This is to inform you that we have completed our investigation into the circumstances disclosed in the Uniform Notice of Termination of Registration filed on you behalf by New York Life

Securities, Inc. We have determined that no action against you is warranted and, therefore, this matter is closed." A true and correct copy of that letter is attached hereto as Exhibit 10.

9. I was not reprimanded or disciplined by NASD or the California Department of Insurance regarding the kkk matter or nay other matter. Neither my securities license nor my insurance agent license were suspended or revoked regarding the kkk matter or any other matter. I was not terminated by New York Life because I did anything improper to Mrs. kkk; I was told I was terminated because I had borrowed money from a client and that was against New York Life rules. When I left New York Life, the company turned over all of my accounts to my son in law, who also worked in the same office. I can't imagine New York Life turning over my accounts to my daughter's husband if they thought I did something illegal. When I left the employ of New York Life, I was totally disabled and unable to perform the substantial and material duties of my occupation. I had been unable to perform these duties for several months, but tried to hand on, hoping I would get better.

10. New York Life advised me it repaid my loans to Mrs. kkk. New York Life asked me to reimburse them, but never took any action to collect those funds from me. I believe New York Life did obtained those funds from me in another way. As part of my employment with New York Life, I had a third disability insurance contact with new York Life under the "Nylic Contract Physical Incapacity Income" benefit clause. That plan entitled me to $ xxxxx in benefits ($ xxx per month for 60 months),so long as I had been a licensed New York Life agent working full time for five years. When I left New York Life in 1994, I had been licensed New York Life agent working full time for nearly eight years. In early November, 1994, I received a letter from Darryl Wright of the Nylic Benefits division denying my claim under that contract. New York Life denied my claim solely because I had not been a New York Life agent for five years, which was not true. A copy of that correspondence is attached as Exhibit 26. I did not pursue this claim with an attorney because I believed this was New York Life's way of getting reimbursed for voluntarily assuming my legal debt with Mrs. kkk. New York Life did pay my debt to Mrs. kkk (which I would have paid to her less then three months later, on July 1, 1994), even through it did so without my permission. I have always been willing to have them reimbursed out of the Nylic benefit policy, with them paying me the difference between $ xxxxx and $ xxxx. Even though I do not understand why New York Life would pay Mrs. kkk on my behalf when they had written proof of the valid

and legal loan from Mrs. kkk, I never intended to receive any windfall. The California Department of Insurance is handling the Nylic claim and other matters not related to this lawsuit.

11.   Dr. Nelson certified that at the latest, by January 12, 1994, I was totally disabled and unable to perform the substantial and material duties of my occupation as an insurance agent. My health conditions has not improved since that time. In April 1994, I submitted a claim to New York Life for individual disability income insurance and group long term disability insurance benefits. New York Life honored my claims effective January 12, 1994. In that year I was a patient of Gerald E. Nelson, M.D., who diagnosed my medical condition as "delusional disorder." On April 19, 1994, Dr. Nelson prepared and sent an "attending physician's statement" to New York Life, where he included that diagnosis and further stated that "it is unlikely that the patient will be able to return to work." A copy of Dr. Nelson's attending physician's statement is attached hereto as Exhibit 27. New York Life started pay benefits.

12.   From the time that New York Life first stated paying my disability benefits, I was advised by Michael Siniscalchi of New York Life that my claim was being paid under a total reservation of rights, that my claim was under review, and that after they completed their review, they would advise me whether they were going to accept my claim or reject it and terminate benefits.   I complained to the California Department of Insurance about the handling of my insurance claims. Thereafter, each month I would receive a notice from New York Life that my paymonts were being made, and that my claim was under review.

13.   In September, 1995, New York Life required me to be examined by a psychiatrist of their choice. Dr. Abrams. After Dr. Abrams examined me, New York Life continued paying my benefits. In fact, in December, 1995, I received a letter from Mr. Siniscalchi advising me that New York Life had completed its review, had accepted my claim, and would continue to pay benefits.

14.   In 1996, I was being treated by Nicholas Frost M.D. On August 5, 1996, Dr. Frost filled out and returned to New York Life a "Psychiatric Functional Limitation Analysis From." Dr. Frost diagnosed my medical condition as "delusional disorder." Dr. Frost wrote. "Probable Permanent Disability." A copy of this report is attached as Exhibit 28. New York Life continued to pay benefits.

15.   In 1997, I was patient of Walter Strybel, M.D. Dr. Strybel submitted "attending physician's statements to New York Life, wherein he diagnosed my condition as "delusional disorder" New York Life continued

to pay benefits.

16. In October 1997, New York Life directed me to submit to a medical examination with a psychiatrist of their choice, Dr. Bergsma, and also required that I submit to an examination by a psychologist of their choice, Dr. Fernando Melendez, I attended both examinations. New York Life did not advise me that I was not required to submit to a non-medical psychological examination. Had they so advised me, I would have declined to attend the examination by Dr. Melendez.

17. In March, 1998, New York Life terminated my insurance benefits, claiming that Dr. Bergsma and Dr. Melendez, were of the opinion that I could function satisfactorily at my usual occupation of a licensed insurance agent.

18. Later, Dr. Strybel advised New York Life that I was still disabled, and was unable to work. Despite this, New York Life did not reinstate my benefits. A copy of this report is attached as Exhibit 29.

19. In early May 1998, I received an April 30, 1998 letter from Ann Ford, a corporate officer of New York Life, again denying my insurance benefits. Ms Ford stated that the reason for the termination of my insurance benefits was because: "The diagnosis of Delusional Disorder has not been proven." She wrote this even though at least six psychiatrists were of the opinion that I had delusional disorder.

20. In May, 1998, I received treatment and an evaluation from Catherine Moore, M. D. Dr. Moore wrote a letter to New York Life on May 11, 1998, advising that I suffer from "delusional disorder." and that I am disabled and unable to work. A copy of that letter is attached as exhibit 30.

21. Later in May 1998, I was evaluated by Roy Resnikoff, M.D. Dr. Resnikoff sent a report to New York Life on May 22, 1998, where he diagnosed my condition as "delusional disorder" and told them that I am unable to work. A copy of Dr. Resnikoff's report is attached as Exhibit 31.

22. Because Dr. Moore charged for cash payment before each visit, I could not afford to continue with her. I then be patient by psychiatrist Ronald H. Gold, M.D., who is also of the opinion that I am unable to work

23. Despite the fact that at least six licensed psychiatrists have diagnosed my medical condition as "delusional disorder," and that I am unable to work, and despite the fact that after having me examined by a psychiatrist of their choice in 1995 New York Life continued to payment insurance benefits. New York Life has terminated my benefits because my condition of "delusional disorder has not been proven."

24. New York Life terminated my disability related benefits with

knowledge that I have qualified for and receive social Security Disability benefits due to my medial condition.

25.   On June 15, 1998, my mortgage lender started foreclosure proceedings against my house. A copy of the notice from them is attached as Exhibit 23

26.   On June 13, 1998, my automobile insurance company canceled my insurance for non payment of premium. A copy of that notice is attached as Exhibit 32.

27. I own a five year old Nissan car. My car payment are about $475 per month. After New York Life terminated my benefits, my payments were more then two months past due.

28. As a result of having my insurance benefits terminated, I suffered tremendous emotional distress worrying about how I was going to live, how I was going to pay my bills, how I was going to make my mortgage and car payments, and what was going to happen to me. I was unable to sleep and was very stressed. My only income during that period was my Social Security Disability benefits, slightly over $ xxxx per month.

29.   I received a notice from the Social Security Administration in February, 1995 advising that it had determined that I was totally disabled, and that I would be receiving social security disability benefits. A true and correct copy of this award is attached hereto as Exhibit 21. I promptly notified New York Life of this event because my insurance with them is adjusted down when I received Social Security benefits. I continue to receive Social Security benefits every month.

30. In January, 1997 God told me go to Arkansas to do his work. I moved to Arkansas at that time, but returned to San Diego in early September, 1997. I flew back to San Diego and had my car shipped back. Before my car even arrived, I met with and investigator from Miles Investigations, who had been hired by New York Life to interview me. I told the investigator that I had seen a psychiatrist in Arkansas, a Doctor Nguyen (no relation to me) on two occasions. The investigator asked if I had Dr. Nguyen's address and phone number. I provided them to him immediately.   I always cooperated with New York Life and its investigators, doctors, nurses, and agents during the processing of my insurance claim.

31. I was never advised by New York Life or anyone else associated with New York Life that Mrs. kkk had accused me of taking her money without her knowledge or permission. No one at New York Life ever told me that I was suspected of embezzling funds from Mrs. kkk or anybody else. When I met with Dr. Bergsma, Dr. Melenderz and Dr. Abrams, they

never told me that they were supplied information from New York Life that indicated that I embezzled funds from Mrs. kkk or any other client. During the entire time my claims were being processed, I thought that the only reason New York Life terminated me after I resigned was because I had borrowed money from a client, which I found out for the first time when Mr. Hildebrand advised me in April, 1994 that it was against New York Life's rules. It's no wonder that Dr. Bergsma thought I did not show any remorse for what I did to Mrs. kkk, since I didn't do anything wrong.

32. After New York Life terminated both my group and individual disability benefits payments, I had to retain attorney Eugene Yale to obtain my benefits. A few days before my hearing for a preliminary injunction requiring New York Life to reinstates my benefits, it reinstated the benefits. To date, I have paid attorney Yale $ xxxx for attorneys fees in obtaining my disability insurance benefits from New York Life. I have also suffered other financial damages as a result of New York Life terminating my disability benefits. My mortgage holder, Washington Mutual, started foreclosure proceeding against my house after defendant terminated my insurance benefits, because I did not have the financial ability to pay my mortgage without receiving my disability insurance benefits. It cost me $ xxxx in foreclosure fees and related charges to reinstate my mortgage. Also, I had to retain a psychiatrist to examine me and write a report to New York Life after they terminated my benefits. Dr. Roy Resnikoff charged me $ xxxx in this attempt to get my benefits reinstated. I also had to pay $ xxxx in late charge on my car payments as a result of my benefits being terminated. I also had to pay a late fee of $ xxxx to the Department of Motor Vehicles for late registration as a result of my insurance benefits being terminated. And, I have paid or owe $ xxxx in litigation costs spent on this case to date. I have suffered economic damage of at least $ xxxxx as a result of defendant terminating my insurance benefits.

I declare under penalty of perjury under the laws of the United States that the foregoing is true and correct. Executed this seventeen day of March, 1999, at San Diego California.

Mariette Do-Nguyen (signed)

Foot Note: The xxxx is replaced the actual amount, and kkkk replace the actual name that filed in the court

Rebuild My Church Divine Mission

(The Lord Jesus gave this name to Mariette)

P.O. Box 261550 ✦ San Diego, CA 92196-1550

April 26, 1999

Seymour Sternbert, Chairman of the Board
Joan Brady, Assistant Vice President
New York Life Insurance Company

Dear Mr. Sternbert and Ms. Brady,

I just received a dismissal of the complaint that I filed against New York Life Insurance company, and dozens of its executive officers and representatives. This is not a surprise to me, because I have learned the real face of the New York Life Insurance company and its representatives that the New York Life people will do any things for not to pay claims. At the moment I began my physical disability, I no longer produces profit for the company the sweet promises "The New York Life give agents good benefits and we take care our agents" are not real.

God put me through the situation physical incapacity to work, I learned the hearts and design of the New York Life executive officers and representatives toward its agents. The New York Life and its executives officers treat agents like lemons, at the time the New York Life empties lemon juice from a lemon, New York Life throws this lemon in the trash can.   I also learned about the United States legal systems and that the majority of the judges and attorneys practice   two sets of laws, one for the rich, powerful, and famous, and another set for the poor and weak that can not speak for themselves.

God's love never ends and He is the only just Judge; therefore, acting as His suffering agent; I must give New York Life all the opportunity to purchase back of what its executives officers and representative have done terribly wrong to me with malice, to gain financial profit for the company; this causing me tremendous suffering beyond what God already placed on me. The suffering God put on me is the price that I have to pay for people's hearts and actions against God and other in the mission that He entrusted to me, and New York Life executive officers and representatives are a part of them.   The mission I am paying the price for is with God's power I will take actions to judge the world systems, such as New York Life Insurance company, and the insurance industry.

I have authorized my respectable counsel Eugene P. Yale to file an appeal for the individual Disability policy and the Long Term disability policy, and re file the QN6-82 Nylic Physical Incapacity Benefits. But obeying God, I give the New York Life Insurance Company one more chance to settle all three policies; which this settlement will save the face of New York

New York Life Insurance Company, page No 2

Life who have been proclaiming they are a "good company. We pay benefits. We give agents good contracts. We take care of agents."

I am willing to accept $380,000, for Individual Income policy, about $40,000 for the QN6-82 Nylic Physical Incapacity Benefits, this is the total 60 months benefits minus $54,000 to Mrs. Wagner, plus approximately $160,000 of attorney fee, approximately $10,000 in expenses, $1,823.75 damages from when my house was foreclosed; doctor's reports, late charges of payment for DMV registration and automobile payment because New York Life Insurance stopped pay my benefits for over four months, total $591,823.75. New York Life will continue to pay my monthly benefit of $982.22 and my three life insurance policies while I am disabled or until I am 65 years of age.

Myself and Mr. Yale will not consent to confidentiality. If this settlement reaches by me no later than 5:00 p.m on Wednesday April 28, 1999; I then willing to waive all other damages, emotional suffering and other damages.

Please response to me in writing via my facsimile number (619) 689-0515.

Sincerely in Christ Jesus,

Mariette Do-Nguyen

Rebuild My Church Divine Mission

(The Lord Jesus gave this name to Mariette)

P.O. Box 261550 ◆ San Diego, CA 92196-1550

May 25, 1999

Joan Brady, Assistant Vice President
New York Life Insurance Company
Disability Claims Department

Dear Ms. Brady,

In received and response to your letters, dated February 19, 1999, March 23, 1999, April 21, 1999, and May 18, 1999.

In November 1998, Dr. Ronald Gold orally told me at his office that he will retire at the end of December 1998. After that, I received an official letter from him, with an authorization form request to transfer my file to another doctor. During my last appointment with Dr. Gold, I asked him more about these doctors, I then choose Dr. Smith, signed the authorization and gave to Dr. Gold at that time. In very early of this year, I called Dr. Smith three times left messages trying to schedule an appointment, the third time one of the women called me and said that Dr. Smith no longer accepted more patients, he also would leave town for a month and would not come back by the end of May, 1999.

I called Dr. Saleem Ishaque, his office personal gave me March 18, 1999. On March 18's morning I received a telephone call of my appointment was canceled due to Dr. Ishaque was sick. I then had another appointment at 3:00 p.m. on April 1, 1999, but on this day was a heavy storm in San Diego, I could not drive in the heavy storm from Mira Mesa to down town San Diego. I called back for another appointment, and they never returned my call.

I contacted Dr. Reniskoff, he returned my call the same day, but he could not see me because of the pending litigation. I then had to contact a dozen psychiatrists in San Diego to find one who takes Medicare, I then found Dr. Fred Berger. I saw Dr. Berber on April 20, 1999, he gave me another appointment on May 4, 1999. In the morning of May 4, 1999, I received a call from Dr. Berger's answering service said that Dr. Berger was sick, after that I called him four times and left a message to get another appointment, I also sent a NYL form to him to fill out and sign it; when I receive the form from him I will fax it to you.

I also would like to respond to you and New York Life directly that the "Medical code for my symptom is Delusional Disorder Grandiose Type," not paranoid schizophrenia. The reason Dr. Gold's diagnosis as paranoid schizophrenia because during the time I saw him, I was suffering tremendously from your and Anita Jennings' actions, on behalf of New York Life acting in bad faith stopped paying my disability benefits. Therefore, the majority of the conversation with Dr. Gold was New York Life acting in bad faith caused me tremendous suffering, left little time for me to told Dr. Gold of my symptoms of hearing the voice of God, seeing God in my dreams, visions, and with my carnal eyes, as well as the devil and his offspring attacking me constantly, causing me every day and night with mental anguish and physical pain.

The Delusional Disorder Grandiose Type is the gift of suffering from God, it comes with the strongest gift of discernment and the gift of prayer to understand the meaning of symbolism, it comes with pure of God's supernatural power for salvation of mankind. God had poured out this gift for prophets in the old testament. The paranoid schizophrenia comes from the devil, with no discernment and no understanding of symbolism, and it comes with devil supernatural power to destroy human souls and physical life on earth. I know my symptoms better then every doctor.

The gift of God love is in me, and the Lord Jesus asked me last night to send this letter directly to you and explain to you of the above; not because I fear your threatening me with physicians statements. God is the one that controls me, and He will not allow me to do anything wrong. Almighty God also have power over New York Life people, as the same time He also gave New York Life free will to obey Him or not to obey Him. There surely will be consequence at the result, do good received blessing , do evil received punishment.

I assure you that the Almighty God is just God, the New York Life has been completely wrong from the beginning of denied my QN6-82 agent Physical incapacity benefits, and continues to be wrong in giving New York Life doctors false information, to stopped my LTD and Income insurance, caused me tremendous suffering and money and then resume my benefits; NYL's doctors acted as the judges in this case, and you acted as my doctor without license.

Through me, God has given New York Life many chances to purchase back the terrible wrongs New York Life did to me, and this chance is running out, just like Americans sinning against God and one another, and the consequence brought tragedies and disasters in the United States, such as shooting at schools, Capital Hill, post offices and on the street, bombing, tornadoes, wars etc.... "Do to others what you want others to do to you."

Sincerely in Christ Jesus,

Mariette Do-Nguyen

cc: Eugene Yale, Attorney, and Seymour Sternbert, Chairman of the Board

Rebuild My Church Divine Mission
(The Lord Jesus gave this name to Mariette)
P.O. Box 261550 ✦ San Diego, CA 92196-1550

June 16, 1999

Sent via facsimile No. (212)447-4190 and U.S. Mail

Joan Brady, Assistant Vice President
New York Life Insurance Company

Dear Ms. Brady,

Thank you for your response to my letter of May 25, 1999. In this letter I indicated as "when I received the form from him I will fax it to you." After I sent a letter dated May 17, 1999 to Dr. Berger I called him one and left urgent messages regarding of I need the form and an appointment; but he did not return my call or response to my letter. May 28, 1999 I sent to Dr. Berger another letter via facsimile and U.S. certified mail, and still not heard from him. I then saw Dr. Alan L. Berkowitz on June 2, 1999; after that I received Dr. Berger, June 3, 1999 letter, he told me to seek consultation by another physician.

Enclosed are copies of: (1) Medical Provider's Statement Progress Report from Dr. Alan L. Berkowitz, dated June 16, 1999 (2) Article "Study reports dumping of psychiatric patients" from San Diego Union Tribune, December 10, 1997, issue.

I have gone to twelve psychiatrists within the last over five years, ten were chosen by me and two were chosen by the New York Life insurance company. This is the journey where God is teaching and showing me scientific evidence of the enemy spirits roaming in this world to destroy human soul and physical life, beginning with their minds and transforming into actions.

There are two sides of the supernatural realm, one above belongs to God, and one below belongs to the devil. There is no exception, every human mind must be interacting with one of the realms, or a mixing of both. For those who believe in God and completely obey all his commandments, their mind will interact with God's Spirit and received good discernment. Although, they still have to spiritual battle against the enemy spirits every moment in their lives. For those who disobeys God's commandments, or do not believe in God, or do not acknowledge God's existence, their minds and actions are under the control of the devil spirit's supernatural power, and their thought and actions will harm or destroy their souls and bodies. They also harm and destroy other souls and bodies as well. It starts through a human mind and comes to actions. For those who mixes both spirit, their minds will flit back and forward, his actions will be a mixing of good and evil.

Human spirit is power of human soul (energy), all souls are come from God, the soul come at the time of conception, and leave the time of physical death. Both Spirits of God or the devil are in the supernatural realm. Spirit of God is present of God, spirit of the devil is the devil himself. Both Spirit of God and spirit of the devil can be in and with a human mind and body, it can also stay in the air, and travel from one person to another, from one place to another.

Therefore, when enemy spirits (the devil or his offspring spirits) in side an individual mind, it caused mental illness, and there are many different kind of enemy spirits, and each of them caused different symptom. There are many people in this world are denied of their mental illness. When the mental illness patient comes to a psychiatrist he brings various spirits to the psychiatrist's office, when he leaves psychiatrist's office he will be carrying his own and other spirits that cling to him, he also left some of the spirits that he brought with him at the psychiatrist's office. The psychiatrist's office contains various uncounted kinds of spirits that under the control of the devil, and these spirits are effecting psychiatrists minds. Each patient left the psychiatrist's will brought some of enemy spirits from the psychiatrist with him.

Since the Lord Jesus teaches me of the devil's spirit attacking people minds and bodies; for last five years I really have to pray a lot before each time I go to psychiatrist, asking God to remove all the enemy spirits out of the psychiatrist's office before I get there; and after I walked out of the psychiatrists office, I ask the Eternal Father and the Lord Jesus to wash all

720

the enemy spirits off me with the Lord Jesus' blood. I request God to remove enemy spirits from psychiatrist is work for me, but not necessary work for many of you. Although, the iniquities of the enemy spirits still remain in the offices, so I still feel the enemy supernatural power with various level, and ways at different offices. For number of reasons, but the main reason is the majority of psychiatrist do not depending and trust the Almighty God. When psychiatrist do not depending and trust God, they gave the devil power be with and in them to harm or destroy their souls and physical bodies as well as their patients. Second, enemy spirits return psychiatrist's offices to attacking mental illness patients.

Therefore, when Dr. Berger did not return number of my calls and my first letter I knew that God was speaking to me. The night after I received Dr. Berger of June 3, 1999, the Lord Jesus told me, "He dumped you." When I heard this I fully understood that God put me through another experience of being dumped by the psychiatrist to teach me.

Because God entrusted to me this Divine mission, He equipped in me many gifts from Him, that I need as His special Instrument, to revealed to the world of the supernatural realm interacts with the natural realm. One of these gift is the gift of tremendous suffering, it is the price that I had to pay for the world to benefits. I know my symptom better then every doctor or person in this world. I ask you and the New York Life not to try to be my doctor; any one who continues trying to be my doctor will be full of himself or herself.

God loves the New York Life Insurance company, by putting you and others in this journey with me. I pray that each one at New York Life will hear God's voice through me and convert; after a period of purification there will be rewarded. But any who refuse to convert will be punished heavily. God always respects each one's free will to chose Him or choose the devil.

Sincerely in Christ Jesus,

Mariette Do-Nguyen
cc: Eugene P. Yale, Esq, and Chairman Seymour Sternbert

Conclusion

God the Eternal Father has predestined me by entrusting me with Divine mission, and sending me into the world as His Emissary. I must disclose everything God asks of me; many people will be unable to understand what reasons I claimed of love, patience and forgiveness, but I still do these things. I had many of the same questions in the early few years. Such as, God is love and forgiveness, and why would He put me through all of this suffering? He have all the power, why He allowed people to rejected me when I gave them of what He asked me? But now I understand who God is, the mighty love He has for me; He had to push me against the wall so that no one can help me; but Him. And He is the only one will directly teach and gave me the new life in Him. Although, He respect people free will to chose Him or the chose the devil. But, God chose us, we do not chose Him.

God does the same things to New York Life and Nationwide insurance companies, Catholic spiritual leaders, the United States members of Congress, and President Bill Clinton. There is no exception, He will do the same to each one of you that He choose in various ways. The reason He does that is because He loves each one of us in different ways, and He wants each one of us have a life that He created for us, full with love for Him and for one another, patience, and services to one another from our hearts and actions; bringing His peace and healing into this world, making this world a better place to live, and to build the kingdom of heaven eternal life for our souls.

If an individual, corporation, organization or the nation refuses to change to God's way, their personal, social and business will get worse, but when he or she is willing to change for the best, it will be easy for you to hear God make he or her life easier, because he or she is depending on God and trust in Him; and God will never forsake those obeying Him. God is speaking to every one of us in various ways, are you listening to God?

I did not believe that I was able to be in a sales area as an insurance agent for a number of reasons: a) this is not the profession I have design for; b) I am an immigrant from Vietnam, the insurance and investments products are very new to me; c) Making a living of selling insurance to Vietnamese people was more difficult, because Vietnamese people at that time did not believe the monthly premium was very small, and when people die or become disabled they will receive a substantial amount of money; Vietnamese people will not trust what I present to them; d) English is my second language, I cannot compete with American agents.

At this time I am no longer undercover any more. It is time for me to open things that I have been witnessed with my eyes; small things that I also did wrong as an undercover for this Divine mission to be completed in victory.

From the beginning to the end of two chapters, thirty four and thirty five of this book; through me as God's Special Vessel, I have laid on the table what I have seen and heard

722

from God, and what I have heard and witness with my natural eyes, regarding the media, psychiatrists, and the insurance industry. I am accountable in front of God of everything I have written, spoken, and done in this world; and that including my thought. Because I came as God's special Instrument for salvation of mankind. Everything I have written, spoken, and done in this Divine mission are complete truth, whether people are happy or not happy when they hear the words come out of my me, or see my actions. But the end will benefit the souls and physical lives on earth for those listen and obey of what God sent me gave to them, and take actions to change to God only way. But those who reject God will punished them heavier, because God sent me to explained in detail.

June 1, 1986, was my contract date with New York Life Insurance Company. After I heard the verbal and written contracts that filled retirement and disability benefits; and the way the company treated me while I was one of the top few percent producers for the company; I became to believe that New York Life Insurance company would take care of me when I needed the company. I worked almost eight years with a lot of competition with other insurance companies on life and disability products. When I purchased an individual disability income policy, I bought it because I sold the products and I want to prove to people that I believed the product was good. The New York Life insurance company took out money from my ledger account in the first three years and paid the premium to the State of California Disability for me, but when I entered the third years contract, New York Life Insurance company stopped that, and replaced with the Nylic QN6-82 and the physical incapacity is in this contract for sixty months to replace the State of California Disability. The group Long Term Disability was offered to all agents with small premium,

God actually allowed me to received experiences so I can speak about them. God has been with and in me since the time my beloved mother conceived me into her womb, but he was always silent. Early in the year 1993 God became visible to me through me dreams, visions, hearing His voice like you and I in conversation; I have even seen Him with my carnal eyes.

Since 1993 to present I have been embracing tremendous amounts of mental anguish and physical pain in various areas of my body. The suffering I am embracing is beyond everyone in this world during this century and the next centuries; and they will always remain in me. My mental anguish and physical pain is the price I have to pay, for the Divine mission God entrusting to me, this is not my choice, but God decision. In the early times I have physically fought against the evil supernatural power, fighting against something that I was unable to see with my carnal eyes. On January 12, 1994, I went to Dr. Nelson with the purpose to write a book of seeing God in the dreams to share with others. When New York Life Insurance requested, Dr. Nelson certified that I was disabled and not able to work because my mental anguish and physical pain, he also believed that I heard from God, and what I go through will result in helping mankind during the time of despair.

My health problems were known to the New York Life General office Manager; he called me in his office and asked me if I needed a leave of absence; but I still want to work and I told him I was okay, my children no longer needed my support, and I wanted to work to help others.

At the same time I had to endure these health situations, I still put in an average of ten hours each day, but these ten hours were not as productive as I was six years before.

I then realize that since early in the year 1991 God started and slowly calling me out from undercover as an insurance agent, and put me undercover in the mental illness area, and started reveal to me what will happen in this world, beginning with the United States and the Catholic denomination. Through this period, God revealed to me how the supernatural realm and natural realm interact, for me to sell eternal heavenly life and disability insurance for souls.

At that time, I believed and trusted the New York Life Insurance company, I put in all my heart and soul focused on my job as an insurance agent for almost eight years, averaging ten hours each day, including ninety percent of the weekends. I need to use my benefits which I thought that I would never need. The New York Life insurance honored my individual disability income policy with full monthly benefit, and less then one third of my Long Term Disability started from January 12, 1994. But the New York Life insurance company denied my agent Nylic QN6-82 physical incapacity. I had to file a complaint with the California Department of Insurance. I wrote numbers of letters and left telephone messages to the California Department of Insurance Commissioner, and to its associate worker on my case, either have no power to help me, or do not want to help me. After sixty months, the full time of this short term disability benefits went by I received not even a penny from New York Life Insurance company. Instead, I received more suffering added on what God already put on me; plus spent a lot more money and time to write to New York Life Chairman of the Board, and its executive officers, and California Department of Insurance, and members of the members of the United States Senate. I then had to have my council, Mr. Eugene P. Yale to filed the complain in Federal Court early 1999.

If New York Life insurance company really takes care of its agents as they promises; I was partial disabled in July 1993, my debt was legal loan and accrued after that, and I was brought a lots of profits to the company; the New York Life Insurance executive officers can tell me in very simple words "Mariette, we pay the loan to your former client for you, pay us with the agent Nylic QN6 disability benefits, (because my 60 months benefit is a lot greater than the amount of the loan. Remember that the loan is legal.) I will be very happy to accept this. But the New York Life Insurance company free will was allowed the enemy spirits under power of the devil to used their minds and bodies, changed legal loan into embezzlement, and feed this information to their psychiatrists.

Their psychiatrists free will were also given to the enemy spirits under the power of the devil to use them.   Dr. Alan Bergma's report was full of legal terms and bold letters focusing on embezzlement, NOT the doctor's report for diagnosis of mental anguish and physical pain.

Dr. Bergma's report was sent to Dr. Strybel, and Dr. Strybel was my physician at that time, he returned the report to New York, and told me it was returned when I asked for a copy. Dr. Strybel action improper. After the complaint against New York Life Insurance company was filed, I obtained this report from my council Eugene P. Yale.

The New York Life Insurance company needed my permission to obtain copy of my medical record; but at the end of Dr. Bergma's report indicated:

"Note: This report should not be directly released to the claimant; it could have deleterious psychological effects. It only should be shared with her by a qualified mental health professional."

On April 13, 1998, I sent a letter to Ron Joseph, Executive Director of Medical Board of California, complaining against Dr. Alan S. Bergma and Dr. Alan A. Abrams. I received two response letters May 5, 1998, issued two control numbers; number 10 98085882 for Dr. Alan Stuart Bergsma, and number 10 98085883 for Dr. Alan Arthur Abrams. On the control number issued letter indicated, "This is to acknowledge your recent correspondence regarding the above named subject. We are presently reviewing the information you have provided and will be conducting a thorough analysis. Our review may require procuring medical records, documents, and obtaining an opinion from expert consultants as to any potential violation of law. This process can take up to six months. If we need any additional information during the course of our inquiry, you may be contacted by a customer Services Analyst." As of June 30, 1999, the date of settlement of this case, I have not heard from the Medical Board of California. From the time I received Dr. Bergma's report, the Assistant Vice President of New York Life, Joan Brady sent request forms asking me to release my medical records to the New York Life Insurance company, but I told Mr. Yale, "The case is in litigation, and I do not trust New York Life Insurance company any more; they will misuse my medical record."

For over five years, I obeyed God to embrace the suffering for the world's to benefit. New York Life Insurance company added more suffering unto me. Obeying God's instructions that I must take the settlement and "not" go through the trials, be patient with them, love them, and do what God asked of me so they can convert to God. After my case was thrown out of court, before filed for appealed, I sent a letter April 26, 1999 to New York Life Chairman of the Board and Seymour Sternbert and Assistant Vice President Joan Brady. Mr. Yale received an offer from New York Life Insurance attorney, with a request the settlement consent be confidential. I told Mr. Yale, "It is the most important for the Divine mission God entrusted to me in this case is the settlement WILL NOT consent to be confidential. I offered a face to face meeting with New York Life insurance to speak to them." Then the arrangement for the settlement was made for June 29, 1999.

On June 29, 1999 conference were two New York Life representative came to their attorney office in Irvine, but they did not face to face with me during the settlement process. I saw them walking in front of me before I entered the conference. After the settlement agreement were signed by all parties, I came to them said hello to them; and gave each of them and their attorney the "God Creation and Healing" audio tape. "God's Creation and Healing" audio tape. (The audio tape contains testimony of Mrs. Kim Salas. Through me at the Lord's Prayer during the Catholic mass, God healed Kim from her shaking hands and emotional distress. She described that both of her hands shook like Parkinson's disease. The tape also explains God's creation of man: his soul, spirit, with and in the physical body; human life starts at the time of conception; and God's healing through this tax petition for the civil right to freedom of religion in the United States.)

After I entered the conference room and greet the mediator, Mr. Viggo Boserup, I laid in front of him, on the conference table: One side was a "New York Life Annual Report 1998," at the center front cover indicated, "Financial Strength / Integrity / Humanity;" next to it was my agent Contract with New York Life Insurance company, dated June 1, 1986, and the "Going the distance in 1992, New York Life, San Diego Agency" performance award given out at 1992 Kickoff Dinner for San Diego agents; a picture of news agents panel, and I was one of the four New York Life new agent who in the panel to glorified New York Life at the conference. On the another side was a stack of eight certified mailing of foreclosure my home notices from California Reconveyance, a letter denied for Discover card indicating the reason "Foreclosure," and the note affecting my daughter's credit because she is the trustee for the house. I told Mr. Boserup: "I have a question for New York Life people. I would like to ask them directly or would you deliver to them." He agreed to deliver to them.

I explained, "Here is the New York Life Annual report doing so well, pointed out the Financial Strength / Integrity / Humanity. Here is my contract with New York Life, and here is my performance contained in the report, and the picture when I was at the panel to glorify New York Life. New York Life claimed takes care of its agents, gave agents good contract, but they are not real. For almost eight years, I put all my heart and soul in the business to profit the company, of course also for my income, averaging ten hours each day, and including weekends. When God pulled me out, I became physically disabled; I needed help the most, New York Life twisted the issue saying I was embezzled client's money while I had a legal loan with documents. They stopped my benefits, almost throwing me out on the street, all my bills were past due, causing me bad credit, and affecting my daughter's credit. I would like New York Life to answer to me of these?" He asked me, "What do you think they will answer?" He then told me that he will deliver to them; and the questions have not been answered to me.

Obeying God, offer to Him as my living sacrifices to save souls. I agreed to put the total amounts of 60 months benefits of the Nylic QN6-82 that was end in May 1999, and my future 11 years and six months individual disability benefits in one pot, minus the loan that New York Life paid to my former client without my permission, I settled the case on June 29, 1999. I calculated my benefit to the end of the term of my disability income policy. The reason I used the end of the contract term because God already told me that I will continue to be suffering as I am now, plus God is the One who is controlling my mind and actions. To satisfied the earthly law, Dr. Nelson and Dr. Frost's statements indicated that I will likely be permanently disabled. After the attorney fee and cost, I ended up with less than half of my benefit, and retained the settlement "will not" consent confidentially, the first Amendment of the United State Constitution, "freedom of speech, or of the press."

It was a surprise to me, when I received the itemized cost from Mr. Yale, there were over three thousand dollars charged to me. These charges were paid for New York Life Insurance company's attorney taking depositions from the psychiatrists of my choice, to obtain information for their benefits. In front of God, these charges must be billed to New York Life Insurance company, not to my attorney.

After I signed the settlement agreement on June 29, 1999, I told Mr. Yale to get a copy and give it to me. When I came to endorsed the settlement check on July 13, 1999, he did not give me a settlement agreement; he only gave me a copy of cost itemizes, and told me, "You read them, if you have any question, ask me on Friday." Then Amber gave me an appointment 10:00 am on Friday, July 16, 1999. When I got home, I remember of I still not have copy of a settlement agreement; I called Mr. Yale's office and spoke to Amber; I asked her to fax a copy to me. She told me that she will fax to me in same day; but she did not. On July 14, 1999, I sent Mr. Yale a letter request for a copy of this agreement and invoices to be ready for me to pick up when I met with him on July 16, 1999. But when I got to his office, he was not there, instead there was an envelope for me to pick up. I went to the bank where Mr. Yale account to turned his business check to the bank cashier check. After I turned Mr. Yale's business check into a bank check, I look inside the envelope there was no settlement agreement. I was very afraid that the settlement agreement would be altered after I signed it. I called his office on my wireless phone while I was standing at the bank, spoke to Amber, I informed her that I will come back in a few minutes to pick up an agreement. I then walked cross the street to his office to pick up an agreement, but Amber, his assistant did not find it for me. I then left a note for Mr. Yale. When I got home I asked the Lord to help me; He told me to call New York Life's attorney in Irvine obtain a copy, but New York Life attorney's secretary informed me that he does not allow them to talk to me. I asked her to fax it to Mr. Yale for me. She promised that she will do it within three hours.

After I did this the Lord instructed me to rush the letter that served as an invoice to the New York Life Insurance company Chairman of the Board. I did as the Lord commanded me.

Therefore, my duty in this Divine mission that God entrusted to me, I must disclose the details of my matter to protect New York Life's agents and the agents at other insurance companies; and to protect the insurance policies holders of the disability policies of all insurance companies; and protect mental illness patients that do not understand the systems of the insurance industry and many psychiatrists, the two set of laws, (one for the weak and poor, another for rich and famous,) and government agencies practice.

In my case, I am directly received instructions from God, and I completely depending in God and do exactly of how and when God told me to do. I strongly advice each one of you to obey God, seek Him for instructions each time you get involve with any of insurance company, psychiatrist, government agency. When a person trust and depending in God, He will never forsake you. God sent me into the world be surrounding of natural things like you; these people did to me; they will do to any of you. Do not trust any insurance company, psychiatrist, government agency, and the legal system, but your God alone. Keep in your mind that people very easy to give their free will be under power of the devil, more or less depending on each individual, I mean the relationship between a person and God; and the devil proposes is to destroy man soul, physical life and financial.

While I was writing this conclusion, the Lord Jesus reminded me of the people on that day who slandered and crucified him on the cross. I am His servant following my Master's footsteps; in this century God entrusted to me this Divine mission, the New York Life changed from legal loan to embezzlement, and Dr. Bergsma's focus on embezzled not the mental anguish and physical pain.

Eternal Father's Judgment

At 3:15pm on July 13, 1999 at the middle of my devotion, the Eternal Father said to me, "The four hundred twenty five thousand I gave you means holiness, discernment, and righteousness of the Creator of heaven and the earth, not New York Life settlement amounts, you are not listening. The settlement amount you received from New York Life is the same formula settlement like every other one received from New York Life. Let's open the truth of the insurance industry practice to the public. Keep the conclusion you did after the settlement. All of these were foretold in Isaiah chapters two and ten."

Isaiah chapter 2: 1-5 "Zion, the Messianic Capital" Isaiah 2:6-22 "The Lord's Judgment against Idols." Isaiah 10:1-4 "Social injustice," Isaiah 10:5-27 "Assyria the Unconscious Instrument of God," Isaiah 10:28-34 "Sennacherib's Invasion."

The Eternal Father's judgment also can be applied to other situations as well beside the New York Life Insurance company and the insurance industry. The biblical pattern meaning for number four is symbolic of holiness, number two is symbolic of discernment, and number five is symbolic of authority over the supernatural power of the devil working through human bodies, and supernatural power in the supernatural realm. It is the power of the Creator of the heaven and the earth.

There are some chapters in this book I wrote that God allowed me to go through things like other ordinary people go through in life; but the difference is I obey God and do everything He wants me to do. From obeying all God's commandments, God bestowed upon me the gift of holiness. From do everything God asks received a gift of holiness. From holiness God controls that me completely. From God controlling me, the works I do, and words I spoke accompany God's power. From God's controlling me completely the gift of discernment is attached to me. When I discern between right and wrong I will reject the wrong and remain firm in the right. The right is to obeying God and do everything He asks of me, my right to retaining the first amendment of the United States Constitution of freedom of speech. Other people may choose to go to trail for greater amount of money.

From I retained the not consent to settlement confidentially; now the Eternal Father using me as His Vessel to open wide to the truth to the world of the insurance industry, psychiatrists and government agency. God will bless them in the future, after they convert to God from their hearts and actions, and all their iniquities being purge by God.

Because my obedience to God took financial loss and embracing suffering for others to gain benefits, God rewards me with other things that money can not purchase. My case of obeying God and doing His will shall apply to any of you, and you will receive a reward in a different way by God. Please refer to Isaiah chapters two and ten for more details of the Almighty God judging and reward.

At 8:30pm on July 14, 1999, the Eternal Father instructed me, "You need to get copies of all the invoices of the cost for the litigation from your attorney; bill the attorney's fee and the other expenses to New York Life insurance company, send it to the Chairman of the Board, and do the same for Nationwide insurance company." The Almighty God means that He is just God, and everyone must pay for the damages that they caused to others; either to the same person or to others, in various ways. This including money, health, business and personal financial heard ship, or great lost, or personal , business relationships trouble, etc....

Rebuild My Church Divine Mission

(The Lord Jesus gave this name to Mariette)

P.O. Box 261550 ✦ San Diego, CA 92196-1550

July 16, 1999

Sent via U. S. Certified Mail

Seymour Sternbert, Chairman of the Board
New York Life Insurance Company

Re: Request for reimbursement of litigation costs.

Dear Chairman Sternbert,

Obeying the Almighty God, the Creator of heaven and the earth gave me instruction on July 13, 1999. The fault of New York Life insurance terminated my benefits from March 1998 to July 1998, caused these costs. Therefore, this letter is to serve as an invoice to you, as the Chairman of the Board for New York Life insurance company. Also enclosed are copies of itemized costs that were caused by the New York Life insurance company that God asked me to bill to you. Please pay the amounts on the invoice to me upon received.

I am sending you chapter 34 and 35 edited manuscript that is ready for layout in the book "God's Purification - Not Easy;" together with an outline of it. This book will be published parallel with the book "The Only Tax Petition at the United States Tax Court."

Please find the reason of the caused of cost on both chapters. If you need more details of the reason, please do not hesitate to contact me.

Sincerely in Christ Jesus,

Mariette Do-Nguyen, Founder & President

Rebuild My Church Divine Mission

(The Lord Jesus gave this name to Mariette)

P.O. Box 261550 ✦ San Diego, CA 92196-1550

July 26, 1999

Sent Via U.S. Certified Mail Returned Receipts

Mediator Viggo Boserup, Esq., 1801 Century Park East, Ste 2400, Los Angeles, CA 90067

J. Ronald Ignatuk, Esq., Law Offices Barger & Wolen LLP 19800 MacArthur Blvd. Irvine, CA 92612

Seymour Sternbert, Chairman of the Board New York Life Insurance Company.

51 Madison Ave. 13th Floor, New York, NY 10010

Eugene P. Yale, Esq. 501 W. Broadway Ste. 1350, San Diego, CA 92101

Re: Contesting against incorrect information on Settlement Agreement
dated June 29, 1999
Mariette Do-Nguyen vs. New York Life Insurance company,

Dear Gentlemen,

At the time I offered a face to face with New York Life representative for the purposed of explain to them of how terrible wrong they did me before I take any settlement amount, with condition of I will not consent of the settlement to be confidential. Mr. Yale advised me of renting a judge to be a mediator. I agreed with him, I thought that since I suggested this and because my health situation is very difficult for me to make a long drive. I cannot go more than an hour long without rest and prayer. Because of these, a judge would be from San Diego area, and meet in San Diego.

But when I received a letter from Mr. Yale, dated June 14, 1999, that a conference will be at the Law Offices Barger & Wolen LLP, New York Life attorneys, and the conference started at 9:00 am on June 29, 1999. The mediator will be Viggo Boserup, and Mr. Yale will meet me a half hour prior to the mediation hearing. I fear I will not be able to drive there and return with almost three hours driving and hours conference. I asked the Lord Jesus, He told me, "The Father allowed it to happen." Obeying God, I asked Him to strengthen me.

I left San Diego at 7:00 am on June 29, 1999, because traffic was heavy and jammed, I arrived at the Law Offices of Bager & Wolen LLP about five minutes before 9:00 am. After being there for the conference of over four hours and two hours driving to get there, I was very exhausted; although when I be exhausted very heard for people to tell, because Spirit of the Almighty God shadow me. After I signed two different documents, while Mr. Ignatuk's secretary was still making changes on the agreements. After I signed them, I told Mr. Yale that I must go, and asked Mr. Yale get the agreements and give me copies.

Around noon, Mr. Boserup asked me and Mr. Yale while we were in the conference room if it would be okay for us that they order lunch and bring it there, while we continued the discussion. I agreed with his idea, and reached into my pack to get the money to pay for Mr. Yale's and my portion; but Mr. Boserup told me that he thinks Mr. Ignatuk's office would treat us.

While Mr. Yale was sitting at my left, and Mr. Boserup was sitting across the table eating our lunch. When Mr. Boserup and Mr. Yale just finished eating, and I was still eating, Mr. Ignaturk came to the left side of Mr. Yale and gave him the first part of an agreement, and said some comments of the changes that the secretary was still typing. Mr. Yale turned to me, laying this part of agreement on the conference table and explained to me, and I was focused on not consenting to confidentially. After Mr. Yale finished explaining to me this portion; I asked, "Where is the part that I will not consent to confidentially?" He replied to me, "You are not consenting to confidentially. It will not be on the agreement."

Through the dialogue between Mr. Ignatuk and Mr. Yale when Mr. Ignatuk came the second time, gave Mr. Yale more pages and told Mr. Yale that there were more pages still typing changes, and these more pages were not the same wording of the pages that Mr. Yale just finished explained to me. I found out that the agreements were pre-prepared by the New York Life attorney, and Mr. Yale read them and made corrections. Then Mr. Ignatuk came to Mr. Yale the third time with few pages of the end of a settlement agreement. Mr. Yale took them and continued to finished them, and asked me to sign.

While I was signing this agreement Mr. Boserup still sitting across the table, I thought "Mr. Yale explained to me very fast, I could not take time to read them word by word and think of them, but I trust that he had already read them, and he was representing me. I will read them later after they finished changes, before I leave."

Then Mr. Ingatuk brought to Mr. Yale more pages, and Mr. Yale explained to me another agreement of mediation procedures; this agreement had less pages than the one before. When I read the about a half way of the papers, I saw some thing confidential, and I protested, "I do not agree with confidential." Mr. Boserup and Mr. Yale told me that the mediation is confidential, not the settlement. The second agreement was already signed by Mr. Yale and Mr. Ignatuk before it was brought to me, the two named as Joan Brady, and Carol O'Driscoll had not signed. Again, I thought, "I will read both of the actual agreements when the changes are finished, before I leave." After I signed both of them, while I was still waiting for actual agreements, Mr. Boserup, Mr. Yale, and I engaged some conversation. Through this conversation, the God the Father silently smeared my memory of getting these agreements before I leave, and I told Mr. Yale to make sure to get an actual agreement and give me a copy and I left.

A few minutes after I left the parking lot, while I was driving, I felt very tired and sleepy; I prayed and asked the Lord to help me to drive home safely. I did get home safely and fell asleep immediately after I got home. But when I was on the freeway, I was very tired and a few times almost hit other cars.

Since, I agreed with everything on the agreement it must be the truth, and I agreed to settled the case for $xxxxx; but I must always obey the Almighty God's instructions of sent an invoice New York Life Insurance Chairman of the Board Sternbert. On July 16, 1999 I prepared an invoice and sent to New York Life Chairman of the Board. After I mailed this letter I went to the bank to deposit my check. When I got home I received a copy of the settlement agreement, dated June 29, 1999, that broke into two parts during faxing, some parts were unable to be read, some parts were blank. I also received phone messages from Amber at Mr. Yale's office, I returned her call, and told her of the trouble of the agreement sent through facsimile, and asked her to send a copy through the mail service for me. She said that she already did.

On July 17, 1999, I received the original letter unsigned from Mr. Yale, dated July 16, 1999. I would like to respond to Mr. Yale's letter as follows:

a) On July 14, 1999, I sent to Mr. Yale a letter, thanking him for helping me. The New York Life company I served for almost eight years acted in bad faith, broke their promises, intended to harm me. When I needed the most Mr. Yale advanced all the cost for me without asking me to pay or sending me any bills. He only let me know how much approximately at the time we discussed of the amount of the settlement demand. I owe to Mr. Yale of he understanding of how suffered I went through because New York Life's people done terribly wrong to me. Although, When God asked me to tell him anything, I still have to do the right things when God asks me; the things God asked me to do for him through the matter of he represented me. He is not understand it now, but he will understand them later; like God did to me, I did not understand before, and I understood them now.

b) I have questions for the amounts paid to the psychiatrists of my choice for New York Insurance company to take their depositions, none of other expenses.

c) The Eternal Father instructed me to send a letter that served as an invoice to New York Life Insurance company Chairman of the Board Seymour Sternbert, dated July 16, 1999, of God's judgment against New York Life Insurance company in the matter when they were terribly wrong to me. It is symbolic of the Almighty God judging against them on other cases before and after my case; and it also symbolic of God is judging against insurance industry. Everything God asks me to do is coming with His supernatural almighty power.

d) Again, I thank to Mr. Yale for warning me that the New York Life may seek and obtain an anti-harassment restraining order prohibiting any communication with them. They have free will which allowed the devil to use their minds and bodies to do this. But I must do what God asked of me. The world is a temporary home to generate good deed (s) for every one to carry to eternal life in heaven. They have their free will to reject eternal life in heaven and blessing on earth.

In response to Carol M. O'Driscoll on behalf of the New York Life Chairman of the Board Sternbert, on her letter of July 21, 1999 indicated, "The Company is not obligated to reimburse the costs allegedly arising out of the temporary cessation of the payment of benefits in 1998. Please be advised that on June 29, 1999, you with the advice of your own counsel executed a Settlement Agreement and Mutual Release. In paragraph 6 of that agreement, you released New York Life from, among other things, any claim or demand of whatever nature that you might have had to... costs, expenses, attorneys fee....."

Paragraph 6 of the settlement agreement was over one page long, and it indicated that I, as the plaintiff to release New York Life Insurance company of millions of things, and paragraph 7 indicated, "Pertaining solely to and limited to the DO-NGUYEN RELEASED MATTERS, it is understood by DO-NGUYEN that there is a risk that subsequent to the execution of this AGREEMENT, DO-NGUYEN may incur or suffer loss, damage or injuries which are in some way caused by or related to matters which are the subject of paragraph 6 of this AGREEMENT, but which are unknown or unanticipated at the time of the execution of this AGREEMENT."

Therefore, the New York Life insurance company had planned to strip me of requiring the Psychiatrist certification to cover their evil plan by having me sign these agreements while they were still changing the corrections that Mr. Yale corrected on the agreements that they prepared early. Beyond that I did not read the entire agreement word by word to fully understand the entirely agreements.

I have executed in perjured of a declaration my loan is legal, and I have legal documents for them; how can I agree that the amount $xxxx had been misappropriated in the settlement agreement? The New York Life people gave their free will to the devil and his offspring, and the devil gain permission from God to use New York Life and its representatives to place the loan was misappropriated in the settlement; in the same format of other cases to harm me. The enemy spirits works through New York Life's people mind and actions. The New York Life's own stick hit against its back. Yes, I do suffer a great deal caused by New York Life in these matters, but the reward God has for me is in heaven, which to me no one in this world can compare.

I AM CONTESTING THE FOLLOWING UNTRUE INFORMATION ON THE SETTLEMENT AGREEMENT:

a) On settlement agreement page number 3, (DO-NGUYEN's NYLIC TRACT Claim): This paragraph indicated inaccurate loan information that should never be in this agreement. The loan I borrowed from Mrs. kkk is a legal loan; and New York Life acted wrongly by paying her without my permission. This loan had no connection with my agent physical incapacity QN6-82. These two are two different issues; I have provided the legal note and trust deed to Mr. Hilderbrand on April 7, 1994. After that I wrote to New York Life chairman of the Board and other executive officers giving them numbers of letters and explaining to them. These legal loan documents I also provided to Mr. Yale, and Mr. Yale provided them to the court as an exhibit on my declaration. Therefore, I request to separate this legal loan from my agent Nylic QN6-82 physical incapacity, and completely remove this legal loan, and Mrs. kkk's name from the settlement.

b) On settlement agreement end of page s and beginning of page number 3, (in RECITALS, DO-NGUYEN's POLICY Claim). New York Life changed the legal term into embezzlement and fed this information to Dr. Alan Bergma. Dr. Bergma allowed the devil to use his mind and body to go along with New York Life, focusing on embezzlement and issuing false report, to profit New York Life.   New York Life people rejected Dr. Strybel's statements containing true information report. I had explained to New York Life personnel of the time I first went to Dr. Gold that my mind was filled with pain caused by New York Life. Dr. Gold and others spent the majority of the time talking about New York Life, very little of my mental anguish, and physical pain.   I have explained to Dr. Gold, Mr. Yale, New York Life people, and many others of the "Delusional disorder, grandiose type." This is a gift from God, and it comes with the strong gift of discernment.   This is the gift for prophets in the old testament, and Saint John who stood at the foot of the Cross. The delusional disorder is comes with spiritual battle. The spiritual battle is a tremendous amount of mental anguish and body pain daily.   This generation, God entrusted this gift to me together with the Divine mission. The things I saw in my dreams and visions are symbolism; and many times God's words speak to me in symbolism. I must spend a lot of time in prayer to understand the meaning of them. Psychiatrists, and the medical field do not understand the meanings of symbolism, they name "delusional disorder, grandiose type." The paranoid schizophrenia is the mental illness caused by the spirits under the power of the devil, it comes with no discernment, fear, causing destruction like the man who killed the two security guards at Capital Hill. Many mental illness patients came to psychiatrists and agreed to take medication without praying to the Almighty God, and the situation gets worse. Without God, the devil will work strongly within the minds and bodies of man. Therefore, I request to remove the false medical evidence from Dr. Alan Bergma's report and the incorrect diagnosis from Dr. Gold's statement of my symptoms.

c) On settlement agreement page 12, paragraph 16, indicates, "THE PARTIES acknowledge that certain of the agreements which relate to the subject matter of this AGREEMENT may purport to require the application of the laws of states other than the State of California." My loan is obtained in the State of California, and they are legal documents. Therefore, any words related to this loan are void in this settlement agreement.

As of July 26, 1999, the day I executed this letter I still have not received a copy of an agreement regarding the mediation confidential. I will acknowledge when I receive it, and comment on it, with the same reason that I had not thoroughly read them on June 29, 1999, because I signed it while Mr. Ignatuk's secretary still typing changes.

I request these changes to be made immediately upon your receiving this contest request.

Sincerely In the name of the Almighty God,

Mariette Do-Nguyen

36

GOD REVEALED TO HIS CHURCH LEADERS

The First Deacon Receives the Gifts of Healing and Deliverance

March 9, 1997, at midnight, during my devotion, in my vision I saw the middle aisle, after entering the front double glass doors of the Cathedral of Saint Andrew. There was a square wooden chair facing the sanctuary; in front of it a man was wearing a white alb, and kneeling while leaning his lower back against the chair. From up high in the foyer, I saw the glow of a bright light shining on his face; it seemed as if this light came from an invisible candle held in his right hand. He covered the other side of the light with his left hand, making it shine more powerfully between his face and hand as it radiated onto his face. I asked, "Lord, who does this man symbolize? Why is he not at the sanctuary?" I then saw, in the middle of the air, the left side is Deacon Gary's face. Then the Lord said to me, "I bestowed the gifts of healing and deliverance upon him alone."

I then saw Deacon Gary was standing in front of his wife, at the end of the second pew, to the right of the sanctuary, facing me. I was kneeling, facing the sanctuary, as the Lord encircled both the deacon and his wife, and He said to me, "Because he is a deacon, the vision is at the beginning of the middle aisle."

On one occasion in the past, Deacon Gary actually was standing and talking to me with his wife behind him, at the end of the second pew to the right, in the Cathedral of Saint Andrew, just as the Lord showed me in this vision.

The bright light is symbolic of God's presence. Wearing white represents a pure heart. His hand covering the light is symbolic of God's presence dwelling within him, which has not yet radiated to others. My seeing his back symbolizes that this revelation will reveal other deacons; but the face of Deacon Gary at the side, supporting the kneeling man is symbolic of God actually revealing to me the bestowal of His gifts upon Deacon Gary. His kneeling and leaning against the square wooden chair is symbolic of his willingness to carry his own cross and the Cross of the Lord Jesus, the cross of obedience to all God's commandments and following in the Lord Jesus's footsteps. The deacon and his wife standing at the second pew of the right section symbolize God helping them to discern and understand His commandments. My kneeling represents my obedience to God's instructions and my promise to deliver the exact content of His messages.

The actual scene of the deacon and his wife standing and the Lord encircling them, means the Lord chose both of them to assist with marriage and child counseling, because the grace of God has given them both marriage and a life of serving God; therefore, they are better prepared to assist in these areas than a priest. And this commandment will protect His priests from the devil who causes marital troubles, leading women to seek out priests for advice, then using these women to attack the priests and bishops.

The word "alone" after he was commanded by the Lord, who bestowed the gifts of healing and deliverance, means that God only bestowed these gifts to the deacon, not to his wife; but His encircling both of them means that he married to God of responsibility to serve people.

The Lord Jesus loves us; He is not willing to lose a single soul. He has shown His love for us by dying on the Cross to save us. He is now asking us, "Do you love Me? show Me that love in your heart and in your actions."

Jesus the Lord has told me, "My Father said, 'It is time for My Church to unify and My wounds will be healed.' "

In this revelation, the Lord Jesus also revealed His message by commanding me, Mariette, and all spiritual leaders with the loving and simple words, "Obedience to Him."

He said, "Pastors, reverends, bishops, and your wives; I chose both of you to come closer to Me. Obey all my commandments and serve Me. The devil has been blinding your eyes to make you eliminate the four most important commandments that I gave to you before I went home to heaven. I have bestowed this glowing light to open your eyes and your hearts that you might see the truth. Unify God's Church; honor your Holy Blessed Virgin Mother, she is your spiritual mother and she is always there to assist you. Do not ignore her any longer." By obeying these four most important commandments you will be in full communion with God

Spirit of The Church Urgently in Need of Holy Priests

March 19, 1997. In my dream, I saw myself standing on the ground in the open air during the day, and looking up to heaven. In front of my feet was a glow of bright light. On the other side of this glowing bright light was a man kneeling and bending his head down, looking at a 9 x 12 inch paper pad, in between his knees and the glowing light. On the ground to his right was a gold pen placed inside a square white marble holder. While I was busy in communion with God, this man interrupted me and said, "Tell me about the

Holy Eucharist healing and altar call at Saint Andrew Cathedral." As he said this, I knew he was anxious to know about the altar call service more than the Holy Eucharist healing. The location changed, now I was inside the rectory of the Cathedral of Saint Andrew, inside the same room that I had the appointment with Father Scott the day before. I saw the Cathedral of Saint Andrew to my left, outside the rectory.

In understanding this dream, I am myself, and my looking up to Heaven means I am completely dependent on God for works in the mission that He called me to fulfill. The glowing bright light is the presence of God.

The man kneeling is symbolic that church people must be humble. Bending down is symbolic of embracing the virtue of love, serving God by loving Him first and secondly one another then ourselves. Left is the weak side and it is symbolic of human weakness allowing the devil to gain. Cathedral means the firm foundation; Saint Andrew was the first apostle that the Lord Jesus chose is symbolic of me. In this revelation the Lord revealed that everyone of us must fight against the devil, and go back to the foundation that the Lord Jesus teaches us to serve God in love from our hearts.

The man anxious to hear about the Holy Eucharist healing services and altar call is symbolic of the church urgently needing more holy priests to lead people to eternal life; and now is the time that the Lord Jesus will heal His church by blessing it with more holy priests.

In this revelation, God revealed to the church in many areas. Serve God from our hearts, serve one another with love from every heart, not just externally. Be humble before God.

When Does Seminarian Life Begin?

January 17, 1998. In my dream I was inside an empty huge house with several people, these people were my helpers. While I was standing opposite my helpers, suddenly a lot of dirty laundry dropped down from the air. My helpers responsibility was to bundle the laundry, but there was nothing to bundle them with. I then was standing in front of an empty open closet. At the end of the wooden rod, to my right, were several metal hangers. I took them out of the closet, and used my gardening iron scissors to cut these hangers at their shoulders, straightened them out, and gave the wire to the helpers for bundling the dirty laundry.

The laundry now turned into dry jack fruit, and these helpers crushed them to pieces, small pieces like come out of a grinder. Then they strained the fruit with a Vietnamese bamboo rice strainer. The parts that fell through the strainers were put in large cloth bags, and set in a dark corner of the house. While these flower bags were in the corner, they condensed themselves, a midget priest came and said something to me. I then said to him, "We have a family living here that has several small boys. Would you put two of them in seminary for me?" He replied, "Putting the small children at their ages in seminary costs too much to raise them. We only accept them after high school." Then he left.

The laundry is symbolic of purification. Vietnamese bamboo strainers are round in different sizes, normally about 36 inches in diameter and five inches high. They are used to strain unshelled rice, separating whole rice from broken rice. A person holds the strainer in both hands and turns it until all of the broken rice falls down the holes at the bottom. The strainer in this dream is symbolic of God separating the good and evil like goats and sheep to His right and his left. Those staying on the top of the strainer are symbolic of those who endure to the end. Those in the rice bags and set in the dark corner of the house and condensed are those rejecting cooperation with God.

The helpers are symbolic of angels. The midget priest is symbolic of spiritual leaders who made church rules not in accordance with God's commandments. The metal hangers to bundle is symbolic of strict rules will be applied. God revealed cutting the metal hangers with my iron gardening scissors and the words I spoke to the midget priest spoke symbolic of each one of us must obey all God's commandment from the time our souls came down from heaven, it is the time of conception, and to endure to the end. The midget priest's statements is symbolic of majority people in this world want to live in the life that benefits flesh, damaged the souls, and will convert when get old age before the physical die.

At 2:15 p.m. the Lord Jesus told me, "You go to the pastor of Good Shepherd parish for confession today. Confess the sin you committed for almost twenty five years in the invalid marriage in front of God. Then your children will understand everything you said."

I entered the Blessed Sacrament Chapel at 3:00 p.m. and felt God's power so strongly upon me that I was hardly able to open my eyes. I had to try very hard to look for the priests names at the doors of confession boxes; I saw the pastor's name on one of the two doors. I then went to the side, kneeled facing the Tabernacle and continued to examine myself. There were three people sitting in three chairs in the line waiting, when they moved up and left the last chair empty, I moved to this chair, continuing to keep my eyes closed, opening them just a little when I had to move. During this time the Lord Jesus told me, "You are here today, while you are in the confession box, facing the priest, I will be above both of you, bestowing discernment, with holiness to prevail over the devil upon the priest".

I entered the confession box, made sure the door was tightly locked and got ready to kneel down. I found out that the priest was not the pastor, but the young priest. I silently asked, "Lord, what do I do?" I then knelt down. The priest and I discussed the invalid marriage in front of God, but the church authorities denied the annulment. He then said to me, "For your penance you say one Our Father, and pray for God's will be done."

For my contrition I said, "Father, Lord Jesus, Holy Spirit...I ask you to pour out Your grace of discernment and holiness to prevail over the devil upon the church minister in this confession box."

While I was praying for God's grace upon the priest, I saw the number "02 04....." up high in the sky. This means God was telling me that my prayer was not only for the priest in this confession box, but for other priests who cooperate with God. The invalid marriage in front of God and committing sexual intercourse in this revelation is symbolic of priests who violate their vows, and are married to the devil's works like men and women having sexual intercourse outside of marriage in front of the Almighty God. God's commandments are in the Book of Leviticus Chapter 18. The pastor of the Good Shepherd parish is symbolic of God bestowing His grace upon church ministers to lead His people to Him. My children are symbolic of those who convert, daily exam and repent for heavenly eternal life.

January 18, 1998. Among other dreams that support the interpretation to this dream, in one dream I saw a cup of iced tea. The ice melted and stayed on top of the tea. The cup was sitting on top of a black and white striped area rug, between the foot of my bed and the wall between the closet and bathroom.

In the morning before I woke up, the Blessed Mother taught me like a mother teaching a teenager, she said, "You need to be very careful of everything; and understand the way God speaks to you. For an example: You are saving time to serve God by eating in front of the television to watch the news. The Lord told you that you can watch television some time, but do not eat and watch every day. You do not have to eat and watch TV, you just sit and watch it little. When the Lord told you this, He meant that you should not watch television, the enemy spirits use television broadcasts to attack people. Or when you see something that needs to be done, even a little, you should do it right the way. Do not put it off for later, the enemies will come and make you forget it. Like the cup of iced tea, if you do not pick it up and dump it in the sink, you will trip it over, even though you said, 'I know that I will not knock it over.' "

She then told me to dress in the sky blue three-piece dress, wear pearl earrings, and anoint myself with blessed holy oil before I go to the Sunday 8:30 a.m. mass. She also instructed me to sit in the right section, at the end of the third pew and next to the baptismal fountain.

As I was walking up, the first four rows were reserved for the faith initiative. I silently said, "Lord, I can not sit at the third pew, it is reserved." I took the fifth end pew.

The first few sentences of the visiting priest's homily and his body language troubled me. I was trying to think if the Lord wanted me to hear his sermon, and the Blessed Virgin Mother told me, "Just listen to what he is saying." He interpreted the Lord Jesus turning water to good wine at the wedding at Cana as the sign, and he said people should look for signs.

It was time for Catechism candidates to leave for their class and give some empty seats in the reserved area. I heard the voice say to me, "Move to the second pew." As I heard this, I said, "Lord, if this is not from You, I will destroy this voice. If it is from You, it will happen." I meant that God is the only one who has power to move my physical body; and I remained in the same spot. The voice tried to convince me three times, and I repeated the same pleading to the Lord.

At the sign of peace, the Lord told me, "The boy in front of you, give him My peace." I looked at the boy in the seat in front of me, and waited after he finished hugging his mother for peace; I then touched his shoulder with both of my hands; he turned his face to me. Both of my hands were holding his right hand, and I said, "Peace of the Lord Jesus be with you. Jesus the Lord loves you." He nodded his head. I asked him, "Did you understand what I said?" He replied, "Yes." I then said to him, "Be a good boy."

Immediately after I kneeled down from receiving the Holy Eucharist, the Lord told me, "You are not far from being in front of the public. You only need to distinguish the voice tone at the first sound." I asked the Blessed Virgin Mother, "Mother, I think the Lord is teaching me something new; how to discern supernatural voices quickly." She said, "In the natural, when a person receives an order, he sees the evidence in a body form so he can recognize where the order comes from. In spirit you do not see, you have to discern the voice."

After the mass, I asked the boy, "How old are you?" He replied, "Nine." I said to him, "You will be a good priest." As his mother heard me say this, she immediately turned to me and said, "You really feel that? I have been encouraging him." I said, "You need to find a seminary for him, put him in there and pray for him. Do not wait until he gets out of high school, at that age that they know girls, and are in love, have sexual relationships, then they go to seminary. After ordination, the devil uses their past experience to attack them easier. Just look at many priests having sexual misconduct, the devil attacks them a lot heavier than laity, because they are the ones who will assist people to God." She agreed with me. I then asked her, "What is his name?" She said, "Matthew." I said, "The tax collector will watch over him." I meant the apostle Matthew is his patron saint.

The cup of iced tea that had been there for too long is symbolic of things that we know, but ignore, and put them aside. The closet is symbolic of a place to put things away and forget about them. The sink is to dispose trash. If a person keeps collecting small wrong actions, each action will not harm anything, but other things added to that will cause big trouble. For example, when a child goes to the store and takes a piece of gum and eats in the store. No one can see this child's action. This is stealing and will grow within him to expensive shoplifting, bank robbery, and committing murder for money. The Blessed Virgin Mother telling me how to dress to be in front of the Almighty God is symbolic of God choosing His priests, but the parent must cooperate with God in His salvation when the child is little. Plant the seed of grooming him to be a priest at the time he learns God's word for the first Holy Communion. When the seed becomes a plant, the parent must take it and plant in a bigger pot, and that pot is seminary, if not, this plant will not be able to grow in God. Then the time of harvest is the priest's ordination. All of these must come from the heart. The third row was reserved. I sat at the one that was closest to the one in her instructions, symbolic that I do my best to fulfill the order. The voice trying to trap me is symbolic of very careful discernment, and standing firm to support decisions to the end. Do not let the devil interfere in your thoughts and actions. Nine years old is the best age for parents to get the child ready for seminary, eleven or twelve is the most effective ages for beginning seminary. Starting when the child is this young will produce a holy priest, from his holiness the power of God will work through him.   Matthew's situation was arranged by God for this revelation. By his name "Matthew" God is calling priests for conversion, the congregation must help priests in their road of conversion. When God's power works through a holy priest, his daily services will be focused in God to benefit souls, not on formal good looks, or a professional speaker style in the homily.

Spiritual Leaders Concealed God's Commandments

March 3, 1998. In my dream I was entering the aisle of a dark, dried food store, but a rope was blocking the entrance. I walked over it. While I was looking around, I found a jar of sesame cookies. I was on my way out close to the check out counter; this area had little light, and some other people were about to leave, because store would be closing.

God revealed that spiritual leaders lack understanding of the scriptures. They believe and teach their congregation to believe some things that do not exist, or cut off some of the benefits that God has promised for them. Through me, God will reveal the meaning oorrootly.

I then saw a group of people practicing formal dance in a large room for an upcoming event soon. I found out from the market that I also needed to be practicing this dance, but I did not get a notice. Looking through the group practicing the dance, on the opposite corner was a man responsible to distribute the notices to all members in the group for practice. When I saw him, he also saw me, he drew his strength about to run, and I yelled at him, "When you receive information, you must distribute it, not keep it for yourself only."

I saw another dream that I had seen before, some living heavy medium dark spirit next to the throne said in Vietnamese, "Bi chui phai can rang chiu." In English it translates to "men can not say any thing back while being yell at."

In another dream, I was in a room with another person. He asked me to go outside and help a few others unload stuff from a moving trailer. When I got close to these two man unloading the trailer, I heard a voice coming from that stuff saying in Vietnamese, "Du ma, chang dang gi ma phai tra gia qua mac" In English it means, the four letter word that starts with an F and mother, what we did was little, but the punishment was heavy."

God revealed that people will scolded spiritual leaders when they found out that majority of spiritual leaders are not teach their other the correct meaning of holy scriptures.

God Purifying High-Ranking Spiritual Leaders

February 9, 1998. In my dream I was lying on the floor like a log, in prayer. God's Spirit was going through my muscles and bones, shooting out sparks of power. On the other side of the room, some distance from me was a midget door. The top of it was an oval, the same kind of entrance to the restroom I saw in a dream over week ago. The back of the entrance was blocked with clay; the side of the entrance had an oil lamp with no foot. The lamp was on the floor and its light was very tiny. I was fighting against the oil lamp. I prayed harder and harder, the more I tried, the more sparks shot out from my body; then suddenly the oil lamp exploded like a light bulb.

The other side of the entrance being blocked is symbolic of the world's systems no longer growing. Myself lying down on the floor is symbolic of how I laid down my life for other. Through God's power I fight against the enemy spirits that work through humans, with my living sacrifices to God and complete obedience to Him. The tiny light of the lamp symbolizes God's present in His Church on earth. When it exploded is symbolic of God's present will suddenly appeared in the temple.

In my dream of February 10, 1998 I stood in the open air, looking at the huge tunnel. This tunnel was filled with water, and there was an iron beam with a twisted blade built from one side of the tunnel to the other. The corner close to me had a very tiny oval-topped entrance; this was the only entrance to the tunnel. I saw the iron beam was turning and the blade cut through the water.

The tunnel is symbolic of God's purification, and there is only one gate that every one must go through to enter eternal life in heaven. No one can escape God's power.

> *Lo, I am sending my messenger to prepare the way before me; And suddenly there will come to the temple the LORD whom you seek, and the messenger of the covenant whom you desire. Yes, he is coming, says the LORD of hosts. But who will endure the day of his coming? And who can stand when he appears? For he is like the refiner's fire, or like the fuller's lye. He will sit refining and purifying [silver], and he will purify the sons of Levi, Refining them like gold or like silver that they may offer due sacrifice to the LORD. Then the sacrifice of Judah and Jerusalem will please the LORD, as in the days of old, as in years gone by. I will draw near to you for judgment, and I will be swift to bear witness. Against the sorcerers, adulterers, and perjurers, those who defraud the hired man of his wages, against those who defraud widows and orphans; those who turn*

aside the stranger, and those who do not fear me, says the LORD of hosts.

–Malachi 3: 1-5

Appointments Revelation

July 31, 1997. In my morning devotion, the Lord Jesus told me, "I want you to place an e-mail address on My web site, on the internet, saying 'If you need assistance to heal your emotions and your soul for eternal life in Heaven, or more information regarding priesthood and religious life or supporting seminarians, please e-mail to the Rebuild My Church Mission."

I asked, "Lord, what do I do with their responses? There is no one assisting me now."

The Lord said, "I chose the Abbey of Gethsemane monastery, Seminaries in Vietnam through Cardinal Tung, and Charity order in India, to take over these responses after you mail out the opening letters." These three orders is symbolic of obedience, suffering and charity.

Before the 12:05 p.m. mass, in the Cathedral of Saint Andrew, the Lord Jesus told me, "When you receive their responses, you send out to them the opening letters. I will dictate these letters to you. Afterwards, the prospective priests will be interviewed by Fathers Peter and Scott only, until I give you new directions. The prospective deacons will be interviewed by Deacon Dollar, through the pilot program, unless they are already approved by their dioceses. I want you to contact the charity order in India, to get their representative to interview the prospective nuns." These are symbolic of step by step on the road of purification.

The Lord Jesus continued, "Open a trust account to deposit all donations to support seminarians. All requests for funding must be approved from the Holy See, this includes the requests from Abbey of Gethsemane order. Send this instruction to: Bishop Andrew, Abbot of Abbey of Gethsemane order; Father Peter, Father Scott, Cardinal Tung, Deacon Gary Dollar; the head of the Charity order in India, and a copy of complementary to the Roman Catholic church officials in Vatican." These are symbolic of the level of God's grace working through God's chosen ones on earth.

When He Changes Our Name His Power Come with It

August 30, 1997. In my morning devotion, through the Lord Jesus, the Father said to me, "The thunder has sounded in the ears of the church leaders. You forgave the false witness. You renewed your vows promising even to die for the love you have for your Savior."

He continued, "In spirit, I have changed the Peter Hero like Jacob of Israel. Please put the name Hero in the mission Bylaws. You are the head of the mission; I changed your name to Suffering Servant of God, especially for Jesus's mission, to prepare for the Second

Coming of Christ, also to Michelle. You will continue to suffer and fight. [The Father means that suffering and battle will accompany the names.] Scott's name is not changed, he as a church leader will follow in your footsteps. [The Lord means following in the Lord Jesus's footsteps]. The name Hero is President of the Mission in the bylaws".

Spiritual Leaders Refuse to Cooperate with God

On June 21, 1997, the tobacco companies agreed to pay 368 billion dollars in a settlement with the attorney general. A judge sentenced three teenagers to 15 years each in prison, for stealing a stop sign that caused three deaths in an accident. In my devotion, the Lord told me, "The attorney general is symbolic of Me. Tobacco companies are symbolic of church leaders. The judge is symbolic of Me, putting these three teenagers in prison. Now I have the case to transform God's supernatural into the mission. I have promised you before, but I did not have substance to transform the power. Through you, these two cases are a natural substance for me to transform my power into the mission."

Cigarettes cause cancer, and cancer is a disease of the lungs, and we need air to breathe. But the devil poisons the air through spiritual leaders. Stealing a stop sign is illegally taking away the traffic law, and causing death. Spiritual leaders cut short God's commandments, bringing people to spiritual death. There are huge punishments for spiritual leaders misleading people on earth.

Spiritual leaders must be very careful in everything and actions. Many time these things do not look big, like stealing the stop sign or smoking a cigarette. But these little thoughts or actions can cause major destruction.

God gave every one of us free will to chose Him or to chose the devil. When a person's actions focus in obeying God's commandments, she chooses God. But when a person's actions are evil, he chooses the devil.

God respects everyone's free will, but the devil continues to pull everyone of us toward him. One time the Lord told me, "I give the church leaders free will, they have that free will to some point. If they do not obey me, I take that free will away from them." God spoke of pre-destined chosen ones.

God has pre-destined me, Mariette, for this calling. Coming with this calling is the authority in the supernatural realms. During the night of June 20, 1997, in my devotion, the Lord gave me permission to exercise my authority, to take away the free will from many of the spiritual leaders, and government officials that He loves.

On June 21, 1997, God asked me to distribute the gift of faith and discernment on church leaders who obey to all His commandments, and June 25, 1997 the Lord asked me to distribute God's grace of repentant upon church leaders.

Rebuild My Church Divine Mission

(The Lord Jesus gave this name to Mariette)

P.O. Box 261550 ♦ San Diego, CA 92196-1550

June 17, 1997

Most Reverend Andrew J. McDonald
Bishop of Little Rock Diocese

Re: "God the Father's house is not a den of thieves. "

Dear Excellency,

God would not allow me to come to the Holy Hour of Adoration in the chapel on June 17, 1997, at the Cathedral of Saint Andrew.

While I was looking for a parking place, I saw some people wearing name tags in front of the Cathedral, standing around and talking. I entered the cathedral, and there were a few groups standing inside the church socializing, some of them had their backs turned to the tabernacle that contained the Blessed Sacrament.

I wondered what are these people doing in here? I felt fearful and unsafe. I continued proceeding to the seat that I normally sit in; I saw there was a man setting up a projector and a screen, with a notebook computer at the right side of the altar, up to the middle of the sanctuary.

Immediately after I kneeled, the Lord Jesus's Spirit came upon me powerfully. This is the first time I ever felt His Spirit this way: the Spirit of love was very angry. The love and anger of the Lord Jesus was controlling me, He said to me, "They are turning my Father's house into the den of thieves." I continued trying to pray, but I could not, because the Spirit of the Lord was so angry. I called Tony Thompson, and asked him, "Tony, what are they doing here?" Tony replied, "I don't know." I asked, " Are we still having Communion service?" He replied, "Yes, at 12:05."

When Tony departed from me, the Lord Jesus said to me, "Go tell him [the man setting up the equipment], My Father's house is not a den of thieves." As the Lord said this, my thought was, "This Cathedral belongs to the bishop, and Father Scott is Rector," I said to the Lord, "Lord I will tell Father Scott when he comes back from retreat." The Lord said again, "You go tell him. My Father's house is not a den of thieves." I said, "Jesus, Lord, I will tell Tony and have Tony to tell him." But the Lord insisted, "You, get up and go tell that man, My Father's house is not a den of thieves."

He then dragged me to the sanctuary. Standing at the second step of the sanctuary, facing the equipment, I said to the man doing the set up, "Excuse me, what are you doing here? What is this equipment set up for?" He replied, "I'm setting up for the concert at 12:45, after the service." I said to him, "The Lord Jesus is very angry. He said, 'My Father's house is not a den of thieves. I know that you have permission from the Bishop, but Father Scott is the one who will get all the blame." The man replied to me, "Thank you for giving me the message."

They came to Jerusalem, and on entering the temple area he began to drive out those selling and buying there. He overturned the tables of the money changers and the seats of those who were selling doves. He did not permit anyone to carry anything through the temple area. Then he taught them saying, "Is it not written: 'My house shall be called a house of prayer for all people'? But you have made it a den of thieves.

–Mark 11:15-17.

Even though in this concert the music words are to glorify God, it is wrong. The churches are for worship, especially when there is Blessed Sacrament in the church. Therefore, at no time can the sanctuary be used for concerts. Concerts are to please human ears, not to focus on God like the time of worship. And concerts are to glorify the musicians. And the most thing against God today, June 17, 1997, was moving the Blessed Sacrament Adoration to the small chapel, and using the church for the concert.

The Lord asked me to serve Him as Eucharistic Minister at the Cathedral of Saint Andrew. On June 10, 1997; after I entered the church, I signed for June 11, 13, 18, 20, 23, and 25, 1997.

Sunday, June 15, 1997. I found that all the priests in the diocese will be on retreat this week, and there is only Communion Service. After consulting with the Lord Jesus Monday 16, 1997, I told Tony that I will serve for the Communion Service on June 18, 1997. But this morning, after the Lord dragged me to the sanctuary to talk to the man who did the equipment set up for the concert, He told me, "You will not serve the Communion Service tomorrow; go tell Tony, and cross off your name from the paper. I went to the back of the church to let Tony know what the Lord told me, but there was no pen next to the volunteer service paper sheet; I went back to my seat, and the Lord told me, "Get your pen, and go cross off your name from that paper. I will not let you touch the muddy morass." I did as He asked of me. I then returned to my seat, and the Lord said, "When you get home, write a letter to Bishop Andrew, tell him what happened today."

At this time, I did not understand why the Lord instructed me to cross off my name, but I obeyed Him in faith, and I believed that there was major teaching that He had me cross off my name.

A few weeks ago, on Sunday, after the 12:03 p.m. mass, while the final song was still being sung, people were standing singing and praying. There was a woman, a man, and two of the altar boys competing with each other to turn off the candles. I then heard the Lord Jesus say, "They are treating the sanctuary like a supermarket." I then repeated out loud what the Lord said, and there were a few people around who also saw the incident and heard the words I repeated of what I heard from the Lord.

And last Sunday, June 15, 1997, during the vigil mass on Saturday, another incident happened. Sitting at the front pew was a lector and the man accompanying her. Their actions were very distracting to the people behind. I believe that lectors and Eucharistic ministers must set a good example for others to follow, not exposing evil actions to distract others from focus on God.

We must focus on what comes from our hearts to God, to glorify God, not the external things that glorify man. I have enclosed "Church Manners" that the Blessed Mother taught me. I passed them on to others, too.

I must say everything the Lord asked me to say. I know these words will not please you, but these things are good for your soul and the souls of others that you shepherd.

In Christ Jesus,

Mariette Do-Nguyen

Pay Back to the Community What You Owe

The Third Annual Red Mass in observance of Law Day, at 11:00 am at Cathedral of Saint Andrew.

Normally I am in the church thirty minutes before the mass, to be with the Lord. The main celebrant was the Most Reverend Andrew, Bishop of Little Rock Diocese. There were reserved rows in both front sections of the pews for judges, attorneys, and legislators. At the time the procession began from the back of the church, I felt the Spirit of the Holy Trinity descend above the altar very powerfully; especially the spirit of the Father with powerful command of authority.

The Spirit of the Holy Trinity today was completely different from the Chrism Mass.

The Spirit of the Trinity descended at the Red Mass with the power of ruler of the world. The Spirit of the Holy Trinity at the Chrism Mass came with a lot of love as the Father toward His little children. The glory of the Holy Trinity affected my body differently from before. At the Chrism Mass I felt soft and resting in the middle of the Spirit of the Holy Trinity; at the Red Mass I felt in the middle of the Holy Trinity, powerful and ready to fight, not at rest like at the Chrism Mass.

At the consecration, in my vision I saw Calvary in the movie "Jesus of Nazareth." Jesus was hung on the Cross, and turned his face to the man that hanging on the cross to His left and said to him, "Today, you will be with Me in the Paradise." I then saw a crowd standing afar from the Cross.

On the same day, in my late afternoon devotion, in my visions I saw a holy water pot. It was up in the air, between the sanctuary and the front section, to the left side of the Cathedral of Saint Andrew. It was a gold colored pot and inside the pot was Coca Cola with a top layer of melted ice water, together with cast.

I then saw Bishop Andrew at his throne, he was facing the congregation. To his right was a lower chair, on this chair was clear holy water inside the holy water pot, with cast. This is symbolic that in faith, through this holy water, God can destroy the devil.

I then saw the holy water pot containing Coca Cola and melted ice water. Above these, judges were sitting in the two and half front pews to the right section in the Cathedral of Saint Andrew. Human judge decisions sound good, but these decision are filthy inside like the ice water looking clean. At the bottom was Coca Cola, it contained sugar and is sweet, but when it gets on people's skin, it is very sticky and dirty.

May 2, 1997, 3:12 a.m. In my sleep I heard God the Father say to His priests in the United States, "Fathers [priests] you must obey all my commandments. I love you, but you must obey all my commandments." God the Father continued, "The authorities of the nations are not obeying my commandments."

I then said to the Father, "Father forgive them, they do not know what they are doing."

While I was on the way to the 12:05 p.m. mass on May 2, 1997, The Lord reminded me of the five dollar fine for the parking on May 1, 1997. Just the moment after I kneeled down in church, I asked the Lord, "Lord, God show me what I need to do. I must obey what the owner put on the sign at the parking lot, but that lot belongs to the church, I park there to come here. If I am wrong, I ask you to forgive me, and show me what I need to do."

I then heard the Father said, "Pay back everything you owe." I tried to calculate seventy five cents per hour, by being here an hour a day, six day a week, since January 12, 1997.

In my vision I saw the sign of an hour parking $.75[AU1] with the cent sign instead of a dollar sign; and added a comma in between the seven and five, then made an "X" on top of my open check book. I understand that the Father doesn't told me to pay back the money to the owner of the parking lot.

The Father continued, "It is time for you to pay back to the community that accepted you. The people who come to mass here every day watch you, Father Scott, the Bishop Andrew, the Diocese of Little Rock, the city of Little Rock, and the state of Arkansas."

The Father continued, "The Bishop needs you, Father Scott needs you, the people in this parish need you, the city of Little Rock, and state of Arkansas needs you. Through you, they will see the glory of God."

I said to the Father, "Father, I am just only your instrument, they need You."

The Father continued, "Your Blessed Mother will be happy to see you stand at the Gospel podium to speak the first time, she will stand next to you; she will follow you like she followed Jesus on the way of the Cross."

The Lord Jesus then asked me, "Do you understand of what the Father said?" I replied, "Kind of, but I am not sure that what I understand is the same as what the Father said to me. You know my thoughts and understanding. You help me to understand in spirit and in the nature, so I can take actions according to Your being in me."

The Lord Jesus said, "Father Scott wants to greet you when he sees you come in the church, but you are so quiet. He understands that you are following the Spirit of the Lord. On the way out today, stop to say Hello to him, before you say goodbye and go." The bishop symbolic of the Father. Fr. Scott symbolize of the Lord Jesus. People symbolic of angels and saints.

After the mass, on the way out I stopped and shook Father Scott's hand, and said to him, "The Father said to me 'pay back to the community," He stood still and tried to understand what I said. By looking at his face, I knew that he did not understand what I just said. I repeated, "Father told me to pay back to the community of what I owe." He then understood.

2:01 p.m., May 2, 1997. Because I did not understand the revelation, a little later, after I arrived home, in my devotion the Father said to me, "The Bishop Andrew, Father Scott and the Diocese of Little Rock all accept you. You must pay back to the community for them accepting you. Father Scott must pay back the Cathedral of Saint Andrew parishioners for accepting him as the rector of the Cathedral. Bishop Andrew must pay back to people in the state of Arkansas for accepting him. These judges must pay back to the community of the honesty from their hearts."

Then the Blessed Virgin Mother said to me, "Get your tape recorder. The Father is going to speak to you."

God the Father said to me, "Look at the book of Malachi, chapter three from verse six to verse ten." He continued, "I want you to look at it right now, before I continue to speak."

The Father asked me, "Have you looked at it yet?" I had not read it yet, so I replied to the Lord, "Lord, I have not read it yet, I am still drowning in the Spirit of the Lord."

He then asked me, "What did you just do?" I responded, "I just scratched the back of my head."

The Father asked me, "Why have you have the chance to scratch the back of your head, but you not have not had a chance to read my words?" I responded to the Father, "Father, what is my answer? I do not have the answer for You."

The Father said, "That is the reason the people in this world give today. They have time to do everything, except to learn My words, and obey my commandments." I said to the Father, "Father, what do You want me to do to serve You?"

The Father said, "I want you to read the book of Malachi chapter three, verses six to verse nine."

> *Surely I, the LORD, do not change, nor do you cease to be sons of Jacob. Since the days of your fathers you have turned aside from my statutes, and have not kept them. Return to me, and I will return to you, says the LORD of hosts. Yet you say, "How must we return?" Dare a man rob God? Yet you are robbing me! And you say, "How do we rob you?" In tithes and in offerings! You are indeed accursed, for you, the whole nation, rob me. Bring the whole tithe into the storehouse, that there may be food in my house, and try me in this, says the LORD of hosts: Shall I not open for you the floodgates of heaven, to pour down blessing upon you without measure?*

> –Malachi 3:6-10

I got up and read the verses, then I said to the Father, "Father, I did, I just read them, Father." The Father asked me, "Do you understand what I said?" I responded, "Yes, Lord, but that is only one meaning; I am very sure there are a lot of hidden meanings behind these words." The Father asked me, "What do you do to understand other meanings of them?" I replied, "Lord, I need to seek You, and You will give me more of the meanings about what you said are contained in these words." The Lord said to me, "When you understand every meaning of these words; come back and tell me, I will reward you in heaven and on earth." My beloved Blessed Virgin Mother called me, "Mariette, Mariette." At the second of her calling, I responded to her, "Mother, yes." She asked me, "Do you understand of what the Lord said?" I answered to her, "Mother, I am not sure that I understand what He said." My beloved Blessed Virgin Mother said to me, "Those are the very same scriptures that the Lord gave to me before, when I was on earth." I said to the Blessed Virgin Mother, "Mother, I am not sure that I understand what the Lord said; I am drowning in the Spirit of God. Mother, did you ever understand them before you went home to heaven?" She said to me, "I understood very little. The time that I fully understood was the time that the Lord crowned me as the Queen of Heaven and Earth." I said to her, "Mother, I am not expecting to understand until I go home." The Blessed

Mother asked me, "How you can explain to people. You can not leave them dry." I said to her, "I do not know. What would you want me to explain to them? Should I tell them to follow in your footsteps of obedience to all God's commandments?" I continued, "Mother, have you ever come back to the Lord and given Him the answer of your understanding of those words that He gave you?" She said, "Yes, I went back to the Lord several times, but every time I gave Him the answer; He always said 'yes, your answers are correct, but you have not answered to all my words."

I now finally understand that God's words are almighty words; and no one in this world will understand all His words.

She asked me, "Look at verse number nine, "You are indeed accursed, for you, the whole nation, rob me." The Lord Jesus said, "The spiritual leaders are not the only one that I am speaking to; I am speaking to the whole world. They are accused, and robbing Me." The Lord Jesus spoke of the judges, attorneys, and legislators at the Red Mass and others in the whole world.

God revealed to the spiritual leaders, lawmakers, attorneys, legislators, governments' officials, and God's chosen ones; everyone must pay back what they owe to the community with sincerely and honesty from the heart to the communities, because the community accepts them as their representatives, leaders, shepherds, and models.

God Revealed Spiritual Leader's Hearts and Mariette's Obedience to God

May 7, 1997, 5:54 a.m. In my dream I saw myself standing on the lower level of a large house, it had two levels; on the lower level were some heaps of flat, big, long wooden bars; and there was a man who picked up one small bar and got up on the higher level. This level was higher to the level of my shoulder. This level seem like a dark stock room without a divider to the lower level. The man embraced this wooden bar and entered into a spot that look like dark high shelves. Somehow just as he entered, the wooden bar turned into a bow and arrow branch. This bow and arrow branch was in the way and stuck to the shelves, it looked like the window to me. He could not got in or get out, because he embraced the branch so he stuck there with his bottom showing to the public on the lower ground.

I then saw myself standing on the ground of the upper level. This level now had some light, there was one shelves that covered one side of the wall; the very same man was still caught in the middle of the shelf, with the bow and arrow branch held at his right chest, his bottom showing to the public on the high floor.

In my right hand, I had a huge, long hunting knife. I raised my arm and chopped one top side of the bow and arrow branch; this man then fell down to stand on the floor, facing the shelves and looking at his thin, small chopped branch that I was holding at shoulder level in my hand, in the way of speaking to him, "You were holding onto the things that you thought were big and important to you; but look at it; they are skinny, just dump it in the trash; what you have in your thought is not what you are thinking."

As I got up the Lord said, "This dream I revealed to you will go in a letter that you will write, and deliver to Bishop Andrew and Father Scott today. I am speaking about the church high authorities holding on to what they thought were from God, but they are not from God. The part that they are holding on to from God is a very small percents, the larger percent of what they are holding belongs to the devil. The devil is protecting their earthly crowns. This revelation and the letter will make them suffer, because what they thought was truth and completely from God, is not the truth completely from God. I the Lord struck down Pharaoh and his servants. I, now do the same to them. They shall listen to my commandments and obey all of them, to serve Me, through services to others in truth and love."

The Lord then said to me, "I instruct you to place this revelation and letter to Bishop Andrew in the chapter of high church authorities in the book 'God's Purification - Not Easy, with the title God Revealed High Church Authorities' Hearts,' so they will understand that I am speaking to them. Through this letter, symbolically for other, the Bishop Andrew McDonald and Father Scott are following in the footsteps of the martyrs." The Lord continued, "I am surely not turning a staff into a snake, but I turned wind into tornadoes; water not into blood, but water into floods; not frogs on the ground, but suffering on earth." The Lord continued, "Scott wants the 'over all picture.' I gave them the 'over all picture.' They said 'that was part of the discernment.' Put trust in God. Everyone must walk in faith, God will discern for them; they do not need the over all picture." The Lord continued and said to me, "I am speaking to you, the Princess of Heaven and Earth. When I first called you, you saw no picture; but you obeyed Me from your heart said 'I do not know anything to do, so I did what God told me to do.' By your saying that you have no understanding of the plan; I have planned everything out for you. At this point in time, I have given you eighty percent of the plan. You have another twenty percent that you need to seek Me for the rest. I the Lord know everyone's hearts. I know that you have given your free will to Me, to do My will. I then pour out My power unto you to control your actions. But for them, they have not, and some of them will never surrender their free will to Me. They continue do their own things."

Two persons in this revelation, Bishop Andrew and Father Scott are symbolism of the gift of discernment.

The Gap between God and His Priests

August 10, 1994. I flew from San Diego to Carthage, Missouri for the Marian days. This annual feast was organized by the priests and seminarians of the Our Mother of Coredemtrix, to honor the Mother of Our Lord Jesus. I then returned to San Diego on August 14, 1997.

August 17, 1994. In my vision I saw the Seminarians building at Our Mother of

Coredemtrix. Facing the entrance of the building, I saw myself wearing a white wedding gown with a white veil.

The gown and veil were formed by a white cloud. I was standing in front, to the left side of the building; behind me, at the hem of my veil, many priests wore white chasubles with some red design lines in front, they were standing like one group, quietly, facing my back. I turned right, went forward around the back of the building, to the right side of the building, and entered a high stage at the middle side of the other side building. While I was entering the stage, a Priest joined me, and both of us stood in front, facing the altar, this priest was on my left side.   While I was walking around the building, the end of my veil stayed still at the began spot, the body of my veil was stretching. The more it stretched, the more clouds filled into the body of the veil. Because the hem of my veil did not move forward, this veil gave the group of priests no ground to walk on, so they stood still with their hands joined at their upper belly.

God Closed the Gap Between God and Man for Obedience

August 19, 1997. Before mass, at the Cathedral of Saint Andrew, the Father said to me, "I will no longer be with you. I give you to Jesus, but I will manifest in you. The devil will fight against you, because he recognized you as the Princess of Heaven and Earth, by your seeing Me, the Eternal Father. Michael will fight against them for you." Then the Lord Jesus told me, "You still see the Father in Me. There will be times you will see the Father. I am in Him." The Lord Jesus continued, "The Father and I are in you, and my mother, in different ways. There is a gap between God and man; this gap was created by Eve, and will not close, because Eve never repented. There was a gap between God and His priests, this gap was created by Peter, but Peter repented. Therefore, this gap was closed on the day the priest, Scott walked behind you, in procession to the altar. [May 24, 1997, the feast of the Holy Trinity]"

May 24, 1997. The morning before the feast of the Holy Trinity, the Lord brought this vision back in my devotion and gave me the interpretation which is different from what I was understanding.

The Lord told me the seminarians' building is symbolic of the clergymen. The veil formed with white clouds is symbolic of glory, power, and the grace of God. This veil on top of my head means I place God above all things. The wedding gown and a dark shadow of the group of priest standing to my left symbolizes the Mission that God called me, I married to God. The front and one corner of the seminarians building not covered by my veil, means it is not covered with glory, power and the grace of God; this symbolizes a gap between God and His priests. God has blinded their eyes is symbolic of not moving my veil for these priests to walk forward in faith; meaning clergymen lack of faith in God. Faith is a gift from God.

After the Lord explained the vision to me, He then told me, "Today is the vigil mass of the Holy Trinity. I have scheduled you to serve as the Holy Eucharistic Minister today, to walk in front of the celebrant, Father Scott. He represents all the priests of My church, to walk behind you in procession to the altar; this procession will close the gap between God and His priests. Alter servers are symbolic of the angels, readers are symbolic of apostles.

At about 4:00 p.m. that evening; after I entered the Cathedral of Saint Andrew, I felt the glory and power of God start pouring upon me, coming through my bones.

A few minutes before the time of procession to the altar; I got up and stood behind the lector, and the Spirit of the Trinity increased. When I had walked one third of the aisle, the Lord said to me, "It is over. You are in a new level." After He said this, I suddenly physically felt my spine stretching, I got taller, my face lifted up, my shoulders stretched, and my chest raised up.

After the sign of peace, I entered the sanctuary to deliver the Holy Eucharist. I was standing next to an altar boy, behind the celebrant, and facing the altar. The other side of the altar had the congregation. I felt the power of God coming down upon the entire sanctuary, pushing down on my head and my shoulders. I was afraid that I might fall, so I said, "Jesus, help me here, keep my body standing firm and peaceful to serve You." He kept me from not falling to serve Him, to deliver His body and blood to people, while God's power, glory, and grace ran through my bones and in the sanctuary.

After the mass, I talked to Father Scott, and shared with him what I felt during the celebration of the Holy Eucharist. I saw the power of God raised from the priest's Holy Eucharist, on May 13, 1997, the eightieth anniversary of the Blessed Virgin Mother's appearance at Fatima, and the first time I served as Holy Eucharist Minister.

I saw a globe of strong heat waves, rising up and spreading around from the blessed priest's Holy Eucharist, inside the gold paten, on top of the corporal, in front of the celebrant, Father Scott Marczuk. I knew it was God's power, from the Spirit of the Holy Trinity; I blinked my eyes so I could see it more clearly. Even though I was standing a few steps away, after I blinked my eyes I felt God's power pushing against my forehead and my chest. God's power was gentle and powerful. I feared that I might fall, and I said in my thoughts, "Jesus keep my body firm and strong." I then stood still, and continued to see the power of God spreading over the altar and the sanctuary. I also felt it through my body.

Later in the same day the Lord Jesus said to me, "Since I returned to the Father, today is the first time the glory of the Father descended upon the altar."

I also explained to Father Scott that I fully understood the reason the Lord commanded me to put the Lord Jesus's website on the internet the night before Pentecost Sunday. Father Marczuk, Bishop Andrew and I are stuck, the Lord did not let the Bishop speak;

that's why he was so quiet. We are just God's instruments, we are now waiting to hear from the Vatican, the Archbishop CacciaVillan, apostolic ProNuncio. While I was sharing this with him, two other women and a boy also listened. Father Scott listened very attentively, accepting what I shared with him.

At night, after my devotion, in my vision I saw the hem of my veil pushed forward to behind my feet. In front of the altar, the group of priests standing behind my veil now turned dark, and walked forward to the foot of the altar, following step by step after my veil was pushed forward, and gave them room on the ground to walk.

The Lord said to me, "By your speaking to Father Scott, and walking in front of him to proceed to the altar today, that means the gap between God and His priests now is closed." The Lord meant, the gap between Him and His priests, as a community gap was closed. Because this gap was closed, for those priests who live the life of holiness and put their faith in actions, they will feel that God is within them, and be more visible through their services to Him. For those who are disobedient to God's commandments and have no or little faith in Him, the devil will put the personal gap between them and God.

The Gift of Steadfast Faith: I share with you the beginning of the time I realized God called me. Close to the time my youngest daughter, Tuanh graduated from the University of California at Berkeley, I felt that all my children would not need me to support them financially. I found the way to help others by organizing the "Americans Helping Asian Children" foundation. I struggled with others on the board of directors because they were not performing as a charity foundation. Later I found that it was not what God called me to do.

April 7, 1994. God took me out from work completely in a very painful way. He then told me to pursue the freedom of religion in Vietnam, minister to priests, and unify the church. I thought that God did not know what He was doing by telling me to do these things. But I still followed His instructions very carefully. I knew very little of operating a computer, because I had a secretary at the time I worked as a field underwriter at a large insurance company.

When the Lord Jesus told me step by step to take action to restore the freedom to worship the true God in Vietnam, I had too many troubles. The great problem was the Lord Jesus told me a number of times, "Go see the bishop." I tried many times to see Bishop Robert Broom, the Bishop of Catholic Diocese of San Diego, but his secretary prevented me by not giving me an appointment; she gave me to the director of the Office for Social Ministries. This director gave me an appointment, then canceled on me. I called and left a number of message, but he did not return my call. I then sent a letter to Bishop Broom, by certified mail, and sent him a copy of complement. He then finally returned my call, and told me to send all the papers to him. I sent the materials that the Lord Jesus instructed me to him.

I asked the director of the Office of Ministry to support me in bringing this petition that I was going to mail to congress and senators into the public, and if there were donations received to support seminarians in Vietnam, they could be donated to the Catholic Diocese of San Diego. In turn, the Diocese of San Diego, would send the money to the Catholic church in Vietnam to support seminarians. Back and forth twice, the Director of the Office of Social Ministry approved to support me by circulating papers in the diocese to gather congregation signatures to send to congress and senators; for the donations he told me to ask the pastor of the Good Shepherd parish.

I then went into the Good Shepherd parish office and asked to see Father Fernando Ramirez, but he was not in, so I left a message. Later in same day Father Ramirez called me, I asked him for donations made out to Good Shepherd parish's name, which in turn the church could forward to Vietnam to support seminarians, but he said, "No. What does Congress have to do with Vietnam? Mariette, you're just wasting your time and money." I cried and told him, "Father Fernando, I must obey God."

Father Fernando Ramirez, Pastor of Good Shepherd Parish is proud of himself and look down on me a sinner; he does not believe that God could called me a sinner for this mission. He forgot that the Blessed Virgin Mother is very simple and lowly young girl. He also forgot what he leaned and preaching of Saint Mary Madelene and Saint Paul were conversion, and became great saints in God's Church, and in the history of Catholic canonized saints, majority of them were conversion; and that God can turn bad to good.

The Lord Jesus instructed me to print on the letterhead, "Initiated by Mariette Do-Nguyen with the sponsorship and approval of the San Diego Diocese, and seeking the support of U.S. Catholics through prayer." These words are symbolism. Jesus instructed me to date the letters to congress and senators July 4, 1997, and mail on July 7, 1997, giving the final printed materials to the Director of the San Diego Diocese, the Office of Social Ministry. Early in the morning on July 6, 1997, I picked up materials from the printing company and went directly to the Diocese of San Diego and left the complete packet for the Director of Social Ministry. I went home, and while I was trying to put them in envelopes to mail out the next day, I received a telephone called from a woman who identified herself as a worker for the Diocese of San Diego. She told me, "The Diocese is not an official sponsor, you can not use its name at all, because priests would call and complain."

There was no way I could reprint 139 pounds of documents, and get them ready to mail out the next day, but more importantly I must obey God, no matter the cost. I called one of my closest friends at the time to pray with me, seeking for direction. The voice of God spoke out from my heart saying, "Mariette, no one can harm you, not even one hair on your head. You are being protected. I have already given you My words."

The actions from the Diocese of San Diego have no faith in God, are disobedient to

God's commandments, they do not cooperate with God to save souls, and they please man to protect their earthly crowns.

The Lord Jesus just told me today, May 26, 1997, while I was in the middle of transcribing this message in the book, "These actions are also at many other dioceses. God knows that clergymen will contain these kind of actions against Him. He then put the gap between Him and His priests.

God knows everyone's hearts. He knew the Diocese of San Diego would reject me, His faithful Servant, but He allowed me to go through. There are a lot of clergymen, and some people serve God with no faith in Him, are disobedient to many of His commandments, and they please man to protect their earthly crown, thus preventing the works of God to save souls. Because the enemy spirits lives in them, and among them. God also knows there are some willing to go extra miles for him, faithful to Him to embraced His Servant. God is a just God, there are rewards and punishments for every action each one takes, every word that comes out from the mouth, or in the thoughts.

The second problem was on July 4, 1994. I needed to enter five hundred thirty eight names and addresses of the congress on the computer, and print them out on labels. I had very little experience operating the computer, so I was stuck. But God is good, He had my son, James stay home with me on that day to help me.

My family is a victim of the misconduct of the Catholic leaders, so my son believes in God, but he does not trust the leaders of the institution. But he loves me, and saw the suffering the people in Vietnam have undergone, and he helped me with many things in the area of computers. At the time I started writing this book, 1999, he is a Computer Programmer Analysis at UCSD, but back in 1994 he was not. For the love he has for me, his mother, he spent all day assisting me through this process. I bought the wrong kind of mailing labels, and could not print out the way that I wanted to fit with the letter. I told him to go to Office Depot to buy a different size to fit, and he told me, "Mother, today is July 4. Office Depot is not open today." I picked up the telephone to find out if they were open. While I was asking an employee for the time that store closes, he looked at me, and thought that I was kidding him by pretending to talk to a person. He said, "Mother, there is no one there." I replied, "Yes, they are open, let's go get the labels." I got my purse, then he believed that the store was open. He said something like, "Normally these kind of stores are not open July 4. But this one being open is very odd." I said, "God wanted them to be open today just for His works to be done." This problem was taken care of by my son.

The third problem was the Lord Jesus instructed me to mail them out on July 7, 1997. About 2:00 p.m. on July 6, 1997 the woman called from Diocese of San Diego and told me not to use the Diocese of San Diego name. At this hour I still had 139 pounds of materials to be put in five hundred thirty eight nine by twelve inch envelopes, and put the labels on them; 331 business envelopes were to Vietnamese priests in the United State. I then called Natty Nannane and asked her for help, at about 6:00 p.m. she came with her friend Rose Williams. By 11:00 p.m. we were almost finished, we then prayed the rosary to offer all these works in the hands of our Lord, before Natty and Rose went home. The next morning, July 7, 1997 after the 8:30 a.m. mass, Natty and I finished the rest, we then left for the post office about 1:00 p.m. to mail them.

It was surprised me at that time, when I received letters from United States senators and the United State President in response to the freedom of worshipping the true God in Vietnam. But God kept His promised me that, "No one can harm you, every hair on your head is being protected." And my obedience to God and steadfast in Him. At this time, I reviewed this page before this book publish, March 29, 1999, I saw mighty God's blessing upon the works that He called me to do, and I have seen no harm.

He then told me to move to Arkansas, to go see Bishop Andrew and bring copies of everything for the freedom of worshipping the true God in Vietnam to the Bishop. I obeyed Him, called the bishop for an appointment and purchased an airline ticket to meet with him, and gave the bishop the file. My uncle, Father Dominic Nho Do, who serves God in the Diocese of Little Rock, could not understand my actions. My uncle called my son-in-law, Huy and asked him, "The bishop is very busy; what is the purpose your mother wants to see the Bishop?" My uncle called my children behind me, later my daughter, Thuy-Trang told me.

These are just very little actions that I share with you, there are many more major things that God told me. I believe everything He told me to do will be completed before I go home to heaven.

The gift of steadfast faith in God has been bestowed upon me. The devil has no power over my actions, because God the Almighty is the only one who has control of my soul, my spirit, and my physical body, He will never abandon me, He will always answer to my petitions. He answers me when I have questions, or when I need Him, and I know that I will fly directly to heaven on my last day on earth.

You are not hear God's voice in same dialogue like I hear from Him. Even though I directly hear His voice, and have dreams and visions, I also saw God with my carnal eyes, and I always base on scriptures. I still base on the scriptures. God speaks to everyone of us, through His words in scriptures, our wisdom, and dreams, but we must place Him above all things, seek Him through daily prayer, and living sacrifices. When a person completely surrenders his free will to God, obeying all His commandments, He will bestow up on you the gift of faith. Service to God in faith does not demand proof or evidence, or an overall picture to discern. Seek God, He will discern for you, He will not fail you.

Priests are married to the Lord Jesus's Church. The virtue of love is above all other virtues; the love of priests toward God, the spouse relationship. The Lord Jesus loves us, and freely came down to earth, to die on the Cross to save us. Priests are spouse of responsibility to the Lord Jesus's church. Priests must empty themselves into God, and sacrifice everything for God. The priest's responsibility is to serve God, their spouse, by service to other people, because God is in the poor, the sick, the lonely, and elderly.

Faith is a gift from God; priests must labor to God for the gift of faith. To receive the gift of faith, the priest must always obey all God's commandment. Service to God in faith is like a life of a good little child, doing everything the parents ask, there is no question or argument, but there are questions for directions. God will not give you any specific plan, or any understanding of His works, except what He has said in the Bible. When a priest or a person that obeys God is like a little child, completely obedient to his parents, God will never abandon them, instead, He will carry them in His arms.

God Revealed to His People

In this revelation, God indirectly spoke to the congregation, and directly to spiritual leaders.

July 1, 1997, 2:25a.m. The Lord woke me up with my thought, all day yesterday my body hurt so badly that I had to take several Tylenol. In my dream I saw the Red Mass at the Cathedral of St. Andrew on May 1, 1997, Monsignor Royce was giving the homily; and judges were sitting in some front pews at the right section of the Cathedral. I then saw some activities from the last few days on televisions regarding the Hong Kong handover. I said to the Lord, "Lord I did not choose this calling. You chose me, I only obey you. My soul is wounded badly; I ask you to heal my soul." I then asked, "Lord, is the Hong Kong handover good or bad?" The Lord said, " It will be good for the world, but it will be bad for the kingdom of God." I said to the Lord, "Lord, speaking out loud to the world is part of my job that You called me." The Lord said to me, "Be peaceful and calm. I allowed this to happen. How could the church leaders say 'remove the splinters from your brother's eyes, while the beams remain in their eyes.' " I said to the Lord, "My Lord, my Lord, may God forgive them, have mercy on them." The Lord said, "Their actions against you are very little, but their actions to their congregation is major in front of the Almighty God. "I asked, "Lord, why are they against me?" The Lord said, "You're bringing their sinfulness into the public, giving them no choice, they must obey Me. They then kneeled down at your feet to worship Me." When I heard this I asked, "Lord, do you really want me to record this?" The Lord said to me, "You say what I said. Give them a part of yourself, the humbleness before Me." The Lord continued, "One is paying for the sins of many." When I heard this, I did not want to record it, because I was so weak, I was barely able to lift up the recorder. The Lord continued, "Say what I just said to you." I said to the Lord, "My Father, my Father, my Father. The sins of the world are so high, and everyday, they continue to put on more and more. Jesus the Lord is suffering, and this suffering continues to add more and more on the Lord Jesus." I then saw Prince Charles get on the boat, and sail away from Hong Kong after handing over Hong Kong to China, that I saw on CNN yesterday. The Lord said, "The British Prince is sinfulness himself, how could he lead the people in the life of holiness?" I said, "Lord, what do You want me to do with all this that You just said?" The Lord said, "Just let it set there for a time, and I will tell you what to do with it." I said, "Lord, I am like a lamb in the middle of a jungle of wolves." The Lord said to me, "The wolf will become the lamb of God." [The Lord means wolf is symbolic of His actions upon the world, to discipline people.]

The Lord called me by name, "Mariette, the church leaders, they think that they do everything for My will; many give their free will to the devil, so they are in trouble with Me now, and they sit and talk to one another with shamefulness. Their shamefulness that they thought they would never have to deal with in their lives as bishops, priests, and cardinals. They thought that they are dealing with you, but actually, they are dealing with Me, the Lord, their God. They like and they dislike what you are saying. They are mixed up. They are lack of discernment. They are still looking for the future of the church, by embracing you and persuading you. The devil sifts them like they sift wheat. They said to Me in their words 'I love you Lord', but their actions do not prove to Me that they love Me." The Lord then said to me, "Place this revelation in the chapter that you were working on for Archbishops, cardinals, and priests."

Like other revelations, when the Lord spoke out His words, there are hidden meanings in each word He spoke out, in the same way the Lord Jesus spoke to John of seven churches in the Book of Revelation. Therefore the name and title also symbolic like triple six in the Book of Revelation.

Priest's Homily Leads God's Children in Wrong Direction

One day after Easter Sunday, Michelle called me and shared a priest's homily, she said something like, "I went to church with my husband Tony; the Gospel was regarding the Lord Jesus appearing to Mary Madelene. But this visiting priest's homily was an insult to Saint Mary Magdalene, in that the homily was nothing about Jesus, it was all was about Mary Madalene, he called her a "hoax." Priests must be a good example for others to follow. Tony was sitting next to me. He is not Catholic, and this priest was saying all these insults about Mary Madalene." I told her, "You should write to the Bishop of San Diego." She said, "I called the church pastor, but he was away, I left the message."

A few days later, she shared with me that she called Bishop Broom, so she did speak to the Bishop. The bishop said that he was an ordained priest, he has a psychologist office in San Diego, he only helps with saying mass.

Through the church, God has bestowed authority upon bishops. Although, beside the bishop pray for priests, these bishops must monitor priests actions, and discipline them. If bishops do not do their job correctly, they then are liable in front of God for that priest and the congregation that the priest leads.

God chose Mary Madelene to embrace the foot of His cross, and appeared to her first. It means God loves the converts. Jesus the Lord was telling the world in actions, "Follow in the footsteps of Mary Magdalene. I love each one of you."

But, if any one has thoughts like the priest giving the sermon in the church in San Diego regarding Saint Mary Madelene, you are in deep trouble, you are exalting yourself, and this action is controlled by the devil.

Many people think: Oh! Well, I have been going to church every Sunday; I have put a lot of my time in to help the church functions; I have joined many prayer groups, I have donated a lot of money to the churches.

But, God is asking every one of us, "I came down to take flesh, die on the cross to save the world. Do you really love me? What is in your heart? Prove to me your love. Can you give up everything for me? Do you obey all my commandments?"

Eucharistic Ministers and Lectors

I am testifying: I have seen through my spiritual eyes the glory, power and grace of the Almighty God cover the sanctuaries a number of times; and with my natural eyes, I saw the power of God elevated from the Holy Eucharist, like a heat wave in front of the priest. I feel the presence, the power of God powerfully at the sanctuary; and have heard God's voice at the time I was standing at the sanctuary. These things also occur during the nights and in my devotions.

It you live the life of placing God above all things, it means you will pay God's church bills before your own bills, you keep your heart pure and serve God with all your heart, your mind, your soul, and your strength. In faith you must believe that God is present at the sanctuary, and you must feel God's glory and His presence when you are standing in the sanctuary. If you have not felt God's presence when you stand in the sanctuary, and that there are many things in your life against God's commandments. Do not let the devil control your mind any more, admit the truth and convert. If you take offense at my testimony, and refuse to convert, you will not be saved. I was in your spot before, but I obeyed God and converted.

Throughout the Book of Exodus, God commanded Moses of the sanctuaries, altars, priests, deacons, and altar servers uniforms. Beyond the physical dressing, every word God spoke to Moses has more meaning than what it sounds. The church has been obeying God's commandments to dress the physical sanctuaries and priests. Churches training must prepare the priests interior above the outer formal to serve God through seminary training.

The church leaves the laity sanctuary servers to the bishop of each diocese. The sanctuary is not a beach to wear shorts, sleeveless dresses, or not a party place to advertise clothes. It is not for joining hands, shaking hands, and not a street corner for sloppy clothes. As a Eucharistic minister and lector, everyone must be a good example for others to follow. We are in the presence of the almighty God, serving Him through services to others. Priests are dressed for God, we then must look at how the priests dress, and we dress accordingly, to worship God.

In the presence of the almighty God, to worship Him; we must always join our hands at our chest, not at the lower belly, behind us, or straight down.

Beyond the outer looks, each one must prepare his heart, and pray for those they are serving. Eucharistic ministers pray for those that they deliver the body and blood of our Lord to; ask the Lord to help them receive Him in pure heart. If they receive the Lord without a pure heart, even those you do not know, you are participating in delivering punishments to them. For the lectors, pray for those who are going to listen to the words of God that you are going to deliver to them; not just only praying for you to read well, and leave the listener like water poured over the duck's head.

Women Services in the Church and Rectories

The Catholic component honored the rule of priests taking the vow of celibacy. When a priest takes the vow of celibacy it means he completely surrenders himself to God. The devil is trying twenty-four hours each and every day and night to attack priests, by bringing women in front of priests, and interfering in priest's thoughts.

You, as women must remember to serve God, not to serve the priests, or to serve God because of the priest. If any of you have intended to serve in the church because of the priest, and not repented fast, you are on your way to the place that humans call "hell', because the devil is finding the way for you to break the priest's vow of celibacy, directly or indirectly.

Keep your communication with the priests by telephone or in very minimum presence; keep a physical distance from the priests, do not reach over and hug him; but, instead, pray for him. Receive assignments, instructions, and refer the questions to whoever has the authority over the matters, follow the instructions at all times, be obedient. Once you follow these instructions you will serve God in the correct direction, serving God because you love God, not because of the priests, and also to protect your soul and your marriage.

God gives every one free will. Bishops, pastors, and priests have the free will to choose a female or male secretary and maid. I give a big red flag for those churches that have one priest and one female secretary in the office, this includes priests who use female maids. If there is any woman who says it will not happen to you, you are wrong; it could be happen to any body, if not outer then is in your mind, but you are lack of discernment, you can not discern it. If there are any priests who say that will not happen to you, you are wrong, you will be the one who falls before the others.

Nuns: As a nun you must put more distance away from priests than lay women, because of your vow of celibacy. You should never hug priests, or show any alluring action in front of priest or through business talk. If you really love that priest in God's love, then pray for him, not hug him. Because you and the priest are both committed to the vow of celibacy, the devil works even harder to stimulate the sexual design.

Protect the Lord Jesus, Priests and His People

Do not accept a woman without her husband to help in the church alone. It is okay for women in a group. When a priest loves a person in God's love, he does not have to spend time with a woman. Priests who council woman with marital trouble is the most danger to priests as well as to that woman. Limit to the minimum of meeting and talking to any woman; do not hug women, or nuns, except your mother and your sisters. Do not hire a female secretary, maid, or cook. Never go to dinner or lunch alone with a woman or women only. Set rules that woman can not enter the sacristy while the priest is changing before and after the mass. Woman only enter for business, and get out fast. At all times, do not allow women into your bedroom. The spirit of sexual intercourse controlled by the devil will interfere in priest's thoughts, concerning women friends or parish troubles. Priests can do nothing for them, God is the only one who can heal them. Immediately turn to the Lord Jesus for deliverance, and protection. The devil will continue to try again and again. But if you have faith in God, He will not forsake you.

The Feast of Assumption of the Blessed Virgin Mother

August 15, 1997. While I was about to get ready to go to 12:05p.m. mass, the Lord told me, "Bring two bottles of annointment oil, have Father Scott bless them."

In the church, when they started the first song for the procession for the holy mass, the Lord told me, "move to the front row." As He said this, the glory of the Blessed Virgin Mother surrounded me while I moved from the third row to the front row. Her glory continued surrounding me throughout the mass.

I offered this holy mass to the Father, the Lord Jesus, and the Holy Spirit, in honor of the Blessed Virgin Mother, mother of the Lord Jesus, my beloved mother, and mother of all man; praying for the "Mission" that the Lord God trusted in me.

During the mass I had to fight against the counterfeit worshipping spirit; who indirectly denied the Lord Jesus, by denying the Blessed Virgin Mother as their spiritual mother.

After I received the body and blood of the Lord; the Father said to me, "The Church is in danger. Church leaders are afraid of being corrupt. They will come to you, (you do not have to come to them) and clap on your shoulders, persuade you. But you are not to do what they say. Stand firm and do what I tell you to do, [help then convert, daily exam and repent."

After the mass, I was on the way to have Father Scott to bless the oil, the Lord said to me, "You give him one bottle." The Lord meant that after Father Scott blessed the two bottles of annointment oil, give him one bottle. After Father Marczuk blessed them outside the front door of the cathedral, I gave him one bottle, I said to him, "Jesus said this one is for you for protection, it is the faith." I meant that when you put it on yourself with faith, that God protects you.

The blessing of the oil symbolic of God pour out His power upon me and upon spiritual leaders who obey all His commandments.

The Blessed Virgin Mother Teaches Her only Daughter

May 23, 1999, During the night in my dream, my beloved Blessed Virgin Mother told me, "Do not let the enemies attack you. All the letters to Catholic leaders are fine; all you need to do is read them again to correct spelling if needed, and publish them in the book "God's Purification - Not Easy." Your are publishing the Catholic leaders letters of response in the Tax Petition book; and if you do not publish the letters you sent to them; people will question where are the letters are that Mariette wrote to them. Show the readers of the letters to Catholic leaders is you love them; you do this for them to convert to God."

Letters to the Roman Catholic High - Ranking Leaders

Rebuild My Church Divine Mission

(The Lord Jesus gave this name to Mariette)

P.O. Box 261550 ✦ San Diego, CA 92196-1550

March 25, 1996

Most Reverend Andrew
Bishop of Little Rock Diocese

Dear Excellence,

I thank God the Almighty for having arranged for me to meet with you on October 18, 1995. I also thank you for answering God and accepting me with love and His blessings. God has His plan and He does things His way. The Blessed Virgin Mother just obeys God and is moved by the Holy Spirit. I am following in Her footsteps in obeying God, and accepting His calling. Now is the time for more of the chosen ones whom God brings in the boats; and you are the next step in the boat as the Church authority who will guide me.

I pray to Father God, the Lord Jesus and the Holy Spirit to constantly guide, protect, and bless you, and to shepherd me and your congregation, as well as the future He is sending you.

Enclosed is the completed manuscript of "My Patient - God's Gift." The Lord's revelations have brought me to the final stages in publishing this book, and He has instructed me to mail you this copy. The book is now being printed, and 70% of its profits will go to support seminarians in Vietnam and other countries where help is needed, and 30% will go to Dr. Gerald E. Nelson.

I would like to make an appointment to meet with you after the book's first printing, perhaps in late April or early may of this year.

Please pray for me to be the servant that God has ordained me to be, that I may accomplish His will.

In Christ Jesus

Mariette Do-Nguyen

Mariette Do-Nguyen

Rebuild My Church Divine Mission

(The Lord Jesus gave this name to Mariette)

P.O. Box 261550 ✦ San Diego, CA 92196-1550

September 19, 1996

Cardinal Joseph Ratzinger, President
of the Pontifical Bible Commission
Prefect Congregation for the Doctrine of the Faith

Via: Federal Express

Dear Cardinal Ratzinger:

First of all, I give prayers and thanks to the Lord our God who chose me to carry out His works, and to write this letter to you.

Enclosed are: (1) a copy of my first book, "My Patient—God's Gift," published on April 12, 1996; (2) the overview of the second book, "Not Easy—God's Purification," which is in the process of being edited; (3) Abortion and tax benefits that work against God's commandments; (4)

God's covenant, Unification of the Church; Ark of the Covenant - The Lord Jesus and the Holy Eucharist.

On July 30, 1996 I presented over two hours of sworn testimony to a panel at the Tribunal Office at the San Bernadino Diocese, lead by Monsignor Robert E. Lawrence. But yesterday the Lord Jesus instructed me to submit this letter to you myself, along with accompanying documents.

I write this letter as God's servant, nothing else, to you, the Roman catholic Church authority, to request your permission, to testify in the Church to what I hear and see from the Father, the Lord Jesus, God the Almighty, that the truth to unify the Lord Jesus' Church on earth.

I hope to hear from you soon, to serve the Lord Jesus who told me, "My urgent is Conversion and repentance."

In Christ Jesus

Mariette Do-Nguyen

Rebuild My Church Divine Mission

(The Lord Jesus gave this name to Mariette)

P.O. Box 261550 ✦ San Diego, CA 92196-1550

October 15, 1996

Most Reverend Andrew
Bishop of Little Rock Diocese

Dear Excellency,

Today I followed up on my letter of September 19, 1996, to Cardinal Joseph Ratzinger, President of the Pontifical Bible Commission. After graciously listening to my query, the secretary at his office told me, "The Cardinal does not answer private members of the congregation. He replies to the Bishop, and the Bishop answers to congregation. Go see your Bishop."

As you know, God works in strange ways. He called on me in 1991, when I knew nothing, and allowed the San Diego Diocese to reject me so that people in other churches will believe that my words are from God. In the beginning I told God, "Jesus, why don't you call a priest or a nun who has been with You since baptism? I am a sinner."

But He said to me, "I want you. I do not want a nun or a priest for this calling." Now I understand that the clergy's responsibility is to instruct their congregations to do God's will, not to engage in politics.

Because Jesus was not accepted in His own native land, God has told me to move to Arkansas, that I might follow in His footsteps of obedience. And now God has instructed me to ask you to bring me to the public; through me He will speak to the world, because people can see me with their carnal eyes, whereas they cannot see Him.

The Lord Jesus urgently wants conversion and repentance. The United States of American is the most powerful country in the world, and He wants to cleanse the United States as a mirror for other nations to follow. This country's presidential election will take place on November 5, 1996.   Revelations about abortion and about tax benefits that work against God will effect the decision of the voters. In the tax benefits revelation, God the Father commands against the issue of same sex marriage, sacrifices used for purposes that are against His will, such as abortion clinic, research and training that oppose His laws, and weapons of destruction. The Lord holds these sins against almost all of us.

I am obeying God and begging you to bring me to the public before this election date, to let the citizens of the United States, the tax payers, know that if their government continues to use tax dollars for purposes that go against God, they must demand that lawmakers pass laws according to God's commandments or they will refuse to pay.

It is nearing the time when I need to physically move to Little Rock to be more effectively under your direction, because Jesus told me that you are my shepherd, next to the Holy Father.

Please respond as soon as possible. I am prepared to travel immediately. My heart and soul are praying for the Father's will to be done. Please pray for me.

In Christ Jesus,

Mariette Do-Nguyen

Foot note: The holy father is symbolic of the Eternal Father, bishop Andrew is symbolic of the Lord Jesus. Father Hung is symbolic of the high priest, or hero. The town of Little Rock is symbolic of the Divine mission in Mariette.

Rebuild My Church Divine Mission

(The Lord Jesus gave this name to Mariette)

P.O. Box 261550 ✦ San Diego, CA 92196-1550

November 10, 1996
Most Reverend Andrew
Bishop of Little Rock Diocese

Dear Excellency,

I would like to offer prayers and thanks to the Lord our God, and honor our Mother, the Blessed Virgin. I also thank you for seeing me and approving the revelations that come to me are from God.

Enclosed are copies of: (1) the Lord's instructions to me and list of the Roman Catholic Church high authorities (2) the revelation about the Principality spirit ruling the United States of America, and (3) my letter to Father Timothy, Abbot of the Abbey of Gathsemani.

God has placed you as the Bishop of the Diocese in Little Rock, Arkansas—President Clinton's hometown—for a reason. He then sent me to you, Father Peter Joseph Hung Tong and others, to place an even heavier burden on your shoulders. But the reward that God has reserved for you in Heaven is mighty.

I am in the process of renting an apartment in Little Rock, and will be moving there in early January, 1997. I pray to God that at that time, the Lord Jesus will have gathered all His main servants in Little Rock to serve Him before His second coming.

I know that our calling will become increasingly difficult for both of us, but Jesus is the one who performs His works through you and through me. Please pray for me.

In Christ Jesus,

Mariette Do-Nguyen

Rebuild My Church Divine Mission

(The Lord Jesus gave this name to Mariette)

P.O. Box 261550 ♦ San Diego, CA 92196-1550

November 10, 1996

This letter address to the list of 36 cardinals and archbishops in the U.S

Tax benefits that work against God's commandments, and abortion laws that permit the murder of innocent children who are unable to speak for themselves.

Dear ....

I have previously mailed to you the Abortion Revelation in June 1996. Enclosed are copies of: (1) Revelations about Tax benefits that Work against God's Commandments, and Principality spirit Ruling the United States of America, (2) the book "My Patient—God's Gift," and a table of contents for the book, "Not Easy—God's Purification," to be published before Easter, 1997, (3) letters to first lady Hillary Rodham Clinton, June 21, 1996, and from her, June 25, 1996.

On the night of November 10, 1996, God the Father said to me, "All cases of abortion and birth control are murder, except in instances where the life of the mother is threatened."

The lawmakers, high ranking government officials, and others who profit from tax benefits that work against God's commandments are committing direct sins against God, and the taxpayers are sinning against Him indirectly. Whether sin is mortal or venial is determined by God, and depends on the purposes for which the money is used. Church authorities have a responsibility to God to instruct their congregation to obey God's commandments, because human laws can be deceiving. The citizens of the United States must demand that lawmakers pass laws according to God's commandments; if not, they must refuse to pay taxes in order to save their souls. The Lord Jesus has told me many times over the last few years, "Things will look bad for the earth, but good for Heaven."

In Saint Peter's Square, Simon is the big rock, the Holy Father in the Vatican. The Lord Jesus established it two thousand years ago. Saint Andrew's Cathedral in Little Rock, Arkansas, is the "little rock." this land also the hometown of the President Bill Clinton. This is the place God is gathering His servants to prepare for His second coming to execute judgment and reward his followers at the end of the world. The Lord Jesus shepherds His Church through the Holy Father, and the Bishop of Little Rock Diocese is supervising His servants in Little Rock to prepare for His second coming.

I will pray for you to hear God the way He speaks to you. I also ask you to pray for me to serve God the way He wants, and to please Him always.

In Christ Jesus,

Mariette Do-Nguyen

Mariette Do-Nguyen

Foot note: Big rock is symbolic of the Lord Jesus; Saint Peter's Square is symbolic of heaven. Little Rock, Cathedral of Saint Andrew refers to Mariette and the Divine mission God entrusted to her.

Rebuild My Church Divine Mission

(The Lord Jesus gave this name to Mariette)

P.O. Box 261550 ✦ San Diego, CA 92196-1550

February 7, 1997

Most Reverend Andrew
Bishop of Diocese of Little Rock

Dear Excellency,

Yesterday I went to the doctor at the Medical Towel next to the Baptist Hospital. I do not know what God does in the supernatural, but after this visit the snares' spirit attacked me almost all night. My mind and my entire body were fighting against the snares' spirit, to the point where I said to the Lord, "Father, Lord Jesus, everyone has ignored what You told me to tell them, including the Roman Catholic Church authorities. The Catholic newspapers published a small article about the cardinals' and bishops' announcement, but they ignored what You told me to say. I ask You to take me home [in heaven], and have these cardinals and bishops speak for You, because the Catholic newspapers will print their words, but not mine." Then the Lord said to me, "They can stand at one side of the earth and yell to the other end, but will no one will respond to them. But people will respond to you, because your say what I tell you to say."

After I received Holy Eucharist today, my body was still in pain because my soul was wounded from my spiritual battle of last night. I said to the Lord Jesus, "Lord, I do not know what to say now, You know everything." Suddenly the Lord allowed me to share His suffering; He then said to me, "They [38 Roman Catholic cardinals, archbishops, and bishops] heard what you said, but they are silent and say to themselves 'If God speaks through her [Mariette], what will happen?' I gave everyone free will; they chose to please man, and not to respond to what I told you to say. They either have little faith or no faith in Me."

He also reminded me of those cardinals who stand in front of government building with boxes of post cards against partial -birth abortion to override President Clinton veto. This is political action, God chose clergymen as spiritual leaders to teach their congregations to obey God's commandments in their thoughts and actions. But they, the clergymen, must not become involved with politics. The devil is very slicky, if a clergyman lack of discernment, he easily confuse the two.

In the early morning on February 7, 1997, during my devotion, the Lord told me, "Go see Bishop Andrew on February 28, 1997, regarding the Holy Eucharist healing for bodies and souls, and the celebration honoring the Holy Father John Paul II." I replied to Him, "Lord, will a new abortion law be passed according to Your commandments before that day? If not, they will not listen to what You told me to say." I then asked Moses, "Moses pray to the Lord for me, Moses pray to the Lord for me ." I then asked my beloved Blessed Virgin Mother, "Blessed Mother pray to the Lord for me." She said to me, "Jacob obeyed Rebekah and went out to get choice kids to made food for Isaac. He then received a blessing from Isaac. You do what the Lord told you; the Lord God will go before you."

I obeyed the Lord and our Blessed Virgin Mother; I spoke to Liz Parker, and she gave me an appointment with you on March 4, at 10: a.m.

God instructed me that His plan is now in action, and He wants to begin in this land of with milk and honey, the Cathedral of Saint Andrew, Little Rock, Arkansas, by healing His people, and reopening Saint John's seminary in Little Rock. He also instructed me to distribute this letter to 36 cardinals, archbishops, and bishops, stating that clergymen should not be involved in politics. Instead they must honor their responsibility to their congregation's souls by teaching them to take actions against human laws by only obeying laws that are passed according to God's commandments.

The Lord Jesus told me, "My Father said, 'It is time for the church to unify so my wounds can heal.' " The celebration to honor the Holy Father

John Paul II as God's precious servant at St. Andrew's Cathedral, is the event where the Lord Jesus will say to the world that He is shepherding His church through the Holy Father. The Roman Catholic Church is Jesus' only Church in front of God; Christians [other churches] must obey the Holy Father's teachings to be in full communion with God; if not, they are rejecting the presence of the Lord Jesus through the Holy Eucharist, and their souls will lack nourishment.

I ask you to seek the Lord Jesus, and ask Him to show you those whom God has chosen to take beginning steps with us as a team, with the Lord Jesus is our team master. And, if possible, they can join us at our meeting. The Spirit of God will lead us through the entire meeting, to plan for these two services to serve Him.

I will see you at 10:00 a.m. March 4, 1997. Please pray for me.

Sincerely in Christ Jesus,

Mariette Do-Nguyen

Foot note: Saint John's seminary is symbolic of the Rebuild My Church Divine Mission, to preparing people for returning to God, being God's faithful servants to help one another from their heart and actions to serve God. Holy Father John Paul is symbolic of God the Father. Roman Catholic is symbolic of God's only Church on earth.

Rebuild My Church Divine Mission
(The Lord Jesus gave this name to Mariette)
P.O. Box 261550 ✦ San Diego, CA 92196-1550

February 18, 1997

Most Reverend Andrew
Bishop of Diocese of Little Rock

Dear Excellency,

Enclosed are copies of: 1) the letters to Cardinal Ratzinger and the Holy Father John Paul II, dated February 18, 1997; 2) "Obedience Results in Victory Revelation."

Neither you or I know the next step God wants us to take as we serve Him, or what tragedies will come down upon the earth. Therefore, we must take actions accordingly to God's will, and not to please man, that God might limit some of the tragedies upon the world

Sincerely in Christ Jesus

Mariette Do-Nguyen

Mariette Do-Nguyen

Rebuild My Church Divine Mission

(The Lord Jesus gave this name to Mariette)

P.O. Box 261550 ✦ San Diego, CA 92196-1550

February 7, 1997

This letter mailed to over 270 United States Roman Catholic cardinals, archbishops, bishops, and high - ranking officials in Vatican

Dear ....,

Per the Lord Jesus' instructions; I am enclosing a copy of a letter to Bishop Andrew, dated February 7, 1997; and letters to President Bill Clinton, to all members of congress, and to Vice President Gore], dated February 3, 1997; the reopening of Saint John's Seminary and the Celebration honoring the Holy Father revelations, and information about the Holy Eucharist healing of souls and bodies services at the Cathedral of St. Andrew.

As an Ambassador to Christ Jesus, I must always say everything He instructs me to say. I pray to God to increase your faith in Him. And please pray for me that God's will shall be done.

I also would like to invite you and your congregation to join us in Little Rock, Arkansas, part of our as a team, with the Lord Jesus as our team master, in the celebration honoring the Holy Father John Paul II, the precious servant to the Lord Jesus; and to reopen Saint John's seminary in Little Rock and other seminaries throughout the world. You can respond to me or to Bishop Andrew at Rebuild My Church Mission - P.O. Box 1077 - Little Rock, AR 72202.

Sincerely in Christ Jesus,

Mariette Do-Nguyen

Mariette Do-Nguyen

What good is it, my brothers, if someone says he has faith but does not have works? Can that faith save him? If a brother or sister has nothing to wear and has no food for the day, and one of you says to them, "Go in peace, keep warm and eat well," but you do not give them the necessities of the body, what good is it? So also faith of itself, if it does not have works, is dead.

– James 2:14-17

Rebuild My Church Divine Mission

(The Lord Jesus gave this name to Mariette)

P.O. Box 261550 ✦ San Diego, CA 92196-1550

February 18, 1997

Cardinal Joseph Ratzinger, President
of the Pontifical Bible Commission
Prefect Congregation for the Doctrine of the Faith

Via: Federal Express

Dear Eminence,

Enclosed are copies of: 1) The manuscript of "Not Easy - God's Purification", to be published around Easter 1997; 2) letters to Most Reverend Andrew, the Bishop of Little Rock Diocese, dated October 15, 1996, February 7 and 18, 1997; 3) letter to Holy Father John Paul II, dated February 18, 1997; 4) letter to Archbishop Agostino Cacciavillian, Apostolic Pro-Nuncio, dated December 10, 1996; 5) letters to 36 Roman Catholic Church authorities in the United States, dated February 7, 1997; 6) "The celebration to Honoring the Holy Father and to reopen Saint John's Seminaries Revelations", "Taxpayers Indirectly Murder Babies through Abortion Funding", "Heavenly Court Summons Writ for Mariette Do-Nguyen", and "Obedience Results in Victory Revelation;" 7)letters to President Bill Clinton and 100 members of the United State Congress, February 3, 1997.

When the Lord Jesus told me, "Priests will hate you, they're hate you, and they're hate you; but they think that you are just My servant. If they're hate you, they are like the Pharisees; they then will come back to Me, and then they will love you." The first part of His message, "Priests will hate you, they hate you, and they hate you" is very true. I have been facing some priests who go against God's commandments, and are trying to destroy the works of God as He is calls me to serve Him.

On February 12, 1997, in my dream, I saw the words as well as I heard the Lord Jesus speaking to me, "My words come with the power of God. You are here [on this earth] to finish the work that the Father gave Me when I was on earth."

This is the most difficult job in the world that God the Father has predestined for me; but the gift of steadfast faith in God equips me for the task. I know that God's words come with His power, grace and love; the Lord Jesus does His work through the Holy Spirit, and I am just His instrument; the Father's will shall be done.

I ask you to serve God by rebuilding the Lord Jesus' Church that it to be unified, and by assisting me with the assignments that God gave me before I left San Diego, California for Little Rock, Arkansas: the Celebration of Honoring of the Holy Father John Paul II, the Lord Jesus' precious servant at the Cathedral of Saint Andrew in Little Rock, Arkansas, and the reopening of Saint John's Seminary in Little Rock, and other seminaries throughout the world. We must also announce to Christians, taxpayers that they are indirectly murdering babies through abortion funding.

If you need more information, please contact me at: Rebuild My Church Mission - P.O. Box 1077 - Little Rock, AR 72203; and please pray for this mission, and for me.

Sincerely in Christ Jesus,

Mariette Do-Nguyen

Rebuild My Church Divine Mission
(The Lord Jesus gave this name to Mariette)
P.O. Box 261550 ✦ San Diego, CA 92196-1550

February 18, 1997

Holy Father John Paul II
00120 Vatican City State
Rome, Italy

Via: Federal Express

Dear Holiness,

The Lord Jesus asked me to write this letter to you. These things you already know, but the world does not know them, because the world can only see with their human wisdom, while you see with God's wisdom.

"The Lord Jesus loves you dearly in His heart. Your body is the temple for the Lord Jesus' Spirit; it means the Lord Jesus is residing in you, as He gives you His thoughts, speaks through you, and uses you to take His actions to shepherd His Church. Your health is suffering as you are share the suffering of the Lord Jesus to pay for the sins of people in this world. You have the victory as you embraced the Lord Jesus' cross, and maintained steadfast faith in God; but the world has not, because people allow the devil to blind their eyes as they complain about your health."

Enclosed are copies of: 1) "My patient - God's Gift" and "Not Easy - God's Purification table of contents; 2) letters to Most Reverend Andrew, the Bishop of Little Rock Diocese, dated October 15, 1996 & February 7 and 18, 1997; 3) letter to Cardinal Joseph Ratzinger, dated February 18, 1997; 4) letter to Archbishop Agostino Cacciavillian, Apostolic Pro-Nuncio, dated December 10, 1996; 5) letters to 36 Roman Catholic Church authorities in the United States, dated February 7, 1997; 6) "The celebration to Honoring the Holy Father and to reopen Saint John's Seminaries Revelations", "Taxpayers Indirectly Murder Babies through Abortion Funding", "Heavenly Court Summons Writ for Mariette Do-Nguyen", and "Obedience Results in Victory Revelation;" 7)letters to President Bill Clinton and 100 members of the United State Congress, dated February 3, 1997.

Per the Lord Jesus' instructions, in the letter to Archbishop Cacciavillian, I petitioned to him for a private meeting for Bishop Andrew and me to meet with you during the first week of July, 1997. I am only obeying God's instructions with my request.

My family and I have been victims of Catholic Church authorities' misconduct, but I am following the Blessed Virgin Mary and obeying God, and Saint Mary Madelene by converting and serving Him. Please pray for me, and may God's will be done through me as His lowly servant.

The Lord Jesus told me that I must always obey you. I pray to God that you will accept to meet with us in first week of July 1997 and give us the blessing from God. My new address: Mariette Do-Nguyen - P.O. Box 1077 - Little Rock, AR 72203- Tel. (501) 663-9559.

Sincerely in Christ Jesus.

Mariette Do-Nguyen

Foot note: The Holy Spirit working through the Catholic Pope and spiritual leaders and other people throughout the world, more or less depends on the level of the holiness. The Lord Jesus working through Mariette and her successors.

Rebuild My Church Divine Mission

(The Lord Jesus gave this name to Mariette)

P.O. Box 261550 ♠ San Diego, CA 92196 1990

February 24, 1997

This letter mailed to over 270 United States Roman Catholic cardinals, archbishops, bishops, and High-Ranking officials in Vatican

Re: Holy Eucharist Healing Services & Altar Call. Reopen St. John's Seminaries throughout the World. Celebration to Honor the Holy Father to Unify the Church.

Dear Excellency,

God does His works in strange ways. He called me, a sinner and a convert, and gave me the most difficult job in this world. He gave me the name Rebuild My Church Mission and three tasks, pursue freedom to worship the true God in Vietnam; minister to priests, and unify the Church. At first I denied these tasks, and later resigned many time, but He said "NO" with a double underline the word no. So I obeying God and following the Blessed Virgin Mary, Saints Mary Madelene, Bernadette, Joan of Arc, Francis, and Moses to serve Him; may God's will be done through me as His lowly servant.

The Lord Jesus is the one running this mission; He gives me instructions on everything; how to do His work, what to write in letters, and when I speak, He speaks through me.

The Lord Jesus told me, "My Father said, 'It is time for the church to unify so my wounds can heal.' " The celebration to honor the Holy Father John Paul II as God's precious servant at St. Andrew's Cathedral, is the event where the Lord Jesus will say to the world that He is shepherding His church through the Holy Father. The Roman Catholic Church is Jesus' only Church in front of God; Christians [other churches] must obey the Holy Father's teachings to be in full communion with God; if not, they are rejecting the presence of the Lord Jesus through the Holy Eucharist, and their souls will lack nourishment.

This is the time that the Lord Jesus is raising His iron rod, and ruling the world. God is no longer hiding His face.

Enclosed is a pamphlet so you can review some of the works that the Lord God performs through me. Please read carefully the Holy Eucharist Healing Services - Altar call Revelations and the Information.

You can send in reservations for your diocese and receive more information. Have faith in God and He will do miracles at your diocese.

Sincerely in Christ Jesus,

Mariette Do-Nguyen

If you have faith the size of a mustard see, you would say to [this] mulberry tree, Be uprooted and planted in the sea, and it would obey you.
                                                                            –Luke 17: 6

Rebuild My Church Divine Mission

(The Lord Jesus gave this name to Mariette)

P.O. Box 261550 ✦ San Diego, CA 92196-1550

March 22, 1997

Most Reverend Sam G. Jacobs
Bishop of Alexandria

Dear Excellency,

After reading your letter of March 17, 1997, I feel that God has truly blessed my soul. I asked the Lord, "Jesus, the Bishop answered to your letter. What do you want me to do?"

I am completely agree with everything you stated in your letter. What you know of me and God's calling for me is not even a fraction of whole. Discernment is based on good fruit borne from good trees; plus this calling is based on all God's commandments which I must always obey.

At the time the Lord Jesus began His public ministry, he was about thirty years old. He was fully almighty God in the form of fully man, and it was not easy for Him at that time; He was rejected by His own people, the Pharisees, the elders, and scribers. I am just His instrument, This job that God gave me is the most difficult in the world. But I believe that God always opens the eyes of His chosen ones, and you are one of those rare and special people.

The name Rebuild My Church Mission was given to me by the Lord Jesus; I am compelled by God's commandments to reveal Hi messages. He is the one giving me assignments, telling me what and how to take actions. Almost two thousand years ago, Jesus appeared as fully man to perform His works; but now He has chosen me as His Instrument, and His Spirit is dwelling in me as I take action. (I complete surrender my free will back to the Father.)

The three main elements of the Rebuild My Church Mission are:

1. To unify the Lord Jesus' Church so His wounds will be healed.

2. To train more seminarians throughout the world to serve the Roman Catholic Church, to generate more holy priests; these priests will please God by leading His people to Heaven, not by pleasing human fleshes.

3. To assist people in obeying all God's commandments, as they come to Him from their hearts, pleasing God, not man, so their souls will be saved.

Therefore, this mission is an entity separate from the Diocese of Little Rock; it cannot be under any of the Dioceses, only under the Holy Father. Bishop Andrew is the first one chosen by God, as the Roman Catholic authority to supervise me, to fulfill the Roman Catholic Church's rule and God's commandments that I must be under the Roman Catholic Church, like Jesus was under the Laws of Moses.

The Lord Jesus instructs me to deliver His complete message when addressing the public as well as sharing special revelations with Bishop Andrew for future investigation of my life, after I return home to Heaven.

God has blessed the Diocese of Little Rock and Bishop Andrew by choosing the land of Little Rock as the place to gather His faithful servants to prepare for the Lord Jesus' Second Coming.

Little Rock, Arkansas is also President Bill Clinton's home town; God the Father has allowed the devil to blind his eyes, to act on many things against God's commandments in order to wake up the people.

At the same time God sending many tragedies down to earth to purify the world; human power can do nothing against them. There will more tragedies upon this world that humans have never seen before; the only way to limit the destruction is for people to turn their hearts to God, place Him above all things, worship Him, love Him first, and love one another from their hearts.

The Lord Jesus told me that Bishop Andrew has been praying for this mission and for me. The evidence is: On October 31, 1996, under the Lord Jesus' instructions; after I delivered to Bishop Andrew the revelation "Taxpayers Indirectly Murder Babies through Abortion Funding," and "Christian's Must Stop Contributing to these Actions," he was filled with joy because God is now ruling the United State through His people. He raised both his arms and said to me, "All right, how are we going to do this?" I responded, "Jesus will do this through us; but it will not be easy for me and for you; if it is easy then it will not be from God." Because I did not know the next step God wanted us to take, I remained steadfast in my faith, and depending on the Lord Jesus to give me step-by-step instructions.

On March 4, 1997, after I obeyed God and moved to Little Rock, I met with the Bishop to deliver the Holy Eucharist Healing Service and Altar Call revelations and instructions, with special details of the Lord Jesus' revelations regarding the Diocese of Little Rock had been revealed to me earlier, I told him, "Jesus said 'In your prayers you have been asking for more priests, for over twenty years, since you came to this Diocese, but you have received none. Now is the time when God will answer your prayers. He will bless you and this diocese with many priests, more then you need. You will have more priests to help other dioceses." The Bishop was filled with the joy of blessing and victory, and raising both his arms again, he said, "All right."

Have faith in God, I know that the Lord Jesus will surprise you with many blessings for you and your diocese. I will forward the copy of your letter to Bishop Andrew; and if you write to him or call him, he will share more.

Enclosed is the "Not Easy - God's Purification" table of contents which is its on the way to press. The Lord Jesus instructed me to place your letter in His third book, "The Bride of Christ in Action," showing that I am His instrument.

Please pray for me that God's will shall be done through me as His lowly servant.

Sincerely in Christ Jesus,

Mariette Do-Nguyen

A tree and its Fruits. "Either declare the tree good and its fruit is good, or declare the tree rotten and its fruit is rotten, for a tree is known by its fruit. You brood of vipers, how can you say good things when you are evil? For from the fullness of the heart the mouth speaks. A good person brings forth good out of a store of goodness, but an evil person brings forth evil out of a store of evil. I tell you, on the day of judgment people will render an account for every careless word they speak. By your words you will be acquitted, and by your words you will be condemned.

–Matthew 12: 33-37

Foot note: The mission is symbolic of Mariette. The Diocese of Little Rock in the letter to Bishop Jacob is symbolic of the Catholic denomination. Holy Father is symbolic of God. Bishop Andrew is symbolic of the Lord Jesus as fully man in a glorified body and praying for Mariette. The word Catholic is symbolic of spiritual leaders throughout the world.

Rebuild My Church Divine Mission
(The Lord Jesus gave this name to Mariette)
P.O. Box 261550 ✦ San Diego, CA 92196-1550

March 23, 1997

Most Reverend Andrew
Bishop of Little Rock Diocese

Dear Excellency,

Enclosed are copies of: 1) a letter from the Most Reverend Sam G. Jacobs, dated March 17, 1997; 2) a letter to the Most Reverend Sam. G. Jacobs, dated March 22, 1997; 3) Interpretation of the Book of Revelations Chapter Twelve and Thirteen which the Lord Jesus revealed to me; 4) "The Church is Unified and the Lord Jesus' Wounds are Healed" revelation; 5) Holy Eucharist Healing and Altar Call Information for Diocese of Little Rock.

On March 4, 1997, I had delivered partial of the first revelation to you; today, the Lord Jesus asked me to deliver the last part of the first revelation, plus another two.

- Jesus said, "In your prayers you have been asking for more priests, since you came to this Diocese, over twenty years, but you have received none. Now is the time when God will answer your prayers. He will bless you and this diocese with many priests, more than you need. You will have more priests to help other dioceses." After that date Jesus said to me, "At the Holy Eucharist Healing and Altar Call; I will calling out those young men and women who live in this diocese; they will come forward to commit themselves to priesthood and the religious life."

- Now is the time for the Cathedral of Saint Andrew to open twenty-four hours a day for the Blessed Sacrament exposition, so God's presence in the cathedral will heal those who come to Him with sincere hearts and strong faith in God.

- In the future, ninety percent of the Arkansas population will be Roman Catholic.

Since that first Sunday, January 12, 1997, I have been attending mass at Cathedral of Saint Andrew; and day by day I have seen how few people attend weekdays and Sunday mass. I have seen the cathedral almost empty, and it tore my heart for Jesus, for you, Father Scott, and others devoted to God who serve Him in this holy place.

God sent me here, to use me as His instrument, to feel a small part of the pain and suffering that He feels for His Church; and to have me to convey this feeling to you and others.

I want the Cathedral of Saint Andrew and all of the Lord Jesus' churches to be filled with people of God, as much as you do. And what I want is what God has given to me. Jesus will do everything through us. We must have faith in God, and not limit Him by making it difficult for Him to take action through us.

I met with Father Scott on March 18, 1997 regarding the Holy Eucharist Healing Service and Altar Call in April, 1997. He told me that he needs to talk to you; would you please let me know, through Father Scott.

Sincerely in Christ Jesus,

Mariette Do-Nguyen

Foot note: The Diocese of Little Rock is symbolic of Mariette in this Divine mission. The bishop is symbolic of the Lord Jesus. Priests are symbolic of God's faithful servants. 90% is symbolic of completion.

Rebuild My Church Divine Mission

(The Lord Jesus gave this name to Mariette)

P.O. Box 261550 ✦ San Diego, CA 92196-1550

March 23, 1997

Father Scott, Rector
Cathedral of Saint Andrew

Dear Father Scott,

Enclosed are copies of: 1) a letter to Bishop Andrew, dated March 23, 1997; 2) a letter from Bishop Sam G. Jacobs, dated March 17, 1997; 3) a letter to Bishop Sam G. Jacobs, dated March 22, 1997; 4) Interpretation of the Book of Revelations Chapter Twelve and Thirteen which the Lord Jesus revealed to me; 5) Holy Scriptures that I will base on for Holy Eucharist Healing Services and Altar Call.

Besides on the letter, I had expressed my feelings regarding the Cathedral of Saint Andrew's activities to Bishop Andrew. I would like to share of my feelings with you, of course, with Bishop Andrew, and the world. Today, Passion Sunday, while I was standing on the top step of the side cathedral door, looking directly at the center the Saint Francis's courtyard where the Bishop Andrew were blessing palms, I saw you and Deacon Dollar beside him. From up high I was able to see the entire courtyard, almost to the gate. The number of people attending was so small, I estimate maybe two hundred. It even tore my heart more; I said to the Lord, "Good Lord, Jesus, I have never see any place that has this so few people attending a service that has a bishop, a main celebration. I ask You, next Palm Sunday, to fill this courtyard with people until they stream out through the gate, and on to the street."

Later today, after the mass, in my devotion, I saw the spirits of many people filling the courtyard, through the gate and on to the street in front of the cathedral.

Have faith in the Son of the most high living God, the Son of Promise; He will fulfill all His promises. He has fulfilled many promises to me, and he will continue to carry out everything His has pledged, as He will do for you and for others who have faith in Him. Do not limit Him.

Please let me know regarding the Holy Eucharist Healing and Altar Call as soon as you speak to the Bishop.

Sincerely in Christ Jesus.

Mariette Do-Nguyen

Rebuild My Church Divine Mission

(The Lord Jesus gave this name to Mariette)

P.O. Box 261550 ✦ San Diego, CA 92196-1550

April 28, 1997
Father Scott, Rector
of Cathedral of Saint Andrew

Dear Father Scott,

Thursday , April 24, 1997; after I received the Holy Eucharist, the Lord Jesus told me, "There will be a bomb at the Saint Andrew Cathedral this weekend." I asked Him, "Jesus is this in spirit or in the natural?" He said, "It will be in the natural." I said, "Lord, if so how can the Holy Eucharist Healing Service and Altar Call take place?" He then said, "It will be in the parking lot in front of the church, but your car will be protect. It will cost the church millions of dollars, and take at least five years to rebuild." I thought to myself, "If a bomb explodes and I do not report this to the police, they might arrest me for holding information; but if God allows it happen, I must not say anything, no one will know." I had more conversations with the Lord regarding the bomb after that day, but He did not give me any more details.

Saturday, April 26, 1997; during your homily, the Spirit of God was upon me; through the wisdom of God I partly understood, and after I received the Holy Eucharist, the Lord told me, "The homily was the bomb exploding. There was more than what you already know. Therefore, through My words, I had Father Scott indirectly tell you that he has accepted you to serve God, the Holy Eucharist Healing Services and Altar Call at the Cathedral; he also tells others to follow in his footsteps."

God does His work in strange ways; He only gives us a little at a time; when we completely obey and have faith in Him, He then moves forward. I thought that you would give me the answer directly; but God has His reasons for you indirectly answering me through your homily.

In the presence of the Lord, our God, I give thanks to Him, through His grace. He brought me back to Him, and gave me a new life, and I will never deserve it. I have surrendered my free will back to Him, and the Father accepted it on January 10, 1997, the day I arrived in Little Rock, Arkansas. Beyond this He has chosen you and Bishop Andrew as the second Barnabas [Acts 9:26 27] to take charge of bringing me, His servant, to the public to serve Him. I have no way to repay you and the Bishop Andrew; all I have is my prayers for you and the Bishop; but Jesus has everything for you and the Bishop here on earth, and especial in Heaven.

Please pray for me; I will talk to you soon.

Sincerely in Christ Jesus,

Mariette Do-Nguyen

Foot note: The bomb is symbolic of the early times the Rebuild My Church Divine Mission opened to the public throughout the world. The healing service and altar call are symbolic of God's calling for conversion and serving Him.

Rebuild My Church Divine Mission
(The Lord Jesus gave this name to Mariette)
P.O. Box 261550 ✦ San Diego, CA 92196-1550

May 7, 1997

Most Reverend Andrew
Bishop of Little Rock Diocese

Request to held the Holy Eucharist Healing Service and Altar Call at Cathedral of Saint Andrew, on three evenings, May 27, 28, and 29, 1997.

Dear Excellency,

Enclosed is copy of the "Over All of the Lord Jesus' Mission." God the Father has dictated this to me and asked me to send it to you, a long with the Holy Eucharist Healing Service and Altar Call Agenda, to Father Scott, and Father Hung in Kentucky.

I also enclosed copies of a letter to Father Scott, April 28, 1997, and a note, April 18, 1997.

I will work together with Father Scott. I pray to God that you tell Father Scott what you need. If you have any questions you can summon me directly.

Sincerely in Christ Jesus,

Mariette Do-Nguyen

Foot note: Father Hung is symbolic of those obeying all God's commandment in their hearts and their daily life put in actions without "fear of man." Father Scott is symbolic of those doubt of God.

Rebuild My Church Divine Mission

(The Lord Jesus gave this name to Mariette)

P.O. Box 261550 ✦ San Diego, CA 92196-1550

May 16, 1997

Most Reverend Andrew
Bishop of Little Rock Diocese

Reverend Father Scott,
Rector of Cathedral of Saint Andrew,

Dear Father Bishop Andrew and Father Scott,

God's words always come with His power. Last night Jesus the Lord gave me Nehemiah chapter six and seven.

After I received the instruction from the Lord Jesus, His web site on Internet must be entered before the Pentecost Sunday, May 18, 1997. About twenty pages of the Lord Jesus web site, the Lord Jesus commanded me to include the Holy Eucharist Healing Service and Altar Call to be held in three evenings May 27, 28, and 29, 1997, at the Cathedral of Saint Andrew. I had pleaded with God that I have not received the approval from you and the Bishop Andrew, so I can not put in the web site; I even begged Him to allow me to wait for approval from the Bishop and you. But He has His way of doing His works; He commanded me to put on this information by Saturday night, before the Pentecost Sunday. I have no choice, so I came to you today after the mass.

The Lord Jesus had commanded me that I must always obey all His commandments, the Holy Father's teachings. For the church authorities, if he obeys all God's commandments and the Holy Father's teachings, then I also must obey.

After I had explained to you what God had told me to do, you said to me "The Holy Eucharist Healing can not be scheduled on that day." I said, "I am stuck, I have to obey God, and His has His way of doing His works." You said to me, "You have no authority to schedule any thing in this church. You have no proof of what God told you. On your letter of May something, you said the abortion is allowed when the life of the mother is threatened; but the Church teaches that at any time there is to be no abortion."

I have not directly heard from the Holy Father that there is no abortion at any time. My discernment is: God will allow it if it is very early after conception; and if the only way to save the mother's life is to bring the baby out of the womb. God will not let the mothers die, and the babies die, in the womb.

Millions and millions of the babies have been aborted because of the U. S. legal abortion Laws. What are the church authorities doing to save these babies?

The Roman Catholic Church leaders: The cardinals, archbishops, bishops, priests, and deacons must teach God's commandments, as Jesus the Lord has commanded. They must love God by obeying all His commandments, put their teachings into their daily actions, to benefit their souls and the souls of those they lead, to destroy the teaching of man's doctrine, the doctrine of pleasing man, satisfying flesh and destroying souls.

In obeying God, I had to deliver this message to you, and to two hundred seventy one Roman Catholic Church high authorities, and to the taxpayers who indirectly murder innocent babies. As of May 7, 1997, the mass murder still happens daily, by the United States government passing laws that legalize the abortion, and by using tax dollars to fund abortions and this kind of medical training, to lean and performed abortions, as well as weapons and chemicals that kill innocent people in other countries.

Again, I have clearly stated what God has told me to say to high Church authorities; they have learned of God's commandments of "You shall not kill." Yet they have been taking the wrong actions against legalized abortion law. God had me to point out to them the correct way; but they still either allow the devil to blind their eyes or they hold on to their earthly titles by pleasing man; They refuse to obey God when God has ordained them to teach their congregations to take action according to Jesus' teachings. So now they are more liable for the sins of their congregation who indirectly murder these babies.

Jesus said "Go in the closet to pray, your heavenly Father already knows what you will ask, " He does not teach us to stand in front of abortion clinics and congressional buildings to pray. When cardinals stand in front of congressional building praying for partial abortion to be ended, when priests organize or participate in these marches, they are being led by the devil. These actions are for the laity; they must have a lot of love for these mothers, President Bill Clinton, lawmakers, and doctors, from each ones heart, and pray in quiet areas or in church with pure hearts. God only answers petitions from the pure of heart in His way and His time. When a person prays without a pure heart, the devil will tell him what to say; if we do not pray the will of God, then God will not answer the devil's petitions.

The high Church authorities are now more responsible for the sins of the taxpayers who indirectly murder innocent babies. I must state exactly of what God has told me to say, because I love you, I want your souls to be saved.

The Roman Catholic Church is the only Church in front of God; but church authorities are disobedient to God, they please man to protect their earthly crown. They want every other church to obey the Holy Father, but they are not a good example; many are preaching God's commandments, but not putting their teaching into practice.

I must obey God and say everything that the Lord Jesus asks me to put in this letter, and this letter will be followed under the Holy Eucharist Healing Service at the Cathedral of Saint Andrew, to be held on the three evenings, May 27, 28, and 29, 1997, at the Cathedral of Saint Andrew, 617 Louisiana Street, Little Rock, Arkansas, 72201. Other things I leave in the hand of God.

Sincerely in Christ Jesus,

Mariette Do-Nguyen

Foot note: Holy Father's teaching is symbolic of God the Father's commandments. The church Father Scott spoke of is symbolic of earthly church laws that are set to look pretty. Two year later of the first date God revealed of Holy Eucharist Healing and altar call; the Rebuild My Church Divine Mission incorporated on May 27, 1999, and obtained tax identification the same day. All God revelation are come in symbolism and have no time of manifesting in the natural. Example the Book of Revelations was revealed of Mariette Do-Nguyen as God Servant as the head in the natural for the Rebuild My Church Divine Mission. I, Mariette did not know this until after God removed me from the insurance company on April 7, 1994.

Rebuild My Church Divine Mission
(The Lord Jesus gave this name to Mariette)
P.O. Box 261550 ✦ San Diego, CA 92196-1550

June 2, 1997
Father Scott, Rector
Cathedral of Saint Andrew

Dear Father Scott,

Enclosed is a copy of the Lord Jesus web site: it was entered on the internet the evening of May 17, 1997, the night before the Pentecost Sunday, as the Lord Jesus instructed me.

The Lord Jesus told me, "The web site on the Internet is for the new generation all over the world. I want you to print the same information in a pamphlet for those who do not have use of a computer." For the Lord's instruction, I have Darcy to do the lay out for the pamphlet.

The following is addresses for the Lord Jesus web site:
http://www.Jesusweb.org
The Lord Jesus is connecting His church and the governments of all nations in one law, and that law is to obey all God's commandments.

Jesus the Lord assured me in one of the revelations, "If any one gets in you way, I will sweep them off the concrete ground like a piece of sand down to the dike." The Lord means the people who refuse to cooperate with him or want to wait in their time, He then sweep them away, and chooses others that obey Him.

On the feast of Corpus Christi, Jesus the Lord told me, "You and Father Scott will not stuck that long. He needs your comfort more then you need him." After the mass go see him, I need to speak to him." I hope that you remember what words came out from my mouth after the mass on Sunday June 1, 1997.

Sincerely in Christ Jesus,

Mariette Do-Nguyen

Rebuild My Church Divine Mission
(The Lord Jesus gave this name to Mariette)

P.O. Box 261550 ♦ San Diego, CA 92196-1550

June 9, 1997

This letter mailed to over 270 United States Roman Catholic cardinals, archbishops, bishops, High-Ranking officials in Vatican, and 12 Cistercian of Strict Observance Abbots.

Dear ....

On June 6, 1997, the first Friday of the month, also the feast of the Sacred Heart of Jesus. The Lord Jesus said to me, "Church authorities, government officials, and lawmakers are refusing to cooperate with God's plan for salvation of the world. I need you to listen carefully to all my instructions, and take actions as I tell you. Give them My web site address."

The Lord Jesus, Jesus of Nazareth Web site on the Internet:

http://www.Jesusweb.Org

This web site information is also printed in a pocket booklet reference for those who do not have access to a computer.

But Samuel said: 'Does the LORD so delight in holocausts and sacrifices as in obedience to the command of the LORD? Obedience is better than sacrifices, and submission then the fat of the rams.

−1 Samuel 15:22

Enclosed are copies of a letter to the members of the U.S. Senate and to President Bill Clinton, dated May 23, 1997, and mailed June 9, 1997. While Jesus the Lord emphasized on the first be the last, and last be the first; I enclosed copies of the first two pages, and last two pages of the web site [The Mission Purposes and a letter to Father Scott, Rector of Cathedral of Saint Andrew, and Most Reverend Andrew, Bishop of Little Rock, Diocese, May 16, 1997].

God has ordained you to cooperate with Him, to fulfill His plans for salvation of the world. I pray that you will obey Him, and not go against any of His commandments.

Sincerely in Christ Jesus,

Mariette Do-Nguyen

Rebuild My Church Divine Mission

(The Lord Jesus gave this name to Mariette)

P.O. Box 261550 ✦ San Diego, CA 92196-1550

June 17, 1997

Most Reverend Andrew
Bishop of Little Rock Diocese

Re: "God the Father's house is not the den of thieves. "

Dear Excellency,

God would not allow me to come to the Holy Hour of Adoration in the chapel on June 17, 1997, at the Cathedral of Saint Andrew.

While I was looking for a parking place, I saw some people wearing name tags in front of the Cathedral, standing around and talking. I entered cathedral, and there were a few groups standing inside the church socializing, some of them had their backs turned to the tabernacle that contained the Blessed Sacrament.

I wondered what are these people doing in here? I felt fearful and unsafe. I continued proceeding to the seat that I normally sit in; I saw there was a man setting up a projector and a screen, with a notebook computer at the right side of the altar, up to the middle of the sanctuary.

Immediately after I kneeled, the Lord Jesus' Spirit came upon me powerfully. This is the first time I ever felt His Spirit this way: the Spirit of love was very angry. The love and anger of the Lord Jesus was controlling me, He said to me, "They are turning my Father's house into the den of thieves." I continued trying to pray, but I could not, because the Spirit of the Lord was so angry. I called Tony, and asked him, "Tony, what are they doing here?" Tony replied, "I don't know." I asked, " Are we still having Communion service?" He replied, "Yes, at 12:05."

When Tony departed from me, the Lord Jesus said to me, "Go tell him [the man setting up the equipment], My Father's house is not a den of thieves." As the Lord said this, my thought was, "This Cathedral belongs to the bishop, and Father Scott is Rector," I said to the Lord, "Lord I will tell Father Scott when he comes back from retreat." The Lord said again, "You go tell him. My Father's house is not a den of thieves." I said, "Jesus, Lord, I will tell Tony and have Tony to tell him." But the Lord insisted, "You, get up and go tell that man, My Father's house is not a den of thieves."

He then dragged me to the sanctuary. Standing at the second step of the sanctuary, facing these equipment, I said to the man doing the set up, "Excuse me, what are you doing here? What are these equipment set up for?" He replied, "I'm setting up for the concert at 12:45, after the service." I said to him, "The Lord Jesus is very angry. He said, 'My Father's house is not a den of thieves. I know that you have the permission from the Bishop, but Father Scott is the one who will get all the blame." The man replied to me, "Thank you for giving me the message."

They came to Jerusalem, and on entering the temple area he began to drive out those selling and buying there. He overturned the tables of the money changes and the seats of those who were selling doves. He did not permit anyone to carry anything through the temple area. Then he taught them saying, "Is it not written: 'My house shall be called a house of prayer for all people'? But you have made it a den of thieves.

–Mark 11:15-17.

Even though in this concert the music words are to glorify God, but it is wrong. The churches are for worship, especially when there is Blessed Sacrament in the church. Therefore, at no time can the sanctuary be used for concerts. Concerts are to please human ears, not to focus on God like the time of worship. And concerts are to glorify the musicians. And the most thing against God today, June 17, 1997, was moving the Blessed Sacrament Adoration to the small chapel, and using the church for the concert.

The Lord asked me to serve Him, as Eucharistic Minister at the Cathedral of Saint Andrew. On June 10, 1997; After I entered the church, I signed for June 11, 13, 18, 20, 23, and 25, 1997.

Sunday, June 15, 1997; I found that all the priests in the diocese will be on retreat this week, and there is only Communion Service. After consulting with the Lord Jesus; Monday 16, 1997, I told Tony that I will serve for the Communion Service on June 18, 1997. But this morning, after the Lord dragged me to the sanctuary to talk to the man who did the equipment set up for the concert, He then told me, "You will not serve the Communion Service tomorrow; go tell Tony, and cross off your name from the paper. I went to the back of the church to let Tony know of what the Lord told me, but there was no pen next to the volunteer service paper sheet; I went back to my seat, the Lord told, "Get your pen, and go cross off your name from that paper. I will not let you touch the muddy morass." I did as He asked of me. I then returned to my seat, the Lord said, "When you got home, write a letter to Bishop Andrew, tell him of what were happened today."

At this time, I did not understand of why the Lord instructed me to cross off my name, but I obeyed Him in faith, and I believe that there is major teaching that He had me cross off my name.

A few weeks ago, on Sunday, after the 12:03 p.m. mass, while the final song was still being sung, people were standing singing and praying. There was a woman, a man, and two of the altar boys competing with each other to turn off the candles. I then heard the Lord Jesus say, "They are treating the sanctuary like a supermarket." I then repeated out loud what the Lord said, and there were a few people around who also saw the incident and heard the words I repeated of what I heard from the Lord.

And last Sunday, June 15, 1997, during the vigil mass on Saturday, another incident happened. Sitting at the front pew was a lector and the man accompanying her. Their actions were very distracting to the people behind. I believe that lectors and Eucharistic ministers must set a good example for others to follow, not exposing evil actions to distract others.

We must focus on what comes from our hearts to God, to glorify God, not the external things that glorify man. I have enclosed a "Church Manners" that the Blessed Mother taught me. I passed them on to others, too.

I must say everything the Lord asked me to say. I know these words will not please you, but these things are good for your soul and the souls of others that you shepherd.

In Christ Jesus,

Mariette Do-Nguyen

Foot note: Cathedral of Saint Andrew is also symbolic of an individual, the world, nation, group, organization, or any Christian denomination. The man setting up equipment and concert is symbolic of actions working against God's commandments

Rebuild My Church Divine Mission

(The Lord Jesus gave this name to Mariette)

P.O. Box 261550 ✦ San Diego, CA 92196-1550

July 2, 1997

Most Reverend Andrew
Bishop of Little Rock Diocese

Re: Diocese of Little Rock is God chosen One

Dear Excellency,

Enclosed are copies of: (1) The "Appointments Revelations;" (2) a letter to Cardinal Edmund Szoke, President of Prefecture for the Economic Affairs of the Holy See, August 2, 1997; (3) a letter to Father Timothy, Abbot of the Abbey of Gathsemani Monastery, August 2, 1997; (4) a letter to Father Peter Joseph Tong and Father Scott, August 1, 1997; (5) the "New Books" script.

God's will "must be done" through you, me, and some of the chosen ones in your diocese. I accepted the most suffering to follow in the Lord Jesus' footsteps in salvation of the mankind. You, the Diocese of Little Rock priests, and many people in your congregations have been chosen by God to suffer with the Lord Jesus.

My obeying God, and actions have brought many good things from heaven down to the Lord Jesus' church on earth, specially the Diocese of Little Rock, and they will affect the world. Through you, your priests, and your congregation actions; God will use these actions to pour out His grace and blessings upon your diocese and the Roman Catholic Church.

The predestined God chosen ones have no choice, but obey Him. The Lord Jesus said, "You have not chosen Me, but I am the One who chose you." Therefore, when the chosen one resists God's call, make the situation get worst, He will push him against the wall. God did it to me, He is now pushing you, your priests, the Roman Catholic church leaders and officials against the wall.

In the morning of July 17, 1997, the Lord Jesus told me, "I ask you to hand deliver this letter [God Directly Reveals to the American, and indirectly reveals to the World of Catholic Church leaders a lack of Discernment, and "Despise the Blessed Sacrament."] to Father Scott." I did not want to face Father Scott regarding this letter, I said to Him, "Lord, can I mail it?" He said, "Mariette, you are the one that I use to pour out

My love in him [Father Scott], please do not refuse my request."

About 11:25a.m. while I was getting out of my car, Jesus the Lord told me, Father Scott is in the church, and the door is open for you. I will speak to him a few minutes before you give him the letter."

I then was trying to open the front door of the Cathedral of Saint Andrew, but it was locked; the Lord told me, "Go to the side door." I then went in the church by the side door. I saw Father Scott was walking in the sanctuary; I called him, "Father Scott." He then walking toward me, and said to me, "How did you get in this way?" I replied, "Through that door." He said, "That door should be locked." I said, "It was open." Later that day the Lord told me, "I opened the door for you to get inside the church." I thought of the angel rescuing Saint Peter from prison.

Within about five minutes conversation, these are main elements. Through me, the Lord said to Father Scott, you and others who love God above all things; I said, "Like the father loves his children, he wants his children to be the best; and there are times children disobey him, he has to raise the rod to correct them. God loves His church leaders, he does the same like the father does to his children. Jesus loves you, and the more He loves you, more you suffer." He said, "That is the things that we fear, and do not want to know." I said, "God is using the diocese of Little Rock as the model to purify His church. The Bishop Andrew also suffers very much.

I have seen other bishops have priests served them, carry their bags every time they come to church for service; but for Bishop Andrew, I saw him carrying his own bags entering the church. I can tell you from the scale one to ten, one is the best and ten is the worst." I did not know where the diocese of Little Rock stood, I pleaded, "Jesus, help me here, what number is the diocese of Little Rock?" I then said to Father Scott, "The Diocese of Little Rock is at number three. There is no diocese in number one; many other dioceses are below the number three, some of dioceses are at number ten. Some how, God has me to tell you all these; would you deliver to the Bishop for me?"

Before we ended the conversation, he said to me, "The front door now is open." Because Father Scott will suffer very much, God allows me to tell him of his heart in front of God. To protect the mission, God's works, and me; God reveals people hearts to me; I can not tell anyone's heart to other when God reveals it to me, many times not even to that person.

To serve God by services to others, assist them to convert, daily exam and repent, focus on heavenly eternal life in heaven; I ask you to distribute this "New Books" script to the people in the State of Arkansas; by inserting this flyer to your diocese church bulletins, and publishing it in the Arkansas Catholic papers. This is the way that you are planting good seeds to bear good fruit and last forever.

Please pray for me, the Lord Jesus' mission, and those God chose to serve Him in and through this mission, the mission that sits on your diocese physical land.

Sincerely in Christ Jesus,

Mariette Do-Nguyen

Mariette Do-Nguyen

Rebuild My Church Divine Mission
(The Lord Jesus gave this name to Mariette)
P.O. Box 261550 ✦ San Diego, CA 92196-1550

July 16, 1997

Cardinal Bernardin Gantin, Prefect Congregation for Bishops
Cardinal Joseph Ratzinger, President of the Pontifical Bible Commission
Most Rev. Jorge A. Medina Estevez, Prefect Congregation of the Divine Worship over 270 United States Roman Catholic cardinals, archbishops, bishops

Re: God Directly Revealed to the American, and Indirectly revealed to the World of Catholic Church Leaders are lack of Discernment, and "Despise the Blessed Sacrament"

Dear ....
July 16, 1997; at about 2:00 a.m.; I got up and prayed for over and hour. The Lord Jesus asked me, "Mariette, Just for Me, would you hold off on your July trip to visit your children in San Diego until Christmas. You will be leaving Little Rock on December 20, 1997 and return on January 5, 1998." I replied to Him, "Jesus, Lord, if You want, I will do it for You. I had promised to the Father that I will do everything for You."

I then asked, "The other day, you told me that I will be moving within a few months after I return from my July trip to San Diego, and not to sign the six months leasing agreement, but only signed a monthly agreement. You also told me that the next place I rent will be a house for me to store my car in a garage, and this house will be offered to me by a developer." Jesus the Lord cut me here, He said, "The developer is symbolic of Me."

At this time I knew the Lord was trying to reveal something to me, I said, "Jesus, the Almighty God, You are revealing to me something here." I then continued, "Father, Holy Spirit, open my heart, mind and ears so I can hear, understand, and remember everything that the Lord Jesus shows me. Mother, the Blessed Virgin, Saint Michael, and all the holy angels and saints intercede for me."

In my vision, I saw the Blessed Sacrament chapel at Good Shepherd Church, where one time I found a toy lion at the foot of tabernacle. This toy distracted me from my focus in God; I moved it to the side; I did not want this lion toy to distract others. Before I left the chapel, I took the lion toy with me. I did not throw the toy away at the side of the same road I take every day to church, I went on different road and threw the toy to the side of that road.

I then saw inside the restaurant, at the table that I had lunch with my uncle, Father Dominic, the Roman Catholic priest, , on July 15, 1997; with the conversation we were shared about the American despise to the Holy Eucharist exposition.

I then saw the Sunday, June 22, 1997; a Eucharistic minister, Mary Jo was wearing a sleeveless, short dress. She came to tabernacle to bring out the ciborium, and stood to the right side of the priest to gave the Holy Eucharist.

After I received the Lord Jesus' body and blood, I closed my eyes to be with Him. In my "vision" I saw Mary Jo wearing a short sleeveless dress, and she was standing to the right of Father Scott, exactly in the natural. The lector that was standing in front of the Gospel podium was wearing a tight-at-chest, white short sleeve dress, and the Lord said to me, "They have no respect for their God. The God of all creation." I said, "Lord, forgive them, have mercy on them, they have no knowledge of what they are doing."

After the mass, Mary Jo went to the original altar to took the tabernacle key to put away; on her way out, she made a turn from the left of the sanctuary to the right, through the front pew, as she saw me at the end of the third pew about to go out. She stopped shaking my hand, and with both of my hands holding her right hand, I said, "Jesus is not happy for you to wear a sleeveless dress at the sanctuary; many times we did it without understanding it." Mary Jo heard I said this, she said to me, "I have to go, my family is waiting for me, and I am not receiving any of it." I said to the Lord, "Jesus, she said she did not receive what you have me to tell her." And at the vigil mass on Saturday June 28, 1997, a tall Eucharistic minister was wearing green short and blouse to deliver the Holy Eucharist.

Then I saw the Tuesday adoration of the Blessed Sacrament during the month of June 1997; in the dark sanctuary, with six small blurred candles in a two candle stands, together with Liz in a service for the adoration. I then saw Liz wearing a sleeveless, long white wrinkled robe, the robe seemed like she wore it to sleep, got out of the bed, and come to church to serve the Holy Communion service in the same robe.

Now I understand that the Lord revealed to me the heart; and from the heart is showed out in actions of Eucharistic ministers are despise to the Blessed Sacrament.

I then saw Deacon Gary and Father Scott serving for Sunday's Blessed Sacrament adoration, with incense, in a separate visions.

The Lord then reminded me a revelation, on April 18, 1997, Jesus the Lord said to me, "Tell Father Scott to have Eucharistic ministers and lectors to wear white robes to serve in the sanctuary. I do not want people wearing short in My presence." The Lord God means both inner and outer outfits. I delivered this message to Father Scott on April 20, 1997.

I then saw the Good Shepherd church sanctuary with Eucharistic ministers standing behind the empty altar. The Lord reminded me a Eucharistic minister at the Good Shepherd that He revealed to me of that minister will not enter the heaven. When God revealed to me others hearts, and where they will be after their last breath for the purpose of the calling me to fulfill this mission, as His vessel, and this is between God and me, there is no second person in this world knows these.

Jesus the Lord said to me, "I want people who perform services to Me in physical contact with My body and blood to have "pure hearts". But the church leaders' are lack of discernment, they allowed people against Me [containing grave/mortal sins] in physical contact my body and blood." He continued, "Send this revelation to bishops, and church officials."

I cannot disclose what God revealed to me of the people's hearts; but I can publicly say what I saw. During the first week I attended the cathedral, after a mass, I was talking to the cathedral's secretary, Bobbie, and two other women. One of the woman was Liz. The secretary left to return to work; these two women and I went out the side door. Liz was wearing white long robe, and she told me while she was walking toward the rectory and I was walking to the parking lot, "I am a volunteer, and a very active one." After that I only talked to her few times. I saw her at the church almost every time I went to mass, and 99 percent of the time I saw her, she was wearing a white long robe.

I go to mass every day, and about ninety percent of the time I went to mass, I saw Liz either talking to Father Scott before or after the mass.

After masses; she either went in the vesting sacristy at the back of the church, and stood in front of Father Scott, talked to him, or if she in the church and saw Father Scott went to rectory, she then followed him, over the bridge to another building belong to the Cathedral.

Again, I cannot disclose what God revealed to me of Father Scott's heart; but Jesus the Lord revealed to me many times that the devil is using women to destroy the priest's vow of celibacy, and the devil is using this woman to attack Father Scott.

I then went back to sleep. In my dream, I saw a large toilet bowl, water almost finish running down the bottom of the bowl after being flushed. The entire bottom of a white bowl was thick with a residual stain, and there was a spot that was rusty.

Still in the dream, I then saw I just entered, and was standing in the middle of an apartment similar to my apartment. I saw one large bag of rice, about one ton, unopened laid on the floor with junks; there were four light bulbs in a dinning room ceiling lamp hung on the ceiling, and the dining table was taken away. I wondered why my mother left the apartment while it was such a mess. I then went to the front door, there was no door knob. I thought that the door was reversed from right to left, and left to right. I then looked at the top left corner of the door, I saw the fastener still there; I realized that the door knob was taken off.

I then was inside the apartment next door. A little girl who lived in this apartment came out from her bedroom and told me, "Your mother came here and asked for rice. I gave her some." In my thought, "There was an unopened bag of rice on the apartment floor. Why did my mother come here to get rice?"

I then woke up. I heard the Lord Jesus say to me, "The little girl in the apartment symbolic of Me. You are yourself in the dream. The apartment symbolizes the church. The missing dinning table is symbolic of the altar, the sanctuary. The ton of rice is symbolic of the words of God. The missing door knob is symbolic of no discernment. The four light bulbs are symbolic of the light from God, will open the eyes and hearts of the church leaders and those in service to Me and the Father. The toilet bowl is symbolic of Eucharistic ministers', and priests'/ clergymen's hearts. Stains and rust are their sins and iniquities. Water running down is symbolic of confession without converting and daily repentance from each ones' heart."

After the Lord spoke, he then reminded me of the July 1993 trip I took to Vietnam. I visited the parish that my earthly parents belonged to. I donated two tons of rice for the poor in the parish.

Everything Jesus the Lord gave in this revelation is in the Book of Exodus, especially in three chapters 28, 29, and 30, Exodus 3:5 'God said, "Come no nearer! Remove the sandals from your feet, for the place where you stand is holy ground." And Luke 19:36 "As he rode along, the people were spreading their cloaks on the road."

Jesus tells us very clearly that the church leaders and officials are disobedience to God's commandments, not keeping their hearts pure. From their hearts are not being pure, the devil blinds their eyes, minds and hearts, causing a lack of discernment. Many Eucharistic ministers' and priests' hearts are filled with and sins and iniquities. Going to confession is just external, having no root in God's words. Because their hearts are dirty, they then show it to the outside. But they lack discernment, they can not tell what is from God and what is from the devil; they are mixing God's and devil's works together.

I have enclosed the copies of the letter to Most Reverend Andrew, Bishop of Little Rock, July 14, 1997, and June 17, 1997.

On July 4, 1997, Jesus the Lord told me, "Mariette, you are the custodian for my sanctuary." Plus in this letter, in actions, God is very clear that He sent me down to earth as His sanctuary's custodian. Again, as God sanctuary's custodian, I must say what God tell me to say to protect His sanctuary.

Through the power of God, God sent me down to be the custodian of His sanctuary. I am warning everyone in this world, especially church leaders; church officials, to urgently take actions to correct these sinfulness actions against God the Almighty.

Sincerely in Christ Jesus

Mariette Do-Nguyen

Rebuild My Church Divine Mission
(The Lord Jesus gave this name to Mariette)
P.O. Box 261550 ✦ San Diego, CA 92196-1550

July 17, 1997

Cardinal Bernardin Gantin, Prefect Congregation for Bishops
Cardinal Joseph Ratzinger, President of the Pontifical Bible Commission
Most Rev. Jorge A. Medina Estevez, Prefect Congregation of the Divine Worship over 270 United States Roman Catholic cardinals, archbishops, bishops

Re: God Revealed Catholic Church High Leaders' and Officials Hearts

Dear ....,

At 2:08 a.m. on July 17, 1997. I woke up with some dreams; in the dream, I had my little youngest daughter with me, I dropped her several times on the ground. Every time I dropped her, her face hit the ground, and damaged her nose badly. The bridge of her nose became soft, without blood. While I sat on my ball feet and knees, I held her in my arm, while she was sitting on my thighs; I lifted one of her arm up, and pulled it to maximum, her arm was almost separate from her shoulder, and I prayed, "Lord, do not let me drop my daughter any more. I smashed her nose every time I dropped her." Even though she was very small in body, her voice was like an adult, she said, "Do not drop me any more. My nose is broken."

I then saw a couple who were moving a lots of conference iron chairs and brochure holders from the congressional officials' office. The furniture was very old. While I saw the man and woman standing at the end of the aisle in between these large amounts of furniture, I knew these pieces of furniture were moved from one location to this location.

As I woke up, I went to get water to drink, and to the bathroom; and returned to the bed on the third floor, I prayed, the Lord said to me, "Your youngest daughter is symbolic of the Catholic church's high leaders. Your dropping her face on the ground is symbolic of each time I told you send letters out to the public. In these letters, I unveiled their hearts. Your praying for yourself not to drop your child's face on the ground is symbolic of your prayer to Me, the Lord God, for the Catholic church leaders to convert their hearts. The child asking you to not drop her any more is symbolic of their saying 'do not open their dirty hearts'."

After the Lord said these things, in my vision I saw the two people from the shoulder up. One was in front of another, their heads were very large, hard plastic in wooden brown color, with some black part on the back of their head is their hair, looking like clown masks of Mr. Earth, worn at a Chinese dragon dance. To these two people's left wall was a dark colored curtain; to their right, in front of them were two living human hands waving at their face, seeking them for help, like some pictures I saw of people in purgatory raising their hands, crying out for help. In front of them was a round judge's bench with a judge sitting inside looking at them. These clown people slowly walked toward the front of the judge , in between the judge and these two man was a small open gate, a judge bench's door.

While I was trying to analyze these two people in the nature, the Lord asked me, "What do you see?" I said, "These two look like mannequins While I was saying this to the Lord, I was thinking of purgatory. The Lord said, "They are not mannequins. Can you look at them closer?" I said, " Lord, I can not tell what it is. But in front of them was a judge sitting at his bench." The Lord said, "Those you called mannequins are symbolic of the Catholic church's high leaders and officials. They are on the way to deal with Me. I am the judge sitting in the bench. They are on earth, but their souls are in purgatory, waiving their hands for help, but no one can help them, they must help themselves. Helping themselves by converting their hearts to Me, so they can have the chance to come to the Father. Those two in the vision moving forward to the judge are symbolic of those who come forward embracing you as My faithful and suffering Servant, and assisting you to serve Me in the mission of salvation of mankind."

The Son of the most high living God continued, "Mariette, this part is for you. You were a First stubborn Archangel in heaven. You are now on earth, paying for that stubbornness with your suffering. Stand firm in your suffering. Your suffering will turn many souls into blood. They must be bleeding out a lots of blood so they can be saved."

Jesus the Almighty God continued saying to me, "That was for you, but I want you to add in with the letter to all the government officials of the Catholic church in the Vatican, and in the United State of American; they are inside those mannequins you saw."

At this time the Lord reminded me of the day before: I was working on a letter of what God revealed of "Church leaders lack of discernment, and despise the Blessed Sacrament"; I was very suffering. I rested and fell asleep; in my dream, I saw a dog from the shoulder up to the head, but he looked like a lion's head. His head was covered with a long thick amount of hair. The color of the hair was white, and looked like it had mud in it for long time, then got out and washed. Hiding under and sticking to his hair were many round dog ticks, like heavy gun bullets.

The One who was a live, dead, risen, and lives for ever said to me, "The lion lives in the jungle, the dog is in the house. The ticks is disease. The bullets are from a gun. The head of the lion dog is symbolic of the head of the church's high leaders."

At 2:33 a.m. July 17, 1997; I said, "Lord, the church leaders do not want to hear all this." Jesus said, "That was exactly who they are in front of Me, the Almighty God, the One who was crucified on the Cross, died and rose from the dead. The One they proclaim as their God, they are worshipping. But they are continue to crucify Me to this day. They are those who follow in the foot steps of Judas and betray Me. ."

I then said, "Lord, are they really that bad?" Jesus the Lord said, "They are living a life like Prince Charles in England. He violated His marriage vow, and is traveling in the yacht." While the Lord said this, in my vision, I saw Prince Charles standing in the huge cruise ship sailing away from Hong Kong. The Lord Jesus meant that Catholic church high leaders live the life like a prince, filled with pleasures.

The Lord God said to me, "Do you know what to do with this revelation?" I said, "Lord Jesus, you told me last night to hold on to the letter "Church Leaders Lack Discernment, and Despise the Blessed Sacrament" for this revelation and mail them together at the same time." Jesus is God said, "Go forward, I, myself go before you." I said, "Thank you Lord. I will do exactly what You commanded."

Everything in this revelation, The Lord Jesus foretold through Saint John in the Book of Revelation, contained in the "Letters to the Churches of Asia." My job is God's instrument, I must do exactly what God commands me. I do not know the next step His will takes. I urgently ask every one of you to quickly take actions from your hearts before the worst actions come upon you and the world. You are in the church recognized in front of God; and you are responsible for yourself and the people that God places in your hands to shepherd them.

Sincerely in Christ Jesus,

Mariette Do-Nguyen

Foot note: The decoration of the physical Christ of King church, the main celebrant's behavior and congregation exploding in laughter are revealed in the world these day as focusing on things to please man's flesh, and worshipping idols. People do not have their hearts and actions to show the love for God and for one another; and spiritual leaders are exulting themselves.

Rebuild My Church Divine Mission

(The Lord Jesus gave this name to Mariette)

P.O. Box 261550 ♦ San Diego, CA 92196-1550

July 21, 1997

Cardinal Bernardin Gantin, Prefect Congregation for Bishops
Cardinal Joseph Ratzinger, President of the Pontifical Bible Commission
Most Reverend Andrew, Bishop of Little Rock Diocese
over 270 United States Roman Catholic cardinals, archbishops, bishops

Re: Church Leaders Allowing the Devil to Use God's Church to Perform Evil Works.

Dear Excellency:

On July 17, 1997, the Lord Jesus told me, "This Saturday's vigil mass; I want you go to Christ the King Church, and to Saint Patrick on Sunday, for the 9:00a.m. mass, and Cathedral of Saint Andrew on Sunday evening for the "Spirituality and Anger" talk, presented by Dr. Sam, D. Min, FCOC. Bring your tape recorder with you to record this session; make copies of it and send to the bishops."

July 19, 1997, I arrived at the Christ The King Catholic church parking lot about 4: 20 p.m. I got out of the car, there were two women getting in and out of their cars, I saw two entrances, the Lord told me, "You ask her for the entrance." I thought, "I'll just try the side door first, and if it's not open I will go the main entrance. I do not have to ask her." But while I was walking by her, I asked, "Which door is the entrance to the Blessed Sacrament chapel?" She pointed to the side door, and said, "That door was open, I just saw two people go in. I do not belong to this church, I just came to pick up my daughter."

I then was inside the huge church; newly remodeled, like the end of the oval theater. I looked toward the sanctuary, searching for the tabernacle with sanctuary light, so I can worship the Lord in the correct manner that the Blessed Virgin Mother taught me. I walked to the front of the sanctuary, still searching for the tabernacle. I saw a huge, tall crucifix at the middle of the sanctuary. I then walked to the foot of the oval sanctuary, from one side to another, but there was no tabernacle. What I saw was, on both sides of the sanctuary, in separate cubicles, were two huge round metal art pieces. I was looking and trying to understand what they were, but I could not tell what were these two metal art works speaking. I then asked two women who were sitting at the pew, "Excuse me, where is the Blessed Sacrament?" One of them told me, "Behind that door." While she was saying this, she pointed to the door at the right side of the Sanctuary, (my left side).

I then went in a large Blessed Sacrament chapel, with many chairs in two sections, but only the two front rows had kneelers. I also saw a small table with a few rosaries, and a small note book. The Lord told me, "I want you to write on that book." I opened the book that said on the cover "Rosary prayer request." I asked, "Lord Jesus, what do you want me to put in here?" He said write down, "Please pray for the church leaders to be faithful to their vows; serve God through services to other in love from their hearts, and you sign 'Jesus' Messenger.' " I then went to kneel down for the devotion, in just a few minutes, and the Lord told me, "I want you to go in the church and ask them what are those two huge metal round things you saw in the church, and come back here." I got up and saw a man entering the Blessed Sacrament from another door next to one came in. I asked, "Are you..." He said, "I am one of the ministers for the church." I ask, "I have some questions for those things in the church." I then went in the church with him following me.

We were now in front of the huge metal round art, to the right side of the sanctuary, I asked, "What is this?" He read the metal art for me, he said some thing like, "This is Mary, with Jesus in the womb. We have it this way so people can easily imagine in their thoughts. There some people who do not like statues. We also have Saint Joseph on other side." I asked, "What is your name? Are you a Eucharistic minister or..." He said, "My name is John... I am studying to be a deacon." I asked, "How come the tabernacle is not inside the church?" He explain to me the reasons, but their reasons are against God's commandments. I asked, "How many family in this parish?" He replied, "Over two thousand families."

I returned to the Blessed Sacrament chapel, the Lord asked me to write on that book again, He said, "Please pray for the Christ the King church's congregation to focus on the body and the blood of the Son of the most high living God."

I then go back to the church for the mass. During the reading, I saw the celebrant was sitting in a relaxing form, by leaning his left elbow on the chair arm, and his chin rested on his left hand.

He was walking right to left and left to right, his arm was either straight down or up for the entire time of sermon.

The first part of his sermon made the congregation explode with laugher and applaud, like a comedian and audience.

After the sermon and all the way to the finish of the mass, there was an assistant, this man served the priest, turning pages on the book "The Roman Missal -Sacramentary" for the priest to read, the priest does not have to turn any page on the book, but only to read.

When he elevated the body of our Lord and said, "This is the Lamb of God who takes away the sins...." He used his left hand only raising up the Consecrated host high at his left and swinging over the center to his right.

The entire mass, I was physically batting with the devil's spirit, the spirit of worshipping idols; and almost the entire mass, I looked at Jesus' head with crown of thorns, hanging on the Cross and silently cried out to Him, "I love You.... I love You..." When I said to Jesus that I loved Him, I meant that I am sharing the Lord Jesus' suffering, by obeying Him, and no one can interfere.

After I returned to my seat from receiving the body and blood of our Lord, Jesus the Lord said to me, "I now release you from the suffering that you paid for this priest and the congregation here today." Before I got out the pew, Jesus the Lord told me, "You wait for those people go out first; if you want to go to the rest room, then go first before you go stand in front of this priest. I need to speak to him."

I went to the rest room, and came standing in front of tho prioot juot celebrated mass, with the Christ the King Catholic Church bulletin in my left hand. I asked the priest, "Which one is your name?" with my right index finger moving up and down the two priest names: The Rev. Msgr. J. Gaston , V.G.- Pastor, and The Reverend John. The Priest said, "I am the top one." I said, "You are the big one." He said, "Yes, I am the big one." He asked me, "Where do you come from?" I replied, "My name is Mariette, I originally came from Vietnam, I was residing in San Diego for twenty two years. Jesus then sent me here on mission." He asked, "What are you doing?" I replied, "I am here to serve God. Jesus sent me here on a mission today. I believe that I have done what He sent me." I then asked him again, "You are the big one?" He said, "Yes, I am the big one." I thought that I was about to go; but I did not, I then asked him, "Beside as Pastor for this church, do you do any thing for the Diocese?" He said, "I am a Vicar General." I said, "You are Bishop Andrew's right hand." He said, "Yes. You know where all the power." I then left the church.

I woke up at 2:46a.m. July 20, 1997 with a dream. In my dream I saw a female. This female was talking to another person, a shadow. This female said to that shadow that she was listening to another person's sins when that person confessed his sins to God at the confession box. Then in my vision, I saw the priest who said mass the night before, at the time he gave sermon.

After I recorded the last dream and vision, I went back to sleep. In my sleep, I had several dreams and conversations with God. I then got up at 6:29 a.m. The Lord told me to record this dream: I saw a very tall man; he was twice of the height of a human. He was thin, wearing light colored trousers and shirt. He was walking behind the Christ the King altar, from the right of the sanctuary to the left of the sanctuary. The Lord said, "This is a counterfeit Spirit of God in the sanctuary." The Lord meant the counterfeit Spirit of God as the spirit of worshipping idols; the spirit worshipping of idols is in the control of the devil's spirit.

July 20, 1997; I arrived at the front of the Saint Patrick about 8:25a.m.. In front, to the side of the church, was a table where a brand new Honda Civic was parked on the street. In front of this table, two women were sitting. While I was approaching the church, one of the woman asked me, "You like to win that car?" I replied, "No, it is not for me. I already know what God has for me."   Standing at the table, I saw at the second line to the bottom of the yellow flyer said, "Immaculate Heart of Mary Catholic Church." I asked, "Is this for the church?" She said, "This is for school." I said to them, "Do you know that this is against God's commandments? This is gamble. " She said, "I heard another say that too, but the church does it." I said, "Many church leaders are lack of discernment, and mix the devil's works in with God's works." She said, "Yes, it is gambling, but it does not take food away from the children's table." I said, "But this is gambling. If they care for the children, they donate to the school to train these children to come close to God. They do not need to have this car in return. Because their return will be in heaven. God said "We must take care of His church first." She said, "But people do not want to do that." I said, "If they do not want to take care of God's church, they will miss heaven." I continued, "You must obey all God's commandments and the Holy Father's teachings. For church authorities, you only obey things according to God's commandments and the Holy Father teachings, if the issues are not based on God's commandments, you do not have to obey. Maybe today is the first time you have heard of what I just said." She said, "Yes, I heard that before. I came from a very strict family." I said, "What I said to you today are not from me; but Jesus the Lord speaks through me; and His words come with His power. Your life will be changed."

Inside the church foyer, I went to the rest room. While I was in the rest room, Jesus asked me, "Why did you not take a flyer?" I said, "Do you want me to take one?" He said, "You go out to get a flyer now before you come in the church." I went out for a flyer, and here is what the flyer said:

"AN EXPLOSION OF FUN! Carnival - Friday & Saturday, September 19 & 20, 1997. - Giant Flea Market - Friday & Saturday / 8:00 AM to 9:00 PM - Arts & Craft * Housewears * Toys * Furniture * Tools - Authentic Polish Meal - Friday 4:00PM - Including Kielbasa (Polish Sausage) with all the trimmings - Teen Dance Saturday - Silent Auction Friday & Saturday - All Day Bingo Friday & Saturday - Balloon Rides Friday - BBQ Chicken Meal Friday & Saturday - Midway Booths Friday & Saturday 6:00PM - Midnight Drawing for 1997 Honda Civic Saturday 10:00PM - Immaculate Heart of Mary Catholic Church - Hwy - 365 at Blue Hill Road * North Little Rock." Reference to God's commands to take care of His church first are in the Book of Exodus, especially in 13:1-2; 25:1-9; 27:20-21; 35:4-9. "God does not teach us to gamble for money to take care of His church."

I then went inside the church, I saw the tabernacle to the right side of the sanctuary, on my left side; because I wanted to be close to the tabernacle, I asked, "Jesus, where do you want me to sit?" He said, "Sit at the third pew to your right," While I was walking up to the seat in the middle aisle, I saw a man who was wearing a white long sleeve shirt, black trousers with suspenders, and sat on a chair at the sanctuary. He crossed his right leg over his left thigh. Before the mass started, I found that he was the one who will celebrate mass.

During the mass, some times his hands join at his chest, some times he was walking with both hands straight down. In his sermon, he spoke about taking "vacation". He is going to vacation at a place with about thirty thousand people, to rejuvenate his body and spirit. The Holy Father went to vacation in the high mountain for two to be alone. He also incurred people get away from work, to take vacation to rejuvenate souls and body. While the priest said these; in my thought, "Yes, the Holy Father went to the mountain, to be alone with God. The minister pours out to others when they are on the job, they need to go away to be with Jesus and draw strength from Him, not to satisfy their flesh. I need Jesus, I do not need a vacation."

Before the consecration, I felt that I was distracted from focusing on God; I mean that I still followed the mass, but my focus in God was not there. I said, "Father, Jesus, Holy Spirit, I need you." I was said these over several times. I then said, "Lord, why I did not say I love you, but I said I need you?" I repeated few times I need You, and then changed to I love You.

After I returned to the pew from receiving the Holy Eucharist, the Lord said to me, "I allowed you to feel losing away from Me, so I can reveal to you. I am always in you and with you." I asked, "Lord, do you want to speak to the priest? If not, I'll just go home." He said, "I do need to speak to him, if you need to go to the rest room, go fast, or you can go after I speak to him." I was trying to hurry so I can go to the rest room before I see the priest, I made the sign of the cross so I can get out the pew while the chorus is still singing, the Lord said to me, "Why are you in such a hurry on Me?"

I then was out side, in front of the church; standing in front of the priest shaking his hand, and said, "Hi Father, You are going on vacation to be with Jesus." He said, "Yes, the place I go will have people and God will be there. God is every where." I said, I am a visitor here, I am Father Dominic's niece." He said, "I heard them say that you came picked up him up for dinner." I said, "I came to the rectory and brought him to lunch." I then asked, "Father, during the mass, at the sanctuary, why do sometimes you join your hands at your chest, and sometimes you let them straight down?" His replied, "That is just my personality; I do not want to join my hands at the chest all the time, look holiness." I said, "During the time you are saying mass, Jesus is in front of you, you need to be in the form of worshipping Him."

There was an elderly man who came, and asked the priest, "This is one of the debate. When you give sermons, do you memorize them?" I said, "I have the answer for you." The priest said, "I memorize them." I said, "Priests should pray, and when they speak, the Holy Spirit will speak through them." Then the elderly person left. I then said to the priest, "When a priest lives the life of holiness, when he speaks, the Holy Spirit will speak through him, a priests should not have a sheet of paper and read it at the homily." He said, "God works in different ways." I said, "Jesus said, 'The Spirit of the Father will speak through you.' In theology, if the priest does not live the life of holiness, they will speak something else." I continued, "Jesus the Lord told me I must obey all God's commandments in the Bible, and the Holy Father's teachings; for church authorities, I only obey them for things according to God's commandments and the Holy Father's teachings. If the issues are not based on God's commandments, I do not have to obey." He said, "We must always obey the authorities unless the issue is mortal." I said, "Only obey when issues are according to God's Commandments, and the Holy Father's teachings." I continued, "I came from Vietnam, I lived in San Diego for twenty two years. God sent me here on mission. Through me, He has been twisting Bishop

Andrew's arms. Today He sent me here, for Him to twist your arms. You will receive something." He asked, "From you?" I said, "Yes, what I saw today, I will be sending to the bishops, officials in the Vatican, and put on the Lord Jesus web site on Internet, and in books. I have two books that have been published, all of the books are revelations." He said, "Mariette, I need to go to Saint Mary for another mass." I then shook his hands good bye.

I then was walking to my car, about to cross the street, I said, "Jesus, you know my heart that I wanted to go the rest room, can I wait and go to rest room when I got home?" But the Lord Jesus said, "You go back to the rest room before you go home I was then hurrying back to the rest room before I left the church.

Here is free my will and God's will. God gave me the choice to go to the rest room or not to go to the rest room before I left the church; but for the Saint Patrick's parish, the choice was commanded, because my uncle, the Roman Catholic priest, Father Dominic, has had his residence in this rectory for twenty years; and also Father Paul Worm, the pastor of the church, the Lord Jesus told me in the mass that he is God's chosen one.

Everyone of you must understand that God uses nature to pours His grace and blessing. We must cooperate with God in our hearts and actions to participating with God for salvation of mankind, and that including our own souls.

The rest room is the place to draw out the bad things from our bodies, wash our hands, clean our faces. The Lord uses rest room as the symbol of purification.

The in and out the rest room before and after mass is symbolic that each one of us must come to God sincerely from our heart, seeking Him for conversion, daily exam and repent. This means that each one of us must keep our heart pure when we receive the God supernatural power hidden in the body and blood of our Lord Jesus. If you contain mortal/grave sin and receive the Holy Eucharist, you are receiving the punishment for your soul and body as well.

On July 17, 1997, in a revelation, the Lord commanded me to go to the rest room, because all my actions will affect spiritual leaders of all religion, and other throughout the world.

My action on July 19, 1997's revelation at the Christ the King, God gave me a choice to do or not to do. It means God gave the choice to convert, and for daily exam and repent.   But the Love that God poured unto me; I went to the rest room before and after the mass. Because I went to the rest room before and after the mass, symbolic of and many will convert their hearts to God.

For the Saint Patrick church, I voluntarily went before the mass. Before I left, God gave me the choice, in the way of commanding me; because during the mass, the Lord Jesus revealed to me that the priest celebrated mass, Father Paul Worm, (Father Worm also symbolic of other God's servants) is God's chosen one. Therefore, Jesus made me to go to the rest room before I left.

God then gave me more dreams and spoke to me in my dreams. Through God power, I remember all my dreams and conversation I have with God in my dreams.

July 21, 1997. 6:09 a.m . In my dreams, I was in the highest building in the world, this building had one hundred and one floors. I then was on the street floor; but somehow, I saw the enemies invaded the inside of the middle of the building. The Archangel Michael and His holy angels fought against them. I then was outside, at the back of the building; I saw from fifty floors up a huge body was being lowered down to the ground . This body was wrapped inside a dark, soft coffin. I was fighting and ran to my car that was parked several feet away to the side of the building.

My car only had one seat for the driver; I then sat at the seat; there is no roof, it is an iron vehicle. I then saw a most powerful soldier. This soldier is able to travel to the moon and to the sky. I then saw a running child following me, he wanted to be saved from this fighting. He asked me to be in the same vehicle. I told him, "Get in, and sit on the floor by my right foot." I then drove away from this property. While I was driving away, some how the boy was no longer at my right foot, but was behind my seat.

Then I returned with a huge bus, parked at the same spot I was parked my car, to pick up my youngest daughter. I saw so many were wounded from the fight. I also saw my younger son. My daughter told me, "I want to go home." I told her, "Get in the bus." While my daughter walking toward the bus, my son was still standing with a group of boarding school students on the second and third floor of the building, looking toward the bus; I also saw a person that was responsible for processing paper for students to move out from the dormitory. This person went inside the building from the back door to process my daughter's papers.

My son in this dream symbolic of earthly priests, he stay behind at the building symbolic of many spiritual leaders refuse to conversion.

While my daughter was stepping on the bus; many of her friends were mourning, and standing outside the bus door. The principal also was standing in the midst of these student, at the same time some of her friends looked at each other and cried. The principal asked them, " Why you are crying," They responded, "We will miss TuAnh?" The principal said to them, "Why do you miss her? Do not miss her at all."

Tuanh is my youngest daughter, she is symbolic of the people received improper meaning of God's commandments. She stepping on the bus is symbolic of start the road of conversion, and leaning the correction meaning of God's commandments in the holy scriptures.

The dream changed again. I was laying on my bed, I heard my voice speak to Lord Jesus, the Father and the Holy Spirit. My voice did not came out from my physical body, but it came out from the invisible body, level at my waist. My voice said to God, "Lord God, come and save all those advertised for the anger, they are teaching the systems of the world, these systems are against Your commandments. They are leading people's souls and bodies down to the place that human call the hell. Father, Lord Jesus, do not let them come in to Your church any more. They are trying every place to organize one ministry to another. They are working inside Your church, persuading Your priests; operating their systems inside Your church. Lord Father, Jesus, open the hearts and minds of Your beloved priests, fill them with Your discernment and love so they can serve You firmly taking the true actions, to save Your people. Jesus the Lord, You told me yesterday that You chose not to take the form of a human body, for You returned to prepare your people to come to heaven. But You are choosing me as Your vessel instead, so I can enter the places without people knowing that I am serving You in the dangerous road. The road, that if these people knew I was there, they would call on the devil to hurt me. But You told me after I went on this journey that You have blinded many other eyes to recognize that I was there. I give thanks to You, Jesus Lord.   Lord Father, Jesus,   I believe that I have finished the silent dangerous road job that You entrusted in my hands."

The Lord said to me and to you, those who want to go to heaven. Jesus the Lord said, "I came in flesh, I died and rose from the dead. I am no longer walking on the street in a human body. I am in the Blessed Sacrament to heal the souls; so they may be saved. But the devil, Lucifer is in human bodies fighting against Michael the Archangel on the top part of the building. The devil is using human bodies to teach My people live life against My commandments, and they come to receive Me with mortal sins; so My people receive punishment. This punishment is eternal death to souls and bodies. The top part of the building is Michael the Archangel fighting against the spirit of the devil. On the street of the floor is my faithful Vessel fighting against humans in this world for my sake, to save souls of those who want to enter heaven."

God then said to me, alone, "My little poor Servant. You have been obedient to Me, step by step, and entered into a room that was filled with the devil's spirit, and you came out with victory; as a champion for Me, the Lord Your God, who won this champion. Continue to go forward; if there is any one trying to harm you, they will be dead before they come close to you; I am speaking of the physical death and death to their souls. But if any one comes to you for the will of the Father, they will be blessed and saved for eternal life in heaven. I give you the choice, whether to share with others of what I was warning to the world." Jesus the Lord is referring to the last part of the revelation, "Little poor Servant...."

The revelations seem like stories, but every words are mean of something that God revealed to us of His future actions. Enclosed is copy of the cassette tape which was recorded on July 20, 1997, recorded with permission from the speaker, the "Spirituality and Anger", presented by Dr. Sam, FCOC. Dr. Sam is a Chaplain at St. Vincent Infirmary Medical Center; sponsored by the Cathedral of Saint Andrew parish health ministry, at Malone hall.

I pray to the Lord Jesus, the Father and the Holy Spirit for everyone of you to seek God for discernment on everything that you are allowing in His church. As the church leaders, you are the first one responsible in front of God for all organizations, and their activities in the church, church hall, church properties, or using the name of God's church.

Sincerely in Christ Jesus,

Mariette Do-Nguyen

Rebuild My Church Divine Mission
(The Lord Jesus gave this name to Mariette)
P.O. Box 261550 ◆ San Diego, CA 92196-1550

August 7, 1997

To God's Chosen High-Ranking Leaders

Dear ......,

Enclosed are copies of: (1) The "First Wine and Last Wine" revelation; and (2) a letter to Most Reverend Andrew, for correction of the date from July 2 to August 2,1997.

On August 1, 1997; the day before the fifth anniversary of the Lord Jesus appearing in my dream, in New Orleans; I said to the Lord, "Jesus, tomorrow is five years from the first time You entered in my dream. For last over three years, I have sent out many words [letters] to 287 high Catholic church leaders, but no one accepts what You told me sent to them." The Lord Jesus said to me, "The letters responded from those archbishops, bishops, and cardinal means that they are accepting what I told you to say." I said, "Lord, but those letters are very vague." He said, "That is all they can said in the letters; because you are in the Diocese of Little Rock."

August 7, 1997: The Lord Jesus said to me, "Prepare the 'First wine and last wine' revelation, send it to Bishop Andrew, and other archbishops, bishops, and cardinals. When I asked you to sent the 'The Lord Jesus Glorified Body is Hidden in the Consecrated Hosts' revelation, the 'News Books' script, the 'Appointments' revelation, and letter to Bishop Andrew to these church leaders, I was silently telling them that their dioceses are indirectly God's chosen ones dioceses. There is only one directly God chosen diocese, for the final phase of My mission, and that is the Little Rock Diocese."

I have been done everything God asked of me; and I will continue to do exactly every thing He is going to tell me. God had pushed me against the wall, I had no choice, but to obey Him. I am telling you, God is doing the same thing to you and to all the Roman Catholic Church leaders and officials. It is suffering for Him and for you, because He loves you, He does these things to save your soul. The more Jesus loves you, the more you are suffer with Him, and in Him. Trust me on this one, do not go against Him, He will not let you go on your way, but you must go His way. Jesus said, "You are not the one who chose Me; But I am the One who chose you."

I pray to the Lord for your faith, be firm and strong in God's commandments, and serve Him. Jesus the Lord is always with you to the end.

Sincerely in Christ Jesus,

Mariette Do-Nguyen

Rebuild My Church Divine Mission

(The Lord Jesus gave this name to Mariette)

P.O. Box 261550 ✦ San Diego, CA 92196-1550

September 30, 1997

This letter mailed to over 270 United States Roman Catholic cardinals, archbishops, bishops, and High-Ranking officials in Vatican

Dear ....

Enclosed are copies of: (1) Eternal Father appeared to Mariette in His Son's image at the cathedral of Saint Andrew, (2) God changed the direction to fulfill His will, (3) The only exception to no-abortion in God's commandments, (4) Mariette saw the Lord Jesus glorified body with her carnal eyes, (5) Mariette is Servant to the most high living God.

I also enclosed a copy of my letter to Vice President Al Gore, September 30, 1997. This letter was also mailed to President Bill Clinton and 100 U.S. Senators.

On September 29, 1997, in my devotion, the Lord Jesus told me, "You ask the Church officials and leaders to announce to their congregation of the 'only exception to no-abortion in God's commandments,' and have them take actions against their state and federal representative of the legal abortion law."

I pray that you will take actions to limit some of the tragedies upon the world.

Sincerely in Christ Jesus,

Mariette Do-Nguyen

Rebuild My Church Divine Mission

(The Lord Jesus gave this name to Mariette)

P.O. Box 261550 ✦ San Diego, CA 92196-1550

October 24, 1997

This letter mailed to over 270 United States Roman Catholic cardinals, archbishops, bishops, and High-Ranking officials in Vatican

Dear ....

Enclosed are copies of the "World Mission Sunday" Revelations, it also the conclusion of the book, "God's Purification - Not Easy."

The messages in this I do not put in the book, because the Roman Catholic Church is my older brother Jesus' Church. I share with the church officials and high ranking leaders; but I still cannot guarantee that this letter will not go into the book, because I must obey God.

After the Lord Jesus gave me dreams on October 24, 1997; when I got up He said to me, "My church is short of priests, but I am unable to ordain more, because church leaders, officials, and priests hearts and actions are not in the way I taught My apostles. They are disobeying God's commandments, violating their vows, misconduct. They please men to protect their positions, use the position to benefits their flesh. If they continue to protect their title, benefits their flesh, they will miss the heaven. Many of them preach but do not put their preaching into their hearts, minds and daily actions. Many of them even preach their own doctrine. As of now, I see none of them following John's footsteps; to stand at the foot of My Cross without fear of the Pharisees and scribes; because they are Pharisee and scribes; they are teaching others to become like them." Matthew chapter 23.

I must said exactly of what I heard. I urgently warn everyone of you to reform your hearts, minds and actions, so the Fatima's sun dancing may come down with blessing instead of the punishment. Each one of you have the free will to choose blessing or punishment from Fatima's sun dancing on earth.

I pray that you will obeyed God so the world can be better place to live, and building the kingdom of heaven.

Sincerely in Christ Jesus,

Mariette Do-Nguyen

Foot note: The title of Catholic clergymen symbolic of all spiritual leaders.

Rebuild My Church Divine Mission
(The Lord Jesus gave this name to Mariette)
P.O. Box 261550 ♦ San Diego, CA 92196-1550

November 4, 1997

Most Reverend Robert Brom
Bishop of San Diego Diocese

Dear Excellency.

The Vietnamese Martyrs Shrine was built in the land of California for a reason. On November 3, 1997, in the Blessed Sacrament Chapel at Good Shepherd Church in San Diego, the Holy Spirit instructed me: "You write a letter to members of the U.S. Senate, President Bill Clinton, Ambassador Peterson, and the Secretary of State Albright, and ask them to assisting you in contact the Vietnamese government about your request for a pilgrimage of about two hundred persons to Lavang, Vietnam, in June 1998. During this pilgrimage at Lavang, people will worship the Lord Jesus, through the Blessed Sacrament adoration, offering to the Father, praying for healing, peace, and blessing upon Vietnam and the world."

Then in the church before the mass, He told me, "Ask Monsignor Tien and the Bishop Driscol, as the church leaders to assist you." The Monsignor and Bishop name is symbolism of the Roman Catholic Church leaders, officials, and its congregation.

Enclosed are copies of: (1) a letter to President Bill Clinton, Madeleine Albright, Secretary of State; Ambassador Peter Peterson, U.S. Ambassador to Vietnam, all members of U.S. senate, dated November 4, 1997; (2) a letter to Prime Minister Phan Van Khai, Nguyen Manh Cam, Minister of Foreign Affairs, Le Van Bang, Vietnamese Ambassador to United States, November 4, 1997; (3) a letter to Charlene Byrd, owner of

House Travel & Cruises Inc.

As you already know, that June 16, 1998 is the 200 anniversary of the Lavang's apparition. I ask you to serve God, following in the footsteps of 117 Martyrs (105 Vietnamese, 12 others), who were canonized on June 18 & 19, 1988, by assisting me as I gather people whom God has chosen join in this pilgrimage, and in seeking Roman Catholics to pray for peace, healing, and blessing upon Vietnam and the world.

If you need more information or have any questions, please contact me.

Sincerely in Christ Jesus,

Mariette Do-Nguyen

Rebuild My Church Divine Mission
(The Lord Jesus gave this name to Mariette)
P.O. Box 261550 ✦ San Diego, CA 92196-1550

November 17, 1997

Most Reverend Robert Brom, Bishop of San Diego Diocese

Dear Excellency,

Enclosed are copies of: (1) a letter to President Bill Clinton, Vice President Al Gore, and all members of the U.S. senate and its attachments, dated October 31, 1997. This letter is regarding why I have refused to pay taxes, because tax monies have funded abortion clinics, family planning clinics, and generated destructive weapons to create war. Also, (2) I am including an outline of the "Spiritual Pilgrimage to Vietnam: Urgent Need for Conversion." In the outline I have explained clearly the Blessed Virgin apparitions at Lourdes, Fatima, and Lavang. The Lavang's apparition has not been approved by the Church in the Vatican, but it was acknowledged by Vietnamese bishops. The healing of people at Lavang about two hundred years ago was an act of God. This action was revealed to Saint John in the Book of Revelations, Chapter Twenty two, verses one through five .

Parallel with the Spiritual Pilgrimage's outline are the books "My Patient - God's gift" and "Bride of Christ in Action" subtitled "God's Purification is Not Easy." The "Bride of Christ in Action" will be published the first quarter of 1998. I ask you to assist me to announce this pilgrimage by inserting it in your parishes' Sunday bulletins, and the Diocese of San Diego newspapers, and bring these books to your congregation. The purpose is through the Holy Eucharist, the Lord Jesus will be visible to the world, so the world will be a better place to live, and build the kingdom of heaven. All profit from the book "My Patient - God's Gift" will benefit seminarians wherever help is most needed in countries throughout the world, and all profit from the book "Bride of Christ in Action" will benefit God's works.

November 15, 1997, during the night, the Lord Jesus said to me, "You go see the bishop"; I told Him "Bishop Brom does not want to see me", But He insisted for me to go see you. I understand that you have the reason to refuse to see me, because I am a sinner, and a lowly woman, but at least you see me because Jesus the Lord is in me. He is the one who insisted on my contacting you for this appointment, there are reasons for this appointment. Please pray for me.

Sincerely in Christ Jesus,

Mariette Do-Nguyen

Rebuild My Church Divine Mission

(The Lord Jesus gave this name to Mariette)

P.O. Box 261550 ✦ San Diego, CA 92196-1550

November 22, 1997

This letter mailed to over 270 United States Roman Catholic cardinals, archbishops, bishops, and High-Ranking officials in Vatican

Dear ....,

Enclosed are copies of: (1) a letter to President Bill Clinton, Vice President Al Gore, and all members of the U.S. senate, dated October 31, 1997. This letter is regarding reasons I have refused to pay taxes, because tax monies have funded abortion clinics, family planning clinics, and generated destructive weapons to create war. Also, (2) I am including an outline of the "Spiritual Pilgrimage to Vietnam: Urgent Need for Conversion." In the outline I have explained clearly the Blessed Virgin

Mother apparitions at Lourdes, Fatima, and Lavang. The Lavang's apparition has not been approved by the Church in the Vatican, but it was acknowledged by Vietnamese bishops. The healing of people at Lavang about two hundred years ago was an act of God. This action was revealed to Saint John in the Book of Revelations, Chapter Twenty two, verses one through five .

Parallel with the Spiritual Pilgrimage's outline are the books "My Patient - God's gift" published April 12, 1996, and "Bride of Christ in Action" subtitled "God's Purification is Not Easy." The "Bride of Christ in Action" will be published the first quarter of 1998. The purpose of the pilgrimage is through the Holy Eucharist, the Lord Jesus will be visible to the world, many will convert, so the world will be a better place to live, and build the kingdom of heaven. All profit from the book "My Patient - God's Gift" will benefit seminarians wherever help is most needed in countries throughout the world, and all profit from the book "Bride of Christ in Action" will benefit God's works.

I ask you to assist me to announce this pilgrimage by inserting it in your parishes' Sunday bulletins, your Diocese's newspapers, and bring these books to your congregation. I hope to hear from you in the near future.

Sincerely in Christ Jesus,

Mariette Do-Nguyen

Rebuild My Church Divine Mission

(The Lord Jesus gave this name to Mariette)

P.O. Box 261550 ✦ San Diego, CA 92196-1550

November 25, 1997

Cardinal Joseph Ratzinger, President
Pontifical of the Bible Commission

Via: Register Mail

Dear His Eminence,

On November 3, 1997, in the Blessed Sacrament Chapel at Good Shepherd Church in San Diego, the Holy Spirit instructed me: "You write a letter to members of the U.S. Senate, President Bill Clinton, Ambassador Peterson, and the Secretary of State Albright, and ask them to assisting you in contact the Vietnamese government about your request for a pilgrimage of about four hundred persons to Lavang, Vietnam, in June 1998. During this pilgrimage at Lavang, people will worship the Lord Jesus, through the Blessed Sacrament adoration, offering to the Father, praying for healing, peace, and blessing upon Vietnam and the world."

After I sent letters to the Vietnamese and United States government high-ranking officials request for visas, the Lord then told me it was also Spiritual Pilgrimage with interpretation.

Enclosed is copy of an outline for the "Spiritual Pilgrimage to Vietnam: Urgent Need for Conversion." I also enclosed copies of:

(1) letters to Vietnamese and United States government officials, dated November 4, 1997;

(2) letters from and to Ambassador Le Van Bang, Vietnamese Ambassador to Vietnam, dated November 12, 1997 and November 21, 1997;

(3) letter from Ambassador Pete Peterson, United State Ambassador to Vietnam, dated May 28, 1997;

(4) a letter and its attachments to President Bill Clinton, Vice President Al Gore, and all members of the U.S. senate and its attachments, dated October 31, 1997. This letter is regarding the reason I have refused to pay taxes, because tax monies have funded abortion clinics, family planning clinics, and generated destructive weapons to create war.

(5) a letter from Senator Trent Lott, United States majority leader, dated October 21, 1997.

On the outline I have explained clearly the Blessed Virgin apparitions at Lourdes, Fatima, and Lavang. The Lavang's apparition has not been approved by the Church in the Vatican, but it was acknowledged by Vietnamese bishops.

The healing of people at Lavang about two hundred years ago was an act of God. This action was revealed to Saint John in the Book of Revelations, Chapter Twenty two, verses one through five .

Parallel with the Spiritual Pilgrimage's outline are the books "My Patient - God's gift" published April 12, 1996, and "Bride of Christ in Action" subtitled "God's Purification is Not Easy." The "Bride of Christ in Action" will be published the first quarter of 1998. All profit from the book "My Patient - God's Gift" will benefit seminarians wherever help is most needed in countries throughout the world, and all profit from the book "Bride of Christ in Action" will benefit God's works.

I ask you, as high-ranking Roman Catholic Church official for the certification to testify in the Roman Catholic Church. The purposed of my testimony is to being the Lord Jesus be visible to the world, in the Holy Eucharist, many will convert, so the world will be a better place to live, and build the kingdom of heaven.

Please pray for me, and I hope to hear from you in very near future.

Sincerely in Christ Jesus,

Mariette Do-Nguyen

Foot note: Vietnam is symbolic of the world. The members of United States congress and government officials symbolic of all other nation congress and government officials.

Rebuild My Church Divine Mission
(The Lord Jesus gave this name to Mariette)
P.O. Box 261550 ✦ San Diego, CA 92196-1550

February 20, 1998

Most Reverend Mario Pompedda, Dean
The Tribunal of the Roman Rota
00120 Vatican City
Rome, Italy

Via: Registered Mail

Re: Appeal of Annulment Decision

Dear Excellency,

Enclosed are copies of: (1) a letter from Rev. Msgr. Robert E. Lawrence, J.C.L. Judicial Vicar for Diocese of San Bernardino Tribunal, dated December 13, 1996; (2) a letter from Rev. Msgr. Mark A. Campbell, J.C.L., Judicial Vicar for the Diocese of San Diego Tribunal, dated March 31, 1995; (3) my letter to Rev. Msgr. Robert E. Lawrence, J.C.L. and receipt for registered mail, dated July 10, 1997; (4) Appeal for Annulment Decision, May 5, 1995.

Also enclosed are evidence letters and English translation copies of: (1) letters from Nguyen Thi Hoa, dated April 10, 1995, (2) Nguyen Thi Thuong, dated April 12, 1995, (3) Vu Thi An, dated April 18, 1995, (4) Nguyen Thi Dau, dated April 8, 1995, (5) Nguyen Manh Hoan, dated April 9, 1995.

The people at the San Diego Diocese Tribunal placed a curse and denied my request for annulment because I spoke the truth about misconduct of the church leaders. When I asked for an appeal, Ms. Greatsinger, who worked on my case, told me that I would be wasting my money.

When I appealed to the San Benardino Diocese Tribunal, the curse from the San Diego Diocese followed, they denied my appeal, and told me if I want to appeal, I must appealed to Monsignor Cornellius O'Leary, Ph.D. at Diocese San Bernardino Roman Rota. This Monsignor is one of the three on the panel of the previous appeals court that denied my appeal.

Because I lacked of knowledge of the responsibility of the wife and mother, and the Sacrament of Marriage, the Lord Jesus told me that this marriage is invalid before the Almighty God. God allowed for me to serve as the undercover for the mission He entrusted in me; to prepare for the Second Coming of Christ to judge the living and the dead.

I request that this marriage be grand deemed invalid on paper; I also request that the church authorities in the Tribunal Court come to God with pure and sincere hearts, designed to served God by servicing others according to their vows at the time of ordination, so they may receive proper discernment on each case.

I will pray for you, and all church leaders and officials.

Sincerely in Christ Jesus,

Mariette Do-Nguyen

Foot note: The Catholic officials also symbolic of other religions and Christian denomination.

Rebuild My Church Divine Mission

(The Lord Jesus gave this name to Mariette)

P.O. Box 261550 ✦ San Diego, CA 92196-1550

June 29, 1998

Archbishop Fx. Nguyen Van Thuan, President, Pontifical Council for Justice & Peace
Monsignor Dennis Schnurr, General Secretary, U.S. National Catholic Conference
Monsignor Joseph Finnrty, Pastor, Saint Michael's Parish, Poway, California

Re: Restored Freedom of Religion and bring God's Peace to United States

Dear................,

Obeying God, for over four years, I was alone in God, communicating with President Bill Clinton, Vice President Al Gore, and all members of the U.S. Senate, helping them to understand the soul and spirit with and in the human physical body, and that the civil right to freedom of religion in the United States is restricted. God has actually used me as a tool for

His works.   In response, I have received over a hundred letters from the dignitaries.

Enclosed are copies of: (1) a letter to the Honorable Mary Ann Cohen, chief Judge at the United States Tax Court, dated June 29, 1998, (2) a letter to President Bill Clinton and all members of the Senate, dated June 12, 1998, (3) an outline the history of God Summoned me and His works through me compelling in two books.

In God's power I am writing to ask you, and U.S. Catholics to assist me in serving God in the mission that belongs to the Lord Jesus, that He entrusted to me.

The Rebuild My Church Mission is the Lord Jesus' Mission; through this mission, God works through His obedience servants, to implemented of what His prophets and apostles bequeath to mankind.   To day is the feast of Saints Peter and Paul; the Lord Jesus commanded me to write this letter, to ask you, and all Catholics in the United States to assist me in serving the Father. Through Him, the Holy Spirit will work through us; (we must be in obedience to God's commandments, in truth and love), to improve the following areas of the U.S. government, local states, and cities that are now being improperly served:

a. The safety of children at schools: Students need focus for high grades to ensure their future benefits themselves and the nation. The root for prevention of shooting and violence in school begins with each student's family.   The parents teach through their actions, friends, entertainment, sports, hobbies and values. Family is the foundation of a child's future.

b. We must educate adults so they can teach children; the first place children learn is from parents and grandparents. We must void birth control and abortion; women must have self-discipline and responsibility result from their actions. This begins with her choice of man, whether in public or in private, what kind of body language and words she uses; one must be careful with thoughts; for hugging, kissing, touching, and stimulation lead to sexual intercourse. A man with is responsibility the same as a woman. Parents and grandparents teach children through their actions.

c. We must bring God's presence and His grace to patients with diseases not able to cure, long term sickness, mental suffering and pain of the elderly, through Bible reading, Sacraments, and the Holy Eucharist.

d. Through God's power we must bring love, comfort, and assistance to homeless teenagers, and bring gang members in from the darkness. We must bring God into their lives by teaching them God's words and obeying

God's commandments, and materials assistance in transit for them to go back to school and to work, so they can achieve a good future ahead of them.

I need volunteers for:

1. The contents of this letter to be announced to the general public

2. Two laity spokespersons: The Spirit of God will speak through them; therefore, these two persons must very spiritual, obedient to God, understand the holy Scriptures, and be willing to spend quality time in devotion to the Blessed Sacrament, and often receiving the Holy Eucharist.

3. Programs organizers: one leader for each state, and many assistants in different cities.

I ask that all volunteers send their profile directly to me with preference of the area of service; choose one that fits best; and send to me at Rebuild My Church Mission, P.O. Box 261550, San Diego, CA 92196.

God appeared to me and summoned me as he did to Moses. Therefore, all the services through this mission are completely dependent on God's power, (not human power). All of us are God's instruments. Through Moses, Israel responded to God. I pray to God, and request that you, your congregation, the general public answer to God's calling, and respond to me.

If you need more information or have any questions, please let me know.

Sincerely in Christ Jesus,

Foot note: The three various positions in this letter also symbolic of many other spiritual leaders titles.

Rebuild My Church Divine Mission
(The Lord Jesus gave this name to Mariette)

P.O. Box 261550 ✦ San Diego, CA 92196-1550

October 5, 1998

Archbishop Fx. Nguyen Van Thuan, President
Pontifical Council for Justice & Peace

Sent via facsimile Number (011)396-69887205 and air mail

Re Life on Earth Revelation, and Spiritual Leaders misleading congregations

Dear Excellency,

Enclosed are copies of: (1) Answer to Amended Petition, and the Reply to Amended Petition, dated September 14, 1998, filled in U.S. Tax Court. (Petitioning for civil right of freedom of religion in the United States); (2) a letter to Professor Adolf Seilacher, Geology Department at Yale University, dated October 1, 1998, and an article from San Diego Union Tribune "Fossil wormholes could she light on evolution of life on Earth; (3) a letter to Vice President Al Gore and eight members of the U.S. Senate, dated October 1, 1998.

On October 9, 1997, I sent the "God Reveals Evolution is the Process of His Creation" to 291 high-ranking Catholic leaders, (copy enclosed). Two nights ago, the Lord Jesus asked me to send this letter to you and to a young priest at the local church in San Diego, together with an article from the San Diego Union Tribune, and letters to Professor Aldolf Seilacher, and eight U.S. lawmakers.

In the letter to the eight U.S. lawmakers, the Lord instructed me to tell them that lawmakers have given license to murder unborn babies, through passing a legal abortion law. In this same letter the Lord asked me to tell them that the spiritual leaders are misleading their congregations.

At the same time the Lord instructed me to send this letter to you, He was very firm of charging you as the "President of the Pontifical for Justice and Peace;" You must strive to lead the Catholic leaders to deal with truth, as the model to other religions. Fear not man, but God alone, and obey all His commandments. He also revealed that these U.S. high-ranking Catholics are protecting their images, please man, misleading people they are leading by not saving the life of all unborn babies that have been aborted. Instead, they go along with lawmakers, fighting for unborn children of 20 weeks age. They well know that life starts from the time of conception, but they are intentionally participating in the murder of these unborn babies. They are liable for these babies that have been killed through abortion, committing an indirect sin of participating in murder, through misleading their congregations. These spiritual leaders think that they do not need the conversion.

Jesus came down calling us for conversion. The spiritual leaders must take the first step to conversion, for their congregation to follow. Everyone in this world must convert with daily exam and repentance, except for the Lord Jesus as fully man; because God is only one is perfect. There is only one way for Justice and peace into this world is each one must come to conversion. "If no conversion, dealing with the truth, no justice and peace."

You may be think that I am nuts, like the over 291 high-ranking Catholic leaders are thinking of me. In the Bible recorded, the members said of Jesus, 'He is out of his mind.' Therefore, it is nothing new of people saying that I am nuts. This mentality I inherited from my Lord, my God, my brother Jesus, to obey all of God the Father's commandments. I pray that you will obey God and fight for these unborn babies being killed through abortion. If you do obey all God's commandments, fight for all the unborn babies; and do not wait 20 weeks later, you will inherit the "out of mind" from the Lord Jesus.

I must deliver to you what God asked of me. If you need more information or have any questions, please let me know.

Sincerely in Christ Jesus,

Mariette Do-Nguyen

* Continued in the book "Fifth Sense."
* Spiritual leaders response letters printed in the book "The Only Petition at United States Tax Court" [AU1]

37

UNIFY GOD'S CHURCH

The Meaning of God's Words and Unify His Church Revelations

February 27, 1998. In my dream I saw a seven-by-ten inch white business envelope, on the top front side of the envelope I saw an invisible hand of God sewing twelve stitches along the edge. Each stitch he sewed down, then lifted the thread up to the top of the next one; those stitches from bottom to top were connecting the straight edges together. After He finished I asked, "Lord, why did You connect these twelve together?" The Lord said, "Twelve religions in one God, twelve components in one faith, the Father, the Son, and the Holy Spirit."

I then woke up in the middle of the night; in spirit, the Lord Jesus, with the Blessed Virgin Mother, explained to me as follows.

1. The meaning of the twelve tribes of Israel in the Old Testament, and the 144,000 sealed in the Book of Revelations that the Lord revealed as twelve components: the number twelve has two meanings: ten is symbolic of the Ten Commandments, two symbolizes discernment which arrives God's people obeys all God's commandments will do good and reject evil.

The number 144,000 is broken into three parts: one hundred thousand is symbolic of the extended number for the Ten Commandments. The Bible, speaks of the four corners of the sanctuary or square; this symbolize holiness. Four for natural and four for spiritual equal eight, symbolic of when a person obeys all God's commandments, receiving good discernment to do good and reject evil, being transformed to spiritual life, and benefiting the soul. The 144,000 sealed in the Book of Revelations refers to those who will inherit heavenly eternal life. Twelve stitches down and twelve stitches up arrives as twenty four. These twenty four are the twenty four elders; symbolic of those obeying all God's commandments will have good discernment, and living a life of holiness, they will be respected like respected elders. The 144,000 is symbolic of everyone in this world, with no difference of color, skin or nation, who worship the Creator of the Heaven and Earth, the true God, the One who gives life and takes it away, the One who created heaven and earth, made the winds and rains.

All in "ONE" faith trust in Almighty God, Creator of Heaven and Earth, the Father, the Lord Jesus, and the Holy Spirit. The three persons in One God, have power over all the Heaven and Earth, and accept the Blessed Virgin Mary, the Mother of our fully-man Lord Jesus as our spiritual mother. These twelve components include those who worship the Almighty God, but have not accepted the Lord Jesus as Son of God, the Messiah, and that they must accepted Him as the Son of God.

2. Each component is like a nation or a large family, with rules of practice to lead their congregations to heaven; these rules must always come under God's commandments. When a person disagrees with his component rule, he moves to another component, but the original component is still in his blood, like a person who moves from one country to another. He is still bonded to his original country. A child who moves from his parents' house still belongs to that family, the move is for a better life, or in some cases for the worst; when a child or a person fails to avoid wrong actions, he or she will be punished. A person moves from her component to another component for a better opportunity to serve God. Transformed into soul, all souls are in spirit, and all come from heaven. All souls came out of heaven in a pure state; when we return we must be pure and bring back with us good deeds, or if not we will be punished. God sent each one of us down to earth with a purpose to build the kingdom of heaven

Remaining in one component or moving to another must always involve helping others in other components. Acting from the heart, loving one another, means each individual will build a component, and components will build the kingdom of heaven.

In Matthew 26: 31-46, Jesus the Lord is very clear on how He judges us in detail according to our love and service to one another. But when any individual or component works against another, competing against others, pointing fingers at others, are filled with hatred, jealousy and serving God for their sake of their own name or their own benefit, such as a position in the component, helping them for their business purposes or reputation, when a person's heart or actions go against God's commandments, the devil will gain his power to ruin that person, his components and others as well. What you send out you will receive back, to a greater degree than what you sent; that includes thoughts, words, and actions.

When an individual disobeys God, it will affect that component; many components will affect the kingdom of heaven. In the Book of Revelations, chapters two and three, God revealed to Saint John by having him send letters to seven churches in Asia. The number seven is symbolic of the beginning of the end; and churches symbolize the twelve components.

836

3. Catholic component's priests, deacons, pastors, or other pastors from other components, reverends, laity or any title are ministers. Each component has different ways of taking their vows to serve God; whatever vows that person takes then must be fulfilled. When a person breaks any of his or her vows, he must convert, and not do it again. God forgives us, but we must always fulfill our vows whatever they may be. If one does not fulfill that vow on earth, it will be pay in lieu of fulfillment by being retained in purgatory, or the person will be in the place humans call hell.

4. The Catholic component chose for their clergymen to take the vow of celibacy, so that the minister can give all his time to God, and not financially burden the component. Other components are willing to support clergymen's families, allowing them to marry to limit some other breaking of their vows; because the devil uses women to attack clergymen who take the vow of celibacy. On the other hand, the devil uses their wives and children as weapons to attack the clergymen in other ways.

5. God is Spirit, He already knows everything in our hearts. He forgives us at the time we come to Him from our hearts, and promise not to sin again. He has already forgiven us. The Catholic component Sacrament of Reconciliation serves two purposes: Priests have more knowledge of God's commandments than laity; God's presence at the time of the Sacrament of Reconciliation; through God's power, priests are able to discern their congregation sins and minister to them. There is a secrecy vow that priests must to take at the time of ordination; God's anointing comes with this vow. But if priests live in sin the devil will take control of them, or interfere in their thoughts; and the priests will damage their congregations. If a priest is in sin, however, the Sacrament of Reconciliation is still valid for his congregations. (Through the Sacrament of Reconciliation, priests serve as spiritual directors to their congregation). But priests will be liable in front of God for the damage that they bring to their congregations. It is also an example of when congregations are true to the priest and being true to others.

6. In Jacob's testament for his son Judah in the Book of Genesis 49: 8-12, Jacob's words described the Lord Jesus in symbolism used by Judah; Judah's father is symbolic of the Eternal Father, the sons of your father are symbolic the of human race.

> *After this I saw four angels standing at the four corners of the earth,*
> *holding back the four winds of the earth so that no wind could blow on*
> *land or sea or against any tree.*
>
> — Revelation 7:1

This verse describes the holiness and power of the Lord Jesus over the earth.

> *And so I say to you, you are Peter, and upon this rock I will build my*
> *church, and the gates of the netherworld shall not prevail against it.*
>
> —Matthew 16:18.

When I caught sight of him, I fell down at his feet as though dead. He touched me with his right hand and said, "Do not be afraid. I am the first and the last, the one who lives. Once I was dead, but now I am alive forever and ever. I hold the keys to death and the netherworld.

–Revelations 1:17-18

The rock is symbolic of standing firm, immovable; but Peter denied the Lord Jesus three times; therefore, Jesus the Lord used Saint Peter to reveal of Himself that the gates of the netherworld shall not prevail against Him, not Saint Peter.

When they had finished breakfast, Jesus said to Simon Peter, 'Simon, son of John, do you love me more than these?' He said to him "Yes, Lord, you know that I love you." He then said to him, "Feed my lambs" He then said to him a second time, "Simon, son of John, do you love me?" He said to him, "Yes, Lord, you know that I love you." He said to him, "Tend my sheep." He then said to him the third time, "Simon, son of John, do you love me?" Peter was distressed that he had said to him a third time, "Do you love me?" and he said to him, "Lord, You know everything; you know that I love you," [Jesus] said to him, "Feed my sheep.

–John 21:15-17

The Lord Jesus told Peter three times: Feed my lambs, tend my sheep, feed my sheep. The word "lambs" refers to the Lord Jesus, the Lamb of God. The word "Feed" refers to Jesus, the bread coming down from heaven for nourishment for our souls; this was revealed again at the Last Supper. "Tend my sheep" refers to the Lord Jesus, the Good Shepherd. Three times "Son of John" is symbolic of the Holy Trinity.

While they were eating, Jesus took bread, said the blessing, broke it, and giving it to his disciples said, 'Take and eat; this is my body.' The he took a cup, gave thanks, and gave it to them saying, 'Drink from it, all of you, for this is my blood of the covenant, which will be shed on behalf of many for the forgiveness of sins.

–Matthew 26:26-28.

Jesus the Lord commanded us to partake of His suffering and death through the Holy Eucharist. Jesus took bread and cup and gave thanks to the Father; that bread became His body, and the wine became His blood; through His word at the time of consecration the priest repeated the words spoken by the Lord Jesus, the bread and wine also became Jesus the Lord's body and blood.

Do you not believe that I am in the Father and the Father is in me? The words that I speak to you I do not speak on my own. The Father who dwells in me is doing his works. Believe me that I am in the Father and the Father is in me.

–John 14: 10.

Through His word, when we receive the Holy Eucharist, we receive the Lord Jesus's body and blood together with the Spirit of the Holy Trinity, because the Holy Spirit is the One who does the work, and also received the new covenant. The Holy Eucharist is the spiritual nourishment for our souls, guiding, healing, and blessing.

7. Almost two thousand years later, through my dreams, Jesus the Lord laid keys and rock on my hand and placed a white shroud around my neck. I am a lowly woman, a sinner, a convert; the rock and keys mean that through God's power I became immovable, fighting for the kingdom of heaven.

Then I saw another angel come up from the East, holding the seal of the living God. He cried out in loud voice to the four angels who were given power to damage the land and the sea, "Do not damage the land or the sear or the trees until we put the seal on the foreheads of the servants of Our God." Revelation 7:2

Lo, I am sending my messenger to prepare the way before me; and suddenly there will come to the temple the LORD whom you seek, and the messenger of the covenant whom you desire. Yes he is coming, says the LORD of hosts. But who will endure the day of this coming? And who can stand when he appears? For he is like the refiner's fire, or like the fuller's lye. He will sit refining and purifying [silver], and he will purify the sons of Levi, Refining them like gold or like silver that they may offer due sacrifice to the LORD.

> *Lo, I will send you Elijah, the prophet, before the day of the LORD comes,*
> *the great and terrible day.*

–Malachi 3: 1-3,23

Through the Lord Jesus, and the work of the Holy Spirit, the Eternal Father entrusted me to a head a mission. I am a Vessel, acting as an instrument for the Holy Trinity. Through the Lord Jesus also revealed this mission through His teaching the apostles. This Mission was revealed in several chapters of the Book of Revelation. The shroud that the Lord placed around my shoulders symbolic of God bestowed upon me the gift of dead to self to serve Him as the natural founder of this mission.

God's Righteousness Comes through Embracing Suffering

March 14, 1998. In my dream I came to the side of the Church, it was crowded with human spirits. The Church and ground around were build with concrete, but there were no trees. These human spirits were on the way to a retreat. Five days of retreat cost one thousand five hundred U.S dollars. I said to them, "One thousand five hundred dollars is very expensive." They responded to me, "This is cheap."

The number one thousand is symbolic of extended Ten Commandments. Five hundred is symbolic of the righteousness of God over the devil's power. The retreat is symbolic of

839

the life serving God is constant learning, obedience to God, embracing the cross of suffering, and love. The Blessed Virgin Mother was the first one who was completely obedient to God, steadfast in faith. Her example is for us to follow. Many people are not understand that in order to earn God's power over the devil, that individual must completely obey all God's commandments.

Obedience is in the heart, mind and actions, not just in the words that speak out to the public. Many times I felt that I was ready for heaven, there was nothing for me in this world; I pleaded to God to take my life; and I know that this will continue in my life until I get home in heaven. Asking God to take our life and personally taking our own life are opposite. We can come to God with everything in our hearts, which He already knows. When a person takes his own life through human design, because of any reason, it is a mortal sin, and he will not enter heaven. But a person asking God to take her life gains good deeds for heaven. She completely depends and trusts in God alone. When a person trusts in God alone, she carries many crosses, the cross of herself, her own family and God's family; and these crosses are different from one to another, no one is same. The life of God's true servant costs everything of her life on earth, following in the footsteps of our Lord Jesus.

The Lord Jesus is the Only Teacher, We are Students

After this, God gave me another dream. In my dream I was in an upper large room with another two persons. This room was divided into two sections; one side for three of us as students doing our home work, the other side was for the teacher.

The home work had three parts, when I finished my first part, I looked at the other two. One of them had finished all three parts, I saw his handwriting was careless and loose, the other one finished the first part and gave up on the rest, although I knew that he finished the first part without seeing his paper.

I had another two parts that I did not know what to do. I got up and stepped to the other side where the teacher was. I was sitting across the long table in front of him, showing him my homework; looking on the white paper for a sign "#" for the next step. I asked the teacher to help me with the homework.

The one who finished the first part that I did not see his text is symbolic of many who broke their vows they promised to God. The one who finished the all three parts in careless loose writing is symbolic of those who believe in something that is not there, they cut off God's commandments, and lead others to be like them.

I am myself in the dream and symbolic of those who carefully observe all God's commandments.

When we seek God in our prayers, and the holy scriptures, through the Holy Spirit, Jesus the Lord teaches each one of us. When a person is insufficient in prayer and living sacrifices, and keeping his heart pure, the devil will pull that person to his ways.

The Blessed Virgin Mother and holy angels and saints only can pray for us. Spiritual director or advisor only can help to some point. God is living God, we must directly come direct to receive His teaching, not the spiritual advisers or directors. There are time very dangerous to people when the spiritual directors or adviser live the life that not complete obey all God's commandments; the enemy spirits will interffer in their minds and actions. The evidence are very obviously that priests and ministers involving sexual relationship with people came to them for advice.

Spiritual Leaders Lack Responsibility

March 3, 1998. There were several dreams to support the meaning of this dream. I saw a group of people practicing a formal dance in a large room for an event coming soon. I found out from the market I went to in the dream before, that I would also be in this dance group, and I needed to be with them to practice, but I did not get a notice.

Looking through the group practicing the formal dance, in the opposite corner was a person who was responsible to distribute the notice to all members in the group for practicing the dance. When I saw him, he also saw me, and he drew his strength about to run, and I yelled at him, and said "When you receive information, you must distribute it, not keep for yourself only."

The group practicing the dance is symbolic of people in this world learning to be formal in routines before God, not coming to Him with their heart. The person that saw me and was about to run is symbolic of over 270 Roman Catholic components who received revelations that God instructed me to mail to them in the past year, their responsibility was to make these public to their congregations, but they did not fulfill their responsibility, especially in the case of abortion, and tax monies funding programs working against God's commandments, such as generating destructive weapons and teaching medical students how to perform abortions.

Time to Proclaim the Gospel

October 19, 1997: In my dream, I was sitting on the ground in an open supermarket, at the side of a long open wall shelter, with two people. I told these two people, "At the time I was beginning to serve God, Father Binh An told me a real story of a woman. Her husband died, leaving her with four children. She entered a convent, and later she became a mother superior of the convent. Her order performs service all over the world." These two persons said, "We must go." I said to them, "I can sit here for a long time, but I do not want to sit here alone." I meant that if these two people go, I would go with them.

These two persons left, and I followed them. While we were walking, they said to me, "You need to do whatever needs to be done. You are not doing that, you have been leaving the chores aside, waiting for too long and not doing them." I defended myself, saying, "Eventually, I will do them, I do not want to do anything in a hurry."

I then was in a house like the rectory. A large woman was there, she was the maid in this house. She was standing in front of an open closet, I was standing to her right. This closet had several cloaks in it, she pulled out the tail of the "V" neck red cloak, and said to me, "These belong to the Cardinal, the King before he was raised up to a higher title." I then saw a part of the book "God's Purification - Not Easy," the part where the Lord Jesus commanded me, "You will found the Priest's order, and name it Jesus's Servant." I then saw the words "Freedom to Worship God in Vietnam". The spirit of Monsignor Tien was sitting on a chair on high platform, he was wearing a black cassock with a red belt around his waist. I then saw the corner of the restaurant where I meet with the owner of Cong Luan newspaper, and his friend, Mr. Son on October 13, 1997.

Then the Lord Jesus said to me, "Now is the time for you to take actions to pursue the freedom to worship God in Vietnam. There is a new government. I will send people to assist you. You need to make a trip to Orange county next week."

As I got up, the Lord told me, "The book of Exodus chapter 4." He then continued, "The two people in the dream are symbolic of God's discernment telling you it is time to take actions. You are delaying and waiting for a miracle from God before you take action; you have faith in God that eventually God's work will get done. The woman who pulled out the red cloak from the closet is symbolic of My Spirit telling you it is time for you to go out to the public, fight against the devil and his offspring spirits that are hidden inside people's minds and hearts. The red "V" neck cloak is symbolic of the mission the Father gave Me, in flesh, to die, and rise. This mission I entrusted in you, you are my Vessel, Instrument, and Ambassador."

Number four is symbolic of holiness; the mother of four children is symbolic of me, Mariette. I must completely trust and depend on God and always live a life of holiness, for God to use me as His Vessel. Mother superior is symbolic of the head of the mission. Four hundred nuns are symbolic of holiness upon the world. The Lord God did not tell me to be a nun like a women in the story that a Navy Chaplain told me in the third quarter of 1992. God used the Navy Chaplain to share that story with me to open my mind, thoughts, and actions that God calls people in very strange ways, so He can reveal that He called me to be His messenger. But every one of us must know that we are always sinners until we enter heaven.

In the year 1994, God used another priest in another town. After I met with him and shared what I have seen and heard from God, and how I felt, this priest told me, "Be God's messenger."

After 8:30 a.m. mass, while I was in the Blessed Sacrament chapel, I asked, "Blessed Mother, pray for the mission that the Lord entrusted in me, for me and teach me to pray;

842

holy angels and saints intercede for me" I then prayed, "Father, Lord Jesus, Holy Spirit; I am no longer myself, I belong to You. The works I do are not mine, they are Yours. I ask You Lord God to go before me all the time in this mission. This mission will not end at the time I go home to heaven, it will continue until the end of the world." The Lord Jesus said to me, "Victoria, Victoria, Victoria, the Father is very pleased with you and all your actions. He sends holy angels and saints before you, and I am in you in this mission. There are times you have not heard my voice, but My Spirit is in you to do the works." Filled with God's Spirit, I then said, "Victoria, Victoria is my name; every one must call me Victoria."

October 21, 1997. After seeking the Lord of what He wants me to do, He told me, "You go see the priest you saw yesterday [Father Lai Van Khuyen, Associate Pastor of the Holy Family parish], the Vietnamese Monsignor in Orange County [Monsignor Nguyen Duc Tien, President of the Vietnamese Center], and the earthly priest, pastor at Good Shepherd parish [Father Fernando Ramirez]."   I then got an appointment with Father Khuyen for 9:30 a.m. October 22, 1997.

Revelation Meanings

Father Khuyen is an associate pastor of the Holy Family parish. The name Khuyen has two meanings; "Khuyen khich" in English means encourage; and "Khuyen cao" means warning. The Lord telling me go see Father Khuyen is symbolic of ministering others, to assist them to convert, daily exam and repent; and warn them of the Fatima's sun dancing coming down on earth. If they are disobedient to God's commandments they will receive punishments. Monsignor Nguyen Duc Tien is President of the Vietnamese Catholic Center. The name "Duc Tien" in the English biblical translation means go forward and live in the life of holiness. The president is symbolic of being the head, with services to others to help them to convert, daily exam and repent. Father Ramirez is the Pastor of the Good Shepherd parish. The Pastor of the Good Shepherd parish is symbolic of church leaders and officials following in the footsteps of the Lord Jesus, and being an example for others to follow.

On October 22, 1997. At the beginning of the 8:30 a.m. mass, I prayed to the Lord, "Father, Lord Jesus, Holy Spirit; I offer this Holy Eucharist celebration to You, I pray for the meeting with Father Khuyen. I ask You to go before me and be in me. You have promised me many times that you will get me candies and cookies, but I have not see any candy or cookies. I claim that this meeting you will give me candy or cookies on earth." I also submitted this petition at the consecration.

Then when the priest placed a consecrated host in the palm of my hand, I looked at it and said, "Lord Jesus, I receive Your real body and blood. This mission is Your mission, not mine. I did not want to go see them, but You told me to go because they cannot see

You, but they can see me." When I finished saying this, I got to my seat, kneeled down, and the Lord Jesus said to me in the way of being angry at church officials and leaders refusing to cooperate with God, "What you think is human thinking, God's thinking is different from humans." I asked, " Lord, what is my thinking? My thinking is disappointed." The Lord Jesus said, "You come to him [Father Khuyen] to command him to do the will of the Father, you are not asking him. If he obeys, he will receive blessing. If he disobeys, he will receive punishment. Same as the one in Orange County; you come to command him and others to do the Father's will, you are not asking him. If they obey, they will receive blessing, if they disobey they will receive punishment. Also the priest here. You come to command him and those under him to do the Father's will. If they obey, they will receive blessing, if they disobey, they will receive punishment." He continued, "Didn't I tell you to ask the Father for Fatima's sun dancing to come down on earth? And you did ask the Father for it." I said, "But your time is different from the earthly time."

There is Only One Church, the Lord Jesus is Head

God's anointing comes to each individual to build the kingdom of heaven. When Church leaders and others are disobedient to God, they serve their own will, not the will of God. Then God's power is no longer with them.

God then sent the Blessed Virgin Mother to appear to Vietnamese Roman Catholics, at the time that they ran away from those who persecuted their faith. They gave up everything they owned, and evacuated to the middle of the jungle to worship God. When these Vietnamese Roman Catholics placed God above all things on earth, He was with them to protect them, heal them, and bless them.

God then chose a lowly girl, Bernadette, and sent the Blessed Virgin Mother to appear to Her. He gave Her a mission to carry out the announcement of the Blessed Virgin Mother as the "Immaculate Conception." Her word repeated of all man are immaculate conception was revealed in the Book of Genesis chapter two.

Then the third time, God sent the Blessed Virgin Mother to appear to three children at Fatima, and gave a very clear warning to pray the rosary and convert to God with the sign of the sun dancing, and souls crying out to God, from the middle of fire with the dark shadow. This warning is symbolic of souls that refuse to convert, exam daily and repent will be chained in the darkness of the devil, be punished for their sins, and be tortured by the devil.

For the last time, before the earth goes back to before it was created, the Eternal Father, in the image of His Son, and the Lord Jesus appeared to me revealed to me that I am a sinner, a convert, and that I was pre-destined by the Father on this mission.

When God sent me down to earth, He had me born in the Roman Catholic family. My family is a victim of the Catholic church authorities, I left the church for nine years.

Because I was undercover, I returned to Catholic component for God to use their daily worship and activities to teaches me. After over four and half years God removed me from the Catholic component, be neutral to speak of what asks of me; finish the mission that belongs to the Lord Jesus, that God entrusted to me.

Revival of the Souls

Before I went to sleep at night on January 8, 1998, I read several chapters of 1 Kings, 2 Kings, 1 Chronicles, and 2 Chronicles. While I was asleep, I heard the front door bell ring. I jerked myself up, I knew it was a spiritual bell and not the earthly house door bell. Then the Lord Jesus told me, "Say to the Father, 'Father, my soul's door is opening for You to enter and stay forever." The Lord broke this sentence into three parts, each time He said it, I repeated after Him. I then repeated it for the second time, "Father my soul's door is opening for You to enter and stay forever."

I then went back to sleep, while I was half asleep I heard the Lord Jesus explained to me of my son. He then asked me, "Do you understand Elija entering the boy?" I said, "No." He said, "That was not a physical death of the boy, it was spiritual death; through Elija's prayer the boy's soul revived." He continued, "The oil is symbolic of anointing. Flour to make cake and bread transformed to the new testament is bread at the last supper; and to My glorified body; the Holy Eucharist. The widow is a poor sinner, the boy is a great sinner, Elija now is you in the case of your son and others. Through me, you will bring many to return to the Father. That mother and son are like Saints Monica and Augustine."

The scripturoo tho Lord explained to me was 1 Kings 17.17-24.

Before I got out of bed in the morning of January 9, 1998, the Father said to me, "Jesus came down with His mission; He then gave power to [Saint] Peter to shepherd His church. After [Saint] Peter went to heaven, the church leaders got in the flesh, and miscarried their mission by disobeying My commandments. You came down as a Vessel to the Holy Trinity, special to Jesus with another mission."

The Church on earth is a copy of the Church in heaven. For God's Power to work through each person, that person's heart must constantly focus in God and live a life holiness. When Lucifer wanted to be like God, God cast them out of heaven, at the time Lucifer left heaven, He took one-third disobedient angels with him, they now became fallen angels. When spiritual leaders and officials are disobedient to God, refuse to convert, they live in the life without God's present.

When spiritual leaders are holding a title in the church, disobey God, the physical body will still be working there, but God's power is not there or there very little, depending of the level that they are disobedient to God.

God measures each one heart and actions of holiness to pour out His power to work through each individual, and many individual will build the church. When a person's heart is focused on holiness, it will result in the life of holiness. When a person's heart is focused the least on holiness, it will result in less holiness. Many people use the excuse that humans make mistakes, and God always forgives; yet, God forgives every sin, but if that person continues using any kind of excuse to short God, then that person will very easily fall; if a person focuses on evil or material things, he will do things against God.

Measured by percent, more or less when the level of holiness decreases the devil gains his power in that person.

> *Some time later the son of the mistress of the house fell sick, and his sickness grew more severe until he stopped breathing. So she said to Elijah, "Why have you done this to me, O man of God? Have you come to me to call attention to my guilt and to kill my son?" "Give me your son," Elijah said to her. Taking him from her lap, he carried him to the upper room where he was staying, and laid him on his own bed. He called out to the LORD: "O LORD, my god, will you afflict even the widow with whom I am staying by killing her son?" Then he stretched himself out upon the child three times and called out to the LORD: "O LORD, my god, let the life breath return to the body of this child." The LORD heard the prayer of Elijah; the life breath returned to the child's body and he revived. Taking the child, Elijah brought him down into the house from upper room and gave him to his mother. "See!" Elijah said to her, "your son is alive." "Now indeed I know that you are a man of God," the woman replied to Elijah. "The word of the LORD comes truly from your mouth.*
>
> *–1 Kings 17:17-24*

Stimulation vs. Faith

January 28, 1998. In my dream I saw a man that I had known for some time, who came to church very often on weekdays. I was standing inside the door of my family room, I also saw the garage door was open, and I knew that he just came from garage door. I said to him, "Get out of my house, get out of my house, get out of my house." I then pleaded to the Lord, "Father, do not let this man in my house. Lord Jesus, get him away of my house. Holy Spirit, get him away of my house." I then saw I was in the middle of the air in a classroom. This was an extra room at the side close to the entrance of the Good Shepherd Church. The classroom was filled with students, and one teacher. Looking down, I said to the teacher, "You get out. You are a false teacher; get out of the church. You are a false teacher." He then walked out of the room; on his way to the door, he shrunk to a midget. I knew that he was trying to get in the church, so I said to him, "You are not going in the church, get out at the door." I then pleaded to the Lord, "Jesus, Lord, I ask You to get this

846

midget man out of the door for me."

The man in my house is symbolic of those who come to church often, without daily exam and repentance. The students in the class are symbolic of Christians. The teacher is symbolic of those who mislead people, disobey God's commandments, and teach others to disobey God as well; and of those who preach, but do not put their preaching into their daily life.

All of these people believe what they practice will save them for eternal life. What they believe is stimulation, not faith in God. One must have faith in God and obey all God's commandments; completely surrendering his life to God; living a life in holiness; embracing suffering with Jesus and not complaining, enduring to the end.

Faith will Bring Victory

January 27, 1998. In my dream I was standing in front of my house, by the main entrance door. To my right was a two-level rack of clothes. I turned my face to the rack of clothes. A woman who came to church almost every day was there. The Lord prohibited me from talking to her; she was doing something with the clothes at the lower level. I said to her, "You, get away from here, do not touch these clothes!" I then turned around and saw in the sky, thick clouds with light like flashing thunder moving fast up to the center; then after I blinked my eyes, the sky turned dark. I walked inside the house, when I passed the center of the house, I turned around and saw the same woman who was standing in front of the clothes rack. I told her, "You, get out of my house, get out of my house; you, get out of my house." When I finished the third time of my demanding she went out the door.

The woman is symbolic of those who go to church frequently and refuse to convert and repent. Clothes are symbolic of people spiritual life. The devil is hidden under others who refuse to convert; the woman doing something with these clothes is symbolic of the devil attacking people through other people. We must discern and avoid the devil's actions, many times it appears like they are from God, but they are not from God. Thick flashing light clouds moving fast are symbolic of God's will being visible to the world, pour out tragedies to purify the world system For those He chose must go through great suffering so they can see the living God and convert. The woman then in the house is symbolic of the devil going and coming back, we must constantly battle.

Through God's power, in faith, I obeyed God to accept this mission. In faith, I obeyed God and moved to Little Rock, Arkansas. In faith, I obeyed God and moved back to San Diego. In faith I communicated with President Bill Clinton and all members of the United States Senate, delivery to them of what God asked of me, including freedom of religion in Vietnam. In faith I obeyed God to filled the petition in United States Tax Court, through this petition, I request the taxpayers civil right to freedom of religion to be restored. Although some of the Catholic leaders were spoke evil behind me, and some were trying to stop me from do the Eternal Father will.

The Road of Purification to Received the Healing Righteous of God

July 22, 1998. In my dream I was standing inside the door of a large section of the house, it was like a small apartment. My right hand held a door. This door was open a little and was I trying to close it tight. There was a person outside the door pushing against it, so she get in. But my hard stool went out my bottom down close to behind my left knee. I needed to take care of this, therefore, I told the woman to come back later. I then closed the door tightly. Immediately I closed the door, my soft stool following the hard stool, then both of them went through my trousers leg and were laying on floor. I grasped a paper towel from the top of a lamp table, and put many layers over to cover the top, and was about to pick it up with my left hand; but the same woman returned to open the door, and went in the restroom in my apartment. (This restroom is same the restroom the dark, big woman went in few nights ago, and was trying to save the marriage.) While she was in the restroom, I left the house, took my stool to the kitchen, a Vietnamese kitchen style, the burners are set on the ground . I just entered in front of the ash area, the stool fell on the ground. I took a metal kitchen spoon and scooped it up and buried it in front of the main wood stove ash. I had to do it twice to complete the job.

This was a continuation of the dream. I saw myself in the driver's seat in an automobile. There was a very dark person sitting in the front passenger seat, and another dark person sitting on the spot that had no seat between me and the passenger. Under the person who had no seat, a big round cord was sticking out. The top had a round lock, this lock was a control of the automobile, and I had a key for it. The person with no seat pulled out a CD player from the dashboard that had a CD in it. Just after he did this, I told him to get out of the car. He climbed over the driver's seat and stood outside the driver's door. I then got in the car, put the CD tray back under the center of the dashboard, and as I did this the cord got more visible to me. I was about to let the person with no seat get in the car, but he had not gotten in yet, and the dream changed.

Then I saw this car close to the right front corner of the large stage, next to the wall. This wall covered the car from the audience, but suddenly the car disappeared, and I was there alone toward the stage. I saw the left side of the stage and in front were very crowded with the audience. I saw my former life insurance company general manager from behind his left back, he was flying at the right side of the stage and entered the door into the chamber behind the stage, and there were several people accompanying him. I then saw this general manager and his companion get out the chamber door and do and stand at the second step in front of the stage. While his companion stood at his side, he made some kind of announcement.

This is the third part of the dream. I sat on the ground with a person to my left. Son, my cousin came to me, with his younger brother, Hiep following behind him. Son gave me a small white piece of paper, it had hand writing, and served as an invitation, "The band will play at UCSD at 9:15 tonight." I knew that my oldest daughter gave Son this piece of paper to give to me. I turned to a person at my left and asked her, "Would you like to come with me, to see my daughter sing. She will sing with the band." I then thought that I needed to go home to rest before I went to hear the band tonight. I knew that my cousins Son and Hiep came from where my daughter and her husband were from the left, far in front of me.

The dream changed, I just entered a house built with four building connecting at it corner, and a center was open a garden. This building had many rooms. In the house I saw my daughter's friends in the band, the two rooms I just entered had some tables with cut watermelons displayed on the tables. It seemed like the band was about to practice. I past the corner into another room, this room was bigger, there was a round table at the center, with three people around the table. I took a seat at the table; while I was sitting there, one was busy decorating a watermelon, another was eating, and another sat quietly looking at me while I was talking. After I was talking for few minutes with them; the one who was busy decorating said to me, "She (quiet person) can not hear you." I replied, "If she can not hear me, she can read my lips."

The dream changed to the conclusion of the revelation. I was in small room, in front of me was a tall wooden stereo case, with double clear plastic doors. This stereo case was being used as a file cabinet. Looking through this double clear doors. I saw the case was divided into three compartments, one on top of another, and all three compartments were filed with files. One on top of another, all the front files faced the front double clear doors.

Then a doctor wearing a white lab coat came from the room at my right, and with his key, opened the cabinet. While He was taking some of the files out and laying them on top of the cabinet with his invisible key, a nurse came from a room at my left to assist him. At the moment the doctor handed the first stack of files to the nurse, the Blessed Virgin Mother told me, "Mariette, take that key." I spoke out loud, "I'll take that key." Now, I have the key to the victory road.

The next morning, when I woke up, the Holy Spirit told me, "All prophets are living in an environment that will happen again in future. Those prophets in the old testament are alive like the way you are. John saw the beasts. You saw the beasts in the dream; the first beast is symbolic of the world's system, they are in the house; the second beast is symbolic of false miracle workers and prophets, they are in morass." The Lord mean from the man-made ocean.

The dark person in the passenger seat changing to former life insurance general manager is symbolic of Executive officers. A dark person with no seat changing to those accompanying life insurance general manager is symbolic of those advisers. The doctor is symbolic of the Lord Jesus. The nurse is symbolic of God's faithful servants and ministers. The stage is symbolic of God's throne. This general manager and his companions making an announcement is symbolic of admitting the wrong and proclaiming the truth and converting to God. The automobile is symbolic of me. The key symbolic of righteous of God work through the mission that God entrusted to me. The dark person pulling out the CD from the dashboard is symbolic of the advisers digging into more trouble for others.

UCSD is symbolic of a place to teach God's words. My daughter, her husband, two of my cousins, and people in the band are symbolic of people in the world. The band playing at UCSD is symbolic of those converting to God will learn all His commandments, and praising God.

The one eating the watermelon and the one busy decorating the table is symbolic of Martha in the holy scripture, the one deaf listening to me is symbolic of Mary Madelene. The watermelon is symbolic of works looking good, but not benefiting the souls.

Unity in God, Win over the Devil

January 28, 1998. In my dream I was walking in an open field. I saw from the distance a few people putting a snake, but it looked like two bodies, into a round sewer tank gate. Closer to me, a woman from behind was doing something. I walked a few more steps in front of her. I saw a young female had just finished cleaning the scales off a globe fish. One side of its body was slashed twice, she then cut its head off from the body. The head of the globe fish belonged to an elderly woman, but she refused to accept the entire head, she asked the young woman to cut the head in two. The young female cut its head in two parts, the part closer to the lady was smaller than the part next to the elderly women. The small part was for the young female, the bigger part was for the older woman.

When I got up the Lord told me, "The elderly woman is symbolic of the spiritual leaders. The young woman is symbolic of you. The fish head is symbolic of responsibility on the spiritual leaders. Now the fish head divided in two parts means sharing responsibility; the small part is yours, and your responsibility is to hear from God and deliver messages to spiritual leaders. Their responsibility is to teach their congregation, and lead them to eternal life." The snake is symbolic of the devil. Putting it down the sewer gate is devil is lost.

Battle to the End and Win Victory

When I woke up and was still laying on the bed, the Lord Jesus said to me, "In your dream, you have not lost your sandals, they tried to take your sandals and give you their sandals. You fought against them to get your sandals back. When you felt the spirit like a ghost out in the open air, you cast the devil out, that woman told you, 'she did it already.'

You responded to her, 'must do this with pure heart.' Your daughter is not herself, she is symbolic of those false worshippers. Go back and label the revelation as 'false worshipping' not 'counterfeit'. Look at Elija in the Bible, he ran away from over two hundred false prophets, you are in the same way. They abandoned you in the dream, they adjusted their convoy vehicle seat, moved their vehicle forward and backward, got out of the morass, then took off without you, and left you to walk alone on bare feet. Your walking barefoot to your car in the large parking lot is symbolic of them choosing luxury, and you are being a humble Servant to the Father, so they rejected you. Your children do not understand you now, but they will understand in time. They believe God spoke to you, you heard and obeyed Him. You car had an engine, the engine generating energy, it symbolic of God's power. You have obeyed little things, you will obey big things. The devil uses people not obeying God in little things and leads them to disobey big things. The Catholic leaders will accept you and ask you to serve God their way; but you are fighting against them, they then abandon you."

I said, "Lord Jesus, please do not be silent to me. I need You more visible to me at all times. Give me instructions of how and what to do, and when I am wrong, you correct me and forgive me."

He said, "When you are in the place filled with evil, like the time you were at Cathedral of St. Andrew, I will be silent, but I am always in you. The Blessed Mother and Archangel Michael will be visible and speak to you, and give you directions."

He continued, "Put in the revelation that the Blessed Virgin Mother explained to you of your adoption to the Holy Family. You do not have to speak about your son, just say, 'My family is a victim of the Catholic authorities, and now my son is still against them. That was the beginning of the Blessed Mother being visible to you."

Immediately the priest placed the Body and Blood of the Lord in my mouth. I felt the enemy spirits attack me, and I said, "Lord Jesus, the devil is attacking me. Protect me." Getting back to my seat, I knelt down with the consecrated host laying on top of my tongue. The Lord Jesus said to me, "The way you understand the word 'silent' that I said last night is not what I mean. It was a revelation, it means humble, not exalted, completely obeying God, not obeying man. You will be hearing from the Father, Me, and the Holy Spirit more. That revelation revealed the Blessed Virgin Mother is your Mother, she is with you; she is also the spiritual mother to all human race." I replied to him, "Lord Jesus I am opposed to this." I meant that I wanted the Father, the Lord Jesus, and the Holy Spirit more visible to me, the same as my Blessed Virgin Mother and the Archangel Michael.

He continued, "An example: The three piece shingle on the roof of your house was blown away. While El Nino was in town, people prepared for it, your son told you to repair the roof of your house. But you trusted and obeyed Me not to fix it yet. While rains, snows, and floods happened all over the nation, very little water came in your one window. This little water was the Father testing you." While the Lord was saying this, I had not swallowed the Holy Eucharist, but when He finished I knew that the Eucharist was no longer in my mouth.

He continued, "Church leaders abandoning you is spiritual, it is in their heart. You and others will not able to see with your natural eyes, that means they still serve God with you. Their hearts do not trust God, they depend on human power. But after you go home to heaven, they will convert."

God revealed of obeying all His commandments. When a person obeys all God's commandments, they will live a life of holiness. Living a life of holiness will increase faith. When Jesus the Lord told me that the Father and He will be silent, He meant that people do not hear God's voice like a human voice. But they must believe that when a person lives the life completely obeying all God's commandments, and pleasing him, He is always within that person.

He then said that when a place contains an evil spirit, He will not be there. He means that in a place where the devil stays, there will be no presence of God. When a person lives a life in grave sin, God will not be within that person. Instead, through God's power, the Blessed Virgin Mother is the spiritual mother of human race, she is there to assist them to convert to God. There is a gap between God and man. Therefore, those who refuse to convert, exam and repent daily will not encounter the presence of God in this world, and will not see His face in heaven.

Through receiving the Holy Eucharist, we are in one with God. But being one with Him is only for those who receive the Holy Eucharist with a pure heart. Vice versa, when a person receives the Holy Eucharist with grave sin, they will receive punishment. You may find that God speaks to me frequently immediately after I receive the Holy Eucharist.

Over three years from the date of this revelation, the wind ripped off two pieces of shingles from the roof of my house, leaving a hole on the back side. Water came through the back wall window of the family room. A roofing company did an estimate, but I did not fix it, not because I did not have the money. Later the storm ripped off another piece. Water came in at the time the two pieces ripped, and then it stopped. The Lord Jesus told me it is not time to fix it yet, when He said this to me, I knew that God was going to use these holes for His works.

When the weathermen notified us of El Nino, my sons told me a few times to fix the roof, but I did not do it, because the hole is for God's works. This hole stayed for three rainy seasons without water coming in the house. During the El Nino season in December 1997 and January 1998, people got ready to protect themselves from El Nino. Here I am praying to the Lord, "Jesus, you told me not to fix the hole on the roof, please do not let the water come in the house." The El Nino storms came with heavy rain, snow, floods and other bad weather. But I obeyed God by not fixing the roof. There is a hole on top of my roof, yet while the rain was heavy for days, water did not get inside my living room, and there was no flood in my backyard.

Lucifer has been vacuuming the world of good deeds and replacing them with his evil actions. Bad weather, heavy rains, snow, and floods are God's warning upon the world to purify its system. But for those who obey all God's commandments, remain steadfast in faith, and completely depend on Him, He will protect them. Those who refuse His commandments will perish.

After the Lord took me out from work in April 1994, He asked me to write letters to all members of the U.S. Senate, and the House of Representatives, requesting assistance for freedom of religion in Vietnam. At the time, I thought I did not have anything to do, so I did it. Father Ramirez, Pastor of the Good Shepherd parish told me not to, but I did what God asked me, not what the Pastor of the church asked. At the time I write this chapter, January 1998, I understand that not only Vietnam does not have the freedom of worshipping God, but the United States and all over the world does not have freedom to worship God, because these countries pass laws against God's commandments.

God's power only works through those who have faith in Him, and live a life of holiness. Keep in mind that every one in this world are sinners, except the fully man Jesus.

Give Thanks to God for the Victory

January 29, 1998. As the Holy Eucharist celebration began, I prayed, "Father, I offer this Holy Eucharist to give You thanks for rewarding me with victory in this mission. Lord Jesus, I offer this holy mass to You, I give You thanks for bringing victory to me in this mission. Holy Spirit, I offer this holy Eucharist celebration to you, I give You thanks for winning the victory for me in this mission. Blessed Virgin Mother, I give you thanks for always pleading to the Lord God for me, and being with me at all times to protect me, remind me, and do things for me. Archangel Michael, Saints Peter and Paul, Saints Joseph, John the Baptist, Saint John, prophets, martyrs, and all holy angels and saints that constantly pray to the Lord for me, fight against the devil to win this victory for me in this mission."

After I received the Holy Eucharist, I bent to put down the kneeler; while the consecrated host was still hard, I used the top of my tongue and turned the consecrated host over and quickly swallowed it. I kneeled down, and the Lord said to me, "You have turned the world upside down. Swallow your suffering. Other people suffer a little, and they complain. Your suffering is high like a huge mountain, you swallowed it just like you swallowed My body and blood."

Re-register at Good Shepherd Church Revelation

March 12, 1998, 7:30 a.m. mass at Saint Michael's temple. Immediately after I received the body and blood of our Lord Jesus, the Holy Spirit told me, "You go and re-register at the Good Shepherd Church." After I heard this in my thought, knowing that my natural family is still on the Good Shepherd Parish's record, I realized in that the Good Shepherd Church, the word "Church" is only Church and Jesus the Lord is the Head of the Church.

I said, "Lord God, I registered myself Mariette Tin Do-Nguyen, my daughter Theresa Thuy-Trang Do, her husband Vincent Huy Quang Cao, along with my son John the Baptist James Linh Do, his wife Amanda Hanh Nguyen, and my granddaughter Madelene Mai Do; also my son, Joseph Chau Dzuy Do, and my daughter Theresa Tuanh Do." Then I saw the words written, "Approved by Eternal Father, the Creator of Heaven and Earth," the end of the letter "h" was trailing down a few inches. The Lord then told me, "Send a copy of this registration to the Monsignor at Saint Michael's Parish."

God revealed that after conversion, each one of us must re-register to His Spiritual Church, the re-registered symbolic of renewed our covenant with God.

Celebration of Conversion

March 15, 1998. In my dream I was standing in front of the Good Shepherd Church, facing the parish office. I heard a voice come out from the parish office and say, "Mariette, we built a house for you." Then the voice said to the others, "Get the trumpets, drums and flyers to notify for the celebration."

I then heard the Lord Jesus tell me, "The Church celebrates their conversion. Building the house means they are accepting you. Who accepts you, accepts Me. Who accepts Me, accepts the Father. Who rejects you, rejects Me. Who rejects Me, rejects the Father."

The parish is symbolic of parents or spiritual leaders. The voice coming out from the parish is symbolic of the conversion that must start from both roots. The family's root are parents who must be an example for their children, and the church root is the spiritual leaders for their congregation.

From Generation to Generation, the Older Shall Serve the Younger

January 13, 1998. Late in the evening during my communion with the Lord, Jesus told me, " El Nino will spread throughout the world, it will be stronger in San Diego. Rain will come down harder, flood all over, trees and power poles will fall on ground and there will be no electricity. Water pipes will break. All of this was revealed in the Gospel of Matthew, this is just the beginning.

He continued, "Tomorrow, I want you go buy a portable gas stove and several gas bottles, so you can cook food in the house. Your daughter can use her stove, but she has to move it to the inside corner of the patio. Buy two more large trash cans, the same kind you bought two day ago. Do not use these two new trash cans, use the one you bought two days ago. Put plastic a bag inside the can before putting the trash in it, so when El Nino comes you can wash inside the can easier. That time you will use a plastic sheet to receive water from the rain into these three trash cans. Use the water to cook and drink. You and your members can wash bodies with it, but very little."

He continued, "I will tell you when and what kind of food to buy before the day. You need three large cardboard boxes of food. At that time I will have your youngest daughter come back from Oakland, your son, Chau, Thuy-Trang and her husband, Huy will be in your house, together with you, your son James Linh, Hanh, and your granddaughter Madelene. Suddenly it will happen, your children can not go to their houses, they will sleep upstairs in those two bedrooms. You children's cars parked outside will perish, but insurance will cover it. Your car and Hanh's car in the garage will not perish.

The supernatural power of El Nino symbolic of God, Rain symbolic of purification. Food symbolic of God's words. My children symbolic of those will be save and inherited eternal life. Trash can symbolize of the physical body.

January 14, 1998. In my dream I was on the ground of a very dark area, it had some poor houses. The people did some kind of work like casting stars for movies. I told a child, "You go over there to apply." The dream then changed, I saw two small children kneeling behind the back of the pew in the church, there was another pew behind them. They were shoulder to shoulder sharing a prayer booklet, the light was shining between their faces, on the booklet, down to the upper part of their chest. The dream changed, I saw a corpse wearing dark clothes. The hands, feet and head were uncovered, the left leg bent up, with white skin, and it was laying face up the rain. I then looked to my right, several yards away there was another one exactly the same. I knew that these two corpses were the two children I saw praying together. I then heard the Lord say, "These two are symbolic of Peter and Scott."

Then I had another dream. I went out of my bedroom, this bedroom was the master bedroom for the house. I made a right turn, around the stairway with the wooden-topped, iron bar handrail. While I was walking, I saw an ex-spouse's brother sitting on a stool in the loft, outside the corner of my bedroom, playing a drum. On the way down the stairway, I said to him, "You are playing the drum again."

The next morning, immediately after I kneeled down in the Blessed Sacrament chapel, in front, up high, to my right I saw the Spirit of God, in the same position that I saw in a dream, before the first time I saw the last vision of Fatima. His Spirit was a powerful, sparking loose fire. This loose fire was shooting out heat waves. I prayed, "Father, Your will be done through Jesus, Your begotten Son, and through the works of the Holy Spirit. Father open my mind so I can understand the dream You showed to me last night. I pray for conversion of my son, and all my children, for Chau to move back home, his conversion being like another Saint Francis."

I then saw a large, heavy darkness formed at the foot of the Spirit of God, replacing the actual natural tabernacle. I prayed, "Lord Jesus, I am Your only sister, hold me, keep me safe; help me to stand firm and strong to serve the Father, You, and the Holy Spirit."

I saw to my right, on the ground, a smaller, same kind of spirit taking over the tabernacle. I then heard a voice coming out from the Spirit of God, saying, "The real apple you saw will now turn to real gold, it is coming in front of you. In your dream, at this time, the two corpses are symbolic of Peter and Scot. The older shall serve the younger, and they are your descendants. The man playing a drum symbolizes church leaders. The violet will serve the purple is symbolic of revelation of heaven, who want to be the greatest in heaven must serve the least on earth. Example Jesus is the Son of God, He is the King of kings, the royal family or purple; He took flesh and die on the Cross to save us.

He Lord God continued, "You favor the younger son, and bestowed upon him what the Father pre-destined for you, just like you inherited from your Blessed Mother. Jesus is dwelling in you, He gives you everything the Father gave Him."

The Lord continued, "Victoria, Victoria; I give you My peace, the same peace I gave to the apostles. I sealed you with Jesus's blood. Stand firm and be strong in faith. Hold on to what you have and ponder it in your heart like your Blessed Mother."

The name Peter symbolic of the Lord Jesus and Scott symbolize of me. The violate is symbolic of me Mariette. Purple is symbolic of the Lord Jesus as fully man in glorify body. The real meaning is through this mission the Lord Jesus is with me and in me to do all the works.

Understanding the Sacrament of Reconciliation

Jesus said to them again, "Peace be with you. As the Father has sent me, so I send you." And when he had said this, he breathed on them and said to them, "Receive the holy Spirit. Whose sins you forgive are forgiven them, and whose sins you retain are retained.

– John 20:21-23

When I got up, the time was after 3:00 a.m. on Easter Sunday, April 4, 1999; the Lord Jesus told me, "There is no man who can forgive sin. God is the only one who forgives sins. The scriptures you asked me about last night means the priests sitting in the confession box are God's disciples; God's disciples are everyone who does the will of the Eternal Father. Forgiven sins in the scriptures are symbolic of those receiving the present of God through God's disciples and convert to God. For example: One disciple commanded that a person must stay away from an evil person or place do evil, that person refused, meaning whose sins are retained. When God's disciple comes to an individual or a village to preach God's commandments and they convert, this mean whose sins you forgive are forgiven. The Sacrament of Reconciliation is the way that Catholics use priests as spiritual directors or advisors."

This is the way that God allowed Catholics priests to acting as spiritual directors or advisers, because priests understand scriptures more than laity; but many Catholic understand that they must come to priests to confess their sins before their be forgive. There are many catholic misunderstand, they believe that each person must have priest as spiritual director, and they must have private appointment for spiritual adviser; they forgot that God is living God; and Jesus is the living Teacher through the work of the Holy Spirit. They also do not understand that when a priests live in the life of disobey God's commandment, the devil interfered priests' minds then the priests gives them the advise to benefit the devil's will.

March 21, 1998. At 9:00 a.m. Saint Michael's held a Parish Penance Service, preparing for the memorial of the Lord Jesus siren from the dead. After Monsignor Joseph announced all priests stations, I asked, "Lord, which priest would You want me to go to?" I heard the angel of the Lord say, "Reverend Larry." I then heard another opposite voice say, "Today, you are here to pray for them [people coming to reconciliation with God through the Sacrament of Reconciliation]. You will set a private confession with Father Larry for your penance." In my thought, "My last confession was one month and four days ago. I need to receive the regular Sacrament of Reconciliation." I quickly said, "In Jesus' name, I rebuke you; get under my feet." I then rapidly got up and walked fast toward where Reverend Larry was sitting. I was the third one that received the Sacrament of Reconciliation from God through Reverend Larry.

My turn, after the priest proclaimed the sign of the Cross, with my head bowed down, I proclaimed "the Father, the Son and the Holy Spirit. Lord God forgive me all my sins." I then lifted my head up a little, to speak to Reverend Larry, "Father, my last confession was one month and four days ago. I have examined myself. I confess the sins that I am unaware of them." He said, "If you are unaware of them, and there are no sins." I replied, "Father, there are many times we commit sins without knowing that they were sins." He then explained to me the three elements to commit sin........" While he was explaining to me, silently in my head I said, "Lord, the priest doesn't know the calling that you gave me." Even though I asked the Lord, I still heard everything Reverend Larry said. He then asked me, "Do you have any of that?" I replied, "Father, I do not have any of those, but I want to please God." He then said, "For your penance say two Our Fathers and two Hail Marys." Then through Reverend Larry, God blessed me.

At the moment I got up from the chair, I repeatedly said, " Father, I claim your righteousness. Father, through the Lord Jesus, I claim Your righteousness. Lord Jesus, I claim Your righteousness." While I was repeatedly claiming the Eternal Father's righteousness, I passed the front corner of the sanctuary at my right.

Kneeling down, I continued, " Father, I claim to be at your right. Through the Lord Jesus no one can interfere, or invade Your right side that You have for me. Lord Jesus, I am at your right side."

I then heard the Holy Spirit say to me, "The Father's righteousness that the Lord Jesus requested, through the Lord Jesus, the Father's righteousness is your." He then continued, "Repent." I then said the two Our Fathers and two Hail Marys.

Priests must minister to their congregation, and help them to understand God's commandments in detail according to the sins that they confessed. I personally have some experience when one time I was trying to tell a priest in the confession box of my sins, he told me, "Just confess your sins." I then told him of my sins, he then told me, "It is that easy." But there was also another time when a priest told me, "Is that sin little like a big rock on the street? or like a little rock in your shoes?" For me I understood what he meant, because I knew that a small sin was still a sin, but for others, he or she may not understand. Therefore, spiritual director or adviser must help people in depth the meaning of their questions is very important.

When priests do not advise to their congregation correctly, they are partial liable to their congregation for any future confusion. Yet, God knows all sins and forgives, but priests are God's chosen ones, and God's instrument for Him to speak through. When a priest is God's instrument, the priest must do everything God instructed them to in their vows, even beyond their vows.

Priests, you must obey all God's commandments, so God can work through you. If priests mix thoughts and or actions, then the devil will either interfere or control that priest. This mix can be part or all of your thoughts and or your actions. Priests, do not hurt or destroy your soul and souls of others, by confiding that you only depend on God fifty percents and you are fifty percents, and your are okay. The highest level of holiness, we are completed depending on God, and there are time still unsure if our action is a sin or not a sin. But our faith that we "completed depending and trust in God," He will not for sake us.

The righteousness of the Father is supernatural power over the devil power. The devil's power is hidden under the carpet, and lawn. Each one of us must cut out our carpet and lawn daily. Carpet is in the house, it is in your heart. The lawn is outside the house, and it is your action. That could mean good talk and no action, good actions with evil thoughts, or evil thought and actions.

Understanding the Disagreement Among Spiritual Leaders and Unity in God

You shall not have other gods besides me. You shall not carve idols for yourselves in the shape of anything in the sky above or on the earth below or in the waters beneath the earth. You shall not bow down before them or worship them.

–Book of Exodus 20:3-5

Jesus the Lord commanded: "You shall love the Lord, Your God, with all your heart, with all your soul, and with all your mind. This is the greatest and the first commandment. The second is like it: You shall love your neighbor as yourself. The whole law and the prophets depend on these two commandments.

–Matthew 22:37-40.

If you keep my commandments, you will remain in my love, just as I have kept my Father's commandments and remain in his love.

–John 15:10

If you love me, you will keep my commandments

– John 14:15

There is only ONE true God, the maker of heaven and the earth, One who gives and takes away life. One who pours out winds and rain. This is the only God that we must love, worship, and obey above all things.

The meaning of the foot of the Cross' revelation: Saint John was the only apostle there, and after the Lord Jesus returned to the Father, Jesus the Lord revealed to Saint John His future ministry. Mary Magdelene was symbolic of conversion. The blessed Virgin Mary, mother of Jesus as fully man, and the Blessed Mother's sister Mary were there. The Jesus Christ is fully God in the fully man body. Hanging on the Cross He spoke as fully God to His fully man Mother, "Woman, behold, your son." Then He said the Disciple John, "Behold, your mother."

Saint John is symbolism of: (a) our becoming brothers and sisters of the Lord Jesus as fully man in God's family, and the Blessed Virgin Mother becoming the spiritual mother of the human race. (b) God revealed to Saint John the future of His ministry. Mary Magdelene, a convert, was the first one the Lord Jesus appeared to. Mary was the sister of the Blessed Virgin Mother. These characters at the foot of the Cross reveal a special adoption of a female convert into the Lord Jesus as fully man, a sister, to be God's Servant, God's Vessel to continue the Lord Jesus' mission.

Jesus as fully man is King of kings; therefore, the Blessed Virgin Mother became the Queen of Heaven and the Earth. We are to honor (not worship) her as our spiritual mother: Her responsibility is to go after heavy grave sinners and pick us up; through God's power, she helps us return to God. Even after we return to God, she is always there to pray for us, and remind us.

Holy saints are those who gained good deeds while they were on earth, and returned to heaven before us. They are our brothers and sisters, they are in the line with holy angels. They pray to God for us, and act on orders from God. We honor (not worship) them, and ask them to pray to God for us. The words "holy saints" mean everyone who left this world before us, they could belong to any denomination or religion. They are those who obeyed all God's commandments, did good and rejected evil with discernment, gaining good deeds in front of the Almighty God.

We are sisters and bothers in one God's family. We love God first, and love one another the same as our earthly brothers and sisters. As brothers and sisters in the same family, we must help one another in our time of need. Love from each one's heart comes to actions.

God is love, obedience, forgiveness, patience, and peace. The devil is hatred, disobedience, division, anger, temper, and violence. The spirits of division and hatred lead to protests, violence, and bombing among Catholics and Protestants in Ireland. The fighting between one country, from one nation against another is in the realm of the devil. The spirits of exalting oneself and controlling work among spiritual leaders and government leaders is also in the control of the devil himself or his offspring, it depends on the level of exalting and controlling. When a spiritual leader or government official filled with love and responsibility, he or she placed other people interests above their own; and he or she is very humble before God in truth.

God is calling everyone to conversion. When people refuse conversion, they give more power to the devil to win more cases, in receiving more permission from God, the Creator of the earth to damage the world. These damages are eternal punishment for souls, and physical death through disaster. During the course the devil destroyed souls and bodies of those who refused to convert, others who have converted have to sacrifice their lives for others, such as in bombings, air crashes, and shootings. God purifies the world's systems with heavy rains, storms, floods, fire, hurricanes, earthquake, and there are sometimes deaths.

To limit tragedies and disasters upon the world, each one in this world has the free will to answer God's calling to convert, and daily exam and repentance. The tragedies and disasters will not go away, indeed they will get worse if people refuse to convert. But they will be limited when each one of us returns to God. The quicker each one of us unifies in love with one another in God from our hearts and actions, the sooner God's peace will come upon the world. Although the iniquities must be purged by God.

> Jesus the Lord commanded us to love enemies: *"But to you who hear I say, love your enemies, do good to those who hate you, bless those who curse you, pray for those who mistreat you. To the person who strikes you on one cheek, offer the other one as well, and from the person who takes your cloak, do not withhold even your tunic. Give to everyone who asks*

of you, and from the one who takes what is yours do not demand it back. Do to others as you would have them do to you.

–Luke: 6:27-31

Jesus teaching about anger: *Therefore, if you bring your gift to the altar, and there recall that your brother has anything against you, leave your gift there at the altar, go first and be reconciled with your brother, and then come and offer your gift.*

– Matthew 5: 23-24

Jesus teaching about judging others: *Stop judging, that you may not be judged. For as you judge, so will you be judged, and the measure with which you measure will be measured out to you. Why do you notice the splinter in your brother's eye, but not perceive the wooden beam in your own eye? How can you say to your brother, 'Let me remove that splinter from your eye,' while the wooden beam is in your eye? You hypocrite, remove the wooden beam from your eye first; then you will see clearly to remove the splinter from your brother's eye.*

–Matthew 7:1-5

Jesus teaching of the Greatest: *Whoever wishes to be great among you shall be your servant; whoever wishes to be the first among you shall be your slave. Just so, the Son of Man did not come to be served but to serve and give this life as a ransom for many.*

–Matthew 20: 26-28

Spiritual leaders must be humble before God and completely obeying "all" God's commandments. When spiritual leaders obeying "all" God's commandments, he will be full with love, discernment, he will no longer sat on the high throne and pointed his finger to judging other religion or denomination; and all of this will started from he heart and come out to his actions.

As the Father loves me, so I love you. Remain in my love. If you keep my commandments, you will remain in my love, just as I have kept my Father's commandments and remain in his love.

–John 15:9-10

In the name of the Almighty God, through God's power and above God's commandments, as the Vessel and Servant to the Eternal Father, the Lord Jesus, and the Holy Spirit, I call each one of you, the spiritual leaders to convert your heart and actions to God, obey "all" His commandments, and to unify with each other, in God's only Church.

Rewards: *Whoever receives you receives me, and whoever receives me receives the one who sent me. Whoever receives a prophet because he is a prophet will receive a prophet's reward, and whoever receives a righteous man because he is righteous will receives a righteous man's reward. And whoever gives only a cup of cold water to one of these little ones to drink because he is a disciple - amen, I say to you, he will surely not lose his reward.*

–Matthew 10:40-42

38

ON THE WAY TO OUR LAST BREATH

The Lord Jesus Promise Comes to Fulfillment

I offered the 9:00 a.m. mass on March 17, 1998 to the Eternal Father for the Lord Jesus' attention.   Shortly after the beginning of the mass, the Lord Jesus showed me His attention to the Father. After I received the body and blood of our Lord Jesus, I pleaded, "Father, let them come to me, and through me, they will see You, the Lord Jesus, and the Holy Spirit. The powerful works of the Holy Spirit come from you, through the Lord Jesus."

The Father said to me, "What you just asked is the same thing Elisha asked Elijja." I said to the Father, "Lord, Father, I have faith in this. But if there is something behind my head, or hidden at the bottom of my heart that does not have the same faith as I just proclaimed to You, I ask You to bring it up and help me change it."

The Father said to me, "I will build Michael's hands and sword. You come to nine o'clock mass each day, until the end of the week." In the natural world, in front of Saint Michael's physical church in Poway was a statue of Saint Michael that had no hands or sword. I emphasized, "Saturday." I meant the end of the week was Saturday. The Father then said to me, "You are a living example."

After I sent out breaking news of "The Meaning of Saint Peter's Key and Unify the Church" and the "Restore Freedom of Religion in the United States" to the media, in my afternoon devotion the Lord Jesus told me, "John chapter ten, verse six."

"Although Jesus used this figure of speech, they did not realize what He was trying to tell them."

He then told me, "The Book of Revelation, chapter Ten."

The Angel with the Small Scroll: *Then I saw another mighty angel come down from heaven wrapped in a cloud, with a halo around his head; his face was like the sun and his feet were like pillars of fire. In his hand he held a small scroll that had been opened. He place his right foot on the sea and his left foot on the land, and then he cried out in a loud voice as a lion roars. When he cried out, the seven thunders raised their voices, too. When the seven thunders had spoken. I was about to write it down; but I heard a voice from heaven say, "Seal up what the seven thunders have spoken, but do not write it down." Then the angel I saw standing on the sea and on the land raised his right hand to heaven and swore by the one who lives forever and ever, who created heaven and earth and sea and all that is in them, "There shall be no more delay. At the time when you hear the seventh angel blow his trumpet, the mysterious plan of God shall be fulfilled, as he promised to his servants the prophets."*

Then the voice that I had heard from heaven spoke to me again and said, "Go, take the scroll that lies open in the hand of the angel who is standing on the sea and on the land." So I went up to the angel and told him to give me the small scroll. He said to me, "Take and swallow it. It will turn your stomach sour, but in your mouth it will taste as sweet as honey." I took the small scroll from the angel's hand and swallowed it. In my mouth it was like sweet honey, but when I had eaten it, my stomach turned sour. Then someone said to me, "You must prophesy again about many peoples, nations, tongues, and kings."

–Revelation Chapter 10

After I read it, the Lord Jesus told me, "You are in the place of John. The angel is symbolic of Me, your brother."

One foot on the sea and another foot on the land: the sea is symbolic of heaven, land is symbolic of the earth, the word "on" symbolizes of above the heaven and the earth. The angel is symbolic of the Lord Jesus as fully God and fully man; heaven and earth are under Him.

March 18, 1998. Among many dreams during the night, I saw the words printed, "The angel of God put one foot on the sea, another foot on the land. This angel is the Son of God, in fully God and fully man. He works through His Servant. The work was sent out on March 17, 1998 and will be on public record July 4, 1998." The date, month and year in this revelation are symbolism.

Today the Lord asked me to send this breaking news to several of the Church leaders who responded to letters He asked me to mail out over the last few years. These Church leaders are those who do not belong to the Diocese of San Diego and Vatican, although the Church leaders and Vatican were notified earlier.

That afternoon in my devotion I said to the Lord, "Lord, I will build three houses in my soul, one for the Father, one for the Lord Jesus, and one for the Holy Spirit. I will build another three houses in my heart, one for the Father, one for the Lord Jesus, one for the Holy Spirit. I will build three more houses in my physical body, one for the Father, one for the Lord Jesus, and another one for the Holy Spirit."

The Lord Jesus said, "Second Kings, chapter ten, verses one through eleven." After I finished reading it, He then said to me, "Jehu is you and the seventy princes and their descendants are symbolic of all Church component denominations." The church component also symbolic of religion.

March 19, 1998, the feast of Saint Joseph, chaste husband of the Blessed Virgin Mother. In my dream I saw a man a little to my right. In front of me, up high, his face was covered with white plaster, down to both of his ears and some part of his neck. I was angry and said to him, "You used all my stuff." Then the Lord said to me, "They wanted to have the same kind of anointing as you, but there is no one who has all the anointing that the Father poured upon you. It is in spirit." The words "It is in spirit" is the Lord reminded me of this revelation will take for while to manifest on earth.

Today I prayed to the Father of the Lord Jesus of intention during the mass. I then prayed to the Father for the Lord Jesus' intention of praying for His Church to be unified, so His wounds can heal.

During the Gospel and the homily the Lord brought back to me the dream where I saw Saint Joseph kneeling with a staff in his hand, in front of the manger filled with hay. This dream is written in the book "My Patient - God's Gift." Chapter 8, "What is the Holy Eucharist?"

With Carnal Eyes - Mariette Saw the Living God's Spirit at Saint Michael's Temple

After I received the Holy Eucharist, and while Father Joseph was giving the Holy Eucharist to others, I was kneeling at the end of the fourth pew, next to the center aisle of the right section. In spirit, with my carnal eyes, I saw in the air, God's throne covering two-thirds of Saint Michael's temple sanctuary. The Throne was formed by God's living Spirit, mixing fire and clouds, and moving up in the air. On the ground, around the sanctuary were reporters with cameras, choirs were wearing blue long gowns with white stoles at the quiet area next to the left of sanctuary. I then heard the Lord call, "Abraham", and the response, "I am ready." He then called, "Mariette," and I responded, "Lord, I am ready." As I said this, in my vision I saw the words "Mariette" and "I am ready." The letter "M" at the top, and letter "e" at the bottom. The letter "e" was laid on top of the letter "I" and made a corner. The way these letters made a corner is symbolic that I am ready as God's Servant, calling people to conversion, daily exam and repentance.

The Lord then said to me, "You come back this temple on Sunday, hide from the evil doers. Have Monsignor Joseph bless those anointing bottles of oil, and you keep both of them."

When I got home, in my devotion the Lord Jesus said to me, "Your keeping both bottles means the special God's grace is for you 'only', and not for others."

In Part I of this book, without my knowing anything, God revealed to me the physical structure of Saint Michael's Temple in Poway. At that time, it was foretold, and this time is fulfillment. Saint Joseph in my dream stretching his right leg is symbolic of prayer harder. Hay is food for sheep, symbolic of the Blessed Sacrament of the Altar. The Blessed Virgin Mother is symbolic of me, Mariette, a Vessel to God, as a head of the mission that God entrusted to me.

Then the angel showed me the river of life-giving water, sparkling like crystal, flowing from the throne of God and of the Lamb down the middle of its street. On either side of the river grew the tree of life that produces fruit twelve times a year, one each month; the leaves of the trees serve as medicine for the nations. Nothing accursed will be found there anymore. The throne of God and of the Lamb will be in it, and his servants will worship him. They will look upon his face, and his name will be on their foreheads. Night will be no more, nor will they need light from lamp or sun, for the Lord God shall give them light, and they shall reign forever and ever.

–Revelations 22:1-5

March 20, 1998, about 10:15 p.m. In my dream, the Lord Jesus told me, "After the confession tomorrow; you go to Wal-Mart to have the oil changed in your car. This will reverse the curse. At the time you heard Me tell you to move back to San Diego, you went to Wal-Mart in Arkansas and bought nothing. Bring fifty dollars to buy two chairs, to replace the two chairs that you returned to Wal-Mart before you left Arkansas."

I replied, "Lord, I do not have fifty dollars." He then said, "Bring one hundred dollars." I then said, "Lord, I had those kinds of beach chairs before, and I gave them to my oldest daughter. Why do you want me to buy two more chairs of that same kind?" The Lord then said to me, "The two chairs are the two bottles of anointing oil that were blessed yesterday." He then continued, "The scroll that John swallowed, sweet in his mouth and sour in his stomach is symbolic of the mission that the Father entrusted to you."

In the book "My Patient - God's Gift" the Lord Jesus promised that he will read the scroll to me.

The Righteousness of the Father

On March 21, 1998. After I saw some dreams, the Lord then told me, "When you go to mass in the morning, dress yourself in purple." That morning, when I put my purple dress on I said, "Lord Jesus, I put my purple on. I put my sash cloth on."

Before the Holy Eucharist celebration, the Lord Jesus told me, "After you received the Holy Eucharist and while Father Joseph was giving the Holy Eucharist to others, you saw the throne of God take over the whole upper sanctuary. People with movie cameras are those who heard the words of God but did not retain them in their hearts, and are like seeds that fall on the rocks and die. The choirs are symbolic of listening to God's word, thinking about it applied to their life, but when tribulation comes they turn their backs to God. They are like seeds that fall on bad soil, when they grow and do not have enough fertilizer they die. Those receiving the Holy Eucharist are symbolic of those who heard God's words, put it in their hearts and proclaim it. Father Joseph is symbolic of Church clergymen and laity ministers." He continued, "Fourteen John three." The Lord meant the Gospel of John, verse three."

"And if I go and prepare a place for you, I will come back again and take you to myself, so that where I am you also may be."

Diamond Necklace and Steel Heart Containing Holy Eucharist

March 25, 1998. In my dream I saw a man walking to the back of the altar. Following him was an altar boy, both were formed with clouds. While they were walking, the altar boy raised his right hand, and gave me a small, steel heart containing the Holy Eucharist. I received it with both of my hands. The dream changed, I stood at the end of the altar and was about to put that box on the altar, but I decided to keep it for myself.

I then saw my neck, I was wearing my Italian gold "V" necklace, on top of it was another pure gold necklace that half of it filled with diamonds. While I looked at it, I saw the twenty four diamonds sparkling out glints; these twenty four diamonds were laid from the center of my neck over my right shoulder, then an invisible hand moved them to the center. The night of March 26, 1998, I saw the Father's finger touch the part of gold that did not have diamond yet. When He lifted His finger up there was a diamond. He touch it many time, after finished, the entire necklace was filled with diamonds on top of gold.

That evening at 10:30 p.m. the Lord Jesus told me, "The suffering you went through for the last two days with the insurance company and the Church leaders are the beginning of your business. The last time you started was when you went to theology school. Now you are graduated with a master's degree in theology [the Lord meant that I am His Vessel]. After your graduation you have to go to work in the public. Church leaders will come to you, but you have to tell them what you want. You already told the bishop and the pastor here in San Diego, you need to call the cardinal and the other two bishops and a archbishop. The cardinal's office worker asked you to put your messages in writing. I will dictate to you what to send to them."

"Dear....As I have sent to you in the past, there is no freedom of religion in the United States, and you already know that the Lord Jesus' Church is divided into many parts. As long as His Church is divided, His wounds continue to increase.

I formally request that you and the assistants in your diocese assist me to restore the freedom of religion in the United State and throughout the world, and unify the Lord Jesus' Church. The restoration of freedom of religion includes ending the legal abortion law, stop generation of destructive weapons, and for lawmakers to pass laws under God's commandments.

The Lord Jesus told me that the reconciliation with God is the gate to the Holy Eucharist, and the Holy Eucharist is the road to heaven.

I ask you for a one-time service to the Father with Blessed Sacrament Exposition for thirty minutes. During the time of adoration, God will bestow His grace of conversion and repentance. Offer some time to assist people to examine themselves. You will provide priests for Sacrament of Reconciliation, and the Holy Eucharist celebration. All collections during this service will benefit seminarians at your diocese." The Lord words is full of symbolism; you now read my books to this part, I leave it up to you to seek God for the meaning of them because the Lord is speaking to you.

Our Lady of Carmel Visible to Mariette

Jesus the Lord told me go back to Good Shepherd church on March 24 and 25, 1998. March 25, 1998, was the Catholic component solemn feast of Annunciation of the Lord. Obeying the Lord, on this day, I contacted three of the Catholic component leaders, requesting the services to pray for unification of the Church and restoring freedom of religion in United States and throughout the world. One denied my request, the highest authority assistant passed it on to the pastor. The Lord then told me, "Tomorrow, you go to mass at Our Lady of Mount Carmel."

I went to mass at Our Lady of Mount Carmel on March 26, 1998. At the prayer of the faithful I requested to pray for the unity of the Church. On March 27, 1998, after the homily, Father Paul, presiding over the mass asked the congregation, "Does anyone have any questions?" I submitted, "Why are you different from other priests by breaking in the middle of the mass and let the congregation ask questions?" Father Paul gave his explanation, and I then said to him, "You are on the right road to serve God, and He will bless you, and I join you on this road. These are prophetic words." He said, "Thank you."

When he asked the congregation to pray for the sick, after several people submitted their petitions, I began to submit mine, but Father Paul said, "We are praying for the sick."

I said, "This is a prayer for the illness." He said, "Okay" I then continued, "[Eternal] Father, our illness is that we have not served You correctly. I ask you to help us to serve You and heal the illness of our hearts." While Father Paul gave assignments to five Eucharistic ministers before giving the Holy Communion, in spirit, with my natural eyes, I saw thick white cloud formed as the Blessed Virgin Mother sitting on an invisible chair, holding the infant Jesus in her left arm, and the infant Jesus was raising in front of Him a scapular with both of His hands. It started from high over the main altar and descended to above the Eucharistic minister who stood next to the right of the altar. Later that night in my vision, I was a child who came up in front of infant Jesus, and Jesus the Lord placed a scapular over the child's head.

The apparition is symbolism that God revealed to me that the power of God keep me stand firm, more quality of devotion to seeking God; and through all of these God protecting me; and through the Lord Jesus, the righteous of the Father conquer the devil will be visible on earth in God's Church

Guava Tree Needs Fertile Soil

March 17, 1998. I was close to the back corner of a large building, the building was filled with people like a Church's special feast. Every one faced the side of the building, and even though I did not see, I knew they were facing the altar.

I then saw several people around me get out their seat and form a line waiting to receive the Holy Eucharist. I came out and was the last one in the line. I saw a priest wearing a white alb with a purple stole approaching where we were stood in line. He then stood at the middle of the three way aisle and gave us the Holy Eucharist. After he gave me the flesh of our Lord, he turned to his left, I followed him by walking at his side to cross the building. Behind the people to my right, directly across from the altar was an entrance, although I did not see the altar.

The dream changed. I was entering the driver's seat of my car, there were several people sitting in the front bench, and these people left me very little room. I got in and pulled the door to close it, but the seat belt buckle laid in the way so I could not close the door. I opened the door wider, put the seat belt inside, at the same time I told those people, "All of you go to the back bench, so I can move in and close the door." These people opened the passenger door and went to back bench behind me.

I then saw my very healthy guava tree with big leaves was cut at the foot. People stood it on the concrete ground, next to the outside front corner of a small building, and tied it to the wall with a rope so the tree could stand straight. I looked at the foot of the tree, it was cut and had no root. I then look at the fertilized wet garden soil parallel with the building's side wall. Half of the garden had a trellis above and some things were planted under it. The other half did not have anything planted yet. I then said, "Put my guava tree in the good garden soil so it can stay fresh.

I then stood at the middle of the walkway between the building and the garden. Looking at my guava tree, I saw the side branch was missing. I was very angry that people had cut it off, I yelled at them. After I yelled at them I saw the top of the branch was missing on the roof, at the center, and on top of the building entrance.

The garden was in front of me while I was standing and holding three small healthy guava branches. I said, "I need a vase of water to put these in, so they can root."

People inside the building are symbolic of humans. The priest is symbolic of the Lord Jesus. People receiving the Holy Eucharist is symbolic of those who preach but do not put their preaching in their daily lives, or cut short on God's commandments. I was myself dwelling in God's Spirit through this mission.

An automobile is symbolic of the Lord Jesus' Church. People in the front bench moving to the back bench are symbolic of spiritual leaders incorrectly leading people to God. My getting in the driver's seat is symbolic of my being just God's vessel. Through me, the Lord Jesus is the one who shepherds His people. Putting the buckle back in the car and closing the door tight is symbolic of reconnecting the protection from God. People moving to the back bench is symbolic of the old teaching the meaning of God was incorrect

Fertilized wet soil is symbolic of God's grace. The guava tree standing on concrete and tied to the wall is symbolic of spiritual leaders exalting themselves not rooted in God's words. My anger and demanding to put the tree in the garden is symbolic of Church leaders exalting themselves. One branch being cut off is symbolic of those who already separated from these spiritual leaders. My holding all three small branches and finding a vase of water to put them is symbolizes through the power of God, I will help spiritual leaders and others come to God, become rooted in His words, and put God's words in their daily life.

Heavenly Insurance Agents are Visible

March 27, 1998. I was in the middle of folding two baskets of my clothes that I took out from the dryer and I felt the anointing upon me so that I could not do it any more, and I had to go to the foot of the altar. I took two bottles of holy water and sprayed throughout the house asked the Father to bless the house. After I finished, I went and laid at the foot of the altar praying. The Father said to me, "Now it is four thirty, from this hour in this world, your time, Highly favored Daughter, no one can touch you. Go on to your job, bring the Light to the world. Your business cards were given out to the public. Wait and they will come to you in the ways that I have for you. Through you, the world will see My begotten Son, who suffered and died for them."

March 28, 1998. While I was sleeping during the night, the Lord Jesus told me, "When

I came to Judea, there was a woman possessed by the devil for eighteen years. I set her free and I possessed her." He then continued, "The world depends on earthly life insurance. You go sell heavenly life insurance. You are the Debra sitting at the palm tree and summoning spiritual leaders to do the work; you assist them, but stay behind. The prophet stayed behind, he did not have to go in the field."

Before the 8:00 a.m. mass, while I was walking toward the Our Lady of Mount Carmel temple, I pleaded, "Father, Abraham's faith made him the father of many nations. In faith, I believe that I have been adopted in Jesus' fully man family." I then was in the Blessed Sacrament chapel, after I finished my devotion, still kneeling at the back of the tabernacle without my shoes, I was about to get up and put my shoes on, and get out to the main area of the temple for the Holy Eucharist celebration. The Lord told me, "Sit down, I need to speak to you." It took me several seconds to sit on the Blessed Sacrament chapel floor.

I then said, "Father, I believe that I am Jesus' only sister, this relationship is firm and no one can interfere with it. The steel heart box with the Holy Eucharist, I was about to put on the altar, but Jesus told me to keep it for myself. Father I need tools to serve You. Lord Jesus, send me tools so I can serve the Father and You. Holy Spirit help me with these tools." While I was saying this, I saw the dream on March 25, 1998.

The Lord said to me, "John, chapter thirteen." I then read John chapter thirteen to the end of verse twenty "Amen, amen, I say to you, whoever receives the one I send receives me, and whoever receives me receives the one who sent me." The Lord Jesus said to me, "Whoever receive you receives me, and whoever rejected you rejected Me."

In the old testament many times God spoke to Abraham, Isaac, and Jacob. He blessed them and their descendants from generation to generation. These three earthly names are also symbolic of the Holy Trinity.

The two baskets of dry clothes I was folding and putting away are symbolic the Lord Jesus teaching two thousand years ago was dried out and replaced with human designs and man lack of discernment.

The Father said to me, "Highly favored daughter, no one can touch you" is symbolic of God assuring me I am the Father's highly favored daughter, and through God's power I, a sinner, and convert will be adopted to the Holy Family and inherit the Highly favored status from the Blessed Virgin Mother, and the Lord Jesus as fully man's sister. Through God's power, this inheritance put on me the responsibility to enforce God's commandments.

Selling earthly insurance symbolizes earthly business expanding from generation to generation, to provide earthly products. Your selling Heavenly insurance is symbolic of God sending me down as an undercover agent to understand the earthly insurance products. After my conversion I showed the world the different between two products. The heavenly insurance business also needs to grow through the human race. Through this undercover action, the Lord placed me in an invalid marriage so my four children, two boys and two girls, will expanded the heavenly insurance business.

Through this adoption the heavenly insurance products will continue to visibly expand from generation to generation.

Understand God's Judging the World

Then Peter said to him in reply, 'We have given up everything and followed you. What will there be for us?' Jesus said to them, 'Amen, I say to you who have followed me, in the new age, when the Son of Man is seated on his throne of glory, will yourselves sit on twelve thrones, judging the twelve tribes of Israel.'"

–Matthew 19:27-28

Then he said to me: Son of man, these bones are the whole house of Israel. They have been saying, 'Our bones are dried up, our hope is lost, and we are cut off.' Therefore, prophesy and say to them: Thus says the Lord God: O my people, I will open your graves and have you rise from them, and bring you back to the land of Israel. Then you shall know that I am the LORD, when I open your graves and have you rise from them, O my people! I will put my spirit in you that you may live, and I will settle you upon your land; thus you shall know that I am the LORD. I have promised, and I will do it, says the LORD.

–Ezekiel 37:11-14

August 21, 1996, before sleeping. In my vision I saw a cloud form the throne of God, like a huge rock. Standing to the right of the throne was a little girl about nine years old, with dark blond hair, bound into tresses. She was wearing a short-sleeved dark, navy blue dress, with white polka dots, and both her hands held a pile of large size computer paper sheets with names. The Lord Jesus said to me, "Princess, hold tight to the Book of Life and read their names to Me."

August 27, 1996. As I prayed after receiving the Holy Eucharist, in my vision, I saw that the little girl remained in the same position, but the rock had changed into the front of the Good Shepherd's Image of the Lord Jesus, with a staff in His right hand (next to the girl.)

The cloud forming a rock and the Good Shepherd's image is symbolic of the Lord Jesus as fully man and fully God. He is the spiritual shepherd of His sheep until the final judgment. The computer paper represents the assignment that God assigned to me . The Lord saying to me, "Princess, hold tight to the Book of Life and read their names to Me," is symbolic of my responsibility to delivery to each one of you needing to hold tight to the

Lord God's teachings, to keep our name in the Book of Life, for these names will be called after each one's last breath. At the Judgment everyone will be judged according to his life on earth.

God's Just Judgment: *"Therefore, you are without excuse, every one of you who passes judgment. For by the standard by which you judge another you condemn yourself, since you, the judge, do the very same things. We know that the judgment of God on those who do such things is true. Do you suppose, then, you who judge those who engage in such things and yet do them yourself, that you will escape the judgment of God? Or do you hold his priceless kindness, forbearance, and patience in low esteem, unaware that the kindness of God would lead you to repentance? By your stubbornness and impenitent heart, you are storing up wrath for yourself for the day of wrath and revelation of the just judgment of God, who will repay everyone according to his works: eternal life to those who seek glory, honor, and immortality through perseverance in good works, but wrath and fury to those who selfishly disobey the truth and obey wickedness. Yes, affliction and distress will come upon every human being who does evil, Jew first and then Greek. But there will be glory, honor, and peace for everyone who does good, Jew first and Greek. There is no partiality with God.*

–Romans 2:1-11

Triumph of the Elect: *"After this I had a vision of a great multitude, which no one could count, from every nation, race, people, and tongue. They stood before the throne and before the Lamb, wearing white robes and holding palm branches in their hand. They cried out in loud voice: "Salvation comes from our God, who is seated on the throne, and from the Lamb."*

– Revelations 7:9-10

Who Receives the Servant Receives the Master

After I received the Holy Eucharist on March 28, 1998, Jesus the Lord told me, "Go say hello to the presiding priest at the mass today; and ask him if he would receive you."

After the mass, I was standing at the sacristy door and said to the priest, "Father, I just want to say hello to you. Father, what is your name? You are the Monsignor?" He turned facing me and said, "I am Father Frank, Monsignor, Pastor." I then said, "Would you accept me?" He asked, "Accept you for what?" I said, "Accept me to serve God." He said, "Yes, of course." I said, "You accepted me, you accepted Jesus, because Jesus is in me"

Before I meet with Monsignor Frank on March 30, 1998, the Pastor of Our Lady of Mount Carmel parish, I went in the Blessed Sacrament chapel. Kneeling in front of the tabernacle, both my arms held a file at my chest, a file containing several letters of God's commandments that were mailed out early to Vietnamese and United Governments officials, lawmakers, and Catholic leaders, and over one hundred letters of their responses. I prayed, " Jesus, Lord, God, I am alone with you. I renew my vow to the Father that I will do everything that Jesus asks me, even if I have to physically die. I only ask the Father to give me tools. I pray for my son Chau to pass the exam on Tuesday; my children to convert, and the world come back to You, Lord Jesus, and You lead them to the Father. Also for my daughter Tuanh and my son Chau to move back home." The Lord responded to me, "They [insurance company] have not sent your check out yet; they will automatically deposit it into your account. Your son will not pass the exam this time; but when his scores come back, he will understand why he did not pass, and he will pass the exam next time with high scores."

The purpose of the meeting was for me to deliver God's commandments of combining the three most important services into One service. The Blessed Sacrament exposition for about thirty minutes, followed with God's words calling for conversion, exam and repentance daily, and the Holy Eucharist celebration, plus praying for Unity of the Lord Jesus' Church and restored freedom of religion in United States and throughout the world.

But like me and many others being called by God in a special mission, Monsignor Frank (Henry) denied to received of what God asked me to delivery to him. After he denied three times, he then said to me, "All these things you said, I do not see them coming from the devil, they are good. They either came from you or from the Lord." I said to him, "I am here to deliver what God asked of me, you pray and the Lord will speak to you. I have denied this calling, and I know that if I continue to deny it, I suffer." He then said to me, "I will walk out with you."

The insurance company symbolic of God, check symbolic of God's power. My son is symbolic of myself; and he not pass the exam this time is symbolic of Monsignor Frank rejected to receive of what God asked me to delivery to him. The next time my son will pass the exam symbolic of I must seeking God more and be patient, God will full fill His promises.

Twin Men in Red Uniform

April 1, 1998. In my dream I saw twin men from behind, they were wearing fresh blood-red albs, the alb high collars were strong and bent out like a priest's chasuble. I put on a blended mixed purple and red colored dress, the outer layer was like a rain coat. The front of the dress was buttoned from the neck down to the hem. At the time I put it on, two thirds of the top buttons were open, I held it touching the ground to step inside. I saw the back collar was the same as the chasuble collars, and the front was tied with a scarf, both ends triangular shaped. These two ends of the handkerchief were the same as the two ends of the handkerchief I saw the Lord Jesus wearing over His head at the time He appeared to me in my bedroom, in Little Rock, Arkansas. That time I saw him with my natural eyes. Later in the same day I saw the right part of the collar under my jaw, and the right end of the collar was moving very fast.

The two symbolic of discernment. Red symbolize of spiritual battle. My dress is red mixed with purple symbolic of I must spiritual battle for kingdom of heaven.

Right Hand Palm Grows a Water Sprayer

April 4, 1998. In my dream I saw a water sprayer growing out of my right hand. From a distance, I shot water out to the left side of a dark man while he was walking. When he got behind a house, the water no longer shot out strongly, it got weaker and close to stopping. I turned to my left while I was sitting on my feet on the ground, passing the outside corner of the building where the man was hiding behind. After I turned and passed the outside building corner, I raised the water sprayer up and pulled the trigger again. Water shot out in a triangle, sparkling with light. Through this light, I saw three men swimming in the dark man-made ocean. Two men were black, following each other, and one man at the middle was closer to me than other two. The light from the water I shot out was shining down on the man-made ocean, so that I was able to see his human skin.

There were several dark people sitting at my left side. Behind me, in the distance was a white mobile home with a bright light inside. I knew that my daughter-in-law just moved in that trailer. She then came and sat next to me. I said to her, "You married my son and moved in the house when I left the city the last time."

After I received the Holy Eucharist in the next morning mass, the Lord Jesus told me, "Oh! Princess, everything you asked for is already there. The Word became flesh. God's words become actions."

The man made ocean symbolic of the world system. Three men symbolic counterfeit good actions. Water shedding out from my right hand symbolic of the righteous of God working through me in this mission to purify the world systems. The mobile home symbolic of heavenly army compound on earth. My daughter-in-law symbolic of people who either do not believe in God or do not know the real Creator of heaven and the Earth; they will learn and convert to God.

Star Landed on Top of University Mall Commercial Buildings

April 7, 1998. After I received the Holy Eucharist, in my vision I saw a huge star land on top of the roof of a commercial building at La Jolla Triangle Center, North University shopping mall. This star was formed with a white cloud, and its tail had seven flat bars and covered the entire dark sky.

The next day I saw sevens bands of its tail blended in one huge tail covering the entire dark sky. The Lord Jesus said to me, "In the old testament it was a seven year cycle; but for me it is a four year cycle.

Number seven is symbolic of the beginning of the end, seven is symbolic of holiness. White clouds are symbolic of God's existence, and refers to the star at Bethlehem when the Lord Jesus as fully man was born. April 7, 1998 is the fourth anniversary of the Lord taking me out from work to serve Him. That was my first transition from serving mammon to serving God. The way God called me to serve was very painful. This fourth anniversary of God putting me in a another painful situation purifies me more in depth.

Seeking understanding of the purification of the revelation, refer to the Book of Leviticus 16:28-29.

"If she becomes freed from her affliction, she shall wait seven days, and only then is she to be purified. On the eight day she shall take two turtledoves or two pigeons and bring them to the priest at the entrance of the meeting tent. The priest shall offer up one of them as a sin offering and the other as a holocaust. Thus shall the priest make atonement before the LORD for her unclean flow."

Restaurant Full of Customers, But No Food

April 7, 1998. In my dream I entered a deep rectangular restaurant. While I approached from the back, I saw all the chairs were filled and people were sitting, waiting for food to be served. I saw a counter that paralleled the back wall. Behind this counter was a Chinese man standing up high at the middle of the counter. When I saw this thin man standing on something high, I was able to see him from his lower belly up, I knew he was the owner of the restaurant. To his left sat a dark woman. I was saw her from her shoulder up, and to his right was his son. His son was a little higher than the woman.

I then stood in front of the owner and said something to him, after I finished speaking, he turned to his right, to the kitchen and said something to the people working in the kitchen at the back of the restaurant. He then returned to where he was and looked at the customers again. I talked to his son, this young man was a little over thirty five years old. I reached over the counter and saw under the counter, this young man was spreading his cards, like people showing playing cards. I said to him, "I used to have some of those cards, but I do not have them anymore."

I then walked to my left, I saw inside the kitchen door that the owner was there talking to his employees. I saw the inside was very dark; even though it was dark, I knew the cooking equipment was military equipment.

I was at the side of the kitchen, in the court yard talking to two man. I heard another sitting near by me say, "Someone is poor, they only have two thousand and want to purchase something that costs more than two thousand. I did not respond to this comment.

876

I stretched my spine straight, raised my face up, my chest forward, with both of my hands at my waist and said to these two men, "I am not afraid like them."

The dream changed, while I was standing to the right of a man, a person handed me a healthy green grape cluster.

God's Servant Riding on a Square Iron Bar

April 9, 1998. In my dream I sat on top of a square iron bar up in the air. In front of me was a little child, this child was facing me, and a driver was a young man, who sat behind the child facing the same direction as me. The light was shining at the spot where the child was sitting, and helped me to see the square iron bar very clearly between the child and the driver, and between me and the child.

Then both of the child's legs were moving down, I lifted up both of my thighs straight to the child's thigh level.

The driver is symbolic of the Lord Jesus. A child is symbolic of His mission that He entrusted to me. The square iron bar is symbolic of God enforcing His all commandments to purify people's hearts, minds and actions.

1998 Holy Wednesday

April 8, 1998. I was inactive as a Eucharistic Minister since I returned San Diego from Little Rock, Arkansas. Today I walked over to a man who did the set up at weekday mass. I said to him, "I told Monsignor Frank that I want to serve as Eucharistic Minister at this temple. I have been trained and served at the Diocese of Little Rock in Arkansas. He told me 'Sure, whenever you ready.' After that I registered at this parish [Our Lady of Mount Carmel]. Father Paul called me, he will have someone to call me." He said to me, "You talk too softly, I can not hear you, because my of hearing aid." He then called a woman nearby to come, I said to her the same as I said to the man. She then told me, "Can you serve the cup this morning?" I replied, "I am not dressed to be serving at the sanctuary." She said, "You are dressed beautifully to serve." She then continued, "If you stand at the left go to the left of the sanctuary, if you stand at the right then go to the right side of the sanctuary." I paused for the Lord Jesus' instruction, I then said, "Okay." I asked, "What is your name?" She responded, "My name is Francis." Immediately I left her and I thought of Saint Francis, she has her name.

There were two at each side, I was the one next to the host minister at the right. Francis went to me for the cup, through God's power, I said, "This is the blood of Christ." and handed a cup to her, while she was drinking, I said to her, "God blessed you."

During my afternoon devotion the Lord Jesus told me, "First Kings, chapter three for you from now until end of Easter Sunday."

After I read it, the chapter contained "Wisdom of Solomon and Solomon's judgment."

Jesus the Lord said to me, "The world has a dead child, you have the living one. The Father judged this case in the morning by your coming to that man, telling him you are a Eucharistic Minister. The woman trusted your words, and said to you, 'You serve the cup this morning.' If not from what the Father gave to her, how could she believe you. Francis put you in her place to serve God, and she came to you for God's blessing." The Lord continued and said to me, "You have not received my flesh in your hand for awhile, but for the custom, you received by hand today. While you looked at the consecrated host and believed in faith that it was my flesh, and finished the last drop of consecrated wine, knowing that was my blood. Suffering showed on your face, you stepped down three times to get closer to those who received the cup." While the Lord spoke, in my vision I saw the scene of my serving the cup at Our Lady of Mount Carmel in the morning.

Holy Saturday

April 11, 1998. During my afternoon devotion, I saw from inside the Our Lady of Mount Carmel temple, at the area for choice, several adults wearing colorful clothes in line, facing to the south. I asked, "Lord who are they?" I then saw from the center of the foot of the sanctuary, in the same spot, were the same number of adults in line, this time they were not sharp in body, but instead, they looked like they had been in the desert for a few days. Their hands were one on top of another at their waists, waiting to receive the Holy Eucharist, while the eternal Father formed with white cloud laid the Holy Eucharist in their hands. I moved closer to the right hand of the Eternal Father, these people now changed to teenagers, and the Eternal Father placed the Holy Eucharist on each of their hands quicker, and each of them received more than one.

I then saw at the right of the sanctuary, a black music iron stand. Behind it was a small teenage girl, standing on top of a shining, light wooden square box dais. This young girl's face looked like my face when I was her age. She was wearing a Vietnamese traditional formal outfit: a big gold turban and a gold ankle-length cloak. Also on the dais, to her left was a child wearing exactly the same outfit she wore. I then saw a child walking in between her and the music stand. Somehow the child was blended in one with her.

Easter Sunday

April 12, 1998. I went to the Blessed Sacrament Chapel before the holy celebration of the risen Christ mass, during this devotion the Lord Jesus told me, "The six seals were opened. You must prophesy against many peoples and nations. You are one of the two witnesses" He continued, "Enter the temple and sit at the first seat to the right."

When I got there, the front four seats were reserved. I obeyed the Lord and sat at the second center end seat to the right of the altar. To my left was a five year old girl, her mother was to her left, and her brother to her mother's left.

In Monsignor Frank's homily, he said that all the apostles were murdered, except Saint John. When he said this, I remembered the two witness that the Lord Jesus has revealed to me for last the four years. God kept Saint John from being murdered, and through Saint John, Jesus the Lord revealed Himself to the world, and what would happen next. Saint John is one of the two witness to testify of what he heard and saw after the Lord Jesus went home to the Father.

He was speaking of Saint John's spiritual life, because he stood at the foot of the cross. The others apostles spiritual life was death, they feared to be prosecuted, and scattered away from the Lord Jesus.

Almost two thousand years later, God revealed to me that God is a living God, the Holy Trinity. I have seen and heard from God and His power, through my dreams, visions, and with my natural eyes. Jesus the Lord is the only Son of the Father. He died and rose from the dead. His glorified body lives among us. The meaning of God's words are symbolism throughout the Holy Scriptures. God's words are living words and they come with His power.

While I was kneeling, after I received the Holy Eucharist, the Blessed Virgin Mother, my beloved Mother told me, "Ask the Father of what you want, He will give to you." I then said, "Mother, help me for what to say; holy angels and saints pray with me. Holy Spirit, help me to ask the Father. Lord Jesus, you know what the Father will give to me, help me of what to ask the Father, and help me to remember of what I am going to ask." I continued, "................. This petition is too long for me to remember."

The Father said to me, "Everything you asked is not for you, but for others to build the kingdom of heaven. Your throne in heaven is yours, earth is copy of heaven." When the Eternal Father said this, I saw the back of chair that was higher than the head, the top was triangular shaped and it had two poles at both sides. It was formed with a mix of gold and white living spirits. I then said, "Father, keep me humble."

Rebuild My Church Divine Mission

(The Lord Jesus gave this name to Mariette)

P.O. Box 261550 ✦ San Diego, CA 92196-1550

April 9, 1998

Armand Subia
KIEV 870AM Radio Station
Glendale, California

Re: Commercial to be air on 1998 Easter Sunday

Dear Armand,

Thank you for assisting me through KIEV 870 radio station. Per our telephone conversation today; enclosed is a check for $400.00 and four scripts, for four commercials of sixty seconds each time to be aired on Easter Sunday. The amount left over, use for another slot on the air to benefit the U.S. citizens. The times on Easter Sunday are around 8:45 a.m, 11:00 a.m, 6:00 p.m., and 8:30 p.m. as we spoke on the phone; if there are any changes, please let me know.

I also enclosed some copies of letters to President Bill Clinton as an individual and as the President of the United State, first lady Hillary, and the U.S. Senate. We are together as God's servants to make this nation be better a place to live and to build the kingdom of heaven.

I continue to pray for you, your family and the KIEV radio station employees. If you need more information or have any questions, please contact me at (619) 689-0445.

Sincerely in Christ Jesus,

Mariette Do-Nguyen

Commercial Scripts air on 1998 Easter Sunday

In spirit, several times during the past years, with Mariette Do-Nguyen's carnal eyes, she saw the Eternal Father in His Son's image and the Lord Jesus in glorified body several times. Over the past several years, days and night, through Mariette Do-Nguyen, dreams, visions, and the voice of God, God revealed the systems of the world go against Him, and the future of the next centuries. Tragedies such as heavy rains, storms, floods and

880

tornadoes are God's warning to purify its systems. These tragedies are just beginning, and will not end until people convert to God. Mariette is co-author of "My Patient - God's Gift"

A. When the U.S. government uses tax moneys to fund programs against God's commandment, such as generating destructive weapons, supporting abortion and training for abortion, to destroy human race, and investigating leads to dead ends, these actions violate human rights and freedom of religion. Each U.S citizen must stop this government spending, to restore the freedom of religion in the United States, by a peaceful solution for the right of each citizen to determine how tax dollars are to be spent.

B. Jesus the Lord said, "Let the one among you who is without sin be the first one to throw a stone at her." Let us change the face of the Nation: President Bill Clinton is standing at the White House front porch, God calls the U.S citizens, "who has no sin throw a first stone at him." God calls government officials and lawmakers to unity in one with Him in love, not to judge one another.

C. Most Christians think that the Lord Jesus gave the authority in heaven and earth to Saint Peter, by giving him the key. The sacred scriptures means that the rock is symbolic of standing firm. The other said, "feed my lambs, tend my sheep, feed my sheep." The Lamb is the lamb of God; Feed is bread coming down from heaven to nourish our souls; tend is symbolic of the Good Shepherd. Jesus the Lord used Saint Peter to revealed Himself, not Saint Peter. God calls us to Unify His only Church, and He is the head.

D. Mariette's second book "GOD'S PURIFICATION - NOT EASY" is approximately 500 pages in large size, and will be published in the third quarter of 1998. This book explains in detail of God's purification, and is a guide to understanding God's commandments hidden in the scriptures, and the symbolism in the Book of Revelations, anointings, UFOs, discerning visions and voices; and how the power of the devil works through people's minds and actions, plus how to heal and prevent mental illness, and fight against the devil's power. The bookstore price is $45.00, but if you order in advance of the printing without sending money, you will be billed a discount price of $40 just prior to the book's mailing.

KIEV. 870 AM aired at 7:00 a.m; 7:30 a.m, 2:00 p.m., and 2:30 p.m. on Easter Sunday April 12, 1998.

39

FIRST DEATH, SECOND DEATH AND FINAL JUDGMENT

When is the Final Judgment?

Blessed and holy is the one who shares in the first resurrection. The second death has no power over these; they will be priests of God and of Christ, and they will reign with him for [the] thousand years.

–Revelation 20. 6

The first death is death to self, the second death is death to the physical body. Death to self means converting to God, surrendering your life to God, and obeying all His commandments; to die for the Lord Jesus and live with Him. When a person gives death to self for the Lord Jesus, that person will live with Him in both natural and spiritual life. God's power will work through this person; therefore, the death of the physical body will not cause death to the soul. Instantly, when the soul enters heaven, his or her soul will receive a glorified body. This body is like an angelic body, sometimes here and sometimes not here.

December 31, 1997. In my dream I was in an open area with some other people, between an iron fence and in front of a huge building that had a cathedral ceiling like a church. I saw the inside of the building was on fire under the ceiling, and the people were trying to evacuate. This fire was getting larger and larger, and huge, then it was all over on the floor. The people were trying to evacuate, but they could not do anything.

I turned to my right and walked to the front left corner of the fence. Just as I turned, I saw my mother walking from the corner of the fence toward the front of the building. When I saw her, I was concerned about my family's jewelry. I was about to ask her about it, but there was little distance yet, and another person was walking to the corner in between us. I then walked faster to pass this person, and ask, "Mother, where is our jewelry?" She said, "Our jewelry, I separated it from the building and put it at the park."

As she said this, I saw the living spirit at the park, afar on the other side of the building, higher than the level of the top of the building.

I then was walking on top of a fence. This fence was built with many black iron square bars standing up, four long bars were on top of them, and made four corners around the building. When I got to the back of the building, there was a small security guard booth, but it was built only like a fence, with three sides of it connecting to the fence that I was walking on. One side was a building fence. I said to this person, "There is a fire inside the building." I then continued my walking. When I got to the middle of the last side of the fence, I saw water running on the ground and light shining on the water.

I then saw my living room, in front of the altar, at the foot of the Christmas tree an invisible hand of the Lord lifted up a visible square box. The box had two parts, the deep bottom and a lid, sparkling silver with green Christmas color wrapper paper, with yellow ribbon around, and a bow on the top.

The house is symbolic of the earth. Fire is symbolic of the God's power purify the world systems. Mother is symbolic of God, with Jesus the Lord coming down to judge. People standing outside the building are symbolic of souls in purgatory. A person in the security square booth at the fence is symbolic of holy angels. The park is symbolic of heaven. The gift box is symbolic of good deeds sent to heaven before we go to heaven.

God Revealed Sending Mariette on a Mission in the Field, and She Must Remain in Her Realm

In the Blessed Sacrament, in the evening of June 20, 1998, immediately after I went out from confession, the Lord told me, "God blessed you to go in and out with pastual. Proverbs chapter four for you and chapter seven for the priest."

During the night of June 21, 1998. In my dream I was outside a front door of the last room to the right of a one story building. I faced up to the sky, and around me was a large crowd of people. I saw in the sky, to my right, three faces. These faces were carved into a huge tree, the light mingled with gold fire shining on their faces, making their noses and eyes more clear on their faces. The body of the tree was their face, three noses and six eyes formed a triangle. One set of eyes and nose was on top, the second set of eyes and a nose was below to the right, and the third set of eyes and a nose was to the left of the second, and it was a little lower than the second. When I saw this, I knew I was seeing God in my dream.

I then looked below this image and there was a large aircraft formed with white clouds, parked on the ground. The largest percent of the people on the dry dirt ground with me were following a large tall man going toward where the aircraft was parked. I went with them a few steps, but I separated from them and walked to my left. When I started to separate from the large group, both my arms held my green covered Vietnamese-English dictionary. I then followed behind a small group of people in the dark area. I was the last one entering their security gate, this gate was a dark rectangular shelter. Although there was no security guard, inside was a rectangular, dark, high table. I left my dictionary on the table corner, the corner next to the other side of the entrance. While I was walking in their rectangular compound, I saw the compound was secured with eyes wire fence. To my right was a row of several pick-up trucks, side by side, heading toward the fence. These were empty pick up trucks, they had no camper, no back seat, and each of them only had one front bench for drivers and passenger. I tried to get in one of these trucks twice. The first time the truck was full, I then walked forward deep into their compound, and tried a different truck. When I reached this truck and was about to try to get in the passenger seat, I saw a man was already there. He was trying to get in the drivers seat, but there wasn't enough room for him and for me.

I then picked up my dictionary, and left out the same gate I entered, to return to the one story building. I crossed the dry dirt ground and entered a door in the center room of this building. Inside the door of the dark room I saw some light shining on a table, this table had two black books laying next to each other. The books were the same side and thick as the Bible I have in the natural world. I had to pick up these two books, but I wanted to make sure these books were mine. With my right hand, I opened the book to my right, the second page inside the front cover was printed in black ink, in a large title "Jew and denominations." I then left the room by the same door I entered, with both of the books. The open book was in my right hand, and the sealed book was in my left hand. I then made the right to the next door, the last door to the right of the building.

When I entered the door, to my left was a wall, about ten feet directly from the door, and close to the wall was a rectangular table. To my right was the large group of people and the leader who had just returned from the trip, all of them faced the table. I then stood at the table covered with white linen and laid my big green dictionary at the beginning top corner (my top left corner), and the two black books, side by side, on the center table.

The dream changed. I then saw inside a twenty five gallon, round bamboo planter basket. The bottom around the side was lower than the center, at this lower part was some fertilized wet soil, and a new clear plastic water holder covered the entire bottom of the basket.

Before I got up in the morning of June 21, 1998, the Archangel Gabriel brought back to me four visions I saw more than two years ago, the Blessed Virgin Mother statue at Good Shepherd. Her station was at the corner, and in front of her was a hall. One vision showed small dry branches all over the floor, and another vision was to her left, where the glass window was covered with black iron square bars fence. Both ends of the hallway were also protected with the same kind of black square iron bars. I stood looking inside, it felt like a prison.

Another two were in my dreams: I saw up high in heaven, several angels were looking up and blew their trumpets; another angel holding a lighted candle landed at the parking lot in front of the restaurant. All of these angels were formed with thick white clouds. He said to me, "The Father created a special realm for you. He boxed you in a box. You have very little room to move in the nature, (the discipline in natural). Below the Blessed Virgin Status was a snake, and on the ground were dry branches, these dry branches are symbolic of the devil's trap in front of you, if you step out of the discipline, you will be hurt. The youngest (Tuanh) blowing her trumpet is symbolic of you, and this was revealed in the Book of Revelations, the number seven angel blew his trumpet. The angel landing with the candle is you, God's Servant bringing light to the world."

The man trying to get in the driver's seat and the leader of the large group is symbolic of the Lord Jesus as fully man in glorified body. The three faces carved into the tree are symbolic of one God in three persons, the Holy Trinity. The white cloud aircraft is symbolic of the God pour out His Spirit to save the world. The compound with empty trucks are symbolic of the one third of the human race that will not enter heaven. They are rejecting the Lord Jesus, they also rejected me, Mariette, God's Servant. The middle room I went in to pick up the two books is symbolic of the Holy Trinity's throne on earth. The sealed books are symbolic of those who have not believed or worshipped the true God, the Creator of heaven and Earth, His only Son, and the Holy Spirit, and they will converted. The room to the right with the table and filled with people returning from the trip is symbolic of those convert to God. The people following the leader is symbolic of those who believe and worship the true God, the Holy Trinity. The green dictionary is symbolic, I understand the meaning hidden under stories of the Holy Scripture, and the symbolism in the Book of Revelation, Daniel, Ezekiel, and in my dreams and visions, and the voice of God; I then deliver to others.

Through God's power, the Blessed Mother adopted me, Mariette as her only daughter, and she bestowed all her estate unto me. Therefore, when I saw the Blessed Virgin Mother, she is symbolic of me, that I am following in her footsteps as God's Servant. The iron bars around her are symbolic of the Father boxing me in with discipline. The dry branches on the hall floor are symbolic of the devil's traps working through human bodies.

After the 9: a.m. mass on Sunday, June 21, 1998, I went in the Blessed Sacrament Chapel. While I was praying, the Pastor of Saint Michael's temple came and opened the tabernacle, emptying the consecrated host from one ciborium to fill another ciborium. The Archangel Michael said to me, "You are receiving the Father's glory, this glory will shine upon the world. You are receiving the Father's power. You are receiving the grace of conversion from the Father, and distributing it to the world. You are receiving the Father's peace through the Lord Jesus, give this peace to the world."

God Sent Mariette to Washington, District of Columbia on Mission

At the end of June 1998, Father Thuy shared with me the Commemoration of the 200th Anniversary of the LaVang's apparition at the National Shrine Immaculate Conception Basilica in Washington, DC. This commemoration also had a three day discussion conference, and he encouraged me to attend it. I responded to him that I did not know if the Lord Jesus would allow me to go. After that, during my devotion, I knew that I would be able to go without details. I called Father Long, the Chairman for commemoration organizer committee to make a reservation. Immediately after I introduced myself, he asked me, "Mariette, are you Father Dominic's niece?" I replied, "Yes." At this time it was about 11:00 a.m. Pacific time, and his time was about 2:00 p.m. Father Long said to me, "There is too much work to do, I have been working since this morning, and have not eaten anything today. I have been working very hard, but I do not know that I please the Blessed Mother."

After I called Father Long for the reservation, the Lord Jesus asked me, "What are you going to do when you attend that discussion conference? I have been teaching you. You will be able to come to that discussion conference one or twice, but not all the sessions." At this point I knew that I would be in Washington DC during this time, but was not sure of how and what the Lord wanted me to do. I quickly sent a letter to Father Long to cancel the reservation. During this devotion, the Lord also told me, "Do not tell Father Long on the phone, but wait until you see him, tell him that he is busy Martha." I then called Father Long again and told him that I would be unable to attend all the meeting, but I will attend the convocation for four nights. He told me to send him $300.00 to cover the hotel bill, and that did not include food. I could not stay in the same hotel with those attending the conference, because they must attend all of the meetings, but I was not. Therefore, he put me at the Holiday Inn with others. I did as Father Long told me, but when I called the hotel for a reservation, they wanted my VISA credit card number, so I gave the VISA number to them.

After the Lord told me this, I felt that the priests and people in this conference would reject me in some way. I then refused to go, but the Lord told me, "I can have you meet Archbishop Thuan when he comes to California, or send you to the Vatican. But I have designed this commemoration for you to meet with the Archbishop, Senator Ashcroft's Liaison , and several other people that I call to assist you in this mission." Hearing there are will be people to assist me gave me courage. After I got everything ready, I heard Father Thuy tell me that Monsignor Luong told him not to go, instead, to stay at the parish to serve the congregation while the Monsignor and other priests go. I was sad, but I accepted that God did this for a reason.

Father Long offered to provide transportation from and to the airport, and between the hotel and the Catholic University (places for discussion conference) and National Shrine Immaculate Conception Basilica, with no meal. I told him that due to my arrival at Baltimore Washington Internal Airport being very late (12:10 a.m;) I would get my own transportation to the hotel. But two people from the commemoration committee, Deacon Huong and Ms. Kim Nga called to verify information of my arrival so they could pick me up. Obeying God of telling me to let them pick me up from the airport, and asking them for transportation to and from visiting Senator Ashcroft's Liaison, Kris Ardizzone, regarding the petition for civil right to freedom of religion and regarding tax money benefits program against God's commandments, I asked Father Long, Deacon Huong, and Ms. Kim Nga for transportation to and from the Senate building in Washington, DC.

I left San Diego after 2:30 p.m. on August 19, 1998, and arrived at the Baltimore, Washington airport at 12:10 a.m. the next day. Mr. Lien and Mr. Cuong waited to pick me up and welcomed me in such happiness. It took over thirty minutes to drive to the Our Lady of Vietnam parish rectory. Entering the rectory, we passed one open door at my left where a man worked in front of a notebook computer. We went into the dining room, and Father Long was working there. When Father Long saw me he was very happy of my arrival and welcomed me. I said hello to him in Vietnamese with a very respectful manner. He repeatedly asked me to have a seat across the dining table. While I was standing at his right smiling, I silently asked the Lord Jesus for instruction. I then said to Father Long, "The Blessed Mother told me to tell you that you work like Saint Martha. You know the holy scriptures. You know what that means." He replied, "I am doing bustle works." He gave me a refund for the hotel check of $300.00. In turn I gave him two checks, each one hundred dollars, one hundred for a donation to the commemoration of 200th Lavang's apparition, and one hundred for musical brunch tickets honoring Archbishop Thuan's visit (seventy dollars for the musical and thirty dollars for brunch). Then Mr. Cuong dropped me at College Park Holiday Inn at 1:30 a.m. .

August 19, 1998. In my dream I saw an old priest, over fifty years old. He just returned from someplace. When I saw him, I knew that before he left, he took my treasury with him and used it to build his credit. He now returned, and did not appreciate my treasury that build his credit; his actions made me very angry. I said, "Lord, why I am so angry at him? Forgive me." The Lord Jesus told me, "When you gave church leaders information that I revealed to you, they took it, crossed your name off, and used it for their own purposes." He continued to say to me, "You came down to serve others. Do not get angry at them, when your book is published, people will know where the information came from."

August 20, 1998. It was very hard after losing three hours in the time zone change, and I woke up at 6:00 a.m. for the 8:15 a.m. mass. After I returned from mass at Saint

Joseph's temple, I was not sure how to get to Washington DC for the 2:00 p.m. appointment at Senator Ashcroft's office. I asked the hotel to either get a cab or a rental car. But the Lord told me, "You do not know the roads; ask the hotel clerk for a shuttle to the rectory, ask the priest for a ride to the Senator's office." I then arrived at Our Lady of Vietnam's parish rectory about 11:00 a.m. I asked Father Long for a ride, but he was too busy, and unable to help me. I went to the next room, asked another man, he was also unable to help me, but he brought to me Mr. Tuan, the parish committee chairman. Mr. Tuan told me that he would find someone to give me a ride. Then another man came and told me that they could not give me a ride. I then followed this man downstairs where more people were. At least three people had authority for transportation but they told me that there would be no one who could drive me to Washington DC at the time of my appointment. If I could change my appointment early then they would help me. (The important thing was for me to get to the U.S. Senate building for the meeting that the Lord sent me). I went upstairs and tried to call Senator Ashcroft's office, but there was no phone available for me to use. I then went downstairs and asked them to give me a ride at that time, about 11:30 a.m. They then allowed Mr. Thien to give me a ride. On the way to Washington DC, Mr. Thien and I talked a little of how I was going to return to the hotel. I told him that if he could return, to pick me up between 3:30 and 4:00, otherwise I would take a cab.   Before Mr. Thien left he told me that because he had no way to call me, he asked me to wait at the corner from 3:30 to 4:00. If he was unable to come then I would take a cab. Indeed, I got out of the appointment at 3:00 p.m. and waited until 4:00 p.m., then took a cab to the hotel.

(See the meeting with Senator Ashcroft's Liaison in "Restored Freedom of Religion in the United States" chapter).

I got to the hotel around four thirty; I then prayed. The Lord told me, "A little later you will go to eat, get dressed and go to meet the Archbishop tonight.   After I prayed, I went to the hotel restaurant for dinner, took a shower, got dressed, and arrived at the Catholic University in Washington DC by cab a little after seven that evening.

When I entered the auditorium, I saw people attending the discussion conference and about a dozen priests already there.   Deacon Huong handed me a red folder with a blue pen.   Facing people when I was walking in, I asked the Lord, "Jesus, where do you want me to sit?" I then took a seat up high in the back, at the same entrance door side aisle.

In Archbishop Thuan's speech was a story that had the strongest of God's commandments hidden under them, and a sermon:

Story: "There were two ball teams, the Lutherans and the Catholics were playing against each other. The Lord Jesus was in the audience. When Lutheran team wins, the Lord Jesus raised up with joy; then the people in the audience said to each other, 'He must be a Lutheran team fan.' When Catholic team wins, the Lord Jesus also raised up with joy and the others said, 'He must be Catholic fan.' They then said, 'He is crazy.'

Sermon: He told the audience to speak the truth without fear. From speaking the truth they will open up, and come to conversion. After the Archbishop spoke, I went out and said hello to him for a few minutes for the first time. I also asked to meet with him during this pilgrimage, he did not give a specific time, but he said, "we will meet again."

The meeting was over about 10:00 p.m. I looked for Father Long to ask him to assist me in finding someone to give me a ride to the hotel, but I could not find him. I then asked Deacon Huong, he told me that I must call a cab. I thought this late inside the university, and I am a woman in a strange city, how can I find a cab? I then asked a few others, but everyone was going to Hampton, while I was going to Holiday Inn. I ran across a friend, she is a citizen of Virginia, and asked her if she could help me. She turned around and asked a priest that give her a ride, but the priest did not want to help me. She told me that she rode with them, so she had to go.

I asked the Lord, "Jesus, I need a ride back to the hotel." He told me, "Go outside the auditorium, there is someone who will give you a ride." I then went out the door, to my right was an Episcopal priest who came from San Diego on the same flight with me. I asked, "Father Mai Bien, would you give me a ride to the hotel?" He replied, "I need to ask Father Tinh, who is also an Episcopal priest. He lives nearby and has a car." He then went inside the auditorium, then came out and told me, "Wait until after he pays for the book." He then came inside the auditorium again trying to ask Deacon Huong, but I ran behind him and told him, "Do not ask him, he does not want to help." When Father Tinh came out, Father Mai Bien asked Father Tinh, and Father Tinh asked me where the hotel was. He then consented to give me a ride to the hotel.

While we were walking away from the auditorium, I told them, "God's words are true: The priest and the Levite saw a person being beat up, and did not want to help, but the Samaritan man cleaned up the victim and took him to the inn." We met Archbishop Thuan, after Archbishop Thuan shook Father Mai Bien's and Father Tinh's hand, I walked between the Archbishop and the two Episcopal priests, and I said to the Archbishop, "Catholics do not want to give another Catholic a ride, but the Episcopal priest gave me a ride."

When we got in the car, Father Tinh and Father Mai Bien looked on the map for Baltimore Blvd., College Park, Maryland, but was unable to find Baltimore, because the map did not have street details. We then left after everyone else. Going for several minutes, Father Tinh stopped on a side road and looked on the map again, but still could not find Baltimore Blvd.. Father Tinh then pulled into the shopping parking lot to seek directions. We crossed the shopping center security patrol car and asked them, they told us to follow them. We followed the security car to the Baltimore Blvd. exit, and they left.

A few minutes after they began to look on the map, I repeatedly said, "God's words are true, the priest and the Levite did not want to help, but the Samaritan helped. The man being beat up at the side of the road is the Lord Jesus, priests and Levites ignored him." But the Blessed Mother told me, "Let them find the way." She meant for me to be quiet, so they could find the way and take me to the hotel. I then stopped speaking out loud, and started praying for direction.

When I got back to the hotel, I was really hurt for being rejected. Even though it was midnight, I called the airline and tried to change my flight to return to San Diego, but I was not successful. Since trying several times did not work, I thought that the Lord did not want me to return yet. I then went to sleep. While I was asleep, the Lord Jesus told me, "You are fighting against them (people attending the discussion conference spirits). You do not understand in spirit; and you will understand later. Tomorrow they will come and pick you up. You will not attend the discussion conference. You need to go to the District of Columbia" But I did not believe Him that people would come to pick me up.

The next morning I did not go to join the group for the 7:00 a.m. mass at the Catholic University, instead, I went to Saint Joseph for an 8:15 a.m. mass. I returned to the hotel to have breakfast. After I finished my breakfast, I went to talk with some people in the hotel restaurant. There was Ms. Hanh, an Our Lady of Vietnam parishioner, she also was quiet, and related that Father Long would come to pick up the family for a drive. One of the young girls in the family asked me if I want to join them. I asked where they would go, but they had not decided. Hanh was the driver, so I asked Hanh to give me a ride with them. We then ended up at the National Shrine, Immaculate Conception Basilica, next to the Catholic University.

When I got there, I separated myself from them. I went in the Blessed Sacrament Chapel to pray, and walked inside the Basilica to look at some images. I then went down to the gift shop, and I saw the family I drove with. I was making a decision of either going to the Capital or taking a trolley tour in the District of Columbia. I asked the girl who invited me to join her family if they wanted to go with me, but they did not want to go.

I took a cab to Union Station to get on the Old Town Trolley Tours of Washington for two and a half hours. During this two and a half hour tour, the trolley stopped eighteen times for tourists to get off and see the sights, and every thirty minutes a trolley would come to pick up the tourists at the stop. When we got to the White House, I got off the trolley, walked away a few steps, then changed my decision and reentered the trolley to continue the tour. At the time the trolley stopped at the National Cathedral, I got off and entered the Cathedral to check out the inside of the National Cathedral. (I was very careful with the supernatural power in every temple that I enter. The decorations and activities in the temple are the things that spirits attach to.) I saw several tourists groups, and in the front center was a sign, "Eucharist Service at noon," and in front was "The house of prayer." These signs gave the purpose that this temple was built for worshipping God, and believed in Jesus the Lord's resurrection, His body is hidden in the Holy Eucharist as nourishment for souls.

I walked toward the sanctuary, and entered the area reserved for children. I was looking at images of the Lord Jesus with other holy saints. While I was looking at the Lord Jesus' image, he reminded me, "Do not be late for the trolley." I then quickly got out of the Cathedral, on the way out I understood that He used this trolley to remind me not to be late for the work that God entrusted to me. After finishing the tour, I had my dinner at the Union Station, and took the train back to College Park, Maryland. This was the first time in my life that I remembered riding the train.

The night before Saturday, August 22, 1998, the Lord Jesus instructed me, "Tomorrow, you will attend the mass at the Immaculate Conception Basilica, but do not participate in the procession. While they are in procession, you will be at the Blessed Sacrament Chapel. There will be many people remaining inside without participating in the procession. You will not attend the musical program and lunch for honoring the Archbishop."

I went to the Blessed Sacrament chapel before and after the Holy Eucharist celebration, to worship God, and honor my beloved Blessed Virgin Mother. I then had lunch, and after lunch I was in the lower level of the Basilica, talking to a few people from other states. When I got to the public telephone in front of the gift shop to call the cab, there was a young lady waiting for other people using telephone. When a phone was available she told me to go ahead because she needed a hotel to stay overnight, and would catch the early flight tomorrow to return to Florida. When I was searching for coins, she asked me, "Could you help me with calling this phone number? I'm going to a hotel." I replied, "Father Long, the Chairman for this event reserved two hotels in Maryland, Hampton Inn and Holiday Inn., they charged us a group rate, lower than the regular rate. I am staying at the Holiday Inn. If you want to stay at the Holiday Inn, here is their telephone number." She asked me, "Would you call the hotel for me, I am here with a close friend of advanced age." I then covered my forehead with my left hand and silently prayed, "Lord, what would you want me to do?" (I know that Jesus as my Lord and my God, as well as my dearly beloved brother always answers me immediately, either in voice or silently.) I then said to her, "My room has two beds, there is an extra bed, you and your friend can stay overnight. But I pray a lot." She was extremely happy, and said, "me friend wants to stay for the musical program." But I told her, " I bought the ticket for seventy dollars, but I am not attending." She then said to me, "I will tell my friend not to go, too. Instead, we will go with you to the hotel." She then quickly found her friend within a minute.

During the time Thien Nga Nguyen and Nhiem Nguyen stayed with me, Thien Nga told me that on Saturday morning, she and her friend were be on line at the Capitol Hill for a ticket to see the Capital at 7:00 a.m. After two hours, by 9:00 a.m. it was their turn and there were no more tickets for that day. There were a few other people who promised Thien Nga and Nhiem to stay with them, but they all got lost.   She also shared that last year, 1997, her parish organized an Our Lady of Lavang pilgrimage, and there were about fifty people, but this year was no one went, except her and her friend Nhiem. We had dinner together at the hotel restaurant, Thien Nga poured out twenty dollars and insisted to pay for the cab, but I did not let her do that, she then laid a twenty dollar bill inside one of my books, but I gave it back to her. She also insisted on paying for the stay, but I said no. At the dinner, Thien Nga got up and tried to pay for my dinner, but I did not let her do that.

August 23, 1998. After I ordered a cab for Trina Nguyen and Nhiem Nguyen, I went to the 10:00 a.m. mass at the local Catholic temple. I then went back to my room and prayed and rested a little before I went to the airport for returning to San Diego.

It is a Biblical pattern, a Virgin with a child and bearing a son in Isaiah 7:14. The child is symbolic of a mission, the Virgin is the Blessed Virgin Mary called by God on the mission to be Mother of our Lord Jesus. The Lavang apparition is the action of the river giving living water in the Book of Revelations 22:1-5, a woman with the child in chapter 12, and the seventh angel blowing his trumpet.

The parable of the Good Samaritan in the Gospel of Luke 10:29-37 has symbolism. The beat up man in this Gospel is symbolic of the poor, sick, widowed, homeless, lowly, and children, and all those who need help. Jesus the Lord is with or in them. The priest is symbolic of spiritual leaders and government officials in high positions. The Levite is symbolic of the second ranking in the church and governments title. Both of these ranks are a comfortable position, and they are denying to help the needy. The Samaritan traveler is symbolic of those have no title, and need no title in earthly church do help other when they needed assistance.   God teaches each one of us must obey "all" God's commandments, applying the virtual of love from our hearts to actions in our daily life. When there is no human watching, only God knows our hearts and actions. The virtue of love is above all other virtues.

For this reason, Jesus was born in the stable and in cold weather, instead of in an expensive home or hotel, and during His earthly life He lived in a poor village, wearing sandals. His ministry was with sinners, the poor, and those who needed Him the most.

God knows the hearts of His chosen ones, those who are willing to convert and follow His footsteps.   Indeed, during the trip when He sent me to Washington, on the commemoration of the 200th anniversary of the Lavang apparition, God put me in both positions, the man beaten by robbers, and the Samaritan traveler to have experience so I can speak about the need, the responsibility of spiritual leaders in their vows, and other people to following Jesus' footsteps at any time and every places. The truth God's servants are those services to other when no one watch him or her; and give thank to God when He answered to our request.

People respect the Seven Holy Orders Sacrament that is given to priests, bishops, archbishops, and cardinals. It is easy to find help for themselves and for others in their local parish, diocese, and in strange cities. One of the most important vows for those receiving the Holy Order Sacrament is to serve God; and serving God is giving service to others. Therefore, the "obligation" for the priests vow is to help people at all times, even when they are at home, traveling, attending conferences, or at convocations. There is no executive that priests, bishops, archbishops, and cardinals in strange cities with no transportation, or who do not know the road, should not give assistance. In fact, they must find those who need assistance to help them. This is one of the reasons the Lord Jesus chose male instead of female. The vow to serve God through service to others is also the obligation for deacons as well.

Jesus the Lord came down to serve, He washed the apostles feet. We are following in His footsteps of service to others. The word "others" means no difference in religion, color, nationality, poverty, handicapped, widows, homeless, or beggars. Therefore, each time they organize a convocation, the local parishes and dioceses congregations, we as children born by God, have an obligation to serve God through services to others that come from other cities. We also have to serve God in services to others at any time in our daily life.

We must have faith in God, when a person completely surrenders his or her life to God, and completely depends on Him, He will provide guidance and protection at all times.

White Writing on Purple Banner

August 24, 1998. After I returned from the Mission trip to Washington, District of Columbia, in my dream I saw banners formed with fire covering the horizon in front of me. A little distance to my right, a young woman was making these fire banners. Off in the distance to her right was her spouse in a dark shadow . I went to her and stood at her left to ask her to help me make a banner. At the moment I reached her left side, my long large purple banner was already in front of us. I then took her hand and showed her where to put the white writing on this purple banner. After she finished three letters, I let her continue to do it herself, she dropped a line down below the three letters we just finished. I then told her, "White writing on purple will be very clear to read the words." She then told me to wait because she is busy helping other making those fire banners. Immediately when she said this, I heard the voice of God say "crush down all those fire banners." All the fire banners disappeared, and left only the purple banner with three letters written in white paint in front of us.

The young woman is symbolic of church leaders. The dark shadow next to the woman is symbolic of the devil attacking church leaders minds, hearts and actions. Raised banners formed with fire are symbolic of church leaders raising up works mixed of good and bad, causing hardship to souls in the supernatural realm. These souls' hardship will cause tragedies in the natural. The purple banner is symbolic of continuation of the Lord Jesus' Mission entrusted to me, through the adoption. White is symbolic of purity.

The Price the Chosen One Pays on Earth

February 2, 1998. In my dream I saw a small and unusually dirty black skinned man. He was a little higher in front of my face, he had short curly hair, and wore eyeglasses. Immediately after I saw him, his eyeglasses fell down on his nose, the spot where his eyes should have been had no eyes, just two dark spots lower than his cheeks.

Eyeglasses are symbolic of discernment; black in this dream is symbolic of the darkness of evil. The black man is symbolic of people in the world who believe that they know good and evil and are proud of themselves when they do good things. When the glasses fell down, no eyes are symbolic that they have eyes but can not see the truth, they are just like the blind.

The next morning, I was in the Blessed Sacrament Chapel before the mass like I normally was every morning. I kneeled down, but could not pray like I normally do, my mind and body was exhausted. I repeatedly prayed, "Lord God, I am exhausted. I ask you to take my soul to heaven, and leave my physical body, my children will come and get me, and bury me under the ground." Exhausted to the point that I could not kneel any more, I sat on the chair, leaned to the back, and continued, "Father, Lord Jesus, take my soul home to heaven, leave my body here and bury it under ground. You gave me this job, but it is too big for me. I am very weak, and the responsibility so huge, I can not do it. Take it back and give to other people who are strong [at this time I meant the cardinal who marched to protest abortion in January 1998]."

(In the middle of 1994, the Lord removed me from a job earning a living on earth to serve Him with full responsibility to God. One morning I was on my way home after mass, while I was driving alone; Jesus the Lord told me, "Mariette, I want you to pursue freedom of religion in Vietnam." I quickly said out loud, "Lord, I cannot do that. I do no know anything about politics. I don't even know scripture. Why don't you chose a priest or a nun?" He said to me, "I do not want a priest or a nun. They are proud of themselves. I want you." Another day after that I was also on my way home after mass. I was driving alone, Jesus the Lord said to me, "I want you to unify the Church." I said out loud, "This is even worse than your telling me to pursue the freedom of religion in Vietnam. You chose the wrong person. The Pope, cardinals and bishops of different churches have been trying to do this, they can't achieve it and now you told me to do this. You are wrong. I can't do them." At that time my knowledge of God was very little, so God asked me to do this works instead of told me as His instrument; God told me Vietnam is not the world because Vietnam is a communist country, but actually God speaking of the world, not. He had to use the words churches, not denominations or religions so I He can related to messages to me. It was also at that time I thought that clergymen and religious people knew a lot of God and His commandments, I respected that they would be the right people for the job; therefore, I kept the major part of the conversation in secret, but as I finish this book, after God taught me, and I find out many actions of clergymen and nuns have done, I knew that God is right, because the majority of them lack discernment. They allowed the enemy spirits to use their minds and actions, and they are misleading God's people.)

I sat for over twenty minutes. I then got inside the church, and I continued repeatedly, "Father, when I am weak, I am strong in You like Saint Paul said in the scriptures. I ask you to strengthen me, help me to listen, understand, and deliver what You reveal to me to the world."

After I received Holy Communion the Father said to me, "Your suffering saved a hundred thousand, a million thousands souls." I said, "Father, I think what You said did not mean what I understood." The Father said, "What I revealed to you is in the spirit, when it comes to nature, it is a hundred thousand times, a million thousand times bigger. Your walking on top of the iron fence around the house is symbolic of your spirit around the world, a spiritual battle. The one where you held the pile of large size computer paper sheets with names, and not understanding the meaning, is about gathering these names like earthly records. But instead, your responsibility is to hear, understand, and teach others of what you hear and see so they can be saved."

Tickets to Super Bowl and Wedding Feast

January 4, 1998, the feast of Epiphany of the Lord. In my dream I was sitting on my knees, to my right was the dark shadow of a man standing. In front of me was the President of the United States in a large dark body. He was a little off to my left. There was another man on the right in his early fifties.

The President was giving out tickets to the super bowl and to the banquet after the super bowl. The top ticket he had was five thousand dollars, and he gave this ticket to the dark shadow man, he also gave some tickets to members of my family, each of these tickets were valued at three thousand five hundred. He told me that those who do not have a ticket can come to the wedding feast [not the super bowl], and when they come ask for the feast organizer. The President meant that the man with him is the wedding feast organizer. While the President said this, the man with him came forward to my left side, and pulled out from his black, double-pocket business card wallet, two business cards, and showed them to me. He said, "These are the addresses, tell them to come to this address. I looked at them, these two business cards had two different addresses.

The dark shadow person and I had our full body and legs. The dark shadow stood on a cloud and I kneeled on the cloud. The President and the other man only had the upper part of their bodies, they were flying on the cloud, not walking.

When I got up the Lord gave me this interpretation: The dark shadow to my right is symbolic of the Holy Trinity dwelling within me through this mission. The President of the United States is symbolic of the Eternal father, who is giving out the super bowl tickets and wedding banquet tickets.

The values of the tickets being different is the differences of God's power. Number five is symbolic of authority over the enemies power. God revealed the difference in His power in five thousands and five hundreds. Number three is symbolic of the Holy Trinity.

The Holy Trinity dwells within the pre-destined Servant, then the fully God's power is within me, Mariette. God sent me down to earth on this mission as an undercover person, to open the devil's actions through human bodies.

The family members are my four children and other chosen ones on earth. These chosen ones are not pre-destined; they still have their free will to choose to completely obey all God's commandments or to partial obeying. When these chosen ones do not completely obey all God's commandments, God will change His mind and replace them with others. The wedding feast is symbolic of heavenly reward as the Lord Jesus revealed in the Book of Revelation 22: 12 "Behold, I am coming soon. I bring with me the recompense I will give to each according to his deeds." The super bowl is symbolic of serving God with all our hearts, our minds and our strength, or in other words He is the top of everything in our life.

The man handing me two business cards is symbolic of holy angels. The two business cards are symbolic of the two set of books. The book of life contains the names of those who will inherit heavenly eternal life, and these souls bodies will be resurrected on the last day. This group are others that God sent down to earth for the purpose of fulfilling His will, but not the chosen ones.

The other book contains those who will not inherit heavenly reward, these souls' bodies will not be resurrected. The Lord told me that their souls are half man and half animal, and they have no faith in God, do not believe in God, and they worship idols. They will be chained in the darkness of the devil, being punished for their evils actions during the time they were on earth; they refused conversion, daily exam and repentance. (Book of Revelation chapter 20).

I then saw a man, he was an auditor, sitting on a cloud. He was writing some numbers in a large ledger book on a clip board. To his right, a little toward the front, was my mother in dark shadow. While I was standing in the middle of the cloud in front of him, I saw the number 822,000. I did not want to be nosy so I lifted my eyes up. In my thought, "My mother may give all of this money to my sister, she may not give me any. But I have over one million dollars." I then told my mother, "You should put this money in the bank to earn interest, and keep it safe, do not keep cash with you." Immediately after I finished this, I saw her pull out from her pocket a savings account pass book. She said to me, "I will put it in the bank."

The auditor is symbolic of the Lord Jesus. Number eight is symbolic of spiritual life, the number two is symbolic of discernment, choosing good and rejecting evil, and living a life of holiness. My mother, her saving book, together with 822,00 symbolic God's power works through this Divine mission God entrusted to me.

During the time the Lord gave me the interpretation, He kept saying, "Lo, I will send you Elijah." This scripture in the book of Malachi, chapter three, God gave to me before, on November 6, 1996. After the Lord said, "Lo, I will send you Elijah," He then said, "By what kind of authority are you doing these things?" The Lord Jesus revealed to me that the chief priests and scribes with the elders questioned Him before, and in this century the spiritual leaders will also asked me the same question that the priests and scribes asked Jesus on those day, because the Servant is not greater than Master.

In this revelation, the Lord Jesus revealed to me that I was sent down by the Eternal Father on the Divine mission to as my beloved brother Jesus, and my Lord and my God's Vessel.

Funeral is Time to Pray for Soul and Mourn

October 1997. I attended the funeral announcement of one of my extended earthly family members. After I arrived inside the mortuary I immediately knelt down at the back of the room, separated from the late person's immediate family, and focusing in God, I prayed with the rosary for the soul. After I finished my prayer for the soul, I went up to the front where the soul's family was. I said, "Now your mother can no longer speak to you in words. I am now the oldest one and I speak to all of you on her behalf. The most important thing is to pray for her soul, not only today, but every day. Each one of you should silently reconcile with her, ask her to forgive you for things you have done against her. Even though she is your mother, there were times she did things that were wrong to you; you must forgive her. And all of you must forgive each other, convert, exam and repent daily, and pray for her.

The Vietnamese have a custom when an adult passes away from the earth. Each member of the immediate and extended family receive lengths of white sackcloth. These sackcloths are blessed at the time of the announcement of the death ceremony by the priest, and distributed to family members. This ceremony normally takes place next to the corpse. Whoever wears this white sackcloth symbolically pays respect to the late person with love. The manner of wearing the white sackcloth depends on the relationship between the person wearing the cloth and the deceased. The children of the deceased cover their entire head, grandchildren and the extended family members wear the sackcloth around their head like a band, with both ends to the back. Males of the extended family normally wear it on their upper arm.

After the blessing of the sackcloth and distribution to all the members of the immediate family, one of her sons brought me this white sackcloth while I was standing at my seat. I received it and asked, "Lord Jesus, in God's family I am a Princess of Heaven and Earth, but in my earthly family, this person was my aunt. What do you want me to do with this sackcloth?" I then hung it on my left shoulder, one end at the front, another at the back. When I placed this white sackcloth over my right shoulder, this gesture was symbolic of the love and respect I have for her.

On the day of her funeral, when I entered the Holy Family church, her body was in the foyer waiting to proceed inside the church. I stayed there as a member of the family. The funeral director asked her children, "There are two ways to decorate her casket for proceeding into the church. We can lay flowers on top or cover it with white cloth." I said to him, "We want it covered with white cloth." The white cloth covering her casket is symbolic of wearing white robe in front of God. The funeral director then said, "The flowers can be put at the foot of the altar."

The young men of the family were working on a speech to give after the mass. He asked me, "What should we say?" I replied, "At the beginning you must give thanks to God for creating her and taking her away. Give thanks to the Blessed Virgin Mother, our spiritual mother that assisted her during the time she was on earth, then to the priest of the ceremony, and others."

During the entire funeral, all members of our family were very peaceful, and quietly prayed for her soul. No picture taking, video taping or other flowers, besides the ones at the foot of the altar, and her picture at the end of her casket with incense were involved. Incense is symbolic of prayer offerings to God, and flowers are symbolic of the last offering on earth.

The Enemy Spirit Manifesting through Human bodies during the Funeral Service

January 10, 1998. When I got into the Church parking lot, I saw the funeral vehicle parked outside the left entrance of the Good Shepherd Church. While I was parking my car, I saw a Vietnamese man who formerly served in the same square with my earthly Father, and he was carrying the American flag. He passed the entrance to the Blessed Sacrament Chapel and went toward the right entrance to the church. I thought this was a Vietnamese funeral.

After I finished my devotion in the Blessed Sacrament; on my way to the restroom, I saw a young priest whom God loves, and to whom God had me deliver His words at Christmas. When he heard that I was going to deliver God's words to him, he corrected his form, stood up straight and looked directly at me to receive God's gift for him, "Jesus loves you, you are very special to him. The more Jesus loves you, the more you suffer." He replied, "I believe that." He was sitting in the chair next to the left side of the sanctuary. I knew that since he sat there, he would not be the main priest to celebrate the Holy Eucharist today.

I just got out of the restroom and passed the small hall. While I was walking in the foyer, I saw many people wearing black coming in the church for the funeral. In the middle of them to the left side of the church, on the same side with the casket, there was the middle aged priest wearing his priest's uniform, he was on his way to the sacristy. I knew he would be the main celebrant for the mass today.

I entered the church and I saw that the front right part of the sanctuary, the center section where I normally sit, was empty. On the front row of the opposite section were some women wearing black. I took my seat on the fifth row, at the end of the middle aisle.

While I was praying with scriptures, out of the corner of my eye, I saw the middle aged priest come and talk to those women at the front row. Immediately after the priest left, the second woman from the middle aisle cried out loud. People around her leaned to her and comforted her, but she made more noise while these people were comforting her. Then the young priest walked toward her, and took a seat to this woman's right, to quiet her down. I also heard the voices crying out loud outside the sanctuary, where the coffin was.

The mass started with holy water being sprayed over the coffin. The woman in the front row cried again. I then saw an altar boy holding incense come with the priest following behind him.

After the priest kissed the altar, I saw the coffin being rolled up toward the altar. At the end of the coffin was a woman wearing a tight jean, with dark brown animal feathers hat, and a short jacket. She leaned her stomach behind the coffin. When the pallbearers found their seat, this woman was still laying her stomach on the coffin. One man came and talked to her, removed her from the coffin, and lead her to the front seat with the other women.

When the priest started the mass, the actions and voices of the women in the front row interrupted the priest, and distracted others from focusing on the mass. When priest gave his homily, these women again cried out loud, others around them leaned over to comfort them. These women's actions and voices were louder than the mass celebrant.

When I saw many people wearing black outside, I felt the spirit of the enemies coming to the church. When I heard the woman in the front seat cry; I knew the Lord use this funeral mass to revealed to me something for His works. I then stopped reading the scriptures, took the blessed holy anointing oil and put on myself, and prayed for protection and guiding to hear God well.

When the priest started the beginning of the mass, the Lord told me, "You will get out of the church after the consecration." I said, "Lord, if I leave the church at that time, how could I receive the Holy Eucharist?" He said, "You will go to the 5:30 p.m. mass to receive the Holy Eucharist." Now I really had to seek God to discern these instructions.

I prayed, "Father, Lord Jesus, Holy Spirit, if these words are not from you, I am not receiving them. I ask You to take them away from me. Increase Your peace in me. If this instruction is from You, please help me to hear You exactly of how, and what you want me to do. I know that the devil has no power to move my physical body. Father, Lord Jesus, Holy Spirit, you are the only one that has power to move me. Blessed Mother protect me, pray to the Lord God for me. All the holy saints and angels, surround me above, go before me, praising the Lord God."

When the nun did the reading, I was trying to listen to the reading, but I could not listen to her words clearly. I knew that the Lord was showing me something. I then focused on the Holy Trinity, and said, " Lord, what would You want me to do?" I heard no response.

When the priest started his homily I said, "Lord God, would you want me to listen to his homily, or would You want me to focus on You?" I normally ask the Lord this question when I feel uncertain, or when the Lord is going to tell me something, or when I am seeking direction. Or sometimes when I have heard that priest's homily before, and his homily lacked discernment. After a short time in communion with Him, I said to the dead soul, "You are an evildoer. In the name of the Lord Jesus, I send you down to the bottom of the abyss, to be tormented forever. I punish you for your evil actions." When I said this with closed eyes, in spirit, I saw below the ground of the sanctuary a huge hole with a dark loose cloud. I knew that this dark loose cloud was symbolic of souls being chained in the darkness of the devil after their death. I then heard the Lord say, "You judged for this soul."

I then said, "Father, I finished exactly what you told me. Lord Jesus, You are the only Judge, I did what you commanded me. Holy Spirit, You are the witness."

At this time, except at the altar, I felt the enemy spirits fill the church, specially at the two front rows in the left section. I prayed for protection, and I then felt peace because God protects me. Even though I know that God is protecting me, I still wanted to hurry after the consecration so I could get out of the church. In my thoughts I wanted to make sure that the Lord wanted me to leave early, because if I left at this time, I would distract people, and also the priest would see me. I asked, "Lord, will the priest ask me 'why you did not stay to the end?" He said, "He will ask you when the time comes. It is done, now is just the ceremony"

During the consecration, I asked, "Father, are You here? Lord Jesus, are You here? Holy Spirit, are You here?" He said, "I am not with the dead, but I am with others."

The young priest that I was concerned of his asking is symbolic of the Lord Jesus. The Lord said, "It is done, now is just the ceremony." He meant that after a person breathes his last breath, the body is dead, it is nothing to hold on to; the funeral is just the final ceremony before burying his corpse underground. I was there to receive a revelation. The

5:30 p.m. service that day would be the time for me to celebrate the daily mass and receive the Holy Eucharist obligation that the Lord Jesus commanded me four years ago. The two women crying out loud and those leaning to them and comforting them were actually being attacked by the devil's spirit to distract others from focusing on and worshipping God.

God reveals to the world, there is no exception, every person on earth will be judged after each one's last breath. Jesus is the only Judge sitting at His throne, and He sends His servants to be judged according to each one's life on earth.

3:05 p.m. During my devotion, the Lord Jesus told me, "Princess, you were not the one who judged that soul today, because you are still on earth, that was a revelation. Peter was the one who judged that soul." I asked, "Lord Jesus, what about 'you judged the soul'?" I meant what I heard during the mass. He said, "It means, after you return to heaven, you will be judging people after their last breath."

The funeral is the ceremony for the corpse before being buried underground. It is the last time family members will be with his corpse and pray for him. For God to hear our prayer, each one must focus in Him, and pray for the soul. Video taping, picture taking, and crying will distract people's minds from focusing on praying for the soul. Family member's speeches need to be cut short, giving thanks to God for His creation, and to the Blessed Virgin Mother for Her assistance. Others do not need to be thanked, God will bless them for prayers for the soul with all their heart. Flowers should be kept to a minimum. Every time someone leaves the face of the earth, God reminds us that our physical life on earth is temporary, your soul is the most important because it is permanent. If you get to heaven, you will see God face to face, and see each other again.

God's Judgment Will Be Declared in Three Categories

A. The souls who go directly to heaven to inherit eternal life. These are those who convert, daily exam and repent for their thoughts and actions, keep their hearts pure, focus on God, embrace all suffering and offer it to God; obey all His commandments, and serve Him with love from their hearts, minds and actions, build the kingdom of heaven, and endure to the end. After the judgment, their guardian angel, patron saint, and saint that intercedes for them in their life will accompany them to heaven.

B. The souls who go to purgatory to be purified. These are those who at their last breath do not contain great sin. They will be there to pay the damages for things they did on earth by disobeying God's commandments. These sins could be directly against God, or indirectly through sins against others. Like on earth when the court judges against a person for his or her actions, he or she must pay that judgment in full. This called iniquities.

D. The souls who go to the place of the devil, where he and his fallen angels control the souls. These souls will be chained in the darkness of the devil in torment. This is the punishment for their crime of evil works while on earth. This is the second death, because they refused to convert, examine themselves and repent daily while they were on earth.

Books Order Form

Quantity discount of 30% is available for orders over 50 books of any title. Please indicate the book(s) that you would like to order, and send the proper payment with the order. Please allow 4 to 6 weeks for receipt of shipment. No credit cards please.

______ Volume I, "My Patient - God's Gift" by Mariette Do-Nguyen & Gerald Nelson, M.D. U.S. $25.00. International order add $7.00 for postage.

______ Volume II, "God's Purification - Not Easy" by Mariette Do-Nguyen: Part one, 274 pages, U.S. $25.00. Part two, 654 pages U.S. $35.00. International order add $ 12.00 postage for part I, and $20.00 for part II.

______ Volume III, "The Only Petition at United States Tax Court" Petitioner and author: Mariette Do-Nguyen. U.S. $35.00. International order add $20.00 for postage.

______ Please send me information of the forthcoming book "Fifth Sense" when it available. This book is volume IV of the series.

Please make check payable to: **Rebuild My Church Divine Mission**
P.O. Box 261550
San Diego, CA 92196-1550

Please visit the mission web site www.jesusweb.org for more information and publications.

Enclosed is payment of $__________. Order will be shipped to: (Name and address of receiver

Name: ____

Address: ____

____

City:_______________________________State: __________ Zip: ____________

Telephone: (________) _______________________________